Arabia, the Gulf and the West

J. B. KELLY

Arabia, the Gulf and the West

 **BasicBooks**
A Division of HarperCollins*Publishers*

The author and publishers would like to thank Mr. Philip Larkin
and his publishers, Faber and Faber Limited, for kind permission
to quote from his poem, 'Homage to a Government'; and Lord
Trevelyan and his publishers, Macmillan and Company, for permission to quote from his memoirs, *The Middle East in Revolution*.

First published in Great Britain by
George Weidenfeld and Nicolson Limited
91 Clapham High Street, London SW4
1980

First published in the U.S.A. by Basic Books, Inc.

Contents

Maps

Preface

When Great Britain withdrew from her political and military position in the Gulf at the close of 1971, thereby relinquishing the responsibility she had borne for 150 years for the maintenance of peace and security in the region, the occasion was little remarked by a world intent upon other preoccupations. There was slight disposition in the West, and certainly none in Asia or Africa, to question the expediency of a decision whose correctness was taken as self-evident in an age which had seen the dismantling of Europe's overseas empires. Even among the few who harboured doubts about both the wisdom and the propriety of Britain's action there was a certain resigned acceptance of the fact that, in the light of the general infirmity of will which characterized much of the Western world, it was more or less inevitable. Less than two years after the British withdrawal the world had good reason to mark its consequences, as the Arab oil-producing states of the Gulf imposed an embargo upon the export of oil to some Western countries, demanded assurances of political sympathy from others as a condition of sale, and in company with the shah of Persia raised the price of oil to exorbitant heights.

With the loss of even the tenuous strategic control over the Gulf's oil reserves which the British presence provided, the nations of the free world have had to rely for their continued access to these reserves upon the goodwill of the governments in power in the Gulf states. The price of this goodwill has been the acquiescence by the Western powers and Japan in the repeated raising of the price of crude oil, a process to which there seems no foreseeable end. Apart from its adverse effects upon their economies, this policy of appeasement, like all policies conceived in a similar spirit, affords the nations of the West no guarantee whatever of the security of oil supplies from the Gulf. On the contrary, by confirming the governments of the Gulf states in their estimation of their own importance and, conversely, of the flaccidity of the West, it disposes them even more to believe that they are free to act in the wilful fashion which has consistently marked their conduct in the past.

For all its gloss of recently acquired modernity, which so beguiles the foreign eye, the Gulf today is very much as it has always been – turbulent, backward, intrinsically unstable – and it is this instability which poses the greatest threat to Western interests in the region. The causes of this instability are manifold: some – dynastic rivalries, racial differences, sectarian antipathies, tribal vendettas – are endemic in the Gulf; others – the impact of oil wealth, the ramifications of the Arab–Israeli conflict, the influence of radical political ideas – are of recent occurrence or alien origin. When to these circumstances are added the great array of deadly weapons with which the Gulf states have equipped themselves of late years, the attraction which their oil wealth exerts for predators of every kind, and the interest which the Gulf's economic and strategic significance cannot fail to generate among the great powers, the result is to make the Gulf one of the most potentially dangerous areas in the world today.

Yet the general drift of public comment in the West on Arabia and the Gulf over the past half-a-dozen years, whether by governments, the press, institutions or individuals, has been in the opposite direction, towards a view of the Gulf in which its material transformation is seen as being accompanied – the occasional economic follies of its governments notwithstanding – by steady progress towards political maturity and a sensible appreciation of the region's close economic, and perhaps political, interdependence with the Western industrial world. To sustain such a view has necessitated the depiction of the regimes in power in Arabia and the Gulf in colours more flattering than their true ones. It has required, also, the obscuring or misrepresentation of their basic attitudes towards the West, and the portrayal of their questionable behaviour over oil supplies and prices as nothing more than the proper pursuit of legitimate self-interest.

One of the purposes of this book, perhaps its main purpose, is to offer another interpretation of the recent history of Arabia and the Gulf, and of Western relations with the area, which may serve as a partial corrective to the orthodox and, I believe, dangerously complacent version of that history and those relations which has been propagated in the Western world for the past decade. Because it is intended as a corrective it may on occasions have overstated its case, an offence to which I can only plead guilty for I do not pretend to be impartial about the issues with which this book deals. All that I can offer in extenuation of those opinions expressed here which may be found disagreeable is that they have been arrived at after a good deal of thought and are put forward in all sincerity.

In general I have dispensed with footnotes. The origins of quotations and statements, where they are not indicated in the text, will be apparent from the bibliography. There are a few instances, however, where I have thought it desirable to append a footnote, either to remove any obscurity concerning the source of a quotation or to register a debt to a particular author. The various acronyms used in the text are explained in the index.

I have been greatly helped in the collection of material for this book by the librarians and staff of the library and press library of the Royal Institute of International Affairs, and by the librarian and staff of the London Library. It gives me a great deal of pleasure to be able to express here my deep appreciation of the courteous assistance they have given me at all times. I owe a considerable debt of gratitude to Jo Binns for having skilfully typed a barely decipherable manuscript; to David Pryce-Jones for his encouragement and advice; and to Patrick O'Ferrall for his generosity in allowing me to benefit from his knowledge and experience of the oil industry. To those friends and colleagues who over the years have afforded me amiable counsel and criticism, and in Arabia and the Gulf liberal hospitality, I offer my warmest thanks.

J.B.K.
London
July 1979

Arabia, the Gulf and the West

CHAPTER I
The Abandonment of Aden

Our remedy and safeguard will be to trend continually 'left'.

T. E. Lawrence, 1919*

*Our job was somehow to untie the knot and release ourselves
without disaster.*

Lord Trevelyan, 1970

*That the regime [we] backed should have been overthrown by
terrorists and has forced our speedy withdrawal is nothing but good
fortune . . . we shall get out of Aden without losing a British
soldier, chaos will rule soon after we've gone, and there'll be one
major commitment cut – thank God.*

Richard Crossman, 1967

Aden in the summer of 1967 presented a bleak and melancholy picture. Its
cosmopolitan population of Arabs, Indians, Somalis and Europeans suffered
under a reign of unrelenting violence imposed by gangs of Arab terrorists and
only partially mitigated by the exertions of the British security forces. Commercial life in the town and port, once the hub of a thriving entrepôt trade, had
sunk to a low ebb, as a consequence both of the closing of the Suez Canal by the
Arab–Israeli war in June and of the incessant, politically directed, strikes
which were paralysing Aden's industry. Rival Arab nationalist bands fought a
running battle with each other through the streets and houses of Crater, the old
town inside the walls of an extinct volcano which was the mercantile heart of
Aden. At gunpoint they compelled a frightened population to afford them
shelter and sustenance, as well as money with which to finance their grisly
games and their hit-and-run attacks upon the British authorities. From the
beginning of 1967 until the end of August there were no fewer than 2,600
incidents of terrorism in Aden as a whole, murders, robberies, bombings and
shootings, and most of the victims were ordinary citizens.

* *The Letters of T. E. Lawrence* (ed. David Garnett), London, 1938, p. 293, to Lord Curzon, 25 September
1919.

Beyond Aden, in the hinterland, the primitive structure of law and order that had been sustained by the sultans, shaikhs and amirs of the former Aden Protectorate (since 1963 the Federation of South Arabia) was falling apart. British troops had been withdrawn from the up-country districts in June and concentrated inside the Aden perimeter. The duty of upholding the authority of the federal rulers now rested wholly with the federal army, which was in the process of being hurriedly enlarged and placed under Arab command. But the army was racked by discontents and jealousies among its officers, by tribal factionalism, and by nationalist sedition within its ranks. There was even greater disaffection in the federal armed police, who had at one stage broken out in open mutiny. Deprived of any support from the federal armed forces, the hereditary rulers of South Arabia stood little chance of holding out against the nationalist guerrillas and the tribesmen they had won over to their cause. Before the summer was out nearly every ruler had been toppled from power, the hinterland had been overrun by the nationalist revolutionaries and their cohorts, and the federal government had completely collapsed.

All this was taking place in a country which was still, in name at least, under British protection, and part of which, the colony of Aden, had been a British possession for nearly 130 years. Yet while the tribal Caliban prowled unchecked in the interior, and the British Army strove gallantly to give to the people of Aden some measure of that protection which it is the first duty of a civilized government to accord to its subjects, the British administration was packing its bags and counting the days to its final departure. How, it might well be asked, did such a lamentable state of affairs come to pass? To answer this question with any degree of thoroughness would require an extensive examination both of the history of Aden colony and protectorate since the First World War, and of the course of British imperial and foreign policy during the same period, an undertaking which lies beyond the scope and purpose of this book. Yet some account of the last years of British rule in South Arabia, and of the reasons for its dismal end, is essential to that scope and purpose; for what happened in South Arabia in those years, and especially between the formal inauguration of the Federation of South Arabia in January 1963 and the British withdrawal in November 1967, cast its shadow across the rest of the Arabian peninsula in the succeeding decade, and may well help to determine the shape of events yet to unfold in that corner of the world.

For nearly a century after its acquisition in 1839 Aden was administered from India as an outpost of the Indian empire. Its consequence and its prosperity derived from three sources: its strategic position on the world's sea lanes, commanding the passage of the Red Sea and the routes to India and the Far East; its function as a bunkering port for shipping; and its role as a mart for the trade of Ethiopia, Yemen, South Arabia and the Horn of Africa. The hinterland behind Aden was a harsh and desolate land of jagged mountains, stony plateaux, ravines, wadis and deserts. Few cultivable areas existed in these parched wastes, and they were mainly to be found in the upper reaches of the Wadi Hadramaut and in the vicinity of Aden. The tribes of southern Arabia were as wild and as primitive as the land itself. Wretchedly poor, harried by famine and disease, riddled with superstition and religious fanaticism, they spent their energies almost as much in feuds among themselves as they did in wresting a meagre living from the hostile earth. To the miscellany of sultans, saiyids, shaikhs and amirs that ruled over them they accorded only a perfunctory obedience, changing their allegiances as the impulse seized them. It is little wonder, therefore, that the British Indian authorities set their faces against any involvement in the interior of South Arabia in the nineteenth century, other than what was required to ensure the security of Aden. The policy was much the same as that followed throughout the century, and for many of the same reasons and reservations, towards the tribes and principalities along the Arabian littoral of the Persian Gulf.

Turkish expansion in south-western and eastern Arabia in the last three decades of the nineteenth century and down to the outbreak of the First World War forced a modification of this policy of non-involvement. A series of treaties was concluded with the rulers of both the Gulf shaikhdoms and the South Arabian principalities from 1880 onwards which placed the conduct of their foreign relations in British hands and required them not to alienate any portion of their territories without British permission. The First World War led to further British intervention in the affairs of Arabia. Troops were committed to the defence both of Aden against the Turks and of Muscat against insurgents from the interior of Oman; alliances were concluded with the sharif of Mecca and with his arch-rival, Ibn Saud, the ruler of Najd; and Kuwait and Qatar were brought formally under British protection. After the war the pace of involvement slackened, though less so in South Arabia than elsewhere. There responsibility for the conduct of British relations with the assorted sultanates, amirates and shaikhdoms with which treaties had been concluded was transferred in 1921 to the Colonial Office in London. A tug-of-war then ensued between the Colonial Office and the government of India for control of Aden itself. Delhi wanted to keep Aden within the Indian orbit. Its character and distinctive flavour were Indian, its historical ties were with India, much of its trade was in Indian hands, it was still, as it had been since its annexation, an outpost of India's defensive system. The Colonial Office would have none of this. Aden, in its view, was part of Arabia, the majority of its population was Arab, its future lay in integration with its hinterland, with the rest of the Arabian peninsula, and with the Arab world at large. Analogies with Gibraltar, Hong Kong or Singapore were brushed aside as irrelevant. The Colonial Office had its way, and in 1937 Aden became a Crown colony under the direct authority of Whitehall.

Thereafter it was governed along customary Crown-colony lines, by a governor appointed by the Crown and assisted by an executive and later a legislative council. While important in itself, the change of status was perhaps even more significant because of the fresh impetus it gave to the efforts which, under Colonial Office stimulus, had been going on for some years before 1937 to create a closer, even symbiotic, relationship between Aden and the protectorate states of the hinterland. It had been recognized from the start that the policy could not succeed if these states were left, as by and large they had been left, in their natural condition of turbulence and lawlessness. They would have to be tamed, and British control exerted over them, in fact and not just in name. There were other reasons in the 1930s for making British authority effective in the hinterland. To the west the imam of Yemen, despite his apparent acknowledgement of the frontier between his country and the Aden protectorate laid down in a treaty concluded with the British government in 1934, still asserted claims to paramountcy over the protectorate tribes and rulers. To the north Ibn Saud, having consolidated his authority over the northern half of Arabia, was endeavouring to extend his southern frontiers as far south as he could. With these considerations in mind, the authorities in Aden pushed forward the work of pacification in the protectorate during the 1930s. It was slow work, since neither the men nor the funds were available to make more rapid progress, and in any case the task of persuading the tribes to forgo their simple pleasures of blood-letting and rapine was a delicate one, calling for much skill, patience and tact. For administrative convenience the protectorate was divided into western and eastern regions: a British political agent was stationed in each and made responsible to the governor at Aden for the implementation of the pacification policy.

The process continued after the Second World War along the lines laid down before 1939. Advisory treaties were concluded with the rulers of the couple of dozen sultanates, amirates and shaikhdoms that composed the two protectorates, and political officers were appointed to supervise the implementation of the treaties. Local security forces were created, either for service throughout the hinterland, like the Aden Protectorate Levies raised in 1928, or to police particular regions, like the Hadrami Bedouin Legion raised in 1939, or to keep the peace in their own districts, like the tribal guards. The rulers were kept to the observance of their obligations by the judicious distribution or withholding of government support and favours, especially in the provision of money and arms, the two commodities most needed by the rulers to retain the fickle allegiance of their unruly subjects. Efforts were also made to reform the *daulah*s, or tribal councils, upon which the hereditary rulers relied for advice and support and which often, in the case of an incompetent or feeble ruler, ruled in his stead. As instruments of government the *daulah*s were at first sight inefficient, arbitrary and corrupt; but they were effective in controlling the restless tribesmen, for they were, along with the rulers themselves, the source of patronage and protection, and in any case they were the only form of political institution, however crude they might be in concept and operation, to have emerged in South Arabia. As an ultimate sanction for obtaining compliance with British wishes, the governor of Aden had the power to depose a recalcitrant or ineffectual ruler and to replace him with a more competent or pliable member of the ruling family, one who, as often as not, would be subservient to the more powerful *daulah*. The sum effect of this policy of intervention, especially when reinforced in the 1950s and 1960s by an increasing though hardly munificent provision of economic aid, educational and medical services, and improvements in agriculture and communications, was to undermine the standing and influence of the hereditary rulers, and the traditional structure of authority throughout the protectorates. Unwittingly or not, it paved the way for the débâcle of 1967.

The stirrings of political discontent were not much in evidence in Aden colony before the end of the Second World War. In the next few years the colony began to feel the ripples from the dismantling and partition of the Indian empire, from the communist insurgency in Malaya, and from the beginnings of the general movement within the British tropical dependencies towards national independence and an end to imperial rule. A legislative council composed of nominated members was introduced in Aden in 1947 to give the Adenis a share, however circumscribed, in their own government. The innovation whetted their appetite for further participation in politics, and in 1955 the first elections were held in the colony to fill four new elective seats on the council. Up until this time political activity had been almost exclusively confined to the upper layer of Adeni society, the wealthy merchant families who controlled most of Aden's commerce. They were for the greater part Arab, though there were a few prominent Indian families among them. The population of Aden in 1955 was 138,234, of which Adeni Arabs numbered 36,910. There were, however, 18,881 Arabs from the protectorates living in the colony, and 48,088 Yemenis, so that the total number of Arab inhabitants was 103,879, or over 75 per cent of the population. The next largest group was the Indians (15,817), and after them the Somalis (10,611) and the Europeans (4,488), most of whom were British. Before 1948 there had been a Jewish community of more than 7,000 in Aden; but after the anti-Jewish riots which occurred in that year as a consequence of the war in Palestine all save some 800 had left the colony.

Political activity, as just mentioned, was for all practical purposes restricted to the hierarchy of wealthy and educated Adeni Arabs. They conducted their activities through the Aden Association, a body they founded in 1950 to campaign for a greater measure of self-government for the colony and for its eventual independence within the British Commonwealth. The Aden Association was, by any standards, and especially by those prevailing in most of the Middle East at the time, an organization of impeccable respectability.

There were, however, nascent political forces at work within the colony of a very different kind, whose influence was to prove far more significant in the long run than that of the Aden Association. Because the Aden Association was dominated and controlled by the richer Adeni families, Adeni Arabs from lower down the social and economic scale were virtually excluded from political activity. They found an outlet for their political urges in the organization of trades unions, whose introduction into the colonies had been the inspiration of Sidney Webb (Lord Passfield) during his tenure of the Colonial Office from 1929 to 1931. Thereafter the fostering of trade union activity had become an established feature of British colonial policy. The first trade unions in Aden were organized in 1953 from among the white-collar workers, most of them Adeni Arabs. The great majority of manual labourers and artisans in Aden came from outside the colony – from Somaliland, from the protectorate states, and from the Yemen – and as a group they lacked any natural cohesion. Not only were they divided by ethnic and sectarian differences but their presence in Aden was a transient one: most of them returned home after working in the colony for two or three years. Such political interests and loyalties as they had were directed towards their homelands and their own tribes and hereditary rulers.

Little or no political leadership or support for these migrant communities was forthcoming from the Yemenis, protectorate Arabs and Somalis long settled in Aden. They, and more particularly the wealthier merchants among them, identified themselves and their futures with the colony: they had become, or were on the way to becoming, Adeni citizens, with little or nothing in common with the immigrants. It is doubtful in any case whether the migrant communities would have accepted their leadership. The transient Yemenis were themselves divided by tribal affiliations, diversity of origin and religious particularism, being either Shafi or Zaidi Muslims. It was much the same with the Arabs from the protectorates. Most of the leading merchants in Aden who had originated in the protectorates came from the Hadramaut. The protectorate Arabs, who came from dozens of tribes in the protectorate states and who acknowledged a wide assortment of shaikhs and sultans as their rulers, would have rejected any suggestion that they look for leadership to the Hadramis. There was, therefore, a political vacuum in the large immigrant community, and it was this vacuum that the young and politically ambitious Arabs from the middle ranks of Adeni society moved to fill.

In the elections held in 1955 to fill four seats on the legislative council the franchise was restricted to Adeni and Commonwealth citizens, which meant that Adeni Arabs and most Indian and Pakistani inhabitants were entitled to vote but not the Yemenis or the majority of the protectorate Arabs and Somalis. The result was a foregone conclusion: three Adeni Arabs put up by the Aden Association and a Somali who had the Association's blessing were elected. A more interesting feature of the elections was the surfacing of a radical political opposition in the shape of the United National Front, a loose coalition of trade unionists, Baathists, crypto-Marxists, and individual members of the South Arabian League, a political party based on Lahej in the Western Protectorate. It was far from being the United National Front's intention actually to contest the elections: instead, its aim was to make an ostentatious and vociferous display of boycotting them on the grounds that the franchise was too restrictive and the degree of political advancement they represented derisory.

The UNF's boycott was a failure, its only effect being to demonstrate to the young radical Adenis who had tried to organize it their lack of an effective political base. They learned their lesson, and thereafter they set out to secure such a base through the medium of the trade union movement. An Aden Trades Union Congress was established in March 1956, bringing together under a central directorate some thirty-odd unions, large and small. Control over the Aden TUC was quickly and easily asserted by the white-collar unions, to which most of the Adeni political activists belonged. The first secretary-general to be appointed was Abdullah al-Asnaj, one of the leading figures in the 1955 UNF coalition. Another founder-member of the Aden TUC, and a participant in the UNF, was Abdullah Badhib, an unavowed communist. From the very moment of its inception the Aden TUC was regarded by those who rapidly came to dominate its councils as a political instrument with primarily political aims and objects. The advancement of trade unionists' interests, the redress of their grievances, and the promotion of their social and economic welfare through improved pay, working conditions and security of employment were all subordinated to political ends – or, to put it more accurately, were used as means to the attainment of political ends. Several of the leading lights in the Aden TUC had learned the theory and tactics of trade union agitation while studying or working in Britain, and they were particularly aware of the value of the strike as a coercive measure. The number of strikes that Aden was to experience from 1956 onwards, the great majority of them for political reasons, was of an order to make the British TUC blush with pride at the precocity of its protégés.

Modern Arab politics depends in large measure upon a 'street', an urban mob that can be summoned at will and given its marching orders, whether these be to provide a demagogue with a vocal and approving audience, to intimidate political rivals, to lend colour to a regime's claims of popular support, or alternatively to lend force to its opponents' allegations of popular disaffection. For the ambitious young radicals of Aden, the thousands of Adenis, Yemenis and protectorate Arabs enrolled in the trade unions constituted a ready-made 'street', whose activation merely required a suitable catalyst, something that would override their mutual antagonisms and spur them to concerted action. The catalyst found was Arab nationalism. Many young Adenis who had travelled to Egypt or Syria or the Lebanon for business or education returned in high excitement over what they had seen and heard of the resurgence of Arab power, of the growing sense of Arab unity, and of the impending triumphs that awaited the Arab peoples once this unity had been achieved. Similar impressions of the desirability and irresistibility of nationalism as a political force in Asia were brought to Aden by young Hadramis who had derived these impressions from their travels to and from the Hadrami communities in India, Malaya and the East Indies. Striking confirmation that nationalism's hour had come was held to be afforded by events in Algeria, where revolt had broken out against French rule, and in Egypt, where revolution had swept away the monarchy and brought to power a young and vigorous republican government under Gamal Abdul Nasser, committed to the expulsion of the British from their base in the Suez Canal zone.

A constant theme of the Aden demagogues was the 'artificiality' of the separation of 'south Yemen' (Aden and the protectorates) from the Yemen proper, and the inevitability and the sublime propriety of their unification. To this insistent invocation of the spirit of pan-Arabism were linked denunciations of British 'imperialism' and demands for swift independence from British rule, couched in terms to appeal to racial and religious prejudices. Particular stress was laid upon the unfair operation of the franchise in Aden, which gave the vote to Europeans, Christians, Jews, Indians, Hindus, and other lesser beings of God's creation, while denying it to the far greater numbers of Muslim Arabs from the Yemen and the protectorates. The question of the franchise lay at the very heart of the political situation in Aden and the direction its future development would take. With the introduction of elected members to the legislative council the first step had been taken away from purely representative government of the type normally associated with Crown colonies and towards the attainment of fully responsible government in which all members of the legislature would be elected. To have extended the franchise during this transitional period to the Yemenis and the protectorate Arabs would have been to resign Aden's political destiny into the hands of transient foreign labourers who enjoyed no such political or civil rights in their own countries. Moreover, since the campaign mounted by the leaders of the Aden TUC from 1955 onwards for the extension of the franchise to the Yemenis and the protectorate Arabs was conducted in the name of Arab nationalism, it was subversive of the very foundations of Adeni society. For the inhabitants of Aden, a multi-racial, polyglot community imbued with a mercantile and cosmopolitan outlook, subjection to the constraints implicit in a narrowly conceived nationalism could spell nothing but ruination.

The political climate in Aden in the early and middle 1950s was further unsettled, and the Aden nationalists correspondingly encouraged, by disturbances in the hinterland, where a campaign of harassment against the Western Protectorate rulers was being conducted by the neighbouring imam of Yemen, Ahmad ibn Yahya al-Hamidi. Like his predecessors in the Hamidian line,

Imam Ahmad cherished pretensions to suzerainty over the tribes of the Western Protectorate and, indeed, over South Arabia as a whole. When the British authorities in Aden began in 1950 to exert more control over the states of the Western Protectorate, in an endeavour to bring some semblance of order, coherence and security into their internal affairs, the imam complained that such a forward policy was a violation of the *status quo* in the protectorate and prejudicial to his sovereign rights. He vented his pique in a series of armed incursions across the border into the protectorate, simultaneously intimidating and subverting the tribes with arms and money. To counteract his activities, and at the same time facilitate economic co-operation and progress among the treaty states, the governor of Aden, Sir Tom Hickinbotham, proposed to the Colonial Office that the rulers of the states be invited to combine in a federation. The Colonial Office agreed, and in January 1954 a plan for a federation was put before the rulers. They rejected it out of hand, which was not surprising since the plan envisioned the setting up of an administration similar to those which had developed elsewhere in the British colonial dependencies and which were entirely unsuited to conditions in South Arabia. The idea of some kind of association, however, persisted with the rulers, and the events of the next two years lent it additional attraction.

Subversion from the Yemen continued, and was supported from the closing months of 1954 onwards by Egypt. Britain's agreement in October of that year to evacuate the Suez Canal base in two years' time was interpreted by Nasser as evidence of British feebleness and a prelude to a British withdrawal from the Middle East in general. To hasten that withdrawal he supplied Imam Ahmad with arms and technical assistance, while Cairo Radio and the other organs of Egyptian propaganda portrayed the rebellion being stirred up among the tribes of the Aden hinterland as a revolt against British colonial rule, inspired by Arab nationalist feeling and a desire for union with the Yemen. Needless to say, it was nothing of the kind. The tribesmen, who were Sunni Muslims of the Shafi rite, had no wish to be brought under the rule of the imam, who was head of the Zaidi sect of Shii Islam. Nor were they affirming their natural political affinity with the distant masses of Syria, Iraq, Algeria or Egypt – least of all the Egyptians, who on every occasion when they had appeared in south-western Arabia had come in the capacity of invaders and would-be conquerors. Far from rebelling against British colonial rule, which they had never directly experienced, the tribesmen were expressing their distaste for the political and economic reforms which were being pressed upon their rulers and *daulah*s by the British authorities in Aden, reforms which they resented as an unwarranted interference with their accustomed way of life, a life ruled by cupidity, disaffection and xenophobia (not nationalism). They cared not in the least that the *daulah*s struck Europeans as hopelessly ramshackle and corrupt, and the protectorate rulers as capricious, grasping and inept. The *daulah*s were the only political institution that existed in South Arabia, and together with the rulers they constituted for the tribesmen the chief source of patronage, largesse and, most important of all, protection. They objected to being recast in an unfamiliar mould, and they expressed their objection in the way that they had always expressed it – by armed uprising.

Wisely the Colonial Office took the hint and accepted that any further interference with traditional and tribal institutions should be tempered with patience and discretion. It also accepted that, while the aggression from the Yemen was undoubtedly impelling the protectorate states towards some kind of association for purposes of mutual defence, any move towards a formal union would have to be made by the rulers of the states themselves, and the actual form of the union dictated by their own experience and traditions. Yet federation, even in prospect, automatically raised the question of Aden's continued status as a colony and its future relationship with the federated states. Any alteration in Aden's status, i.e. towards full self-government, depended in turn upon consideration of its place in existing British strategic calculations. The colony functioned as a staging post on the military air routes to Malaya, Australia and the Far East, as a dispersal point for V-bombers, and as an operational base and acclimatization area for troops who might have to be used in defence of British interests in the Persian Gulf. Too much was at stake, it was concluded in Whitehall in the spring of 1956, for direct British rule over Aden to be relinquished for some time to come. Lord Lloyd, the under-secretary of state for the colonies, visited Aden in May 1956 to announce the decision to the Aden legislature. 'For the foreseeable future', he told its members,

it would not be reasonable or sensible, or indeed in the interests of the Colony's inhabitants, for them to aspire to any aim beyond that of a considerable degree of internal self-government. . . . Her Majesty's Government wish to make it clear that the importance of Aden both strategically and economically within the Commonwealth is such that they cannot foresee the possibility of any fundamental relaxation of their responsibilities for the Colony.

It was as inept a decision as it was untimely. To quote one experienced observer:

As a statement of policy it was already verging on the unreal, for the planning of a federation of South Arabia was under way and was firmly fixed in many minds as the next stage of development. It was hardly possible that a federation could exist without Aden, and it was equally unlikely that Aden could remain a colony or constitutional advance be unduly delayed if it joined.*

Contrary to much that has been written on the subject, both at the time and since, there was no great opposition in Aden or the Western Protectorate to a merger of the two. The seeds of dissension lay rather in the differing views of the form the merger should take, the area it should embrace, and the distribu-

* Tom Little, *South Arabia*, p. 35.

tion of authority within it. To the protectorate rulers it seemed only right and natural that the federation should be a loose grouping, expressive of their interests, and over which they would wield ultimate power in association with leading merchant families of Aden. The external defence of the federation would remain Britain's responsibility for some years to come. To the radical nationalists of the Aden TUC, on the other hand, such a prospect was complete anathema. They wanted power for themselves, first of all in the colony, which they could only achieve legally through the enfranchisement of the transient Yemeni and protectorate-Arab proletariat, and later in the protectorate, which they could only obtain by the overthrow of the hereditary rulers. Ultimately, they wanted union with the Yemen, after the imam had been swept away and the country purged of the evils of theocratic rule by the tide of revolutionary Arab socialism.

Six of the states of the Western Protectorate combined in February 1959 to form the Federation of Arab Amirates of the South. Another half a dozen joined in the next three or four years, and the federation eventually numbered seventeen member states. A treaty of advice and protection was concluded at the same time with Britain, which made the defence of the federation and the conduct of its foreign affairs a British responsibility. The British government also undertook to provide the federation with financial aid, to improve social and economic conditions and to ensure internal security. Naturally the federation was at once condemned by devout anti-colonialists everywhere as a sinister device to keep South Arabia in subjection, as a means of perpetuating feudal rule by the hereditary sultans and amirs, as a barrier to Arab unity and as a crime against Arab nationalism. None of the criticism was particularly thoughtful or well-informed, but what it lacked in sagacity it more than made up for in vehemence, especially as voiced in Cairo and only slightly less so in left-wing circles in Britain. The latter particularly objected to the lack of any provision in the constitution of the new federation for popular elections to the federal legislature, membership in which was restricted to the rulers, their *naibs* (deputies) and their nominees. What the latter-day Rousseaus of the British political scene overlooked in their infatuation with the visionary figure of the noble democratic tribesman was that the federation had to build upon whatever political tradition was at hand; and the only basis of authority that existed in South Arabia, the only stabilizing element in a chronically unstable society, was the *daulah*. Far from being instruments of oppression, the *daulah*s were restrained in the arbitrary exercise of their power by custom and prescription, and by the tribesmen's ingrained contumacy. 'To anyone who has worked with South Arabian tribesmen', observed Kennedy Trevaskis, who was political agent for the Western Protectorate at this time,

it would be hard to imagine any people less amenable to authoritarian government or one upon whom any dictatorship could be less easily imposed. With bullets in their cartridge belts they had the most effective means of influencing their rulers and so long as tribalism persists and they have guns in their hands, they are unlikely to be converted to unintelligible principles of the ballot box and the majority vote.

The erection of the federation raised anew the twin issues of Aden's constitutional advance and its relationship to the federated protectorate states. Elections to the legislative council, where the number of elected seats had been raised from four to twelve, were held in the colony in 1959. Again, as in 1955, and for the same reasons, they were boycotted by the Aden TUC and its allies. There were only 21,554 registered voters in Aden, out of a population of some 180,000, and barely 5,000 of these voted. As the Aden Association was the only political organization to contest the election, it won eleven out of the twelve seats (the twelfth went to an independent). To mark its displeasure at this result the Aden TUC launched a series of strikes, which before the year was out had reached the impressive total of eighty-four. Within the TUC there was a running battle for influence between the Adenis, who held most of the key posts, and the leaders of the United National Front, who were a mixture of Adenis, Yemenis and protectorate Arabs. The contest between the two factions for influence over the Yemenis and protectorate Arabs who made up the largest part of the colony's labour force generated a progressive militancy, as each faction strove to outdo the other in protestations of devotion to Arab brotherhood, Arab socialism, Arab nationalism, and the goal of union with 'Mother Yemen'. (Interestingly enough, the theme of Yemeni unity was not echoed in the propaganda put out from Cairo, which habitually and deliberately referred to Aden and the protectorate as the 'Occupied Arab South', not as 'South Yemen'.) The growing militancy led inevitably to a boycott of the 1959 elections on the grounds that they were a worthless charade, a piece of British perfidy which denied participation in Aden's political life to brother Arabs from the Yemen and the protectorates.

Aden's constitutional development was being delayed as much by the colony's increasing strategic importance to Britain as it was by the tantrums and antics of the Aden TUC. The long-drawn-out terrorist campaign in Cyprus, which had recently ended with the grant of independence to the island, had cast a shadow of doubt over the usefulness of the British bases there. Kenya, where an alternative base had been developed, was to become independent within three or four years, which left Aden as the only British sovereign territory in the Middle East. On the eve of his departure in the autumn of 1960 to become political resident in the Persian Gulf, the governor of the colony, Sir William Luce, recommended to the Colonial Office that it grant Aden autonomy and allow it to negotiate its way into the Federation of Arab Amirates of the South. In Whitehall's eyes, however, the retention of British sovereignty over the colony was essential to the security of the base and the enhanced strategic role which was foreseen for it in the years ahead. The principal task of Luce's successor as governor, therefore, would be to devise a formula that would satisfy this requirement and at the same time provide Aden with both a further measure of self-government and a concrete link with the federation.

The imminent possibility of such a link, however, provoked a split in the leadership of the Aden Association and among its representatives in the legislature. While some members approved of the colony's merger in the federation, others were against it, preferring independence for Aden and a relationship with the Federation of South Arabia (as it was henceforth to be called) similar to that of Singapore with the Malayan Federation. It was not an arrangement that appealed to the federal rulers, who foresaw an independent Aden falling rapidly under the domination of the Yemeni 'street', which was bound subsequently to seek some kind of union with the Yemen, thereby outflanking the federation. At a constitutional conference held in London in the summer of 1961 their objections carried the day, and it was resolved that full self-government for Aden would be conditional upon its entering the federation.

A predictable outcry arose from the leaders of the Aden TUC who protested that the merger would subordinate the progressive, dynamic, modern and enlightened inhabitants of Aden to the arbitrary and archaic rule of the backward shaikhs and sultans of the protectorate. Before any merger took place, they declared, the wishes of the Adenis must be consulted, and this could only be done by holding free elections in which all Aden's residents, the 70,000–80,000 Yemenis included, would be entitled to vote. It was an argument destined to awaken an instinctive, sympathetic response in progressive political circles in Britain. The cry for Aden's separate development towards independence was echoed by British liberals and socialists with a fervour and vigour which must have astonished as much as it delighted the Adeni nationalists. For their goal was not and never had been an independent Aden. Abdullah al-Asnaj, the secretary-general of the Aden TUC, had himself publicly avowed in February and again in April 1960 that what they wanted was 'one nation, one Yemen and one struggle only. No North, no South, but one Yemen. No Legislative Council. No Federation ... There is only one Yemen, the occupied part of which must be liberated.' The Aden TUC had pledged itself to 'march forward towards our Arab Socialist Society and its unity and to free it of all means of exploitation and Colonialism'. Independence for Aden, then, like the professed reverence for the principle of free elections, was a sham. The only reason why the Aden radicals wanted free elections was to use them as a plebiscite in favour of Arab nationalism, to attract the attention and support of the world outside, and to hasten the end of colonial rule. Once independence had been attained, free elections would disappear, as they have disappeared in every Arab land, into a limbo from which they would never reappear. Moreover, as Sir Charles Johnston, the new governor of Aden, was later to point out:

It would have been a strange application of our principles to insist that the Adenese, being urban and relatively sophisticated, should be allowed to decide the question of merger by their own vote, while the inhabitants of the original Federation, although five times as numerous and no less vitally concerned, should not be consulted at all – presumably on the theory that as illiterate rifle-carrying tribesmen they somehow counted as second-class human beings.

No one, in fact, except the rump of the Aden Association, wanted independence for Aden alone. All knew that Aden was the natural leader of the federation: half the seats in the new federal legislature were allotted to it, and its wealth, its experience, its mercantile and technical resources, all ensured its eventual primacy. But for the young, frantically ambitious nationalists of Aden the idea of sharing power with the traditional rulers of the hinterland was abhorrent. They wanted power for themselves alone, securing it first in Aden through the diversionary campaign for the colony's independence, and afterwards in the protectorate, by calling in the Yemenis and Egyptians to crush the hereditary rulers. What was more, they wanted nothing to do with Britain, with British constitutional proposals, and least of all with British defensive guarantees. These sentiments only endeared them more to their champions among the British left, who were further gratified when the Aden TUC spawned a political party in 1962 with the pious title of the 'People's Socialist Party' (PSP) to fight for the colony's independence from British rule. What its sympathizers and apologists in Britain failed to grasp about the Aden TUC, however, was that it and the People's Socialist Party were one and the same thing, in leadership, membership and programme, and that its aims and methods were a long way removed from those of Transport House. Instead, they looked benignly upon the Aden TUC as something akin to the British trade union movement, and upon Abdullah al-Asnaj as a kind of fledgling Ernest Bevin. Two Labour members of Parliament, George Thomson and Robert Edwards, who accepted an invitation from the Aden TUC in June 1962 to ascertain for themselves the state of opinion in the colony about the merger, found themselves on arrival being paraded about Aden by their hosts and inveigled into making speeches to the Yemeni workers. They were then taken surreptitiously across the frontier into the Yemen to meet some exiled, nationalist 'patriots' – all without realizing that their presence was being advertised as evidence of the British Parliamentary Labour Party's support of the People's Socialist Party.

On 26 September 1962, against a background of riots and street demonstrations organized by the PSP, the Aden legislature voted for Aden's accession to the Federation of South Arabia. That same night in Sana, the capital of the Yemen, a group of army officers, financed, indoctrinated and armed by the Egyptians, overthrew the government of the imam and proclaimed a republic. The old Imam Ahmad had died a week previously, and his son and successor,

Muhammad ibn Ahmad al-Badr, had not yet properly grasped the reins of power. It was as well for the Colonial Office's plans that the vote on Aden's merger in the federation was taken when it was. 'If the Yemeni revolution had come one day earlier,' Sir Charles Johnston drily observed afterwards, 'or the Legislative Council vote one day later, I feel pretty certain that [the merger] would never have obtained the support of a majority of local members.' As it was, there were eruptions of violence and strikes in the colony as soon as the news of the revolution broke. The PSP threw off the mask of reasonableness and gleefully prophesied the coming of revolution to South Arabia, and the liquidation of all its enemies in Aden and the protectorates. Four of its leaders, exiles from the former imam's rule, flew off to Sana to become ministers in the republican government, and they were followed in the next few weeks by a stream of Yemenis in search of pickings and preferment from the 'new order' that was being established in the Yemen with the help of the Egyptian army.

From this moment forward the future of South Arabia depended upon the outcome of a contest between the British, on the one side, who were trying to integrate Aden with the federation and strengthen that body sufficiently to enable it to stand upon its own feet, and the Yemeni–Adeni nationalists, on the other, who were determined to bring Aden to its knees by chaos and bloodshed, and then, with Egyptian help, destroy the federal structure in the protectorate. Two conditions were vital to the federation's survival: one was adequate financial aid, the other was effective protection from its enemies, within and without. Neither was immediately forthcoming in the months following the formal inauguration of the Federation of South Arabia in January 1963, mainly because the Colonial Office was lulled into a torpid sense of security by the initial setbacks suffered by the Egyptians in the Yemen, and by the consequent dying down of disruptive activity by the PSP in Aden. Up-country, however, a new and more ominous insurgency was in the making.

Among the host of returning exiles, tribal freebooters and assorted desperadoes who streamed northwards from Aden and the protectorates into the Yemen after September 1962 were several bands of political *condottieri* from the various clandestine organizations which had come into existence in the colony and the hinterland over the previous few years. Generally speaking, their strength and consequence were in inverse proportion to the grandiloquence of the names they gave themselves, e.g. 'the Secret Organization of Free Officers and Soldiers' and 'the Revolutionary Organization of the Youth of Occupied South Yemen'. Not a great deal is known about them even now, and it is not likely that much more information on them will emerge in the future. All that one can reasonably say about them at this stage is that a number of the leading activists in them, who had decamped to the Yemen after the revolution, came together under Egyptian auspices at Sana in May and June 1963 to form the National Liberation Front for Occupied South Yemen.

Although the National Liberation Front was a coalition of some ten organizations of varying sizes and strengths, paramount influence within its leadership was exercised by the Aden branch of the Arab Nationalists' Movement. The Arab Nationalists' Movement (*harakat al-qawmiyyin al-arab*) had been founded by a group of Palestinian students at the American University of Beirut in the early 1950s. Its leaders were George Habash and Wadi Haddad. Among its non-Palestinian recruits, who, along with Habash and Haddad, were later to achieve international notoriety, were Hani al-Hindi, a Syrian, and Nayif Hawatima, a Jordanian. The ANM, which masqueraded in its initial phase as a literary club, was a secret society, organized in cells. Its numbers were never large, its members regarding themselves as an élite who would achieve their purposes by influencing Arab governments. Within a short time it had established cells in most of the Arab states, through the agency either of Palestinians who went to work abroad or of nationals from these states who came to study in Beirut and were recruited into the movement.

The ruling obsession of the movement, at least in its early stages, was the unification of the Arab lands, which the ANM believed to be the only efficacious remedy for the maladies that had so long afflicted the Arab peoples. Already, so its adherents asserted, the Arabs were united in spirit, but the Arab 'fatherland' was still broken up into artificial political units by the frontiers drawn by the former European imperial powers. To restore the Arab 'nation' to its former greatness required, among other measures, the attainment of four basic ends: the political integration of the Arab countries, the subjugation of the Zionist state of Israel, the eradication of Western imperialist influence from the Middle East, and the social and economic regeneration of the Arab peoples. In practice, most of the ANM's energy, or its propaganda at least, was directed towards the second of these aims. No distinction was made between the state of Israel and Jewry as a whole, or between Zionism as a politico-religious movement and Judaism as a religion. It was the duty of all Arabs, so the ANM zealots argued, to participate in a war of vengeance against Israel for her 'rape' of Palestine, and to confront her Jewish inhabitants eventually with a choice between expulsion and extermination.

Almost from the start the ANM pinned its faith and hopes for the fulfilment of its dreams upon Nasser. Nasserism, that elusive compound of Arabism, nationalism and Muslim exclusivism, became its guiding philosophy. It hotly and sometimes violently disputed the claims of the only other current pan-Arab movement of any significance, the Arab Baath (Resurrection) Socialist Party, to pronounce with authority upon matters of political faith and morals. There was an air of unreality about these doctrinal conflicts, for the formulations of the Baath's theorists in Damascus and elsewhere were as nebulous, and their abstractions as woolly, as those of the Nasserists and the ANM themselves. Perhaps the only feature worth remarking of the ANM's early years, in the light of the movement's later development, was its antipathy to the socialist element in the Baath's programme. While the ANM was prepared to accept *étatisme* on the Egyptian model, it refused to concede that 'Arab socialism' could achieve any substantial amelioration of the condition of the Arab masses. The union of Egypt and Syria in the United Arab Republic in 1958 and the overthrow of the Hashimite monarchy in Iraq later in the year, were hailed by the ANM as turning-points in Arab history. Rejoicing turned to dejection, however, when Iraq failed to seek unification with either Egypt or Syria, and to even greater dejection when the United Arab Republic broke up in 1961. The ANM's spirits were revived by the revolution in Yemen and the Egyptians' intervention in the civil war between republicans and royalists that followed. To the ideologues of the ANM the Yemeni revolution was the expression of a fundamental inter-Arab conflict transcending the frontiers of Yemen, between revolutionary and unitary Arab nationalism (of which Nasserism was the obvious manifestation) and reactionary Muslim integration (of which the Saudi Arabian regime was the personification). A republican victory in Yemen, it was believed, if accompanied by the expulsion of the British from South Arabia, would render inevitable the union of north and south Yemen. It was not a vision, as indicated earlier, that was necessarily shared by Nasser himself.

From 1960 onwards there developed a definite drift to the left within the ANM, a drift accelerated by the formation in 1964 of the Palestine Liberation Organization, which stole some of the ANM's thunder. A few of its radical theoreticians, notably Nayif Hawatima and the Lebanese Muhsin Ibrahim, began to argue that the movement's failure to achieve any real progress up to this time had been due to its insistence upon achieving its first three aims – the integration of the Arab states, the subjugation of Israel and the eradication of Western influence – before proceeding to the fourth aim, the social and economic regeneration of the Arab peoples. If unification were ever to be achieved, so the argument went, this theory of the 'separation of stages' would have to be abandoned, and the support of the Arab masses enlisted in the struggle. The ANM lacked a popular following, its membership being composed solely of intellectuals and quasi-intellectuals. To attract a mass following it would have to adopt the cause of the Arab masses against capitalism, feudalism and reaction. The overthrow of the traditional, conservative regimes in the Arab world would have to proceed side by side with the campaign to eliminate Zionism and imperialism. Habash and his associates were not convinced by the argument, nor did they accept that a mass movement was either desirable or necessary at this stage. To counter the influence of the Hawatima–Ibrahim faction, as well as to cock a snook at the PLO, Habash in May 1964 organized the Palestinian members of the ANM into the National

Front for the Liberation of Palestine. Thereafter the two wings of the ANM continued in uneasy harness until the outbreak of the Arab–Israeli war of June 1967.

A branch of the ANM had been set up in Aden in 1959, and by 1962 several of its members had secured a foothold in the trade unions, notably in the union controlling the workers at the British Petroleum refinery. Among them was Abdul Fattah Ismail al-Jaufi, a former schoolteacher from the Yemen who had been employed for a time by British Petroleum before being dismissed as a troublemaker. He and two other ANM activists in the trade unions, Mahmud Abdullah Ushaish and Muhammad Salih al-Aulaqi, were to figure prominently in the government of South Arabia after independence. There were ANM cells also in Aden College, where the sons of tribal leaders were educated, in the sultanate of Lahej and the Fadhli sultanate, and in two or three towns in the Hadramaut. The Lahej cell was headed by Qahtan Muhammad al-Shaabi, a former supporter of the South Arabian League who had been a dour and intense Arab nationalist since his student days at agricultural college in Khartum. His counterpart in the Fadhli sultanate was Salim Rubayyi Ali, who operated in the Abyan district.

Most of the Aden adherents of the ANM went north to the Yemen after September 1962, and it was they who were largely instrumental in creating the National Liberation Front of South Yemen. With the emergence of the NLF the struggle that had been joined in South Arabia not only intensified but it also underwent a marked transformation, broadening out from what had so far been almost exclusively urban agitation in Aden colony into widespread guerrilla warfare in the hinterland, a development which the NLF was later to claim was an adaptation of the Maoist strategy of the encirclement and investment of towns by rural insurgents. Whether it was or not, its objectives were unmistakable: to drive the British out of South Arabia altogether, and to destroy the traditional structure of authority in the protectorate, replacing it with a revolutionary political order.

For the opening of its campaign the NLF chose the Radfan mountain area in the amirate of Dhala. Here the tribes had an impressive reputation for insurgency and lawlessness, acquired through centuries of preying upon caravans and travellers passing along the Dhala road, which skirted the foothills of the Radfan on its way from Aden and Lahej to the Yemen frontier. The amir of Dhala exercised only a nominal suzerainty over the Radfan tribes: they were a law unto themselves, considering it their immutable right to raid at will and to levy tolls upon travellers and merchandise on the Dhala road in return for safe passage. Much to their indignation military measures were taken against them by the British authorities in 1961 to force them to give up these agreeable pastimes, and the tolls on the Dhala road were replaced by customs dues collected by the federal government. Angry and disconsolate, the Radfan tribesmen were only too ready to respond to the approaches made to them in the summer of 1963 by emissaries of the National Liberation Front. Hundreds of them slipped across the frontier into the Yemen to receive arms, money and instructions from the Egyptians. Returning with equal stealth, they prepared the ground for a full-scale uprising in the Radfan. On 14 October 1963 the first shots in the campaign of insurgency were fired.

Although in the years that followed the date 14 October 1963 was to be celebrated as the day on which the 'South Yemeni Revolution' began (the 'revolution' itself being styled, after the dreary fashion in such cases, 'the Movement of 14 October 1963'), there was little in the Radfan uprising to distinguish it from the other tribal outbreaks which were a familiar and enduring feature of the South Arabian landscape. While it may have been co-ordinated by a member of the NLF's political directorate, Ali Ahmad Nasir al-Bishi (whose identity was concealed behind the sobriquet of 'Ali Antar'), and while the tribesmen may have parroted some of the slogans about 'nationalism' and 'imperialism' which had been dinned into them, they were at heart inspired by their age-old passions and grievances – a hatred of authority, resentment of their poverty, a delight in fighting and a voracious appetite for plunder. Where the Radfan outburst was significant was in its revelation of the extent of money, arms and effort the Egyptians were prepared to expend to spread disaffection throughout the protectorates. The new governor of Aden and high commissioner of the federation, Sir Kennedy Trevaskis, who had succeeded Johnston in August 1963, grasped the import of this immediately. He had spent years in the Western Protectorate as a political officer, he knew what moved and disturbed the tribes, and he realized that the struggle for South Arabia's future would be decided in the protectorates. He put the issue squarely before the secretary of state for the colonies, Duncan Sandys, three months after becoming governor. If the campaign of subversion instigated and backed by Nasser was to be defeated, and the future of South Arabia to be decided by its own people, Trevaskis argued, Britain would have to cede sovereignty over Aden immediately and begin negotiations to confer independence upon South Arabia. British strategic interests could be protected, as in Cyprus, by the retention of sovereignty over the base areas.

Sandys accepted the recommendation *in toto*. It was the culmination of all that Trevaskis and his fellow political officers had aimed at and worked for over the previous decade, and, what is more, it was a remarkable act of far-sightedness, trust and generosity on the part of Sandys himself. If self-government and national independence were the true goals of the Adeni nationalists, their triumphant cries should have echoed from the walls of Crater to the mountains of Radfan. But although Abdullah al-Asnaj and his associates might have been willing to accept the decision (at least for the moment) if the choice had been theirs alone, they were no longer in control of events or even of themselves. During 1963 Asnaj had paid extensive visits to Cairo, where he had been instructed about the course of conduct he should follow, not only in the interests of the pan-Arab cause but also in conformity with the extensive propaganda campaign which had been launched earlier in the year by the professional anti-colonialist lobbies, both at the United Nations and in the capitals of Europe, to compel Britain to withdraw from South Arabia. So Sandys's decision was greeted by the PSP not with approval but a general strike. An attempt was also made upon Trevaskis's life in December as he was about to board an aircraft at Khormaksar airport, with the federal and Adeni delegations, to attend the constitutional conference being convened in London to fix a date for independence. The grenade that was intended to kill Trevaskis and his wife instead killed George Henderson, his deputy, and an Indian woman bystander.

As a result of the incident the plan to surrender sovereignty over Aden and to grant independence to the federation was shelved for the time being, and a state of emergency was declared in the colony. Henderson's assassin, a member of the PSP by the name of Khalifah Abdullah Hasan al-Khalifah, was put on trial in April 1964, but the case against him failed because the chief prosecution witness had conveniently gone off to Cairo. Khalifah was kept in detention, however, under the emergency regulations. Naturally the proclamation of the emergency was greeted by an orchestrated outcry from the usual quarters abroad, and a delegation of Labour MPs flew out from Britain in the new year as the guests of the PSP to protest against the detention of political prisoners and the suppression of civil rights. The MPs refused to accept Trevaskis's patient explanations that these were dangerous times, and that even a Nasser could not rule South Arabia without the power of preventive detention. (The Egyptian president could not even rule Egypt without it.) It was all too evident that the governor's knowledge and experience counted for nothing in the eyes of these newly minted authorities on Arabian affairs, although as he himself wryly reflected at the time, they were unlikely to allow him to tell them in return how to run the Union of Shop, Distributive, and Allied Workers.

By June 1964 the tribal uprising in the Radfan mountains had been crushed, after some hard campaigning by British and federal troops. The outcome of the campaign proved conclusively that, with determination and adequate military strength, such Egyptian-inspired tribal insurrections could be defeated. For, whatever myths have since been woven by the Marxist regime in Aden and its sympathizers abroad about the 'glorious beginnings' of the 'people's revolution' in the Radfan uprising of 14 October 1963, the fact is that the Radfan tribesmen were fought to a standstill and forced to sue for peace. It remained now for the British government to make plain its resolve to defeat every uprising that might occur in the protectorates in the same way. The calculated purpose behind the Federation of South Arabia had been to hold down the radical nationalists of Aden by the weight of the traditional rulers and tribal *daulah*s in the protectorates. With the Egyptians in the Yemen backing them with arms and money, the nationalists were able to extend their activities into the protectorates, making it all the more essential that Britain should strengthen the protectorate rulers and give them whatever military support they needed to defeat the nationalists and to cut their supply lines from the Yemen.

When the delayed constitutional conference convened in London in the summer of 1964 a date for independence for South Arabia, 1968, was fixed. It now became a race against time to make the federation strong enough to stand on its own feet when independence came. To do so required both a financial and a defensive commitment from Britain of a substantial kind. Whatever chance there may have been that a British government would commit itself to taking this hard road, however, faded from sight when the Labour party was returned to power in the general election of October 1964. Every pronouncement made by the Labour party on South Arabia before it assumed office had been marked by delusion and prejudice, and these two elements were to figure prominently in nearly every decision taken by the Labour government from 1964 onwards which affected the future of Aden and the protectorates. The party's doctrinal convictions about the evils of Western imperialism and the foreordained emergence of socialism in Asia and Africa had led it automatically to sympathize with the Aden nationalists from the start, seeing them as progressive social democrats anxious only to achieve national independence for Aden and social and economic justice for its people. The federal rulers, in contrast, were held to represent all that was abhorrent in the socialist creed – tradition, privilege, inheritance and absolutism. That these simple categories scarcely defined the tangled web of politics, religion and race in South Arabia did not seem to enter the minds of the Labour party's doctrinaires, or if it did, it troubled them little. For they had, without overmuch difficulty, come to the conclusion that the federation was nothing other than a device to perpetuate the rule of the hereditary sultans, shaikhs and amirs of the protectorates, to subordinate the interests of Aden to the latter's selfish ends, and to stifle the legitimate nationalist and socialist aspirations of the colony's radical politicians and trade unionists.

From the moment the Labour party came to power the fate of the Federation of South Arabia was sealed. The day before the general election in Britain elections had been held in Aden so that a new legislature with a fresh mandate could negotiate with the federation and with the British government for the transfer of power by 1968. As in the past, the nationalists demonstrated their attachment to the principle of free elections by boycotting them. On this occasion they had somewhat better grounds for doing so, as the electorate had been reduced from around 21,000 to 8,000 in an attempt to ensure the election of responsible candidates. Both the election and its outcome were a farce. The Aden Association had been in ruins since 1959, and the two parties which had emerged from the wreckage were still at daggers drawn over Aden's accession to the federation. Not only did the People's Socialist Party and the South

Arabian League hold raucous demonstrations in the streets, denouncing everything in sight, whether it be the legislative council or the governor or the
federation, but they were joined by the National Liberation Front, which
coolly represented itself as just another political party – something it was able
to do because its connexion with the campaign being waged in the protectorates
from the Yemen was as yet unknown to the British authorities. Despite the
nationalist parties' ostentatious boycott of the elections, several of their supporters stood as 'independent' candidates, winning seven out of the sixteen
seats in the legislature. One of them was the murderer, Khalifah Abdullah
Hasan al-Khalifah, who was still being held in gaol under the emergency
regulations. On his election a clamour immediately arose for his release.
Trevaskis refused to heed it, but the new colonial secretary, Anthony Greenwood, decided otherwise. It would be a gracious gesture of goodwill on the part
of the new Labour government, he thought, if Khalifah were to be set free. He
was, and promptly took his seat on the legislative council.

Aden, it was clear, had taken a long step backwards in its constitutional
development. There was little possibility that this regression could be halted in
the interval remaining before the date of independence. When that day came,
Trevaskis warned Greenwood, there would be three contenders for power in
South Arabia – the federal government, Nasser, and anarchy. The British
government had only two paths open to it: either to support the federal
government to the hilt or, in a phrase much in vogue in Labour circles in those
days, 'to come to terms with Nasser'. Greenwood thought he saw a third path –
'to come to terms' with the People's Socialist Party and its leader, Abdullah
al-Asnaj, in whom he discerned the lineaments of another Archbishop
Makarios. Believing, with sublime simplicity, that all Aden's troubles sprang
from its 'unnatural' alliance with the federation and from the 'unrepresenta-
tive' character of the Aden legislature, Greenwood set out to court the PSP and
the Aden TUC. Because Trevaskis had not the stomach for such a policy,
which he was certain would only result in victory for the third contender for
power, anarchy, he was sacked by Greenwood at the close of 1964. The colonial
secretary's foolish delusions about the reasonableness and devotion to democratic ideals of Asnaj and the other PSP leaders persisted for several months
afterwards, despite a barrage of insults and humiliations from the nationalists.
What Greenwood could not, or would not, grasp was that they had not the
slightest interest in peaceful and constitutional progress to independence or in
sharing power with the federal rulers. What they wanted was what they had
wanted all along – to destroy the authority of the rulers and the *daulah*s, and to
rule South Arabia themselves, whether as a separate state or in some form of
association with the Yemen. Furthermore, they were well aware that if their
rule was ever to receive the imprimatur of nationalist legitimacy from the
revolutionary Arab regimes, their coming to power would have to be preceded,
if not actually accomplished (for in these matters the appearance is all), by an

armed struggle, in accordance with the acknowledged canons of the anti-colonialist movement. From a practical viewpoint, too, harassment of the British was necessary to secure the continuance of Cairo's support in money and propaganda.

To some extent Asnaj and the PSP were driven to resort to greater violence by their need to compete with the National Liberation Front for the allegiance of the Aden 'street'. The NLF had instituted a campaign of terrorism in Aden in August 1964, and in the next twelve months it made considerable headway in recruiting followers not only among the labourers and artisans of the trade unions but also from the ranks of government servants, police, schoolteachers, office clerks and skilled tradesmen. Much of the NLF's appeal lay in its espousal and propagation of socialist beliefs, its insistence that the nationalist revolution to expel the British was only part of a wider social revolution which would destroy the power of the traditional ruling and merchant classes and pave the way for the emergence of the proletarian state. Whether the labourers from the protectorates who composed the NLF's principal constituency really appreciated the dialectical subtleties being strewn before them is highly doubtful; but they grasped only too well the opportunities for booty and blood-letting being offered them, and this was enough to win their allegiance.

The strongly revolutionary content of the NLF's propaganda in Aden was evidence of a growing rift in its leadership, which in turn was a reflection of the pressures being exerted upon it from several directions, not least from opposing factions within the Arab Nationalists' Movement. As has already been indicated, a conflict had been building up for some time within the movement between those who wanted to keep it an élite group, philosophically wedded to Nasserism, and those who, increasingly influenced by Marxist doctrines, wanted to seek mass support so as to accomplish a sweeping social revolution as well as the destruction of Israel and the elimination of Western influence from the Middle East. At a full-scale conference of the ANM in Beirut in May 1964, to which the NLF sent four delegates led by Qahtan al-Shaabi, the quarrel was brought into the open. Qahtan al-Shaabi's group sided with the Nasserist faction led by Habash, Haddad and al-Hindi, against the Marxist faction led by Muhsin Ibrahim and Hawatima, as much out of a concern to demonstrate their adherence to Nasserism and Nasser, who was, after all, the source of arms and funds for their struggle in South Arabia, as out of personal or political conviction. The NLF cells active in Aden and the protectorates, however, inclined the other way, towards the radical wing of the ANM, and the difference in outlook was made apparent at the first congress of the NLF held at Taiz in the Yemen in June 1965. Although the politburo set up by the congress to direct the NLF's campaign was dominated by Qahtan al-Shaabi and the Nasserite group, the political manifesto that was adopted reflected the influence of the NLF radicals. It declared, in the indigestible prose characteristic of such crypto-Marxist pronunciamentos:

The armed insurrection which has swept the South as an expression of the will of our Arab people and as the fundamental means of popular resistance to the colonialist presences, its interests, its bases, and its institutions of exploitation, does not only aim to expel the colonialists from the area. This revolutionary movement is the expression of a global conception of life which aims basically at the radical transformation of the social reality created by colonialism through all its concepts, values and social relations, which are founded on exploitation and tyranny, and to determine the type of life to which our people aspires and the type of relations which it wants to see installed on the local, regional, national and international levels.*

Whether this turgid stuff was intelligible to the labourer on the Aden docks or the up-country tribesman is highly improbable; but it was not really intended for their ears, except perhaps as a background chant to the acts of terrorism to which they were being exhorted. It was mainly designed to serve as ammunition in the propaganda battle which the NLF was fighting to discredit its ideological adversaries and to secure recognition (especially in Cairo, Damascus and Baghdad) as the sole, legitimate champion of Arab nationalism and revolution in South Arabia. Chief among these adversaries was Asnaj's People's Socialist Party, which in the spring of 1965 had decided to commit itself to a terrorist strategy in Aden and the hinterland, as much to compete with the NLF as to harry the British. Under Egyptian guidance and sponsorship the PSP combined with the South Arabian League in May 1965 to create the Organization for the Liberation of the Occupied South, a hybrid coalition of deposed sultans, politically progressive saiyids, and disaffected minor shaikhs and amirs from the protectorates, linked incongruously with the trade union rabble-rousers of Aden. Obviously it was destined to have a short life. To the NLF the new organization was nothing more than an alliance of 'bourgeois nationalists' – which was precisely why Nasser had been its *accoucheur*. For he was growing very tired of the costly and bloody struggle in the Yemen, now nearly three years old, and was anxiously searching for a way of reducing the scale of the Egyptian involvement. At Jiddah in late August 1965 he reached agreement with King Faisal of Saudi Arabia about the cessation of Saudi aid to the Yemeni royalists in exchange for a cease-fire between the royalists and the republicans and the withdrawal of Egyptian forces within twelve months. Having achieved this measure of disengagement, Nasser was determined not to be drawn into new commitments by the exuberance or miscalculations of the nationalist guerrillas in South Arabia. While wanting the terrorist campaign against the British to continue, indeed to be intensified, he also wanted it to be under his control. Hence the creation of the OLOS, with its headquarters in Cairo.

After its congress at Taiz in June and the public declaration of its aims, the NLF was banned by the government of Aden as a subversive organization. Up to this time the British authorities had known little about the movement, and

* Quoted in Fred Halliday, *Arabia without Sultans*, p. 194.

they were not destined to learn a great deal more about it in the next two years. Because the NLF dwelt a long way underground, its proscription by the Aden government did little to hamper its operations. The reaction in London to the formation of OLOS was one more of sorrow than of anger. Greenwood, the colonial secretary, still persisted in the pathetic fallacy that the PSP, the driving force in OLOS, could be coaxed back to the path of moderation. With this object in mind he invited Asnaj and his lieutenants to a conference in London in August 1965. The conference ended in disarray when Asnaj showed what he thought of the colonial secretary's Fabian forbearance by ostentatiously flying off to Cairo to take personal charge of OLOS's subversive operations. In Aden the nationalists celebrated the failure of the conference by murdering the speaker of the legislative assembly and the superintendent of police. Greenwood responded, again in a spirit of regret, by suspending Aden's constitution and reimposing direct rule upon the colony. The nationalists were delighted, for they saw the action as a further milestone on the road to ruin for the Federation of South Arabia. The federal rulers were correspondingly dismayed, for they interpreted Greenwood's action, rightly, as evidence of the Labour administration's underlying hostility to them and to the federation itself. Had it not been for this hostility, the British government might have adopted the only logical, if drastic, course open to it – now that it had barred any further constitutional advance for Aden in the form of transferring power to the colony's merchant classes – which was to surrender sovereignty over Aden (other than the base areas) immediately, hand over the colony to the federal government and leave the latter to impose an Arab solution in a night of long knives. Instead, by choosing to restore direct rule, the British government was saying that it and it alone would be responsible for the maintenance of law and order in Aden for an indefinite time to come. Since this required the suppression of nationalist-inspired terrorism, the British decision was tantamount, whether the government fully realized it or not, to a declaration of open war upon the nationalists, a war that would have to be fought through to the end.

In February 1966 the secretary of state for defence, Denis Healey, announced a sweeping revision of British defence policy which involved the severe reduction of British military commitments outside Europe, especially in the region east of Suez. Britain was to withdraw from Aden colony by the end of 1968 and to abandon all intention of retaining a base there. The treaties of protection with the states of the South Arabian Federation would be terminated at the same time, and since there was to be no British base at Aden no treaty of protection would be concluded with the federation. It was a total betrayal of all past undertakings, a betrayal of the trust placed in British steadfastness, a renunciation of an imperial power's recognized responsibilities to its subjects. It betrayed, among others, the traditional rulers of the protectorates, the moderate Arab citizens of Aden and the colony's religious and racial minorities, all of whom had been led to believe, by promises renewed many times over, that Britain would defend the federation from its enemies until it was strong enough to defend itself. By this abject abdication of responsibility the British government destroyed in an instant the basis of its authority in South Arabia; for there was no point in the Aden people's continuing to profess allegiance or even obedience to a government which, a few months after throwing down the gauntlet to the nationalists, was tremulously retrieving it. Who would now be so foolhardy as to co-operate with the British when in less than two years they would be gone, leaving the colony at the mercy of the more fanatical nationalists? What purpose was there in any further deliberations or negotiations over the transfer of power when the issue, as everyone knew, would be decided by force of arms? The shape of what was to come materialized quickly in the weeks following the statement on defence policy, when Aden suffered a spate of indiscriminate killings, including that of a woman tourist from a visiting ship. Terrorist incidents, which had risen from merely one in 1963 and 36 in 1964 to 286 in 1965, now rose to 480 in 1966, with the British security forces hampered in their campaign against the terrorists both by the lack of co-operation from the inhabitants, fearful of future retribution, and by the restrictions placed upon their efforts by the government in Britain, fearful of the strictures of the anti-colonialist lobby at home and abroad.

Nasser and the nationalists were jubilant over the British decision. It brought an immediate reversal of Nasser's previous aversion to any further involvement in South Arabia; for the impending British withdrawal placed a far more attractive strategic prize within his grasp than the rugged highlands and remote plateaux of the Yemen. The agreement he had reached with Faisal at Jiddah the previous August had allowed him to withdraw from north Yemen and to concentrate his forces in the Sana–Taiz–Hudaida box. It had also enabled him to reduce the strength of these forces, and the burden they imposed upon Egypt's finances, from a peak of 70,000 men in the autumn of 1965 to about 20,000 the succeeding May. The Jiddah agreement having served its purpose, Nasser now denounced it, declaring that Egyptian troops would remain in the Yemen for five years if necessary to ensure the 'liberation' of South Arabia. There was no question, however, of these troops being used in South Arabia while the British were still there: only after the British had departed would they assume an active role. In the meantime, to impress upon the British government the costliness of the British presence in South Arabia, perhaps even to hasten the day of its removal, Nasser decreed an intensification of the campaign of subversion.

To exercise greater control than hitherto over the campaign, and at the same time to create a more effective instrument of subversion, Nasser attempted to bring about an amalgamation of Asnaj's OLOS with Qahtan al-Shaabi's NLF.

The first step had been taken in January 1966 when some of the more pliable members of the NLF politburo had been flown to Cairo, there to announce their support of a merger of the OLOS with the NLF in the Front for the Liberation of South Yemen. The South Arabian League was more or less forced out of the new organization on the grounds of its being too 'bourgeois', even 'reactionary'. To win over the more militant factions in the NLF to the idea of a joint command under Egyptian guidance, Nasser enlisted the aid of some of the leaders of the Arab Nationalists' Movement. George Habash, Hani al-Hindi and Muhsin Ibrahim were flown down from Beirut to Taiz in March 1966 to preach to the unregenerate the message of brotherly love and the seemliness of expediency. They had only a fleeting impact. The NLF's suspicion that the Front for the Liberation of South Yemen was no more than a stalking-horse behind which the Egyptians were manoeuvring for eventual control of South Arabia was too deep-rooted to be dispelled by mere rhetoric. While he remained in Egypt Nasser might pose and be accepted as the paladin of Arab nationalism; but once he set foot in Arabia, armed and accoutred for war, as he had in the Yemen, he became in the eyes of the peninsula's inhabitants a Pharaonic figure, reviving memories of Egyptian conquests down the ages. So the alliance of the NLF with OLOS in FLOSY was never more than a paper one, and even this fragile link existed only because the NLF stood in need of Egyptian money and arms. The link snapped in November 1966, after months of bickering between the two groups and ideological and personal squabbles between opposing factions of the NLF. At the second congress of the NLF in June 1966 a number of rabid nationalists of distinctly Marxist complexion had been appointed to the politburo. They included Abdul Fattah Ismail, the spoiled pedagogue, who was directing the terrorist campaign in Aden, Salim Rubayyi Ali, who was in charge of subversion in the Abyan district, Ali Ahmad Nasir al-Bishi, the guerrilla commander in the Radfan, and Muhammad Ali Haitham, who was engaged in suborning Dathina tribesmen in the federal army. It was the influence of this faction in the NLF that brought about the final rupture with FLOSY, a rupture which the NLF ultras held to be inevitable since they were engaged as much in a socialist revolution as they were in a nationalist war of liberation. FLOSY was the enemy in the class struggle, the very embodiment, as the NLF ideologues phrased it, of 'the opportunist bourgeoisie, ready to compromise with imperialism and support neo-colonialism', while Abdullah al-Asnaj was categorized as a representative of the 'worker aristocracy denounced by Lenin'.

Having signified its intention to hand the Federation of South Arabia over to its enemies, the Labour government was now without a policy of any kind except to await the day of release at the close of 1968. It drifted about on a sea of vacillation, occasionally stirring itself to utter Pharisaical rebukes to the security authorities in Aden about their treatment of terrorists and the way in which they were attempting to suppress them. Naturally the only effect of such admonitions was to hamper the security authorities in their efforts, and to demoralize the federal rulers even further, thereby destroying whatever slight chance of survival the federation may have had. George Brown, the British foreign secretary, wrote cajoling letters to Nasser, appealing to his better nature for help in keeping the peace in South Arabia, while George Thomson, his minister of state, who had got on so well with the nationalists in 1962, flew backwards and forwards between London and Aden to try to salvage something from the wreck. The final ignominy occurred when the British government appealed for help to the United Nations Special Committee on Colonialism, a body whose malicious and mischievous interference in previous years had contributed not a little to the turmoil in South Arabia as well as to disturbances in other dependent British territories. In May 1963 the Special Committee had sent a commission to investigate conditions in Aden and to report upon the iniquities of British rule there. Refused admission to the colony, the commission had adjourned to Cairo, where it composed a report describing the situation in Aden as 'likely to threaten international peace and security'. The following autumn the UN General Assembly passed a resolution demanding self-determination for Aden (by means of elections based upon universal adult suffrage, regardless of origin), the release of political detainees, the rescinding of all emergency security measures, and the removal of the British base. (A few weeks later, it may be recalled, came the attempted assassination of the governor of Aden, and the killing of his deputy.)

These demands were repeated in a resolution of the General Assembly two years later, in November 1965, which further stipulated that the elections should be held under UN supervision. At the time of its adoption the resolution had been rejected by the British government as a gratuitous attempt to usurp its legal responsibility for South Arabia. By its decisions on future defence policy in February 1966, however, the British government had effectively abrogated this responsibility itself, and it confirmed the finality òf its act by subsequently urging the federal rulers to accept the UN resolution. Reluctantly they did so, in May 1966. If the nationalists had meant one syllable of all their ceaseless rhetoric about free elections, democratic rule and constitutional liberties, they would have done the same. They did not, for the reason that they were fighting for absolute victory over the rulers and the British, absolute control of South Arabia, and, in the case of the NLF, absolute rule by a Marxist politburo. Against such driving passions the tactics of conciliation were useless, and worse than useless. Constitutions, elections, civil liberties, entrenched safeguards – the nationalist fanatics disclaimed them all. It was futile even to discuss them, and worse than futile, for it served only to inflate the nationalists' contempt for those who discussed them.

Nevertheless, throughout 1966 and 1967 the British government persisted in its belief in the inevitable predominance of reason and moderation. In the autumn of 1966 the British ambassador to the United Nations, Lord Caradon, himself a veteran campaigner in the anti-colonial crusade, informed the General Assembly that his government now accepted the resolution of November 1965 *in toto*, and that it would be grateful if the General Assembly would consent to dispatch a mission to South Arabia to help effect the transition to independence. The mission, after a certain amount of delay, was duly appointed. It consisted of a Venezuelan, an Afghan, and a delegate from Mali, none of whom enjoyed a personal reputation for impartiality on the subject of European colonial rule. The proceedings of the mission brought some comic relief to the grim drama being played out in South Arabia. Arriving in Aden at the beginning of April 1967, the trio announced that they would not talk to the federal ministers but only to the nationalists, i.e. to the NLF and FLOSY. The latter, in their turn, refused to talk to the commissioners unless a number of impossible conditions were first met. FLOSY organized a general strike to make things more uncomfortable for the trio from the UN, and when the latter visited NLF and FLOSY terrorists held in Mansura prison, the terrorists heaped abuse upon them. Finally, when they were refused permission to broadcast over Aden radio and television a speech reviling the federation and refusing to recognize the legitimacy of the federal government, the commissioners departed in a huff for Geneva, five days after their arrival. Even this *opéra bouffe* episode, however, failed to deter the British government from continuing to solicit the mission's advice and assistance in the months to come.

Bereft of all ideas, the Cabinet sent Lord Shackleton, a minister without portfolio, out to Aden in the second week of April 1967 to seek enlightenment on the spot. He returned with the highly original suggestion that an effort should be made to bring the federal rulers, the moderate Adenis and the nationalist organizations together to work out an agreed programme for the peaceful attainment of independence. As the high commissioner and governor, Sir Richard Turnbull, who had succeeded Trevaskis some two years previously, refused to accept that such co-operation was possible, believing that the only practicable as well as proper alternative left was for Britain to throw her weight behind the federal government, it was decided to replace him.

The man chosen as his successor was a recently retired diplomatist, Sir Humphrey Trevelyan, whose service abroad had included spells as ambassador to Cairo, Baghdad and Moscow. Trevelyan arrived in Aden on 21 May and immediately issued a statement explaining how he viewed the task before him. The principal points he had to make were these:

Our purpose is to withdraw our military forces, as we have undertaken to do, and to bring into being an independent state with a stable and secure government.

We start from a position of support for the Federal Government which is the legal government of South Arabia and with which we shall work in close co-operation.

What we should like to achieve is a central caretaker government, broad-based and representing the whole of South Arabia.

Our central task is to ensure that South Arabia will come to independence under the best conditions possible and will be able to defend that independence and develop the economy for the benefit of the people.

Three years later, when he published his recollections of his service in the Middle East, Trevelyan revealed that his mission had been constructed upon much narrower premises than these remarks suggested. Although Britain was still publicly committed to remaining in South Arabia until the end of 1968, George Thomson, the minister of state at the Foreign Office, had gone to Aden in March and proposed to the federal rulers that the date of withdrawal be advanced to November 1967. If this were agreed to, Thomson said, a naval force, including an aircraft carrier, would be stationed in South Arabian waters for six months after independence to deter any attack upon the federation from the Yemen. The rulers refused to accept the proposal, demanding instead that independence should not be conceded before the spring of 1968, that it should be accompanied by a defence agreement, and that British troops should remain behind to carry out the agreement. A month later they were told by Lord Shackleton, when he came out to Aden, that their demands could not be met. All that could be conceded was a two-month delay in the date of withdrawal, to January 1968.

Small wonder, then, that Trevelyan in his memoirs infuses a sense of urgency into his account of his first few weeks in Aden. His brief, he says, was 'to evacuate the British Forces and their stores in peace, including the large Middle East Headquarters, and, if possible, to leave behind an independent government which could assure peace and stability in the tiny country of South Arabia, so poor and so ravaged by age-long tribal warfare and revolution'. Before he is half-a-dozen pages into his narrative Trevelyan has narrowed his aim still further. 'Our job was somehow to untie the knot and release ourselves without disaster.' He goes on to record his conviction that the Federation of South Arabia had been a failure, that Aden colony had been brought into the federation 'by methods which were dubious and widely criticised', and that what confronted him was 'not a strong and coherent nationalist movement but a prospect of anarchy'. What, then, was his prescription for these serious ills? Search though one may through his recollections, one can find little substantial discussion of suitable remedies. Instead, again and again, we are told that the high commissioner's overriding concern was to get the British troops out safely. 'We could not leave British troops to face the alternative of either being drawn into a civil war with an uncertain outcome or of sitting helplessly and dangerously while the place crumbled round them.' In brief, it would seem that Trevelyan saw his mission in terms of a rescue operation, something along the lines of the evacuation of Gallipoli in 1916 or the retreat from Burma in 1942.

Having determined upon a withdrawal from South Arabia by the end of the year, the Cabinet was momentarily embarrassed when, in the third week of May 1967, King Faisal of Saudi Arabia, who was in London on a state visit, expressed concern about the consequences that would follow a British withdrawal. If Britain pulled out of South Arabia altogether, Faisal warned the prime minister, Harold Wilson, at a meeting on 19 May, the Gulf would be subverted within months. Not only should British forces remain, he urged, but Britain should also enter into a binding military commitment to defend South Arabia against Egyptian-inspired nationalist attacks. It was an awkward, as well as unexpected, complication to have to cope with, especially as Britain had just completed the construction and equipment of a highly expensive air-defence system for the western region of Saudi Arabia, and could expect further valuable arms contracts to follow. To add to the Cabinet's predicament, it was confronted with the developing crisis between Egypt and Israel over the international status of the Straits of Tiran, an issue in which Saudi Arabia was more than peripherally involved. Some kind of response, however, was called for from the British government, whether with respect to its responsibilities in South Arabia, its interests in the Middle East, or its relations with Saudi Arabia. All that was forthcoming was temporizing, empty rhetoric and feeble compromises.

While indecision prevailed in London the NLF in South Arabia was growing bolder and more dangerous. Its break with FLOSY the previous November had cut it off from Egyptian support, and to finance itself it had resorted to armed robbery and extortion, particularly within the confines of Aden town. Merchants of substance and petty shopkeepers alike were robbed at gunpoint and forced under threat of death or maiming to hand over money and goods to the NLF gangs that infested the streets and alleys of Crater. The same means were used to force the inhabitants of Crater to shelter the terrorists in their homes and to conceal their whereabouts from the security forces. Violence was used indiscriminately – against the British, against the supporters of FLOSY, against innocent citizens, even against children. In the first six months there were nearly 1,500 incidents of terrorism, compared with less than 500 in the whole of 1966. The NLF was fairly certain that it had the British government on the run, and it interpreted the change of governor as confirmation of British irresolution. When, on Trevelyan's recommendation, the proscription imposed upon the organization two years earlier was lifted, the feeling of certainty became absolute conviction. Henceforth, so the leaders of the NLF reasoned, it would be a contest of wills between them and the British government, a contest which they had no intention of losing.

Then, in the first fortnight of June, it and FLOSY both suffered a crippling blow to their morale – the defeat of the Arab armies by Israel in the Six Day

War. Overnight the strategic circumstance which had dictated the pattern of politics in South Arabia for nearly five years, viz. the Egyptian presence in the Yemen, began to disintegrate. Here, if ever, was an opportunity for the British government to arrest the slide into chaos, to repudiate its earlier abdication of responsibility, and to restore the rule of law to South Arabia. An Egyptian withdrawal from the Yemen was now unavoidable, and any doubts on this score were removed at the Arab summit conferences at Khartum in August, when Nasser himself volunteered to reactivate his agreement with Faisal of two years earlier and to evacuate his troops from the Yemen without delay. He knew very well the constraints under which he now had to act: Egypt was defeated, bankrupt and shaken by internal unrest. Saudi Arabia, Kuwait and Libya had agreed to come to Nasser's rescue financially, with Saudi Arabia putting up the bulk of the money. Faisal had wanted the Egyptians out of the Yemen ever since they had arrived there, and he had no hesitation in making his financial aid to Nasser contingent upon a prompt Egyptian evacuation. With the Egyptians gone, the NLF and FLOSY would have lost their principal source of moral and material sustenance; for although the NLF had ceased to receive Egyptian subsidies, it was still procuring arms and supplies from the Egyptian army in the Yemen, paying for them with the proceeds of robbery and extortion in Aden. A collapse of the NLF and FLOSY would not automatically have followed an Egyptian withdrawal, especially as the NLF, pursuing its Maoist strategy in the protectorates, would have been able to continue guerrilla operations for some time to come. But at least a deferral of the date for Britain's departure from South Arabia, and a resolute statement of intent to defeat the terrorists, would have put some heart into the federal government and given it time in which to find and assert its authority.

As it was, the British government shied away from the chance it had been offered, preferring to keep on with the usual medley of half-measures and weak expedients. On 20 June the foreign secretary, George Brown, informed the House of Commons that the date of independence had been fixed as 9 January 1968, to coincide with the end of Ramadan, the month of fasting, in the current Muslim year (AH 1387). Additional arms and military aircraft would be supplied to the federal armed forces, and a British military mission would remain after independence to help with training and advice. To protect the country from external dangers during the first six months of its independence, Britain would keep a naval force, including an aircraft carrier, in South Arabian waters, and a force of Vulcan bombers at the RAF airfield on Masirah Island, off the coast of Oman. The strength of the Wilson administration's determination to quit Aden, come what may, can be measured by their refusal to allow the disaster to the Egyptian army in Sinai, and the Egyptian evacuation of the Yemen which was to follow that disaster, to influence their course of action. It can also be measured by the nature of the defensive obligations they were prepared to undertake towards South Arabia after independence, which, one suspected, had only been adopted as a sop to King Faisal's susceptibilities. The battle for South Arabia was being fought, and would continue to be fought, on the ground. While strikes by seaborne aircraft might make a limited contribution to the winning of such a battle in the hinterland (assuming that liaison and communications between the naval force and the federal troops were efficient – a very large assumption to make), they could hardly be used within Aden itself. Nor could the Vulcan bombers, whose function was predominantly that of strategic offence, be employed in the counter-insurgency campaign in South Arabia, indeed against anything less than a full-scale invasion of the country by a modern army, an extremely remote possibility, and one which, if it had ever materialized, would have removed the South Arabian question to another, more serious, dimension. What, in fact, the proposed defensive undertakings signified, when taken in conjunction with their limitation to a period of six months, was a desire to be rid of the troubles of South Arabia and to avoid the risk of being drawn into them again. Trevelyan, in his memoirs, states it plainly. 'If things went wrong, at least the ships could sail away, the aircraft could fly away and at worst we should look rather foolish.' Would that it had been so simple.

On the very day that Brown unfolded his proposals to the House of Commons they were being rendered more or less irrelevant by events in Aden. At the beginning of June the federal army and the federal guards (the *gendarmerie* which policed the protectorates) had been reorganized into the South Arabian Army and the South Arabian Police. The reorganization and the appointments and promotions which accompanied it had aroused strong tribal jealousies among the officers and other ranks in both forces, especially as tribesmen from the Aulaqi sultanates, which had traditionally supplied a high proportion of recruits, seemed to be particularly favoured. Feeling was also running high in both the army and the armed police over the Arab defeat by Israel, a defeat which Cairo and Sana Radios mendaciously and insistently proclaimed had been facilitated by British assistance to Israel. The armed police, and to a lesser extent the lower ranks of the army, had been partially penetrated by the NLF, so that the two forces, although still disciplined and competent, were becoming increasingly disturbed by the emotional tug-of-war created by their sympathy for the Arab nationalist cause, on the one side, and their fealty to their oath of service to the British and federal governments, on the other. Their mood was not improved by the deterioration of confidence between them and the British security forces brought about by nationalist propaganda and infiltration, or by the affront to their pride caused by the British Army's assumption of responsibility for internal security in Aden.

These several discontents came to a head with the nomination of an Aulaqi colonel of doubtful military ability to be the first Arab commander of the South Arabian Army. Four non-Aulaqi colonels protested directly to the federal minister of defence about the choice of commander, and were suspended from duty for acting improperly. A rumour that they had been arrested and dismissed sparked off a brief riot in the cantonments of the South Arabian Army on the morning of 20 June. The noise of the riot in turn alarmed a South Arabian Police detachment in a neighbouring barracks. Taking the sound of gunfire to mean that British troops were being used to subdue the rioters, the police detachment ran amok and fired on a passing British army vehicle, killing eight soldiers. Word of the mutiny quickly reached Crater, where a state of hysteria, brought on by the terrorists' campaign and mortification at the Israeli victory over the Arab armies, already reigned. The Aden police in Crater promptly threw in their lot with the mutineers and ambushed two patrols of the 1st Battalion, Royal Northumberland Fusiliers and the Queen's Dragoon Guards, who were responsible for security in Crater. A dozen British officers and men were killed, and further casualties were inflicted upon the troops sent in to try to recover the bodies of their slain comrades. When the day ended, a total of twenty-two British soldiers were dead and thirty-one more had been wounded, not in open battle but as a result of treachery.

Two courses were now open to the high commissioner. One was to let the federal forces – the South Arabian Army and the Armed Police – restore order in Crater, where the terrorists had come out into the streets and were in control of most of the town. At the request of the federal government, British troops had subdued the rioters and mutineers in the army cantonment and police barracks within hours, and they had done so with such disciplined skill and restraint that although they suffered a few casualties themselves they inflicted none upon the federal soldiers or police. So impressed were the latter by the forbearance shown them, and so smitten were they with remorse for what had occurred on 20 June, that they badly wanted a chance to redeem their honour and their reputation. Within Crater only a minority of the police (and they were mainly NLF sympathizers) had taken part in the slaying of the British troops. The majority, frightened and dismayed by the bloodshed, were still loyal. One Arab police officer had saved the life of a British soldier caught in an ambush, while another had recovered the bodies of the slain officers and men and handed them over to the British authorities. To rely upon the South Arabian Army and Police to recapture Crater with or without British assistance, was certainly a risk; but if one of Trevelyan's aims was, as he had said it was, to support and strengthen the federal authorities, it was a risk that was well worth taking.

The second course was to order the British Army to re-enter Crater immediately and reassert British authority. This would have been the most natural action to take, not only in military terms but also for the sake of the troops' morale. It was the course of action favoured by the overwhelming majority of the British officers and men in Aden, and notably by Lieutenant-Colonel Colin Mitchell, the commanding officer of the 1st Battalion, Argyll and Sutherland Highlanders, which was in the process of relieving the 1st Battalion, Royal

Northumberland Fusiliers. During the previous twenty years Mitchell had seen service with his battalion in Palestine, Korea, Cyprus, Kenya and Borneo. As a great deal of the 1st Argyll's campaigning had been concerned with the suppression of outbreaks of internal violence or guerrilla activities in British colonies and territories before and after independence, the battalion was probably the most experienced in the British Army in the mounting and maintenance of internal security operations. An officer and two men of the Argylls had been killed in the ambushes in Crater on 20 June, and Mitchell was understandably anxious to see that their deaths did not go unpunished. Though he knew little of the intricacies of the situation in Aden, he was convinced from past experience of similar disturbances that prompt, sharp and firm military action would not only succeed but it would also prevent worse bloodshed. He had no doubts that the Argylls would quickly gain the upper hand: the wail of the pipes alone, he predicted, would suffice to frighten 'a lot of third-rate, fly-blown terrorists and mutineers'.

Faced with these alternatives Trevelyan chose a third course – to stay out of Crater for the immediate future. He had an assortment of reasons for his decision. Though the federal ministers pressed him to be allowed to send in the South Arabian Army and Police to clear Crater, he did not feel he could entrust the town to them. 'The Khormaksar airport was in mortar range of Crater. We had to keep control of Crater to protect the evacuation.' The alternative of sending in the British Army did not appeal to him either: it would almost certainly alarm and provoke the South Arabian Army and Police, causing them either to mutiny or to fall apart. 'If they did,' Trevelyan solemnly avowed,

it would ... have meant our early withdrawal, the victory of the dissidents, the abandonment of most of our stores and, most important, a civil war and the probable massacre of many British still in an exposed position up country or in the Federal capital.

Consideration had also to be given to the probability of heavy casualties among the inhabitants of Crater if British troops had to fight their way into the town, and to the inevitable outcry this would arouse at the United Nations and other resorts where the arbiters of international morality are accustomed to congregate.

So Crater was left in the hands of the NLF and FLOSY gangs, who spent their days in hunting down and killing each other, when they were not robbing and abusing the frightened populace, while the police stood idly by. To Mitchell, as to many others, it appeared a 'fantastic, nightmarish situation, where in the middle of a British Colony in peacetime the rule of the Queen is abandoned. And worse,' as he noted bitterly, 'it was about to be condoned by Her Majesty's Government with twenty-two dead British soldiers to prove it.' It was, indeed, a most peculiar state of affairs, with the high commissioner apparently allowing his understandable anxiety for the safety of British soldiers

and officials in the protectorates to obscure what one might reasonably expect
to be the foremost duty of the governor of a British colony, viz. the protection
of the lives and property of the local population. So far as the inhabitants of
Crater were concerned, this meant their prompt liberation from the rule of the
terrorists who now held the town in their grip. While Trevelyan acknowledged
the necessity to recover control of Crater, his reason for doing so, as we have
seen, was to protect the eventual evacuation of the British forces from Aden.
Throughout his account of his governorship, in fact, he appears to subscribe to
a most unusual interpretation of the respective roles of diplomatist (or
governor) and soldier in conditions of limited warfare or civil insurrection. One
would have thought that the prime function of military forces in such conditions would have been to uphold the civil power and support it in its
endeavours to restore and maintain peace and security. Trevelyan, in contrast,
seems to consider that the diplomatist's (or governor's) first task is to rescue the
military forces from the very disorders they are sent to quell. It was not an
interpretation which commended itself to the British Army in Aden in 1967,
however much it may have accorded with the outlook of its political masters in
Britain.

On the night of 3 July the Argyll and Sutherland Highlanders re-entered
Crater, and by the early hours of the next morning they were in full command
of the town. There was only one casualty in the entire operation, a suspected
Arab terrorist. None of the inhabitants of Crater was injured, there was no
massacre of Britons up country, and the South Arabian Army and Police
neither mutinied nor disintegrated. All the dire predictions had proved false.
For the next four-and-a-half months the Argylls kept the peace in Crater so
effectively that the NLF and FLOSY terrorists went to ground or moved out
altogether. The Argylls received few thanks for their efforts. They had embarrassed their own government by recalling it to its duty and showing how it
should be performed, and for this Mitchell and his men were in due course to
suffer retribution. The Wilson administration, while shirking its responsibilities to its colonial subjects and flinching from its enemies in Arabia, could
be magnificently petty in its treatment of its own servants. When the list of
honours and awards for the Aden campaign was published Mitchell's name was
conspicuously absent; and in July 1968 the Ministry of Defence announced
that the Argylls, the original 'thin red line' of the British Army, were to be
disbanded as a regiment. Wilson himself, Shackleton and Trevelyan (who
received a barony as well), were all later to become Knights of the Garter, the
premier order of chivalry. The wheel, it would seem, had turned full circle
since the day when Lord Melbourne, the young Victoria's prime minister, had
quipped, 'I like the Garter; there is no damned merit in it.'

After the reoccupation of Crater Trevelyan urged the federal ministers to
grasp the reins of government more firmly, to initiate reforms, and to try to
broaden the basis of their government, perhaps by coming to terms with the

nationalists, the NLF and FLOSY. Though the ministers, most of whom were federal rulers, were reluctant to follow this advice, which was hardly surprising seeing that the two terrorist organizations were dedicated to their overthrow, they empowered the federal minister of information, Husain Ali Bayumi of Aden, to form a more broadly-based cabinet. He found the task well-nigh impossible, for the NLF and FLOSY threatened to kill anyone who co-operated with him. In the last week of July the federal ministers instructed Bayumi to abandon his efforts. For Trevelyan this was the last straw. 'Our attempt to strengthen the Federal Government had failed. We could do no more for them.'

All British troops had been withdrawn from the protectorate states by the end of June. Henceforth the federal rulers were to be left to fend for themselves, which was just as Trevelyan thought it should be.

We had no responsibility under the Treaties which we were unilaterally abrogating on independence, except to support the Rulers against attack from outside the country. Internal security was the Rulers' responsibility. . . . We had to stick to the decision to withdraw. We were not going to create a little Vietnam.

What is missing from this prim summation is any indication that towards the close of June the date of the final evacuation from Aden had been quietly advanced, on Trevelyan's recommendation, by two months, to 20 November 1967. Though Whitehall wanted the decision kept secret (on the grounds that its publication would hasten the disintegration of the federation), it leaked out within weeks, as Trevelyan had foreseen it would. He took a rather idiosyncratic view of the consequences of the disclosure. 'So we were able to put the dissidents on notice that they could not go on indulging in the luxury of shooting us and avoiding responsibility for much longer.'

Now that the NLF was certain that the British were really withdrawing and would not venture again into the interior, it opened its final offensive to topple the federal rulers. The offensive met with astonishing success. One after another, throughout the month of August, the protectorate states were overrun by the NLF guerrillas, until by the close of the month no fewer than twelve of the amirates and sultanates of the Western Protectorate were in NLF hands. To this day it is impossible, for want of detailed and reliable information, to account for the NLF's success. Several of the rulers were absent from their states at the time: some were in Geneva, at the request of the British government, to talk to the UN special mission (which was still wandering vaguely about); one was in hospital in London; another was in Saudi Arabia seeking support. The South Arabian Army refused to stir from its cantonments and outlying garrisons in the protectorate to help the federal government or its own rulers. It remained inert, presumably awaiting the call to a nobler destiny. Certainly it received no prodding to bestir itself from the higher British military and civil authorities, who seemed to be preoccupied with adhering to the timetable laid down for the army's assumption of duties from the British forces. Thus the hinterland was left to cope as best it might with the NLF guerrillas. When the young ruler of the Wahidi state returned from abroad and was flown up to his capital in a RAF helicopter, only to be abducted on landing and the helicopter pilot and a British army officer with him killed by insurgents, the British authorities in Aden did nothing. 'There was nothing we could do,' Trevelyan explained afterwards. 'We had left all that country and could not go back.'

With unnerving suddenness, the collapse of the federal rulers' authority in the Western Protectorate had brought the threat of chaos to the very doors of Aden. 'We now faced that situation which we had tried to avoid,' Trevelyan recalls.

There was no Government, only an army and civil servants with no authority over them. There was serious danger of anarchy. The British and Arab servants from the Federal capital [Al Ittihad, a few miles from Aden proper] urged an immediate British move. Everyone was looking to us. The NLF were not far from Aden and might at any moment take over the Federal capital.

The most obvious British move would have been for Trevelyan to take a firm grip on the situation and assert his dual authority as high commissioner of the Federation of South Arabia and governor of Aden to suppress disorder and rebellion and maintain peace and security in the protectorates and the colony. Trevelyan did not do so, presumably because it would have run counter to the spirit of his instructions and to the wishes of the government at home. He was also, it should be recalled, a diplomatist, not a colonial officer, and there was (as we shall have occasion to notice more fully later in connexion with the Gulf) a considerable difference in outlook between the British foreign and colonial services, the guiding spirit of the one being accommodation, that of the other, consolidation. So Trevelyan flew off instead to London at the beginning of September to talk to the foreign secretary. As a result of this consultation he announced on 5 September that, the federal government having ceased to function, he was prepared to recognize the NLF and FLOSY as representatives of the people of South Arabia and to discuss with them the transfer of sovereignty.

That same week the NLF openly set up headquarters at Zinjibar, about twenty-five miles up the coast from Aden, where Qahtan al-Shaabi called a press conference to announce his refusal of the high commissioner's offer of joint negotiations. He was ready, however, he said, to discuss the immediate handing over of power to the NLF as the sole representative of the South Arabian people. To back up his claim to paramountcy the NLF launched a fierce attack upon FLOSY's supporters in and around Aden. A pitched battle lasting several days took place at Shaikh Othman, a satellite town of Aden, in the first half of September, under the astonished gaze of British troops who had been instructed not to interfere. The FLOSY terrorists got the worst of the fight, despite the arrival of a thousand Yemenis to reinforce them, and they were only saved from complete defeat by the intervention of officers of the South Arabian Army who arranged a cease-fire. The affray at Shaikh Othman was the beginning of the end for FLOSY, and the start of what was to prove to be the fateful involvement of the South Arabian Army in the terrorists' struggle for supremacy.

For the next few weeks FLOSY and the NLF fought a hit-and-run campaign against each other while marshalling their forces for a final requital. It came in the first week of November, when the most savage encounters again took place at Shaikh Othman. At first, the South Arabian Army did nothing but hold the ring. Then, after the fighting had gone on for three days, it intervened on the side of the NLF to bring the conflict to a close. FLOSY was defeated and destroyed as a political movement, not so much by the arbitrament of war, for it had given as good an account of itself in conflict as had the NLF, as by the collapse of its logistics base in the Yemen. The government of Abdullah al-Sallal had fallen on 5 November and the Egyptians, who had underpinned both his regime and the activities of FLOSY, were packing their bags and leaving. Shorn of their support, the FLOSY organization fell to pieces. Its supporters in South Arabia were hunted down and killed or imprisoned, while those who escaped fled to the Yemen to join their exiled leaders.

Nothing now stood in the way of the NLF's ultimate triumph except the possibility that the British government might raise difficulties at the last moment. It was an extremely remote possibility, especially as the actions of the British authorities in Aden in the intervening weeks had seemed almost consciously directed towards facilitating the NLF's accession to power. When, for instance, the most redoubtable of all the federal rulers, Sharif Husain of Baihan, was reported to be gathering support from the Yemeni royalists and the Saudis to fight his way back into his amirate, which had been seized by the NLF with the aid of a battalion of the South Arabian Army, he was warned by the high commissioner that if he crossed into Baihan from the Yemen his force would be attacked by the RAF, since it was British policy to support the South Arabian Army, including the rogue battalion encamped in Baihan.

It was an incident almost beyond belief, yet Trevelyan in his recollections makes it all too comprehensible.

So we had come to threaten the use of British aircraft against an attempt by a man, who was still nominally under British protection, to recover his State by attacking from across the frontier the rebels who had usurped his power with the aid of a battalion which we were helping to pay and arm and which was still nominally under British command. We were right to do so. We could not compromise our main objective to leave in peace and leave the country at peace.

Again, some weeks later, after the bulk of the South Arabian Army had declared for the NLF and begun a purge of FLOSY adherents in its ranks, its commanders asked for RAF support against a FLOSY force raiding across the Yemen frontier. The British authorities obliged by ordering the RAF to strike at it.

Away to the east, in the three sultanates that made up the Eastern Protectorate, the NLF was also gaining the upper hand with disconcerting ease. None of the sultanates – the Qaiti and Kathiri sultanates of the Hadramaut and the sultanate of Qishn and Socotra, which also nominally embraced the Mahra country – had joined the Federation of South Arabia, either at its inception or subsequently. In the case of the two Hadrami sultanates the reasons were partly economic: their receipts from customs dues, a principal source of revenue, would have been reduced by being brought into conformity with the lower level of federal duties. Their hesitation, however, was also attributable to the distinctive character of the Hadramaut, to its relative isolation from the states of the Western Protectorate, and to its comparative immunity from intimidation by the Yemen (which had been primarily responsible for persuading the western states to federate). As for the Mahra sultanate, its nominal boundaries contained the wildest and most inaccessible region in southern Arabia. Only in the town of Qishn and among the scattered settlements along the coast was there any display of authority by the ruling sultan. Inland, among the tribal nomads and cultivators, a kind of formalized anarchy reigned. To have tried to bring this desolate, untamed land into the federation would have been futile. Yet although the Hadrami and Mahra sultanates were not members of the ill-fated federation, Britain still had residual obligations to them, arising from the treaties of protection which were now on the verge of being unilaterally abrogated. George Brown had recognized this in his statement on South Arabia on 20 June when he said that Britain would continue to pay for the upkeep of the Hadrami Bedouin Legion, which, together with the armed retainers of the individual sultans, was responsible for the preservation of security in the Hadramaut. The payment was to run for three years after independence, and would be conditional upon the sultans' agreeing to a system of joint command of the Legion and to its close co-operation with the South Arabian Army. In a forlorn attempt to induce the three sultans to join the moribund federation, Brown further stipulated that any financial aid that might be forthcoming from Britain would be channelled to them through the federal government.

It was all too little, too late and too hastily contrived. A network of NLF cells already existed throughout the Hadramaut and in the ranks of the Hadrami Bedouin Legion, and between late August and the middle of October, by means which are still obscure, the NLF's supporters took control of the principal towns along the coast and in the Wadi Hadramaut. The Qaiti and Kathiri sultans, who were out of the country at the time, found when they tried to return that their lives would be forfeit if they ventured to set foot in their former capitals. So they chose exile in Saudi Arabia instead. The sultan of Qishn and Socotra suffered a similar fate.

Throughout September and October, while the British Army tried to afford to the distracted populace of Aden the protection and security which it is the duty of any civilized government to afford its subjects, even those it is about to forsake, the representatives of the British government scurried backwards and forwards between FLOSY and the NLF, frantically trying to decide to which of these rival terrorist gangs they should transfer the symbols of authority and sovereignty over Aden. Their choice fell upon the NLF, even before the final defeat of FLOSY in the first week of November. The Foreign Office had expressed itself in favour of approaching the NLF as early as the beginning of September, when Trevelyan paid his flying visit to London. The high commissioner, it may be recalled, had recommended soon after his appointment that the proscription on the NLF as an illegal organization be lifted, especially as it was doubtful, he believed, that the NLF had any communist affiliations. The idea of handing over Aden to the NLF, which would automatically cancel the commitments made earlier to the federal government to keep air and naval forces in South Arabian waters for a period after independence, appealed to more than one member of the Cabinet. Richard Crossman, the lord president of the council and leader of the House of Commons, thought it 'first rate' and so, too, if he is to be believed, did other members of the Overseas Political and Defence Committee of the Cabinet. George Wigg, the paymaster general, and George Brown thought otherwise. To Wigg the impending abandonment of Aden was a 'disaster', a betrayal of everyone who had put his trust in Britain. Brown was unhappy that the plans he had put forward in June were to be scrapped, now that the federal government no longer existed. Yet despite this nagging sense of disquiet at leaving Aden in the condition it was in, he did not hold out against his colleagues and insist upon a reconsideration.

On 30 October the Cabinet confirmed the decision to evacuate Aden during November and to enter into negotiations with the NLF – if they could be enticed to the conference table – for the transfer of power. Crossman was delighted: 'Really we've been miraculously lucky in Aden – cancelling all our obligations and getting out without a British soldier being killed.' Trevelyan echoed the sentiments:

It was by this time obvious that we only had the choice to hand over to the NLF or to nobody. We were lucky in at last finding someone to whom we might be able to hand over in peace. . . . Our stores were all away. There was nothing to keep us. It was better for us to go as soon as possible.

On 2 November Brown announced the Cabinet's decision to the House of Commons. Its immediate effect in Aden was to provoke the final, bloody struggle for supremacy between FLOSY and the NLF already described. The victors, the NLF, promptly called upon Brown to name a place and date for discussions on the transfer of power. Brown proposed that talks should begin at Geneva on 16 November, and that the last British troops should leave Aden on the 22nd. This did not suit the NLF, who asked for a week's delay. Brown obliged. Further concessions were made during the talks which opened at Geneva on 22 November between a NLF delegation led by Qahtan al-Shaabi and including his cousin, Faisal Abdul Latif al-Shaabi, and Abdul Fattah Ismail al-Jaufi, and a British delegation led by Lord Shackleton. The islands of Kamran, Perim and Socotra were handed over to the NLF, even though Brown had wanted Perim to be internationalized to prevent it from being used to blockade the entrance to the Red Sea. A sum of £3 million in the treasury at Aden was made over to the NLF, with the promise of a further £12 million after independence. Despite protests from the NLF delegates, however, the Kuria Muria Islands, which had been administered from Aden ever since they had been granted to Queen Victoria by the sultan of Oman in the mid-nineteenth century, were returned to Omani authority.

Trevelyan left Aden on 28 November and the last British troops departed on the 29th. The next day Qahtan al-Shaabi and his delegation arrived from Geneva and the NLF entered upon its inheritance. 'It all happened', Trevelyan recalled afterwards, 'in perfect peace. . . . The local boys had made good. . . .' 'A wonderfully lucky and fortunate result', exulted Richard Crossman.

That the regime [we] backed should have been overthrown by terrorists and has forced our speedy withdrawal is nothing but good fortune. It now looks as though we shall get out of Aden without losing a British soldier, chaos will rule soon after we've gone, and there'll be one major commitment cut – thank God.

Sic transit imperium . . .

It is doubtful whether in the entire history of the British empire there has been such a shameful end to British rule over a colonial territory as the abandonment of Aden in November 1967. Yet it was not for the want of ability, experience or dedication on the part of the political agents, advisers and governors who served Britain in Aden and the protectorates in recent times that British rule in South Arabia foundered. Rather was it the lack of spirit and resolution on the part of politicians and officials in London. A sequence of remarkably able governors and high commissioners was appointed to Aden in the thirty years between 1937 and 1967 – Bernard Reilly, Tom Hickinbotham, William Luce, Charles Johnston, Kennedy Trevaskis and Richard Turnbull – and if their masters had been as true to them as they were to their commissions, nearly 130 years of British rule in Aden would not have terminated in the surrender of the colony into the hands of terrorists. Looking ahead at the end of his term as high commissioner in 1963, Charles Johnston commented tersely, 'Frankly, the main question-marks as I saw them were not in Aden but in London.' That Britain was not driven from Aden but elected to leave is confirmed by Humphrey Trevelyan's testimony. 'We left without glory but without disaster. Nor was it humiliation. For our withdrawal was the result not of military or political pressure but of our decision, right or wrong, to leave. . . .'

The fatal blow at the Federation of South Arabia was struck by the statement on defence policy of February 1966, which gave full rein to the Labour party's aversion to residual imperial responsibilities and overseas military commitments by reducing Britain's political and defence obligations east of Suez to a cipher. The architect of the policy of retrenchment and retreat, the secretary of state for defence, Denis Healey, was impenitent when Kennedy Trevaskis went to see him to protest against the decision to remove the British base from Aden at the end of 1968 and to default on the undertaking to conclude a defence treaty with the Federation of South Arabia after independence. The decision, Healey said, was irrevocable. 'Surely I must see', Trevaskis records of his conversation with the defence secretary, 'that to undertake a defence commitment which had only been proposed . . . as a complement to a British base would be nonsensical? I did not. I saw only a long line of Arab friends whom I, and others, had led up the garden path.' Colonel Colin Mitchell formed much the same opinion of Healey:

He was a shadow without substance. He had all the apparent qualities, the appearance and the methods of a statesman. But I suspected he was entirely dominated by his colleagues in the Socialist Cabinet and their useless dogma, later demonstrated by his series of utterly contradictory defence policies. There must have been a terrible cynicism in him to be party to the Labour government's fundamental allergy to monarchical institutions in the Middle East whilst having the intelligence to realise that the only long-term alternative was for South Arabia to look towards Egypt and Russia for support.

Much of the criticism of the hereditary rulers of South Arabia voiced in Britain in the decade up to 1967 was as uninformed as it was ill-intentioned. The sultans and amirs of the protectorate states, far from conforming to the standard caricature of them as avaricious, callous and feudal despots (albeit, also, effete, timorous and incompetent), were men of widely differing characters and abilities, ranging from the wise to the foolish, the enlightened to the backward, the able to the inept, the strong to the infirm, the noble to the disreputable. In this they were like the generality of mankind, including their own people. It was as pointless for their distant critics to rail against them for their defects as it was to deplore the existence of hereditary rule itself. South Arabia had never in its history developed any form of government beyond that of the sultan and his *daulah*. If the rule of the sultans was to be replaced, then it would have to be replaced by one equally, or even more, authoritarian; for the very nature of South Arabian society (primitive, violent, riven by tribal feuds) required the constant application of coercive power for its effective government. In the case of the hereditary rulers, this power was sanctioned by tradition, by tribal custom and by Islamic prescription. Lacking such sanctions, a revolutionary regime would have no recourse but to rely upon superior force to compel obedience to its decrees.

The campaign of denigration against the federal rulers was not confined to left-wing political circles and publications. It was carried on also, albeit more urbanely, in what were, by repute, the more responsible organs of the press. Much of the criticism was inspired by nothing more than a frivolous desire to be fashionable. In the shallowly cynical and infinitely knowing intellectual atmosphere of Britain in the 1960s all that was traditional, long established or revered was deemed fit only for mockery, contumely or relegation to oblivion. In an Arab world dominated by progressive, socialist regimes headed by dynamic and astute colonels, South Arabia, with its sultans, amirs and saiyids, its rifle-carrying tribesmen, British political officers and isolated up-country garrisons, was deemed hopelessly *démodé*, an anomalous survival from the nineteenth century. As Trevelyan put it in his memoirs, 'It was all very romantic in the old way'. Men who should have known better, ex-diplomatists and colonial officials, lent their voices to the orchestrated chorus of denunciation of the Federation of South Arabia, or joined in the modish chatter about the necessity for the termination of the *ancien régime* in Arabia, the inevitability – and hence the desirability – of a new political order, and the ineffable blessings which it was bound to confer upon the Arabs at large.

The collapse of the federation, and the abdication and flight of the protectorate rulers under the assaults of the NLF, were afterwards held up as ample vindication of all that had been said in condemnation of them. There was particular rejoicing among the British left, accompanied by sneers at the ease with which the federal rulers had been deposed and the rapidity with which they had fled their ancestral lands. Neither the satisfaction nor the sneers proceeded from any searching analysis or prolonged reflection. The deposition of rulers is not exactly a new or unusual occurrence in the Middle East or elsewhere, nor is flight from the certainty of death an unnatural human response. Even today, more than a decade afterwards, we are without reliable and adequate information about the sequence of events in the protectorates in the summer and autumn of 1967. What is certain is that the overthrow of the hereditary sultans and amirs was not accomplished by widespread popular revolution against their rule. Nothing in the character of this rule had altered for the worse in the years up to 1967, no sudden heightening of its severity had occurred such as to make it oppressive beyond endurance. It was not, in any case, in the make-up of the tribesmen of South Arabia to suffer misrule patiently. As Trevaskis summed it up: 'With bullets in their cartridge belts they had the most effective means of influencing their rulers.' The fact is that in these years the lot of the tribesmen had grown easier, with the provision of economic aid and technical services by Britain, improvements in agriculture, communications, health and education, and the application of pressure upon the more backward rulers by British advisers to reform their administrations. It was the very effectiveness of this interference, however well-intentioned, in conjunction with the amelioration of his material circumstances that was in large measure responsible for unsettling the ordinary tribesman. For innovations, especially those designed to curb his anarchical behaviour, were resented by him; while at the same time his predatory instincts were sharpened by the economic benefits which were beginning to accrue to him and his fellows.

In such a frame of mind the tribesman was, if not exactly ripe for sedition, at least highly vulnerable to nationalist propaganda, especially of the skilful kind broadcast from Cairo and, after 1962, from Sana and Taiz. The spread of this propaganda was greatly facilitated by the ubiquity of transistor radios throughout the protectorates, again the consequence of economic progress. Its success in arousing the tribesmen (as well as the proletariat and intellectual *sans-culottes* of Aden) was undeniable, and this success was seized upon by the federation's critics in the West, where the irresistibility of the advance of Arab nationalism was one of the pillars of the current political orthodoxy, as conclusive evidence of the essential rottenness of the whole federal structure and of the rulers in particular. Whether the tribesmen appreciated precisely what Arab nationalism was or meant is highly improbable. What they did understand was its appeal to their xenophobic and Muslim sentiments, and it was precisely these elements in Arab nationalist ideology that Egyptian and Yemeni propaganda was at pains to emphasize. It sought, by playing upon the tribesmen's Muslim prejudices, already excited by British interference in their accustomed ways, and by portraying the federal rulers as tools and allies of the infidel British, to condemn them as traitors to Islam. Needless to say, the propaganda was also charged with rancorous denunciations of the principle of hereditary and princely rule, coupled with vehement exhortations to the tribesmen to put their rulers to the sword and set up a people's republic in their place.

The contribution of the NLF to the coming *auto-da-fé* was to provoke the tribesmen's endemic blood-lust and avarice by harping upon the contrast between their comparative poverty and the wealth of the rulers and the more prosperous saiyids. That the NLF's incitements derived from a quasi-Marxist source was neither known, nor of any consequence, to the great body of the tribes. Their lives were lived by the blood-feud and the razzia; any pretext would serve for them to take up arms in pursuit of plunder and blood-letting. But what won them over to the NLF more than anything else was the quantity of arms and money supplied by the organization, which was far greater than anything the tribesmen had encountered before. Thus primed, they went on the rampage, and before they had time to discover that they had been manipulated, they had gone further than they had ever conceived of doing, disrupting the elementary but serviceable system of customs, prescriptions, loyalties and duties that had upheld the rough-and-ready political order in South Arabia for centuries, and plunging the country into a maelstrom of violence, the grim consequences of which they were themselves shortly to experience.

South Arabia swiftly slipped below the horizon of British interest after November 1967. There was little disposition on the part of the British government or people to be reminded of the disastrous end to British rule over Aden colony and protectorates, or of the fate to which they had consigned their erstwhile subjects and protégés. Some indication of the nature of the regime to which Britain had surrendered power in South Arabia can be gathered from the fact that within eighteen months of the British departure the population of Aden had shrunk from 220,000 to fewer than 80,000 souls. At least a further 100,000 people had fled the up-country areas to find refuge in Saudi Arabia and elsewhere; and in the next few years another 100,000 at least were to follow them. This mass flight was a crushing indictment of the new People's Republic of South Yemen, and one which gave the lie to all the easy assertions and glib sophistries uttered by the anti-colonialist lobby in Britain up to the end of 1967. Whatever view one takes of Britain's retreat from empire since 1945, it is impossible to avoid the sombre conclusion that Britain betrayed her trust and ran away from her responsibilities in South Arabia. Faced with a terrorist movement which was determined, ruthless and implacable, the British government of the day displayed none of these qualities in return. In a contest of wills it proved spineless.

It is, of course, needless to remark that the members of that government hardly viewed their conduct in this light. Remorse held little savour for them, least of all for Harold Wilson, who had few words to spare for the abandonment of Aden in his lengthy published recollections of his administration. And even in these few words he managed, by means of a parenthetical device, to convey the implication that the abandonment was actually something of an accomplishment. 'We announced that the final withdrawal from Aden would be in 1968. (It was, in fact, achieved in 1967.)'

CHAPTER II
The Retreat from the Gulf

Next year we are to bring the soldiers home
For lack of money, and it is all right.
Places they guarded, or kept orderly,
Must guard themselves, and keep themselves orderly.
We want the money for ourselves at home
Instead of working. And this is all right.

It's hard to say who wanted it to happen,
But now it's been decided nobody minds.
The places are a long way off, not here,
Which is all right, and from what we hear
The soldiers there only made trouble happen.
Next year we shall be easier in our minds.

Philip Larkin, *Homage to a Government*, 1969

On 30 October 1967, the day that the Cabinet confirmed the decision to quit Aden the following month, the minister of state at the Foreign Office, Goronwy Roberts, left London for the Gulf to inform the local rulers of the decision and to reassure them that it did not entail any similar abandonment of Britain's responsibilities in the Gulf. The reassurance was highly necessary, for the Gulf shaikhs had watched the development of the débâcle in Aden with mounting dismay and apprehension, being well aware that the principal justification offered by successive British governments for holding on to Aden had been that it was needed to underpin the British position in the Gulf and to enable Britain both to safeguard her considerable oil interests there and to honour her treaty commitments to the Gulf rulers. Some attempt had been made earlier in the year to dispel their misgivings. In April the secretary of state for defence, Denis Healey, had stated in the House of Commons: 'The Gulf is an area of such vital importance not only to the economy of Western Europe as a whole but also to world peace that it would be totally irresponsible for us to withdraw our forces from the area.' The statement was echoed by George Brown in the course of a debate in the House of Commons on 20 July.

In the present disturbed situation in the Middle East we must be particularly concerned about the stability and security of the Gulf area, for which we still have treaty responsibilities. . . . Our forces are not in the Persian Gulf simply to protect our oil interests as such, but to maintain stability in the area.

This was the burden of the message that Roberts took to the Gulf in the first fortnight of November. He visited the various Gulf shaikhdoms – Kuwait, Bahrain, Qatar and the Trucial States – and then went on to Tehran where he saw the shah and the Persian prime minister and foreign minister. After his final discussions on 13 November he gave a press conference at which he said firmly: 'Britain will stay in the Persian Gulf as long as necessary to maintain peace and stability, and the states on both sides of the Gulf understand and appreciate this policy.' The impression that this was the confirmed intention of the Labour administration was maintained through November and into December. On 8 November Healey had assured the House of Commons, 'We have formal treaty obligations to certain States in the Persian Gulf, and we intend to carry them out so long as they exist.' A month later, on 7 December, the prime minister, Harold Wilson, in reply to an inquiry in the House about what plans had been made for a withdrawal from the Gulf, referred the questioner to Brown's statement of policy on 20 July. He went on to say: 'I do not think that there is anything that can be added at this stage to what was said . . . last July. There has been no change in the situation since then.'

But there *had* been a change in the situation, of quite remarkable proportions, only the previous month, when Britain's deteriorating economic condition had precipitated a crisis of confidence in sterling. The deficit in Britain's overseas trading account had grown alarmingly great, leading to a run on the pound and a rapid dwindling of the country's foreign currency reserves in an effort to halt the run. It was palpably evident that sterling would have to be devalued and that an application would have to be made to the International Monetary Fund for a loan to halt Britain's slide into bankruptcy. The devaluation of sterling (from $2.80 to $2.40 to the £) was announced on 18 November, and the Cabinet at the same time began the task of deciding upon the cuts that would have to be made in public expenditure to meet the conditions of the IMF loan. The chancellor of the exchequer, James Callaghan, resigned on 30 November and Roy Jenkins, the home secretary, was appointed in his place. Jenkins calculated that some £850 million would have to be taken out of the economy in the form of additional taxation and a reduction in public expenditure, if some semblance of financial equilibrium was to be restored. At once the Cabinet fell to bickering over where the cuts in public expenditure should fall, the arguments and the haggling being destined to continue throughout December and into January.

For the left wing of the Labour party and their adherents in the Cabinet any reduction of expenditure upon the social services was anathema. When Jenkins proposed that savings in expenditure upon education and health services might be achieved by postponing the planned raising of the school-leaving age and by reimposing charges for medical prescriptions, the left-wing members of the Cabinet were outraged by what appeared to them a betrayal of socialism. If expenditure upon the social services was to be pruned, then, they demanded, there must be even greater economies than those already tentatively suggested in areas which were equally anathema to them – defence and overseas commitments. The bargain within the Cabinet was struck at a meeting on 4 January 1968. The concurrence of the left in the trimming of expenditure on the social services was bought by the abandonment of Britain's defence commitments in the Far East and the Persian Gulf, and by the cancellation of the intended purchase for the Royal Air Force of F-111 military aircraft from the United States. (Richard Crossman, and, if he is to be believed, others in the Cabinet, wanted to go further and abandon the British independent nuclear deterrent as well.) Only the question of timing delayed the sealing of the bargain. Those on the left, naturally, wanted the withdrawal from east of Suez to take place as soon as possible, but in any case before the next parliamentary general election, which had to be held by March 1971 at the latest. The more responsible members of the Cabinet held out for as long an interval as possible before the withdrawal was complete. Eventually the two sides agreed upon March 1971.

Now those countries and governments affected by the decision had to be consulted – or, rather, informed – about it before it was made public. George Brown flew off to Japan and the United States; George Thomson, now secretary of state for Commonwealth relations, left for Malaysia, Australia and New Zealand; while Goronwy Roberts set off again for the Gulf, to tell the rulers that Her Majesty's government had had a new inspiration. He saw the shah in Tehran on 7 January, the principal Trucial Shaikhs on 9 January, and King Faisal in Riyad on 10 January. Financial stringency, he explained to each and all, now compelled Her Majesty's government to rescind the assurances he had given them only two months previously about the continued maintenance of a British military and naval presence in the Gulf to fulfil Britain's treaty obligations and to help preserve peace and stability in the area. The explanation was received with scepticism. The sum required in non-sterling currency for the upkeep of the British forces in the Gulf was some £12 million per annum. It was a sum of almost paltry proportions when set against the value of British oil investments in the Gulf region and the annual return received upon those investments by the British companies concerned and by the British exchequer. Nor, if economy were the order of the day, need Britain even continue to find the money. The shaikh of Abu Dhabi, Zayid ibn Sultan, told Roberts that he would be happy to contribute the funds himself from his oil revenues to secure the continuance of the benefits he and his fellow rulers derived from the British presence in the Gulf. His neighbour, Shaikh Rashid ibn Said of Dubai, made a like proposal a fortnight later. The four oil-producing shaikhdoms under

British protection – Dubai, Abu Dhabi, Bahrain and Qatar – would be per-fectly willing, Rashid said, to meet, in proportion to their respective means, the annual cost of retaining the British forces in the Gulf.

Roberts's report on his travels was conveyed to the Cabinet on 12 January. By this time George Brown had returned from the United States where, he informed his colleagues, the news of the British decision had been received (so Crossman noted sardonically) with 'horror and consternation'. It was not so much the effect that the withdrawal might have in the Far East, where American power was so much greater than that of Britain, that made the Americans apprehensive, as the possible repercussions in the Gulf. Although Brown had told the Americans that to remain in the Gulf after withdrawing from Singapore and Malaysia would involve Britain in 'colossal expense', nevertheless he strongly advised the Cabinet to put back the withdrawal from the Gulf by at least a year. That same week Lee Kuan Yew, the prime minister of Singapore, alarmed by the news George Thomson had brought, flew to London to urge the Cabinet to reconsider the whole decision. On 15 January some members of the Cabinet made an effort to have the decision reversed, but all they achieved was a concession, tossed out by the prime minister, to extend the terminal date for the withdrawal to December 1971. The next day Wilson broke the news of his government's intention to Parliament.

The trivial considerations and shabby horse-trading that went into the making of the decision, so far-reaching in its foreseeable consequences, to withdraw from east of Suez are still a cause for wonder, even in an age which has afforded so many examples of wretched incapacity on the part of British governments. It was given out at the time that financial necessity, occasioned by the flight from sterling and the widening balance-of-payments deficit, was the overriding reason for the decision. But the financial crisis that arose in the final months of 1967 had been brought on in no small measure by the partial reduction in oil supplies from the Gulf during the Arab–Israeli war in June. Instead of heeding the warning, the Wilson government, with that peculiar logic it was so often to display in its conduct of domestic and foreign affairs, now proposed to make it easier for oil supplies to be cut off in the future at the whim of Arab governments by relinquishing whatever control Britain might have exerted over them through her presence in the Gulf. Moreover, whatever dubious merits the argument for withdrawal on the grounds of financial stringency might possess, they were nullified by the offers made by the shaikhs of Abu Dhabi and Dubai. Yet the Labour government not only brushed these offers aside but it also managed to be boorish in the manner of its refusal. Asked in a television interview in late January why the offers had not been taken up, Denis Healey retorted that he was not 'a sort of white slaver for Arab shaikhs'. 'It would be a very great mistake', he went on, 'if we allowed ourselves to become mercenaries for people who like to have British troops around.' Strangely enough a like sensitivity was not evinced in the case of contributions from either the West German government towards the cost of supporting the British Army of the Rhine, or the government of Hong Kong towards the maintenance of the colony's British garrison. Healey's gratuitously offensive remarks were also an odd way of rewarding the Gulf oil shaikhs for their loyalty in retaining their sterling deposits in London throughout the financial crisis in the autumn of 1967. It was a loyalty which cost them dearly when sterling was devalued without advance warning. Bahrain alone, which could least afford a loss, suffered a fall in the value of her holdings of £2.5 million.

Afterwards, in his memoirs, Harold Wilson was pleased to describe the 'package' of proposals adopted by his Cabinet in January 1968 as having 'as a whole . . . an impressive integrity and balance'. 'Integrity' seems a singularly inapt word to apply to the planned repudiation of solemn treaty engagements and defence commitments. It has even less applicability to the series of shabby manoeuvres that attended the assembly of this 'package' and which were later to become public knowledge through the publication of Richard Crossman's diaries. Though the diaries must be approached with circumspection, they are nevertheless an intimate record of the way in which the Labour Cabinet dealt with great affairs of state, at home and abroad, in the weeks that elapsed between the onset of the sterling crisis in October and the fateful decision-taking of the following January. Here, it is clear, was no searching and far-reaching analysis of Britain's foreign, imperial and defence policies, with all their grave implications and perilous imponderables, but an unseemly squabble among ministers of the Crown for private advantage, factional ascendancy and ideological or financial priority. Every consideration, it would seem, was subordinated to the narrow interests of party and doctrine, and the fate and consequence of Britain in the world was made to revolve around such mighty issues as whether or not the reimposition of medical prescription charges would be a blot upon the name of British socialism.

For a time after the announcement that British forces were to be withdrawn from the Gulf some uncertainty prevailed as to whether the withdrawal automatically meant the termination of Britain's treaties with the Gulf shaikhdoms. Shaikh Rashid of Dubai publicly complained in late January that although he, along with the rulers of Bahrain and Qatar, had asked for clarification on this score, he had so far received none. Britain's legal position in the Gulf rested upon the trucial system and the special treaty relationship with Bahrain, Qatar and the seven shaikhdoms of the Trucial Coast. The trucial system had its beginnings in the first half of the nineteenth century when Britain, in an effort to stamp out piracy and maritime warfare in the Gulf, persuaded the ruling shaikhs of the principal tribes dwelling along the southern shore of the Gulf from Abu Dhabi to Ras al-Khaimah to observe a truce among themselves at sea during the months of the annual pearl fishing, the tribes' principal source of income. In return Britain undertook to police the truce and to maintain the maritime peace of the Gulf. The truce was extended in stages until 1853 when it was made permanent. Eight years later Bahrain, which had been excluded from the trucial agreements because of conflicting claims to suzerainty over the shaikhdom by the Persians, Turks, Egyptians and Saudis, was brought within the scope of the agreements and her independence recognized and guaranteed by the British government. During the first half of the century a series of agreements was also concluded with the Trucial Shaikhdoms and Bahrain, as well as with the sultan of Oman and the governments of Persia and Turkey, for the suppression of the slave trade in the Gulf.

In the 1880s and 1890s Bahrain and the Trucial Shaikhdoms entered into further engagements requiring them not to alienate any portion of their territories to other powers, and to place the conduct of their foreign relations in the hands of the British government. An undertaking along similar lines was given by the shaikh of Kuwait in 1899, and shortly after the outbreak of war between Britain and the Ottoman empire in November 1914 the shaikhdom was formally taken under British protection. The war was also responsible for the integration of Qatar into the trucial system: in 1916 the ruling Al Thani shaikh subscribed to the various undertakings which had earlier been given by Bahrain and the Trucial Shaikhdoms, and in return he was assured of the defence of his territories against attack by sea. A final series of engagements, covering the arms traffic, the grant of oil and other concessions, and the exercise of extra-territorial jurisdiction by Britain, was concluded with the various shaikhdoms in the early decades of this century.

At the heart of the trucial system lay an obligation upon Britain not merely to maintain the maritime peace of the Gulf but also to preserve the independence and territorial integrity of the shaikhdoms which subscribed to the truce. Without the existence of such an obligation there would have been no justification for the restrictive engagements which Britain had taken from them regarding the slave trade, the arms traffic, the conduct of their foreign affairs and the grant of oil concessions. The obligation had been made explicit in the case of Bahrain because the shaikhdom's frontiers were defined by the sea and could therefore be defended by naval means. A similar explicit undertaking, as just mentioned, had been given with respect to the maritime frontiers of Qatar, but not with regard to its landward frontiers, the limits of which were undetermined when the treaty of 1916 was concluded.

No such formal guarantee had been extended to the Trucial Shaikhdoms of the lower Gulf, primarily because such a guarantee would have been counter to the principle upon which British policy in the Gulf in the nineteenth century was based, that of non-intervention in the affairs of the Arabian mainland. In any case, the absence until well into this century of any firm notion of where the inland frontiers of the shaikhdoms lay would have made such a guarantee unrealistic. At the same time, however, it was acknowledged that an implicit responsibility for the defence of the shaikhdoms against external aggression devolved upon the British government as a consequence of the relationship it had established with the shaikhdoms through the trucial system and subsequent engagements. Though unsanctioned by treaty, the commitment existed, and its existence was never denied. It was embodied only once in a formal undertaking, in 1952, when for reasons of local politics which need not detain us here a promise of protection was given to the ruler of Fujairah, the only one of the seven Trucial Shaikhdoms which did not lie within the Gulf proper but faced upon the Gulf of Oman.

Kuwait was the sole shaikhdom along the Arabian shore of the Gulf whose frontiers had been the subject of international agreement and definition, and the defence of these frontiers by Britain was covered by the assurance of protection given in the agreement of November 1914. With the discovery and exploitation of Kuwait's great reserves of oil in later years, the shaikhdom rapidly outgrew its status as a British-protected principality, and in 1961 the agreements of 1899 and 1914 were terminated by mutual consent. Kuwait became wholly independent, and the only vestige of her former treaty relationship that remained was a provision in the instrument of abrogation which required Britain to give friendly consideration to any future request for aid from the shaikhdom. Kuwait's wealth, the size of her population and the international recognition accorded her all made her transition to independence untroubled as well as inevitable. The transition was aided also by the fact that Kuwait had never been included in the trucial system, nor had her relationship with Britain been as intimate or as long-standing as that of Bahrain and the Trucial Shaikhdoms. So far as Kuwait was concerned, therefore, Britain was under no active obligation in January 1968, as a consequence either of past undertakings or of established policy, to protect the shaikhdom against external aggression. It was a different case with the Trucial Shaikhdoms, Qatar and Bahrain, and it was the question of their continued protection that lay at the heart of the inquiry from the rulers of Dubai, Bahrain and Qatar in January 1968 whether or not Britain's military withdrawal from the Gulf also implied the dismantling of the existing treaty structure.

An answer of sorts was given the following month when the Foreign Office suggested to these rulers that they should combine with the other lower Gulf rulers in a federation which would make the passage to independence easier, and at the same time afford them some measure of mutual protection. Despite the all-too-recent and unhappy example of the Federation of South Arabia, the rulers of Bahrain, Qatar and the Trucial Shaikhdoms signed an agreement on 27 February 1968 to establish a Federation of Arab Emirates. (The change of designation from 'shaikhdoms' to 'emirates' was presumably intended to bolster their morale and endow the embryonic federation with a little more consequence.) The agreement, which was supposed to take effect on 30 March 1968, was as yet nothing more than a hesitant statement of intent, a restrained

avowal of hope rather than a *fait accompli*. It was enough, however, to excite the
feelings of the shah of Persia, who was already nervous about suggestions that
had been floating around in the British and American press about a possible
regional security pact between the major local powers, perhaps supported by
Turkey and Pakistan, to preserve the peace of the Gulf after Britain's departure. On 27 January the Persian prime minister, Amin Abbas Hoveida, had
declared:

As the most powerful nation in the northern coast of the Persian Gulf, Iran is naturally
very much interested in the security and stability of this area. The Imperial Government
can protect, with the utmost power, its interests and rights in the Persian Gulf and will
not permit any country outside the region to interfere ... Britain's exit from one door
must not result in America's entrance from the other door – or in British re-entry in a
new form.

Much the same view was expressed by the Russian government in a statement
published in *Tass* on 3 March:

The Soviet Union, loyal to its policy of protecting the national interests of sovereign
countries and peoples against the encroachments of imperialists, and realising that these
plans of neo-colonialism are directed against the security of the southern frontiers of the
USSR as well, comes out resolutely against the new attempts by aggressive circles in
the United States and Britain to interfere in the affairs of the countries in the area of the
Persian Gulf, and to dictate their will to those countries.

Encouraged by this selfless assurance, Muhammad Reza Shah breathed a
measure of fire in the second week of March, on the occasion of the inauguration of work on a new steel mill at Ispahan which was to be constructed with
Russian assistance: 'I warn our current friends, the British and Americans,
that if they do not respect all the interests of Iran, especially its interests in the
Persian Gulf, they must expect that we will treat theirs in kind.' Two months
later he was still complaining about the projected Federation of Arab Emirates,
calling it 'a colonialist and imperialist manipulation and an attempt by Britain
to come back through the back door after announcing plans to withdraw from
east of Suez by 1971'.

What was really arousing the shah's ire was the inclusion of Bahrain in the
new federation and the tacit ignoring of Persia's long-standing claim to
sovereignty over the island. The claim itself had a very dubious foundation,
deriving from Bahrain's occasional submission to provincial governors in
southern Persia from the seventeenth to the late eighteenth century, and from
the spasmodic attempts of Persian officials in the nineteenth century to make
good the Persian government's pretensions. The British government had never
recognized the claim as having any validity, and it was repeatedly rejected by
the ruling dynasty of Bahrain, the Al Khalifah, who had conquered the island
in 1783 and ruled it uninterruptedly ever since. Despite their inability to

substantiate the claim on legal or historical grounds, and their even greater inability to enforce it, the Persians had persisted with it as a matter of *amour propre*. Appearance being all in such matters, Muhammad Reza Shah had kept up the performance since he came to the throne during the Second World War. Bahrain was regularly listed in official publications as a province of the Persian empire, legislation purporting to apply to it was solemnly enacted by the Persian parliament, or *majlis*, and diplomatic protests were frequently voiced against supposed violations, especially by Britain, of Persia's sovereign rights in Bahrain. Thus it hardly came as a surprise when, less than a fortnight after the shah's speech at Ispahan, the Persian claim to Bahrain was formally reasserted in a note to the British government.

Over the next two years a series of exchanges over Bahrain took place between the two governments which it would be tedious as well as unrewarding to describe here. Saudi Arabia, Kuwait and Bahrain all at one time or another joined in the diplomatic manoeuvring without exerting any decisive influence upon its outcome. The shah was playing for advantage, knowing full well that he could not make good his claim in law, still less by force of arms. What he was really seeking was a way to disencumber himself gracefully of the claim and at the same time to reap some reward for doing so. In his pursuit of this aim he was greatly abetted by the British government, which was equally bent upon making an untroubled exit from the Gulf and did not want to be impeded in the attainment of this goal by any awkward obligation to defend the territorial integrity of Bahrain against the Persians. A number of meetings in Geneva, that city of murky compromises, led at the close of 1969 to the devising of a formula which would save face on both sides. The Bahrain question would be referred to the secretary-general of the United Nations, who would in turn appoint a mission of inquiry to determine the 'true wishes' of the people of Bahrain regarding the future status of the shaikhdom.

Thus far the shah's reassertion of the Persian claim to Bahrain had been more or less successful in its object, which was to impede any progress that might be made by the Gulf shaikhdoms towards federation. While the claim hung in the air the rulers of Qatar and the Trucial Shaikhdoms were loath to enter into any form of association with Bahrain that might require them to support the shaikhdom against the shah. They were also extremely wary of the possibility that Bahrain's more advanced economy, her longer mercantile experience, her more sophisticated society and her much larger population would combine to give her a preponderant position in the projected federation. At first the Bahrainis did what they could to stifle these apprehensions on the part of their prospective partners, whose moral backing, at least, they were anxious to secure in their resistance to the shah. As time went by, however, their efforts slackened, as they came to acknowledge the fruitlessness of continuing to deny the obvious. Bahrain, with a population of well over 200,000, greater than that of the seven Trucial Shaikhdoms combined, and a large proportion of which was educated, technically skilled and politically alert, simply could not be equated with a Trucial Shaikhdom like Ajman, for example, with a population of 5,000 illiterate fishermen and goatherds. Notional parity might be conceded in principle among the rulers of the nine Gulf shaikhdoms, but if, as seemed inescapable, representation in any federal legislature was to be based upon population, then the Bahrainis would inevitably predominate – a situation which the other shaikhdoms were not prepared to tolerate.

Old quarrels and antipathies also divided one shaikhdom from another and made the chances of political union, however rudimentary, seem exceedingly remote. The Al Khalifah rulers of Bahrain had once exerted supremacy over the Qatar peninsula and over its principal clan, the Al Thani, as tributaries. Although the tributary relationship had been terminated a hundred years earlier (since which time the Al Thani had ruled Qatar more or less uninterruptedly), the two ruling families were still on bad terms. Much of their hostility derived from conflicting claims to ownership of the Hawar Islands, a cluster of islets between Qatar and Bahrain, and to Zubara, on the north-western coast of Qatar, the site of a former Al Khalifah settlement, built when the latter migrated to Qatar from Kuwait in 1766. It had been retained by them after their conquest of Bahrain from the Persians in 1783 until the 1870s, when it was captured and razed to the ground by the Al Thani. The passage of time, however, had not operated to diminish the Al Khalifah's sense of grievance over its loss.

Dynastic animosities, tribal feuds and territorial disputes also divided many of the other Gulf shaikhdoms. The Al Thani of Qatar had been at odds with the ruling family of Abu Dhabi, the Al Nihayan, for a century at least, and one of the principal objects of their rivalry was a winding inlet at the base of the Qatar peninsula, on its eastern side, known as Khaur al-Udaid. The dispute over ownership of the *khaur* (inlet) was complicated by the presence of a third contender for its possession, Saudi Arabia, which had originally put forward a claim to the inlet, and to a considerable slice of the hinterland behind it, in 1935. After the Second World War the Saudi claim had been enlarged to take in the greater part of Abu Dhabi shaikhdom, along with a portion of the adjoining sultanate of Oman; and although the claim had been rejected by the British government as having no valid foundation, the Saudis were still persisting in it. More will be said about the origins and development of this frontier dispute shortly. What needs to be remarked at this point is that its presence in the wings exerted the same deadening influence upon the desultory negotiations going on among the shaikhdoms to establish a federation as did the shah's claim to Bahrain. For none of the rulers concerned was anxious to place himself in a position where, as a member of a Gulf federation, he would be obliged to support Abu Dhabi in resisting Saudi Arabia's territorial claims. The reluctance was particularly strong in the case of the rulers of Bahrain and Qatar, both of whom were on friendly terms with the Saudis and did not want the relationship to turn sour. For the Al Khalifah, the virtual certainty of Saudi assistance in opposing the Persian claim to sovereignty over their shaikhdom was a much more reassuring consideration than the remote possibility of support from the other Gulf rulers. In the case of the Al Thani of Qatar, their connexion with the Al Saud had increased in intimacy over the previous half-century, and it was reinforced by their profession of the same sectarian beliefs.

As if these mutual antagonisms, rivalries and disputes – of which there were still more, which we can safely pass over here, among the various Trucial Shaikhs – were not enough to bedevil the prospects of federation, they were further confused by the course of domestic politics in Britain between 1968 and 1970. At the time of the announcement in the House of Commons in January 1968 of the intended British withdrawal from east of Suez, the former Conservative prime minister, Sir Alec Douglas Home, who was now his party's principal spokesman on foreign affairs, had condemned the decision to withdraw 'as a dereliction of stewardship, the like of which this country has not seen in the conduct of foreign policy before'. He went on to upbraid the Labour government for having damaged Britain's honour in the eyes of the world, and his condemnation was echoed by Iain Macleod, the shadow chancellor of the exchequer. 'To break our word, solemnly pledged and reaffirmed only a few months ago, is shameful and criminal,' Macleod declared robustly. The Conservatives, he affirmed, would keep Britain east of Suez if they were returned to power. Reginald Maudling, the deputy leader of the Conservatives, gave much the same pledge when he spoke in the debate in the House which followed the announcement, describing the decision to withdraw from the Gulf, in particular, as 'a breach of solemn undertakings'. Macleod, Maudling and, after them, Home and Edward Heath, the Conservative leader, assured the House of Commons that a future Conservative government would ignore the timetable laid down by the Labour government for withdrawal from east of Suez. Instead it would work out, in consultation with the local governments concerned, the most helpful and practicable way in which a British presence east of Suez might continue to be maintained.

The pledge was repeated at intervals over the next two years. In a speech in December 1968 Maudling described a continued British military presence in the Gulf as 'infinitely important', and he went on to remark, 'If we can maintain our position as a token of our determination to maintain our influence we will have an effect for good in the future of the world.' After a tour of the Gulf in March and April 1969 Heath expressed himself as 'even more convinced than before that it would be in our interests' to retain a British presence in the area. Nine months later, in January 1970, while on a visit to Australia and the Far East, he spoke of a 'reversal' of the Labour government's decision to withdraw, especially in view of increased Russian activity in the Indian Ocean, should the Conservatives be returned to power.

It is not to be wondered at, therefore, that those of the Gulf's rulers who preferred to retain the protection which the British treaty relationship afforded them tended to drag their feet in the negotiations towards federation. Who knew but that the turn of the wheel of political fortune in Britain might yet save them from having to accept the unpalatable necessity of federal union by bringing the Conservatives into office before December 1971? So the negotiations drifted along in their somnolent way, each ruler allowing himself to indulge as he pleased his dislike for his neighbours or his apprehensions of how federation might adversely affect his own fortunes. The uncertainty over Britain's departure, however, was not much to the liking of the shah or King Faisal of Saudi Arabia. Muhammad Reza Shah believed (not without justification after the abandonment of Aden) that Britain was finished as a Middle-Eastern power – indeed, as any kind of power at all. It was high time, therefore, so he reasoned, that the British quit the Gulf and left it to him and the other Gulf rulers to sort out the question of its future for themselves. With somewhat less justification he believed that Persia was perfectly capable of taking Britain's place as the arbiter of the Gulf's destiny and the guardian of its peace.

What was very much on his mind, and which made the chances of a reversal of the British decision doubly distasteful to him, was the awkward situation he had got himself into by the outset of 1970 over Bahrain. He had originally opposed the Federation of Arab Emirates because it was to have included Bahrain, to the detriment, if not the complete demolition, of Persia's claim to sovereignty over the island. At the same time he acknowledged that there was a strong possibility that the British departure might be delayed until the federation was actually in being. Hence his willingness, expressed in the agreement reached at Geneva at the end of 1969, to allow the question of Bahrain's status to be resolved through the agency of the secretary-general of the United Nations. By this concession, he reasoned, he had deprived the British of their principal excuse for delaying their departure, viz. the necessity to assure Bahrain's security and independence; for he was well aware that the most likely outcome of the secretary-general's mission of inquiry would be a recommendation that Bahrain be recognized as an independent Arab principality. But what if, after he had for all practical purposes renounced the Persian claim to the shaikhdom, the Conservatives should return to office and redeem their pledge to retain the British presence in the Gulf? The thought was too painful for the shah to entertain, so on 9 March 1970 he requested the secretary-general of the United Nations to implement the Anglo-Persian accord of the previous December with all dispatch.

The secretary-general complied with the request promptly, since the British government was just as anxious as the shah to have the matter settled. He appointed an Italian diplomatist from his secretariat, Vittorio Winspeare Guicciardi, to head the mission of inquiry, and before the month was out Winspeare (as he preferred to be called) was on his way to Bahrain to sound out its inhabitants on their attitude towards the Persian claim. He reported in late April that the overwhelming majority of Bahrainis were in favour of the recognition of their island as a 'fully independent and sovereign state'. His finding was endorsed by the Security Council on 11 May, the British representative on the Council, Lord Caradon, marking the occasion with one of his ecstatic effusions about international co-operation and amity, which he was prone to utter whenever his country nervelessly surrendered yet another segment of its power or patrimony in the world. 'So the favourable factors have converged and met', Caradon rhapsodized, '– Iranian magnanimity, United Nations impartiality, Italian fairness of judgement and Arab dignity and self-respect. An irresistible combination!'

It was not quite as innocent and jolly as all this. There was, in the first place, no merit at all in the Persian claim to Bahrain – though perhaps Caradon should not have been expected to know this. The Foreign Office, however, was well aware of the fact; yet it chose to represent the settlement of the Bahrain issue as a diplomatic triumph, the product of a hard and prolonged negotiation selflessly undertaken and steadfastly pursued in the face of every discouragement and setback. All that such unwarranted self-congratulation demonstrated was that British diplomacy had become a mere shell, a shadow play in which posturing and gesticulation were reckoned of greater consequence than the rights and wrongs of the issue at hand, and where the prime purpose of the performance was to permit as graceful an escape as possible from the uncomfortable shackles of responsibility. As for the shah, he had brought off his finesse with some skill, earning plaudits for his wisdom and forbearance both from Western governments (themselves ignorant or uncaring of the worthlessness of his claim to Bahrain) and from Asian governments eager to curry favour with him. In brief, he had stored up indulgences to draw upon at a later date.

There was only one small cloud on his horizon. In London, Parliament was dissolved in the third week in May and a general election was called for the following month. Although the signs were propitious for the return of the Labour party to power, there was a possibility that the Conservatives might upset the current predictions, in which case there might be a reversal of British policy in the Gulf. The shah was not alone in experiencing a certain unease at the thought. Earlier in the month King Faisal, who had so far abstained from any serious move to influence the course of events in the Gulf subsequent to the British decision of January 1968, had taken the occasion of a visit to him by the ruler of Abu Dhabi to make it crystal clear that he had no intention of accepting the Federation of Arab Emirates until and unless his territorial claims in eastern Arabia had been satisfied. With this pronouncement he brought to the forefront of affairs a problem of far graver significance to the minor states of the Gulf, and to Britain in her role as tutelary power, than the trumped-up Persian claim to Bahrain had ever been.

South and east of the Qatar peninsula stretches a desolate region made up of sand dunes, salt flats and gravel plains. On the north it is bounded by the waters of the Gulf, on the south by the Rub al-Khali (or Empty Quarter), the great sand sea that extends from the highlands of the Yemen and the Hadramaut in the south-west to the edge of the Oman steppes in the north-east. The northern and larger half of the Rub al-Khali is made up of towering sand hills, known to the Bedouin who frequent them simply as 'al-Rimal' – 'the sands'. A northward extension of the Rub al-Khali, the Jafurah, thrusts up towards the Gulf coast to the west of Qatar, and is marked off from al-Rimal in the south by a great depression, the Jaub, which runs eastwards from the Jabrin Oasis almost to the southern edges of the Sabkhat Matti (see map pp. 62–3). The coastline for about sixty miles south and east of Qatar is low-lying and deeply indented with *khaurs*, or inlets, all of them very shallow. Inland there is a rolling expanse of sand with several wells and some sparse vegetation, and further east a gently rising gravel plateau, which falls away in a sharp escarpment to the Sabkhat Matti, a great salt plain which stretches for some thirty miles along the sea's edge and inland for about sixty miles. Much of the *sabkhah* (salt-flat) is impassable, though across its southern arms there are a few trails suitable for motor vehicles, and of late years a highway has been constructed along its northern rim.

Beyond the Sabkhat Matti the coast as far as Abu Dhabi – and beyond, for that matter – is, for the most part, low-lying and marshy with frequent patches of *sabkhah* and occasional limestone ridges. Off-shore an intricacy of islands, reefs and shoals makes navigation in these waters extremely hazardous. The region lying between the coast and the northern rim of the Rub al-Khali goes under the general name of 'al-Dhafrah'. Towards the coast it is made up of low-lying, undulating sand dunes, with a number of brackish wells and some meagre vegetation. Further south there are successive belts of dune country, the dunes growing progressively higher as they approach the great sand hills of al-Rimal. In the centre of the dune country lies the Liwa oasis, a succession of gravel depressions with sweet-water wells and palm groves, extending in an arc for some forty to fifty miles from south-west to south-east. Scattered among the dunes are a number of tiny settlements, only a few of which are inhabited throughout the year, the rest being occupied only during the date harvest in the late summer. No European had ever set eyes upon the Liwa until the end of 1946, when Wilfred Thesiger, the last of the great Arabian explorers, arrived on its southern outskirts after his epic crossing of the Rub al-Khali from Mughshin in the far south.

It was across this desolate region that raiding parties from Najd, the highland area of central Arabia, began to make their way at the turn of the nineteenth century to plunder the villages of inner Oman and exact tribute from their inhabitants. The Najdis' incursions were made under the spur of a movement of religious revivalism known as Wahhabism, of which a fuller account will be given later, in the chapter on Saudi Arabia. It is sufficient here to notice that the progress of the movement was intimately linked to the rise to power of the house of Saud, of Dariya in Najd, the ruling members of which, from the late eighteenth century onwards, also filled the office of *imam* of the Wahhabiya. The Wahhabis made their first appearance east of the Jafurah at the outset of 1800, when a force of horsemen and camel-riders rode 500 miles across the desert to seize the oasis of al-Buraimi, hard by the foothills of the Hajar mountain range of Oman. Buraimi was the key to inner Oman and to the neighbouring shaikhdoms along the Gulf coast. The oasis measured about six miles across and was roughly circular in outline. It had perhaps half a dozen settlements and a plentiful supply of good water, brought from the nearby hills in underground channels. The soil was fertile and grew a variety of fruit and crops, as well as providing pasturage for livestock. South of Buraimi ran the tracks to Nizwa, Bahlah, Izki and the other ancient towns of central Oman. To the eastward a pass wound its way through the Hajar mountains to another major town, Sauhar, on the Gulf of Oman. To the north and west the tracks led to Ras al-Khaimah, Sharjah and Abu Dhabi, a hundred miles away. Whoever held Buraimi in force could overawe these shaikhdoms and much of inner Oman besides. The point was not lost upon the Wahhabi invaders from Najd, who garrisoned the oasis for several years on end at intervals during the nineteenth century.

To a large extent the Wahhabis' successive occupations of Buraimi were made possible by their ability to exploit the numerous feuds, factional rivalries and sectarian differences that divided the tribes of northern Oman and the adjacent coast of the Gulf. Among those they attracted to their standard or converted to their interpretation of Islam were the Qawasim of Sharjah and Ras al-Khaimah, the strongest of the seafaring tribes of the southern littoral of the Gulf, whose piratical exploits over the years had won for this stretch of shoreline the name among European mariners of 'the Pirate Coast'. Under the spur of Wahhabi teachings, the Qawasim in the early years of the nineteenth century launched what amounted to a seaborne *jihad* against European and Indian shipping, not only within the Gulf but further afield. A British expeditionary force was dispatched from India against them in the winter of 1809–10, and again in the winter of 1819–20; and at the conclusion of the second expedition the Qawasim were compelled, along with the other tribes of the Pirate Coast, to subscribe to a treaty (the General Treaty of Peace of January 1820) outlawing piracy forever. Thereafter the British authorities in the Gulf kept a close watch upon the degree of influence exercised by the Wahhabi or Saudi rulers of Najd over the maritime shaikhdoms of the Gulf, so as to ensure

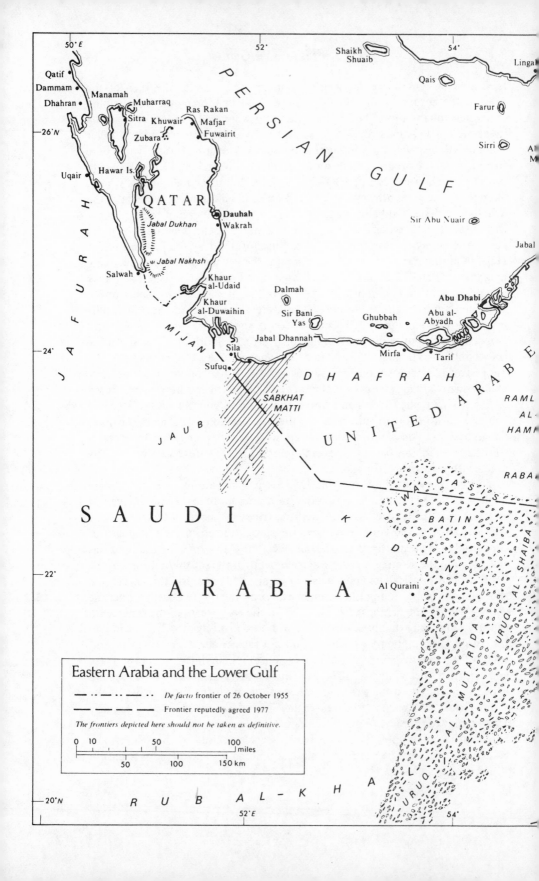

Eastern Arabia and the Lower Gulf

- - · - - · - - ·   *De facto* frontier of 26 October 1955
- - - - - - - - - -   Frontier reputedly agreed 1977

The frontiers depicted here should not be taken as definitive.

0   10   50   100
|__|__|_____|_____| miles
    |_____|_____|_____|
    50   100   150 km

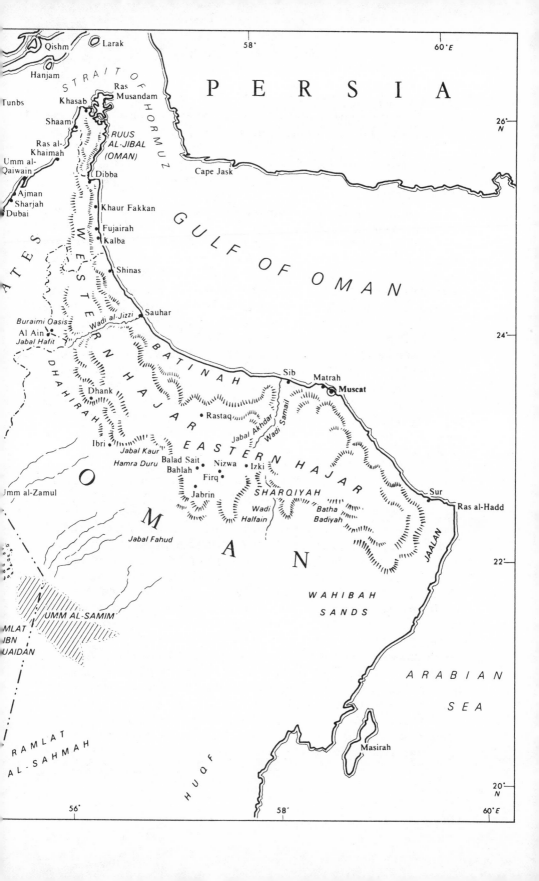

that there would be no renewed outbreaks of piracy on a large scale. As the century wore on, and Britain entered into a closer relationship with these shaikhdoms, it became an abiding principle of British policy to resist the assertion of a Saudi paramountcy over them lest it impair the proper observance of their treaty engagements. In effect, by resolving to uphold the independence of the littoral shaikhdoms against the Al Saud, Britain set her face against the expansion of Saudi power in eastern Arabia beyond the limits of Najd and Hasa.

The last Saudi occupation of the Buraimi oasis in the nineteenth century ended in 1869 when the Najdi garrison was expelled by the ruler of Muscat. Thereafter the oasis fell more and more under the domination of the Bani Yas tribal confederation of Abu Dhabi. The territory of the Bani Yas (who were a confederacy of some twenty sub-tribes) stretched from Buraimi westwards across the Dhafrah to the foot of Qatar, and southwards, beyond the Liwa oasis, to the edges of al-Rimal. They shared the territory with the Manasir, a powerful nomadic tribe who acknowledged the leadership of the ruling shaikhs of the Bani Yas, the Al Nihayan family of the Al Bu Falah section, who resided at Abu Dhabi and had extensive holdings in both the Liwa and Buraimi oases. The Bani Yas and the Manasir alike had remained inveterately hostile to the Wahhabis throughout the period of the Wahhabi occupations of Buraimi, and they invariably turned back or slew any Wahhabi force which attempted the passage of the Dhafrah in insufficient fighting strength. As a consequence the Saudi governor in Hasa was forced to maintain communication with the Wahhabi garrison at Buraimi, 500 miles away, by the sea route from Qatif or Uqair to Sharjah or Ajman on the Pirate (or Trucial) Coast. It was the Al Nihayan shaikhs of the Bani Yas, also, who on more than one occasion had organized the tribal coalitions which had at intervals driven the Saudi garrison from Buraimi.

For more than half a century after their expulsion from Buraimi the Saudis made no attempt to venture again beyond the Jafurah. Indeed, they were in no position to do so, for the Saudi state itself collapsed in the last two decades of the century, and it was not fully restored until (as we shall see in a later chapter) Abdul Aziz ibn Saud proclaimed the kingdom of Saudi Arabia in 1932. Only then did Ibn Saud feel free to turn his attention southwards and eastwards in the direction of the maritime shaikhdoms of the lower Gulf. The resumption of his interest in the region beyond Hasa coincided with his award of a petroleum concession in the summer of 1933 to the Standard Oil Company of California (SOCAL). The concession was restricted to the 'eastern portion' of the Saudi kingdom, which immediately raised the question of where the limits of Saudi Arabia in the east lay. When the United States embassy in London put the question, on SOCAL's behalf, to the Foreign Office early in 1934 it was informed in reply that the frontier was that laid down in a convention concluded between the British and Ottoman governments in July 1913, which defined the eastern limits of Najd and Hasa as a straight line (the 'Blue Line' as it was called from the colour used to denote it on the map accompanying the convention) beginning on the Gulf coast to the west of Qatar and running due south, roughly down the middle of the Jafurah desert, to the Rub al-Khali (see map p. 70). Ibn Saud refused to accept the Foreign Office determination, insisting that his authority now reached well beyond the Blue Line. There was some merit to his argument, especially as the convention of July 1913 had never been ratified. How far to the east of the line his authority extended, however, was uncertain; so discussions were initiated between the Saudi and British governments in the early summer of 1934 to decide the location of the Saudi frontier with Qatar, the Trucial Shaikhdoms, the sultanate of Oman and the Eastern Aden Protectorate.

The Saudi government put forward its proposed frontier (afterwards known as the 'Red Line') in a memorandum of 3 April 1935. It was in three sections. The boundary with Qatar began on the western side of the peninsula, about fifteen miles north of Salwah, and ran across the peninsula to end on the eastern coast north of the Khaur al-Udaid. The boundary with the Trucial Shaikhdoms started on the coast about sixteen miles south of Khaur al-Udaid (somewhere along the shore of the Khaur al-Duwaihin) and ran south-eastwards through the Sabkhat Matti before turning eastwards and continuing on south of the Liwa oasis. Beyond the Liwa its course was obscure, for the next point of reference mentioned in the memorandum was the intersection of longitude 56° E with latitude 22° N, which lies to the north of the Umm al-Samim (see map p. 70). The final stretch of frontier, which purported to define the landward limits of eastern Oman, Dhufar, the Mahra country and the Hadramaut, consisted simply of straight lines arbitrarily laid down by reference to lines of latitude and longitude and devoid of any named topographical features. Evidently Ibn Saud had a greatly inflated notion of the limits of his authority, for the bite he was proposing to take out of the southern half of Arabia amounted to something between 150,000 and 200,000 square miles.

Most of the claim, of course, was mere bluff, especially that part of it which related to Oman and the Eastern Aden Protectorate. After due consideration the British government rejected it and proposed instead a frontier which corresponded more closely with reality. The Riyad Line (so called because it was put to Ibn Saud at Riyad on 25 November 1935) began at the western foot of Qatar and ran south-eastwards to the southern tip of the Sabkhat Matti, and thence eastwards along the northern edge of the Rub al-Khali to longitude 55° E at its junction with latitude 22° 30' N. From there it continued southwards and south-westwards along the marches of Oman, Dhufar and the Eastern Aden Protectorate, assigning a good deal less of the fringes of the Rub al-Khali to Ibn Saud than he had claimed. In its northern section – that from Qatar to longitude 55° E – the Riyad Line differed from the Saudi Red Line in that it retained the whole of the Qatar peninsula for that shaikhdom, denied the

Saudis access to Khaur al-Udaid, and preserved the land bridge between Qatar and her neighbour, Abu Dhabi. Ibn Saud rejected it within twenty-four hours of its being proposed to him. There were two reasons for his rejection – Jabal Nakhsh and Khaur al-Udaid. Jabal Nakhsh was a low hill in the southern part of Qatar which was suspected of forming part of an oil-bearing structure, and Ibn Saud was determined to have it for this reason. He wanted Khaur al-Udaid for strategic purposes – to gain access to the coast east of Qatar, thereby separating that shaikhdom from Abu Dhabi and placing himself in a position to put pressure upon both, as well as upon the Trucial Shaikhdoms as a whole. It was for these very reasons that the British government had rejected his proposed frontier and put forward the Riyad Line instead.

No further discussions on the frontier took place for more than a year. They were resumed in March 1937, by which time the British attitude had undergone a change. The Foreign Office was worried about the deterioration of Britain's position in the Middle East as a consequence of increased Italian and German diplomatic activities and the Arab rebellion which had broken out in Palestine in 1936. The officials of the Eastern Department of the Foreign Office, having convinced themselves that Ibn Saud was a figure of some consequence on the Middle-Eastern stage, were anxious to remain on good terms with him, in the hope that his influence might be brought to bear to help to resolve the difficulties into which Britain had got herself in Palestine. To procure his goodwill the Foreign Office suggested to the Iraq Petroleum Company, which held the oil concession for Qatar, that it might consent to surrender that part of its concession which included Jabal Nakhsh to Ibn Saud and SOCAL. IPC flatly refused to do so, so the Foreign Office turned its attention to Khaur al-Udaid as a means of appeasing Ibn Saud. Here it ran into firm opposition from the India Office, which had charge of British relations with the lesser Gulf states as well as overall responsibility for the British position in the Gulf. Khaur al-Udaid, the Foreign Office was informed, was indisputably Abu Dhabi territory, and had been formally recognized as such by the British government on more than one occasion. The objection did not strike the Foreign Office as insurmountable, and so throughout the latter half of 1937 and much of 1938 it continued to press the India Office to reconsider its stand on the issue.

The arguments it advanced in support of its aim are of some interest and importance, for they were to be used again in 1970–71 in an endeavour to persuade Abu Dhabi to gratify Saudi Arabia's territorial claims. According to the Foreign Office, it was as much in Abu Dhabi's interest as it was in Britain's to reach a settlement on the frontier. Within a few years the situation in eastern Arabia might well have changed radically, Ibn Saud's authority could have spread among the various tribes inhabiting the disputed areas, and Abu Dhabi would be in a much weaker position to resist what would probably be a much larger territorial claim. If Abu Dhabi refused to accept the logic of this line of reasoning, then, the Foreign Office suggested, she might have to be reminded that her existence as an independent state depended upon British protection, and that this protection would only be continued on British terms, which meant accepting a British definition of her frontiers. If a frontier were not agreed upon, the British government might find it extremely difficult in the future to uphold Abu Dhabi's rights to the hinterland, where oil might possibly be found. It was therefore greatly to Abu Dhabi's advantage, so the Foreign Office contended, to reach an agreed settlement of the frontier by ceding Khaur al-Udaid to Saudi Arabia – even more so if Ibn Saud were subsequently to undertake not to claim any territorial rights beyond that frontier.

The validity of the argument, and of the premises on which it was based, was strongly questioned by the India Office. In its view Ibn Saud had already been offered in the Riyad Line a reasonable frontier – in fact a most generous one considering the actual extent of his effective jurisdiction in eastern Arabia. The British government, the India Office believed, should stick to this offer and not allow Ibn Saud to use it as a basis for extracting new concessions. He had no right to Khaur al-Udaid, and even if it were to be transferred to him as a sop to his ambition, there was no guarantee that in return he would agree to a definite frontier with Abu Dhabi and respect it afterwards. Appeasement was both objectionable in principle and unavailing in practice. From the evidence of Britain's past dealings with Ibn Saud it was patently clear that he would inevitably use any concession made to him as a lever with which to try to obtain further concessions. Even if he were to be induced to give an undertaking to respect an agreed frontier, the worth of such a pledge was open to serious doubt. Oil and revenue were what he was seeking, and if he failed to find oil at Khaur al-Udaid or in its vicinity, he might well decide to advance claims to territory further afield – wherever, in fact, along the southern shores of the Gulf oil companies might show an interest in prospecting for oil.

Unabashed by the India Office's strictures, the Foreign Office pressed ahead with its plans to buy Ibn Saud's co-operation over Palestine. A change of direction in the conduct of British foreign policy took place after Halifax replaced Eden as foreign secretary in February 1938 and Sir Robert Vansittart's appointment as adviser on foreign affairs to the Cabinet was terminated. At the insistence of G. W. (later Sir George) Rendel, the head of the Eastern Department, the question of Khaur al-Udaid was removed from the normal processes of interdepartmental consultation from March 1938 onwards and dealt with by the Foreign Office alone. In July 1938 the Foreign Office's proposals for settling the issue were put before the Cabinet. No decision was taken upon them, but the Foreign Office did not lose heart. Two months later, at the time of the Munich crisis, it made another effort to obtain the Cabinet's approval. This time its attempt was frustrated by the opposition of the secretary of state for India and by the personal intervention of the viceroy. Still the Foreign Office was undismayed, and early in April 1939 it marshalled its arguments once more in an endeavour to overcome what it regarded as the India Office's wilful and unjustifiable obduracy. The nub of the Foreign Office's complaint against the India Office and the government of India was that they should ever have recognized Abu Dhabi's title to the Khaur al-Udaid, let alone have guaranteed her rights there. It was ludicrous, so the Foreign Office thought, that trifles such as recognitions and guarantees dating from the previous century should be allowed to stand in the way of reaching an amicable understanding with Ibn Saud concerning matters of much wider interest and importance. The sentiments were very much in keeping with the times: indeed, they were expressed only three weeks after the extinction of Czecho-slovakia's independence, and a matter of days after the giving of the British guarantee to Poland on 31 March 1939.

The reply from the India Office to the Foreign Office's latest submissions said all that needed to be said on the subject. On the practical plane, it was pointed out, the calculation which had led the Foreign Office to propose the cession of Khaur al-Udaid to Ibn Saud, viz. the desirability of securing his friendship and possible co-operation in view of the troubled state of the Middle East, might prove to be ill-founded. What if Khaur al-Udaid were given to Ibn Saud and he then proved unwilling or unable to make any positive return? What if he merely used the cession of Khaur al-Udaid as an excuse to demand further territory? If the safeguarding of British interests in the Middle East was the decisive reason for seeking to win over Ibn Saud, what effect did the Foreign Office think the use of compulsion upon the ruler of Abu Dhabi to hand over Khaur al-Udaid would have upon Britain's standing and reputation in the Middle East? Presumably the effect would be as deplorable as that which, according to the Foreign Office, British policy in Palestine was having upon Arab opinion, and which had led the Foreign Office in the first place to propose the cession of Khaur al-Udaid to appease Ibn Saud. The India Office considered the whole idea of alienating the territory of one of the Gulf shaikh-doms, to which Britain had stood in a tutelary relationship for more than a century, to gain some advantage in Palestine or in the Middle East at large equally repugnant and unprincipled. It was also self-defeating. Any advantage that might be gained in Palestine or elsewhere was bound to be transient: the mere passage of time would see to that. But the damage done in the Gulf would be permanent; and the same passage of time would act to perpetuate the memory of the injustice, to the certain and ultimate detriment of Britain's position there.

War intervened in the late summer to bring discussion of the frontier question to a close. It was not raised again for another decade, by which time the India Office had vanished into oblivion, along with the Indian empire. When the war ended the exploratory activities of the oil companies in eastern

Arabia were resumed and intensified. The California Arabian Standard Oil Company (CASOC), the affiliate set up by Standard Oil of California to exploit its concession in Saudi Arabia, had been enlarged by the accession of the Texas Oil Company, Standard Oil of New Jersey and Socony Vacuum (Mobil) as partners, and renamed the Arabian American Oil Company (ARAMCO). On the eve of the war CASOC prospecting parties had made a swift reconnaissance of the region at the foot of Qatar and further east, at about the time that the Iraq Petroleum Company was awarded a concession by the shaikh of Abu Dhabi. Following the war, ARAMCO surveying parties again began probing east of Qatar and beyond the Sabkhat Matti. At the same time the Arabian research division of ARAMCO at Dhahran embarked upon an intensive study of the topography, tribes and history of the southern coast of the Gulf and its hinterland, and of the sultanate of Oman as well, with special attention being paid to past Saudi contacts with these regions.

The not unexpected upshot of these activities was the assertion by the Saudi government in October 1949 of a new frontier claim. It was vastly different from the Red Line put forward by Ibn Saud in April 1935, not so much in relation to Qatar as in what it implied for Abu Dhabi. For the new Saudi Arabia–Abu Dhabi frontier began on the coast only sixty miles west of Abu Dhabi town, whence it ran south-west for some fifteen miles, then east and north-east to end just north of the Buraimi oasis (see map p. 70). The claim was tantamount to a demand for the forfeiture to Saudi Arabia of four-fifths of the Abu Dhabi shaikhdom, including areas which in 1935 Ibn Saud had specifically recognized as belonging to Abu Dhabi, notably the Liwa oasis, the ancestral home of the ruling Al Nihayan shaikhs. All too clearly, the new claim had less to do with any actual accession of authority to Saudi Arabia in the region since 1935 (there had been none), or, alternatively, any diminution in the effectiveness of the jurisdiction exercised there by the shaikh of Abu Dhabi (again, there had been none), than with the renewal of oil prospecting in the western areas of Abu Dhabi and the environs of Buraimi by Petroleum Concessions Limited, the IPC subsidiary which held the concessionary rights for the shaikhdom.

The British government's initial response to the new Saudi frontier claim was to dismiss it as totally unrealistic. It was recognized, however, that an early settlement of the frontier question was highly desirable in view of the increased operations of the oil companies in eastern Arabia, especially as a settlement would be so much more difficult to obtain if oil were discovered in any part of the region in dispute. Exchanges took place between the two governments, therefore, to try to reach a measure of agreement on the constitution of a joint commission to determine the frontiers, and the principles upon which such a commission would operate. It was in the course of these exchanges that the Foreign Office, in an attempt to make a placatory gesture to the Saudis, and particularly to the Amir Faisal ibn Abdul Aziz, Ibn Saud's son and foreign

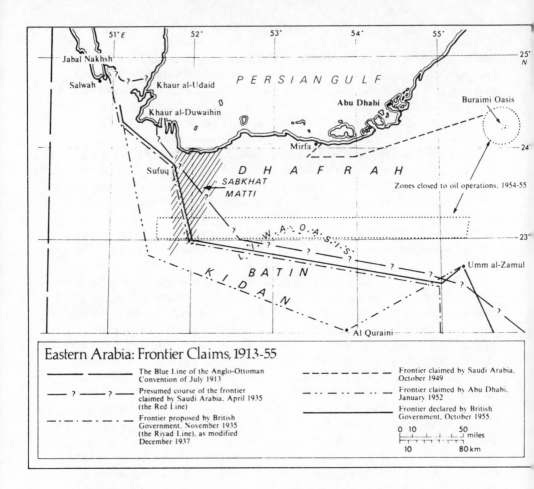

Eastern Arabia: Frontier Claims, 1913-55

⎯⎯ · ⎯⎯	The Blue Line of the Anglo-Ottoman Convention of July 1913	
⎯ ? ⎯ ? ⎯	Presumed course of the frontier claimed by Saudi Arabia, April 1935 (the Red Line)	
⎯ · ⎯ ·· ⎯ · ⎯	Frontier proposed by British Government, November 1935 (the Riyad Line), as modified December 1937	
⎯ ⎯ ⎯ ⎯	Frontier claimed by Saudi Arabia, October 1949	
⎯ ·· ⎯ ·· ⎯ ·· ⎯	Frontier claimed by Abu Dhabi, January 1952	
⎯⎯⎯⎯	Frontier declared by British Government, October 1955.	

0 10   50
├┬┬┬┼╌╌┴╌╌┴╌╌┘ miles
10   80 km

minister, made a fundamental error of judgement which was to have unfortunate repercussions for twenty years afterwards.

During talks in London in August 1951 Faisal suggested that while the projected frontier commission was doing its work all activities by oil companies in the disputed areas should be banned. The same suggestion had been made by Ibn Saud in 1935 concerning exploration by CASOC and IPC in the areas then in dispute. To have acquiesced in it would have been to acknowledge, however implicitly or indirectly, that CASOC actually possessed concessionary rights in these areas, which, of course, it did not. Acquiescence would also have conceded, albeit again by implication, that Saudi Arabia had some kind of parity (or even priority) of title to the disputed areas, since CASOC operated under the concessionary authority of the Saudi government. Finally, and perhaps most ominous of all, acquiescence would have been tantamount to admitting that IPC's concessionary rights were themselves ill-founded. IPC refused point-blank to entertain the suggestion in 1935 and the Foreign Office, with evident reluctance, was forced to reject it. Now, in August 1951, when the suggestion was again put forward, the Foreign Office accepted it. It also agreed to Faisal's demand that movements of the Trucial Oman Levies (later Scouts), the British-officered force of tribesmen under the command of the political resident in the Gulf which was responsible for internal security in the Trucial Shaikhdoms, should be restricted to areas which were not in dispute. For their part the Saudis undertook to refrain from activities which might prejudice the work of the proposed frontier commission.

No sooner had they given this undertaking than they set about bribing and inciting the leaders of tribes in and around the Buraimi oasis to declare themselves Saudi adherents. The success of their efforts led them in August 1952, a year after the Amir Faisal's visit to London, to dispatch an armed party across the Dhafrah to seize and occupy one of the villages in the Buraimi oasis. As the force was led by a former governor of Ras Tanura, the oil-loading terminal on the Hasa coast, no one was greatly surprised that the party travelled in transport provided by ARAMCO. When the sultan of Muscat, who controlled three of the villages in the oasis, gathered a large force of tribesmen to eject the interlopers, the Saudi government hastily appealed to the American ambassador in Jiddah to intervene. He in turn suggested to the Foreign Office that both sides should remain where they were and refrain from acts of provocation. The Foreign Office agreed, and told the sultan of Muscat to disband his tribal levies. It was the second fundamental error of judgement made by the Foreign Office, and the sultan in particular (as we shall see), was to pay a heavy price for it. The Saudi force remained in Buraimi for the better part of two years, doing its best to suborn the local shaikhs and tribesmen into denying their traditional allegiances and pledging fealty to the Al Saud.

By now the outlines of the Saudi government's strategy were becoming clear. Its principal target was the western areas of Abu Dhabi, especially the Dhafrah, the Liwa and the adjacent districts, where oil was believed to lie. Because Saudi Arabia had never exercised jurisdiction in these areas, the Saudi government was directing its attention towards the Buraimi oasis, where it had evidence of a past connexion, even if this amounted to nothing more than a series of armed occupations in the preceding century. If it could buy or force its way into possession of the oasis, or even part of it, and if it could put up some kind of legal or historical case, however spurious, for claiming title to it, the Saudi government might then hope that in the fullness of time the intervening western areas would fall to it. Buraimi itself, in any case, would be a valuable acquisition, for it was perfectly sited to act as a springboard for further penetration of Oman, with the eventual aim of securing control of the Oman steppes, where IPC survey parties had lately started operations.

The Anglo-Saudi negotiations culminated in an agreement in July 1954 to submit the dispute to arbitration by an international tribunal. The tribunal was to decide upon the location of the frontier between Saudi Arabia and Abu Dhabi, and to determine the question of sovereignty over the Buraimi oasis and its environs, which were defined as the area contained within a circle having as its centre Buraimi village and its radius a line from there to the terminal point of Saudi Arabia's 1949 claim (see map p. 70). In reaching its conclusions the tri-bunal was to take into account not only legal arguments and historical facts but also the traditional loyalties of the tribes in the disputed regions and the exercise of jurisdiction over them. Certain conditions were to be observed by both sides while the tribunal went about its work, and it was in the framing of these conditions that the Foreign Office repeated its previous errors of judgement by conceding more than it need have done. Thus, in exchange for the withdrawal of the Saudi force from Buraimi (where it had no right to be in the first place) the Foreign Office undertook to keep the Trucial Oman Levies out of the disputed areas, where they had every legal right to be. The immediate effect of this concession was partially to compromise Abu Dhabi's rights of sovereignty over its own territory. But the Foreign Office went even further in compromis-ing these rights, and IPC's concessionary rights with them, by concurring in the retention of the ban on oil exploration in the disputed areas first conceded to the Amir Faisal in 1951. However, under pressure from IPC, it confined the area covered by the ban to the Buraimi circle and a strip of territory to the westward, some 240 miles long and seventeen miles wide, north of latitude 23° N.

While the arbitration was in progress the two sides also agreed to abstain both from interference in the lives of the inhabitants of the disputed areas, and from any activities which might prejudice the conduct of a just and impartial arbitration. A small police force, made up of fifteen men from each side, was stationed in the Buraimi oasis to help keep order there. As soon as the Saudi police detachment arrived in August 1954, it picked up and carried on the work of bribery and subversion that the previous occupying force had been engaged in since 1952. Large sums of money, running into millions of rupees, were disbursed to the various shaikhs and tribesmen, and equally large supplies of arms and ammunition were smuggled in and distributed to the surrounding tribes with the object of provoking a 'spontaneous' uprising in favour of Saudi Arabia. On several occasions the money and arms were brought from Saudi Arabia in the aircraft which the Saudis were permitted to use for the supply of the police detachment. By far the Saudis' boldest move, however, was that made in August 1955, when they tried to persuade the Abu Dhabi governor in the oasis, Zayid ibn Sultan, the brother of the ruler, to throw in his lot with Saudi Arabia in return for a promise of 400 million rupees, to be paid out of the proceeds of any oil subsequently found in the disputed areas.

The Saudi operation at Buraimi was controlled by the governor of Hasa, the Amir Saud ibn Jiluwi, and directed by the Saudi deputy foreign minister,

Shaikh Yusuf Yasin – who was also Saudi Arabia's representative on the international arbitration tribunal. Much of the bribery and some of the other *louche* activities had as their object the manufacture of evidence for incorporation in the memorial which the Saudi government intended to submit to the tribunal in support of its case. Although the memorial was compiled in the main by American advisers not wholly unconnected with the Arabian research division of ARAMCO, the Saudis were uneasy about entrusting their chances of success solely to the skill and inventiveness of their advisers. So in Geneva in September 1955 they took the logical step of trying to bribe two of the members of the tribunal itself. At this the British member resigned, and his example was followed by the tribunal's president, a distinguished Belgian jurist and former judge of the International Court of Justice. A month later, on 26 October, the British government informed the Saudi government that it considered the arbitration to have been wrecked by the Saudis' behaviour. Henceforth, it added, it would regard the Riyad Line of 1935, subject to a couple of minor modifications, as the frontier between Saudi Arabia and Abu Dhabi. That same day Abu Dhabi and Omani tribesmen, supported by the Trucial Oman Levies, expelled the Saudi police force from the Buraimi oasis. A substantial sum of money found in the police post was returned to the Saudi government with the comment that, as it seemed an unduly large amount for the upkeep of fifteen men, it could only have been intended for illicit purposes. The Saudis accepted the money but rejected the accusation. 'It is not part of the traditions of the Saudi Arabian government', they asserted, 'to make colonies of nations, whether by force or by buying their loyalties with bribes.'

A year later, at the time of the Suez crisis, the Saudis broke off diplomatic relations with Britain. They offered several times in the next few years to reopen relations in exchange for a substantial concession on the frontier issue. Each time they were told that this was not possible. 'We cannot consider "buying back" . . . our diplomatic relations', the Foreign Office stated publicly in July 1959, 'by making concessions at other people's expense.' Diplomatic relations were eventually resumed in January 1963, when it was agreed to resume discussion of the Buraimi question under the supervision of the UN secretary-general, acting in his personal capacity. Little progress was made, not least because the Saudis kept insisting, as they had since October 1955, that the arbitration was still in force. Oil had been discovered in Abu Dhabi territory in 1960 – the Murban field in the northern quarter of the Dhafrah – and production began a couple of years later. It had the effect of intensifying the Saudi government's protests, which had been going on at intervals since 1955, against the operations of the Abu Dhabi Petroleum Company (as the Abu Dhabi division of the IPC subsidiary, Petroleum Concessions Limited, was now called), on the grounds that ADPC was violating Saudi territory, appropriating Saudi oil and contravening the arbitration agreement of 1954.

To remove any doubts about its attitude to these protests, especially in the light of the defence statement of February 1966 announcing the intended British withdrawal from Aden by 1968, the British government informed the Saudis that same month that it intended to honour its obligations to the Trucial Shaikhs. At the same time the ruler of Abu Dhabi, Shaikh Shakhbut, was told that the pledge applied also to the frontiers of his shaikhdom, and that he would be afforded any support that was deemed necessary to uphold them. A few months later, in August 1966, Shakhbut was replaced as ruler by his brother Zayid. The following April Zayid travelled to Riyad, as a matter of courtesy, to pay his respects to King Faisal. He was greeted, not with fraternal pleasantries but with a new frontier claim (see map p. 211). Although it was not quite as spectacular as that of 1949 – it demanded only three-quarters as opposed to four-fifths of the shaikhdom – it was, like the earlier claim, connected with oil exploration, its intention being clearly to deprive Abu Dhabi of two oilfields which had lately been discovered in the southern Dhafrah. Zayid told Faisal he would have to discuss the claim with his family and took his departure. He never sent a reply.

Throughout the 1960s ARAMCO had been surveying along the northern edges of the Rub al-Khali and in the Kidan, the high dune country south of the Liwa. ADPC had likewise been exploring in and around the Liwa, and southwards through the Batin-Liwa, the tract immediately below the oasis, to the edges of the Kidan further south. Both companies had observed the Riyad Line as the boundary between their spheres of operation. ARAMCO had detected the existence of a large, possibly oil-bearing, structure in the Uruq al-Shaiba, to the south of the Riyad Line and extending up to it. ADPC's surveys had revealed the existence of a northern extension of the structure above the Riyad Line, to which the company had given the designation of the Zarrara structure. Early in 1968 ARAMCO commenced drilling on the Shaiba structure, and continued drilling until late in 1969. ADPC commenced drilling on the Zarrara structure in January 1970. The results of the drilling on both sides revealed the presence of a large oilfield under the structure. It did not require a great deal of prescience to realize that a reassertion of Saudi Arabia's frontier claim was now only a matter of time.

In the first week of May 1970 Zayid again visited Riyad. He went on his own initiative with two principal objects in mind – to obtain from Faisal some definite expression of his attitude towards the proposed federation of the nine Gulf shaikhdoms, and to express to him his own apprehensions, and those of his fellow shaikhs, about the growing menace of subversion in the Gulf, especially in view of the Marxist rebellion currently going on in Dhufar (the southernmost province of Oman), a menace which, Zayid believed, could only be effectively countered if the Gulf rulers, including Faisal, acted in concert against it. Faisal listened with half an ear to what Zayid had to say, then abruptly asked him what proposals he had brought with him for ending the frontier dispute. Zayid replied that he had brought none, since he had not journeyed to Riyad to discuss the question. Thereupon Faisal produced his own plan, which consisted of yet another version of the Saudi Arabia–Abu Dhabi frontier and a proposal for putting the Saudi claim to sovereignty over the Buraimi oasis to the test. The new frontier began on the coast at the eastern edge of the Sabkhat Matti, ran south by south-west in a straight line to the 23rd parallel, then eastwards along the parallel to the end of the zone of no oil operations laid down in the 1954 arbitration agreement (see map p. 211). From there it ran north by north-east to the terminal point of the Saudi 1949 claim, travelled around the Buraimi circle and dropped down longitude 56° E. To solve the question of ownership of the oasis, Faisal proposed that a plebiscite be held among its inhabitants, after the manner of the plebiscite just held in Bahrain. Before such a plebiscite could be held, however, it was essential, Faisal insisted, that those tribesmen and their leaders who had fled to Saudi Arabia in 1955, when the Saudi police detachment was expelled from the oasis, should be permitted to return and resettle there.

To leave Zayid in no doubt about the seriousness of his intentions – or, for that matter, about his motives – Faisal demanded that ADPC cease its drilling operations on the Zarrara structure. Zarrara, he said, lay in Saudi territory. ADPC had no right to operate in the Batin-Liwa or in the Kidan, i.e. below the 23rd parallel. If the company did not halt its activities between that parallel and the *de facto* frontier (the Riyad Line) he would stop them by force. Zayid asked for time to consider both the ultimatum and the new frontier claim. Faisal gave him two weeks to halt ADPC's operations, and two months in which to reply to the frontier proposals. When Zayid pointed out that the sultan of Oman exercised jurisdiction over part of the Buraimi oasis and would have to be consulted, Faisal waved the matter aside as of no consequence.

What did the new claim imply? It was a retreat, certainly, from the sweeping claim of 1949 and the only slightly less sweeping claim of 1967. But it still proposed to annex to Saudi Arabia the westernmost portion of Abu Dhabi, i.e. the Sabkhat Matti and the region west of the salt flat as far as Qatar. Saudi Arabia and Qatar had more or less agreed upon their common frontier in bilateral negotiations in 1965, but the settlement had not been recognized by Britain because it infringed Abu Dhabi's rights to the Khaur al-Udaid. Now, by claiming the coast from the Sabkhat Matti up to and including the *khaur*, Saudi Arabia was in effect cutting Abu Dhabi off from Qatar at a time when the two shaikhdoms were trying to form a federation with Bahrain and the Trucial Shaikhdoms. If the claim were conceded, the Saudis would acquire an outlet on the lower Gulf from which to overawe the federation in the future, even to disrupt its actual functioning. The claim also infringed the concessionary rights over the western areas of Abu Dhabi held by ADPC and others, including Phillips Petroleum Company, ENI (Ente Nazionale Idrocarburi), and two Japanese companies, the Middle East Oil Company (MEOC) and the Abu Dhabi Oil Company. It also rode roughshod over the agreement concluded between Qatar and Abu Dhabi only the previous year for the definition of their common maritime frontier. The frontier, which ran out to sea from just off the entrance to the Khaur al-Udaid, roughly in a north-easterly direction, was designed to facilitate exploitation of the Bunduq offshore oil structure, which extended into both Qatar and Abu Dhabi territorial waters. The concessionary rights, which again were jeopardized by the Saudi claim, were divided between the Japanese Middle East Oil Company and Abu Dhabi Marine Areas, a consortium of British Petroleum and Compagnie Française des Pétroles (CFP).

In the south the projected frontier along the 23rd parallel deprived Abu Dhabi not only of the Zarrara structure but also of the Shah field and part of the Asab field. It violated ADPC's concessionary rights in the territory between the 23rd parallel and the Riyad Line, as well as the rights of Phillips Petroleum, ENI and MEOC in the same stretch of territory. In its course from south to north through the eastern marches of the shaikhdom the frontier again infringed the concessionary rights of all four companies. The demand that ownership of the Buraimi oasis, where Zayid himself had been born and raised, be determined by plebiscite was both impertinent and cynically conceived. Not only did it sweep aside all the normal determinants of sovereignty, such as historical title, legal jurisdiction and prescriptive usage, but it also presaged a repetition of the bribery, sedition and intimidation which had characterized Saudi activities in the oasis and its vicinity from 1952 to 1955. By brushing aside the sultan of Oman's legitimate interests in the area, Faisal was arrogating to himself the right not only to decide to whom the Omani villages in the oasis belonged, but also to determine unilaterally the whereabouts of the Saudi Arabia–Oman frontier by declaring it to lie along the 56th meridian. In so doing, he both violated the territorial integrity of the sultanate and trespassed upon the concessionary rights held by Royal Dutch Shell and CFP, the principal concessionaires in Oman.

Finally, Faisal had thrown out a direct challenge to Britain as the protecting power in Abu Dhabi, a challenge that struck at the very basis of Britain's legal position in the Gulf and her historical connexions with the littoral shaikhdoms. That position, as we have seen, rested upon the trucial system and upon the subsequent exclusive treaties with the shaikhdoms. The trucial system had evolved out of the need to keep the peace at sea, and this, in turn, had required that the independence of the shaikhdoms be upheld against potential conquerors, which in effect meant setting limits to the expansion of Saudi power. The containment of Saudi power implied the delineation of the eastern frontier of the Saudi state, which Britain had been attempting to bring about since 1935. As things stood in May 1970, the *de facto* frontier was the Riyad Line of 1955, as modified and reaffirmed in 1955. Saudi Arabia and Abu Dhabi, as well as the other Trucial Shaikhdoms, had been informed in February 1966 that Britain intended to uphold her obligations respecting the frontier, and as late as August 1969 the Foreign Office had stated that it still regarded the Riyad Line as the frontier.

The decision to leave the Gulf at the end of 1971 brought the frontier question into sharper focus. With the formation of the Union of Arab Emirates, Abu Dhabi's frontier with Saudi Arabia would, in effect, become the federation's frontier. At the same time, however, Britain's withdrawal meant the dismantling of the trucial system and the treaty structure. Without the treaty structure Britain had no *locus standi* to act for the shaikhdoms to determine the frontier with Saudi Arabia. But the treaty structure was still standing in May 1970, and Britain therefore had both the right and the duty to act for Abu Dhabi over the new Saudi frontier claim. If she failed in this obligation, then she would herself undermine the treaty structure and the trucial system, and along with them the legal basis of her own position in the Gulf. Whichever way one looked at it, Britain was under an obligation to retreat from the Gulf in good order, and to ensure that the treaty structure was dismantled in a reasonable and fitting manner, which involved settling the frontier issue in the interests of the shaikhdoms. Yet if Britain was to discharge this responsibility properly, she could not set a time limit to her efforts. This, however, she had done, and the fact of having done so was to condition the British response to Faisal's challenge.

Word of what had passed at Riyad between Faisal and Zayid reached the Foreign Office quickly. Evan Luard, the parliamentary under-secretary for foreign affairs, had been received by Faisal in the same week as Zayid's visit had taken place, and he had been told both of the new frontier claim and of Faisal's determination to compel ADPC – by force, if necessary – to cease operations in the disputed zone. The response of the Foreign Office to the news was hesitant, a hesitancy which may have been due in part to the impending general election. On the other hand, the permanent officials had long exercised more influence over policy in Arabia and the Gulf than had any of their ministerial superiors; so it is unlikely that they were constrained in their actions over the next few weeks by any lack of ministerial direction. The issue was a straightforward one. ADPC was a British-controlled company, operating under a concessionary agreement with the ruler of Abu Dhabi, the terms of which had been approved by the British government. The limits of the company's concession on the Arabian mainland – leaving to one side those areas which ADPC had relinquished to other oil companies at intervals during the previous five years – were the territorial limits of the Abu Dhabi shaikhdom. These had been affirmed by the British government in 1955, and reaffirmed since then, as the Riyad Line. ADPC, therefore, had every reason to expect that its right to continue its operations on the Zarrara structure, and in the rest of the concessionary area remaining to it between the Liwa and the

Riyad Line, would be firmly upheld by the Foreign Office, especially as, whatever Faisal might pretend, Saudi Arabia had never exercised the slightest particle of jurisdiction in the area.

The Foreign Office, however, equivocated, and in the absence of an unqualified expression of support Zayid informed Faisal on 18 May, at the end of the fortnight's grace which the latter had given him, that drilling had ceased on the well site on the Zarrara structure closest to the Riyad Line. Dissatisfied with this reply, Faisal peremptorily demanded the immediate cessation of any and all drilling in the Zarrara field. Zayid replied on 2 June that he had understood the original demand to refer only to the well site nearest the frontier. Faisal refused to accept the explanation: he had made it perfectly clear, he told Zayid on 4 June, that the prohibition applied to all operations below the 23rd parallel because they were taking place in Saudi territory. No drilling had, in fact, taken place since 18 May: what Zayid was hoping to achieve by these exchanges was simply a breathing space, to allow the Foreign Office time in which to reach some firm decision. All that he received for his comfort was a message from the Foreign Office on 15 June advising him not to allow drilling to be resumed lest it rekindle Faisal's anger. Zayid had little option but to accept the advice for the time being; but ADPC kept its drilling rig on the Zarrara site so as to demonstrate both its conviction of the validity of his title to the area and its determination to stick by its own concessionary rights.

Why did the Foreign Office hedge over Faisal's ultimatum, especially as its officials knew – or should have known – that it was an open challenge to Britain's treaty rights and obligations regarding the Trucial Shaikhdoms? The answer is that the officials had by this time come round to the view that the policy of withdrawal from the Gulf by the end of 1971 should be adhered to. They had only just cleared the hurdle presented by the Persian claim to Bahrain following the shah's renunciation of the claim, and they blenched at the thought of another long-drawn-out attempt to resolve the Saudi Arabian frontier problem. The advent of the Conservative party to power in the June election did not alter their conviction in the slightest. Whatever the Conservatives might have in mind regarding the Gulf, the Foreign Office had formed its own conclusions and did not intend to alter them.

What were the Conservatives' views in June 1970, as compared with those they had expressed while out of office? The Conservative election manifesto had been forthright in its denunciation of the damage done to Britain's interests abroad by the Labour government's decision to withdraw from the Far East and the Gulf. 'By unilaterally deciding to withdraw our forces from these areas by the end of 1971', so the manifesto proclaimed, 'the Labour government have broken their promises to the governments and peoples of these areas and are exposing these British interests and the future of Britain's friends to unacceptable risk.' The argument was restated in the Commons debate on the address in reply to the Queen's Speech on 6 July by the new foreign secretary, Sir Alec Douglas Home. 'The rupture of the theme of coherent foreign policy', Home told the House,

has been most vividly illustrated in the Persian Gulf. The announcement of precipitate withdrawal has had two results. It has let loose a spate of claims and counter-claims between the countries and States of the area, and it has made it virtually impossible in an orderly way to create the Union of the Arab Emirates on which the future security of that area depends. There has been no time for those States to adjust themselves to change. The urgent tasks now are first to create a climate favourable to the settlement of the local disputes, some of them far-reaching and important. The second is to consult the leaders of the Gulf as to how Britain can best contribute to the pattern of stability in that area. We shall go into such consultations with a completely open mind.

On the surface it seemed a very definite and unambiguous statement, a resolute avowal of the new government's intention not to shirk Britain's responsibilities in the Gulf or to be constrained in its efforts to resolve existing difficulties (especially those created by conflicting territorial claims) by the timetable for withdrawal laid down by its predecessor. Whether the statement reflected the government's real sentiments, however, is, in the light of the events of the next few months, a matter for conjecture. Four days after making it, Home hastened to Brussels to attend upon Muhammad Reza Shah, who was then in the course of an extended progress through Europe. Only three weeks earlier the shah had publicly expressed his displeasure at the idea that the new Conservative administration might reconsider the question of withdrawal. The withdrawal, he declared, must go forward as planned. Britain must not try to perpetuate 'imperialism in a new guise' by retaining troops in the Gulf beyond 1971. 'Britain cannot decide alone on these troops because the time of colonialism is over.' His prime minister, Amir Abbas Hoveida, faithfully echoed him in a public statement on 22 June. Any indication by Britain of an intention to remain in the Gulf, he said, would be 'reminiscent of a much despised colonial past'. He went on: 'The security of the region must rest only in the hands of the littoral states and emirates of the Persian Gulf and no outside interference should be allowed.' It was, presumably, to soothe any ruffled feelings on the shah's part that might have been caused by his speech in the Commons that Home hurried to Brussels in the second week of July. The foreign secretary refused, when questioned, to disclose the nature of his talks beyond offering the curt comment that 'their purpose was to help me consider the problems of the Gulf and the political stability of the area in which we, Iran, Saudi Arabia and the rulers are concerned'. He vouchsafed the further sibylline utterance that it should not be assumed either that the policy of withdrawal would be changed or that it would not be changed.

Whatever Home may have said to the shah, or whatever Muhammad Reza Shah may have understood him to say, the Persian monarch was taking no chances. His foreign minister, Ardeshir Zahedi, was already in Saudi Arabia to drum up support for a joint warning to the British government. The warning was duly issued at Riyad in the second week of July, when Zahedi declared, 'Iran and Saudi Arabia want Britain to leave the Gulf on the date already announced', and the Saudi deputy foreign minister, Omar Saqqaf, echoed him, saying, 'We are not interested in keeping British troops in the Gulf or any other part of our region.' Considering what both parties were up to at the time, it was rather like a conclave of burglars calling for the removal of the police from the neighbourhood. From Riyad, Zahedi went on to Kuwait to seek further backing. The Kuwaitis readily obliged. 'Kuwait is strongly opposed to the stay of British forces in the area, and insists on their withdrawal within the identified period', announced the foreign minister, Sabah ibn Ahmad Al Sabah. On 15 July the crown prince and prime minister, Jabir ibn Ahmad Al Sabah, told the national assembly, 'We in Kuwait do not welcome or accept any foreign presence in our area, be it British or anything else.'

At the end of his tour Zahedi happily summed up its results:

The views of Iran, Kuwait and Saudi Arabia are identical in . . . opposition to a British military presence in the Gulf after 1971. All the States of the Gulf maintain the view that Gulf affairs must be handled by the countries of the region without outside interference.

All the states of the Gulf? Or only those three who, by mere coincidence, had the largest populations, the greatest wealth and, in addition, no treaty relationship with Britain? What of the nine lesser states of the nascent Union of Arab Emirates who stood to benefit least from Britain's departure? Their rulers were reluctant to express their true feelings in public, since outwardly they were required to conform to the dictates of Arab nationalist dogma regarding Western 'imperialism' and 'colonialism'. But there is little doubt that Shaikh Rashid ibn Said of Dubai spoke for them all when, in mid-July, he tersely replied to a correspondent of *The Times*, who had asked him whether he wanted British troops to remain in the Gulf, 'Who asked them to leave?' 'Abu Dhabi and Bahrain', he went on, 'and in fact the whole coast, people and rulers, would all support the retaining of British forces in the Gulf, even though . . . they may not give a direct answer out of respect for the general Arab view.'

At the close of July Home announced that he was appointing Sir William Luce, who had formerly been governor of Aden and afterwards political resident in the Gulf, as his special representative to examine the situation in the Gulf, to consult with the rulers and governments involved and to report his findings in due course. Since his retirement in 1966 Luce had expressed himself publicly about the current and future course of British policy in the Gulf, more particularly in two articles in the *Daily Telegraph* and the *Round Table* in April and July 1967 respectively. Luce's principal theme in both articles was that the Gulf was 'inherently a highly unstable power vacuum' where peace and stability were maintained by Britain's presence. While it was unrealistic to think that Britain herself would remain in the Gulf indefinitely, she had a continuing interest in the maintenance of peace in the area, particularly in view of the operations of Western oil companies there and the security of oil supplies for the industrial world. There was no single local power, in Luce's opinion, 'reasonably well disposed towards a Western oil industry, which could fill the vacuum effectively and continue to ensure the peace of the area'. 'If the present equilibrium were destroyed by our early withdrawal from our commitments to the Gulf Rulers', he continued, 'the whole area could rapidly become a jungle of smash-and-grab, and the scene of conflict would not be confined to the Gulf States only . . .'

Time, therefore, was required for Britain to do what had to be done before she withdrew. 'The first requirement is an understanding between the two principal powers concerned, Saudi Arabia and Iran, regarding the territorial inviolability of the Gulf States, for without this there could be little hope of avoiding Arab–Iranian conflict.' The minor states of the Gulf should combine in some kind of union which would accept the leadership of Saudi Arabia in foreign affairs and defence, and co-operate with her in economic affairs. The breach between Saudi Arabia and the sultanate of Oman should be repaired, and the Gulf states made to abandon their feuds with one another. Thus, Luce went on (and it should be recalled that he was writing in July 1967), the timing of Britain's withdrawal 'should not be determined by any arbitrary or unilateral decision designed to effect a small saving in British defence costs or to satisfy opinion based on the artificial division of the world into east and west of Suez'. On the contrary – and he laid great stress on the point – Britain should strive 'to terminate honourably our special treaty relationship with the Gulf States and to withdraw without undue risk to the peace and stability of the region'.

The events of the next two years caused Luce to modify his views slightly. Writing in the *Round Table* of October 1969, he again described the Gulf as 'an unstable power vacuum', and he still held to the belief that 'there is no country within the region which is strong enough to take over control and ensure peace in the whole area'. Of the decision in January 1968 to leave the Gulf by the end of 1971 he observed:

That so important a decision was taken without prior consultation with the rulers of these states [Bahrain, Qatar and the Trucial Shaikhdoms], or with our other friends in the Gulf region, and apparently for reasons irrelevant to our and their interests in that area, can only be regarded as morally wrong, unwise and unnecessary.

Nevertheless, now that the decision had been taken, it could not, in Luce's view, be reversed, or the withdrawal postponed. The creation of the Union of Arab Emirates meant the end of the treaty system and of Britain's special position in the Gulf. Any show of hesitation on Britain's part about leaving would only reduce the urge among the shaikhdoms to proceed with the federation. However, Luce insisted,

it is one thing to relinquish our special and exclusive position as the protecting power of the Gulf states, which would happen in any case within the next few years; but it is quite another thing to leave not only the Gulf itself but the whole of the western Indian Ocean wide open to uncontested Russian influence.

To counter that influence, Luce advocated the retention of a Western, preferably British, naval force in the Indian Ocean, which would pay frequent visits to the Gulf. An assurance of support should also be given to the Union of Arab Emirates. The naval force would be tangible evidence of the West's intention to back this assurance.

In the latter half of August 1970, some three weeks after his appointment by Home, Luce set off for the Gulf on his first tour. By the last week of September he had visited all the Gulf states, and had called at Cairo as well. Considering the nature of the statements on the Gulf made by leading members of the Conservative administration at various times during the previous two and a half years, one might reasonably have expected the Cabinet to have thrown the engine of withdrawal into neutral, if not into reverse, while Luce was conducting his investigations. Caution was also called for in view of the highly disturbed state of the Middle East in September 1970, with a civil war raging in Jordan between the government and the Palestinians, and American, Swiss and British airliners being hijacked and destroyed by Palestinian terrorists. No such standstill occurred. While Luce delved, the wheel of withdrawal spun in the Foreign Office's adroit hands. There was hardly an official to be found in London or the Gulf in the late summer of 1970 who was prepared to entertain the possibility of postponing, even for a day, the date of withdrawal. Nor, it would seem, were their political masters any more anxious to face harsh decisions or tread the stony path of duty, if their timorous response to Palestinian terrorism was any guide. It would have been difficult in the extreme for Luce to avoid being influenced by the atmosphere he found around him, especially as he had himself already expressed the opinion that a reversal of policy in the Gulf was impracticable.

Luce made his preliminary report to the foreign secretary at the end of September. What he recommended needed little surmise – withdrawal from the Gulf on schedule and the stationing of a naval force in its vicinity afterwards. The diplomatic correspondent of *The Times*, who could normally be relied upon to reflect the Foreign Office's viewpoint, wrote at the time: 'Sir William will return to the area after the British Government's decision to leave has been taken. A firm date for withdrawal should act as a spur to induce the rulers to drop their rivalries and make their federation into a going concern.' Luce duly returned to the Gulf on 15 October. No word was vouchsafed by the government, however, that the decision had in fact been taken. Instead, at the

Conservative party conference the previous week, the prime minister, Edward Heath, had resoundingly proclaimed to the assembled delegates:

We were returned to office to change the course of history of this nation – nothing less. . . . Overseas, we face the limitations of the broken pledges of the last six years and above all of defeatist attitudes after continuing retreat. . . . We are leaving behind the years of retreat – we are determined to establish the reputation of Britain once again, a reputation as the firm defender of her own interests and the skilful and persistent partner of all those working for a lasting peace.

The foreign secretary also addressed the conference on the theme of resoluteness in discharging Britain's responsibilities in the world. 'It is not Britain's way to stay the course only when we are in a clear lead, and this government has no intention of dropping out', he informed his audience.

We do not propose to reap the benefits of a peace kept by others without making such contribution as we can afford to make ourselves. Limited resources we have; but those resources can be used to good effect. We shall, therefore, use them in areas which Britain knows and where we have had experience.

It would be natural to assume that, if Heath's and Home's remarks had any substance to them, if they had any applicability anywhere in the world, they applied above all to the Gulf. Yet it is far from certain that either minister intended his statement to be construed in this sense. So far as the Gulf was concerned, Home in particular was given to pronouncements of a truly Delphic kind, though whether he deliberately intended them to be so it is impossible to say. In any case, the test of the sincerity of his and Heath's declarations to the Conservative party is the action they took subsequently.

Lord Carrington, the secretary of state for defence, had made no reference to the Gulf in his speech on defence policy at the party conference. On 28 October his junior minister, Lord Balniel, placed before the Commons the government's interim statement on defence and the supplementary estimates of defence expenditure (Cmnd 4515 and Cmnd 4521). These laid down, categorically and specifically, the intended expenditure upon defence for the next four financial years. There was no provision in them for the upkeep of British forces in the Gulf beyond the current financial year. Asked in the House to state what percentage of the defence budget was earmarked for use in the Gulf beyond 1971, Balniel replied: 'No decision has yet been taken about our future policy in the Persian Gulf, but the costs will be met within the framework of Cmnd Paper 4515.' His own ministry, however, was in no doubt about the situation, for in mid-November, when the resident infantry battalion stationed at Sharjah on the Trucial Coast, the 1st Battalion Scots Guards, completed its tour of duty, the ministry of defence stated publicly that the battalion would not be replaced. Instead, two companies from the only infantry battalion left in the Gulf, the 2nd Battalion, Royal Irish Rangers stationed on Bahrain, were to be assigned to Sharjah on rotation.

Luce and the Foreign Office now had little more than twelve months in which to make the Union of Arab Emirates a reality, and to persuade the major Gulf states to accept it. The major obstacle to Saudi Arabia's acceptance was, obviously, the frontier dispute with Abu Dhabi. Following Zayid's submission, in the absence of British support, to Faisal's ultimatum over drilling, the two rulers had agreed to open discussions on the frontier at the beginning of September. Before these could start Luce visited Faisal at Taiz, the king's summer residence in the hills above Mecca. As a result of their talks the Foreign Office urged Zayid not to negotiate directly with the Saudis but to allow the British government to use its 'good offices' to see if an accommodation could be reached. It was easy to see why the Foreign Office recommended this course. If direct negotiations over which the Foreign Office had no control took place between Saudi Arabia and Abu Dhabi, they might well create difficulties which would delay the British departure from the Gulf. It was much less easy to see what benefit Zayid would derive from accepting the Foreign Office's advice. Accommodation implied concessions by both sides, and the Foreign Office made it clear that it considered that Faisal had already made his concession by not claiming as much of Abu Dhabi shaikhdom as he had in 1949 and 1967. The question that the Foreign Office now left hanging in the air was – what concession was Zayid prepared to make in return?

Despite his reservations, Zayid agreed to let the Foreign Office act for him. (If he had refused, then the Foreign Office was prepared, ironical as it may seem, to insist upon its right to do so under the existing treaties with Abu Dhabi.) In the next few months a number of suggestions were floated for the resolution of the dispute, most of them of obscure provenance but all of them earnestly taken up and pressed upon Zayid by the Foreign Office. Faisal, it was hinted, might be prepared to give up his claims to the Buraimi oasis by means of some kind of face-saving device akin to that which had permitted the shah to withdraw his claim to Bahrain. He would do so, however, only on condition that he received full satisfaction of his claims to the western and southern parts of Abu Dhabi shaikhdom. Again it was suggested that the territory south of the 23rd parallel might be transferred to Saudi Arabia, with ADPC retaining its concessionary rights in the area but paying revenue for the oil it extracted from the Zarrara field to Saudi Arabia instead of Abu Dhabi. Alternatively, the territory between the 23rd parallel and the Riyad Line might be designated a neutral zone, with ARAMCO and ADPC jointly exploiting the Zarrara-Shaiba structure, sharing the revenues proportionately between Saudi Arabia and Abu Dhabi. A refinement of this proposal – put forward because the Saudis were ill-disposed to the concept of neutral zones after their experience with the neutral zone they had shared with Kuwait – envisaged the territory in question being placed entirely under Saudi Arabia's control, with ARAMCO alone exploiting the Zarrara-Shaiba field and Faisal making an *ex gratia* payment from the revenues to Abu Dhabi. On more than one occasion, so it was said, he had emphasized that he was not interested in further sources of revenue but only in recovering his ancestral territory.

Much the same kind of fanciful suggestions were made with regard to the western areas of Abu Dhabi. The Saudis, so the Foreign Office told Zayid, wanted possession of the Sabkhat Matti and the coast region to the west of the salt flat so that they could run a pipeline up from Shaiba and the other oilfields on the northern rim of the Rub al-Khali to the coast, where they proposed to build an oil-loading terminal. Zayid countered this argument by repeating an offer which his elder brother, Shaikh Shakhbut, had made when he was ruler of transit rights for an ARAMCO pipeline across Abu Dhabi territory to ADPC's terminal off Jabal Dhannah. The offer was rejected by the Saudis because, it was said, of the difficulties they and ARAMCO had encountered in the operation of the Trans-Arabian pipeline (TAPline) through Syria to the Mediterranean. When, in reply, it was pointed out to them that the coastal waters to the west of Jabal Dhannah were too shallow to allow tankers of any size to load there, the Saudis simply ignored the argument. They also ignored it when it was applied to their ostensible reason for wanting possession of Khaur al-Udaid, viz. to build a port and naval base there. What they really wanted, as everyone involved knew, was an outlet on the lower Gulf which would enable them to counter Persia's growing influence and extend their own influence over the emergent Union of Arab Emirates (UAE).

The Foreign Office came up with other suggestions for the western frontier of Abu Dhabi, all of them designed to give the Saudis Khaur al-Udaid and the adjacent coastline. None of the suggestions was accepted by either side. In December a Saudi delegation arrived in London, led by two of Faisal's brothers, the Amir Fahad and the Amir Nawwaf. Although they had come ostensibly to discuss a whole range of questions affecting Anglo-Saudi relations, they soon made it obvious that they were interested only in the frontier dispute. Nawwaf ibn Abdul Aziz also made it abundantly clear, in language of a kind not normally heard in the decorous corridors of Whitehall, that his government intended to have its way over the frontier, and that if the territory it was demanding was not made over to it promptly, it would revert to the far more sweeping 1949 claim. No hint of the roughness of the amir's discourse was vouchsafed, however, in the communiqué issued by the Foreign Office at the end of his visit, which spoke, in accents of surpassing banality, only of the common desire of the two governments for peace and stability in the Gulf.

If the Foreign Office's conduct smacked of the methods of the bazaar, or *suq*, it was no more than an accurate reflection of its underlying attitude to the frontier dispute. 'It will not be a question of rights and wrongs but a *suq* bargain', was how one official in the late summer of 1970 defined the character of the frontier negotiations. Though the Foreign Office professed to see itself in the role of honest broker in the haggling that went on over bits and pieces of Abu Dhabi territory, honesty was hardly the outstanding feature of its performance. It knew full well that Saudi Arabia had not a shred of right, legal, historical or otherwise, to the territory it was claiming. The Foreign Office also knew, however, that it possessed no real influence with the Saudi government to persuade it to modify its claim. The issue at stake resolved itself, therefore, in the Foreign Office's eyes into one of inducing or compelling Abu Dhabi to concede the Saudi claim, if not in its entirety, at least to an extent that would satisfy the Saudis. That the British government had time and again solemnly affirmed the Riyad Line as the true frontier of Abu Dhabi seemed to trouble the Foreign Office little. Nor did it appear to feel itself constrained by the fact that the treaty of 1892, which provided the legal justification for Britain's intervention in the frontier dispute, also bound the ruler of Abu Dhabi not to alienate any portion of his territory except to the British government. Instead of interpreting this clause in the treaty as interposing a legal barrier to prevent it from doing what it was attempting to do, the Foreign Office sought in effect to prove, as an implicit corollary to this undertaking, that the ruler was also required to cede territory to another state at the behest of the British government. If any implicit corollary resided in the non-alienation clause of the treaty, however, it was that the shaikh was under no requirement whatever to cede any part of his territory to another state, even if urged to do so by the British government.

None of these considerations counted for anything in the eyes of the Foreign Office, which proceeded at the outset of 1971 to bring renewed pressure to bear upon Zayid to induce him to yield to Faisal's demands. All the discreditable arguments which had been employed in the 1930s to justify the appeasement of Ibn Saud's expansionist ambitions were dredged up and used again. Faisal, the Foreign Office insisted, had made concessions by retreating from his earlier immoderate claims: Zayid must reciprocate. If he did not reach an accommodation with Faisal now, while he still enjoyed the 'good offices' of the British government, by relinquishing a reasonable portion of his shaikhdom, he would be forced after Britain's withdrawal from the Gulf to agree to a far less favourable settlement and to surrender a much larger slice of territory than was at present being demanded. When the obvious objection was raised that the Saudis might well, as they had in the past, use any concession as an excuse for further demands, and, furthermore, that there was no guarantee but rather the opposite, to judge from their past conduct, that the Saudis would continue to respect any agreement on the frontier once the British were gone, the Foreign Office brusquely replied that Zayid had no choice but to trust Faisal to keep his word. If he failed to satisfy Faisal's demands and to conclude a settlement with him before the end of 1971, he would have to face the Saudi ruler on his own afterwards. In this event, he would be able to count himself fortunate if he was left with a sand-dune to call his own.

Such being the Foreign Office's attitude, it was obviously in Zayid's interest to provoke a crisis with the Saudis before the British left the Gulf and while they were still under an obligation to defend him. The Foreign Office, however, had provided against this contingency by pointing to the absence of any explicit commitment in the existing treaties to defend the integrity of the shaikhdom. That such a commitment implicitly resided in the trucial system, that it had been acknowledged in the past, and that it had been confirmed by precedent and practice, was of no consequence in the brave new world of 1970–71. Not only did the Foreign Office make it plain that there was not the slightest chance that any assistance would be forthcoming if Zayid were so foolish as to provoke Faisal's wrath, but it even went so far as to express indignation with him for having placed the British government in 'an acutely embarrassing position' in May 1970 by failing to respond with sufficient alacrity to Faisal's ultimatum over the cessation of ADPC's drilling operations below the 23rd parallel. It is not too much to say that there was at the beginning of 1971 a disposition among officials at the Foreign Office – though not, to their credit, among all those concerned – to contemplate Zayid's predicament with a certain degree of relish. There was even an attempt at *suggestio falsi* by hinting that Zayid may well have given unspecified undertakings to Faisal when he visited him in Riyad, undertakings which he had not communicated to the British government and which he had afterwards gone back on. In this case, it was primly observed, since he had originally been cautioned by the Foreign Office against making the visit, Zayid had only himself to blame for what had subsequently befallen him.

The atmosphere of the *suq* also hung over the Foreign Office's transactions with the Persians at this time. Muhammad Reza Shah was determined to exact a price for his acceptance of the UAE, yet he had, through an accident of timing, already used up his major bargaining counter – the withdrawal of his claim to Bahrain. Annoyed at his own miscalculation, and alarmed that he might miss his share of the spoils after the election of a Conservative government, he had, as we have seen, done a good deal of huffing and puffing about the impossibility of the Conservatives' reversing the policy of withdrawal. His alarm, needless to say, was unfounded: the Conservatives were only too willing to placate him, and the only question that concerned them was how they might do so without antagonizing his Arab neighbours across the Gulf.

Fortunately, the shah's requirements seemed to be modest – the transfer to Persia of three small islands, Abu Musa and the Tunbs, which lay just inside the entrance of the Gulf, roughly equidistant from the Persian shore and the northern Trucial Coast. According to the shah, his reason for wanting possession of the islands was to safeguard the Gulf's main shipping channel, which, he said, would be endangered if hostile forces, especially Arab revolutionaries, were to seize the islands and fortify them. There was only one slight impediment to the extension of Persian sovereignty over the islands and this was that Abu Musa had hitherto been regarded as a dependency of the shaikhdom of

Sharjah, and the Greater and Lesser Tunbs as dependencies of the shaikhdom of Ras al-Khaimah. The impediment, however, in the shah's view, could easily be overcome, since Persia was able to show proper legal and historical title to the islands – as she could indeed, if required, to nearly all the islands in the Gulf.

Was this actually the case? Abu Musa and the Tunbs had for two centuries been in the possession of the Qawasim ('Qasimi' in the singular), a tribe which had established itself in a paramount position at Sharjah and Ras al-Khaimah in the first half of the eighteenth century. From there their power had spread across the Gulf to Lingah on the Persian coast (which they occupied in 1747) and to the intervening islands, Abu Musa, the Tunbs and Sirri, a few miles west of Abu Musa. Twenty years later the Qawasim were expelled from Lingah, only to return and reoccupy it about 1780. Thereafter they remained in control of the port for a century, periodically paying tribute to the Persian court whenever it was thought judicious to do so or when, which was less frequent, the Persian authorities were strong enough to exact it. Much the same situation prevailed in the other ports along the Persian littoral where the inhabitants were predominantly of Arab descent. (Bandar Abbas, for instance, was ruled by the sultan of Oman until the second half of the nineteenth century.) The Persian government ultimately exerted its authority over Lingah in 1880, and seven years later it expelled the Qasimi shaikh from the port and occupied the island of Sirri. Abu Musa and the Tunbs, however, remained in the hands of the Qasimi shaikhs of Sharjah and Ras al-Khaimah respectively.

The Persians made no serious attempt to annex Abu Musa or the Tunbs until the 1930s. It was a time when the shah's father, Reza Shah, was seeking to make his country's weight felt in the politics of the Gulf by the creation of a Persian navy. The assertion of Persian sovereignty over Abu Musa and the Tunbs, so Reza Shah reasoned, would serve to promote this object and at the same time challenge Britain's naval supremacy in the Gulf. While the Foreign Office was inclined at the time to humour his pretensions, under the plea of advancing Britain's wider Middle-Eastern interests, the India Office was not. So he was told that, although Sirri was acknowledged to be a Persian island, Abu Musa and the Tunbs had since the previous century been considered by the British government to be attached to Sharjah and Ras al-Khaimah. There the matter more or less rested until the announcement in January 1968 of Britain's impending withdrawal from the Gulf. Muhammad Reza Shah lost no time in demanding the transfer (or, as he would have it, the reversion) of the islands to Persian control, so as to safeguard the passage of oil tankers and other shipping through the Straits of Hormuz. Why or how the passage of shipping would be endangered by the islands remaining in Arab hands – or, conversely, be safeguarded by their being transferred to Persia's – was not, for all the shah's dark references to potential guerrilla activity, immediately self-evident.

Abu Musa is only a few miles square, with one tiny port and no land flat enough to serve as a site for an airfield. It has never had more than a few dozen semi-permanent inhabitants, except on the occasions when gangs of Arab labourers have been brought over to mine the island's deposits of iron oxide. Otherwise it has been frequented mainly by fishermen from the Arabian shore. The Greater Tunb (Tunb-e-Buzurq) is little more than a desolate rock, visited occasionally by fishermen. The Lesser Tunb (Nabiyu Tunb) to the west is even smaller, having no significance except as a hazard to shipping. If the shah had wanted to control the main shipping channel, then he already had Sirri, which was equally suitable – or unsuitable – as an outpost. More to the point, the Persian islands of Qishm, Hanjam and Larak were much better placed strategically to command the Straits of Hormuz. There was obviously some motive behind the shah's demand other than the one he had declared, and one didn't have to look far to discover it. Oil prospecting had begun in the waters around Abu Musa, and there were promising indications of the existence of a submarine oilfield. Oil also was behind the shah's claim to the Tunbs. On every occasion that attempts had been made to define a median line down the Gulf for the purpose of oil exploration, the question had invariably arisen whether islands were to be taken into account in fixing the baseline from which the median line was to be calculated. In the case of the median line between Saudi Arabia and Persia, for instance, the Persians had wanted Kharq Island, off Bushire, to be designated the baseline on the Persian side for dividing the waters of the upper Gulf. If the Tunbs were to be acquired by Persia, they could serve eventually to increase her share of the continental shelf in the lower Gulf.

In October 1970 the Persian government formally informed the British government that it would not recognize the existence of the UAE unless its demands over Abu Musa and the Tunbs were satisfied. The warning was repeated publicly in late December by the Persian foreign minister, Zahedi: 'Iran will never abandon her legal rights to sovereignty over the islands of Abu Musa and the Tunbs and unless these rights are completely recognized there can be no peace and security in the Persian Gulf.' Here, then, was a situation comparable to that created by Saudi Arabia's claim to Abu Dhabi territory, with the same implications for Britain's legal position in the Gulf and her treaty responsibilities to the Trucial Shaikhdoms. In fact, the implications could be said to be more significant in this instance, since the British position had rested *ab initio* upon the sea (i.e. upon the trucial system and the maritime police of the Gulf) and the Persian demands posed an overt threat to the maritime peace. Furthermore the implicit obligation upon the British government to defend the Trucial Shaikhdoms from aggression was even more marked in the case of attack from the sea than it was in the case of assault by land. The existence of the obligation had been recognized virtually from the very inception of the trucial system in 1835, and by the time of the conclusion of the treaty of maritime peace in perpetuity in 1853 it was accepted without question. Time and again in the years that followed the commitment to protect the shaikhdoms from seaborne attack was fully admitted – most pertinently in the present context in the instructions given to the senior British naval officer on the Gulf station in November 1928 to resist, by force if necessary, any move by the Persians to occupy the Greater Tunb.

The mood in Whitehall in 1971, however, was very different. Towards the end of January Sir William Luce set off on his rounds once more – to Jiddah, Bahrain, the Trucial Shaikhdoms, Qatar, Muscat, Kuwait and Tehran. The message he bore was that British troops would be out of the Gulf by the end of the year, by which time the British government expected that all the outstanding problems attendant upon Britain's withdrawal, whether concerning the formation of the UAE or affecting the federation's relations with the other Gulf states, would have been solved. There was more hope than faith in the soundness of the prophecy. The negotiations for a federation of the nine shaikhdoms were foundering. Bahrain and Qatar, for their own separate and sometimes identical reasons (which have been described earlier), were growing increasingly reluctant to enter into a union with the seven Trucial Shaikhdoms. Abu Dhabi and Dubai, the leading shaikhdoms of the seven, were themselves at odds over old dynastic feuds, territorial disputes and political rivalry between their rulers. The shaikh of Ras al-Khaimah, Saqr ibn Muhammad Al Qasimi, who saw himself as a man of destiny, the Bonaparte of the Trucial Coast, openly expressed his disdain for the federation, which to him was a mere device to promote the ascendancy of Abu Dhabi and Dubai. Circumstances, however, enjoined caution. He needed the crumbs that fell from the two oil shaikhdoms' tables, as well as their support in opposing the shah's claim to the Tunbs. His distant cousin, the shaikh of Sharjah, Khalid ibn Muhammad Al Qasimi, likewise needed what aid the federation might give him in retaining his hold on Abu Musa. A mild and unpretentious man, Shaikh Khalid was on good terms with his two wealthy neighbours and more likely to persuade thém to side with him against the shah than was his truculent cousin to the north. At the same time, however, Shaikh Rashid of Dubai, who was as much an astute merchant as he was an able tribal chieftain, was very loath to tread on the shah's toes, since 60 per cent of the shaikhdom's profitable entrepôt trade was with the Persian shore.

The manoeuvring and bickering among the rulers was viewed with mounting irritation by the Foreign Office. So far as the permanent officials were concerned, the date for Britain's departure from the Gulf had been fixed, and they did not want that departure delayed by protracted deliberations among the shaikhs to resolve each and every dispute that divided them. When Luce returned from his tour of the Gulf in February and reported the misgivings and apprehensions the rulers had expressed to him, the Foreign Office dismissed them as mere quibbles, an excuse for prevarication. What was needed, it was convinced, was the cut of the knife to arouse the shaikhs from their torpor and force them to act with greater urgency to make the federation a reality. On 1 March the cut was administered. Home announced in the Commons that the treaties with the Trucial Shaikhdoms, Qatar and Bahrain would be terminated before the close of the year, and that all British military forces would be withdrawn from the Gulf by the same date. He was prepared to offer the UAE on its formation a treaty of friendship and to hand over control of the Trucial Oman Scouts to serve as the nucleus of a federal defence force. In lieu of a defence commitment by Britain to the federation the foreign secretary proposed that British officers and other personnel should, if desired, be seconded for service with the federal defence forces. British troops might also carry out occasional training exercises and liaison duties in the federation's territories, and the Royal Navy might make regular visits to the lower Gulf.

There was about the whole statement an evasive air, as well there might be. For what in essence Home was saying (however obliquely he might say it) was that, for all the Conservative leaders' bold pledges while out of office, once in power they had chosen to take the easy way out by adhering to a decision which they had denounced when the Labour government had taken it – although, as George Thomson, the former secretary of state for Commonwealth relations, caustically observed after listening to Home's words, 'the Foreign Secretary appeared to be doing his best to obscure that fact from the House'. Thomson went on to ask, with no little justification,

Why has it taken eight months to reach this point...? The party opposite had, as one of its election pledges, the intention to reverse Labour's withdrawal plans. Presumably, that was one promise which they decided to break very quickly after the General Election. How else can one explain the acceptance in October of Labour's ceilings on defence expenditure, leaving no extra money for remaining in the Gulf?

Thomson's point was highly apposite, but what neither he nor anyone else in the House saw fit to question was the sincerity of Home's proposals about the secondment of British officers and men to the UAE's defence forces, and the dispatch of British troops to carry out training exercises and liaison duties in the federation's territories. The government must have been well aware that even the infrequent presence of British troops in the federation would have been received with suspicion or worse by the Saudis, and that the possibility of the troops' becoming involved either in internal disturbances or in border incidents was far from remote. Considering the extreme reluctance – to an extent bordering upon timidity – of the Cabinet up to date to offend the Saudis in any way (least of all by upholding Abu Dhabi's territorial integrity), it is difficult to view Home's proposal other than with considerable scepticism.

With Home's announcement the decision to withdraw became public knowledge, and the Gulf shaikhs were free to break the silence they had diplomatically observed during the period of Luce's consultations. Shaikh

Rashid of Dubai, who had argued all along against the policy of withdrawal, had a few sharp words to say about the Foreign Office's ideas of 'consultation'. 'I am prepared to be frank with them; but they come along at times and say "this is our decision", and you are not given an opportunity to express your own view.' Shaikh Isa ibn Salman, the ruler of Bahrain, was more scathing. 'Britain could do with another Winston Churchill. Today we see her kicked out of everywhere – or leaving. Britain is weak now where she was once so strong. You know we and everybody in the Gulf would have welcomed her staying.' Shaikh Zayid of Abu Dhabi felt even more bitterly about the fickleness of the British government, and with good cause; for not only had he had to contend with Saudi Arabia's continuing efforts to filch half his shaikhdom but he had also to bear with the Foreign Office's incessant nagging of him to give the Saudis what they wanted – not for Abu Dhabi's sake, but in the interests of improved Anglo-Saudi relations and to afford the British government an untroubled departure from the Gulf.

One factor which seemed to play no part at all in the Cabinet's final endorsement of the decision to withdraw was the confrontation which took place at Tehran in January and February 1971 between the major Western oil companies and the Gulf members of the Organization of Petroleum Exporting Countries. The clash was over the fundamental issue of whether the prices for crude oil would in future be determined by negotiation or by OPEC fiat. A detailed account of the nature of the confrontation will be given in a later chapter. What needs to be noticed here is the unconcealed hostility evinced by the Gulf oil-producing states, under the leadership of Persia, towards the Western world, which culminated in a threat to cut off oil supplies if they did not get their way over prices. It was an ominous and unmistakable sign of what lay ahead, and of the insecurity which threatened the West's oil supplies from the Gulf. Yet even though Luce was in Tehran at the time of the crisis, even though he must have recognized its implications and reported them to the foreign secretary, neither Home nor the Cabinet seems to have been deterred by the warning from pressing on with the policy of retreat. It was a miscalculation of immeasurable proportions.

Now that the date of departure had been announced the Foreign Office hastened to tie up or cut off the awkward loose ends of Britain's remaining involvement with the Gulf. The first was the Union of Arab Emirates, the fig-leaf with which the British government hoped to conceal its diminished parts from the quizzical gaze of the outside world. It was all too evident by the spring of 1971 that not the slightest chance existed that Bahrain and Qatar would be drawn into a federation with the Trucial Shaikhdoms. It was equally obvious that the shah would insist upon his pound of flesh in the shape of Abu Musa and the Tunbs if he was to be reconciled to a federation which included Sharjah and Ras al-Khaimah. On 8 May the Persian government handed the

British *chargé d'affaires* in Tehran a note protesting against the alleged flights of Royal Air Force planes over Persian islands in the Gulf, including Abu Musa and the Tunbs, and stating that orders had been given to Persia's warships in the Gulf to open fire if any such incidents occurred again. It never seemed to occur to the Foreign Office to tell the shah that the establishment of the UAE was none of his business but solely that of the shaikhdoms concerned and of Britain as the tutelary power. Instead, every effort was made to mollify him and to treat his pretensions with deference and solemnity. There was, of course, good reason, at least in the Foreign Office's eyes, to pander to his whims in May 1971; for that same month his ministers had signed a contract for the purchase of Chieftain tanks and communications equipment from Britain to a value of over £100 million. The contract had been obtained through the agency of one of the shah's confidants, a Parsee named Shapoor Reporter, to whom the Crown Agents are said to have paid more than £1 million in commissions. Money, however, was not all that Reporter wanted as payment for his services to the British government. He also wanted public recognition, and this was accorded him by the award of a knighthood in the Queen's birthday honours in 1973. If the British government was prepared to go this far to oblige an intimate of the shah, it was hardly likely to offer any resistance to that monarch's ambitions in the Gulf.

Luce was sent out to the Trucial Coast again in June, this time to tell the rulers of Sharjah and Ras al-Khaimah that they could expect no help from Britain if the Persians saw fit to occupy Abu Musa and the Tunbs by force, and that they would be wise, therefore, to seek an accommodation with the shah. The latter, so it was said, was prepared to reach a financial understanding with Sharjah to protect the shaikhdom's oil-prospecting rights in the waters around Abu Musa. Where the inspiration for this proposition came from is not clear, though it bore a distinct resemblance to the offer reputedly made by Faisal to Zayid regarding the Zarrara oilfield. Muhammad Reza Shah refused to treat with Ras al-Khaimah over the Tunbs, since the islands, he maintained, were Persia's by incontrovertible right. Saqr ibn Muhammad of Ras al-Khaimah, for his part, was just as determined to resist the shah, and he had hopes that he might be aided in his resistance by the government of Iraq, with which he had been in close contact for over a year and which was itself at daggers drawn with the Persian ruler. Saqr was hardly to be swayed, therefore, by Luce's admonitions. His fellow ruler, Khalid ibn Muhammad of Sharjah, was, as indicated already, of different metal. He was sorely in need of money and he did not want to be left out of the federation. He stood to lose on both counts if he did not compromise with the shah over Abu Musa, so he allowed himself to be persuaded by Luce's arguments. With this barrier to its formation removed, the federation of six Trucial Shaikhdoms, Abu Dhabi, Dubai, Sharjah, Ajman, Umm al-Qaiwain and Fujairah – henceforth to be known as the United Arab Emirates, *al-imarat al-arabiyya al-muttahida* – was officially proclaimed on 18 July. Much to the relief of his fellow shaikhs, Saqr ibn Muhammad elected that week to play Achilles rather than Bonaparte and remained sulking in his tent up in distant Ras al-Khaimah.

Bahrain declared her independence on 14 August when the existing treaties with Britain were abrogated and replaced by a treaty of friendship to run for fifteen years. Qatar followed suit on 1 September and concluded a similar treaty. The Foreign Office's attention could now be concentrated upon pacifying the shah, whose complaints were daily growing shriller. 'Those islands, Abu Musa and Greater and Lesser Tunb, are ours!' he cried in the last week of September. 'We need them. We shall have them. No power on earth will stop us. . . . I have a war fleet, Phantom aircraft and brigades of paratroopers. I could defy Britain and occupy the islands militarily.' He had no need to distress himself so. The British government had no intention of standing in his way, nor was public opinion in Britain, at least in so far as it was articulated by the press, opposed in the slightest to gratifying his wishes. Almost without exception, British newspaper opinion had been in favour of Britain's withdrawal from the Gulf from the moment that the Conservatives returned to office. Now, in the autumn of 1971, it was equally in favour of appeasing the shah, so as to facilitate Britain's escape from the tiresome responsibilities which she had so inconveniently inherited from her imperial past.

An editorial in the *Sunday Times* argued plausibly on 11 July,

If the Shah is willing to compensate the Shaikhs handsomely for the loss of their islands, they will almost certainly be willing to agree. In that case, the Arabs must be provided with a scape-goat. What better one than Britain, if we can find the formula before December for the transfer to Iran of these miniscule seeds of discord? It would surely not be beyond Britain's capacity to bear the probably short-lived Arab odium that would result.

The diplomatic correspondent of the *Guardian*, a newspaper much given to moralizing about international affairs, commented on 3 November:

Given the military predominance in the area of the forces of Iran, and the very considerable British financial interest in the Iranian oil industry, the path of realism would appear to be to accept the inevitable and recognise the determination of the Shah's Government to occupy Abu Musa as soon as the British forces are gone.

The *Guardian* delivered a further sermon on the theme of 'might is right' on 20 November, in which it earnestly counselled satisfaction of the shah's claim to the islands – which, it went on to observe (with a certainty which no doubt proceeded from expert knowledge of the subject), 'has some historic as well as strategic merit'. Sentiments of a similar kind were voiced by *The Times*, whose diplomatic correspondent airily observed in late November, 'If Iran carries out its threat to seize the Tumbs, Shaikh Sakr has only himself to blame.'

The Foreign Office's efforts to conciliate the shah finally bore fruit in mid-November. A written understanding was concluded between the shah and

Shaikh Khalid of Sharjah providing for the establishment of a Persian military post on Abu Musa in return for the payment to the shaikh of an annual subsidy of $3.5 million for a period of nine years, or until such time as any revenues the shaikh might derive from oil discovered in his territories reached the sum of $7 million annually – after which, presumably, they were to be shared. At the same time the British government informed the Persians that the treaties with the Trucial Shaikhdoms would be terminated on 1 December, and that the UAE would be formally inaugurated the following day, when a treaty of friendship would be signed between Britain and the federation. Only the question of Ras al-Khaimah and the Tunbs remained, and on this, after some delicate manoeuvring at Tehran, a tacit understanding emerged that the British, for their part, would not oppose a Persian occupation of the islets, while the shah, on his side, would take no step to effect an occupation until after the abrogation of the British treaties with Ras al-Khaimah on 1 December, when the British government would be under no requirement whatever to assist the shaikhdom. Moreover, since Ras al-Khaimah was not a member of the UAE, the federal rulers would have no legal obligation to support Shaikh Saqr in resisting any Persian move to occupy the Tunbs.

Everything was now settled, with all parties satisfied – except, of course, Shaikh Saqr, but then he was a notoriously awkward character – and Britain could now retire smoothly and gracefully from the Gulf. The Middle-East correspondent of the *Financial Times*, who was watching approvingly from the sidelines in Kuwait, extended his congratulations on 30 November, both to Luce on his 'considerable triumph' at Tehran and to the shah 'who has acted in a very statesmanlike manner'. The congratulations were a little premature. That same day Persian troops went ashore on both Abu Musa and the Tunbs, inflicting several casualties upon a police detachment from Ras al-Khaimah stationed on the Greater Tunb which opposed the Persian landing. What had gone wrong? Had the shah failed to keep his word? Or had an excess of cleverness in the scheme concocted at Tehran simply caused confusion? Whatever it was, the shah achieved a propaganda triumph with his *coup de théâtre*, which he vauntingly represented to his people as a humiliating defeat for the power which had held sway in the Gulf for 150 years. There appeared to be no conscious realization of any humiliation on Home's part when he rose in the House of Commons on 6 December to announce the termination of Britain's guardianship of the Gulf and to explain the circumstances in which it had occurred. Perhaps it was because he was simply unaware of how such events are viewed in the Middle East, just as he seemed to be uncertain whether or not sovereignty over Abu Musa and the Tunbs had actually been transferred to Persia. 'As for the Tunbs and Abu Musa,' he told the House, 'their sovereignty is left open.' When questioned on the point he repeated what he had said: 'The view of the government of Iran, as I understand it, is that the sovereignty issue has not been raised by either side.' How Home could make this statement is something of a mystery, for he must have been aware that only a few days earlier, on 30 November, the Persian prime minister, Abbas Hoveida, had informed the *majlis* that Persian sovereignty over the islands 'had been restored following long negotiations with the British government'. Hoveida went on to emphasize the fact that Persia has 'in no conceivable way relinquished or will relinquish its incontestable sovereignty and right of control over the whole of Abu Musa island'.

On the day that the Persians occupied the Tunbs by force the aircraft carrier HMS *Eagle*, with No. 40 Royal Marine Commando on board, and the cruiser HMS *Albion* were standing by in the Gulf of Oman. Why were they there? Was it simply to give comfort to the British community in the Gulf by a last showing of the flag? If so, then their mission was pointless, for they remained unseen outside the Gulf and their presence there was largely unknown. Or were they at hand to cope with any complications that might arise over the termination of the treaties and the ending of Britain's naval protectorate of the Gulf? If this were the case, why was nothing done to contest the Persian landing on the Tunbs on 30 November when the treaties with Ras al-Khaimah were still in force, albeit that they had less than twenty-four hours to run? It is, of course, futile to ask such a question. There was never the slightest intention on the part of the British government to run the risk of offending the shah by thwarting his wishes. On the contrary, its views harmonized exactly with those enunciated so confidently by the *Sunday Times* some months previously, that it was far better for Britain to act the scapegoat in the Gulf and to bear 'the probably short-lived Arab odium that would result'.

As had happened so often before, however, it was not the British government that had to bear the severest consequences of its delinquencies. While most of the Arab states did nothing more than make the obligatory noises of protest against the 'rape of Arab soil', the Libyan junta vented its anger at the British government for its collusion with the shah over the occupation of the islands by abruptly nationalizing the British Petroleum Company's concession and assets in Libya. The Iraqi government broke off diplomatic relations with Britain and Persia, forcibly expelled 60,000 Persians from Iraq, and six months later nationalized the Iraq Petroleum Company's remaining holdings in the country. There was at least one more victim of the 'short-lived odium' which was supposed to follow, and this was the amiable and inoffensive Shaikh Khalid of Sharjah. Some six years previously his predecessor, Saqr ibn Sultan (who came from the Bani Sultan branch of the Qasimi ruling family), had been removed from power and sent into exile by the British political resident in the Gulf for conspiring to promote disturbances along the Trucial Coast. Now in January 1972, backed by Iraqi money and arms, he made his return. Sailing by dhow from Basra, he landed clandestinely on the Trucial Coast with a number of followers and made his way to Sharjah town. Calling on the populace to join him in avenging the 'traitorous' transfer of Abu Musa to Persia, he and his band of cut-throats stormed the palace and slew Khalid and several of his retainers. They were soon afterwards overcome by units of the Trucial Oman Scouts and the Abu Dhabi Defence Force and placed in confinement at Abu Dhabi. A brother of the murdered Khalid, Sultan ibn Muhammad, was, by agreement within the Qasimi family and with the concurrence of the other federal rulers, later installed in his place.

No real debate took place in Britain in 1970–71, either within the government or in parliament, still less in the country at large, about whether the British position in the Gulf should be retained or abandoned. Instead there was from the very first days of the new Conservative administration a consensus of opinion among politicians, government officials and publicists, not only that the Conservatives had no option except to adhere to the timetable of withdrawal laid down by the previous administration but also that it was infinitely desirable that they should do so. Most of the fashionable arguments that are the staple of political discourse in our day, especially in the sphere of foreign affairs, were deployed to buttress the consensus, as they had been three or four years earlier in the case of Aden – historical inevitability, the decline of British power, the irresistible advance of nationalism, the incongruity of the *pax Britannica* in a post-imperial age, the growing wealth and maturity of the Gulf oil states, the advent of a new Afro-Asian dispensation in world affairs and so forth. As arguments they had little merit in themselves, politically or historically. All they served to demonstrate was how advanced was the palsy which had overtaken the conduct of British foreign policy, a palsy which owed its origin to a craven view of the world and of Britain's place in it. With a foreign policy that operated from a basis of fear, it is not to be wondered at that the hallmarks of British diplomacy of late years have been vacillation, self-abasement and a profound yearning for 'peace for our time'.

Except on rare occasions, the formulation of British policy in the Gulf since the Second World War had been the exclusive preserve of the permanent officials of the Foreign Office. One does not have to seek far for the reasons. The region, and especially the lower Gulf, was comparatively isolated, more or less unknown to the world outside. Little had been written about it, and the only extensive body of information concerning it resided either in the archives of the Foreign Office and the India Office, which were closed to public view under the fifty-year rule (reduced in 1966 to thirty years) governing access to government records, or in the archives of the oil companies operating in the Gulf, which again were not accessible to outsiders. Members of parliament and ministers, therefore, were almost wholly dependent upon the permanent officials of the Foreign Office for instruction about the Gulf's affairs; and as an understanding of these required an acquaintance with some fairly *recherché* information concerning tribal structures, religious particularism, genealogical ramifications, historical connexions and topographical peculiarities, it was almost inevitable that the officials should be left largely to themselves to make the running in the Gulf. They were not responsible, however, for the most momentous decision taken in the post-war years – that of January 1968 to end the British connexion with the Gulf in 1971. Many of the officials concerned with Arabian affairs were strongly opposed to the decision, although at the same time they conceded that Britain's protectorate of the Gulf had to end some day. Yet once the decision was taken they came round, almost without exception, to the view that it could not subsequently be reversed; and as time passed the initial feeling of dismay which the decision had aroused was gradu- ally replaced by a sense of relief – for reasons which (as Lord Gore-Booth, who was the permanent under-secretary at the time, has since testified) were rather less than incontestable. '... In the Office [so Gore-Booth records] there had been some anxiety about an indefinite prolongation in the Gulf of a "special position" which might involve us in internal struggles in the Arab world.'*

The Foreign Office had never really felt comfortable about its role in the Gulf. It had inherited the custodianship of British interests there from the old Indian political service when the British raj came to an end in 1947. The duties and responsibilities which Britain shouldered in the Gulf were more of a colonial than a diplomatic nature, a fact reflected in the designation of the British representatives there by the titles of 'resident' and 'agent' which used to be current in the Indian political service. The functions of the political resident in the Gulf, whose headquarters had been at Bushire on the Persian coast until 1946, when they were transferred to Jufair on Bahrain, were as much those of a colonial governor as they were those of an ambassador. He had under his command the Trucial Oman Scouts, based at Sharjah, and there were units of the Royal Navy, the Royal Air Force and (from the 1950s) the British Army stationed in the Gulf to assist him if the need arose. His subordinates, the political agents in Bahrain, Qatar, Dubai, Abu Dhabi and (up to 1961) Kuwait, bore more than a passing resemblance to the collectors or district commis- sioners of the former Indian Civil Service and the Colonial Service. Their roles, in short, were of a kind which fitted the officers of the Indian political service more readily and naturally than they did the diplomatists of the Foreign Office, not merely because of the differences in their training and experience but also because of a fundamental divergence in outlook between the two services.

Diplomacy of its nature is a process of bargaining, of the reconciliation of different and often opposing interests, a process in which the completion of a negotiation is all too frequently considered of greater consequence than what transpires during it. In such circumstances, peoples and territories are apt to be regarded somewhat distantly, as concepts or symbols. Imperial or colonial rule, on the other hand, breeds a deep sense of responsibility towards the peoples and lands ruled, along with a habit of authority over them; so that there is a natural resistance among imperial administrators to the notion that the fate

* Paul Gore-Booth, *With Great Truth and Respect*, London, 1974, p. 377.

of these peoples and lands is to be bandied about in transactions in far-off capitals. When the Foreign Office assumed charge of Britain's interests and obligations in the Gulf from the India Office and the Indian empire, it did not inherit along with it the spirit and outlook of the Indian Civil Service. Herein lay the essential difference between the two services in their approach to the Gulf, a region where Britain had always played an imperial rather than a diplomatic role.

This difference of approach manifested itself clearly in the controversy over the location of the eastern frontier of Saudi Arabia and in the negotiations for the establishment of the United Arab Emirates. As we have seen, the Foreign Office was prepared in the 1930s to give away part of Abu Dhabi shaikhdom to appease Ibn Saud in the furtherance of British interests elsewhere in the Middle East, particularly in Palestine. It was only prevented from doing so by the India Office, which was opposed on the grounds of principle to the giving away of territory which was not Britain's to give, territory which, furthermore, had previously been recognized as rightly belonging to Abu Dhabi. The India Office was also opposed on the grounds of policy to the perpetration of an injustice in one area of British responsibility (an injustice which would continue to rankle for years to come to the detriment of Britain's relations with the minor Gulf states) in the hope of securing what would doubtless prove to be a transitory advantage in another – if, indeed, such an advantage was actually secured in the first place. The spirit of appeasement in the conduct of British relations with Saudi Arabia persisted in the Foreign Office in the post-war years, even though it was masked, and even for a time subdued, by the firmer political control of Britain's Middle-Eastern policy exercised during the years of Sir Anthony Eden's foreign secretaryship and premiership. Hence the resolute rejection in those years of Saudi Arabia's more extreme territorial claims and the willingness to follow up this rejection with forceful action.

Among the permanent officials, however, there was a disposition to tread softly, a disposition which expressed itself, for example, in the willingness to compromise Abu Dhabi's rights and those of the Iraq Petroleum Company by agreeing to the Saudi demands in 1951 and again in 1954 for a ban upon all oil operations in the disputed areas for the duration of the frontier negotiations and the subsequent arbitration. The officials concerned had read through the files of the 1930s negotiations in their own archives, and had been impressed by the arguments put up by their predecessors in favour of accommodating the Saudis. They paid less attention to the cogent counter-arguments advanced by the India Office at the time, partly because there was no longer an India Office to press them, but even more because they were considered to represent an outmoded way of thinking, the product of beliefs and principles that had no validity or relevance now that the British raj was no more and the retreat from empire was under way in every quarter of the globe. Far from being immune to the mood of disillusion with the imperial past (not to say revulsion against the burden of empire) current in advanced intellectual and political circles in Britain in the 1950s, the Foreign Office fully shared it. It was thus conditioned to adopt a more pliant attitude towards Saudi Arabia and her ambitions than the India Office had advocated twenty years earlier. It could also point, as it had in the 1930s, to the difficulties which Britain faced elsewhere in the Middle East to justify a conciliatory approach to the Saudis. The Suez crisis of 1956 and the failure of the Anglo-French intervention in Egypt – which, as they were afterwards at pains to make known publicly, the majority of officials had vehemently opposed – only confirmed the Foreign Office more deeply in its defensive and apologetic posture; so much so that by 1970 it was prepared to aid and abet Saudi Arabia's designs upon Abu Dhabi's territory for the sake of an untroubled departure from the Gulf.

The mood was again evident in the exchanges in 1970–71 over the merger of the Gulf shaikhdoms in the UAE. Here the chief sentiment evinced by the Foreign Office was impatience – impatience that the negotiations were so dilatory and protracted, impatience that the shaikhs seemingly could not realize that the die was cast, that Britain was leaving and that the days of her benign tutelage were over. Yet as Sir William Luce had himself publicly pointed out in the *Daily Telegraph* only three years earlier,

We have taught the Rulers to rely on our support and protection, and they have undoubtedly benefited from the relationship; but it would not be reasonable or just to blame them now for sheltering under our umbrella when for generations we have encouraged them to do so.

Yet even Luce, whose experience in the Sudan and later in Aden (where he had brought the initial federation of Arab amirates into being) inclined him to view the Gulf shaikhs' misgivings and hesitations with sympathy, was before long infected himself with the Foreign Office's mood, so that he grew less forbearing and more brusque with the shaikhs as their prevarications threatened to set back the date of the British withdrawal. So anxious was the Foreign Office to be gone that when, in the early summer of 1971, the hopelessness of creating a federation of the nine shaikhdoms was finally admitted, it refused to explore the possibility of some kind of federal link between the Trucial Shaikhdoms and the sultanate of Oman to the east. The concept of 'Greater Oman' was by no means new. Moreover, it was a more natural and logical political arrangement than a federation of the Trucial Shaikhdoms with Bahrain and Qatar. But to have initiated negotiations to this end, and, even more, to have persisted in them, would have delayed the British departure beyond 1971, and this the Foreign Office would not abide.

What was equally distasteful to its officials was the reflection that any encouragement Britain might lend to the creation of a 'Greater Oman' would assuredly arouse the ire of both King Faisal and Muhammad Reza Shah, to the serious detriment of all the Foreign Office's patient efforts of the previous months and years to placate them. Throughout 1970 and 1971 the Foreign Office had been at pains to demonstrate that it accepted these two monarchs at their own valuation, as sagacious and redoubtable rulers who were fully deserving and capable of assuming from Britain the guardianship of the Gulf's coasts and waters. Yet Luce himself, it may be recalled, had as recently as October 1969 reiterated his view that 'there is no country within the region which is strong enough to take over control and ensure peace in the whole area'. Much must have changed, evidently, in the succeeding eighteen months to have persuaded his colleagues in the Foreign Office that Saudi Arabia and Persia were now fit to become the joint legatees of Britain's position in the Gulf – that is, if they really were so persuaded. What was probably far more influential in convincing the Foreign Office, and even more so the Cabinet, of the expediency of pretending that a Saudi–Persian condominium over the Gulf was both logical and practicable was the lure of arms and other contracts dangled before them by the Saudi and Persian governments. All knew that the actual award of these contracts was contingent upon a British withdrawal from the Gulf on the date stipulated. So the date was kept and the *suq* bargain completed.

For Britain to have allowed herself to be persuaded by such considerations to retire from the Gulf when she did was a betrayal of all she had done and stood for in the region for 150 years. Not only did she cease to restrain by her presence the two local powers, Saudi Arabia and Persia, whose conduct and ambitions had throughout that time constituted the principal threat to the Gulf's tranquillity, but she magnified her delinquency by immediately embarking upon the sale of armaments to these states on a scale hitherto unknown in this part of the world. The easy rationalizations advanced in 1970–71 to justify the manner and timing of Britain's departure could not conceal the cynicism and shabbiness of the British government's behaviour. Even if the assumption were valid that Britain could not, in the circumstances prevailing in the Gulf in 1971, have continued to play the policeman there much longer, it was no excuse for her degrading transformation overnight into a pedlar of arms to the peoples among whom she had kept the peace for a century and a half. That other Western powers have done the same – which is the miserable reason usually offered in extenuation of Britain's conduct – is irrelevant: none of those powers has ever borne responsibility for the peace of the Gulf, nor was it by their efforts that piracy and maritime warfare were suppressed, the slave trade and the arms traffic put down, and the rule of law extended to the peoples around its shores.

With opinion in the Foreign Office in 1970–71 almost unanimously in favour of withdrawal, it was scarcely conceivable that the Cabinet would act against it. Nor did it, for the simple and sufficient reason that its members – for all their brave utterances since January 1968 about 'honour', 'duty' and 'obligations' – were in favour of withdrawal almost from the day they took office. Despite the evident sincerity with which Luce undertook and pursued his mission, it was conceived of essentially as a cosmetic exercise, designed to give the appearance of fulfilling the Conservatives' election promises. That this was its purpose was made abundantly clear by the fact that on every one of his trips to the Gulf Luce returned by way of Cairo, so that he might keep the Egyptian government informed of the progress of his inquiries and negotiations. From the murmurs of approbation from the Egyptians which followed in the wake of each visit, it was only reasonable to infer that he had yet again procured their benediction upon his efforts – a benediction which would not have been forthcoming if Luce had offered the slightest hint that the Conservative government was reconsidering withdrawal. It was obvious at the time, and even more obvious in retrospect, that the administration of Edward Heath had only one aim in foreign policy and this was to secure Britain's entry into the European Economic Community. By 1970 the permanent officials at the Foreign Office had also come round to the view that Britain's destiny lay in Continental Europe and not, as in the past, in the lands and seas beyond. Politicians and officials were as one in believing that it was necessary for Britain to go naked to the EEC altar, shorn of her political and strategic commitments outside Europe. It never seemed to have occurred to them (or, if it did, it was swiftly dismissed) that the British position in the Gulf might have constituted an attractive dowry, offering a partial guarantee at least of the security of Europe's principal source of crude oil.

An end to the British presence in the Gulf obviously had to come and before many more years had passed. Even in the circumstances of 1971 it was clear that the treaty system was in need of revision: many of its features were irreconcilable with the age or were impediments to the proper working of the system itself. There was no good reason, however, once the necessary or desirable adjustments had been made, why the defensive obligations implicit in the system should not have been retained, along with the influence that such obligations conferred. Together with the facilities for the use of British forces which they would have entailed, these obligations would have contributed to the stability of an area vital to Western interests. It was argued at the time that Britain could not afford to meet the cost of her defence establishment in the Gulf (some £12–14 million annually), and, furthermore, that the demands being made upon the British Army, particularly since the start of the insurgency in Ulster in 1969, meant that troops could not be spared for service in the Gulf. The objection on the grounds of financial stringency seems pretty threadbare today, in view of the prodigality of successive British governments since 1971. As for the argument on military grounds, the reply it obviously invites is – why not raise more troops? Or are we to take it that Britain's defence estimates and the strength of the British Army are graven upon tablets of immemorial stone? To a great extent, however, the question of a British defence commitment to the lesser Gulf states was academic by the end of 1971, not just because the conventional wisdom about Britain's military and financial capabilities had prevailed but even more because the government of the day had, by its behaviour over the preceding eighteen months, prejudiced beyond redemption the usefulness of such a commitment. Defensive commitments to another country are, *ipso facto*, concerned with the preservation of that country's territorial integrity. By conniving at the Persian occupation of Abu Musa and the Tunbs, and by endeavouring to procure the surrender of Abu Dhabi territory to Saudi Arabia, the Heath administration had subverted this principle and thereby debased the value of any defence undertaking that might have been given the fledgling UAE.

In a way, the manner in which Britain left the Gulf was fitting, if not exactly edifying, for it was comparable to the manner in which she had entered it three and a half centuries earlier. The English East India Company began trading to Persia in the second decade of the seventeenth century, establishing factories at Shiraz, Ispahan and Jask (near the entrance to the Gulf). A century earlier the Portuguese had preceded the English into these waters, and they had made the island of Hormuz the citadel of their power in the region. Shah Abbas I, the greatest of the Safavid rulers of Persia, was determined to expel them from the Gulf, and to this end he enlisted the aid of the East India Company to supply the ships he lacked to transport his army for the assault upon Hormuz. At the outset of 1622 ships of the East India Company ferried the Persian army from the mainland to Hormuz, fought and defeated the Portuguese fleet, and imposed a blockade upon the island. The fall of Hormuz brought the English the rewards they had been promised for their help – a trading factory at Bandar Abbas and lucrative commercial privileges in Persia. *Mutatis mutandis* the same mercenary spirit presided over Britain's retreat from the Gulf in 1971.

CHAPTER III
Tribal Rebellion, Marxist Revolution

Our country will be able to play an effective role in spreading the fire of revolution throughout the entire Arabian peninsula without fearing hostile reactions from the coalition of imperialists and reactionaries.

Programme of the National Liberation Front of South Yemen, March 1968

Intrinsically, though not in terms of present wealth or power, Oman is the most important of the minor states of the Gulf. It is also the most interesting, not only for its geographical diversity but also because it possesses a history, reaching back to antiquity, which none of the Gulf shaikhdoms can match. In area, Oman exceeds Kuwait, Bahrain, Qatar and the United Arab Emirates taken together. Its cultivable regions are more numerous, its mineral resources other than petroleum more substantial, and its potential for natural economic development greater than those of these other states. For two centuries, from the time of the expulsion of the Portuguese from Muscat in the middle of the seventeenth century to the assertion of Britain's paramountcy in the Gulf in the nineteenth, Oman was the principal maritime power in Arabian waters. For much of this time her rulers exercised dominion over Zanzibar and the adjacent East African coast, over Bandar Abbas and parts of Makran, and on occasions over Bahrain and Hormuz. Even after her power and influence began their unremitting decline in the mid-nineteenth century – when Oman turned inwards upon herself, morosely putting up the shutters against the world outside – the ghost of her former greatness, like that of the Venetian republic, continued to haunt the seas and shores around her for generations to come.

The dominant geographical feature of Oman is the Hajar mountain range, which sweeps in a great arc from Ruus al-Jibal in the north, the high, rocky promontory jutting into the entrance to the Gulf, down through Oman to end just short of the headland of Ras al-Hadd on the Arabian Sea. Several valleys cut across the Hajar, the largest of them being the Wadi Samail which splits the range into two halves, the western Hajar and the eastern. Only a narrow ridge separates the head of the Wadi Samail, running northwards to the Gulf of Oman, from the second of the great wadis of Oman, the Wadi Halfain, which runs due south towards the Arabian Sea. Towering above the Samail Gap is the Jabal Akhdar, or Green Mountain, a cluster of peaks rising to over 10,000 feet, while a few miles to the west rises the almost equally impressive height of the Jabal Kaur. Enclosed between the Hajar and the Gulf of Oman is a narrow coastal plain known as the Batinah, which ends just north of Muscat where the mountains reach the sea. On the inner side of the western Hajar the foothills gradually give way to a bare and rock-strewn sand-steppe, scored by numerous straggling wadis. In its northern reaches the steppe is known as the Dhahirah; in the south, where it becomes a broken, rocky plateau, as the Hamra Duru. To the south-west the steppe merges with a series of gravel plains and *sabakha* (the plural of *sabkhah*, a salt-flat), at the southern edge of which lies the tract of quicksands known by the grim name of Umm al-Samim, 'Mother of Poison'. Further westward the gravel plains and *sabakha* give way to the forbidding sandhills of the Rub al-Khali.

East of the Samail Gap the Hajar spreads out in range upon range of steep, jagged hills which continue all the way to the coastline south-east of Muscat. The region is called the Sharqiyah (or 'eastern') and it ends where the hills give way to the sandy plain below Ras al-Hadd known as Jaalan. South of the Sharqiyah the highlands of Oman are left behind, and for nearly five hundred miles, until the confines of Dhufar are reached, the landscape is a dreary succession of dune country, like the Wahibah Sands, of gravel plains, like the Huqf, and of stony steppe, like the Jiddat al-Harasis. Dhufar, a fertile enclave on the Arabian Sea, is doubly blessed – by the brief visit every year of the south-west monsoon, which brings rain, and by the Qara Mountains, which shelter it from the scorching winds that blow out of the Rub al-Khali to the north.

The population of Oman, which has been variously estimated in recent years at anything between 650,000 and 900,000, probably numbers less than half a million. It is still intensely tribal in composition: the main non-tribal elements are the Indians, Pakistanis, Baluchis, Persians and others who form the larger part of the polyglot communities of Muscat, Matrah and the towns of the Batinah. There are some 200 major and minor tribes distributed throughout the country, mostly along the Batinah coast and in the valleys and foothills of the Hajar mountains, especially in and around the towns of Nizwa, Izki, Firq, Bahlah and the other ancient centres of habitation in central Oman. The tribesmen live by agriculture, the raising of livestock and fishing, producing little in the way of an exportable surplus. Centuries of feuding have bred in them a rancorous disposition, and long isolation has made them intensely suspicious of strangers and foreign influences.

The contentiousness which is so marked a feature of Omani life is due in large measure to the inveterate religious discord and factional rivalry that exists within Omani society. Roughly half the tribesmen are Sunni Muslim by persuasion, the other half, Ibadi. Since Ibadism has played so decisive a part in shaping the history of Oman, down to the present day, some notice must be taken of its origins and attributes, as well as of the dissensions to which these have given rise in Omani politics.

Ibadism is the third, as well as the smallest, of the three major divisions of Islam (the others being the Sunni and the Shia). It originated with the *Khawarij*, or outsiders, of the early years of Islam who repudiated the caliphate of Ali and who were, in consequence, put to death for their apostasy. One of the few Kharijite groups which survived was led by Abdullah ibn Ibad, and it was his followers who were largely responsible for implanting Kharijite doctrines in Oman. Ibadism in Oman early acquired a militant character as a consequence of the hostility of the Sunni tribes, and even more as a result of the punitive expeditions periodically sent against the Ibadiya by successive Umayyad and Abbasid caliphs from the seventh to the tenth centuries AD. These harsh visitations had the unlooked-for effect of diminishing the antagonism between the Ibadi and Sunni tribes, so that the survival of the Ibadiya gradually became equated with the preservation of the independence of Oman as a whole.

Doctrinally, the Ibadiya differed little from the adherents of the Sunni schools. They were strict, even fanatical, in their observance of the duties and prescriptions of Islam: no charge of heterodoxy could fairly be levelled against them. Where they parted company with the majority of Sunni opinion was in their attitude to the imamate or caliphate of Islam. They not only refused to recognize any imams or caliphs other than the first two, Abu Bakr and Omar, but they also rejected the notion that the succession to the imamate should be the prerogative of any one family or clan, even that of the Prophet himself. The imamate, they maintained, was not an unconditional necessity; the Muslim community did not require a permanent and visible head, but if one were desired he could be chosen from any of its members, the criterion of selection being his moral and religious attainments, not his lineage or standing. The prime duty of the imam was to direct the community in the ways of the Koran, the *sunna*, or 'customs', of the Prophet, and the example of the early imams. The community, in its turn, had the power as well as the duty to depose incompetent or unworthy imams. If no worthy successor could be found, the imamate could be left vacant and the community revert to a state of *kitman*, or concealment.

For all their insistence upon the lack of necessity for an imam to lead them, the Ibadiya of Oman have for the greater part of their history since the eighth century AD been ruled over, in name or in fact, by an elected imam. Their prolonged struggles against the Abbasid armies in the ninth and tenth centuries made effective leadership indispensable, if the Ibadi community was to survive; and as a consequence the character of the imamate gradually changed, from being primarily a religious office to one in which the secular abilities of the incumbent were as important as his theological attainments. The imamate was suppressed in the middle of the twelfth century, and Oman was ruled for the next two-and-a-half centuries by a dynasty of *malik*s, or kings, known as the Nabhaniyah or Bani Nabhan. When the imamate was revived at some time in the first half of the fifteenth century it led a precarious existence. The Bani Nabhan still dominated the interior of the country, while the coastal towns were, from the early years of the sixteenth century, under the control of the Portuguese. The restoration of the imamate to a central role in Omani life came about as a consequence of the election to office of the head of the Yaaribah clan of Rastaq in the third decade of the seventeenth century. Under the Yaaribah, Oman became a formidable naval power in Arabian and Eastern waters. After driving the Portuguese from Muscat and the other coastal towns of Oman, the Omanis went on to attack the Portuguese possessions in India, and at the end of the century they drove the Portuguese from their strongholds on the east African coast, which thenceforth fell under Omani domination. Unfortunately, while the Yaaribah had introduced the principle of hereditary succession into the imamate, contrary to Ibadi doctrine, they could not ensure the calibre of their successors. By the third decade of the eighteenth century the dynasty was in a state of collapse, and its demise unleashed a series of conflicts over the succession to the imamate which plunged Oman into almost continuous civil war for the next quarter of a century.

It also subjected the country to foreign invasion and occupation, when in 1737 the last Yaaribah imam appealed to the Persians for military aid against his enemies. A Persian army twice ravaged Oman, and Persian garrisons remained in the country until they were expelled in 1744 by Ahmad ibn Said, ruler of Sauhar and head of the Al Bu Said clan. Five years later Ahmad ibn Said was elected imam, initiating the reign of the Al Bu Said dynasty which has ruled Oman down to our day.

One of the lasting effects of the civil wars of the eighteenth century was to emphasize and perpetuate a basic disunity among the tribes which had existed since the Arab settlement of Oman in the pre-Islamic times. The earliest immigrants in the first millennium BC were Yemeni or Qahtani Arabs from south-western Arabia, who settled mainly in the central mountain complex of the Jabal Akhdar, in the Sharqiyah and in Jaalan. By the second century AD the migration of these Yemeni tribes had ceased. It was followed in the fourth and fifth centuries AD by a fresh series of migrations of Nizari or Adnani Arabs from central and eastern Arabia, who settled north of the Samail Gap, along the inner slopes of the western Hajar and on the Trucial Coast. As a general rule, to which a number of exceptions must be admitted, the tribes of Yemeni stock were Ibadi by religious conviction, while those of Nizari origin were Sunni. One of the exceptions to the rule was the Bani Ghafir of central Oman, a Nizari tribe which was Ibadi by religious profession. The *tamimah*, or paramount shaikh, of the Bani Ghafir was one of the contestants for the imamate in the early stage of the civil wars of the eighteenth century. A rival candidate was the *tamimah* of the Bani Hina, another tribe of central Oman, which was Yemeni in origin. Each attracted the support of other tribes, and as the contest between them intensified it drew in most of the tribes of Oman, on either the Hinawi or the Ghafiri side. Even after the deaths in battle of the two main contestants the tribes continued to identify themselves in political terms as Hinawi or Ghafiri. The reason why the differentiation persisted was because it conformed, by and large, to the underlying distinction in Omani society between tribes of Yemeni and tribes of Nizari origin: most of the Yemeni tribes aligned themselves with the Hinawi faction, most of the Nizari with the Ghafiri faction. Although some important exceptions must again be admitted to this rule, the identification of the Yemeni tribes as Ibadi in religious belief and Hinawi in political affiliation, and of the Nizari tribes as Sunni and Ghafiri, is of sufficient validity to serve as an aid to understanding the course of Omani politics since the eighteenth century.

The character of the civil wars had a profound effect upon the nature and significance of the Ibadi imamate. It debased the office by making it a trophy to be won by force of arms, and it brought into contempt the theological qualifications normally required of a successful candidate. What was of equal moment, because the war ended with the accession to power of the Al Bu Said dynasty it transformed the traditional basis of ruling authority in Oman; for Ahmad ibn Said, the founder of the dynasty, relied for his strength more upon his maritime and mercantile resources than upon his standing as a tribal and territorial magnate. His successors in the Al Bu Said line were essentially merchant princes whose interests and energies were directed primarily to enterprises outside Oman – to trade with India, conquest in the Gulf and dominion in East Africa – and who depended substantially upon the fruits of these enterprises to maintain their rule in the country. None of them, with the exception of Ahmad ibn Said's immediate successor who reigned only a few years, assumed the office of imam. Instead they were content to rule as temporal princes with the title of 'saiyid' (in its meaning of 'lord'), a style by which they have since been customarily known to their people, although later Al Bu Said rulers also adopted the title of 'sultan' which was first applied to them by Europeans.

Throughout the greater part of the nineteenth century Oman was subjected to a series of invasions by the Wahhabis or Saudis of Najd, whose puritanical zeal and fierce intolerance matched those of the Ibadiya themselves. The Wahhabi incursions contributed greatly to the estrangement of the inland tribes, both Ibadi and Sunni, from the Al Bu Said rulers. Saiyid Said ibn Sultan, the greatest of the Al Bu Said princes, who reigned from 1806 to 1856, was, like his predecessors, more interested in overseas trade and dominion than in the internal affairs of Oman. From the middle years of his life until his death he passed the greater part of his time at Zanzibar, leaving the government of Oman to one of his sons. He afforded no real protection to his people against the Wahhabis, electing to pay the intruders Danegeld instead, which is perhaps one reason why the Ibadi tribes never pressed the imamate upon him. Another probable reason is that they considered him unfitted spiritually for the office, being tainted by his trafficking with Christians and Hindus, by his penchant for innovations, and by his consortings with Abyssinians and Baluchis. For his part, so far as is known, Said ibn Sultan never sought election as imam. He may simply not have wanted the office, or the responsibilities which went with it, preferring to keep his court at Muscat, with its view upon the open sea, rather than in the interior, at Nizwa, Rastaq or Sauhar, the three towns where, so Ibadi custom decreed, the imam might properly conduct the Friday prayer.

On Saiyid Said's death in 1856 his eldest surviving son succeeded to his dominions in Oman, while another son declared himself independent ruler of Zanzibar and the East African dependencies. The *de facto* division of the sultanate was made permanent in 1861 by the governor-general of India, acting as arbitrator in the dispute between Said's heirs. The loss of Zanzibar, and of the East African slave trade of which it was the centre, aroused great resentment among the tribes of Oman, a resentment which found expression in a movement to revive the Ibadi imamate. The movement culminated in 1868 in the expulsion of the reigning sultan from Muscat and the election of the head of the collateral branch of the Al Bu Said, Azzan ibn Qais, the *wali* or governor of Rastaq, as imam. Azzan celebrated his election a year later by driving the Wahhabis from the Buraimi oasis, to which they were not to return for three-quarters of a century. His reign, however, proved brief: in January 1871 he was overthrown and slain by one of Saiyid Said's sons, Turki.

With Azzan's death and the restoration of the main Al Bu Said line, the heart went out of the imamate movement for years to come. Turki ibn Said ruled with the fluctuating support of a shifting coalition of Hinawi and Ghafiri tribes, whose loyalty he secured by the customary Al Bu Said policy of alternating bribery with coercion. Though both his reign and that of his son, Faisal, who succeeded him in 1888, were troubled by tribal unrest and rebellions, the fractiousness of the tribes was not directed towards the re-establishment of an Ibadi theocracy. The eclipse of the Saudi dynasty in Najd in the last two decades of the century removed the threat of invasion from that quarter, and correspondingly diminished the desire of the Ibadi tribes for the leadership and unity that an imam might have given them. What sentiment for the imamate endured was kept alive by the *mutawwa* class among the Ibadiya, the religious zealots who never ceased to anathematize the Al Bu Said house for its laxity, debauchery and besottedness with foreign ways. With control of the imamate movement falling almost wholly into the hands of the *mutawiyah*, the spiritual nature of the office came to be portrayed as paramount, its temporal functions

as incidental. The heroic imams of Ibadi tradition had been powerful chieftains, more noted for their political skill and military prowess than for their
piety and suppleness in religious disputation. Azzan ibn Qais, for all his
shortcomings, had been cast in this mould, but with his passing the 'pale-eyed
priests' began to reshape the institution.

To these contentious ecclesiastics the reigning sultan, Faisal ibn Turki, was
little better than a *kafir*, an infidel. Although an Ibadi like themselves, he had
failed in his dispensation of justice to apply the *sharia*, the law of Islam, in strict
conformity with the Ibadi interpretation. He could not speak, read or write
literary Arabic, and indeed the language in which he appeared to converse most
easily was Gujerati. He and his dynasty had so intermingled their blood with
that of Africans, Abyssinians, Baluchis and Indians that they could scarce be
looked upon any longer as Arabs. Faisal ibn Turki not only tolerated Hindus,
Jews and Christians at Muscat, but he also permitted the importation of liquor
and tobacco into the capital. He relied upon the British for his continuance in
power, and he looked to India rather than to Arabia for cultural inspiration. He
had flouted the wishes of his subjects by yielding to British demands to curb
the slave trade and the arms traffic, he had been notoriously fickle in his
apportionment of subsidies to the tribes, and he had at the same time increased
the duties on goods passing to and from the interior.

Whether or not this was a fair estimation of the character and government of
Faisal ibn Turki, it was the view taken of that hapless ruler by the *mutawiyah*
and many of the upland tribes in the early years of this century. It required only
a miscalculation of a major order on his part to translate their contempt into
open hostility, and Faisal made that miscalculation in 1912 when, as a means of
more effectively controlling the flow of arms into Oman, he set up a central
warehouse for their distribution at Muscat. At a gathering of tribal chieftains,
mutawiyah and *ulama* (divines) in May 1913 the revival of the imamate was
proclaimed and the standard of revolt raised against the sultan. A month later
Nizwa was occupied, the Al Bu Said *wali* expelled and the town made the seat
of the imamate, as in times past.

The new imam was a little-known shaikh of the Bani Kharus, Salim ibn
Rashid. His patrons were Himyar ibn Nasir, *tamimah* of the Bani Riyam who
inhabited the high valleys of the Jabal Akhdar and the acknowledged leader
of the Ghafiri tribal faction; and Isa ibn Salih, *tamimah* of the Hirth of the
Sharqiyah and leader of the Hinawi tribal faction. The new Hinawi–Ghafiri
coalition was probably the most formidable ever created against an Al Bu Said
ruler, and the fact of its creation, together with the weight of tribal support
which it attracted, testified to the yawning gulf that had opened up between the
Al Bu Said and their subjects. Had it not been for British intervention in the
years after 1913 the sultanate would surely have been destroyed as an institution, and the Al Bu Said line overthrown. As it was, the partisans of the
imamate were eventually forced to accept that, so long as the Al Bu Said sultan

enjoyed British backing, he could not be deposed; while on his side the sultan was driven to acknowledge that his authority over his turbulent subjects in the mountains had been reduced to little more than a fiction.

British interest in the fortunes of the Al Bu Said dated back to the closing years of the eighteenth century, when the landing of the French expeditionary force under Napoleon Bonaparte in Egypt in 1798 led the British authorities in India to secure an undertaking from the Al Bu Said ruler of Muscat in the autumn of that year to exclude the French from his dominions. It remained British policy for a hundred and fifty years thereafter, down to the dissolution of the Indian empire in 1947, to prevent any other power from obtaining a foothold in Oman, lest it should compromise the security of the British possessions in India. The policy could not be pursued in isolation from developments in Arabia and the Gulf in the intervening century and a half; and so the British found themselves upholding the independence of Oman against various attempts by the Saudis, the Turks and others, to subvert it, either by direct assault or by intrigue. The British also found themselves driven by events to sustain the rule of the Al Bu Said within Oman, largely as a consequence of the undertakings given by successive Al Bu Said sultans to prohibit the slave trade to their own people, to reduce the arms traffic and to afford protection to British Indian subjects residing in their dominions. Thus, a sense of obligation, not just self-interest, informed the British attitude to the Al Bu Said, an obligation which was reinforced by a further undertaking given by the Al Bu Said in 1891 not to alienate any portion of their territory to a foreign power.

British Indian troops saved Muscat from capture by the imamate forces at the beginning of 1915, and they continued to guard the capital for the next five years. Faisal ibn Turki died in October 1913 and was succeeded by his son, Taimur, who proved no more acceptable to the inland tribes than his father had been, and for much the same reasons. Nevertheless by 1920 the tribes were ready to make their peace with him, partly as a result of the economic distress they were suffering, partly because they had been thrown into confusion by the assassination of the Imam Salim al-Kharusi in July 1920. The two sides met in September 1920 at Sib, on the coast to the north of Muscat, where, with the assistance of the British political agent at Muscat, a settlement of their differences was negotiated and signed.

In the years following the conclusion of the *modus vivendi* at Sib relations between the sultan at Muscat and the tribes were relatively harmonious, if somewhat distant. So long as the sultan did not attempt to interfere in their territories, the chiefs of the imamate confederacy did not challenge his government elsewhere in the country or his right to conduct its external affairs. A new imam had been elected within days of the murder of Salim al-Kharusi. He was Muhammad ibn Abdullah al-Khalili of the Bani Ruwaihah, a grandson of a notable *mutawwa* leader who had played a prominent role in the election of Azzan ibn Qais half a century earlier. Isa ibn Salih al-Harithi had nominated him, and he was chosen for his piety and his knowledge of Ibadi theology. He possessed no power or authority that did not derive from the backing of his patron, the Harithi chieftain. Taimur ibn Faisal retired to India late in 1931 and abdicated in February 1932 in favour of his eldest son, Said. A young man of twenty-one years of age at his accession, Said ibn Taimur was content to carry on the government in unspectacular fashion, his principal concern in the early years of his reign being to set its finances in order and to secure a slackening of the reins of British supervision. Real power in the interior of Oman in the 1920s and 1930s was wielded by Isa ibn Salih al-Harithi, at the head of what was essentially a Hinawi confederation, the original alliance with the Ghafiri tribal faction having gradually been attenuated, if not completely dissolved, by the fortunes of war and the death of the Ghafiri leader, Himyar ibn Nasir, whose place as *tamimah* of the Bani Riyam was taken by his son, Sulaiman, a youth of morose disposition and dissolute habits.

Isa ibn Salih al-Harithi died in 1946. He was succeeded in the chieftainship of the Hirth and leadership of the Hinawi faction by his son, Salih, then about twenty-seven years of age. The old Harithi chief's death produced two immediate changes in the balance of Omani politics. One was an accession of power to the Imam al-Khalili, who despite his reputation for sanctity, learning and judicial severity, had always lived in the shadow of his patron. The other was the emergence into the political limelight of Sulaiman ibn Himyar, the *tamimah* of the Bani Riyam, now grown more stable if scarcely more congenial or less profligate. Two further developments in this period were to arouse the interior of Oman from its placid introspection and to confound its politics, and these were the beginnings of serious oil prospecting in northern Oman and the concomitant revival of Saudi activity in the region after a lapse of three-quarters of a century.

Petroleum Concessions Limited, the subsidiary of the Iraq Petroleum Company which had secured concessions from the major Trucial Shaikhs between 1937 and 1939, had also obtained a concession for Oman from Sultan Said ibn Taimur in 1937. The company made a brief reconnaissance of the Dhahirah, from Ibri to the Buraimi oasis, in the winter of 1938–9 and then suspended operations for the duration of the war. After the war it recommenced prospecting on the Trucial Coast, and in the winter of 1947–8 it extended its survey to the vicinity of Buraimi.

The appearance of the surveying party prompted the Imam al-Khalili to declare that he would tolerate no oil prospecting in the districts where his writ ran, or even allow Christians to set foot in the imamate domains. The warning, however, did not deter Wilfred Thesiger from setting out from the Buraimi oasis early in 1949, under the protection of Zayid ibn Sultan, the younger brother of the shaikh of Abu Dhabi who served as the Bani Yas *wali* in the oasis, with the object of making his way along the northern edge of the sands to the territory of the Wahibah tribe in the east. When the imam learned of Thesiger's defiance of his edict he was highly annoyed, although he relented to the extent of allowing the explorer to return to Buraimi by way of the Oman steppes. He was less forgiving when Thesiger reappeared the following year and crossed the *dirah*, or tribal range, of the Duru, with the intention of reaching the Jabal Akhdar. Determined that he should not do so, and particularly that he should not make contact with Sulaiman ibn Himyar, the imam sent a hundred armed men to Thesiger's camp with orders to kill him if he advanced any further. Since Thesiger could not reach the Jabal Akhdar, Sulaiman ibn Himyar came down from the mountain to meet him. The reason why the Bani Riyam chieftain was ready to defy the imam's interdict was that he wanted Thesiger to convey a request from him to the British political resident in the Gulf for recognition as independent amir of the Jabal Akhdar, with a treaty status comparable to that of the Trucial Shaikhs. Thesiger passed on the request but it was not granted.

A more promising avenue for the pursuit of his ambitions opened up to Sulaiman ibn Himyar when the Saudis occupied one of the Omani villages in the Buraimi oasis in August 1952. The sultan, Said ibn Taimur, responded to this provocation by assembling a large force of tribesmen at Sauhar, while the Imam al-Khalili declared a *jihad* against the interlopers and gathered several hundred tribesmen at Dariz to co-operate with the sultan's forces. At the last moment (as related in the previous chapter) the Saudis were saved from having to beat a humiliating retreat from Buraimi by the intervention of the British government, which brought pressure to bear upon Saiyid Said to disband his tribesmen. It was, as has already been remarked, an ill-judged act of interference. Not only did Said ibn Taimur suffer a loss of reputation among his subjects for abandoning the expedition but the Saudis were left with a base at Buraimi from which to mount a campaign of subversion among the tribes of inner Oman. Sulaiman ibn Himyar, who had kept well clear of the fray, accepted an invitation from the Saudi commander at Buraimi in November 1952 to journey to Riyad to discuss matters of mutual interest. There was little he or his new-found friends could do in concert, however, while the old imam lived, so the Bani Riyam chief was forced to cultivate the unfamiliar virtue of patience.

In May 1954 the Imam Muhammad ibn Abdullah al-Khalili died, at the age of some sixty-eight years. Although to the world outside he had presented an image of dour intolerance and rigid xenophobia, in fact his tenure of the imamate had been the very embodiment of the spirit of Ibadism – stern, austere, withdrawn, self-contained, while he himself had been respected by all for his piety and saintliness. It was unlikely, as the taint of the twentieth century spread to Oman, that his successor would be of the same metal. Two candidates for the imamate had been spoken of in the years immediately preceding his death, one a son of the previous imam, al-Kharusi, the other a son of a prominent *mutawwa* historian. Both were passed over in favour of Ghalib ibn Ali, a thirty-five-year-old shaikh of the Bani Hina, who was at the time acting as the imam's *qadi*, or judge, at Rastaq. Though much is still obscure about Ghalib ibn Ali's elevation to the imamate, one thing is clear and this is that he was from the first very much under the thumb both of Sulaiman ibn Himyar and of his own brother, Talib ibn Ali, the *wali* of Rastaq.

With Ghalib ibn Ali al-Hinawi installed as imam the way was now clear for Sulaiman ibn Himyar to extend his collaboration with the Saudis. The change of circumstances had come none too soon, for Petroleum Development (Oman) Limited – the Oman offshoot of Petroleum Concessions Limited – was preparing to send a prospecting party into the interior to survey the Oman steppes and the adjacent sands. Since the disturbed state of the Buraimi region made an approach from the north impracticable, PDO decided to work from the south. In February 1954 a surveying party landed at Daqm, on the southern coast of Oman. After spending the next few months exploring the country to the south-west, it turned its attention northward, to the central Oman steppes, with the aim of surveying the tribal range of the Duru. Talib ibn Ali, determined that any oil that might lie in Duru territory or anywhere else in the interior of Oman should come under the nominal control of his brother, the Imam Ghalib, declared the concession under which the company was operating to be invalid, since it had been awarded by the sultan in 1937 without the knowledge or consent of the late imam. To force the Duru to withdraw their permission to the surveying party to prospect in their *dirah*, Talib sent an armed party to seize the tribe's date plantations at Ibri. The tactic rebounded upon him: the Duru appealed for help to the troops of the Muscat and Oman Field Force escorting the surveying party, and with their support the Duru moved on Ibri in October 1954 and expelled Talib ibn Ali's men. A month later the Sultan Said ibn Taimur reinforced the troops at Ibri and appointed a *wali* to the town, bringing it back under direct Al Bu Said authority for the first time in many years.

This manifestation of Al Bu Said authority at this particular time and place threatened to play havoc with Talib's plans. Not only did it drive a wedge between him and the Saudi outpost at Buraimi, upon which he relied for tactical and material support, but it also interfered with his endeavours to secure assistance from abroad. Towards the close of November 1954, he submitted an application in the name of his brother for the admission of the imamate of Oman (described in the application as an 'independent Islamic state') to membership of the Arab League. The application was unsuccessful, the members of the League's political committee being unable, so it was reported, to locate the imamate's territories on any map. A year later, following the expulsion of the Saudi police detachment from the Buraimi oasis, the sultan moved to settle accounts with Talib, Ghalib and Sulaiman ibn Himyar. Starting from his southern capital of Salalah in Dhufar, Said ibn Taimur made a 500-mile journey across the desert to Nizwa, which he entered unopposed in the last week of December 1955. Meanwhile, on the seaward side of the Hajar mountains, troops of the Muscat and Oman Field Force had flushed Talib ibn Ali from Rastaq, though they failed to take him prisoner. Sulaiman ibn Himyar came down to Nizwa from his eyrie in the Jabal Akhdar to tender his tainted fealty, while the Imam Ghalib slipped away to his home village of Balad Sait, where the sultan allowed him to remain on condition that he did not leave it.

Saiyid Said's progress through the interior of Oman in the winter of 1955–6 seems to have exhausted his capacity for vigorous action. Thenceforward he left the government of the country largely to his elderly *wazir*, Ahmad ibn Ibrahim, while denying him the authority, financial resources or administrative freedom to govern effectively. Ahmad ibn Ibrahim coped as best he could, with the help of a handful of British advisers and by recourse to the traditional Al Bu Said methods of persuasion and coercion – money and other gifts for the more influential shaikhs, meaningful references to the sultan's standing army for the ill-disposed or recalcitrant. Neither expedient was very successful: Saudi Arabia could furnish more splendid bribes and the Muscat and Oman Field Force, recruited mainly from the heterogeneous population of the coast, ill-equipped and short of officers, was hardly of the calibre to frighten the mountain badmashes.

Talib ibn Ali had meanwhile made his way to Saudi Arabia to seek solace and plot revenge. Throughout 1956 and the early months of 1957 he occupied himself with training and equipping an Oman Liberation Army at Dammam in Hasa, and with smuggling arms and men into Oman in preparation for an uprising. An 'Imamate of Oman' office was set up in Cairo to disseminate propaganda and promote the concept of a sovereign and independent imamate state, separate from the sultanate. The office was headed by members of the family of Salih ibn Isa, the *tamimah* of the Hirth, and it was in the Sharqiyah, the stronghold of the Hirth, that the first signs of rebellion made their appearance in the spring of 1957. At a loss to know what to do, the sultan invited Salih's brother, Ibrahim ibn Isa, to Muscat. Surprisingly, Ibrahim came, early in June. Less surprisingly, the sultan promptly clapped him into gaol. Another guest of the sultan that month was Sulaiman ibn Himyar, whose disposition and intentions the sultan was anxious to gauge. The Bani Riyam chief noted the imprisonment of Ibrahim ibn Isa, and he also knew that Talib ibn Ali had secretly returned to Oman in the middle of June, landing on the Batinah coast with a consignment of arms. What tipped the scales for Sulaiman, however, was the closing down that month of the Petroleum Development (Oman) base at Daqm in southern Oman. Henceforth the main supply base was to be at Azaiba on the Batinah coast, which meant that the company's supply route to the interior would have to go through the Wadi Samail. Sulaiman calculated that by seizing the western end of the pass he could virtually hold PDO to ransom; and with this in mind he slipped away from Muscat early in July and hurried back to his lair in the Jabal Akhdar.

Talib ibn Ali in the meantime had made his way across the Hajar to the vicinity of the Jabal Kaur, where he assembled the tribesmen he had trained at Dammam. Reinforced by a contingent of Bani Riyam sent by Sulaiman ibn Himyar, Talib moved upon Bahlah with half his force, while the other half made for Nizwa. Ghalib ibn Ali emerged from seclusion at Balad Sait and announced he was resuming the active functions of imam. Bahlah and Nizwa both fell without a fight to the triumvirate's forces, and the white *mutawwa* banner was broken out over the great fort at Nizwa. Said ibn Taimur, who was incapable of quelling the uprising, turned to the British for help. Troops and aircraft were dispatched from Bahrain and Aden, and by the early part of August the rebellion had been suppressed. Talib, Ghalib and Sulaiman escaped to the fastnesses of the Jabal Akhdar, where they went to ground with two or three hundred followers, determined to carry on the fight.

A good deal of fuss was made at the time about the British military intervention in Oman, especially as it occurred so soon after the Anglo-French expedition to Egypt the previous year. Said ibn Taimur was denounced at the United Nations and by the 'non-aligned' Afro-Asian states as a mediaeval despot propped up by British imperialism, while the imamate of Oman was depicted in these same circles as a modern, progressive and enlightened polity whose independence had been snuffed out by the unholy alliance of despotism and imperialism. The 'question of Oman' was placed upon the agenda of the UN General Assembly by the Afro-Asian bloc and remained there for several years, affording occasions for profound disquisitions on Arabian politics by a variety of delegates from the most unlikely countries. There was rather more point, so far as the people of Oman were concerned, to the efforts which were made after 1957 to put an end to the insecurity rampant in the interior and to effect an improvement in the sultan's administration. An agreement was concluded between the sultan and the British government in July 1958, whereby the latter undertook to provide military, financial and technical assistance to reorganize the sultanate's armed forces, to improve the country's communications and agriculture, and to lay the foundations of medical and educational services. A regular British army officer, Colonel David Smiley, was appointed to command the sultanate army, other officers and n.c.o.s were seconded to help him, and the work of directing economic development was entrusted to Colonel (later Sir) Hugh Boustead, lately Resident at Mukalla in the Hadramaut, who before then had spent many years in the Sudan civil service.

The most pressing task was to deal with the hard core of rebels up in the Jabal Akhdar, who since the autumn of 1957 had been carrying out a series of raids and ambushes along the length of the Wadi Samail and elsewhere. At first Smiley and his fellow officers could do little more than contain the rebels and prevent them from mining the roads, while they themselves pushed ahead with the job of getting the askaris of the Sultan's Armed Forces (as the Muscat and Oman Field Force had now been renamed) into shape to assault the Jabal Akhdar. All through 1958 the insurgents were kept supplied with weapons and other requirements by Saudi Arabia, the arms being smuggled into the high Oman by various routes – overland by way of the Buraimi oasis, through the port of Dubai on the Trucial Coast and by clandestine landings on the Batinah coast. Most of the weapons originated in the United States and had been shipped to Saudi Arabia under military aid agreements. British representations in Washington for restrictions to be placed on the use of these weapons, especially the mines (which were killing British soldiers as well as Omanis), met with the reply that it was no concern of the United States government how the Saudis chose to dispose of their weapons. No other answer could have been expected, for, as was later to emerge, the rebels were at this time in regular wireless communication with both the Saudis and the Central Intelligence Agency.

By the late summer of 1958 Smiley had been forced to the conclusion that the assault on the Jabal Akhdar could not be carried out by the Sultan's Armed Forces alone. He asked, therefore, for British troops and got them, despite the apprehensions of the Foreign Office over the impression that might be created in the Middle East and elsewhere. Two squadrons of the 22nd Special Air Services Regiment and a squadron of the Life Guards arrived in Oman in the next few months, and in the last week of January 1959, supported by a squadron of the Trucial Oman Scouts and the Northern Frontier Regiment of the SAF, they scaled the forbidding heights of the Jabal Akhdar and overcame the rebels in a brief but hard-fought action. The wily trinity of Ghalib, Talib and Sulaiman ibn Himyar, however, again escaped capture, made their way through the Sharqiyah to the east coast and slipped away by dhow to Saudi Arabia. Although they continued for the next two or three years to smuggle arms and supplies to their supporters scattered through central Oman, the heart had really gone out of the insurgency with the storming of the Jabal Akhdar. The subsequent programme of development carried out under Hugh Boustead's direction in the valleys and plateaux of the *jabal* gradually banished whatever traces of nostalgia may have lingered among the tribesmen for the good old days of carefree brigandage.

With the rebels for all practical purposes vanquished, and the normal pattern of tribal alliances disrupted by the events of the years 1954–9, Said ibn Taimur was in a position to tighten his administrative hold on the interior of Oman. Where tribal power still predominated, e.g. in the Sharqiyah, Jaalan and the Duru country, he made no move to interfere with the *tamimah*s in the exercise of their tribal authority or the enjoyment of their quasi-independent status. Elsewhere, the overthrow or flight of local magnates allowed him to appoint *wali*s, directly responsible to him, to govern the tribes in his name.

The absence of Sulaiman ibn Himyar meant that the Ghafiri tribal faction was without its customary leadership; and the disappearance to Cairo of the *tamimah* of the Hirth, Salih ibn Isa, had likewise deprived the Hinawi tribes of their accustomed head. What was perhaps as significant for the future of Oman as the disarray in the traditional Hinawi–Ghafiri tribal camps was the uncertainty surrounding the imamate itself, following the flight of Ghalib ibn Ali.

Many of the Ibadiya (*ulama* and tribal shaikhs alike) were troubled by the use to which the office had been put since Ghalib's election in 1954. From the moment he had applied for admission to the Arab League in November of that year, he had begun to divest the imamate of its historic character and its links with the Omani past. Whether or not he intended to do so is beside the point: the consequences are what matter. It was not so much the furtive transactions of Ghalib and his associates with the arch-enemies of the Ibadiya, the Saudis, that brought the imamate into disrepute, as the compromises he had made with ideas alien to the true nature and function of the office, such as Arab nationalism and Arab socialism, and his subordination of the interests of the Ibadiya to the ambitions of other parties, whether Saudi Arabia, Egypt or Iraq (from whom Ghalib's confederates also accepted money and arms in the early 1960s). To the Ibadiya of Oman their imam is *imam al-muslimin*, the leader of the faithful: he cannot acknowledge the spiritual supremacy of any other Muslim ruler or accommodate Ibadi doctrine to the tenets of the Sunni schools or the Shia. As the spiritual and temporal ruler of his people, his prime duties are to guide the community rightly and defend it against its enemies. It was difficult to see how these limited moral and religious concepts could be squared with the behaviour of Ghalib ibn Ali and his backers after 1954; with the spurious submissions of an 'imamate delegation' to the United Nations, seeking international recognition of the political independence of inner Oman; with the portrayal of the imamate to the world at large as an instrument of revolutionary nationalism; with the issuing of pronouncements in Cairo, Damascus and Baghdad about a shared faith in Arab socialism; with public affirmations of solidarity with a weird miscellany of alien governments and causes; and with the soliciting of pecuniary aid in capitals as far apart as London and Peking.

Whether, in fact, Ghalib ibn Ali was entitled to continue to regard himself, or to be regarded, as imam of the Ibadiya after his flight from Oman in 1959 was also open to doubt. Whether the Ibadi tribes wanted him to return was equally uncertain. While many tribesmen were troubled by the absence (as opposed to the absenteeism) of an imam to lead the Ibadi community, only a minority desired a return to an imamate form of government. This did not mean, however, that the tribes, whether Ibadi or Sunni, were particularly enchanted with the government of Said ibn Taimur. As indicated earlier, the guiding principle of his administration was indifference, coupled with a tenacious refusal to entrust anyone else with the authority and material resources needed to effect even the most rudimentary improvements in the lot of the Omanis. Saiyid Said's outlook was governed by mistrust – of his people, of his neighbours, of his servants, of his own family. Considering the history of his dynasty, the mistrust was perhaps not ill-founded. To warnings from his British advisers that he was courting danger by failing to exert himself (at a time of nationalist and revolutionary fervour in the Arab world) to lift his country out of the slough of mediaeval backwardness in which it lay, he invariably pleaded poverty as an excuse for inaction. Yet he had quite substantial revenues from customs duties, he had acquired £3 million from his sale of the Omani enclave of Gwadur, on the Makran coast, to Pakistan in 1958, and he was receiving payments both from oil companies for exploration rights and from Britain for social and economic development. It was not enough, however, to overcome his ingrained parsimony, which had its roots in the struggle he had waged in the first decade of his reign to rescue the finances of Oman from the bankruptcy into which his father had allowed them to slide. For the rest of his life he was to be haunted, however irrationally, by the spectre of another descent into penury.

Saiyid Said was also oppressed by the fear of what the improvements he was pressed to make by the British – rather gentle pressure and consequently rather trifling social and economic improvements – might bring in their train. 'We do not need hospitals here,' he once told David Smiley. 'This is a very poor country which can only support a small population. At present many children die in infancy and so the population does not increase. If we build clinics many more will survive – but for what? To starve?' When Hugh Boustead tried to persuade him to set up primary schools to educate the sons of tribal shaikhs and religious dignitaries, he snorted in reply, 'That is why you lost India, because you educated the people.' He expressed a similar opinion to Smiley:

Where could the teachers come from? ... They would come from Cairo and spread Nasser's seditious ideas among their pupils. And what is there here for a young man with education? He would go to the university in Cairo or to the London School of Economics, finish in Moscow and come back here to foment trouble.

The strength of this last argument could not be denied, especially when one glanced northward to Kuwait and Bahrain, and even Saiyid Said's harshest critics were forced to admit that as often as not he had logic on his side.

Like his namesake a century earlier, Saiyid Said in the latter part of his reign turned his back upon his country and his people. Salalah in Dhufar was to him what Zanzibar had been to the earlier Said, and it was there that he spent most of his days from the late 1950s onwards. He rarely visited Muscat, and he never again set foot in the interior after his progress through Oman at the end of 1955. Seek though he might to shut himself off from the world, he could not entirely escape its importunities. When trouble fell upon him in the mid-1960s it came, by a fitting irony, not out of the turbulent highlands of Oman but from the languid confines of Dhufar itself. The shape it took, however, was determined less by conditions in Dhufar than by what was happening to the westward, in the Hadramaut and the Mahra country, and even more by what was to happen in the late 1960s as a consequence of the British abandonment of Aden in 1967 and the inception of the People's Republic of South Yemen. It is to these developments, in the Hadramaut and the rest of South Arabia, that we must turn first before attempting to trace the origins and course of the revolt which was soon to break out in Dhufar.

The Hadramaut, like the Mahra country to the east, had long led an existence separate from that of the amirates and shaikhdoms of the old Western Aden Protectorate. Like most of South Arabia it was a harsh and forbidding land – its very name means 'death is present' – yet the energies and enterprise of its inhabitants had made it relatively prosperous, at least by Arabian standards. Geographically its most remarkable feature was the great Wadi Hadramaut, which extended for 250 miles into the interior from the coast near Saihat. Between the coast and the upper reaches of the wadi lay the *jol*, a broken, rocky plateau which rose abruptly from the narrow coastal plain and stretched inland for a hundred miles. A thriving agriculture and a number of imposing towns (the best known of which were Shibam, Saiyun and Tarim) were to be found in the fertile regions of the Wadi Hadramaut, while the ports of the coast, the chief of which were Mukalla and Shihr, were the centres of a wide-ranging maritime commerce. It was not the native economy of the Hadramaut, however, that was the main source of its prosperity but the wealth accumulated by the large colonies of *émigré* Hadramis settled overseas, especially in the East Indies, Singapore, the Philippines, India and East Africa. The constant intercourse they kept up with their homeland, and the steady flow of remittances they sent to it, were in large measure responsible for the Hadramaut's progress in the years before the Second World War; and it was through their efforts and initiative that innovations and improvements in agriculture, commerce and transportation were introduced to the country.

Sovereignty over the Hadramaut was exercised by two hereditary rulers – the Qaiti sultan of Shihr and Mukalla, whose territory extended for some 200 miles along the coast and a further 150 miles inland, to Shibam and its related towns and settlements in the Wadi Hadramaut; and the Kathiri sultan of Saiyun and Tarim, whose lands formed an enclave athwart the Wadi Hadramaut with no access to the sea. The writ of neither sultan, however, ran much beyond the environs of the coastal and inland towns. Elsewhere the tribes, and especially those whose *diyar* (*dirah*, tribal range, in the singular) controlled the routes across the *jol* to the coast, acknowledged no authority save that of their own shaikhs and the more influential *sada*. The *sada* (*saiyid* in the singular) were the wealthiest and most prominent class in Hadrami society, claiming descent (and with it social precedence) from the Prophet himself. The ceaseless feuding and brigandage of the tribes was the principal obstacle to the further development of the Hadramaut, and it was not until Harold Ingrams was sent to the region, first as a political officer in 1934 and then as resident adviser at Mukalla in 1937, that a sustained and successful effort was made to curb their habitual violence. With the help of Saiyid Bu Bakr al-Kaff, the effective head of the Al Kaff, one of the richest and most powerful of the *saiyid* families, Ingrams persuaded the Hadrami tribal leaders to agree to observe a truce among themselves, on the model of the maritime truces concluded a hundred years earlier by the shaikhs of the Pirate Coast of the Gulf. 'Ingrams' Peace', as it came to be called, initially ran for three years. On its expiry in 1940 Ingrams again managed, despite the reassertion of the old anarchical spirit among the tribes, to persuade the shaikhs to renew it, this time for ten years.

The Second World War, and more particularly the Japanese conquest of south-east Asia, brought great hardship to the Hadramaut, by disrupting the customary intercourse with the East Indies and curtailing the payment of the usual remittances from Singapore, the East Indies and the Philippines. Famine occurred in 1943–4, following the failure of the annual rains. Hundreds of people died, and the survival of the remainder was due in large measure to British assistance. The aftermath of the war did little to restore the Hadramaut's depleted fortunes. Dutch rule ended in the East Indies, and the new state of Indonesia, by confiscating estates and businesses and restricting the export of capital, reduced the flow of funds from the Hadrami Indonesian community to its homeland to a trickle. The other Hadrami colonies in Singapore and the Philippines suffered extensive losses in the war, and they were never to regain their former affluence. A like fate overtook the Hadramis of Hyderabad, who for generations had taken service in the army of the Nizam. Their traditional occupation was closed to them when Hyderabad's independence was extinguished by the government of India after the end of the British raj.

For a time the inhabitants of the Hadramaut pinned their hopes for a revival of their former prosperity on the discovery of oil in their territory, but their hopes were not realized. Meanwhile, with British assistance and guidance, they made the best of their indigenous resources. Economic recovery was gradual but steady, and the standard of living measurably improved as irrigation schemes were put into operation, more schools and dispensaries were opened, and imports of food and manufactured goods grew in volume. Much of the social and economic improvement was due to the initiative and efforts of the more enlightened *sada* like Saiyid Bu Bakr al-Kaff. He had been instrumental, for instance, in having the first motor road built across the *jol* from the coast to Wadi Hadramaut in the years before the war. Any more rapid progress in improving the Hadramis' lot, however, was impeded as much by their own outlook and traits of character (especially their inveterate suspiciousness, proneness to superstition and rancour and contumacy towards one another) as by the drying up of their external sources of wealth. Tribal razzias,

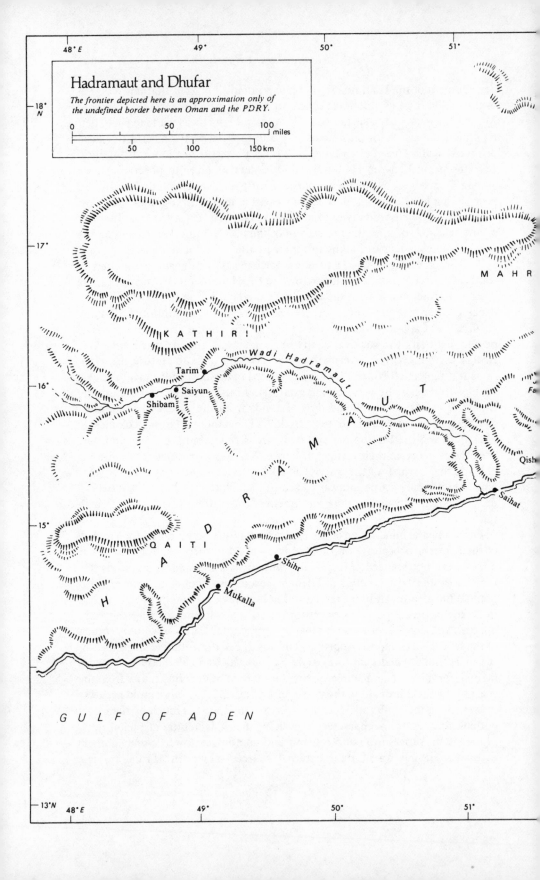

Hadramaut and Dhufar

The frontier depicted here is an approximation only of the undefined border between Oman and the PDRY.

0   50   100 miles

50   100   150 km

18° N

17°

16°

15°

13° N

48° E

49°

50°

51°

M A H R

K A T H I R I

Wadi Hadramaut

Tarim

Saiyun

Shibam

Qish

Saihat

H A D R A M A U T

Q A I T I

Shihr

Mukalla

G U L F   O F   A D E N

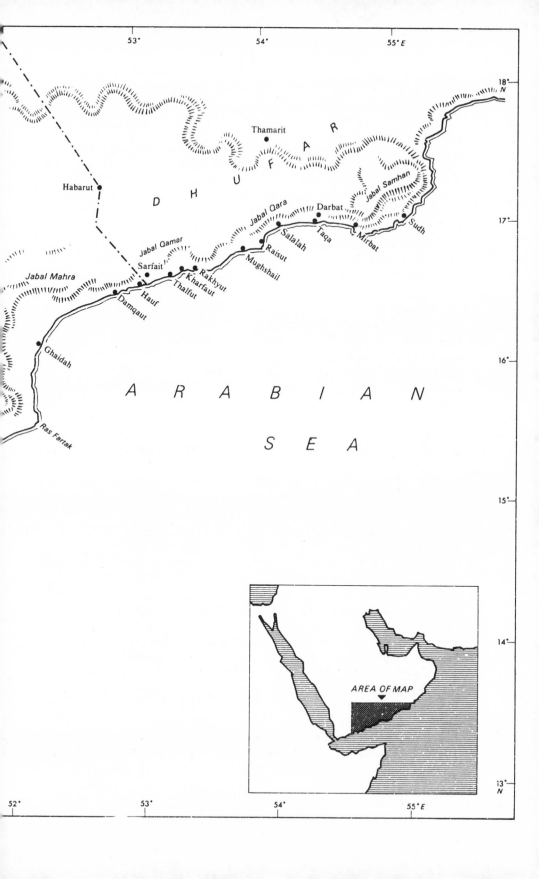

brigandage and blood-letting were still far from uncommon, despite the trucial system; and the Hadrami Bedouin Legion, a British-officered force raised by Ingrams in 1939 to keep the peace, had to maintain a constant vigilance to prevent or suppress outbreaks of tribal disorder.

With their traditional avenues of emigration to India and the East Indies closed to them, many Hadramis in the 1950s began to search elsewhere for work and mercantile opportunities. They journeyed in their hundreds to Aden colony, to the oil states of the upper Gulf, and even to more distant lands. Inevitably they were influenced by the heady notions they encountered, of Arab nationalism, socialism, revolution and the like, so that when they returned to the Hadramaut they were impatient to overturn the existing order of things, more particularly the supremacy of the *sada* and sultans, and the tutelary authority exercised by Britain. Discontent with the privileged position of the *sada* was nothing new among the lower ranks of Hadrami society. It first took organized shape in this century in the Hadrami community in the Dutch East Indies on the eve of the First World War, when the community was split by a controversy over the centuries-old interdiction upon marriage between a woman of the *saiyid* class and a non-*saiyid*. At first the controversy was conducted solely at the level of theological disputation, with each side soliciting judicial opinions in its favour from eminent Muslim *ulama*. As time went by, however, it took on more and more of a secular aspect, assuming the proportions of a popular movement against the social and economic, as well as the religious, ascendancy of the *sada* in Hadrami society, and against the transplantation of this ascendancy by *sada* from the Hadramaut to the Hadrami colonies overseas.

Although the Irshadi movement, as it was called (from the name of the society created by non-*sada* Hadramis in Batavia in 1914 – the *jamiyyat al-irshad*, or 'Religious and Guidance Association'), was restricted to the Hadrami communities in the East Indies and Singapore, knowledge of its existence inevitably penetrated the Hadramaut between the wars. Now that the dominance of the *sada* had been challenged overseas, it was only a matter of time before it was similarly challenged by the non-*sada* majority in the Hadramaut. Whereas religion had been the catalyst which acted to bring the Irshadi movement in the East Indies into being, the anti-*sada* agitation which made its appearance in the Hadramaut in the 1950s was inspired by Arab nationalism. Nationalist precepts were spread through the agency of the social, sports and welfare clubs which sprang up in the principal towns and villages during the decade, and by the ubiquitous transistor radio, which enabled the Hadramis to listen to the revolutionary nationalist propaganda broadcast from Cairo and (after the Yemeni revolution of 1962) from Sana. While nationalism supplied the vehicle for the expression of political discontent in the Hadramaut, the springs of this discontent had little to do with nationalism *per se*. They were what they had always been, viz., the jealousy and resentment felt for the *sada* by the lesser orders of Hadrami society – the *mashaikh*, tribal or religious shaikhs, the *jabail*, or tribesmen, and the *masakin*, the heterogeneous legion of the downtrodden. To them the revolution in the Yemen in 1962 appeared as the harbinger of their own imminent deliverance from *sada* dominance. For the *sada* it was, for the self-same reason, the knell of doom.

Like so many proletarian revolts, the anti-*sada* movement in the Hadramaut depended for its effectiveness upon the defection to its ranks of members of the class whose overthrow it was seeking. A number of the younger *sada*, educated abroad and widely travelled, were among the more vociferous and zealous advocates of the destruction of the existing social and political order. Some of them carried their self-imposed alienation from their own kind to extreme lengths, not only joining forces with its enemies at home but also seeking to collaborate with revolutionary groups elsewhere in the Arab world which were bent upon the overthrow of hereditary and conservative governments. Hadramis, as we have seen, were highly active in the politics of Aden during the 1950s and 1960s, especially at the underground level. The resident colony of Hadramis in Aden was, for the most part, composed either of respectable merchants, whose lively intelligence, commercial acumen and adventurous dispositions had earned them a leading place in the community, or of labourers who had come to earn a living and to support their families at home. There were other Hadramis, however, of a very different kind, young men (as often as not from the *saiyid* class) who were educated, quick-witted, and proud of their superior knowledge of the world, afire with political ambition, and intoxicated from their prolonged imbibing of the strong waters of nationalist and socialist dogma. For them the expulsion of the British and the overthrow of the protectorate rulers were only part of a grander struggle to bring progress, unity and brotherhood to the whole Arab world – and, incidentally, their own ascent to political power.

As we have seen, when the Federation of South Arabia was inaugurated in January 1963 the two Hadrami sultanates, the Qaiti and Kathiri, along with the Mahra territories, were excluded from it. One reason for the exclusion was the apprehension felt by the Qaiti and Kathiri sultans that any revenues they might receive from the discovery of oil in their territories, of which they still had high hopes, might eventually have to be shared with the members of the federation. Another and perhaps more pertinent objection on the part of the Qaiti sultan was that he foresaw a serious decline in his revenues from customs duties, if the rates of duty levied in the Hadramaut were to be lowered to bring them into line with those current in the federation. The Mahra country was the wildest and most inaccessible corner of the Eastern Protectorate. Nominally it was under the suzerainty of the sultan of Qishn and Socotra, who kept permanent residence on the island of Socotra, more than 200 miles away. His authority, however, extended only to Qishn and the other coastal villages: inland a kind of formalized anarchy reigned among the Mahri tribal nomads and cultivators.

No one in power in Aden or the federation quite knew what to do about the Mahra; and as they were in any case more closely related in origins, language and customs to the tribes of Dhufar than to those of the Hadramaut, it was thought best simply to forget about them.

While the political malcontents in the Hadramaut were far from dismayed by its omission from the federation, which they regarded as nothing more than an 'imperialist' contrivance to keep the traditional rulers in power, their goal was far from being an independent Hadramaut. Harold Ingrams and the Dutch Orientalist, Daan van der Meulen (who had been one of the first Europeans to explore the Wadi Hadramaut), both believed that the Hadramaut, with its distinctive society and economy, its sense of singularity and its habitual aloofness, could well survive on its own – indeed, would be better served by independence than by association with a larger political entity. Though many Hadramis thought the same, those of the younger generation who had been indoctrinated with the revolutionary nationalist ideology preached in the northern Arab capitals thought otherwise. Some of them had joined the Arab Nationalists' Movement, others had travelled further along the road to political extremism. Whatever stage their political education had reached, these youthful visionaries were as one in seeking the unification of all the states of South Arabia in a republic which would afterwards merge with the Yemen, and perhaps, in the fullness of time, in a wider union of all the Arab lands. A small and dedicated minority had as their objective the creation of a Marxist state in South Arabia, linked by fraternal bonds with the other communist countries, and dedicated to the cause of world revolution.

Hadramis provided the National Liberation Front in Aden and elsewhere with much of its cannon fodder during the insurgency, and at least two Hadramis, Ali Salim al-Baid and Faisal al-Attas, were elected members of the general command of the Front. The constant coming and going of Hadramis, whether engaged in trade or seeking work, between Aden and the Hadramaut facilitated the establishment by the NLF of a network of cells through the Hadramaut during 1966 and 1967, and paved the way for the overthrow of the Qaiti and Kathiri sultans in September 1967. How exactly the NLF achieved its success in the Hadramaut in the early autumn of 1967 is still unclear. On 17 September, while the Qaiti and Kathiri sultans were holding discussions with the sultan of Qishn and Socotra on a ship of Saudi Arabian registry off Mukalla, the town was taken over by the NLF. The Qaiti sultan never set foot ashore again. At the beginning of October the NLF took control of the Kathiri sultanate and the sultan fled to Saudi Arabia to join his Qaiti neighbour. A fortnight later the NLF occupied Qishn, on the Mahra coast, by flying in men and arms in an aircraft hired in Djibouti. Using the same tactics they occupied Socotra Island towards the end of November, and sent the sultan to join his fellow rulers in exile.

With the establishment of the People's Republic of South Yemen in the closing weeks of 1967 the nationalist revolution in South Arabia was completed. Now the socialist revolution was to follow, to bring about, as the ruling National Front ('Liberation' had been dropped from its title with the end of British rule) phrased it, 'the destruction of the old structure of the state and the building of the proletarian state of the poor'. The ancient boundaries of the former amirates, sultanates and shaikhdoms were abolished, and the country was divided for administrative purposes into six governorates, of which the Hadramaut was the fifth governorate and the Mahra territory the sixth. It was in the Hadramaut that the more fanatical ideologues of the National Front first set about implementing what the Front's propaganda was pleased to call 'the state of workers, poor peasants, soldiers and revolutionary intellectuals exerting their dictatorship over the feudalists, rich peasants and capitalists, local and foreign'. The power of the *sada* and the other privileged classes – the merchants, the tribal shaikhs and the sultanate officials – was destroyed in the way that power has always been destroyed in South Arabia – by the sword. Landholdings were expropriated and broken up, the palaces of the sultans and *sada* taken over, commercial property and funds confiscated, and the former owners reduced to penury, thrown into prison, executed or driven into exile. A people's militia was formed around the nucleus of the former NLF guerrilla bands and organized into units with the grand old Hadrami names of the 'Che Guevara Brigade' and the 'First of May Brigade'. The militia's function was declared to be 'the protection of the revolution by the destruction of its enemies', which meant in effect the pursuit of old feuds and new despoliations under the mantle of political sanctity. Only the Hadrami Bedouin Legion, whose discipline still held, despite the loss of its British officers, stood firm against the tide and resisted attempts to turn it into a political *gendarmerie*.

The pace of the proletarian revolution in the Hadramaut quickly proved too hectic for the South Yemeni president, Qahtan Muhammad al-Shaabi, and the saner ministers of his government. It was too furious, also, for the senior officers of the federal army, who demanded the disbandment of the 'Red Guards' of Hadramaut and a cessation of their 'communist and secessionist' activities. Qahtan al-Shaabi ordered a slowing down of the rate of confiscations and imprisonments until the fourth congress of the NF had met and decided upon the course the republic was to take. When the congress met at Zinjibar in the first week of March 1968 ideological battle was joined between the proponents of 'Arab socialism', led by Qahtan al-Shaabi and his cousin Faisal Abdul Latif al-Shaabi, the minister of the economy, and the 'Marxist socialists' led by the Yemeni, Abdul Fattah Ismail, the minister of culture and guidance, and the Hadrami, Ali Salim al-Baid, the minister of defence. The latter faction emerged from the fray victorious, and their victory was reflected in the programme adopted by the congress for the future. 'Scientific socialism' was declared to be the basis of the South Yemeni state and Marxism its guiding principle. Political power was to be wrested from the hands of the *petite bourgeoisie*, who were deemed incapable of bringing about a national, democratic revolution, and entrusted instead to popular councils in each governorate. These in turn would elect a supreme popular council to govern the country. Until then power would continue to reside with the general command of the National Front. The programme also decreed that, as the burden of protecting the revolution and supporting the government was too heavy for the army to carry unaided, people's militias would be formed to assist it and generally to advance the cause of socialism. To ensure that the army remained obedient to the party's commands, and paid due heed to socialist doctrine, its activities were to be monitored by political commissions. Finally, as the general command saw it, South Yemen constituted on the political map of Arabia 'a revolutionary democratic islet in the middle of a reactionary imperialist sea'. It was the PRSY's bounden duty, therefore, to dedicate itself to the extension of the socialist revolution to Saudi Arabia, Oman and the Gulf shaikhdoms. Beyond Arabia, naturally, it would align itself with the Palestinian resistance movement and with 'progressive' states like Cuba and North Vietnam.

Fired by the triumph of the extreme left at the Zinjibar congress, the NF zealots in the Hadramaut intensified their programme of confiscations and purges. The most rabid of these fanatics were the Maoists, many of whom were refugees from the former Hadrami community in Zanzibar, where they had been converted to Chinese communism some years earlier. Those who survived the general massacre of the Arab population of the island by the Zanzibari Africans in 1964 made their way to the Hadramaut, where they set about recruiting others to their way of thinking. The best known of them was Faisal al-Nairi al-Attas, a renegade from the *sada* class, who had paid more than one visit to China by 1967. In the early months of 1968 he and his fellow Maoists embarked upon a campaign of calculated violence designed to achieve the total transformation of the Hadramaut into something approaching the Chinese People's Republic. The attempt was a failure. The revolutionaries' excesses angered not only many of the tribes but also the remnants of the former federal security forces, so that fighting broke out all over the Hadramaut. In Aden senior officers of the regular army, alarmed and disgusted by the radical programme adopted by the fourth congress, attempted a minor *coup d'état*. Although the attempt misfired, it served to intimidate the Marxist ministers in the government and to strengthen Qahtan al-Shaabi's position. Troops were sent to the Hadramaut to help restore order, and by early June the Maoists and their allies had been subdued and Mukalla and the other principal towns freed from their control.

Disaffection persisted in much of South Yemen throughout the summer of 1968. There were outbreaks of insurgency in the western governorates, which were supported, and in some cases incited, from outside the country by the former federal rulers, along with *émigré* tribesmen and adherents of FLOSY who had taken refuge in the Yemen or Saudi Arabia. The revolts were suppressed, and for a time it seemed that Qahtan al-Shaabi's government was in control of the country. He had dismissed the more radical of his ministers, notably Abdul Fattah Ismail and Ali Salim al-Baid, and they, in turn, had thought it wiser to remove themselves from his reach. Abdul Fattah Ismail went off to Bulgaria for 'medical treatment', while Ali Salim al-Baid went to ground in the Hadramaut. Obviously this was no more than a lull in the battle for power between the two factions of the National Front, a battle which could only result, so intense was the hatred between them, in the total eclipse of the one by the other. Before describing the outcome of the struggle and its significance for the political future of the whole of southern Arabia, it is necessary to turn for a moment to the fortunes of the Arab Nationalists' Movement at this time; for the factional struggle in the leadership of the South Yemen National Front was both a reflection and a part of the ideological battle then being waged in the higher councils and the national branches of the ANM.

The Arab–Israeli war of June 1967 had shattered the faith of the ANM in Gamal Abdul Nasser as the paladin of its cause. Thereafter he and the regimes in power in the other 'progressive' Arab states were anathematized by the movement as 'petty bourgeois' and worse. The more radical theoreticians of the ANM, like the Lebanese Muhsin Ibrahim and the Jordanian Nayif Hawatima, had been arguing for some time that the only way to accomplish their ultimate aims (the elimination of imperialism and Zionism from the Middle East and the restoration of Palestine to Arab control) was to widen these aims to take in the overthrow of capitalism and the traditional social order in the Arab world, and thereby to attract the support of the Arab masses. George Habash, the most prominent ANM leader, had remained unconvinced of the necessity for a mass movement up to the time of the June war. Now, in the aftermath of that terrible defeat, he changed his mind, declaring that henceforth the movement should dedicate itself to leading the armed struggle of the masses against Zionism, imperialism, capitalism and 'Arab reaction' alike. To mark his conversion to this more radical policy he effected in December 1967 a merger of the National Front for the Liberation of Palestine – the organization he had created three years earlier from the Palestinian members of the ANM – with a handful of other splinter groups to form the Popular Front for the Liberation of Palestine. Though Hawatima shortly afterwards joined the leadership of the PFLP, he did not believe that it or the other branches of the ANM had moved far enough leftwards in their political orientation. At the general conference of the ANM in August 1968 his faction within the PFLP, and the radical faction within the movement as a whole, pushed through a programme as thoroughgoing in its Marxism–Leninism as that adopted by the National Front at Zinjibar in March. A bitter feud between Habash's faction and that led by Hawatima ensued, culminating in the defection of the Hawatima faction in February 1969 and its transformation into a rival body, the Popular Democratic Front for the Liberation of Palestine. The schism spread rapidly throughout the entire ANM, splitting its branches in every Arab country beyond hope of repair, and destroying whatever cohesion the organization may once have possessed as a pan-Arab movement.

It was against this background that the struggle for power in the National Front in South Yemen was rejoined in the first half of 1969. The economic distress caused by the drastic decline in Aden's entrepôt trade through the closing of the Suez Canal and the flight of its mercantile classes, together with the armed uprisings and expropriations of agricultural estates and commercial property, had brought the regime of Qahtan al-Shaabi into increasing unpopularity. Confusion and disaffection reigned throughout the army and the civil service as a result of a succession of ideological purges and counter-purges, while the populace at large had grown more and more disenchanted with the fruits of the revolution. It was a situation of which the Marxist–Leninist faction in the NF, most of whose leaders had made their way back from exile in the spring of 1969, were ready to take full advantage. On 22 June 1969 the Marxist–Leninist faction led by Abdul Fattah Ismail, Ali Salim al-Baid and Salim Rubayyi Ali, the former guerrilla commander in the Abyan district, ousted Qahtan al-Shaabi from office and placed both him and his cousin, Faisal Abdul Latif, the acting prime minister, in confinement.

A new government was formed, with Muhammad Ali Haitham, a so-called 'moderate' Marxist, as prime minister, Ali Salim al-Baid as foreign minister, and Muhammad Salih al-Aulaqi, another reputed 'moderate' Marxist, as minister of defence. Actual power, however, was exercised by a presidential council consisting of Salim Rubayyi Ali as president, Muhammad Ali Haitham, Muhammad Salih al-Aulaqi, Ali Ahmad Nasir al-Bishi ('Ali Antar', the one-time NLF commander in the Radfan), and Abdul Fattah Ismail, now designated secretary-general of the party. It was a collective leadership of dedicated Marxist–Leninists, all young, all utterly ruthless and all fiercely determined to turn South Yemen into a full-blown Marxist dictatorship. What followed was an intensification of the repressive measures which had been the lot of the South Yemenis since independence. The army was purged yet again to rid it of any officers or men whose political outlook or tribal affiliations might render them less than abjectly submissive to the regime. At the end of 1969 Ali Ahmad Nasir, who had in the interim succeeded Muhammad Salih al-Aulaqi as minister of defence, was himself replaced in that office by Ali Muhammad Nasir and appointed commander-in-chief of the army, the more effectively to supervise its politicization. To hasten the demoralization of the army, the people's militia (the 'Red Guards') was expanded, to act both as a counterweight to the army and as an instrument of surveillance and intimidation in the towns and countryside. Agrarian reform was pushed forward in a particularly unscrupulous manner by a series of *intifadat* – in essence, government-inspired *jacqueries*, whereby gangs of peasants led by agitators seized landholdings and houses without warning or cause, expelling their owners at gunpoint. Several of the estates occupied in this manner were subsequently transformed into agricultural communes on the Chinese model. The *intifad* method was also used to confiscate commercial undertakings and fishing vessels.

Needless to say, the suppression of all political dissent was pursued with the same ruthlessness. With the *ancien régime* already destroyed, the NF proceeded, after the normal fashion of revolutionaries, to devour its own. Faisal Abdul Latif al-Shaabi was shot dead in April 1970, allegedly while trying to escape from confinement, and others were imprisoned or executed for 'crimes against the state'. Change followed change in the closed circle of the politburo, the reasons for which – personal or factional vendettas, ideo-logical rifts, tussles for office – we can only surmise, since they never emerged into the light of day. If there was any logic to these successive upheavals it lay in their respective outcomes, which was to move the regime politically ever further to the left – as happened, for instance, in August 1971, when the defence minister, Ali Muhammad Nasir, replaced Muhammad Ali Haitham as prime minister.

That the politburo of the NF intended its power to be absolute was made abundantly clear when, on 30 November 1970, the third anniversary of inde-pendence, it changed the name of the country, after the example of Hawatima's PDFLP, to the People's Democratic Republic of Yemen, and promulgated a constitution which purported to vest sovereign authority in a Supreme Council of the People, elected by popular councils or soviets throughout the country. Since such local councils were, for the most part, non-existent and could not therefore elect a supreme council, the members of the council were nominated instead by the politburo. When the council eventually met its sole accom-plishment was to transfer all power, legislative, executive and judicial, to the politburo. Popular participation in government remained as much a mockery as did the lofty declarations in the constitution about personal liberties, basic rights and equality of status.

Towards the world outside the regime behaved in a highly predictable manner. It condemned the conservative Arab states outright as corrupt, reac-tionary autocracies, it sneered at the 'progressive' Arab states for their *petit bourgeois* character (Libya alone was exempted from abuse), and it aligned itself wholeheartedly with the terrorist 'rejection front' of the Palestinian movement. It was regarded in return with loathing by almost every Arab government, even by its closest neighbour, the Yemen Arab Republic to the north, union with which had been one of the ostensible aims of the NLF's struggle to end British rule in South Arabia. Beyond the Middle East the National Front established diplomatic relations with, among others, North Vietnam, North Korea and Cuba, and declared its support for liberation movements everywhere. It courted the Soviet Union and the Chinese People's Republic for the economic and military aid they could furnish, and both were quick to appreciate the strategic advantages of securing a foothold in southern Arabia. The Russians provided arms and technical assistance, the Chinese supplied medical aid and built a road from Aden to the Hadramaut, the Cubans helped with agriculture and the training of the air force, while the East Germans organized the security system. This aid from the communist world played a vital part in enabling the regime to survive and impose its will upon the country. Without it, and particularly without the modern surveillance methods, security techniques and improvements in communications introduced by the Russians, Cubans and East Germans, the NF might well have fallen victim either to those twin scourges of South Arabia, tribalism and anarchy, or to its own internecine quarrels.

The Marxist–Leninist faction now in the ascendant in the NF had insisted, virtually from the start of the original uprising in the Radfan mountains on 14 October 1963, that the theory of the permanent revolution had to be applied in its entirety to South Arabia. If the revolution faltered, if it lost momentum, it would wither and die. The nationalist revolution to expel the British had to be succeeded (if not accompanied) by a social and economic revolution to destroy the power of the sultans, the *sada* and the *haute bourgeoisie*. Any attempt by the *petite bourgeoisie* to appropriate the revolution and inherit its fruits had to be frustrated, and the dictatorship of the proletariat imposed instead. The revolution could never sleep; and while it proceeded at home it should also be extended abroad. To the politburo in Aden the most obvious field for its proselytizing activities was North Yemen, where, exhausted by seven years of civil war, the republicans and royalists were uneasily co-operating in a government of national unity. No matter how fragile their reconciliation might be, however, the Yemenis at least were as one in rejecting the Aden regime's pretensions (as represented by its designation of itself as the 'People's Democratic Republic of Yemen') to political sovereignty over the whole southwestern corner of Arabia. The Yemenis had no wish to subject their ravaged country to a Marxist–Leninist revolution of the kind that was taking place in the south, the true nature of which was attested to by the thousands upon thousands of South Arabian refugees who had fled to the Yemen. All that the attempts of the NF politburo to stir up disaffection in the north achieved was to progressively poison relations between the two countries, until in 1972 they degenerated into open hostilities along the border.

If northwards the outlook for the extension of South Yemen's brand of revolution was gloomy, eastwards the land was brighter. Beyond the Hadramaut and the Mahra country, a fitful rebellion was going on in Dhufar, which promised, if carefully sustained and cultivated from outside, to culminate in the establishment of another Marxist–Leninist enclave in southern Arabia. It was to the cultivation of this exotic hybrid that the Aden regime began, in the spring of 1968, to give serious attention.

Dhufar is somewhat remote from the rest of the sultanate of Oman, both in distance and in character. It is also quite distinct, despite its physical proximity, from the Hadramaut and the Mahra country. Geographically it consists of a coastal plain and a mountain range, the Jabal Qara, both of which are watered by the south-west monsoon. Beyond the mountains, the *najd*, a barren stony plateau broken by ravines, stretches northwards to the southern rim of the Rub al-Khali. The people of Dhufar are of South Arabian stock, with admixtures of eastern Arabian tribes, Africans, Ethiopians and Indians. They speak a language derived from ancient Himyarite. It has no written form, although it is akin in many respects to Arabic, from which it has borrowed extensively. The Dhufaris are Sunni Muslims (mostly Shafi), although their religious beliefs and practices are riddled with animistic superstitions, fetishes and tabus. No accurate figures are available for the size of the population, but a decade ago it would seem to have been between 30,000 and 40,000. The Dhufaris mostly earned their living from pastoralism, agriculture, trade, fishing and seafaring. Like Hadramis, they have a tradition of migrating in search of work and fortune. There are two major tribal confederations: the dominant Qara, who live on the mountain plateau and raise cattle, and who once cultivated frankincense on a large scale; and the Al Kathir, who dwell in the coastal plain and are mainly cultivators and fishermen. (They are distinct from the Bait Kathir who roam the *najd* and the sands to the north of the Jabal Qara.) Mahra, originating further westwards, also inhabit the eastern and western reaches of the *jabal*. Two smaller but important tribes are the Bait Qatan of the western region and the Awamir of the western *jabal* and the western *najd*. Another, rather amorphous, tribal group is the Shahara, descendants of the original inhabitants of Dhufar before the Kathiri and Qara migrations, who exist today in a condition of virtual servitude to the Qara. Dhufari society is divided by other than tribal affiliation. There is a caste system, derived from centuries of intercourse with India, where the Dhufaris went to trade or, like the Hadramis, to enlist as soldiers in the service of Indian princes. Again, as in the Hadramaut, there is also a class of *sada*, or Hashimis, who constitute a religious aristocracy revered by most of the population.

Dhufar came under the nominal sway of the Al Bu Said rulers of Muscat in the second quarter of the nineteenth century, but it was not until the last quarter of the century that the Al Bu Said made any effective display of authority there. Even then successive sultans ruled Dhufar in perfunctory fashion through a series of *walis*, who administered the province by the time-honoured method of setting tribe against tribe. From the time that he took up more or less permanent residence at Salalah, the principal town, in the early 1950s, Saiyid Said ibn Taimur tended to treat Dhufar as his personal domain and its people very much as serfs. Tribal factionalism was encouraged, to make the tribesmen more tractable, and their shaikhs were reduced to mere ciphers. Heavy imposts were laid upon the products of the region and upon imports, and trade in items of any consequence became a monopoly of the sultan. The economy stagnated, driving more and more Dhufaris to seek work in the Gulf, either as labourers or as armed retainers in the service of the Gulf rulers. There was as yet little or no political content in their dissatisfaction: this was to come later, after they had been exposed to nationalist, Baathist and Nasserist propaganda in the states of the upper Gulf.

How and when some of these *émigré* Dhufaris began to contemplate rebellion against the sultan, and to prepare actively for it, is not wholly clear. It would seem, however, from the available evidence that by 1960–61 there were at least three, loosely organized, clandestine organizations in being – a League of Dhufari Soldiers, a Dhufari branch of the Arab Nationalists' Movement, and a Dhufari Benevolent Society (*al-jamiyya al-khairiyya al-dhufariya*). The first, which was largely apolitical, was made up of Dhufaris serving, or who had served, in the armies or police forces of the various Gulf states, including Oman itself. The second consisted mostly of Dhufaris who had been sent to Syria via Kuwait for guerrilla training in 1959, and while there had been recruited into the ANM. The third was an offshoot of this group, which broke away in 1961 to lay the ground for armed revolt in Dhufar under the guise of aiding the poor and raising funds for mosques.

Under pressure from the Kuwait branch of the ANM, and also with encouragement from Cairo, the three groups coalesced in 1964 to create the 'Dhufar Liberation Front'. They were joined by a group of disaffected Dhufari tribesmen under the leadership of a shaikh of the Bait Kathir, Musallim ibn Nufl, who had not only grown tired of the sultan's coercive ways but was also resolved that any oil that might be discovered by the American company then prospecting in Kathiri territory should be used for his benefit and that of his tribe. He made contact with the exiled Ibadi imam, Ghalib ibn Ali (who had some acquaintance with such matters), and Ghalib put him in touch with the Saudis and Iraqis, who were then, for their own separate purposes, supporting the remnants of the imam's following in Oman. To display his mettle Musallim ibn Nufl attacked some oil company vehicles late in 1963 and then fled to Iraq. There, in company with several dozen Dhufaris, he underwent military training at an army camp near Basra. The following winter he and his band returned to Dhufar by way of Saudi Arabia, the Saudi government supplying him with arms, money and transport across the desert, with the promise of more aid to come if they were successful in raising a rebellion against the sultan.

The rebellion was proclaimed at a 'congress' of the Dhufar Liberation Front in the Wadi al-Kabir in central Dhufar on 1–9 June 1965. For the next two years or more it made little progress. There was only a trickle of support from outside, mainly from Egypt and Kuwait, the Saudis having since grown suspicious of the front's political orientation. The insurgents could do little more than carry out haphazard raids, although in April 1966 some askaris in the sultan's service, who had been recruited by the Front, came near to success in an attempt upon his life. The number of insurgents was small, no more than fifty at the start of the rebellion, but it began to grow after the sultan, in reprisal for the uprising and the attempt on his life, forbade all Dhufaris to go abroad to work. Deprived of one of their chief means of supporting their families, many tribesmen took to the *jabal* to join the rebels.

As time went by, differences began to assert themselves within the Dhufar Liberation Front. Most of the tribesmen regarded the rebellion as being directed primarily against the repressive rule of the sultan and the Omani ascendancy in Dhufar. They were concerned to preserve Dhufar's individuality – its linguistic singularity, its religious particularism, its caste system – and consequently they viewed the revolt as fundamentally a domestic affair, possibly, but not inevitably, terminating in the secession and independence of Dhufar from Oman. The ANM faction, on the other hand, wanted to make the revolt part of the wider campaign in which the ANM as a whole was engaged throughout the Arab world. Hence they kept insisting upon the 'Arabness' of Dhufar, upon its identity as part of the 'Arab nation', and upon the role it should play in the great Arab struggle against the forces of reaction, capitalism, imperialism and Zionism. Rhetoric of this kind was unintelligible to most of the rebel tribesmen, and it did not make any discernible impression upon them until events outside Dhufar from the latter half of 1967 onwards tipped the scales in favour of the ANM minority.

The principal event, of course, was the accession of the National Liberation Front to power in Aden, which put it in a position to supply the Dhufar Liberation Front with arms by way of the Hadramaut and the Mahra country. There were other far-reaching results of the NLF's assumption of *de facto* control of the Dhufar rebellion. This was a time, it may be recalled, when the Arab Nationalists' Movement as a whole was breaking in two, with the Marxist–Leninist wing making the running. At a conference in Beirut at the turn of 1968 the Kuwait branch of the movement was deprived of the control it had hitherto exercised over subversive activities in the Gulf region on the grounds that it had exhibited 'bourgeois tendencies'. A strategy of 'revolutionary violence' for the movement was adopted by the Marxist–Leninist majority, and at a further conference in July 1968 the membership of the Kuwait branch was suspended. A new 'Politburo and Regional Command for the Gulf' was set up, and within a brief space of time the intestine quarrels in Beirut were finding an echo in the leadership of the Dhufar Liberation Front. In the contest for power that ensued, the Marxist–Leninist faction in the ANM component of the leadership, backed by the National Front in Aden, carried the day. At the second 'congress' of the DLF held in the Wadi Hamrin in central Dhufar on 1–25 September 1968 a Marxist–Leninist revolutionary programme was adopted.

Dhufar was to be transformed into a proletarian state according to the principles of 'scientific socialism' – whatever the DLF thought these to be. (At the ANM conference on the Gulf in July the Kuwaiti delegate, in an endeavour to rebut the charge of bourgeois recidivism levelled by the Marxist–Leninists, had reasonably but unavailingly argued, 'The Movement has adopted scientific socialism, but we do not yet know exactly what it means . . .'.) The insurrection in Dhufar was declared to be not only part of a wider revolution by the masses of Arabia against 'imperialism, colonialism, Arab reaction and the rotten bourgeoisie', but also part of the national liberation movement throughout the Arab world, and, indeed, of the armed struggle of the peasantry and the proletariat in Vietnam, Cuba and elsewhere. To succeed in Dhufar, so the DLF programme proclaimed, the revolution had to be spread to all parts of Arabia, it had to be unified under the leadership of 'the proletarian left', to be inspired by 'correct ideology', and to follow a strategy of 'constant struggle, multiplying its revolutionary efforts against colonialism and the bourgeoisie, overturning the old social order, and creating a state of poor workers in place of the bourgeois reactionary state'. Such was the language of the communiqué issued at the end of the congress, a document stuffed with the dreary vulgarities and stale tautologies of standard Marxist–Leninist literature yet which nevertheless purported to speak in the name of the simple and untutored tribesmen of Dhufar. To celebrate the transmogrification of a local tribal revolt into an ideological struggle of heroic proportions, the DLF was solemnly renamed the Popular Front for the Liberation of the Occupied Arab Gulf. The old leadership of the movement was dismissed, and several members, including Musallim ibn Nufl, were expelled altogether as 'bourgeois deviationists'. Control over PFLOAG was henceforth exercised by a small Marxist–Leninist politburo, or 'general command', headed by a Qara, Muhammad Ahmad al-Ghassani (who went under the *nom de guerre* of Talal Saad Mahmud), in the post of 'secretary-general'. Others among the twenty-five members of the politburo who were to achieve eventual notoriety were Ahmad Ali Suhail of the Bait Qatan and Salim Musallim al-Awar of the Bait Said.

For operational purposes, PFLOAG divided Dhufar into three commands: the western region adjoining South Yemen, which included the border towns of Madhub and Dalkyut, the coastal town of Rakhyut and the hinterland; the central region covering the capital, Salalah, the port of Raisut and the plateau of the Jabal Qara; and the eastern region, which took in the coastal towns of Mirbat, Taqa, Sudh and their hinterland, along with Darbat and Jabal Samhan. Units of the 'People's Liberation Army' were assigned to each region, and a 'people's militia' was conscripted from the local inhabitants and organized into three groups, with the historic Dhufari names of 'Lenin', 'Ho Chi Minh' and 'Che Guevara'. Camps were set up in South Yemen for the political indoctrination and military training of recruits, the main camp being situated at Hauf, just across the border from Dalkyut. Arms and supplies, as well as propaganda facilities, were provided by the NF in Aden, the arms coming initially from stocks left behind by the British in 1967. Before long, however, the supplying of weapons, medical aid and other equipment was taken over by the Chinese People's Republic. Chinese officers at Mukalla oversaw the transport of these arms and other supplies to the guerrillas, and they also helped with military training, political education, and advice on civil administration in the 'liberated' areas. Occasionally they visited the guerrillas in their operational areas, though how far they were involved in the tactical direction of guerrilla operations is uncertain. Members of PFLOAG were sent to China in batches for instruction in guerrilla warfare and politics for periods of up to nine months. They travelled mostly by way of Kuwait, which acted as the main clearing-house for much of the clandestine movement of revolutionaries and weapons in the Gulf area.

The effects of this flow of aid were made evident in 1969. From their bases in South Yemen PFLOAG guerrillas launched a sustained drive into the western region of Dhufar, which resulted in the capture of Dalkyut, Madhub, and, in August, the port of Rakhyut. The aim of the offensive was to secure control over the routes leading from South Yemen into Dhufar, so as to facilitate the supplying and reinforcement of the PFLOAG units operating in the central and eastern regions of the country. With the capture of Rakhyut the aim was largely achieved, for arms and equipment could now be brought in directly by sea. In the central area the guerrillas concentrated their attacks upon the outlying districts of Salalah and upon the road running north from the capital to Thamarit (or 'Midway', to use its military designation), which was the only land link with Oman proper. Up to the time of the attempt on the life of Said ibn Taimur in April 1966, the Omani regular forces, the SAF (Sultan's Armed Forces), had not operated in Dhufar. Security there had been entrusted to the sultan's armed retainers and to a small detachment of Dhufaris commanded by a Pakistani officer, which confined its activities to the coastal plain. The SAF were unfamiliar with Dhufar in general, with the language and customs of the Dhufaris, and with the peculiar difficulties which Dhufar's climate and terrain posed to the conduct of effective military operations. From June to September the rains brought by the south-west monsoon fell over the Jabal Qara and the coastal plain, hindering the movement of men and vehicles and bringing patrolling to a virtual standstill. In contrast the guerrillas, although hampered also by the monsoon, were not dependent upon motor transport, moving their equipment by camel or carrying it themselves. Movement for the SAF was made doubly hazardous, whether during the monsoon or the dry season, by the guerrillas' extensive mining of the tracks and roads running across the coastal plain and up into the *jabal*.

The guerrillas' raids upon Salalah and its outskirts grew in frequency as 1969 wore on, until by November they had more or less placed the capital under siege. The only safe means of communication in and out of Salalah was by air.

The airfield itself was operated by the Royal Air Force under the terms of the Anglo-Omani agreement of 1958 and guarded by a detachment of the RAF Regiment. To make sure that the field remained operational the guard detachment was reinforced in the closing weeks of 1969. North of Salalah the guerrillas made unrelenting efforts to cut the road to Thamarit (the 'Red Line', as they somewhat enigmatically dubbed it), laying mines, setting ambushes and trying to wipe out the SAF outposts along the road. The main focus of their attacks was the Hamrir (or Hamrin) Pass, where the road climbed the escarpment. From September 1969 until the spring of 1970 they repeatedly assaulted the SAF's positions within and beyond the pass, inflicting substantial casualties upon the troops but ultimately failing in their aim of dislodging them.

By the early summer of 1970 PFLOAG guerrillas were in control of roughly two-thirds of Dhufar. Within these areas the work of 'liberating' the inhabitants proceeded apace. The traditional leaders in each community – the tribal shaikhs, the *sada*, the religious functionaries – were deposed, and their places taken by 'popular councils' manipulated by PFLOAG *apparatchik*s. Private ownership of property, whether houses, land, livestock or wells, was abolished, and villages were reorganized into agricultural communes on the Chinese and North Vietnamese models. Equality of status was decreed for women, who were given the right to participate in the popular councils and to enrol in the militias. To promote the disintegration of the family (which PFLOAG denounced as an outdated 'bourgeois manifestation') children were removed from their parents' care and sent to be educated in revolutionary camps.

While the insurgency in Dhufar was viewed with foreboding by the conservative regimes of the Arabian peninsula, and with suspicion even in Cairo and Damascus, it caused *frissons* of delight among Western connoisseurs of Afro-Asian 'liberation movements'. Here, it seemed, was a miniature Vietnam in the making, a country where the corrupt, reactionary and oppressive regime of the sultan, even though backed by the forces of British imperialism, was rapidly succumbing to the wrath of an aroused and vengeful peasantry, spearheaded by the heroic and selfless cadres of PFLOAG, Maoist breviary in one hand, Kalashnikov rifle in the other. 'Army cannot win war against guerrillas in desert' trumpeted the *Guardian* on 3 August 1970; and the *Sunday Times* on 22 March 1970 published an article by an anonymous correspondent alleging wanton destruction by British troops in Dhufari villages. Even more excitement was generated among French *aficionados* of Marxist-Leninist movements in Asia and Africa, who had already fallen over themselves in acclaiming the emergence of the People's Democratic Republic of Yemen as the first, fully fledged, Marxist–Leninist state in the Arab world. The bolder spirits among them, like Jean-Pierre Viennot of the National Institute of Oriental Languages and Civilizations in Paris, made pilgrimages to South Yemen and Dhufar from

1969 onwards, to mark, savour and report to the faithful the progress of the people's revolution in darkest Arabia.

Tracts and exegetical disquisitions soon began to flow from their pens, earnestly detailing every step in the rise and development of the NLF in South Yemen and its protégés in Dhufar, along with painstaking dissections of every political pronouncement and ideological declaration made by the two organizations since their inception. That neither the NF's nor PFLOAG's pronunciamentos (still less the laboriously contrived interpretations put upon them by the French dialecticians) bore any relationship to the actualities of South Arabia, or to historical accuracy, or even to the character of South Arabian society, did not seem to bother the tractarians or their acolytes in the least. They had a ready outlet for their expositions in *Le Monde*, a journal which took a decidedly indulgent, not to say celebratory, view of Marxist–Leninist revolutions and liberation movements in Asia and Africa, and habitually reported upon them with bemused rapture. Less space was accorded in the 'progressive' sections of the British press to metaphysical dissections of the Dhufar revolt, although the *Sunday Times*'s anonymous correspondent popped up again in *The Times* on 14 June 1973 to deliver a further broadside on behalf of PFLOAG and to ridicule the efforts of the SAF and their British officers to defeat the guerrillas in the field.

It is reasonable to surmise that the identity of the correspondent in question was not exactly light years removed from the person of Fred Halliday, an English Marxist who visited South Yemen and the PFLOAG-held areas of western Dhufar in February 1970 and again in April 1973. Halliday's travels and researches led him in 1974 to publish a book entitled *Arabia without Sultans*, a lengthy analysis of society and politics in the Arabian peninsula presented in uncompromisingly Marxist–Leninist terms. The main purpose of the book would appear to have been to extol the revolution in South Yemen and the insurrection in Dhufar. Beneath its Marxist–Leninist sentiment and jargon there lies a solid layer of information, much of it obtained by Halliday at first hand from participants in both events. It is the sentiment and the jargon, however, which lend the work its particular value, for they reveal with the utmost clarity how the insurgency in Dhufar was viewed in Marxist-Leninist circles in the West.

On his first visit to western Dhufar and the PFLOAG training camp at Hauf in 1970 Halliday was delighted with everything he saw. Wherever he went he found people wearing Mao and Lenin badges, reading socialist works and earnestly discussing the theory and practice of revolution, a favourite text being the 'Thoughts' of Chairman Mao Tse-tung. (Two Chinese visitors to Dhufar a short time earlier had been similarly inspired by what they saw there. On their return to China they wrote an account of their visit for the *Peking Review* under the heading, 'Dhufar Liberation Army Fighters and People Warmly Love Mao-Tse-tung Thought'.) What Halliday found particularly impressive (and about which he waxes lyrical) was the large-scale recruitment of children into the ranks of PFLOAG. At the 'Lenin School' at Hauf children not only received a formal education but they were given political instruction and military training as well. Such was the demand for education, Halliday reports, that on his second visit in 1973 he found that another school, the '9 June School' had been opened at Hauf, the two schools having a combined enrolment of 850, a quarter of which were girls. There was also a so-called 'Revolution Camp' at Hauf for young men and women, where the inmates spent a sixteen-hour day in military training, political instruction and domestic chores. Halliday was greatly moved by what he saw as the devotion and eagerness of all these young volunteers, many of whom, and especially the young women, had made strenuous efforts to reach Hauf and enlist in PFLOAG's ranks.

Such, then, is the view taken by a committed English Marxist of the nature of the insurgency in Dhufar and its consequences for the country's inhabitants. Another view is provided by a British army officer, Sir Ranulph Fiennes, who served with the SAF in Oman and Dhufar from 1968 to 1970, and who recorded his experiences in a book published in 1975, *Where Soldiers Fear to Tread*. Captain Fiennes has many interesting details to impart about PFLOAG's methods of recruitment, training and political proselytizing, as well as about Chinese, and later Russian, involvement in the rebellion, some of his information having been obtained from defectors from the Front who deserted after the proclamation of an amnesty for the rebels by the Omani government in the summer of 1970. What Fiennes has to relate contrasts quite markedly with Halliday's description, a contrast which no doubt can be ascribed to the different perspectives from which they saw the campaign – Halliday as a sympathetic visitor, anxious to ascertain how the revolution was faring, Fiennes as a fighting soldier, stalking and being stalked by PFLOAG guerrillas through the ravines and along the ridges of the Jabal Qara.

The testimony of PFLOAG deserters revealed the recruitment of children to the Front and their indoctrination at the 'Lenin School' in Hauf in a somewhat different light from that cast by Halliday.

In the spring of 1969 [Fiennes records], when child recruits were first sought, it had been with parental consent, but when this brought little response, groups of guerrillas were sent out to bring back a set number of children regardless of the parents' feelings. ... Salim Amr [a PFLOAG adherent] remembered the morning in April when a weeping girl accompanied the latest batch of children into the camp. She could have been no more than twenty. One of the little boys was her son and that evening an *Idaara* [punishment unit] member had caught her attempting to take the lad away from the camp. First they stripped and flogged her. Then, since she still screamed for the release of her child, the Idaara leader caught her up by the ankles and swung her round and round. The uproarious mirth of the onlookers had affected the man's judgement – he later received a reprimand – for he swung ever faster, moving towards a rocky hummock, until with a final swing, he split the girl's head open like an overripe pomegranate.

Whereas Halliday, like the French Marxists, rejoices in the recruitment of women and children into the PFLOAG forces, Fiennes merely remarks laconically, and with greater accuracy, 'The war was getting dirtier.' Again, while Halliday paints a sunlit picture of a pastoral-intellectual idyll up on the *jabal*, with the devoted evangelists of the PFLOAG patiently striving to impart the gospel of Marx and Lenin to attentive tribesmen, Fiennes supplies some rather more down-to-earth illustrations of the way in which the Dhufaris' political education was conducted. Two elderly shaikhs of the eastern Mahra, so Fiennes learned from a Bait Qatan shaikh, had been rather outspoken in their contempt for the new Marxist–Leninist enlightenment, so a PFLOAG *idaara* was sent to show them the error of their ways. Before their assembled tribesmen the two old shaikhs had their eyes burned out with a red-hot knife, wielded by the nephew of one of them, who then went on to upbraid the tribesmen for their adherence to the outmoded beliefs and practices of Islam.

In June 1970 signs of revolutionary activity akin to that in Dhufar surfaced in central Oman. A night attack was made on the SAF garrison at Izki, at the western end of the Wadi Samail, and another at Nizwa, fifteen miles to the west. A statement issued to the press in Beirut proclaimed the emergency of a new revolutionary organization, the National Democratic Front for the Liberation of Oman and the Arabian Gulf. It had been formed, it would seem, by the amalgamation of four small underground groups – Omani adherents of the Marxist–Leninist wing of the ANM, exiles who had returned surreptitiously from abroad, Omani ex-soldiers from the various Gulf states, and disaffected tribesmen. The new organization, so the statement proclaimed, would operate in Oman along the same lines as PFLOAG in Dhufar.

The attacks at Izki and Nizwa, together with the discovery of an arms cache and the arrest of some NDFLOAG adherents at Matrah in July, were to seal the fate of Saiyid Said ibn Taimur. Feeling had been rising against him in the country with each year's passing, and more particularly since 1967, when oil revenues began to flow into his treasury from the fields which had been discovered in the Oman steppes. Very few of these revenues had flowed out again in the form of measures to alleviate the conditions under which his people lived, for Saiyid Said's financial caution was still as excessive as ever. Even in London, where the Foreign Office had for years tiptoed around the question of applying pressure to make him do what needed to be done in Oman, exasperation with his refusal to heed the writing on the wall had finally supervened. The only concession that Saiyid Said would make to the growing murmurs of discontent around him was to announce in June 1970 that ill-health and advancing age would in due course compel him to abdicate in favour of his son, Qabus. The Foreign Office, perturbed by the possibility that the incidents at

Izki and Nizwa presaged the spread of the insurgency in Dhufar to Oman in general, did not believe that the situation could wait upon Said's pleasure. He would have to go, and go quickly, especially if his deposition was to be accomplished, and his successor given time to consolidate his rule, by the close of 1971, which, so far as the Foreign Office was concerned, was the date fixed for Britain's withdrawal from the Gulf.

Qabus ibn Said was then twenty-nine years of age. He had passed out from the Royal Military Academy at Sandhurst and served for a year afterwards with the Cameronians. Since his return to Oman in 1964 he had been cloistered in his father's palace at Salalah, a virtual prisoner. The commander of the sultan's guard, Buraik ibn Hamud, became Qabus's close friend and confidant, and it was with his help that Qabus made his move against his father on 23 July 1970. Although he was later to explain that he had planned the forced abdication of his father for some months, the *coup* when it came was in large measure made possible by the participation in it of the British military commander in Salalah. Said ibn Taimur, who was slightly wounded in the scuffles that took place within the palace during the *coup*, bowed to the inevitable and abdicated in his son's favour. He was flown in an RAF aircraft first to Bahrain and then to London, where he was to live out the remainder of his days in surroundings both fitting and reminiscent of happier times – the Dorchester Hotel. It was there that he died, in October 1972.

Although at the time of his deposition a number of harsh -- and not particularly well-informed – criticisms were made of him in the world's press, along with a good deal of Pharisaical comment about the concubines, slaves, stocks of arms and pornographic films found within his palace, he was by no means the inept, uncaring, capricious and mediaevally-minded ruler that his glib and thoughtless critics made him out to be. He had, after all, ruled for nearly thirty years over a country whose turbulent inhabitants did not take kindly to any show of despotism. The two rebellions he had had to contend with among his subjects had both been instigated from outside Oman, even though they were rooted in the country's politics, religious divisions and economic life. He did not, it is true, move rapidly or even hesitatingly with the times; yet when one contemplates the social upheavals that have taken place in those Gulf states which have so fervently and indiscriminately embraced the fads and fashions of the late twentieth century, one is less readily inclined to condemn Said ibn Taimur for his inaction. It may well be, as most contend, that the temper and exigencies of the day demanded his deposition, and that subsequent developments in Oman have justified it. But it should be borne in mind, in passing judgement upon Said ibn Taimur, that his misfortunes and those of his people were not wholly of his own making. His difficulties in Oman originated in no small degree from the Foreign Office's equivocations in the 1950s and 1960s about discharging the responsibilities it had inherited in the Gulf from British India. The troubles which beset him in Dhufar, although they arose from domestic causes, were greatly exacerbated by Britain's abject surrender of authority in South Arabia in the closing months of 1967.

Shortly after his accession Qabus ibn Said proclaimed an amnesty for all rebels in Dhufar who surrendered with their arms. Among the first to come down from the hills and make their peace with the new sultan were Musallim ibn Nufl and several members of the original Dhufar Liberation Front. In the next few months the trickle of defectors grew into a stream, which the leadership of PFLOAG tried to halt by the summary trial and execution of suspected malcontents. Over 300 Dhufaris were put to death by the Front, either in Dhufar or in the prison camp at Hauf, and their children were forcibly enrolled in the Lenin School for 're-education'. Qabus's declared intention of instituting reforms in the government of Oman, and of using the country's oil reserves for the benefit of its people, angered PFLOAG even more: the last thing the Front wanted was a reforming sultan. What worried it most of all, however, were the steps subsequently taken to intensify the counter-insurgency campaign. A thoroughgoing reorganization of the SAF was set in train, its numbers were increased, its equipment improved, and its quality raised by recruiting fighting men from the hill tribes of Oman instead of Baluchi mercenaries as in the past. To carry through the reorganization of the army and to direct the intensification of the campaign against the guerrillas, the number of British army officers and n.c.o.s seconded to the sultan's forces was greatly augmented. Members of the Special Air Services Regiment were detached on duty to help train both the regular and irregular Omani and Dhufari troops, and to instruct them in counter-insurgency operations, especially behind the enemy's lines. There was an expansion, too, in the number of military officers and pilots, both British and Pakistani, serving on contract with the Omani forces. Additional aircraft, including helicopters, were acquired, to operate from the airfield at Salalah controlled by the RAF.

To describe in any detail the course of the subsequent campaign in Dhufar, or even to compile a reasonably accurate summary of events, is virtually impossible for want of adequate information. Press reports, which are the principal available public source, are generally unreliable, most correspondents being unfamiliar with the Omani and Dhufari background, and, in addition, wholly dependent for their information upon military or governmental sources. A veil of secrecy was drawn over the war in Dhufar, for political as well as military reasons. Although it was in many respects justified, it nevertheless prevented independent observers from making any objective assessment of the war and its conduct. What follows, therefore, should not be taken as anything more than a brief outline, subject to error, of events in Dhufar between 1970 and the close of 1975.

The consequences of the build-up of the Omani forces were not made apparent to any marked degree in Dhufar until 1973. The fact that such a build-up had begun, however, soon forced the PFLOAG general command into a reappraisal of its own strategy and objectives. While its sights, like those of its South Yemeni patrons, remained fixed upon the eventual overthrow of the existing regimes in the Gulf states and the amalgamation of those states into a single Marxist–Leninist Arab People's Republic of the Gulf, the Front was forced to acknowledge that if the revolution did not succeed in Dhufar it would not succeed in Oman; and that if it failed in Oman, it would not only fail in the Gulf states but might well collapse in Dhufar itself. Due expression was given to this reassessment at the third congress of PFLOAG at Rakhyut in June 1971. At the close of the congress a communiqué was issued which, although packed with the usual verbiage about imperialism, capitalism, feudalism, proletariats, peasantry and the like, indicated quite clearly that the Front was drawing in its horns. The Marxist–Leninist content in its programme was played down, the task of raising up local revolts everywhere in Oman and the Gulf states was conceded to be the responsibility of other 'progressive' forces (in other words, it was beyond the capacity of PFLOAG), and a plaintive appeal was made to the British people to stop their government from aiding the sultan of Oman in his efforts to defeat the Front.

Over the next six months PFLOAG was forced to reduce its pretensions even further. Its counterpart in Oman, NDFLOAG, proved to be a damp squib. Although its members had received guerrilla training in Iraq and South Yemen, in PLO camps in Jordan, and even in China, they were seemingly incapable of striking a blow against the Omani government. In December 1971 NDFLOAG acknowledged its impotence by merging with PFLOAG to form the Popular Front for the Liberation of Oman and the Arabian Gulf, a merger which, thankfully, involved no change in the ponderous acronym by which the older organization was known.

The first move in the Omani counter-offensive in Dhufar was made in the spring of 1972 when a strongpoint was established at Sarfait, hard by the border with South Yemen, with the object of interdicting the movement of supplies across the border to the guerrillas. The operation was not a conspicuous success: before long the garrison at Sarfait was under siege by PFLOAG, and its sole accomplishment in the months that followed was to hold on to its position. To prove that its ability to move anywhere within Dhufar was undiminished, PFLOAG shortly after the start of the monsoon season assaulted the town of Mirbat in eastern Dhufar with a hundred men. The gesture proved a disastrous miscalculation. Omani troops closed in on the guerrillas, cut them off and killed more than seventy. Though a hard core of guerrillas remained in eastern Dhufar for the next three years, occasionally making isolated raids or laying mines, the defeat at Mirbat effectively destroyed the Front's capacity to undertake operations in the area again.

To recover the face it had lost at Mirbat (and to impress the representatives of a far more formidable guerrilla movement, the National Liberation Front of

South Vietnam, who arrived in Dhufar on a visit in September 1972) PFLOAG decided to launch an uprising in Oman. The preliminary arrangements for the outbreak were made in Iraq in October 1972 by delegates from the Front and a member of the NF politburo in Aden. Weapons supplied by the Soviet Union, China and Czechoslovakia were to be smuggled into Oman through the port of Sur, on the coast south of Muscat, and distributed to PFLOAG cells in the capital and at Nizwa and Rastaq. The agent in charge of the operation was a political commissar from the 'Lenin Unit' in Dhufar who had slipped into Oman the previous year to set up the underground cells. Unfortunately for him, he was spotted in Matrah by a PFLOAG defector in November 1972, and a watch was kept on his movements. The surveillance led to the uncovering of the cell network the following month, and seventy-seven PFLOAG supporters were arrested. They were brought to trial in January 1973: ten were subsequently executed, thirty-two were sentenced to life imprisonment and most of the remainder were imprisoned for terms of from one to twelve years. Simultaneous and subsequent sweeps in the United Arab Emirates netted several more PFLOAG conspirators in both the Abu Dhabi and the UAE Defence Forces.

Somewhat unnerved by the discovery of the PFLOAG plot, Qabus ibn Said decided that he needed more help than he was already getting if PFLOAG was to be defeated. Since his accession he had received several million dollars in financial aid from Shaikh Zayid ibn Sultan of Abu Dhabi, and when he visited Riyad in December 1971 he was promised further assistance by King Faisal. Two Saudi missions visited Muscat in 1972 and a further offer of money and arms to the value of some $15 million is said to have been made to him towards the end of that year. A Libyan delegation visited Muscat in January 1973, after Qabus had travelled to Libya the previous month to see if he could persuade Colonel Muammar Qaddafi to bring pressure upon the NF regime in South Yemen to cease supporting PFLOAG. This rather quixotic venture had been inspired by Qaddafi's success a short time previously in inducing the PDRY and the Yemen Arab Republic to begin negotiations towards eventual unification. Qabus's plea for the Libyan leader's intercession was as unavailing as were the negotiations Qaddafi had set in train between the two Yemens.

More concrete assistance was forthcoming from Tehran, where the shah had been observing the course of the insurgency in Dhufar with some uneasiness and not a little irritation. In the forefront of his concern was the possibility, remote though it might be, of the overthrow of Saiyid Qabus by the guerrillas and the transformation of Oman into a Marxist–Leninist outlaw state like the PDRY. Other calculations, too, of which more will be said later, may have played a part in determining his attitude towards the Dhufar war. On his side, Qabus was a little wary of accepting help from the shah, lest it should offend his Arab neighbours or his own subjects. The last time Persian troops had set foot in Oman had been in 1810, when 1,500 of them, along with some fifty Russians taken prisoner in the Russo–Persian war of 1804–13, were recruited by Saiyid Said ibn Sultan to help hold the Wadi Samail against an invading force from Najd. The Persians were cut to pieces in the subsequent encounter, though a few Russians survived to tell their tale afterwards at Bombay.

The first tangible evidence that the shah had offered, and Qabus had accepted, military aid from Persia was the arrival in Dhufar early in 1973 of some Persian helicopters, complete with pilots. Later in 1973 (the exact date is obscure) they were followed by a detachment of Persian troops, some 1,200 strong. The Persians were sent into action in the third week of December 1973 to clear the Salalah–Thamarit (Midway) highway and open the overland route to Oman. The action was successful and the road to Thamarit remained open thereafter. Meanwhile, in the western region, at Mughshail, a few miles east of Kharfaut, the SAF had begun the construction of a barbed-wire barrier, equipped with ground sensors and mines, which was designed to prevent camel-borne supplies from South Yemen from reaching the guerrillas in the central and eastern regions. When it was completed in June 1973 the barrier, known as the Hornbeam Line, extended from the coast for about thirty-five miles inland. Its effect was to close off the numerous wadis running up from the coast to the highlands as guerrilla supply routes, thereby forcing the guerrillas to move northwards, onto the inland plateau, where the land was more open and water-holes fewer. From this time forward the infiltration of arms and other supplies by camel became an increasingly hazardous undertaking.

There was no doubt that by the early months of 1974 PFLOAG was feeling the strain. The Chinese government had withdrawn its support in the spring of 1973, mainly, it would seem, out of pique at the Russians' growing involvement in the guerrilla campaign. At this stage the Russians' attitude towards PFLOAG was equivocal. On the one hand they were supplying arms and other military equipment and helping to train PFLOAG guerrillas, a number of whom were sent to the Soviet Union, usually to the Crimea, for instruction in guerrilla techniques and the use of rocket launchers and other heavy weapons. On the other hand, the Russians deliberately held back from wholehearted commitment to the Front, possibly out of distaste for its Maoist leanings.

A new wave of defections was also troubling the PFLOAG general command, especially as many of the defectors were taking the sultan's shilling and enrolling in the irregular fighting units (firqat) which were being raised in Dhufar as part of the counter-insurgency campaign. The general command itself was suffering from internal quarrels, generated by personal and ideological antagonisms, and its ranks had been thoroughly purged at least twice. A new Robespierre, Ahmad Abdul Samaid Daib, had emerged in the leadership to challenge the ascendancy of the secretary-general, Muhammad Ahmad al-Ghassani, and the constant squabbles between the two only served to demoralize the rank and file further. How far this demoralization had gone was revealed in August 1974 when the organization changed its name yet again to the Popular Front for the Liberation of Oman, the change being accompanied by a pronunciamento that 'other forms of struggle' besides armed conflict were legitimate pursuits for devout revolutionaries. To show that it had not entirely lost its bite, the Front set about plotting a new uprising in Oman for the autumn, to be triggered by the assassination of a prominent figure in Omani society. Once more weapons and explosives were smuggled into the country, and an assassination squad was trained by the PFLP in a refugee camp near Beirut. The plot went awry, however, when the assassination squad, which included two members of the Front's general command, was apprehended near Rastaq at the end of October 1974.

It was calculated at this time that the strength of the PFLO amounted to about 800 in the People's Liberation Army and some 1,000 in the People's Militia. Most of the PLA were concentrated in western Dhufar, between the Hornbeam Line and the South Yemen border, and it was in this region that the SAF and the Persians launched a co-ordinated offensive at the turn of the year. The Persian assault was directed at Rakhyut on the coast, the only village of any size in the PFLO's hands. Rakhyut fell, after some fighting, in January 1975. A month later the 9 June (formerly Che Guevara) Regiment of the PLA was brought to battle six miles west of the Hornbeam Line by two battalions of the SAF, supported by irregulars. It was thoroughly routed, suffering heavy casualties and the loss of its stores and ammunition. Immediately after the capture of Rakhyut the Persians began the construction of a second defensive barrier, the Damavand Line, to the west of Rakhyut, some twenty-five miles from the ill-defined border with South Yemen. Its purpose was the same as that of the Hornbeam Line, viz. to interdict the use of the hinterland for the reinforcement and supply of guerrillas up in the Jabal Qara.

The campaign had now definitely turned in favour of the sultan. King Hussain of Jordan announced in March 1975 that he was sending an infantry battalion, an engineer detachment and a squadron of jet fighters to assist the Omani forces. All had arrived by the following June. The Persian commitment in men, artillery and aircraft was also maintained, the number of fighting troops reaching about 3,200 (no definite figures were given out). For all their willingness and good intentions, however, the Persian troops were not as effective as they might have been. Indeed, their principal value was to serve as a tangible demonstration of support for the sultan and as a deterrent to others who might have been tempted to intervene in the campaign on the insurgents' side. It was, in some respects, dearly bought support. When on his state visit to Tehran in March 1974 Qabus was offered by the shah the loan of a squadron of Phantom aircraft for operations against the insurgents, the offer was made conditional on the provision of a suitable air base by the Omani government. As the airfield at Salalah was occasionally waterlogged during the monsoon months, a new airfield with a 4,000 metre concrete runway was constructed at Thamarit. Completed at the close of 1974 at a cost of $145 million, it was little used by the Persians who complained of its inadequacy compared with the more elaborately equipped airfields to which they were accustomed. Although the Persian army was probably, next to the American, the best equipped in the world, it had had no fighting experience. Dhufar provided it with a training ground to gain such experience; and in order to expose as many troops as possible to campaign conditions, the Persian government rotated the Persian contingent every three months. While this may have suited the shah's convenience as a means of keeping his army usefully occupied, it meant that the Persian troops were withdrawn from Dhufar just as they were beginning to learn something about the country and how to fight in it. It also meant that the Persians never remained long enough to begin to understand the Dhufaris, and perhaps, as a result, to moderate the contempt in which they openly held them. On their side the Dhufaris felt considerable bitterness over the damage caused up on the *jabal* by the Persians' excessive reliance upon artillery fire to support their operations. Yet in the final judgement the Persian contribution was not insignificant, and it was paid for in heavy casualties. The total figure for Persian losses in the campaign was never made public, but in the twelve months from March 1975 to March 1976 twenty-five officers and 186 other ranks were killed. Omani military losses for the five years from January 1971 to April 1976 totalled 196 killed and 584 wounded.

By the summer of 1975 the Dhufari liberation movement was virtually back to where it had started from ten years earlier. It was still being supported by the Soviet Union, through the medium of the PDRY, but Russian help was confined to arms and other supplies, and the Russians were shortly to hand over their training and advisory functions to the Cubans. (The PFLO's original patron, the PDRY, had fallen upon such miserable economic times that it could do little to help its protégés, materially or financially.) Defections were also seriously curbing the PFLO's ability to mount any kind of serious operations in Dhufar. By the end of 1974 the number of defectors exceeded 1,000, and by the following July, so it was estimated at the headquarters of the SAF Dhufar Brigade at Umm al-Ghawarif, near Salalah, there were fewer than a hundred guerrillas active in central and eastern Dhufar. The main guerrilla force west of the Hornbeam Line was reckoned to be about 500 strong, supported by 300–400 South Yemenis, most of them from the PDRY regular army. At the end of the monsoon season in October 1975 the Dhufar Brigade began what was to be its last major drive against the PFLO in the west. A two-pronged attack was launched into the border region from Sarfait in the north and the coast in the south. It proved completely successful. By December the main PFLO guerrilla force had been destroyed, and the South Yemeni troops had beaten a retreat across the border. Ninety-four guerrillas gave themselves up in November 1975, another thirty-six in December, and no fewer than 145 in January 1976. Among the last were a member of the PFLO general command, Ahmad Ali Suhail Majauda, and the military commander in western Dhufar, Salim Mustahail Ahmad Sarhan. Both were from the Bait Qatan. A third deserter was Said Salim Huf, the PFLO commander in the eastern region.

For all practical purposes the war appeared to be over. A cease-fire agreement was concluded between Oman and South Yemen on 11 March 1976 through the mediation of Saudi Arabia, which was then on the verge of establishing diplomatic relations with the PDRY. The withdrawal of the Persian military contingent was announced in January 1977, although a year later there were said to be 1,000 Persian troops still on Omani soil, and Persian fighter aircraft were still helping to patrol Omani airspace. Sporadic clashes took place throughout 1976 with the hard core of guerrillas still holding out in the *jabal*, and to a lesser extent during 1977. A former leading member of the PFLO politburo, Salim Musallim al-Awar of the Bait Said section of the Qara, who deserted in October 1977 and made his way from one of the Front's camps in South Yemen to Salalah, estimated that there were then about thirty guerrillas still active in Dhufar and another 200 being trained, mainly by Cubans, in South Yemen.

A good deal of the success of the counter-insurgency campaign in Dhufar was due to the imaginative pacification programme instituted by the sultan's government after 1970. As areas were cleared of guerrillas, government teams set up camp at strategic sites, mostly at watering places which the *jabalis* used for their cattle. If adequate water was not available at the sites chosen, wells were sunk to produce it, much to the joy of the *jabalis* whose economy was based upon cattle, water and pasturage. They were further delighted by the subsequent provision of a medical clinic, school and general store at each location. Security was entrusted to the *firqat* (singular *firqa*), bodies of tribal irregulars numbering anything from 50 to 150 men each. As time went by, the *firqat* came to be composed largely of defectors from the guerrilla forces, who had come in under successive amnesties and received a cash bonus for doing so. They were armed and paid by the government, and trained by British instructors from the SAS Regiment. As the numbers of deserters grew, more *firqat* were raised, until by the autumn of 1977 their total numbers were reported to be over 3,000.

While the *firqat* have no doubt been effective as a *gendarmerie* they are also a potential source of trouble for the government. The fact that their loyalty has been bought is of little account: the tribesman's obedience has always been secured, if it has been secured at all, by bribery or intimidation or the adroit use of both. What is of more significance is the persistence of tribalism throughout the *firqa* system. For all PFLOAG's endless rhetoric about 'a people's revolution', the fact is that tribal animosities played a major part in generating the insurgency and in keeping it going thereafter. One factor which facilitated the setting up of base camps and supply depots by the PDRY government in Mahra territory was the resentment harboured by the

Mahri tribal confederation for the Dhufaris, and its conviction that the border should be located much further east than it was. Few of the Dhufaris who participated in the insurgency did so for ideological reasons: those who were not conscripted by the PFLO joined for reasons of tribal rivalry, for the chance to avenge old wrongs and to profit at the expense of their enemies. The seeds of many new tribal vendettas were sown during the insurgency, and it is far from unlikely that the fruits of them are being harvested by the *firqat* under the guise of peace-keeping. To what degree the former guerrillas in their ranks have been purged of their revolutionary sentiments is uncertain. But even without the stimulus of political ambition or ideology they could still turn against the government, simply because it is Omani and they are Dhufaris. Or they could simply shrug off the restraints of duty and responsibility and become little more than bands of outlaws.

A great deal of money has been poured into Dhufar to improve its economy and render it politically stable. Qabus ibn Said is moved by ties of blood and sentiment as well as reasons of state in lavishing such attention upon the province, for his mother came from the Maashani section of the Qara. Although Dhufaris constitute no more than a tenth, if that, of Oman's population, almost a quarter of the approximately $1,750 million spent on development in Oman in the years 1971–5 was allocated to Dhufar. The current five-year (1975–80) development plan envisages the expenditure of 27 per cent of the budgeted funds upon Dhufar. The principal economic emphasis is being placed upon the exploitation of Dhufar's agricultural potential – its climate, its rainfall and its fertility. The pasturage on the uplands is being improved by the introduction of better grasses, and similar improvements are being made in cattle-breeding. There are plans even to raise crops on the uplands, which may place a dangerous strain upon the region's water resources.

Yet for all that the Dhufaris have benefited and will benefit from these various economic measures, their attachment to Oman remains tenuous, their acceptance of Al Bu Said rule inconstant. Dhufaris are not Omanis. They have their own identity, their own culture, their own past which stretches back over two millennia to the ancient kingdoms of Yemen and Ethiopia. As Bertram Thomas, one of the few Europeans to have ventured among them before the middle of this century, wrote of them forty-five years ago in his *Arabia Felix*:

The people, composed of warlike and rival tribes, have always found law and order irksome. They love unfettered personal liberty more than life, and glory in their hereditary wars. The alternative of an extraneously imposed authority has in the past been acceptable to them only by force, or else as the lesser evil after periods of exhaustion and, as the lessons of one generation had to be re-learned by the next, no dynasty has been able to entrench itself.

As with the other oil states of the Gulf, the story of Oman since 1970 is largely one of lavish expenditure upon development and the rapid gratification of assorted *folies des grandeurs*. At irregular intervals new plans were unveiled with elaborate flourishes by the sultan's government, most of which were fated to moulder thereafter in their pigeon-holes. As with much governmental activity elsewhere in Arabia, the promulgation of intentions was held to be synonymous with their accomplishment. To sift fact from fantasy in estimating what has been achieved in any of the oil states of Arabia is no easy task, and it is not made easier by the plethora of uncritical reporting of these achievements by Western newspapers, which have made a minor industry out of the issuing of endless special supplements in which the feats of development and vast financial expenditures of these states are fulsomely catalogued.

Thus we are told of Oman in the years since Qabus ibn Said came to power that whereas in 1970 there were only three primary schools in the country with 900 pupils, by 1977 210 primary schools and forty-five secondary schools had been built, and 61,500 pupils (a quarter of them girls) enrolled in them. In 1970 there was only one hospital, the American Mission Hospital at Matrah. Now there are thirteen hospitals, eleven health centres and forty-two dispensaries and clinics. Where before there were only dusty tracks straggling through the mountains and plains, now there are hundreds of miles of tar-sealed highways – from Muscat up the Batinah coast to Sauhar, from Sauhar through the Wadi al-Jizzi to the Buraimi oasis, from Buraimi to Ibri, and from Nizwa through the Wadi Samail to Muscat. A new deep-water harbour, Mina Qabus, has been built at Matrah and an international airport a few miles up the coast at Sib. A new town, Madinat Qabus, has been created in the Ruwi valley, next door to Matrah, and the sultan has acquired a couple of splendid new palaces, one at Muscat and the other at Sib. An elaborate electricity generating system and desalination plant have been constructed to supply Muscat, Matrah and adjacent areas.

Where perhaps the largest expenditures have occurred has been in the expansion and equipment of the armed forces and the police. By one of the numerous ironies in which the modern Gulf abounds, Oman, with fewer oil revenues than most of the oil states, has been the only one that has had to expend its revenues in suppressing insurrection. Yet the type and nature of Oman's military expenditure have not been entirely dictated by operational necessities, or by the particular demands of the Dhufar campaign. There are also requirements of face which have had to be satisfied. Qabus ibn Said, after all, enjoys the style and dignity of 'sultan' in his own and the world's eyes. He is, by this token, a cut above the shaikhs and amirs of the lesser Gulf states, more of the company, if not exactly the equal, of the king of Saudi Arabia and the former shah of Persia. While his resources might fall short of theirs, he has by his lights a royal obligation to make a passable show of armed might. To these considerations must be added the fact that Qabus has been heavily importuned by the Western powers, and by Britain in particular, to purchase the trappings of modern military power. So, in addition to small arms, artillery, military transport, naval patrol boats, helicopters and jet aircraft, he has also acquired Jaguar strike aircraft and a Rapier air-defence system. Since his mostly illiterate soldiery are incapable of operating this complicated weaponry, he has had to engage large numbers of expatriate officers from Britain, Pakistan, Jordan and elsewhere for the task. The extensive head-quarters of the SAF near Sib serves as impressive testimony to the central place that the armed forces occupy in the life of Oman, as well as in the country's budget.

The reality behind the programme of economic and social development is not fully reflected in the statistics given a couple of paragraphs back. Although hospitals and dispensaries have been built and equipped, competent staff to run them have not been easy to recruit. There are no more than a score of Omani doctors among the 200 or so that have been engaged. Most of those recruited are Indian or Pakistani, and the quality of medical competence they possess is not conspicuously high. The same might be said of the nursing and dispensary staffs. Enrolment in the new schools opened since 1970 has far outstripped the capacity of the educational system to cope with it. An inspection team from the World Bank reported at the end of 1973 that the standard of the teaching in the schools was abysmally low. Nearly half of the teachers had, of necessity, been recruited from other Arab countries, and two-thirds of the teaching body as a whole were unqualified. Things may improve, perhaps with the help of the new college which is being established to train Omani teachers, although (as experience elsewhere in Arabia has all too unhappily proved) substantial expenditure upon education is no guarantee of satisfactory results. The electricity generating system and the water desalination plant have cost roughly five times as much as they should have cost to construct, while the size of the bills for the sultan's palaces and his beach residence at Sib remains the subject of wild speculation.

Why, it may well be asked, cavil at the cost and effectiveness of Oman's development programme when these are dwarfed by the extravagances and grandiose follies committed by the Gulf oil states as a whole? The Omanis, after all, have reacted to the new prosperity brought by oil in a way that was only to be expected of a people to whom penury and harsh need have been the chief constituents of life for centuries. The reasons for cavilling are twofold. Oman's reserves of oil are limited. Production from the fields peaked in 1976 and since then it has been on the decline. By 1981, it is estimated, it will be down to half its 1976 level. There is oil in Dhufar, discovered by an American company in the 1950s. It is heavy oil, with a high sulphur content, unlike the higher quality light oil produced from Fahud and the other fields on the edge of the central Oman steppes. Its exploitation would not have been considered economically feasible before the price of crude oil was quadrupled in the closing months of 1973. As it is, Royal Dutch Shell, which has a 34 per cent holding in Petroleum Development (Oman) Limited, the principal concessionaire (the sultan's government has a 60 per cent shareholding, Compagnie Française des Pétroles 4 per cent and Partex 2 per cent), estimates that the cost of developing the Dhufar fields to produce the minimum of 30,000 barrels a day required to make the investment commercially worth while would be $200 to $250 million.

Other oil companies have lately begun exploring in Oman. A consortium in which British Petroleum is a partner has been granted a concession for that part of Dhufar not conceded to PDO, and has hopes of discovering a southern extension of the Shaiba field of the northern Rub al-Khali. Elf-Aquitaine of France has an off-shore concession in the Gulf of Oman, and Gulf Oil and another American company are prospecting in northern Oman. Subsidiaries of the Italian ENI are to construct a gas-gathering system in the central Omani oilfields, from which gas will be carried by a pipeline through the Hajar mountains to the coast near Muscat, to provide energy for the electricity generating system, the water desalination plant and the further industrial development that is hoped for. Yet none of these schemes offers a realistic prospect of increasing the revenues Oman receives from oil, or even of making good to any substantial extent the loss in revenue that may be expected from declining production. Already the sultan's government has fallen into the habit of raising loans abroad, and not merely from its richer neighbours, to help meet the cost of its ambitious schemes of development. The habit may well turn into an addiction, and a highly expensive one to satisfy.

The second reason for scepticism about the direction the expenditure of oil revenues has taken is that so little money has been devoted to improving the natural economy of the country. This economy has been sustained throughout Oman's history by agriculture, pastoralism and trade with the world outside. Oman's overwhelming need is to improve its agriculture. It possesses the geography, the climate and even the rainfall, limited though it is, to create a self-supporting, balanced economy, one which, while it may not provide its people with more than a modest standard of living, will endure long after the more spectacular attempts at industrialization now going on in the other oil states have come to naught. Since Oman's oil reserves have all too short a life ahead of them, there is obviously not much time available in which to effect a transformation in the country's agriculture. Yet nothing is at present being done commensurate with the scale of the effort required to complete such a transformation. Instead, the bulk of the oil revenues is being spent upon essentially unproductive undertakings, however worthy they may be, like public buildings, housing, the armed forces and the police, or upon so-called 'prestige' enterprises, whose purpose is to gratify local yearnings after grandeur or to match the splendours that have sprung up in the oil states to the north. Even more regrettable than the misuse of the oil revenues has been the damage done to the country's most precious resource, water, by the irresponsible use of mechanical pumps (by all who could afford to buy them) to draw off far more water from the natural underground reservoirs than could be used productively or the reservoirs could supply without being dangerously depleted. The water table, which throughout Oman's history has been safeguarded by the inability of the population to tap it beyond its capacity to replenish itself, is now sinking steadily. In some places, especially along the Batinah coast, salinity has increased to such an extent as to poison the soil and ruin the wells. It would be a terrible irony if the chief legacy of the riches Oman has derived from oil were to be the reduction of its fertile regions to deserts.

Little real appreciation, as opposed to idle acknowledgement, of the menace that hangs over the country exists at the level of government or, indeed, at most levels of Omani society. Natural temperament, religion, history, social customs, economic circumstances have all made the Omani, like the peninsular Arab in general, both fatalistic and feckless. To him all matters are determined by the will of God. As God has over the centuries willed drought and flood, war and peace, poverty and plenty, disease and health, disaster and fortune, so also has he ordained that riches will flow from the ground into the coffers of the faithful for their delight, enjoyment, pleasure and gratification. To provide against the future, to husband or conserve the present abundance so as to exercise some degree of control over one's fate (and perhaps the fate of generations to come), is tantamount to challenging the will and authority of God, who alone has the power to propose and dispose concerning man and his fate. As God has provided before, so he will provide again. If not, there is naught that can be done about it. God's purposes are inscrutable. It is he who created the desert, and it is the desert that has made the Arab what he is. (There is neither occasion nor sanction for any irreverent speculation about whether it might not have been the Arab and his goats who made the desert what it is.) Against convictions like these the criticism of outsiders is powerless. And it is disarmed further by the reflection that the harsh condition of the Omanis' lives heretofore makes their current, and what is probably fated to be short-lived, plunge into prodigality all too understandable.

Wealth has altered the political structure of the country to some degree, though how far-reaching the changes may be has yet to be seen. Oman is still governed much as it has always been governed: by the disbursement of *douceurs* to the tribal and territorial magnates whose goodwill the sultan feels it necessary to solicit, or by the intimidation of those whom it is impracticable or unnecessary to court. The expansion and modernization of the armed forces, and more particularly of the police, has made the work of intimidation much easier. With the steady and growing movement of tribesmen from the up-country districts to the towns, especially the Muscat–Matrah complex, the police have assumed a central and vital place in the administration of the country. It is they who will be the sultan's and the state's first line of defence if civil commotion follows the decline and eventual cessation of the oil revenues.

For trouble will come not just from the hill tribesmen deprived of their subsidies and other benefits but even more, perhaps, from the rootless, urban proletariat, whose expectations have grown with the advent of transient prosperity, expectations which in the case of the younger townsmen will be further swollen by the smattering of education they have received and the inevitable pretensions and ambitions it has aroused. Said ibn Taimur's prophecy, in short, is all too likely to be fulfilled.

A new and potentially disturbing element was introduced into Omani society after 1970 with the return to the country of numbers of exiles, attracted back by the more liberal regime of Qabus ibn Said and by the opportunities for advancement offered by the country's lack of educated and technically qualified citizens. The largest influx of immigrants, however, was not of returning expatriates but of Zanzibaris, who had either left Zanzibar for the East African mainland before the island became independent in 1962 or who fled after the massacre of its Arab population in 1964.

While Said ibn Taimur lived he refused to grant the Zanzibaris refuge in Oman, though he did allow back into the country most of the Omani tribesmen (some 400 of them) who had fled after the collapse of the imamate revolt in 1957-9. Since the accession of Qabus ibn Said anything from 3,000 to 5,000 Zanzibaris have been permitted to enter Oman, the great majority of whom have settled in Muscat and Matrah. Few if any of them speak Arabic: their native languages are Swahili and English. They are not liked by the Omanis, less perhaps for their origins and their unfamiliarity with Omani ways than for their quick wits and possession of skills the Omanis do not have. These have enabled them to thrive in the conditions created by the economic expansion that has been going on in the capital and its vicinity over the past few years. Prosperity has sharpened rather than blunted their sense of superiority and increased their scorn for the illiterate and unskilled Omani, and the bad blood between the two is further poisoned by the Zanzibaris' lofty references to their ancestral homes and estates in the Sharqiyah, to which, so they say, they intend one day to return. These alleged patrimonies, as they are very well aware, are nothing but figments of their imagination, which is why none of them has been so foolish as actually to set foot in the Sharqiyah.

Among the Omani *émigrés* who have returned are a number who have adopted nationalist, socialist, Baathist or even Marxist ideas and attitudes during their years away from Oman. Some are adherents or former adherents of the Arab Nationalists' Movement, while others have been educated at technical institutions in the Soviet Union or in other countries of the communist bloc. Together with a number of Zanzibaris they now occupy prominent positions in the Omani administration. Although a few members of the Al Bu Said, distant relations of the sultan, have been brought into the government, the dearth of talent and expertise among them has limited their usefulness. Saiyid Qabus likes to have Dhufaris about him, even when, as in the case of one

of his leading ministers, they have been trained in the Soviet Union. Many of
the men he has appointed have proved themselves highly adept at personal
aggrandisement, administrative as well as financial. There is virtually not a
minister in the Omani government who is not engaged in commercial
activities, or who does not exploit his ministerial office for private gain. It is the
same, of course, in all the states of Arabia: indeed, the whole point of holding
office is everywhere acknowledged to be the pursuit of personal profit. So
entrenched are the merchants and entrepreneurs in the Omani administration
that the form of government is a veritable plutocracy.

As the power of the ministers and other nominees has increased, so that of
the sultan has been eroded. In the past, as we have seen, the political balance in
Oman was held by the great tribal and territorial chieftains, by the religious
establishment (the *ulama* and *qadis*), and by the sultanate as the ruling institution. The revolts of the 1950s and their suppression largely destroyed the
power of the great chieftains, while the withering away of the imamate movement sapped the authority of the *ulama*. Today the more prominent tribal
leaders are themselves entrepreneurs, exploiting the opportunities for enrichment thrown up by oil wealth, while the *ulama* have mostly gone to ground,
their influence diminished by the material benefits that affluence has conferred
upon the people. The sultanate and the imamate are the only political institutions that Oman has ever known. The imamate is in eclipse, and whether it will
ever re-emerge it is impossible to foretell. Only the sultanate remains, and its
authority, as already remarked, has declined appreciably, under both Saiyid
Said and Saiyid Qabus. There is no alternative political institution in sight, nor
is one likely to evolve from the oligarchical clique that now surrounds the
sultan.

On his accession Qabus ibn Said made a limited effort to broaden the basis of
government when he agreed to welcome back to Muscat from voluntary exile
his uncle, Tariq ibn Taimur. Tariq was a man of considerable intelligence and
spirit, with a pronounced cosmopolitan outlook. His mother was Turkish, he
had been educated in Germany and his wife was German. At the time of the
imamate revolt he had shown courage and resource as a military commander.
He had also displayed political sagacity in the skilful way in which he dealt with
the defeated rebel tribal leaders, and in his efforts to persuade Said ibn Taimur
to move his capital to Nizwa, so as to be seen by his subjects to be sultan in, as
well as of, Oman. Saiyid Said, of course, did not take the advice, and this and
other political and personal disagreements with his half-brother led Tariq to
absent himself from Oman for the better part of a decade. When he returned
after Said's deposition Qabus appointed him prime minister, without perhaps
understanding the implications of such a constitutional innovation. Tariq's
powers and responsibilities were undefined, though time was to prove that they
did not extend to control over the state budget or even access to the treasury.
Hampered by a lack of direction from the sultan, and impeded by the activities

of the coterie around Qabus, Tariq was unable to accomplish much in the way of administrative reform. He was handicapped, too, by his own inability to attend to the humdrum and repetitive duties of office, to the supervision of his subordinates, or even to the consolidation of his own position.

Where Tariq was more successful was in breaking down the barriers that had isolated Oman from the world outside. Through his efforts Oman entered into diplomatic relations with most of the Arab states and with the major countries of Europe, Asia and America. Oman also became a member of the Arab League and the United Nations. At home, however, Tariq could make no headway against the indifference, perhaps rooted in insecurity and jealousy, of Qabus. He also ran into the hostility of the palace clique who were jealously determined to preserve their own power and to deny him the funds, the resources and even the information he needed to make the office of prime minister a reality rather than a mockery. Few were surprised when, at the end of 1971, he resigned and left the country. He and his nephew were subsequently reconciled, and the reconciliation was sealed by the marriage of Qabus to one of Tariq's daughters in March 1976. Although the relationship between uncle and nephew has since developed cordial overtones, Qabus, who is now over forty years of age, has no heir, and Tariq is the only member of the Al Bu Said family with the stature to be accepted as heir presumptive. Yet he has not been allowed to assume the position on Qabus's right hand for which his talents and experience fit him, and where Qabus, were he but to acknowledge it, has such need of him.

Since his accession Qabus has solicited and accepted a great deal of help from outside. While most of it, especially that given him to conduct the campaign in Dhufar, was necessary, it may yet raise difficulties for him in the future. Of all the aid he has received, that from the ruler of Abu Dhabi, Shaikh Zayid ibn Sultan, is probably the most innocuous. It was Shaikh Zayid, in his capacity as Abu Dhabi *wali* in the Buraimi oasis, who filled the vacuum of power left in the Dhahirah by the suppression of the imamate movement and the subsequent disinclination of Said ibn Taimur to interest himself actively in the government of inner Oman. By the time that Zayid succeeded his brother Shakhbut as ruler of Abu Dhabi in 1966 he was exerting much more authority over the tribes of the Dhahirah than the sultan himself possessed. Since then, by the distribution of cash and material aid, his influence has further increased. Yet though he keeps a watchful eye on the Dhahirah, and has paid for the construction of a modern highway from Buraimi to Ibri, it is doubtful whether he harbours any territorial ambitions in the region. His primary concern, which has expressed itself in grants and loans to the Omani government amounting to well over $300 million in the past half-a-dozen years, has been to preserve stability in inner Oman and to head off potential trouble from political malcontents.

It might be thought that the apprehension of common danger from within and without would draw Oman and the United Arab Emirates into a formal or informal defensive alliance, especially as the sultanate and the former Trucial Shaikhdoms have many historical ties. Trucial Oman used to be numbered among the traditional provinces of Oman under the name of *al-shamal* ('the northern'); while the greater part of the shaikhdom of Abu Dhabi, as far as the Sabkhat Matti, constituted the westernmost province of mediaeval Oman, *al-gharbiyah*. But although the past provides a basis of unity between the two it has also bequeathed a multitude of tribal and religious feuds, political or dynastic rivalries and territorial disputes, which serve to divide, more than their mutual interests operate to reconcile, the rulers of the UAE and the Al Bu Said sultan. While the political and economic developments of the last twenty years would appear, on the surface, to have robbed these historical differences of much of their force and relevance, they still persist in the shape of conflicting claims to jurisdiction over tribes and territories along the divide between the sultanate and the UAE. Two centuries ago, in the aftermath of the civil wars over the Ibadi imamate, the Qawasim of Sharjah and Ras al-Khaimah began raiding across the peninsula to the Gulf of Oman. The consequences of those early forays are to be seen today in the enclaves of Dibba, Khaur Fakkan and Kalba, on the coast north of Sauhar, which are appanages of Sharjah. Similar enclaves belonging to one or other of the northern shaikhdoms lie further south, in the interior. The Al Bu Said sultans never reconciled themselves to the loss of these territories, and the sense of injury has persisted to the present day. Historical causes of dissension aside, personal jealousies and ambitions render the chances of co-operation between the sultanate and the UAE problematical. Saiyid Qabus looks upon the federal shaikhs with condescension, while they, on their side, are unimpressed by his affectations of superiority and majesty.

A strong desire to prevent the spread of revolutionary infection from the insurgency in Dhufar has largely motivated Saudi Arabia's successive grants of money to Oman since 1971. What the Saudi government has given towards the cost of the campaign in Dhufar and to cover part of Oman's growing financial deficit is unknown, but it cannot be less than $150 million. A further $100 million has been donated for road building and other construction work in Dhufar, another $100 million to build a copper smelter near Sauhar, and an undisclosed amount to help pay for arms purchases. It is unlikely, if their past record is any guide, that the Saudis have not exacted some *quid pro quo* for their contributions. Already, it would seem, they may have succeeded, in discussions held in the winter of 1976–7, in pushing their eastern frontier with Oman as far as the 56th meridian, which was the line originally claimed by Ibn Saud in 1935. If so, the concession can only serve to deepen the suspicion with which many Omanis have regarded the exchanges between Muscat and Riyad in recent years. To the Ibadiya of Oman the Saudis have never represented anything but a threat – to their religion, to their security and to their independence. Even those tribesmen who accepted Saudi money and arms in the 1950s did not do so to turn inner Oman into a Saudi satrapy. They were fighting for objects of their own – the preservation of their *de facto* independence, the retention of the imamate as the religious arbiter of their lives, and the acquisition for themselves of the revenues from any oil that might be found in the desert borderlands of Oman. It is improbable that they think any differently today. Reconciled though they may now be to Al Bu Said rule, they would not tolerate its becoming the façade or the instrument of a Saudi ascendancy in Oman.

Suspicions of a like nature, though not of the same intensity, exist with regard to possible Persian intentions towards Oman. While recognizing the usefulness of the shah's contribution to the defeat of the insurgency in Dhufar, the Omanis did not believe that he was acting solely from a disinterested solicitude for Oman's welfare. On the contrary they feared that the Persian intervention in Dhufar might have created a precedent for a second and less welcome intervention at some future date – perhaps in the northernmost portion of Oman, the Ruus al-Jibal, the rocky peninsula, deeply fissured with ravines and fjords, which juts out into the Straits of Hormuz.

Ruus al-Jibal is about forty to fifty miles long and some twenty miles across. At its northern end it narrows into the Musandam peninsula, and finally breaks up into a number of rocky islands, the furthest of which is Ras Musandam. Ruus al-Jibal is inhabited by the Shihu, a wild and solitary people who speak a dialect of Arabic different from that commonly spoken in south-eastern Arabia. Persian influences have in the past been discerned among them, which has led to a distinction being propounded between Arab and Persian Shihu. Their numbers are unknown, though they probably do not exceed 5,000 at most. They live by subsistence cultivation at Khasab and Shaam, on the western side of the peninsula, by fishing and by raising goats. Until recent years they were habitually ignored by the government at Muscat, unless they committed an act of piracy or some other crime, when an attempt would be made to bring them to account, usually with the help of the British naval authorities in the Gulf. A few months after the accession of Qabus ibn Said a *wali* was dispatched to Ruus al-Jibal to take up residence at Khasab. The reason for his appointment was said to be disturbances among the Shihu caused by agitators sent by the recently formed NDFLOAG. It seems highly improbable. The Shihu are as fierce and unruly a tribe as any to be found in Arabia, hardly the type to endure impassively the vapourings of some nationalist or Marxist *jongleur*, still less to show enthusiasm for the cause of world-wide proletarian revolution. What is much more probable is that the Muscat government thought it prudent, while the shah was laying claim to Abu Musa and the Tunbs, to underline the fact that Ruus al-Jibal was Omani territory.

The only other power which at present exercises some influence in Oman is Britain. For the better part of two centuries Britain has helped to preserve the independence of Oman and to uphold the rule of the Al Bu Said dynasty in the country, for reasons largely, but not wholly, of self-interest. Her most recent contribution to these ends has been to help Qabus oust his father and defeat the rebellion in Dhufar. It will possibly be the last time Britain will intervene politically or militarily in Oman. Her interests have become narrower and her capacity to deploy military forces anywhere east of Suez minimal. When Qabus visited London in July 1976 he was told that the RAF would be relinquishing its facilities at Salalah, and its lease of the airfield on Masirah island, by 31 March 1977. Britain's residual military role in Oman is confined to the secondment of officers and n.c.o.s to the SAF (in addition to the ex-officers recruited on contract by the Omani government) and the sale of aircraft, arms and related equipment to the Omani government.

Saiyid Qabus has a considerable liking for ways and things British, and has been anxious to retain the services of British regular and contract officers for his armed forces. They and the other foreign officers in the SAF – mainly Pakistanis and Jordanians – are both a guarantee of the army's continued loyalty to him and a barrier to its possible transformation into a political instrument, as has happened with armies in most other Arab countries. Most outside observers interpret Saiyid Qabus's preference for foreigners in his service as evidence both of his distrust of his own subjects and of his unwillingness to face the realities of the present age. Much the same kind of criticism, of course, was directed against his father during his lifetime, especially for continuing to look towards the Indian sub-continent for inspiration, instead of heeding, as his critics urged he should, the cries of the nationalist muezzins in Cairo and Damascus. So, too, with his son, who is gratuitously advised by his distant critics to replace the British officers in the senior ranks of his armed forces by native, and preferably youthful, Omanis. Such a change, so the critics assert, is inevitable: Saiyid Qabus should yield gracefully and take his chances that the army thereafter will not try to dethrone him.

The assertion raises the immediate question – why should he? It is neither novel nor exceptional for an Arab or Muslim ruler to employ foreigners in his army. The practice has gone on for centuries, and the examples of it are legion, one of the best known of modern times being the army of Mehemet Ali of Egypt, which included in its ranks Albanians, Frenchmen, Algerians, Englishmen, Turks and Scots – one of whom, Thomas Keith, was for a time governor of Madina. As for the realities of the present age, these include such bizarre spectacles as the deployment of Cuban troops in Angola, Ethiopia and South Arabia. There is more than a suggestion of ideological cant in the prim reproaches directed at an Arab ruler of conservative stripe for retaining British officers in his service, while the assistance lent by Russians, Cubans and East Germans to uphold an odious Marxist–Leninist dictatorship in Aden is passed over in silence. For Qabus ibn Said the issue at stake is not the fashionable defeatism of the West but his own ability to survive and to govern his people according to their established ways. No ruler of Oman throughout its history has been able to govern without force of arms: to ensure the reliability of his armed forces is nothing more than mere prudence. Qabus can trust his British officers, who have served him gallantly and well. They are known to the Omanis and their presence in the country is not resented as an imposition. The time for placing the armed forces of Oman under full Omani control will come when the basis of sultanate government in Oman has been broadened, and when there are sufficient qualified and experienced Omani officers of proven loyalty and ability to take command. The last thing that the people of Oman need is a Colonel Qaddafi.

What the future holds for Oman is Oman's secret. The conventional wisdom has it that its long isolation is now ended, that wealth and the influx of new ideas – of nationalism, socialism and the like – will set in train an irreversible transformation of its social, political and religious institutions, so that in due course it will become indistinguishable from the rest of the Arab world. Such predictions are mostly made by Westerners unfamiliar with Omani life and history, who are themselves addicted to change and novelty, and who are inclined to project their own restlessness upon those they affect to study. Whether the Omanis will yield to the 'contagion of the world's slow stain' it is far too early to tell. It is even more difficult to determine how they would react to the radical and revolutionary notions in vogue in some Arab circles. The Omanis have their own conception of how men should arrange their lives, their own theological preoccupations, their own bones of political contention. They also have a tranquil pride which sets them apart from the Arabs of the Gulf and which derives from their long history and the distinctive civilization they developed. It would be surprising if the arid prolixities of nationalist or Marxist dogma were to hold much appeal for them. Be this as it may, however, the Omanis will probably not be spared the attentions of would-be 'liberators' bent upon imposing a regime of more 'progressive' complexion upon them in the years ahead.

What are the chances of such a regime's succeeding in Oman? For guidance, presumably, we should look to South Yemen, where the Marxist–Leninist National Front has been entrenched since 1967. Its accession to power, it will be recalled, was due in large measure to the civil war in the Yemen, to the presence of an Egyptian expeditionary force in that country, and to the smuggling of arms and money to the NLF which that presence facilitated. Above all the NLF's triumph was made possible by the British government's betrayal of its treaty responsibilities for Aden and the protectorates, and its nerveless relinquishment of power to the terrorists. None of these conditions obtains in Oman today. There is no movement there comparable in size or strength to the NLF, nor is the British government in a position to hand over sovereign power to such a movement. Ironically enough, what is possibly of more relevance to the political future of both South Yemen and Oman than the circumstances which enabled the NLF to seize power in South Arabia a dozen years ago is whether in fact the Aden regime will continue to be able to hold down the towns and tribes of the hinterland indefinitely.

'Arabs rule but do not administer,' Wilfred Thesiger wrote some years ago in *Arabian Sands*.

Their government is intensively individualistic, and is successful or unsuccessful according to the degree of fear and respect which the ruler commands, and his skill in dealing with individual men. Founded on an individual life, their government is impermanent and liable to end in chaos at any moment. To Arab tribesmen this system is comprehensible and acceptable, and its success or failure should not be measured in terms of efficiency and justice as judged by Western standards. To these tribesmen security can be bought too dearly by loss of individual freedom.

Political and social life in South Arabia and Oman alike has for centuries been shaped by a trinity of forces – tribalism, factionalism and sectarianism. Tribalism and factionalism today still exert a stronger claim upon the loyalties of the people of South Arabia than does the nebulous concept of the People's Democratic Republic of Yemen. It is one thing to declare tribalism outmoded, as the politburo in Aden has done, and to condemn it as a relic of a past order whose survival is incompatible with the Marxist–Leninist vision of society. It is another thing for the politburo to compel obedience to its ukases from men who neither know nor understand any other arrangement of human affairs than the tribe and the clan, whose very sense of personal identity is inextricably bound up with their tribal affiliations, and who are all too ready to impress this fact forcibly upon others. Detribalization may occur with comparative rapidity and facility in the heterogeneous setting of the towns and seaports of the Arabian littoral; but in the deserts and the mountains beyond the tribe is still the dominant social phenomenon.

Much the same may be said of religious belief and sectarian conflict. Islam has been an inseparable component of men's lives in Arabia for thirteen centuries. However much the regime in Aden may deplore what it sees as the enslavement of men's minds by Islam, and its exploitation by the traditional ruling classes to keep the masses in political and economic subjection, there is little chance that Islam will be displaced in the thoughts and emotions of the people of South Arabia by Marxist–Leninist abstractions, even when backed by the apparatus of a *cheka*. Islam is the only spiritual and temporal order that the South Arabians know; it is the only social and political system that they comprehend. Against this rock the windy pronouncements from Aden beat in vain.

If proof were required of the Aden regime's failure in the past dozen years to wean the people of South Arabia from their attachment to their traditional ways and to convert them to the precepts of Marxism–Leninism, it lies in the monstrous engine of repression (complete with concentration camps for political 'undesirables') which the regime has been forced to construct to keep itself in power and which it is abjectly dependent upon an East German security force, several thousand strong, to operate. As with South Arabia, so also with Dhufar: the only way in which the Marxist–Leninists could gain ground there was at the point of a gun, and it was their own excesses, as much as the counter-insurgency campaign against them, that brought about their defeat. A brutal, ideologically motivated despotism of the kind that now oppresses the people of South Arabia could never arise in Oman from internal causes. It would have to be both implanted and enforced from outside.

For Oman, then, it would seem that the portents are plain: it is infiltration from without rather than agitation from within that is to be feared. And as the PDRY is now thoroughly subservient to the Soviet Union and its Cuban and East German surrogates, there will be lacking neither malevolence of intent nor preponderance in arms to threaten the stability and integrity of the sultanate.

CHAPTER IV
Sorcerers' Apprentices

*Swiftly these pulled down the walls
  that their fathers had made them –
The impregnable ramparts of old, they
  razed and relaid them
As playgrounds of pleasure and leisure,
  with limitless entries,
And havens of rest for the wastrels
  where once walked the sentries.*

Rudyard Kipling, *The City of Brass*

A mere generation ago the peoples of the Arabian shore of the Gulf led a life little different from the one their ancestors had led since the advent of Islam. Society was predominantly tribal in nature, ruling authority was vested in the shaikhly families, and social behaviour was regulated by local customs and usages, by Islamic prescription, and not least by the exigencies of a primitive economy. The population as a whole was divided into sedentary and nomadic groups, the sedentary being made up of cultivators, fishermen, seafarers, artisans, merchants and others, while the nomadic consisted of tribes or sections of tribes which customarily wandered in search of pasture for their flocks and herds. There were also semi-nomadic tribesmen – cultivators or fishermen who grazed flocks in the vicinity of their settlements – and an amorphous category known as *huwailah* (or *muhawailah*), detribalized and semi-Persianized Arabs who roamed the Gulf in search of work or adventure. The layers of Arabian society were traditionally composed of the ruling dynasties, the shaikhly families of tribes, the religious functionaries (*qadis* and *ulama*), the merchants and artisans, nomads, seafarers, cultivators and slaves – much in that order of precedence.

This ordering of society, and the way of life which went with it, has now largely vanished, except deep in the interior of the peninsula or in the mountains of Oman. Along the coast, from Kuwait in the north to Sharjah in the south, carnival reigns – a strident welter of frantic expenditure, heedless waste, conspicuous folly and ceaseless activity, in which it is becoming increasingly difficult to discern (except in perhaps one or two instances) any enduring element of cohesiveness, any basic concept of order and balance, even any valid principle of authority. Masses of money and hordes of migrants have poured into the Gulf states, and with the money and the migrants have come not only novelties and gadgets of a material kind but also political, intellectual and cultural ideas and influences, most of them strange, many of them seductive and some of them eminently disturbing. Altogether these forces have debauched the peoples of the Gulf as severely as they were ravaged by periodic outbreaks of plague and cholera in previous centuries, and to an extent as alarming as the span of time in which the contagion has occurred has been brief.

The process has been going on longest, naturally, in the states which were the first to benefit from oil revenues – Kuwait and Bahrain. Over the past thirty years Kuwait has been a byword for what happens to a small desert shaikhdom when it is inundated by waves of oil money. What has gone less remarked, amid the superlatives and statistics which have become the standard argot for describing the Kuwait phenomenon, is the social and cultural transformation that has overtaken its people. Before the oil boom the population of Kuwait, the bulk of which was Arab, though with a distinct Persian minority, consisted predominantly of Bedouin, fishermen, sailors, craftsmen and labourers, with a small number of merchant families, including the ruling house of Al Sabah, in the ascendant. Within a decade, from the late 1940s to the late 1950s, the population doubled – from over 100,000 to over 200,000 – as foreigners poured in to build and work in the new Kuwait rising by the waters of the Gulf – Egyptians, Lebanese, Palestinians, Jordanians, Omanis, Hadramis, Persians, Indians, Pakistanis, Baluchis and Europeans. Over the next decade the population doubled again, and it went on growing until by 1976–7 it was reckoned to be in the vicinity of a million – of which 55 per cent at least were foreigners. (In 1970 the proportion was 63 per cent.)

With untrammelled access to the oil revenues and the pick of opportunities for mercantile ventures at home and investment abroad, the Al Sabah and the leading merchant families, some two dozen in number, became the richest oligarchy the Gulf has ever known. A good proportion of the oil revenues was spent by the Al Sabah in keeping their subjects happy, the native Kuwaitis becoming, to all intents and purposes, a privileged class of state pensioners. Money was channelled to them by various devices, such as the donation of land which was subsequently purchased by the state at inflated prices; free schooling and medical services were provided on a lavish scale, and housing was made available on terms that amounted to an outright gift. Kuwaiti schools were the wonder of the Arab world for their imaginative architecture and costly equipment, while the Kuwaiti welfare system was ritually extolled by Western newspapermen as the very perfection of enlightenment. As with most of these latter-day wonders, however, and welfare systems in general, there were strong indications that the quality of the education and medical services purveyed was in inverse proportion to the splendour of the surroundings.

As most native Kuwaitis were illiterate and unskilled, except in callings for which there was now little demand, employment was created for them as government functionaries of one kind or another. Twenty per cent of the shaikhdom's labour force is made up of Kuwaitis, and 70 per cent of these are employed by the state. The overwhelming majority of them are still illiterate, or at best semi-literate. They perform no manual tasks, they exercise no useful skills, they provide no necessary services. Yet they, and the small section of their compatriots who possess some commercial, professional or technical competence, alone enjoy the privileges and responsibilities of Kuwaiti citizenship. The immigrants, the *Uitlanders* (to employ the name given by the native Boers to the foreigners who flooded into the Transvaal republic in the late nineteenth century after the discovery of gold), whose labour and skills have created modern Kuwait, possess no rights. They cannot own property or businesses in the shaikhdom and they are effectively denied, through stringent residential requirements, any real opportunity of acquiring Kuwaiti citizenship.

A fundamental disunity, therefore, exists in the shaikhdom between the native Kuwaitis who constitute less than half the population and the *Uitlanders* who outnumber them. There are other rifts in Kuwaiti society. The generation that was adult at the time that the oil wealth began to pour in had lived their lives up to then within the narrow limits imposed by their exiguous resources, their relative immobility and their illiteracy. Their horizons, mental as well as physical, were, except for the comparative few of them who ventured abroad as merchants or sailors, those of their own society and of the immediate sea and desert around them. Affluence enabled them to improve their material circumstances, to taste new pleasures, to divert themselves with novelties, to travel abroad, and generally to acquaint themselves with the affairs of a wider world. If they could not read or write, and were in fact never to learn, they could now inform themselves of men and events far and near through the modern means of communication which had become available to them – the radio, the cinema and television.

The children of this generation of Kuwaitis are now grown to manhood – nurtured by the state, educated by the state, and now, for the most part, employed by the state. Between them and their parents, between those raised in the old Kuwait and those raised in the new, there is a clearly defined gap, tenuously spanned by the ties of blood and adherence to Islam, but more conspicuously marked by differences in political attitudes and style, personal tastes and conduct, and knowledge of the world outside. These younger Kuwaitis grew up at a time when the ideas of Arab nationalism began to penetrate the upper Gulf states, and when the cult of the late Gamal Abdul Nasser was attaining its height in the Arab world. Their education was in the hands of *émigré* Egyptian teachers, and to a lesser extent those of exiled Palestinians. The content of this education was strongly political, and as a consequence the newly educated generation of Kuwaitis, by and large, emerged from their schools in the early 1960s with a much greater appetite for politics than for learning.

Aware of this circumstance, and warned by the disturbances created in Bahrain by youthful agitators in the late 1950s and in Kuwait itself during the Suez crisis of 1956, the Al Sabah took steps to ward off future trouble. Nationalist sentiment was appeased by the termination of the treaty relationship with Britain in 1961 (as being 'inconsistent', so the exchange of diplomatic notes had it, 'with the sovereignty and independence of Kuwait'), and a constitution was drawn up and promulgated at the end of 1962 to serve as a harmless outlet for the expression of political fancies. It provided for the establishment of a national assembly of about fifty members and a council of ministers to conduct the business of government. The first elections were held in January 1963, the franchise being limited, then as since, to adult, male, native-born Kuwaitis, a limitation which scarcely made the assembly a representative body. Nor, since the council of ministers was appointed by the ruler, could it be said to possess any independent authority. The constitution, in fact, was no more than a device to enfranchise the Bedouin (who were by this time mostly settled in or around Kuwait town), to make them into a political prop for the regime, especially against the *Uitlanders*, and to serve as an emblem of Kuwait's modernity in an age infatuated with the trappings of 'democracy'.

It has been successful in this last respect, at least so far as impressionable outsiders are concerned. The authors of a book published in England some half a dozen years ago to celebrate the history of the Al Sabah, and the fair deeds they have wrought, so lost themselves in contemplation of the beauties of the constitution as to declare that it 'set out principles of action and behaviour such as many a country has taken several hundred years to evolve; and not always with so much conviction'. 'Personal liberty, the freedom of the press', they go on to declare,

are guaranteed, and the care and protection of the young and old are the subject of specific requirements. . . . Discrimination on grounds of race, social origin, language or religion invites severe penalties. Freedom to form or join trade unions and other associations, and to contract out of them, is another constitutional guarantee, as is the right to assemble without notification or approval. . . . These freedoms and limitations on the executive power are watched over by an independent judiciary. . . . Few nations can in the nature of things have jumped the wide gulf which separates hereditary tribal rule from universal suffrage with as much alacrity. It was an act of voluntary and enthusiastic faith on the part of successive rulers.*

There is, to put it mildly, cause to doubt whether all the fashionable, contemporary rights and freedoms enumerated here are anything more than an

* H. V. F. Winstone and Zahra Freeth, *Kuwait: Prospect and Reality*, London, 1972, pp. 212–13.

elaborate *trompe-l'oeil*. The prohibition against discrimination would come as a surprise to the *Uitlanders* whose children, among other disabilities, are (or were) forbidden access to the state school system. Likewise, the foreign labourers who perform all the menial tasks in the shaikhdom would be astonished to learn of their right to combine in furtherance of their own interests. All, Kuwaitis and *Uitlanders* alike, would be flabbergasted by the blithe suggestion that 'universal suffrage' has been attained, when the electorate actually consists of the adult, male Kuwaitis who make up about 5 per cent of the population. As for the 'act of faith' on the part of the Al Sabah rulers that the constitution is supposed to represent, it is not quite the bold gesture it appears; for the preliminary articles of the constitution declare Kuwait to be an Islamic state with the *sharia* as the principal source of law, and the *sharia*, as is well known, not only places practically no limits on the power of the ruler but it also enjoins complete obedience to his commands.

Where the constitution is in accordance with the political tradition of Kuwait is that its very promulgation was an expression of that abiding talent for accommodation and judicious appeasement which has characterized Al Sabah rule during the two and a half centuries of the shaikhdom's existence. From the time of its foundation in the second decade of the eighteenth century Kuwait led a precarious existence among its larger neighbours – the Turks in Iraq to the north, the Persians to the east and, later in the century, the Saudis to the south. When, in the early years of the nineteenth century, the British began to make their power felt in the Gulf, the Al Sabah hastened to court them as a counterweight to the other Gulf states. There had been some earlier contacts with the East India Company in the latter half of the previous century, mainly through the company's factory at Basra, and dispatches between India and England via the desert route to Aleppo were occasionally sent through Kuwait. These contacts, however, did not develop into any closer association in the nineteenth century. The Kuwaitis were not given to piracy, which meant that there was no occasion for Britain to enter into treaty relations with them or to bring Kuwait into the trucial system.

Another factor which contributed to Britain's reluctance to have anything to do with Kuwait was the shaikhdom's anomalous relationship to the Ottoman empire. Kuwait earned its living mainly by trade. It served as an emporium for the commerce of the upper Gulf, and Kuwaiti dhows traded as far afield as Africa and the Red Sea. Many goods destined for the Levant or Baghdad were shipped through Kuwait to avoid paying customs dues at Basra, and for this reason the Turks were always seeking to set up customs posts in Kuwait territory. For the greater part of the century the Kuwaitis successfully fended them off. As the Al Sabah shaikhs told successive British political residents in the Gulf, they freely admitted to being Turkish subjects, flying the Turkish flag when it suited them and paying tribute to the Ottoman sultan, from whom, in return, they received occasional honours and gifts. They were adamantly opposed, however, to any actual manifestation of Turkish authority in Kuwait, or to allowing their freedom of action to be inhibited by their status as dependants of the Sublime Porte. Their situation, in short, was very much as the British political resident in the Gulf in 1863 described it: 'The Arabs acknowledge the Turks as we do the 39 Articles, which all accept and none remember.'

Occasionally, however, the Kuwaitis were tripped up by their own cleverness, as in the case of the seaborne slave trade, one of the staples of Kuwait's commerce. At the request of the British government the Ottoman sultan in January 1847 issued a *firman*, or imperial decree, forbidding the transport of slaves by sea into Turkish ports on the gulf. Seeking to evade the prohibition, Kuwait dhows stopped flying the Turkish flag and flew instead their own scarlet ensigns. They discovered, however, when they called to trade at British ports in India, that, since they were not flying the Turkish flag, they were no longer eligible for lower rates of entry duty on the goods they were carrying. Hurriedly, therefore, they ran up the Turkish flag, which at once made them vulnerable to search and detention at sea by British cruisers on anti-slave-trade patrol. Wryly the Kuwaitis acknowledged defeat and thenceforth conducted their slave-trading by clandestine means, after the fashion of the other seafarers of the Gulf.

Kuwait's relations with the Turks and the British continued in much the same fashion for the rest of the century. When the Turks in 1871 occupied the province of al-Hasa, to the south of Kuwait, wresting control of it from the Al Saud, the bulk of the Turkish expeditionary force was transported in Kuwaiti vessels. Later in that year the shaikh of Kuwait, Abdullah ibn Sabah, undertook a mission on behalf of the commander of the expeditionary force to try to persuade the aged ruler of Qatar to acknowledge Ottoman authority. Abdullah ibn Sabah's successor, Muhammad ibn Sabah, was murdered by his half-brother, Mubarak, in May 1896. Immediately on his accession Mubarak ibn Sabah petitioned the Ottoman sultan for recognition as ruler of Kuwait, and investiture, like his predecessors, with the rank of *qaim maqam*, or governor, and the title of *pasha*. The Porte prevaricated, thinking the time might have come to establish its authority more directly in Kuwait; but in the end, through the judicious application of bribes at Constantinople and Baghdad, Mubarak got his way. At the end of 1897 an imperial *iradé* (decree) was issued, appointing him *qaim maqam* and *pasha* of Kuwait, the shaikhdom itself being officially classified as a *qaza* (lesser district) of the *sanjaq* (district) of Najd in the *vilayet* (province) of Basra.

Still fearful that the Turks might try to unseat him, Mubarak made overtures to the British political resident in the Gulf for Kuwait to be placed under British protection. The British themselves were becoming worried by signs of Russian interest in the upper Gulf, by French activities at Muscat, and by the schemes then being put to the Porte by German and Russian entrepreneurs for the construction of a railway from Constantinople to the head of the Gulf. While they were prepared to act to forestall the possible use of Kuwait as the terminus for a railway constructed under German or Russian auspices, the British were not willing to contract any formal treaty relationship with Kuwait (such as they had with Bahrain and the Trucial States), both because of the shaikhdom's legal status as an Ottoman dependency and because of the damage that any interference with that status would do to Anglo-Turkish relations in general. The upshot was that in January 1899 the political resident concluded a secret engagement with Mubarak, whereby, in return for the sum of 15,000 rupees, the shaikh bound himself, his heirs and successors not to alienate any portion of his territory to foreign governments or individuals, or to receive the representative of any foreign power, without the prior sanction of the British government.

For the next fifteen years the British had to exert considerable pressure both to keep Mubarak to the due observance of his bond and to prevent the Turks from tightening their grip upon Kuwait. At length, in the Anglo-Ottoman convention of July 1913, the status of Kuwait as an autonomous *qaza* of the Ottoman empire was agreed by the two powers, and the shaikhdom's frontiers were formally defined. The ratification of the convention, which also defined the status of Qatar and the limits of the *sanjaq* of Najd, was delayed by the Turks, and ratification had still not taken place when war broke out between Britain and the Ottoman empire in November 1914. On the eve of the declaration of war a formal undertaking was given to Mubarak by the British government, recognizing Kuwait as an independent shaikhdom under British protection on the understanding that Mubarak would co-operate in the forthcoming campaign against the Turks in Iraq.

Up until the time of his death the following year Mubarak had done little to fulfil his side of the bargain, and the two Al Sabah rulers who succeeded him in the next three years can hardly be said to have improved on his performance. Their energies were mainly consumed in playing desert politics, in exploiting the struggle between the Saudis of Najd and the Rashidis of Jabal Shammar, and perhaps most of all in capitalizing upon the opportunities that came their way to profit from the war, especially by running supplies to the Turks. So blatant and extensive had the Kuwaitis' smuggling operations become by the last year of the war that the British clamped a naval blockade upon the shaikhdom, which was not lifted until well after the termination of hostilities. The price for Kuwait's double game was paid in 1922 when her southern frontier with the Saudi amirate of Najd was determined by the British government in the Convention of Uqair, signed on 2 December of that year. To compensate Ibn Saud for the loss of the territory he was forced to cede to Iraq in the drawing of the Najd–Iraq frontier, Kuwait's rights to the coastal hinterland south of the boundary allocated to Kuwait in the Anglo-Ottoman convention of July 1913 – a hinterland twice as large as the shaikhdom itself – were abrogated and the area made into a neutral zone in which Najd and Kuwait were to enjoy equal rights of sovereignty.

The new ruler of Kuwait, Ahmad ibn Jabir, who had succeeded on the death of his uncle Salim in February 1921, never forgave the British government for what it had done to him at Uqair. He forgot, or preferred to forget, that if it had not been for British intervention and protection in the two years preceding the settlement of the frontier, Kuwait might well have been overrun by Ibn Saud's forces and annexed to his dominions. He had, in truth, lost little, but there was no convincing him of the fact. As an expression of his resentment he refused for years thereafter to consider awarding an oil concession to a British company, even though he was required by an agreement concluded by Mubarak ibn Sabah in 1913 to secure the consent of the British government to the grant of any such concession. His obstinacy was largely offset by the lack of interest on the part of the main British oil company in the Gulf, Anglo-Persian, in securing a concession in Kuwait, primarily because it doubted whether oil was to be found there in any quantity. What eventually made Anglo-Persian seek a concession was the prodding of the British government and the growing possibility that a concession might be awarded to the Gulf Oil Company of Pittsburgh. The outcome was a compromise: Anglo-Persian and Gulf Oil together formed the Kuwait Oil Company in December 1933, each holding a 50 per cent share, and twelve months later Shaikh Ahmad awarded the company a concession for seventy-five years. He had got what he had wanted all along – the participation of the Americans in the exploitation of Kuwait's oil and the retention of the goodwill of the British government upon whom he depended for the preservation of his independence. Without this protection Kuwait might well have been swallowed up by Iraq and Saudi Arabia in the years between the wars.

Ahmad ibn Jabir died in 1950, by which time Kuwait was on its way to becoming the richest principality *per capita* in the Gulf. Under his successors (Abdullah ibn Salim, 1950–64 and Sabah ibn Salim, 1964–77) the practice of appeasement as the guiding principle of state policy was developed to the level of a higher art form. Kuwait took shelter behind Britain as the protecting power in the Gulf against the boisterous winds of nationalism which blew from Cairo and Damascus in the 1950s; and then, when the moment was opportune in 1961, she trimmed her sails to these same winds by abrogating her engagements with Britain. Iraq immediately preferred a claim to sovereignty over the shaikhdom and threatened to enforce it, whereupon the Kuwaitis swiftly turned to Britain to protect them from invasion. When the crisis was past – it will be described more fully in Chapter 6 below – Kuwait sought to avert any future threat by buying off the Iraqis with a substantial 'loan'. It was thought prudent, however, to retain the assurance given by Britain in 1961 to assist Kuwait should the need arise. The announcement by the British government in January 1968 of its intention to withdraw from the Gulf by the end of 1971 robbed the assurance of whatever value it possessed; which made it easier for the Al Sabah to make a show of independence before the Arab world later in the year – and, incidentally to placate the vociferous nationalist minority in the Kuwaiti national assembly – by publicly repudiating the assurance. Henceforth, so the Kuwaiti prime minister, Shaikh Jabir ibn Ahmad (who was later to become ruler on the death of Sabah ibn Salim in December 1977) boldly informed the assembly in July 1968, Kuwait would neither need nor accept any foreign presence, British or otherwise, in the area. What he omitted to explain was that, while his government had indeed given notice to Britain on 13 May 1968 of its intention to terminate the agreement, it had also been careful to stipulate that the notice was not to take effect for three years, i.e. until 13 May 1971.

A new refinement was added to Kuwait's balancing act by the establishment of diplomatic and trade relations with the People's Republic of China in 1964, a move that immediately drew down upon the Kuwaitis the wrath of the Soviet Union. On a visit to Egypt in May of that year Nikita Khrushchev publicly denounced the Kuwaitis in vehement language. 'There is some little ruler sitting there, an Arab of course, a Muslim. He is given bribes. He lives the life of the rich, but he is trading on the wealth of his people. He never had any conscience and he will never have any.' Though the Al Sabah were no doubt offended by the insulting attack, it did not prevent them from concluding an economic and technical agreement with the Soviet Union in February 1965, by which the Russians undertook to assist Kuwait with the development of its fishing industry as well as with road building, water prospecting and medical services. The establishment of full diplomatic relations followed in due course, the political atmosphere having undergone an improvement after Khrushchev's fall from power.

Trade with the communist world, which had been virtually non-existent before 1964, grew rapidly in the succeeding decade. Other economic initiatives followed. For example, Kuwait joined with Libya in 1975 in financing the construction of a pipeline to take Middle-Eastern oil from the Adriatic coast to Yugoslav refineries, as well as to Czechoslovakia and Hungary. A loan of $40 million was granted to Hungary in December 1974. Two years later Kuwait undertook to meet half the cost of construction of a refinery and petro-chemical complex in Rumania (estimated at $1,250 million), and to supply Rumania with 160,000 barrels of oil a day. A step of potentially greater significance was taken in April 1974 when Kuwait concluded an arms agreement with the Soviet Union. Two further agreements followed, the second of which, signed in Moscow in January 1976 by the commander-in-chief of the Kuwaiti defence force, Shaikh Mubarak ibn Abdullah Al Sabah, covered the provision of arms, military instruction, technical assistance with the local manufacture of arms, and the construction of a naval port and military air base. The total cost of the programme was reported to be in the vicinity of $2,800 million. Why Kuwait, with a defence force of only 10,000 men, should have required the amount of arms said to be involved in the arrangement was a mystery; unless, as was suggested at the time, many of the larger weapons were intended to fill the gaps left in Egypt's armament by the October 1973 war which the Russians themselves refused to fill directly. Some of the smaller arms may also in time have found their way by circuitous routes to revolutionary or terrorist organizations. Whatever the Kuwait government's intentions may have been in contracting these engagements, for the Russians they were a positive windfall. Kuwait still has the finest harbour in the Gulf, and it still possesses a good deal of the strategic significance it possessed at the turn of the century, when it was looked upon as a logical terminus for the Berlin-to-Baghdad railway. For the Russians it offers an attractive alternative to Iraq as an outlet to the Gulf, an alternative made all the more feasible by the latent hostility which exists between the two countries. Small wonder, therefore, that the former shah was reported to have referred with disgust to Kuwait as 'the Finland of the Gulf'.

According to the Kuwait government, these various transactions with the communist bloc are to be interpreted as evidence of Kuwait's desire to establish and preserve her independent and non-aligned status between East and West, and of her need to disarm or placate potential adversaries, jealous of her prosperity and good fortune. If this is so, what then of the other side of the ledger, where Kuwait's relations with the West are recorded? Certainly the bulk of the shaikhdom's trade and financial dealings have been with the West, whether in the sale of her oil, the importation of goods and services or the investment of her surplus revenues. They could hardly have been otherwise. The Kuwaitis have never lacked business acumen, nor have they allowed themselves to be deterred from seeking and exploiting opportunities for profit by the kind of considerations which might inhibit other peoples. What provokes doubt about Kuwait's alleged 'even-handedness' is not her commercial relations with East and West respectively but her political attitudes and conduct. While the Kuwait government has been very free with its censures and anathemas against the West for its supposed misdeeds, it has been remarkably reticent in commenting upon the activities of the Soviet Union and its satellites around the world. Anti-Western diatribes were the standard fare of debate in the Kuwait national assembly, which, until its dissolution in August 1976, fairly rang every day with denunciations of Western, and particularly British, 'imperialism' – an imperialism, it might be remarked, which had profited Kuwait very handsomely in the past and still serves her well today. Kuwait has been in the forefront of those states which have pressed for and obtained astronomical increases in the price of oil to Western consumers, and the voice of its minister of finance and petroleum for most of the decade, Abdur Rahman al-Atiqi, has been one of the most strident and malevolent among those raised in vilification of the West – as will be seen more fully later when we

come to examine the oil question. This readiness to vilify the West at every
available opportunity – a readiness which smacks forcibly of chocolate soldiering, since the West poses no danger whatever to Kuwait – added an unnecessary degree of acrimony to the lengthy negotiations for the nationalization of the
Kuwait Oil Company in the early 1970s. Even when the Kuwaitis achieved
everything they desired in the final agreement signed in December 1975, they
accepted it with the same excess of ill grace that had characterized their
conduct throughout.

Kuwait has also displayed what may be politely termed equivocality in her
attitude to Arab and other terrorists who have sought refuge on Kuwait's soil.
In so doing, she has plainly indicated to the world at large – since the adage that
a man is known by the company he keeps still holds true – just where Kuwait is
believed by the international terrorist fraternity to stand in these matters. That
this should be so is scarcely surprising, since Kuwait has desperately sought to
project (at least in the Arab world) an image of herself as an enlightened
sympathizer with radical movements. The cultivation of this 'radical' posture
has led the Kuwaitis to plumb some murky, at times positively Stygian,
depths. When in March 1973, after the murder of the American ambassador
and other diplomats in Khartum by Black September terrorists, the then ruler
of Kuwait, Sabah ibn Salim Al Sabah, was asked whether in view of this
atrocity Kuwait would continue her financial assistance to the Palestinians, he
replied: 'Of course it is continuing, and it is unlimited.' For the past decade
and longer the Kuwaiti government has allowed the University of Kuwait,
opened in 1964, to become a centre of political agitation, to the inevitable
detriment of its academic purpose. It has also permitted Kuwait to be used as a
clearing-house for the distribution of radical propaganda, funds and possibly
arms in the Gulf, and to serve as a transit point for the movement of
revolutionaries into and out of the region.

By and large Kuwait's appeasement of the political extremists in the Arab
world has paid off. The shaikhdom has been exempted from the revolutionary
targets of the Arab Nationalists' Movement and its offshoots, the Popular
Front and the Popular Democratic Front for the Liberation of Palestine. One
obvious reason is Kuwait's contribution of funds to the Palestinian cause.
Another, less publicized, reason is that for years the ANM branch in Kuwait
served as the movement's politburo for the Gulf region. One of the founding
members of the ANM, and a fellow medical student of George Habash and
Wadi Haddad at the American University of Beirut, was a Kuwaiti, Ahmad
Muhammad al-Khatib. On his return to Kuwait after graduating, al-Khatib
organized a branch of the movement in the shaikhdom and led an agitation for
the grant of a constitution and a representative assembly. When the first
national assembly was elected in 1963 al-Khatib was among its members. A
natural demagogue, he soon came to constitute, along with half a dozen like
spirits, a permanent opposition in the assembly, stridently championing the

cause of the native Kuwaiti 'workers' and the Arab masses generally, and continually inveighing against the evils of Western 'imperialism' and Zionism.

The adoption by the ANM after the Arab defeat by Israel in 1967 of a Marxist–Leninist strategy of the armed struggle of the Arab peoples against Zionism, 'imperialism' and Arab 'reaction' split the Kuwaiti branch of the movement as it split every other branch. At an ANM conference on the Gulf in Beirut at the end of 1967 Ahmad al-Khatib and his comrades were severely criticized for their 'bourgeois' tendencies and for resisting the application of the new strategy to Kuwait. The criticism was not without some point, for the radicalism of the Kuwaiti ANM was all too clearly of the plump and affluent variety. Although at a second conference on the Gulf in July 1968 the Kuwaiti delegate protested that the situation in the shaikhdom did not call for revolutionary violence ('There are no toiling groups in the country', he said, 'except the Bedouins and the Arab workers' – a statement which afforded an interesting insight into his attitude to the non-Arab labourers who performed all the menial tasks), he failed to convince the other delegates, who proceeded to strip the Kuwaiti branch of its responsibility for ANM operations in the Gulf. This decision in turn split the membership of the branch, the majority siding with Ahmad al-Khatib. What the political orientation of the Kuwaiti ANM has been in the years since then it is difficult to determine for want of proper information. It would seem, however, to have kept up a flirtation with extremism, if the reports of Ahmad al-Khatib having remained a member of the central committee (and perhaps of the politburo) of the PFLP are correct.

Just as the Kuwaiti oligarchy has so far successfully bought off potential troublemakers at home, it has also managed to avert threats from outside by the payment of 'protection' money, largely in the form of grants and loans from the Kuwait Fund for Arab Economic Development. Apologists for the fund – and they are many, not all of them disinterested – insist that it is a model of enlightened philanthropy, and that to view it as a 'slush' fund for political purposes is the rankest cynicism. Cynicism, rank or otherwise, however, is difficult to avoid in looking at the record of the fund's disbursements. These fall roughly into three categories: money invested for predominantly financial reasons, i.e. to secure a good return on capital while running no risk that the principal will not be repaid in full and on time; money loaned to Arab states like Egypt and Jordan to help with development projects and to earn political goodwill in return; and money given (sometimes in the guise of loans) to other Arab states and organizations to secure immunity from interference or subversion. There is nothing particularly reprehensible in all this, especially as Kuwait is by no means the first small country to purchase its survival by the payment of Danegeld. What is objectionable is the attempts made by Kuwaitis, or by others speaking on their behalf, to present these disbursements as inspired chiefly by a generous urge to help their less fortunate fellows. The Al Sabah have never been exactly noted for their philanthropy, or for declining to exact their due in any transaction. Nor was it coincidence that the development fund was started in 1961, the year of Kuwait's independence and of the threatened invasion by Iraq. Given these antecedents, and the steady debasement of political standards in the Arab world since then, it is not surprising that the fund has come to be used for some very questionable 'development' purposes. To give money, for instance, as Kuwait has done, to a regime like that of South Yemen, which for the past decade has oppressed its own people, instigated violence and murder abroad and succoured the worst kinds of international terrorist, can only be regarded as futile and worse. Far from placating the regime or persuading it to moderate its excesses, the money merely serves to sustain it while engendering contempt for the donor. Much the same can be said of the subventions to the Palestinian extremists, and the uses to which these are put. Indeed, one of the more bizarre sights among the many incongruous doings on the international stage of late years has been that of the wealthy oligarchs of Kuwait lavishing favours and flattery upon groups bent upon the destruction of the traditional political order to which they themselves belong.

Set beside the annual revenues Kuwait derives from oil, and the surplus that has been accumulated from these revenues, the development fund appears as no more than incidental to the financial preoccupations of the shaikhdom. It is also incidental to the economic well-being of the immigrant community, none of whom, as already remarked, is entitled to benefit from the state welfare system or even permitted to own land, businesses or homes in the shaikhdom. The refusal of the Kuwaiti government to provide housing for the *Uitlanders*, or to allow them to buy houses for themselves, is prompted by the calculation that they should not be given any incentive to settle in Kuwait permanently. But many of the *Uitlanders* have to all intents and purposes already settled there, and others, like the 200,000 Palestinians in the shaikhdom, have no other home. Moreover, Kuwait cannot function without their skills and services. Yet the cost of living, and of housing in particular, has risen so high as to make it barely worth while for foreigners in the more humble occupations to come to work in Kuwait. Even the highly skilled are no longer assured of a decent living.

The *Uitlanders'* resentment of the economic disabilities to which they are subjected is sharpened, in the case of the more educated among them, by their also being denied civil or political rights. While they are aware that the various rights and freedoms enumerated in the Kuwaiti constitution are for the most part illusory, the fact that these rights and freedoms are reserved to Kuwaiti citizens rankles. This is especially so in the case of the educated and technically skilled Palestinians and Egyptians, who believe themselves to be more sophisticated politically than the enfranchised Bedouin of Kuwait. As the Kuwaiti government has imposed almost insuperable obstacles in the way of obtaining Kuwaiti nationality, only a small minority of Palestinians and other Arabs, despite their long residence in the shaikhdom, have become Kuwaiti citizens. Barred from overt participation in local politics, the politically minded among the Palestinians have had to make their influence felt in indirect or covert ways.

Among the younger generation of educated and semi-educated Kuwaitis also there are signs of political unrest. Nurtured by the state, educated by the state, and now as often as not financially dependent upon the state, they are the prototypal *jeunesse dorée* of the Gulf, with all the confidence and self-esteem that their privileged station confers. Naturally they feel that their talents and abilities entitle them to a share – perhaps the preponderant share – in the government of the shaikhdom, though they are not prepared to go so far as to jeopardize their comfortable financial situation by proclaiming their feelings too openly. Some of them, after the fashion of their counterparts in the West, have dabbled in the shallows of revolutionary politics, and for much the same reasons of satiety and boredom. Most of their ideas are of Baathist provenance or are derived from the facile certitudes of the ANM or its Marxist offshoots. Though political parties are forbidden in Kuwait, the ban did not prevent the coalescence of the radical-chic activists, along with some perhaps more sinister figures, into a recognizable political constituency. Their views were expounded in the national assembly by the coterie of ANM deputies and their allies (some dozen all told) led by Ahmad al-Khatib. The bloc acted as a kind of 'Mountain', subjecting the assembly to interminable harangues and histrionics which served mainly to prevent the passage of necessary legislation, including measures which might have afforded some relief to the downtrodden groups in Kuwait whose champions the coterie purported to be.

The bloc's endless and insolent clowning eventually led the late ruler, Shaikh Sabah ibn Salim Al Sabah, to dissolve the assembly on 29 August 1976 while it was in recess, and to suspend several articles of the constitution, including those guaranteeing the freedom of the press and providing for new elections within two months of dissolution. One reason for the ruler's action was the embarrassment caused by the vituperative attacks made in the assembly and in three radical newspapers upon the land and property specula- tion of the previous three years, which had hit the immigrant community very hard. Another and perhaps more influential reason was the Al Sabah's fear that the agitation, if not checked, might lead to a Palestinian-backed *émeute* such as had generated the civil war then going on in the Lebanon. How real the danger of such an uprising was and may still be is not easy to assess. Most of the Palestinians in Kuwait, having nowhere else to go to, are very reluctant to hazard their homes and their livelihoods by antagonizing the regime, let alone rebelling against it. Among them, however, are men of less settled and more reckless disposition, whose political beliefs are of a violent kind and who are, in many cases, adherents or even active agents of terrorist organizations.

Neither they nor any of the native Kuwaiti malcontents who share their views can do much to topple the existing order until they have forged a weapon of popular support, a 'street', a task which may prove more difficult than surface appearances in the shaikhdom would suggest. For instance, the Persians who form the greater part of the labour force would probably be reluctant for religious and racial reasons to join in a revolt led by Sunni Arabs, especially as there is no guarantee, but rather the opposite, that a revolutionary regime would make their lives any more tolerable. On the other hand, they and their fellow Arab labourers (most of them Omanis, Dhufaris, Hadramis or Yemenis) are politically inexperienced and may be fair game for Palestinian or Kuwaiti agitators. Some PFLO cells have been uncovered in Kuwait since the early months of 1973, and a number of South Yemenis and Dhufaris have been deported from the shaikhdom. Doubtless other cells of a similar kind still exist, sustained and encouraged by the South Yemeni embassy in Kuwait, and probably by the Iraqis as well. Yet although the Kuwaiti authorities will occasionally act with dispatch and scant ceremony to expel some troublemakers, they hesitate to undertake a thorough rooting out of all the conspirators, terrorists and other riff-raff that nest in the shaikhdom lest they compromise Kuwait's reputation for 'radicalism' in pan-Arab affairs. The assiduous cultivation of this reputation over the years may prove before long to have been a costly, even fatal, indulgence on the part of the Al Sabah and their fellow oligarchs.

The Gulf state which most resembles Kuwait, although there are great differences between them in wealth and size of population, is Bahrain. Both are city-states with a strong seafaring tradition, both are ruled by merchant dynasties, both in the past achieved consequence and prosperity as trading entrepôts and by mercantile enterprise abroad, and both are today, by the standards obtaining along the Arabian shore, comparatively advanced in political and economic terms. The similarity is by no means coincidental, for the ruling family of Bahrain, the Al Khalifah, is related by blood and common historical traditions to the Al Sabah of Kuwait. Both families belonged to the Utubi clan – a subsection of the far-flung and amorphous Anaiza tribal confederation of north-central Arabia – which migrated to the Gulf coast at some time in the seventeenth century. After settling for a time in the vicinity of the Shatt al-Arab, the Utub moved to Kuwait in the second decade of the eighteenth century and made it their home. Half a century later, in 1766, the Al Khalifah uprooted itself, and accompanied by a third Utubi clan, the Al Jalahimah, it migrated to Qatar. The two families settled in the north-western corner of the peninsula, at Zubara, where they laid the foundations of what was later to be a town of some substance, the ruins of which are still visible today. From Zubara they began trading with Bahrain, which was then under the control of the governor of Bushire on the Persian coast. As time went by the Persian hold on the island progressively weakened, until in 1783 it was broken altogether when the Al Khalifah and Al Jalahimah, backed by a force of tribesmen collected from the nomads and fishermen of Qatar, descended on Bahrain and put its garrison to flight.

Having conquered Bahrain the Al Khalifah had to struggle hard for the next few decades to keep it. Soon after the conquest they quarrelled with the Al Jalahimah, who retired to Qatar and from there waged unrelenting warfare upon Bahrain's trade and shipping. The Persians, unreconciled to the loss of the island, constantly threatened to recover it by force. They lacked the naval means, however, to make good their threats. The ruler of Muscat, Saiyid Sultan ibn Ahmad, invaded and took the island in 1800 and again a year later, though he held it only for a further year before being compelled, after the Al Khalifah shaikhs had appealed for help to the Wahhabis of Najd, to give it up. Wahhabi intervention was bought at a high price: the Al Khalifah were forced to acknowledge allegiance to the Saudi amir and to pay him an annual tribute. After a time the Al Khalifah ceased to pay the tribute, a dereliction which was not taken kindly by the Al Saud. For more than half a century thereafter successive Saudi amirs were to attempt, by menaces and a variety of underhand means, to compel obedience and the payment of tribute from the Al Khalifah. Saiyid Said ibn Sultan of Muscat tried in 1828, with the aid of the shaikh of Abu Dhabi, to repeat his father's feat of capturing Bahrain, only to be bloodily repulsed. Mehemet Ali of Egypt, after his occupation of central Arabia in 1838–9, demanded the submission of Bahrain, and the Al Khalifah obliged him. At the same time, however, they made a vague gesture of acknowledging the suzerainty of Persia, reckoning that one submission would cancel out the other. The ruse seemed to work, and twenty years later they tried it again, submitting in rapid succession to the Turkish *vali* of Baghdad and the Persian prince-governor of Fars.

All these manoeuvres had been watched by the British authorities in the Gulf with some amusement, not unmixed with a certain exasperation. The conflicting claims to sovereignty over Bahrain had been the principal reason why no attempt had been made to bring Bahrain into the trucial system along with the maritime shaikhdoms of the lower Gulf. Yet the very existence of these claims posed a latent threat to the maritime peace of the Gulf, since the claimants, whether Turks, Persians or Saudis, might at any time have tried to enforce them. Since they lacked the naval resources to do so, there was every chance that they would make good the deficiency by enlisting the aid of the maritime tribes of the Arabian shore. On several occasions the British had intervened to prevent such an occurrence, not so much for the Al Khalifah's sake as to keep the peace at sea. The ruling shaikh's dual submission to the Turks and Persians in 1859, however, proved too much for British patience; and when in the next eighteen months he proceeded to harry shipping in the waters around Bahrain and to oppress British Indian traders on the island, confident that his alleged status as an Ottoman/Persian vassal would shield him from retribution, the British government in India decided that the time had come to disabuse him of his illusions. On 31 May 1861 he was made to sign an undertaking to observe the maritime truce in perpetuity, and to honour the engagements he had concluded in 1847 and 1856 to abandon the slave trade. In return, he was recognized as independent ruler of Bahrain and the security of his territories was guaranteed. Later in the century, in 1880 and 1892, as a consequence primarily of Turkish attempts to interfere in Bahrain, further undertakings were obtained from the Al Khalifah, which bound them to have no direct dealings with foreign powers and not to alienate any portion of their territories without the permission of the British government.

From 1861 onwards Bahrain never again had to make the kind of humiliating submission to her larger neighbours that she had been earlier forced to make to keep out of their clutches. Turkish influence in the Gulf was ended by the 1914–18 war, and the Al Khalifah's relations with the Saudis, after Abdul Aziz ibn Saud had re-established their power in central and eastern Arabia in the first two decades of this century, were reasonably amicable, even during the 1920s and 1930s when Ibn Saud was at odds with their kinsmen, the Al Sabah of Kuwait. Only the Persians persisted with their pretensions to sovereignty over Bahrain, using any and every occasion to pursue them, and more particularly when some event or other seemed to them to derogate from their alleged sovereign rights over the island. Thus in 1927 they protested to the League of Nations about the description of Bahrain in the Anglo-Saudi treaty of that year as a state 'in special treaty relations with His Britannic Majesty's Government'; and they objected again in 1946–7 when the British political residency in the Gulf was transferred, without their sanction, from Bushire to Bahrain. Neither the Al Khalifah nor the British government were much perturbed by these complaints, since the Persian claim to sovereignty was exceedingly flimsy and the Persian government could do little to make it good while Bahrain remained under British protection. Eventually, as we have seen, the shah publicly renounced the claim in 1970, though whether his successors have also relinquished it is far from certain.

Oil was discovered in Bahrain in 1932 by the Standard Oil Company of California, operating through its subsidiary, the Bahrain Petroleum Company, and the first shipment of oil was loaded in 1934. The revenues from oil production came at a fortunate moment for Bahrain, for the shaikhdom had been hard hit by the world-wide economic depression and by the collapse of its principal source of wealth, the pearling industry, largely through the competition from Japanese cultured pearls. Because the oil revenues were not large, and because Bahrain already enjoyed a higher standard of living than any of the other minor Gulf states, the added wealth caused no dramatic dislocation of either the shaikhdom's economy or the lives of its inhabitants. The basic situation has not changed radically in the forty years since then, despite the increase in the shaikhdom's wealth of late years. Bahrain's economy is on the whole well balanced. The shaikhdom is a major trading entrepôt and centre of communications, it has a thriving if modest agriculture, and a good proportion of its inhabitants are skilled in some trade. It is less reliant on oil production for its well-being than the other states of Arabia, which is just as well, for the oil reserves, never at any time very great, are running out quickly. Production peaked in 1972 at 70,000 barrels per day, and by the end of 1976 it had dropped to 59,000 b/d. There are quite sizable reserves of natural gas, which are used to fuel electricity generators and water-distillation plants, although a good proportion of the gas has to be injected into the oilfields to keep up the pressure needed for recovery of the oil. A quite substantial portion of Bahrain's earnings from oil come from refining operations: the refinery complex at Sitra, on the eastern side of the main island, has a throughput of some 250,000 barrels per day, most of it piped across from Saudi Arabia.

To diversify Bahrain's sources of income – other than from oil, commerce and associated technical services – a large aluminium smelter has been constructed in recent years (aluminium being a particularly useful material in the type of construction going on in the Gulf), which has so far proved successful. A second major enterprise, the construction of a huge dry dock for the servicing of ships of all sizes, including giant oil tankers, has been undertaken under the auspices of the Organization of Arab Petroleum Exporting Countries. Whether it, too, will prove a success is problematical, since it will have to fit into a much wider economic pattern than that represented by the local economy of the Gulf.

While Bahrain has generally enjoyed prosperity and stability for much of this century, there hangs over the shaikhdom the latent and sometimes active threat of internal dissension. It does not derive, as in Kuwait, from a preponderance of *Uitlanders* in the shaikhdom's population, since the proportion of immigrants is much lower in Bahrain than in any of the other minor states. A few years ago they numbered 38,000 out of a total population of 216,000. The proportion probably remains the same today, even though the population has grown to around 250,000. The menace derives instead from the religious schism in the population between Sunni and Shii Muslims, and from the material division between the wealthy oligarchy which rules Bahrain and the politically conscious and ambitious intellectual proletariat below them. Most of the Baharinah, the indigenous inhabitants of Bahrain before its conquest by the Al Khalifah in the late eighteenth century, were Shii by confession. The Al Khalifah and the tribesmen who accompanied them from the mainland were Sunni, so that with their arrival and settlement a Sunni ascendancy was established in the island. Throughout much of the nineteenth century and into the twentieth there was a steady immigration of Persians into the shaikhdom, most of whom earned their living as merchants, artisans and urban labourers. Though they had little in common with the aboriginal Baharinah (who were in main cultivators and fishermen) they tended as fellow Shia to side with them in religious matters. Persistent discrimination against them and intermittent persecution by the Sunni community only served to strengthen the links between the two groups.

Today, although the Shia comprise a majority of the population, they do not command, in proportion to their numbers, the positions of wealth and power that the leading citizens of the Sunni community occupy. Apart from a handful of well-to-do merchant families and senior government officials, the most prominent and influential individuals among the Shia are the mullahs, the religious dignitaries. The present Al Khalifah ruler, Shaikh Isa ibn Salman, has made considerable efforts to conciliate the Shia. He recognizes, as did his father, the previous ruler, Shaikh Salman ibn Hamad (who died in 1961), that both the Shii mullahs and the Sunni divines possess substantial authority in their respective communities, and he is usually careful to consult them over questions of a politically sensitive nature. Despite his endeavours to identify them with his government and its actions, however, they remain an independent and unpredictable force in Bahraini politics, one that is more likely to be exercised on the side of extremism than it is on that of moderation.

Politics is a livelier business in Bahrain than it is in Kuwait. The percentage of educated and semi-educated citizens is higher, and the revenues of the shaikhdom are not sufficient to allow the Al Khalifah to indulge their subjects in so lavish a fashion as the Al Sabah have indulged theirs, especially by creating lucrative posts for them as government functionaries or by providing them with the funds and opportunities for real-estate speculation. As a consequence, the Al Khalifah have had to contend much more with manifestations of popular discontent in the form of demonstrations, strikes and riots. Though much of the agitation has undoubtedly arisen from economic causes, some of it has been generated by the political ambitions and resentments of the literate or semi-literate younger generation of Bahrainis, who feel that their educational attainments and progressive views entitle them to a decisive voice in the government of the shaikhdom. The urban sophisticates of Bahrain have long been avid consumers of whatever radical political ideas happen to be in vogue in the larger Arab countries, and the various recreational, cultural and sporting clubs which abound in the island have served them as a forum for the interminable political discussions in which they delight. In the 1950s, taking their cue from events in Egypt, Iraq and Syria, they were all wildly republican and nationalist in sentiment, crowding the streets of Manamah and Muharraq, the two main towns, at every opportunity to protest with equal vehemence against the autocratic rule of the Al Khalifah and the continued presence of Britain as the protecting power in the Gulf. The British presence was particularly evident in Bahrain, with the political residency for the Gulf and the Royal Naval base both located at Ras Jufair, and the RAF in charge of the airfield on Muharraq Island. When the demonstrations and riots of the mid-1950s against the Baghdad Pact and the Suez expedition were quelled with British assistance and the ringleaders imprisoned or sent to exile on St Helena, the evidence of Britain's ineradicable perfidy seemed to the young Bahraini nationalists to be conclusive. They also learned, however, to temper their valour with a little discretion, so that their subsequent demonstrations against the ruling family and its British protectors in the 1960s took the form largely of strikes and other trade union agitation over pay and working conditions.

Much of the political agitation in Bahrain over the past twenty-five years can be traced to its roots in the shaikhdom's educational system. The first school was started by American missionaries in the 1920s and the first government school was opened in the 1930s. From these beginnings the educational system developed – under the 'repressive' and 'unenlightened' rule of the Al Khalifah – into the most comprehensive in the Gulf. 'Comprehensive', however, is a relative adjective in this context. Although education is free it is also voluntary, so that as late as 1971 only half the children of school age attended schools, and the proportion of girls among the schoolchildren was even lower. Fifty-three per cent of the whole population was illiterate, and among adults over the age of forty-five, 77 per cent of the men and 95 per cent of the women were illiterate. It is the content of the education provided by the schools that most gives rise to concern. The emphasis is not upon technical and vocational training but upon the social sciences, the young Bahraini having an aversion to earning his living by his hands, especially in an occupation where he might run the risk of soiling them. His ambition is to go into commerce or government service, to be a shopkeeper or a clerk, rather than an engineer, a mechanic, an agriculturist or a veterinarian. The aversion to practical training and careers is shared by the handful of Bahrainis who go abroad each year for higher education. Between 1950 and 1972 426 Bahrainis obtained degrees or diplomas at universities and other institutions of higher education in the Middle East, Europe or North America. The greatest number of them studied one or other of the social sciences, sociology being favoured more than any of the others, presumably because it was considered a soft option. The consequence is that the overwhelming proportion of technical posts in Bahrain are occupied by foreigners (82 per cent in 1971 and 54 per cent of the professional posts as well), while the bureaucracy bulges with so many clerks as to make the government the biggest single employer in the shaikhdom. Whether the recently founded Gulf Technical College will make any appreciable difference to this situation is highly doubtful.

Although Bahrain has more of its own nationals and fewer Egyptians and Palestinians teaching in its schools than is the case in Kuwait, the predilections of the teachers and the nature of the curriculum have combined to produce much the same result as in the more northerly shaikhdom, the students emerging from the schools with their heads stuffed with political fancies and somewhat exaggerated ideas of their own importance, competence, ability and sagacity. Over the past decade, as the pendulum of politics in much of the Arab world has swung further to the left, the expectations of these intellectual *sans-culottes* have grown markedly. When the ruler, Shaikh Isa, announced in June 1972 that the basis of the shaikhdom's government was to be broadened and that elections were to be held for a constituent assembly, they unhesitatingly denounced the move as a meaningless sop and called for a boycott of the elections. The call went unheeded by the great majority of potential voters, so the radicals hurriedly dropped their opposition and joined in the scramble for seats. About a third of the twenty-two candidates elected in December 1972 were moderate or radical nationalists, and the religious division was fourteen Shia to eight Sunnis.

The constitution drawn up over the next six months and promulgated in June 1973 declared Bahrain to be an Islamic state with the *sharia* as the principal source of legislation. It provided for the setting up of a national assembly with legislative powers, consisting of thirty elected members and a council of ministers appointed by the ruler. The franchise was limited to adult, male Bahrainis. Political parties were forbidden, as in Kuwait, so that candidates for the assembly had to stand as individuals. Despite this prohibition, at the elections held in December 1973 candidates with socialist leanings campaigned as the 'Popular Bloc of the Left' and won ten of the thirty seats. They were balanced in the assembly by the elected conservative candidates, some of whom held fairly extreme religious views. As the council of ministers was composed of members of the Al Khalifah family and prominent Bahraini merchants, the overall complexion of the assembly was of moderate or even conservative hue. This did not save its proceedings, however, from degenerating over the next eighteen months into an acrimonious farce. So much time was spent by the members in pursuing personal vendettas or engaging in religious and political polemics that not a single piece of legislation was passed. The climax was reached in August 1975 when, after an outbreak of violence in the shaikhdom instigated by underground Marxist and Baathist cells, the assembly refused to pass a draft internal security law which included a provision for detention without trial. Shaikh Isa thereupon suspended the constitution and dissolved the assembly.

Whether the members of the Bahrain assembly or their supporters have learned anything of the nature of political responsibility from their fleeting acquaintance with representative government is not easily ascertainable. It seems unlikely. Those of them who are not dominated by sectarian or communal passions are befuddled with a hotchpotch of Nasserist, Baathist, Marxist and other ideas which they are incapable of translating into a coherent political philosophy. As we shall have occasion to remark later, the prospects for genuine constitutional and representative government in the Arab world are sombre in the extreme, and in the Arab states of the Gulf, where no political traditions or institutions of any kind other than those of shaikhly rule have ever developed, they are of a positively Stygian darkness. The conservative elements in Bahraini society – and they include the peasantry as well as the merchant oligarchy and the religious notables – do not want any departure from shaikhly rule, other perhaps than an enlargement of the ruler's *diwan* or council into a wider consultative body. Many of the island's self-styled 'progressives' would probably settle for a broadening of the representative and elective component in the present system of government, and for correspondingly greater opportunities for them to display their talents and incidentally add to their store of this world's goods. For the mass of Bahrainis the attainment of the latter goal would probably suffice. The wilder fringe of Bahrain's political life, the putative *enragés* who preach the gospel of Marxist–Leninist salvation, have little hope of acquiring anything more than a nuisance value unless they can raise a 'street' from the urban proletariat. A network for the organization of sedition certainly exists in the trade unions and the miscellany of recreational clubs, and there is equally no lack of demagogues, especially among the *soi-disant* students, some of whom have made the condition into a permanent career. Yet the bulk of the urban proletariat consists of immigrants, mostly Omanis, Baluchis and Persians; while, on the reverse side of the coin, a good proportion of the immigrant community is made up of respectable and law-abiding merchants, clerks and craftsmen – Persians, Indians, Pakistanis and others. To lure any of them to the barricades in an uprising designed to set up a radical regime composed of Marxist–Leninist Arab nationalists would be a fairly tough undertaking.

Few of the political tremors which have disturbed Kuwait and Bahrain have been felt in Qatar. There has always been a certain formlessness about Qatar as a political entity, which might almost be taken as a reflexion of its geographical drabness. It is a barren, featureless peninsula, without even a wadi to break its desolate monotony. Until the coming of oil a generation ago its inhabitants led the meanest and harshest existence of any in the Gulf, surviving by fishing, pearling and the raising of goats and camels. For much of the nineteenth century (and for at least three decades before then) Qatar lay under the authority of the Al Khalifah rulers of Bahrain, who, it will be recalled, had migrated from Kuwait to Zubara in the north-western corner of Qatar in 1766. The Al Khalifah's hold on the peninsula was first challenged by the Saudis of Najd in the first decade of the century. At irregular intervals thereafter, whenever the Al Saud were strong enough to compel compliance with their demands, they exacted tribute from the Al Khalifah in return for an undertaking to refrain from molesting the latter's possessions in Qatar. The Al Khalifah in their turn exacted tribute from the Al Thani shaikhs of Dauhah, on the east coast of the peninsula, then as now the principal town of Qatar. Part of the tribute went to subsidize the Naim, the leading nomadic tribe of Qatar, who were loyal to the Al Khalifah.

Encouraged by the Saudis, the Al Thani attempted in 1851 to throw off their allegiance to Bahrain and to discontinue the payment of tribute. The attempt failed, but the Al Thani tried again in 1867, with somewhat more success. The Al Khalifah retaliated by attacking and sacking Dauhah, Wakra and other ports with the help of the war fleet of Abu Dhabi. The Al Thani and their followers were subsequently saved from further depredation by the intervention of the British political resident in the Gulf. The ruler of Abu Dhabi was required to make reparation for his breach of the maritime truce, and when the ruler of Bahrain refused to make similar reparation he was deposed. It emerged from investigations made by the political resident into the origins of the outbreak that the shaikh of Bahrain had not been remitting the due portion of the tribute he received from Qatar to the Naim tribe, with the result that the Naim had been marauding in the Al Thani domains. An agreement was therefore drawn up by the resident whereby the Naim's portion of the tribute was to be paid directly to them by the Al Thani. The latter, however, were bent upon discontinuing the tribute altogether, and with it their political dependence upon the Al Khalifah. Their chance came four years later, in 1871, when a Turkish expeditionary force wrested control of al-Hasa from the Saudis. Abdullah ibn Sabah, the shaikh of Kuwait, came down to Dauhah on a Turkish steamer in July of that year to persuade the aged ruler of the town, Shaikh Muhammad ibn Thani, to acknowledge Ottoman suzerainty. The old shaikh refused to do so, but his son, Jasim, saw in the adventitious appearance of the Turks a chance to rid Qatar of its Al Khalifah overlords. He promptly accepted appointment as Ottoman *qaim-maqam* of Dauhah and ran up the Turkish flag. No further tribute was paid to Bahrain, and when Muhammad ibn Thani died in 1878 Jasim attacked Zubara and razed it to the ground. The town has never been rebuilt, although the site was occasionally occupied by Al Khalifah subjects in later years, and the Al Khalifah today still look upon it as rightfully theirs.

After successfully challenging Bahrain's supremacy in Qatar, Jasim ibn Muhammad set out to extend the limits of his territory in the south. Here he ran into opposition from the Bani Yas of Abu Dhabi, whose tribal grazing grounds extended to the base of the Qatar peninsula. The contest between the Al Thani ruler and the Bani Yas shaikhs focused upon the inlet of Khaur al-Udaid at the eastern foot of Qatar, which fishermen from the Bani Yas were accustomed to visit. Shaikh Jasim was never able to make good his claim to the *khaur* up to the time of his death in 1913; but he bequeathed the claim to his successors who were to pursue it down to our day.

A short time before Jasim's death the Turks had renounced their suzerainty over Qatar in the Anglo-Ottoman Convention of 29 July 1913. However, as the convention remained unratified up to the outbreak of war in 1914, a Turkish garrison stayed on at Dauhah. It was expelled in the early months of the war, and on 3 November 1916 a treaty was concluded by the British government with the ruler – Jasim's son, Abdullah – which brought Qatar into the trucial system. Shaikh Abdullah agreed to observe all the undertakings given earlier by the Trucial Shaikhs to abstain from piracy, the slave trade and maritime warfare. He also undertook to abide by the exclusive agreements concerning relations with foreign powers and the non-alienation of territory. In return, he was assured of British protection against attacks upon his territory or subjects by sea, and of the good offices of the British government in the event of an attack upon Qatar by land, on condition that such an attack was not provoked by aggressive acts on his part or that of his subjects.

Shaikh Abdullah awarded an oil concession of seventy-five years' duration to the Iraq Petroleum Company in May 1935. The southern boundary of the oil concession was not stipulated, since the landward frontiers of Qatar had never been defined. A month earlier, however, as we have seen in an earlier chapter, Ibn Saud had claimed a frontier with Qatar which, if conceded, would have placed both Khaur al-Udaid and the Jabal Nakhsh, the southern end of the Dukhan range of hills (which was considered to be a promising oil structure), in Saudi territory. It would also cut off Qatar from Abu Dhabi by interposing a wedge of Saudi territory between them. For these reasons, as we have seen, the British government rejected Ibn Saud's claim and proposed instead a frontier further south which would leave Jabal Nakhsh to Qatar and Khaur al-Udaid to Abu Dhabi.

When the onset of war in 1939 brought the frontier negotiations to a temporary halt, Shaikh Abdullah ibn Jasim was greatly relieved. He had no wish to antagonize Ibn Saud, partly out of fear, partly out of religious sentiment (he and many of the Al Thani followed the Wahhabi practice of Islam), and partly because of his family connexions and political links with the Al Saud, which served to strengthen him against his adversaries, the shaikhs of Bahrain and Abu Dhabi. At the same time, however, he was most reluctant either to give up potentially oil-bearing territory or to abandon the claim to Khaur al-Udaid, which over the years had become a matter of honour to his family. Though Jabal Nakhsh, in fact, never proved to be oil-bearing, oil was struck on the Dukhan structure in December 1939. Further development of the field was delayed by the war, and it was not until 1949 that the first oil was exported. Not entirely coincidentally, negotiations were resumed that year to determine the frontier of Saudi Arabia with Qatar, Abu Dhabi and Oman. The Saudi government again preferred a claim to Qatar which embraced a substantial slice of territory at the base of the peninsula. There was reason to doubt, however, that the Saudis were much in earnest in advancing the claim, other than to secure control of Khaur al-Udaid.

Shaikh Abdullah ibn Jasim, now well advanced in years, abdicated *circa* 1950 (accounts vary as to whether he actually gave up power in 1949 or 1951) in favour of his son, Ali. Shaikh Ali, in turn, abdicated in 1960 in favour of his son, Ahmad. Five years later, Shaikh Ahmad ibn Ali reached what was for all practical purposes a definitive agreement on his border with Saudi Arabia. In return for implicitly renouncing his claim to Khaur al-Udaid in favour of the Saudis he was accorded a generous frontier at the base of the peninsula, roughly along the lines that the British had proposed a dozen years earlier. Additional consolation for Shaikh Ahmad for relinquishing the Al Thani claim to Khaur al-Udaid came from the knowledge that by effectively transferring his family's hypothetical rights to Saudi Arabia, he was also impugning Abu Dhabi's title to the inlet.

Oil revenues transformed the life of Qatar from the early 1950s onwards, though rather more slowly than was the case in Kuwait or Bahrain. There was the same influx of immigrants, the same rash of construction, the same mindless extravagances on the part of the principal beneficiaries of the oil wealth. On the other hand, no effort was made to establish a comprehensive system of state welfare comparable to that instituted by the Al Sabah in Kuwait. Gifts and subsidies were doled out to the tribes and their shaikhs, in sufficient amounts to keep them content without unduly sharpening their appetite for more. The evidence of this sparing disbursement of funds could be seen in the early 1960s, a full decade after the oil revenues had begun to flow in, in the depressed and virtually unchanged condition of the fishing villages strung along the coast to the north of Qatar. Discontent with the Al Thani's parsimony combined with a number of other grievances, among them resentment at the truculent behaviour of the ruling family's retainers (and some of its lesser members as well), to bring about a general strike, embracing most sections of the working population, in April 1963. It had its effect, the lot of the ordinary Qatari improving to some degree thereafter.

Most of the oil revenues, however, were still earmarked for the upkeep and enjoyment of the Al Thani and their horde of retainers under a financial regime cynically known as 'the rule of the four quarters' – a quarter for the ruling shaikh, a quarter for the other Al Thani shaikhs, a quarter for the family's reserve funds, and a quarter for the rest of the population. Oddly enough, the division of the spoils was not as grossly one-sided as would appear at first sight; for the Al Thani themselves comprise, if not quite half the population (as the local wits would have it), at least a fair proportion of the native inhabitants. Qatar had a population in 1970 of possibly 90,000 (no accurate figures are available), of which roughly 40 per cent, or about 35,000, were native Qataris. The number of Al Thani shaikhs was reported to be anything between 450 and 700. Their close dependants presumably numbered a few thousand, and their retainers several thousand more – a formidable constituency by any measure, and one which required an equally formidable outlay of money to keep it in a style befitting its conception of its own importance. As an indication of the extent of the expenditure involved, it might be mentioned that every son of every Al Thani shaikh was automatically entitled from birth to an annual stipend of £3,600, rising to £15,600 at the age of thirteen. By the mid-1970s this sum had been increased to £24,000.

Shaikh Ahmad ibn Ali, like his father Shaikh Ali ibn Abdullah before him, ruled largely by a policy of indifference, interspersed with occasional displays of severity. He spent the greater part of his time out of the shaikhdom, preferring to hunt bustard in Persia or Pakistan to shooting snipe in Qatar. His lengthy absences abroad – he often stayed for months on end at his villa near Geneva – led in April 1970 to his being compelled, under pressure from both his relatives and the British authorities in the Gulf, to transfer authority for the conduct of Qatar's affairs to his younger cousin, Shaikh Khalifah ibn Hamad, another grandson of the former ruler, Abdullah ibn Jasim. The change was made by the promulgation on 2 April 1970 of a 'provisional fundamental law', a long-winded document of seventy-seven articles which was apparently designed to serve as the shaikhdom's constitution *pro tempore*. It declared Qatar to be an independent, sovereign, Arab state, with Islam as the state religion and the *sharia* as the fundamental source of legislation. Executive power was vested in the ruler, assisted by the deputy ruler and a council of ministers appointed by the ruler. An advisory council was also to be created, consisting of the council of ministers and twenty-three members appointed by the ruler, twenty of them from a panel of forty candidates to be elected by the adult, male citizens of Qatar.

Shaikh Khalifah ibn Hamad, a much more forceful and energetic character than his cousin, Shaikh Ahmad, had been deputy ruler of Qatar for the better part of a decade. It had long been common knowledge in Dauhah that he aspired to become ruler, without necessarily waiting upon the intervention of mortality to remove his cousin. He had been restrained from gratifying his ambition primarily by factional rivalry within the manifold ranks of the Al Thani. Confirmed as *de facto* ruler by the *démarche* of April 1970, he had only to await a suitable opportunity to transform his position into a permanent one. Shaikh Ahmad unwittingly paved the way for him by failing to return to Qatar for the celebration of the shaikhdom's independence on 3 September 1971, electing instead to issue a formal announcement of the occasion from his villa near Geneva. Six months later, while Ahmad was happily hunting with his falcons in Persia in the last week of February 1972, Khalifah ibn Hamad declared him deposed and proclaimed himself ruler in his place. Shaikh Ahmad, not wholly disconsolate at the turn events had taken, took up residence with his father-in-law, Shaikh Rashid ibn Said of Dubai. Thereafter he divided his time contentedly between Dubai and his villa beside Lake Léman, where at length he died in 1977.

Under Shaikh Khalifah ibn Hamad the shaikhdom has made the familiar strides in construction, education, medical services, housing and the provision of the other amenities characteristic of the system of social welfare now obtaining in the minor oil-rich states of the Gulf. There is no doubt that the lot of the ordinary Qatari has improved considerably in the past half-a-dozen years, an improvement which owes its origin more to the greatly augmented oil revenues since October 1973 than to any remarkable access of benevolence on the part of the Al Thani. The principal beneficiaries of these revenues have been the Al Thani themselves and the merchant community of Dauhah, many members of which have accumulated large fortunes. Yet the benefits have also seeped down through the layers of Qatari society to the lowest levels, where the illiterate Bedouin and fishermen have had jobs created for them in the state bureaucracy. The total population of Qatar is, at most, around 130,000, although it has been placed at a much higher figure, between 200,000 and 250,000, by the Qatari government and by Western publicists anxious to cater to Qatari self-esteem. Native Qataris probably number no more than 50,000, of whom perhaps half are adults of working age. The central administration of the shaikhdom alone employs some 18,000 people, the higher ranks, where technical or professional qualifications are required, being filled mostly by Palestinians, Egyptians and other *émigré* Arabs. Little wonder that the director of the civil service was reported in September 1977 as saying, 'If I were to check at this moment, perhaps only a quarter of those staff would be usefully employed.'

The real work in Qatar, particularly at the lower levels, is done by the immigrants. Pakistanis and Indians, with the former predominant, make up the artisan class, the small shopkeepers and over a third of the labour force. Of the nearly 25,000 Pakistani labourers, half are Pathans, who have a reputation for being strong and hard-working. Roughly another third of the labour force is composed of Persians and Baluchis, while the remainder, again somewhere in excess of 20,000, are Omanis, Dhufaris, Yemenis and Hadramis. None of these labourers, skilled or unskilled, is paid on the scale of the Qatari workers – or non-workers – though all have had to endure the consequences of a grossly inflated cost of living in recent years. Were it not for the dire poverty in their home countries which led them to find work in Qatar in the first place, it would hardly be worth their while to stay there. Northern Arabs – Palestinians, Egyptians and others – who are employed in professional, technical, teaching and clerical posts, some 5,000 or more in all, are paid better, though they, too, have felt the pinch of rising prices.

Oil production, the basis of Qatar's prosperity, has declined of late years, and is now pegged at half-a-million barrels per day. Revenues, however, have increased, running at about $2,000 million per annum in 1975 and 1976. It is reckoned that at the present rate of production the reserves have a future life of perhaps thirty years, mostly in the offshore fields from which 70 per cent of the present production is obtained. There are, however, large reserves of natural gas, again mainly in offshore fields, which may have a life in them of a hundred years at the rate of production that is at present projected. The two principal oil concessionaires, the Qatar Petroleum Company, a subsidiary of IPC, and the Shell Company of Qatar, have both been nationalized, the Qatari government having taken a 25 per cent share in the two companies in 1973, 60 per cent in

1975 and 100 per cent by 1977. Operations, however, are still in the hands of the companies, since the Qataris have neither the skill, the knowledge nor the experience to take them over themselves. As a means of investing the surplus oil revenues and diversifying the shaikhdom's economy within the narrow limits of practicability, the Qatari government has embarked upon several ambitious industrial projects, most of them at the oil port of Umm Said, twenty miles or so to the south of Dauhah. Among them are a nitrogen fertilizer plant; an iron and steel mill being built by the Japanese with a projected capacity initially of 400,000 tonnes per annum; a large natural gas liquefaction plant (the first stage of which blew up in April 1977); and a huge petro-chemical complex for the production of ethylene and its derivatives. This last enterprise, embarked upon in company with a couple of French companies, is associated with the construction of another large ethylene plant at Dunkerque. There is about these vast undertakings, as with their like elsewhere along the Arabian coast of the Gulf, more than a touch of absurdity; yet they appear almost sober (as we shall see shortly) by comparison with what is in the making or in contemplation lower down the Gulf.

Having acquired for themselves over the past two decades a goodly share of the luxuries and necessities the world has to offer, including the obligatory quota of technological marvels just mentioned, the Qataris have of late been equipping themselves with a history and an indigenous culture, both of noble proportions. The showpiece of this particular enterprise is a 'national museum', housed in the former (*c.* 1920) palace of the ruler in Dauhah. Largely the inspiration of a public relations firm in London, the museum has been equipped and adorned at a cost of several millions, despite – or perhaps because of – the fundamental limitation of having very little to put into it. For this reason the museum accords great prominence in its exhibits to the neolithic artefacts unearthed in Qatar by European archaeologists. Since nothing of any note has occurred in Qatar in the intervening millennia, the museum has had to attach profound significance to fishing nets, Bedouin tents, camel halters and saddles in its re-creation of the Qatari past. It is not the fault of the Qataris that they have no history, nor can it be held against them that they would like to invent one – though it is doubtful whether most of them care one way or another about the past. What is objectionable about these public-relations exercises on behalf of the Qatari regime is that they involve the falsification of the historical record over the past two centuries, notably concerning the nature and length of Bahrain's connexion with Qatar, the relationship between the Al Thani and the Ottoman Turks, and the character and exploits of the best-known member of the line, Jasim ibn Muhammad Al Thani, who was far from being the heroic paragon that modern hagiography has made him out to be. The anxiety of the Al Thani to exalt themselves is understandable, since they are undoubtedly the least distinguished – except in their progenitive capacities – of the petty dynasties of the Gulf, and are looked upon with disdain by the other ruling families. It is doubtful, however, whether their efforts at self-glorification – the latest of which is the foundation at Dauhah of a 'University of the Lower Gulf' – will achieve anything more than to confirm their detractors in their present opinion.

The methods of government preferred by the Al Thani have always been rough and ready. Most if not all of them are Wahhabi by religious conviction, and they share the predilection of their fellow sectarians, the Al Saud, for arbitrary and condign punishments, even though they do not always emulate the latter's methods. Although the religious and political restraints to which Qataris are subject are less severe now than they were a decade ago, they are still harsher than those in force in any of the other Gulf states outside Saudi Arabia. Little of the indulgence that is accorded to youthful radicals in Bahrain and Kuwait is evident in Qatar. The Al Thani rule with a tight rein and they intend to continue to do so. Though the advisory council provided for in the temporary constitution of 1970 was brought into being after the accession of Shaikh Khalifah ibn Hamad, it is, like its counterpart the 'national museum', a show without substance, a tame body whose prime purpose is to serve as an arm of the regime. Whether the Al Thani will be able to keep their strict control over their subjects in the years ahead is uncertain. As wealth and education spread, even among limited sections of the populace, as more Qataris travel abroad, and as material comforts and pleasures continue to captivate the minds and spirits of the Qataris, they are bound to chafe under the rigid and cheerless prescriptions of Wahhabism to which they are required to conform.

While some of the shaikhs of other tribes in Qatar resent the dominance of the Al Thani, there is little reason to believe that they would ever express this resentment actively. It is much the same with the bulk of the immigrant population, who are seemingly content to make their living from the country without being troubled by an itch to share in its political life. Of course there are a number of restless spirits about, especially among the *émigré* Arabs and the minority of educated or semi-educated Qataris; but they would have no hope of challenging the supremacy of the Al Thani without the backing of an armed force. Both the small Qatari defence force and the police are firmly under the regime's control. They have few Qataris in their ranks: the police are mostly Baluchis and the defence force is comprised in the main of Omani, Dhufari and Yemeni mercenaries. Some signs of disaffection appeared among them in 1973–4, which resulted in the dismissal of a few score soldiers and their replacement by fresh recruits. If the defence force should become involved in politics, it is more likely to be in support of one or other contending factions of the Al Thani – there are at least three rival branches of the dynasty – than as the spearhead of a revolutionary *coup* designed to overthrow the regime. What may be predicted with some certainty, in view of the close ties that have subsisted for many years between the Al Thani and the Al Saud, is that the Saudi government would not remain indifferent to any attempt to change the internal *status quo* in Qatar.

Affluence struck the Trucial Coast in the later 1960s and began to work its familiar alchemy, transmuting simple metal into dross. The wealth was confined, in the first instance, to two shaikhdoms, Abu Dhabi and Dubai. Oil was struck in Abu Dhabi waters in 1959 and onshore the following year. Production began in 1962. A few years later oil was also found in Dubai waters and production started in 1969, adding to the revenue the shaikhdom already derived from its function as a trading entrepôt.

Before the coming of oil the tribes of the Trucial Coast led lives much akin to those of their neighbours in Oman, subsisting on fishing, pastoralism and limited agriculture. Though privation had been their lot for many decades, they had at times in the past enjoyed marginal prosperity. In the first half of the nineteenth century they had been among the chief carriers of the Gulf's trade, voyaging as far away as India, Africa and the Red Sea to exchange horses and donkeys, fruits and pearls, wool and hides and the other products of Arabia and Persia for rice and grains, sugar and spices, cotton and woollen piece goods, and a wide variety of European manufactures. They supplemented their legitimate commerce with piracy, sometimes on a grand scale, and they controlled much of the slave trade from East Africa and Ethiopia to Arabia and the Gulf. Well before the century was out these pursuits had all been lost to them. Piracy and the slave trade had been suppressed by the British, all but a minute portion of the carrying trade had been taken over by European and Indian steamships, and only the pearl trade, along with some clandestine running of slaves and arms, enabled the tribes of Trucial Oman to earn enough to purchase necessities and lesser luxuries from abroad. When the pearl trade withered away in the 1930s they were reduced to near destitution. Some compensation was afforded their rulers after the Second World War by the concessionary payments made by oil companies for prospecting rights; but the payments went directly to the rulers of the shaikhdoms, and in any case they were not substantial enough to rescue the economy of Trucial Oman from stagnation. So from the late 1940s onwards the tribesmen drifted northwards every year in their hundreds to seek work in the oil states of the upper Gulf and thereby support their dependants at home.

With the discovery and exploitation of oil in Trucial Oman itself the need for such emigration vanished. Fortune was to smile upon the tribes as never before in their history, transforming their existence within the space of a decade from one of penury to one of ease and plenty. At the time that Trucial Oman became independent and was transformed into the United Arab Emirates, the total population of the seven shaikhdoms (or 'emirates' as they now preferred to style themselves) was reckoned to be in excess of 200,000. (Three years earlier, in 1968, the first census ever taken recorded a total of some 180,000 souls.) By the end of 1972 the population was estimated to have risen to 320,000. A second census in 1975 produced a figure, according to report, of 655,937 for the total population. To anyone acquainted with the general level of competence in the administration of the shaikhdoms the precision of this computation comes as something of a surprise. How it was arrived at and what it signifies it is impossible to say, for a blanket of secrecy has since been thrown over the detailed findings of the census. The reason for the secrecy is not hard to discern: it is to maintain the fiction that the original inhabitants of the UAE still outnumber the immigrant population, the *Uitlanders*, a fiction that in its turn is necessitated by considerations of political and economic power and the retention of this power by the native Arab population. Just how much is involved economically may be seen from the figures for oil production and revenues over the past few years. Abu Dhabi's oil output, the majority of it from on-shore fields, rose from 1,302,000 barrels per day in 1973 to 1,414,000 b/d in 1974 and 1,600,000 b/d in 1976, a figure that exceeded Kuwait's production in that year. Dubai's output from its off-shore field rose from 219,000 b/d in 1973 to 276,000 b/d in 1975 and 350,000 b/d in 1976. The increase in revenues was even more striking: Abu Dhabi's and Dubai's combined income from oil in 1971 was something over $800 million. The UAE's income from oil in 1976, by which time Sharjah had become the third oil-producing shaikhdom with an output of 50,000 b/d from an off-shore field, was $8,600 million, more than ten times what it had been five years earlier.

At the time of the 1968 census the population of Abu Dhabi was around 46,000, of whom only half were native tribesmen. Even allowing for a rapid natural increase in the 23,000 or so indigenous inhabitants, they cannot now number more than 30,000 at most. It is much the same story in Dubai, where the population in 1968 was about 59,000, half of them native to the shaikhdom. Again, allowing for rapid natural growth, the indigenous inhabitants probably number under 40,000. In contrast, in the non-oil shaikhdoms of the UAE the native population in 1968 was proportionately much higher, 93 per cent in Ras al-Khaimah and 98 per cent in Fujairah. Of Trucial Oman's (or the UAE's) total population of 180,000 in 1968 roughly 120,000 were native-born. It is doubtful whether it has increased by more than a third since then, which would make it about 160,000 today. If the census figure of 1975 is even remotely accurate, it means that the immigrants outnumber the indigenous population by at least two to one – or even by as much as three to one, as is said to be the case in Abu Dhabi.

Most of the immigrants to the UAE are concentrated in the three wealthiest shaikhdoms – Abu Dhabi, Dubai and, to a lesser extent, Sharjah. The pattern of immigration has been much the same as it was earlier in the oil states of the upper Gulf. At the lowest level are the Persians, Pakistanis (mainly Baluchis), Omanis and latterly Yemenis, who labour on the construction sites and perform all the menial tasks. Above them are the Indians and Pakistanis (other than Baluchi and Pathan labourers) who work as clerks, artisans and shop-keepers; and above them again are the 'northern' Arabs, predominantly Palestinians, Egyptians and Lebanese, who earn their living as government clerks, teachers, doctors, skilled tradesmen and businessmen. Only a handful of the several thousand Europeans working in the three shaikhdoms are employed by local firms or governments. The great majority are employees of overseas firms who remain for only a specified period of service.

As was only to have been expected, the great inflow of immigrants into Abu Dhabi, Dubai and Sharjah, together with the riches derived from oil production and the scale of material consumption which these have permitted, has altered these shaikhdoms out of all recognition, rendering them less distinctly Arabian in character and aspect and more manifestly Levantine. They are, in effect, now city states, and their tribal inhabitants have, to a large extent, become urbanized. (The condition of the other member shaikhdoms of the UAE has not altered so dramatically: for instance, 64 per cent of the population of Fujairah and 40 per cent of that of Ras al-Khaimah are still engaged in agriculture. In Dubai, in contrast, the figure is 2 per cent.) Again, as might have been expected, the rapid inflow of *Uitlanders* has generated racial, religious and cultural tensions, along with a marked degree of economic dissatisfaction, occasioned by the pronounced disparities in effort and reward between the immigrant community and the indigenous inhabitants, and within the immigrant community itself. To keep their subjects contented, the rulers of Abu Dhabi and Dubai, like those of Kuwait and Qatar before them, have disbursed a considerable portion of their oil revenues in the form of social services, factitious employment and straight grants of cash. The native Arab tribesmen are given free or subsidized housing, free education, free medical treatment, and free electricity and water. Jobs are created for them, generally in one department of government or another or by reserving to them a monopoly of particular occupations, such as motor vehicle haulage. Since the tribesmen are nearly all illiterate and devoid of the skills needed for any job above that of watchman or driver, a system of dual appointments has grown up – of foreigners with the required skills and of natives without them. This is particularly true both of the local governments and of the federal government of the UAE, which alone employs over 28,000 people, more or less uselessly.

With minor and trifling exceptions, these various benefits are confined to the indigenous inhabitants of Abu Dhabi and Dubai. The *Uitlanders*, who do all the work that the native tribesmen cannot or will not do for themselves, are denied them. Some of the *Uitlanders*, however, feel no sense of deprivation, since they have profited exceedingly from the careless outpouring of money from the state coffers, especially in Abu Dhabi. Merchants, contractors, entrepreneurs, influence pedlars, consultants and the like all have managed to line their pockets to the full. Of those in paid employment, the northern Arabs in government service, whether professional men or administrative functionaries, receive the highest emoluments, though their contribution to the general economic welfare is of questionable value. At the bottom of the financial scale is the mass of Persian, Baluchi, Omani and Yemeni labourers who do the hardest work and receive the lowest pay. A labourer's basic daily wage in Abu Dhabi in the spring of 1976 was 23 *dirhams* (about £3). For a six-day working week, therefore, he received 138 *dirhams*, or about £18, which came to something less than 600 *dirhams*, or under £80, a month. To emphasize – if emphasis is necessary – the meagreness of this payment, it might be pointed out that, as an inducement to the native tribesmen to send their children to the schools provided for them, the Abu Dhabi government paid parents the sum of 500 *dirhams* a month for every child who attended a secondary school, and the children themselves received from the government a further 100 or 200 *dirhams* a month as pocket money.

The familiar argument put forward in defence of the exploitation of foreign labour in the Gulf oil states is that the labourers earn far more than they would in their own countries, and that it was the very impoverishment of their lives at home that drove them to find work abroad. Hence the swarms of labourers who beat on the doors of the oil states, clamouring to be admitted, and hence, too, the large numbers of illegal immigrants who are willing to run all manner of risks to enter by surreptitious means. There is enough truth in the argument to accord it a hearing, though it is a sorry justification for some of the circumstances in which *Uitlander* labourers are recruited and made to work. Some of the worst abuses arise from the *muqaddam* system, which has for a good two centuries or more operated around the shores of the Red Sea and the Gulf. Essentially it is a system of indentured labour. A *muqaddam* is a broker, a contractor of labour who will for a fee engage to supply a given number of men to work for a specified period of time or until the completion of a project. He is paid both by the employer on a *per capita* basis and by the labourer he recruits. A thriving business is done in the illegal sale of work permits. If a labourer cannot afford the bribe required to obtain a permit at the start of his contract, he may arrange to pay the bribe in instalments as he works; and the bribe is invariably large enough to ensure that he works for a good length of time. As the *muqaddam* usually operates hand in glove with the shipowners who transport the labourers from the Indian sub-continent to the Red Sea and the Gulf, there are further opportunities for profit in the advancing and repayment of passage money. For all practical purposes, the labourer never fully escapes the clutches of the *muqaddam* throughout the length of his contract. *Muqaddams* are also given to squeezing the employer to whom they have contracted to supply men. At one stage or another, usually a critical one, in the construction of a project, a *muqaddam* will demand a higher fee for the continued provision of labour, usually citing as an excuse some wholly imaginary problem that has arisen in the supply of labour from Pakistan, India or Persia. All too conscious of his own contractual obligations and the risk of financial penalties if he does not fulfil them, the employer will almost invariably submit to the extortion. Needless to say, in all these transactions the well-being of the labourer, the alpha and omega of the entire system, is never given a moment's thought.

To what purposes have the oil revenues of Abu Dhabi and Dubai been put over the past decade, other than in providing bread and circuses for the indigenous inhabitants? As in the other oil states of the Gulf, there is simply no way of knowing how much has been dissipated by personal indulgence, extravagance or folly, how much has been corruptly siphoned off in one way or another by the charlatans and carpet-baggers who now proliferate in the Gulf, how much has found its way to distant financial sanctuaries or been used to underwrite political and other activities abroad, some of them of an unsavoury character. The visible evidence of how some of the wealth has been expended is in the transformation of Dubai and Abu Dhabi into smaller replicas of Kuwait. Dubai alone had known some prosperity before the coming of oil, a prosperity based upon its function as an entrepôt for the trade of Trucial Oman and the Persian coast opposite. It had the only port deserving of the name on the Trucial Coast, it had a vigorous merchant class (many of whom were Persians) and the ruler, Shaikh Rashid ibn Said Al Maktum, was himself a highly astute and successful trader. Well before the oil boom his foresight and initiative led him to enlarge Dubai's port facilities, so as to cope with an increased tonnage of shipping, and to build an airport to handle international air traffic. Rashid pursued an equally far-sighted and liberal policy towards foreign merchants, construction firms and banks, thereby ensuring that Dubai would remain the commercial hub and chief market-place of the coast. It has done so, to the extent that 70 per cent of the imports into the UAE in 1976, valued at over $8,500 million, entered through Dubai.

Of late years Rashid seems to have become the prisoner of his own reputation for financial acumen, a victim, perhaps, of the flattery which has been rather indiscriminately heaped upon him by Western *commis voyageurs*. Ignoring, or possibly miffed by, the Organization of Arab Petroleum Exporting Countries' choice of Bahrain as the site for a complex of docks to service large oil tankers, Rashid embarked upon an even larger project of the kind at Dubai. When completed, it will be capable of accommodating the largest tankers yet built – and even larger ones. It remains to be seen whether there will be sufficient work for both dock complexes to justify the cost of their construction. Not content with what has so far been achieved, Rashid has plans for the development of a grandiose industrial and commercial complex at Jabal Ali, to the south-west of Dubai town. At its centre will be an aluminium smelter with an initial productive capacity of 135,000 tons per annum, a capacity which is to be increased until the smelter, like the dry dock at Dubai, is the biggest in the world. Docks will also be constructed at Jabal Ali on a scale designed to make the port the largest in the Middle East. They will be complemented by a new international airport costing $384 million, capable of handling twenty-two wide-bodied jet aircraft at one time. Eventually, so it is said, Jabal Ali will become a mighty powerhouse of industry and commerce, with a population of half-a-million souls. What is perhaps of rather more significance than all this fanfaronade is that Rashid has already borrowed from abroad (mainly between 1967 and 1977) a total of $2,000 million to finance Dubai's expansion. Most of this debt is still outstanding and it requires $100 million per annum to service it. By 1981 the annual charges will have risen to $466 million. If Rashid presses ahead with the Jabal Ali scheme, therefore, he will have to increase his borrowings abroad or his oil revenue, or both. Alternatively, he will have to regain some of his old astuteness and trim his sails to the winds of economic sanity.

Down the coast at Abu Dhabi the hypermania is even more marked, being aggravated by a long-smouldering rivalry between the ruling families of Abu Dhabi and Dubai. Soon after his accession in 1966, the ruler of Abu Dhabi, Shaikh Zayid ibn Sultan Al Nihayan, ordered the construction of a port, so as to avoid having to ship Abu Dhabi's imports through Dubai. The port was completed and then expanded, both times at staggering cost, since the natural conditions of the coastline are not as favourable to harbour construction as they are, comparatively speaking, at Dubai. Abu Dhabi town, which in the early 1960s possessed barely a dozen substantial buildings, has expanded into a kind of Arabian Torremolinos, a bloated, disordered mass of architectural vulgarities and grotesqueries, which it would take a sturdy pen and even stronger nerves merely to enumerate. Such now is Abu Dhabi's importance as the capital of the UAE and a financial centre of the world that the international airport opened in 1970 is now deemed insufficient for its needs, and a second airport, modelled on the lines of Charles de Gaulle airport at Roissy, is now being built at a cost of $200 million. Yet another international airport, costing $75 million, is planned for the town of al-Ain, a hundred miles inland in the Buraimi oasis.

Al-Ain, where Zayid spent most of his life before becoming ruler, has, along with the other Abu Dhabi villages in the Buraimi oasis, had money lavished upon it out of all proportion to the size of its original population, with the inevitable result that its population has now swollen out of all recognition, as tribesmen from near and far and *Uitlanders* of every description have swarmed in to enjoy the cornucopia. Apart from the usual complement of houses, schools, mosques, paved roads, piped water and abundant electricity, the al-Ain scene is now graced by the presence of a 'university', the impulse for which would seem to have been yearnings of the kind that lay behind the creation of the Qatar 'national museum'. There are limits, however, to the development of al-Ain as anything more than an oasis town, albeit the centre of Abu Dhabi's cultural efflorescence.

To match, or preferably eclipse, Rashid's ambitious plans for Jabal Ali,

Zayid has decided upon a similar scheme of industrial development for Abu Dhabi. The site he has chosen as the potential Ruhr of the lower Gulf is Ruwais, a makeshift village on the coast 150 miles west of Abu Dhabi town. Here, according to the local augurs, will rise a giant methane-ethane gas plant (dwarfing that in Qatar), while nearby there will be an oil refinery, a petrochemical complex and a fertilizer plant, all on an impressive scale. Eventually these enterprises will support a city of noble and imposing proportions. As might be surmised, the projected cost of the undertaking is staggering, which is one reason why the oil companies operating in the shaikhdom have in the main resisted pressure upon them to participate in it.

Though the rulers of the other shaikhdoms of the UAE are constrained by limited financial resources, they also cherish ideas and ambitions above their station. Not so long ago there was not a single anchorage up the coast from Dubai that was usable. The anchorages, situated at the mouths of creeks, had all silted up as a result of the steady if imperceptible rising of the land over the preceding century and a half or longer. Now Sharjah, Ajman and Ras al-Khaimah are all constructing harbours in imitation of Dubai and Abu Dhabi; while Sharjah, which receives revenues from the 50,000 barrels of oil produced daily from its off-shore field, plans to build a second harbour on the other side of the mountains at Khaur Fakkan, facing the Gulf of Oman, which was taken from Oman and used as a pirate lair by the Qawasim in the early nineteenth century. Shaikh Sultan ibn Muhammad Al Qasimi, the ruler of Sharjah since the assassination of his brother, Khalid, in January 1972, has, like his predecessor, rather exaggerated notions about the shaikhdom's destiny as another Dubai. On what, in relation to his ambitions, are rather meagre economic revenues, he has tried to push Sharjah forward as a dynamic centre of commerce and finance, a tax haven and a leisure resort – Zurich and the Bahamas in one. To this end he has had an international airport built at a cost of several million dollars, even though the international airport at Dubai is only half-a-dozen miles down the road. All that Shaikh Sultan's activities have so far achieved, it would seem, is to run him into considerable debt. His distant cousin, the ruler of Ras al-Khaimah, Shaikh Saqr ibn Muhammad Al Qasimi, is afflicted by a similar passion for self-exaltation, tinged in his case with Bonapartist aspirations. He, too, has had an international airport constructed, costing $10.5 million, which seems destined to be little used. He opened a casino some time ago in the hope of attracting revenue, only to be forced to close it down in 1977 under pressure from Saudi Arabia, the self-constituted guardian of the Gulf's morals. However, Shaikh Saqr may be able to allow freer rein to his fancies in the near future, as oil in commercial quantities has lately been discovered in Ras al-Khaimah waters.

The economic boom that followed the quadrupling of oil prices in the closing months of 1973 produced a frenzied speculation in land and building in Abu Dhabi, Dubai and, to a lesser degree, Sharjah. (Much the same phenomenon also occurred in Kuwait and Qatar.) Since only the native inhabitants of the shaikhdoms were allowed to own land, almost unlimited opportunities opened up to them, as immigrants flooded in in their thousands, to make rapid fortunes from property speculation. The activity was fully encouraged by the local rulers; for not only did it afford them a convenient means of distributing a share of the oil wealth to their subjects in the form of land grants and building loans but it was also an activity closely attuned to the limited skills and talents possessed by the latter. Moreover, since the native tribesmen had, or were quickly acquiring, a strong sense of their own privileged position *vis-à-vis* the *Uitlanders*, it was a comparatively simple matter, with the money and the opportunities that were thrust upon them, to transform themselves overnight into a *rentier* class.

Having given their subjects a surfeit of bread, the rulers of the three wealthier shaikhdoms are also indulging them with circuses on a grand scale. Again, as might be expected, fantasy reigns unchecked. At Abu Dhabi a sporting complex is being built at a cost of $225 million, capable, so the local Barnums proclaim, of accommodating the Olympic games. Another sports palace being constructed at Dubai at a cost of $120 million includes a traditional feature of the Arabian scene – an ice-skating rink. At Sharjah the ruler has had two grass football fields laid, at a cost that does not bear contemplation. Hundreds of tons of soil were brought across the mountains from Kalba, on the Gulf of Oman, to make the pitches, and 20,000 gallons of water a day are required to keep the grass alive – all this in a part of the world where cultivable land is in desperately short supply and water is still a precious commodity. A similar profligacy in the use of water from the Abu Dhabi villages in the Buraimi oasis has reduced the water table there – which depends upon the run-off from the nearby Hajar mountains of Oman – to such a level that water has had to be pumped back to the oasis by pipeline from the desalination plant in Abu Dhabi.

Politically, the UAE presents a scene no less disorderly than the economic one. For the better part of two centuries the tribes of the coast and hinterland have either been at one another's throats or have co-existed in a state of uneasy peace. The consequences of their numerous feuds and conflicts are vividly illustrated by the boundaries of the seven shaikhdoms, which were defined for the first time by the British authorities in the Gulf in the 1950s for the purpose of oil exploration, and which on a map resemble the pieces of a singularly perverse jigsaw puzzle.

Throughout the greater part of the nineteenth century the politics of the coast was dominated by a contest for supremacy between the Qasimi shaikhdoms of Sharjah and Ras al-Khaimah and the Bani Yas tribal confederacy of Abu Dhabi. Though the Qawasim themselves were a comparatively small tribe, they united under their leadership nearly all the tribes inhabiting the coast from Rams in the north to Sharjah in the south and inland to the Hajar mountains.

The greatest of the Qasimi chieftains was Sultan ibn Saqr, who ruled both Sharjah and Ras al-Khaimah from the first decade of the century until his death in 1866. Throughout his long reign his enmity for his principal dynastic rivals, the Bani Yas rulers of Abu Dhabi and the Al Bu Said sultans of Muscat, never diminished; although in his later years it was restrained by the relationship he and the other Trucial Shaikhs had contracted with the British government. A wily and devious intriguer, unscrupulous in his ways and lacking the nobility of character of some of the other Trucial Shaikhs, Sultan ibn Saqr nevertheless remained true to his treaty engagements, and towards the end of his life he was one of the pillars of the trucial system. He died as he had lived, at the age of ninety-seven. 'I have to report the death of His Highness Sultan ben Suggur, Chief of Ras-el-Khyma,' wrote the political resident in the Gulf to the governor of Bombay in April 1866. 'The late Chief married a young Arab lady of 15 last spring, got paralysis of the loins shortly afterwards, and was meditating a cruise in search of a Doctor when death overtook him.' After Sultan ibn Saqr's death Sharjah and Ras al-Khaimah split into separate shaikhdoms, and they have remained so ever since. None of Shaikh Sultan's successors in either shaikhdom has ever wielded the same influence in the affairs of Trucial Oman as he once did, although two or three have had aspirations to restore the old Qasimi supremacy. Saqr ibn Sultan, the ruler of Sharjah from 1951 to 1965, discovered the gospel of Arab nationalism in the late 1950s and tried in the next few years to promote himself as the Nasser of the Trucial Coast. His increasingly anti-British activities led to his deposition and exile in 1965. As recounted earlier, he returned secretly in January 1972 to slay his successor, Khalid ibn Muhammad Al Qasimi, and to try to seize control of Sharjah. The *coup* failed and Saqr has languished in confinement at Abu Dhabi ever since. Something of the spirit of the long deceased Sultan ibn Saqr still lingers at Ras al-Khaimah, where the ruler, Saqr ibn Muhammad, who has ruled the shaikhdom since 1948, remembers the days of Qasimi greatness and would dearly like to humble the political and economic pretensions of Abu Dhabi.

Although the Bani Yas, like the Qawasim, were seafarers – by the middle of the nineteenth century there were more Abu Dhabi boats on the pearl banks for the annual fishery than from any other port on the coast – they were also, and perhaps more essentially, a pastoral people, who grazed their flocks and herds in the region stretching from the Buraimi oasis westwards to the base of the Qatar peninsula and southwards to the Liwa oasis. Their ruling shaikhs, who came from the Al Bu Falah section, were basically territorial lords, drawing their strength less from their maritime resources than from their tribal domains and the allegiance of the tribes inhabiting them. The rivalry between the Bani Yas and Qasimi confederations had its genesis, at least in modern times, in the increased participation of the Bani Yas in the pearl fishery from the closing years of the eighteenth century onwards. It was heightened, as we have seen, after the Wahhabi incursions from Najd by religious antagonism.

Abu Dhabi underwent much the same economic decline as did the other Trucial Shaikhdoms as a consequence of the dwindling of their maritime trade from the late nineteenth century onwards. It experienced somewhat less distress, however, than did Sharjah and Ras al-Khaimah because its territorial resources were greater. Up to the death in 1909 of Zayid ibn Khalifah, the longest lived of the Al Bu Falah rulers, Abu Dhabi was the most important of the Trucial Shaikhdoms. After Zayid's death its fortunes waned, largely as the result of fratricide within the ruling family and the outbreak of prolonged fighting among the tribes of the interior after 1920. No fewer than four of Zayid ibn Khalifah's sons succeeded him in the years between 1909 and 1928, and only the first of these, Tahnun, died a peaceful death. Hamdan ibn Zayid, his successor, was slain by his brother, Sultan, in 1922; Sultan was killed by his brother, Saqr, in 1926; and Saqr himself was murdered by one of Sultan's tribesmen in 1928. The successor chosen by the shaikhly house was Shakhbut ibn Sultan, an elder son of the late Sultan ibn Zayid. To stop the blood-letting within the family, Shaikh Sultan's widow, Salama, had Shakhbut and his three brothers (Khalid, Zayid and Hazza) vow never to raise their hands in violence against one another. The vow was kept. When Zayid deposed Shakhbut in August 1966 – primarily because of the unrest being generated among the tribesmen by Shakhbut's refusal to spend the oil revenues as quickly as he might – he did so without bloodshed. Shakhbut was first sent into exile at Beirut and then allowed to return four years later.

The deposition of Shakhbut touched a sensitive nerve in the ruling family at large, for it revived memories of the Saudis' attempts in 1955, during their occupation of the Buraimi oasis, to induce Zayid to turn against his brother and throw in his lot with Saudi Arabia. Nor was this the only attempt made by the Saudis at the time to dispose of Shakhbut. Two of the sons of the late Saqr ibn Zayid who had been implicated in the murder of Shakhbut's father, Sultan ibn Zayid, and who had for some years been living in exile at Dubai, were invited to Saudi Arabia in the latter months of 1954 and there given a large sum of money for the purpose of bringing about Shakhbut's overthrow. When the two tried to recruit some tribesmen to carry out the *coup* the plot was discovered and frustrated. So deep was the shame felt by the Al Bu Falah shaikhs that two of their number should have conspired with their hereditary enemies against them that they thereafter adopted the family name of 'Al Nihayan', and dropped that of 'Al Bu Falah', as the official designation of the dynasty.

Aside from the division within the UAE caused by the persistence of the historic Qasimi–Bani Yas rivalry, there is a further enduring source of political friction in the deep-seated animosity that exists between the Al Bu Falah (or Al Nihayan) of Abu Dhabi and the ruling family of Dubai, the Al Maktum. The animosity has its roots in an internal squabble among the Bani Yas nearly a century and a half ago, when one of the principal sections, the Al Bu Falasah, renounced its allegiance to the Al Bu Falah and in 1833 migrated to Dubai, then part of the Qasimi domains. Within a few years the Al Bu Falasah had succeeded both in becoming masters of Dubai and in freeing themselves from the overlordship of the Qawasim, though they continued to side with the latter in their contests with Abu Dhabi. For the rest of the century Dubai had an uneventful history. It remained more or less free from Wahhabi influence, and the Al Maktum family, despite their continuing animosity towards the Al Nihayan, cultivated good relations with the Al Nihayan's allies, the Al Bu Said sultans of Muscat, mainly for commercial reasons. It was commerce which most occupied the Al Maktum, and their energy and application made Dubai the foremost port and market of the Trucial Coast, so that it weathered the economic stresses of the late nineteenth and early twentieth centuries better than any of the other shaikhdoms. The Al Maktum played no significant part in the politics of Trucial Oman in this century, possessing little if any influence among the tribes of the interior, although Dubai often afforded a refuge to tribes from neighbouring territories disaffected with their rulers or disposses-sed of their lands. Dubai itself experienced some upheavals in the 1930s, brought on by disputes within the Al Maktum which degenerated into bloodshed on occasions. These were largely resolved on the eve of the Second World War when the present ruler, Rashid ibn Said, took over the effective government of the shaikhdom as regent for his father, Said ibn Maktum. When Shaikh Said (who had ruled since 1912) died in 1958, Rashid succeeded him.

Throughout these years the Al Maktum's feud with the Al Nihayan of Abu Dhabi continued undiminished, although the two combined in the 1920s to resist attempts by the Saudis to return to Trucial Oman. The enmity between the two families reached its height in 1945, when it erupted into open warfare which continued at spasmodic intervals until 1948. Thereafter the Al Maktum continued to snipe at the Al Nihayan whenever they could, affording refuge and comfort to the latter's renegade subjects and ostentatiously aligning them-selves with opponents of the Al Nihayan, such as the Al Thani of Qatar. Not until negotiations had begun for the formation of the UAE did the Al Maktum see fit to moderate their spite, and even then Rashid ibn Said Al Maktum was the most vehement of the rulers in his insistence that the incipient federation should lend no support to Abu Dhabi in its frontier dispute with Saudi Arabia.

Such, in brief, were the historical legacies which the principal members of the UAE brought to its inauguration, and which still dog its existence today. The federation possesses no innate cohesion, just as it possesses no sound basic economy. The provisional constitution of the UAE is (despite its length and its elaborate provisions) essentially a treaty of alliance among the rulers of the seven shaikhdoms, designed to regulate formal relations among them and to preserve their position as the ultimate sources of authority within their shaikh-doms. It is also constructed to underline the primacy within the federation of

Abu Dhabi and Dubai. The president of the UAE, who is elected for a term of five years, is Shaikh Zayid ibn Sultan of Abu Dhabi; the vice-president, who is elected for the same period of time, is Shaikh Rashid ibn Said of Dubai. Both were re-elected at the end of their first term of office late in 1976. It was never the intention of the framers of the constitution that it should introduce any basic change in the nature of government in the constituent shaikhdoms of the federation, or that it should provide for significant popular participation in the federal government. The only body established by the constitution which possesses real power is the federal supreme council, which is composed of the rulers of the seven shaikhdoms. Its decisions are reached by majority vote, with the rulers of Abu Dhabi and Dubai both possessing the power of veto.

Responsibility for the implementation of the supreme council's decisions lies with the federal council or cabinet. The members of the cabinet – prime minister, deputy prime minister and some two dozen other ministers – are all appointed by the president. As is to be expected, the composition of the cabinet reflects the predominance of Abu Dhabi and Dubai in the federation: the prime minister, deputy prime minister and the ministers of finance, defence, foreign affairs and the interior are all members or close adherents of the ruling Al Nihayan and Al Maktum families. A federal national council was established by the constitution to serve the supreme council as a consultative assembly. It consists of forty delegates (eight each from Abu Dhabi and Dubai, six each from Sharjah and Ras al-Khaimah and four from each of the other three shaikhdoms), appointed by the rulers of the respective shaikhdoms for a term of two years. From the ambiguous way in which the relevant clauses in the constitution are phrased, it would seem that the national council has no power to initiate legislation. Its function would simply appear to be to discuss and approve draft legislation, including the federal budget, presented to it by the council of ministers. Though claims are made for the liveliness of discussions within the national council and the independence of spirit shown by some of its members, it seems on the whole to be nothing more than a tame assembly of placemen and drones.

If the federal government structure so far erected serves any useful purpose, it is as yet another means of distributing cash and sinecures to the native Arab inhabitants of the UAE. There are, as remarked already, some 28,000 federal civil servants. What they do is beyond the power of anyone to identify with any certainty. The federal budget is provided wholly by Abu Dhabi, although in 1977 Sharjah, Ajman and Fujairah promised to pay 2 per cent of it. Dubai, Ras al-Khaimah and Umm al-Qaiwain refuse to contribute a single *dirham*. Shaikh Zayid of Abu Dhabi has from the start been the most dedicated champion of the federation, a dedication which has been interpreted by the other rulers (and by Shaikh Rashid of Dubai and Shaikh Saqr of Ras al-Khaimah in particular) as evidence of his intention to use the federation as an instrument to secure his ascendancy over them. Rashid and Saqr have striven, therefore, as much for reasons of practical politics as from a historical compulsion to offset Zayid's influence in the federal supreme council, though Saqr's opposition has been tempered by his need for the financial benefits that membership of the federation affords him. Zayid's only real ally in the supreme council has been Shaikh Sultan of Sharjah. He, like his brother, the late Shaikh Khalid, before him, has profited from Zayid's bounty, and in turn he has frequently been used by Zayid as a stalking-horse for pushing through new measures to strengthen the federation.

If the federation survives, it will be despite the indifference and contumacy of the rulers of Ras al-Khaimah and Dubai. Shaikh Saqr would dearly like to cut loose from the federation and to recapture for Ras al-Khaimah its past glory as the leading power on the coast. But his resources, economic or otherwise, forbid this course of action, leaving him little option but to continue to look to Zayid as his financial patron. Shaikh Rashid is contemptuous of Abu Dhabi's pretensions as the leader of the federation, and exasperated by the incompetence and financial waste displayed by the federal administration. Yet while he cynically evades his financial and other responsibilities to the federation, preferring to devote himself to the single-minded pursuit of his own interests, he continues to milk the federation for the advantages it affords him. What is true of Rashid is also true of the other rulers: it is only selfish interest and the need for mutual security that unites them, and in the last resort holds the federation together.

Under the constitution of the UAE responsibility for the defence of the federation is vested in a higher defence council, headed by the president and consisting of the vice-president, the prime minister, the ministers of defence and the interior, and the commander of the Union Defence Force. The UDF has evolved from the former Trucial Oman Scouts, an infantry battalion organized in mobile squadrons which was first raised by the British in the early 1950s for internal security duties. Although the UDF has now grown to brigade strength, with roughly 5,000 men supported by artillery and armoured vehicles, its development has been partly stultified by the parallel development of the much larger and better equipped Abu Dhabi Defence Force. The ADDF has a strength of 18,000 men – mobile infantry units, artillery, armoured vehicles, helicopters, fighter and transport jet aircraft and naval patrol boats. Dubai and Ras al-Khaimah have much smaller armed forces, the former's numbering perhaps 2,500, the latter's about 500. Up to the time of its transfer to the UAE the Trucial Oman Scouts had British regular officers seconded from the British army, as well as several dozen British n.c.o.s, and provision was made in the treaty of friendship concluded between Britain and the UAE in December 1971 for the continued secondment of officers and n.c.o.s. In the years since then, however, the proportion of British officers and n.c.o.s in the Union Defence Force has steadily dwindled, and their place has been taken by Pakistani, Jordanian and local Arab officers. Much the same has happened in the Abu Dhabi Defence Force, which formerly was officered almost exclusively by British officers, most of them on contract. The penultimate stage in the severance of the British connexion was reached in 1975, when the task of preparing the ground for the eventual amalgamation of the UDF with the ADDF and other local forces was entrusted to Egyptian army officers.

Amalgamation, however, has proved easier to decree than to achieve – and even the decision to amalgamate provoked a good deal of acrimonious discussion in the federal supreme council. Again the cause of the acrimony lay in the military and financial preponderance exerted by Abu Dhabi. Agreement on the proposed amalgamation was at last reached, at least on paper, in November 1976. Effective control of the unified armed forces was to be shared by Shaikh Rashid's son, Muhammad, the federal minister of defence, and Shaikh Zayid's eldest son and putative heir, Khalifah, the designated deputy commander of the federal forces. Fifteen months later, in the first week of February 1978, Zayid issued a presidential decree while on a visit to Pakistan, ordering the implementation of the merger and the transference of control over the armed forces from their respective governments to the federal defence headquarters in Abu Dhabi. At the same time he promoted his twenty-five-year-old son, Sultan, from colonel to brigadier and appointed him commander of all the federal armed forces. Such was the uproar that greeted his action in Dubai (where Rashid was furious that he, as acting president in Zayid's absence, had not even been consulted beforehand) that Zayid had to hasten back to restore a semblance of tranquillity. It is a fairly safe prediction that a fully integrated command of the federal and local armed forces will never be achieved while shaikhly pride and local sensibilities remain as prickly as they are.

How reliable the several defence forces may be, in terms of both their military capacity and their loyalty, is another question. The potential dangers that the UAE faces are internal as much as external, whether they be subversion within an individual shaikhdom or dissensions among the shaikhdoms themselves. Fighting broke out between Sharjah and Fujairah in the vicinity of Khaur Fakkan and Dibba in the summer of 1972, and was successfully suppressed by the UDF and ADDF acting in co-operation. A year later both forces were found to have a number of supporters of the Popular Front for the Liberation of Oman in their ranks. Most of the soldiers who enlist in the two forces, and in the Dubai Defence Force, are Omanis, Dhufaris or other tribesmen from outside the UAE. The majority of the officers now, as we have seen, are Pakistanis, Jordanians or other Arabs, some of local origin. That they, and more particularly the last, may cherish political ambitions, either of their own or on behalf of others, is far from unlikely in view of what has happened in most Arab countries over the past twenty-five years. Whether they will have an opportunity to pursue these ambitions, alone or in company, depends upon a number of circumstances which do not lend themselves to ready evaluation.

The greatest danger of internal subversion probably exists in Dubai and Abu Dhabi, where the social and economic upheavals of the past decade have seriously disturbed the traditional political order, more noticeably in the latter shaikhdom than in the former. Although the shaikhly system of government still obtains, and the rulers are, in theory at least, the ultimate source of authority, the very complexities caused by the transformation of the two shaikhdoms into replicas of modern states are eroding the foundations of their rule. The chief agents of this process of erosion, more wittingly than unwittingly, are the 'northern' Arabs who staff the growing bureaucracies, the schools, the medical services and other establishments. They, like their counterparts in Kuwait and Qatar, know little about the country or the people they currently serve, and are in the main uninterested in the welfare of either. Their attention is fixed instead upon the countries from which they themselves come, upon the domestic politics of those countries, and upon the labyrinthine twists and turns of the perennial Palestinian question.

The commercial acumen of Shaikh Rashid of Dubai has stood him in good stead in dealing with these interlopers. He has kept their entrepreneurial activities within bounds, and maintained an effective control over those of them who have entered his service as clerks or teachers, or in a professional or technical capacity. There is not a great deal of delegation in Rashid's government, nor does anything of consequence happen in Dubai without its coming to his notice. He is also fortunate in having few dissensions within his own family, and, at the age of sixty-seven or so, no serious problems of succession. His three sons are all men of ability, and of forceful, if not entirely attractive, disposition. Maktum, the eldest and the heir apparent, is nearly forty years of age and has been prime minister of the UAE since its inception. Hamdan, some three years younger, is the deputy federal prime minister, while the third son, Muhammad, in his early thirties, is the federal minister of defence. If none, perhaps, is the measure of his father, any one of them would make a capable ruler of Dubai.

Things are rather different in Abu Dhabi. Whereas Rashid is the quintessential merchant, the haggler over prices, neither renowned for his liberality nor greatly interested in politics – at least not beyond his immediate purview or where his purse is not affected – Zayid's interests and ambitions run in a different direction. He is at heart a Bedouin chieftain, scornful of the ways of merchants, of men with soft hands and a ready abacus. To his mind a ruler is measured by his skills in the arts of politics and war and by his hospitality and generosity to his subjects and suppliants. Zayid's attention and energies are largely engaged by the politics of the UAE and of the Gulf at large, and by the building up of his armed forces. He also aspires to a more prominent role on the

Middle-Eastern political stage and even in the larger theatre of international affairs.

It is precisely these qualities and aspirations that have made Zayid highly vulnerable to the carpet-baggers and mountebanks who now infest Abu Dhabi and the other oil shaikhdoms. Of the hundreds or even thousands of *émigré* Egyptians, Palestinians, Syrians and Iraqis who reside in Abu Dhabi only a minority are men of ability and integrity whose presence confers a positive benefit upon the shaikhdom. The rest are mostly self-seekers who conspire and compete among themselves for position, money, preferment or advantage, constantly warring over the spoils which have so easily come their way, and ceaselessly intriguing to supplant their rivals with nominees or placemen of their own – Egyptians wrangling with Iraqis, Iraqis with Syrians, Syrians with Palestinians, Palestinians with Egyptians. They are particularly numerous in the local and federal bureaucracies, where they have to all intents and purposes taken over the running of the shaikhdom's and the federation's affairs. Towards the ministers who are their nominal masters they exhibit both servility and disdain, their manner outwardly fawning but inwardly mocking. Zayid's court is packed with a host of impostors, intriguers, sycophants and *flâneurs* (most of them northern Arabs), who ceaselessly jostle with one another for his attention and favour. Flattering, wheedling, shamelessly soliciting for personal ends, they swarm about the person of the ruler like so many flies, constantly striving to gain his ear and deny it to others not of their number, shutting him off more and more from his own people, and even from reality itself.

It is the wealth of Abu Dhabi that lures and binds these creatures, whether as a means of lining their own pockets or in order to divert it into political and financial enterprises abroad. The shaikhdom itself interests them not at all. They display a remarkable ignorance of its past, its traditions, its very geography – indeed, not merely of Abu Dhabi but of the Arabian peninsula as a whole. Towards the native inhabitants of Abu Dhabi they act with arrogance and condescension – which makes a mockery of their effusive professions of loyalty to the shaikhdom and their endless cant about Arab brotherhood. To these sophisticates the spectacle of so much wealth, and consequently so much power, in the hands of backward Bedouin is an affront, especially as they feel that they themselves could put it to better use elsewhere. Some of them harbour darker thoughts: they find the very existence of hereditary and shaikhly rule an anachronism and would like to sweep it away, replacing it with a form of government more akin to those to be found in Cairo, Damascus, Baghdad or even Aden.

Just how secure the shaikhly family's position is in Abu Dhabi is unclear, particularly because of divisions within it and uncertainty over the succession. Of Zayid's three brothers only Shakhbut, now aged over seventy, is still alive. Hazza, the youngest of the four, died in the late 1950s; Khalid, the second eldest (some say the eldest), a decade later. Shakhbut had two sons, Said and Sultan, both of whom died in their twenties. Zayid himself is about sixty years of age. His eldest son, Khalifah, who was born in 1949, is the putative heir apparent, although Zayid himself seems to hold his second son, Sultan, born in 1953, in higher esteem. His other sons have not yet reached adult age. A certain degree of jealousy exists between the Bani Sultan (Zayid's and Shakhbut's) branch of the Al Nihayan and the Bani Khalifah branch, the descendants of Khalifah, reputedly the eldest son of Zayid ibn Khalifah. Khalifah's son, Muhammad, a cousin of Zayid and Shakhbut ibn Sultan, sired half a dozen or more sons, who today occupy prominent positions in either the Abu Dhabi administration or the government of the UAE. Two of them, at least, are said to have their hearts set upon achieving greater prominence. Succession in the Al Nihayan line has never been determined by primogeniture; it has been the strongest candidate, or the candidate with the strongest tribal support, who has succeeded, and more often than not the issue has been decided by the sword. Against the background of fratricide and parricide which colours the history of the Al Nihayan, the chances of another bloody upheaval in the family at some future date appear far from remote.

The chief potential threat to the continued rule of the Al Nihayan would seem to be that of a *coup d'état* by the northern Arab *émigrés*. The obvious counter to such a threat, at least at first glance, is the Abu Dhabi Defence Force, which is fully capable of crushing any bid for power by the *émigré* Arabs, if they were acting alone. It is fairly certain, however, that the *émigré* Arabs, effendis to a man, would not act without armed support, and this they do not have, despite the existence within Abu Dhabi, as in the other shaikhdoms, of underground cells of the PFLO and its sister organization, the Popular Revolutionary Movement, another Marxist offshoot of the ANM. The possibility of the armed overthrow of the ruling house, therefore, would seem to depend upon the ADDF itself, or a sizable portion of it, becoming disaffected and attempting a *coup*, either alone or in combination with the subversive elements among the northern Arabs.

Should an *émigré* or army *coup* be attempted in Abu Dhabi it is highly doubtful whether the local tribesmen, assuming their fealty to the ruler to be unchanged, would be as capable as they once were of effectively resisting it. It is also doubtful, given the strains within the federation, whether the other federal rulers would employ the Union Defence Force (assuming that its own ranks had not by then been infected with politics) to try to restore the Al Nihayan to power. Yet if they did not resist the overthrow of one shaikhly house by an *émigré* or military *coup*, the survival of their own houses would be endangered. Amid all these uncertainties one thing is clear, and this is that any revolutionary change in the UAE will be accompanied by considerable bloodshed. The history of the former Trucial Coast is one of raiding and skirmishing, piracy and pillage; the razzia and the blood feud are a way of life among the tribes, and their first instinct in any quarrel is to put it to the arbitrament of the sword. Wealth, and the jealousies it provokes, is more likely to sharpen than to soften that instinct.

The external dangers that the UAE faces are chiefly those of subversion by Iraq, acting alone or with Russian encouragement, and of subjection by Saudi Arabia or Persia. Since Britain's departure at the close of 1971 the UAE has been without any guarantee of protection from a power strong enough to make such a guarantee effective. There seems to be little will among the federal rulers to face the problem of the federation's external security. Instead they appear largely to have ignored it, believing that they will be able, each in his own way, to surmount any crisis that may arise. Only Zayid seems to be oppressed by a consciousness of the latent dangers which exist, just as he is the most anxious of the federal rulers to keep the federation in being. Yet he has no prescription to offer for the UAE's foreign and defence policy beyond the adoption of what he calls 'Arab solutions' for the federation's problems – in other words, appeasement, after the precedent set by Kuwait.

He himself has applied this technique to the resolution of his frontier difficulties with Saudi Arabia. The question of the Saudi Arabia–Abu Dhabi frontier, it may be recalled, was still unsettled at the time of the British withdrawal from the Gulf, when King Faisal made it clear that while his territorial demands upon Abu Dhabi remained unsatisfied he would not recognize the existence or legitimacy of the UAE. Occasional exchanges over the issue took place between Saudi Arabia and Abu Dhabi between 1972 and 1974, and then in August of the latter year a compromise was apparently reached between them. What exactly was contained in the agreement signed on 21 August 1974 is not certain, for the details of the agreement were never made public by either side. It would seem, however, that Zayid gave the Saudis nearly everything they wanted – a corridor to the sea, west of the Sabkhat Matti, separating Qatar from Abu Dhabi and affording Saudi Arabia an outlet to the lower Gulf; a goodly slice of the western part of his shaikhdom; and, in the south, the bulk of the Zarrara oilfield. By capitulating to the Saudis in this way, Zayid in effect set aside the concessionary rights he had awarded earlier to foreign oil companies in the surrendered territories, including the Abu Dhabi Petroleum Company's rights to the Zarrara field, of which only a token portion was left in the company's concessionary area. In return, Zayid secured Faisal's recognition of the UAE and the withdrawal of the Saudi claim to the Buraimi oasis and the corridor of territory leading to it, a claim that was, in fact, as baseless as Faisal's claim to the western and southern areas of Abu Dhabi which Zayid had seen fit to concede.

If Zayid had forgotten what he and previous rulers of Abu Dhabi had learned from grim experience of Saudi ways – or perhaps had deluded himself into believing that these had changed – he was to be given a sharp reminder less than two years later. In the late summer of 1976 the construction company which

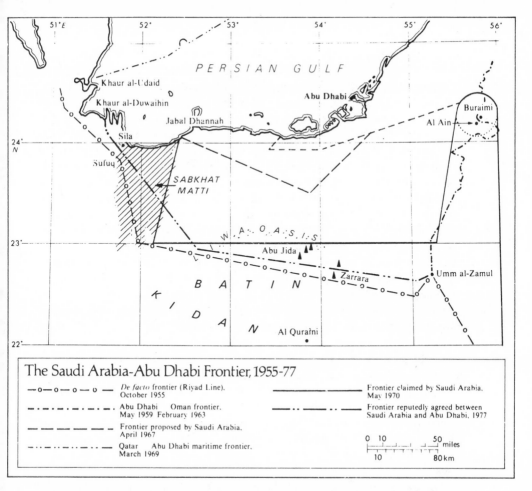

The Saudi Arabia-Abu Dhabi Frontier, 1955-77

was building a new highway to link Abu Dhabi with Qatar reached the vicinity
of Sila, on the coast just west of the Sabkhat Matti. Here its operations were
halted by a Saudi police detachment which claimed that the company was
working in Saudi territory. The upshot was that fresh discussions on the
frontier were begun in the winter of 1976–7, this time with the participation of
the Omanis who had complained about their exclusion from the earlier negotiations. A new agreement was apparently reached in the early summer of 1977,
although again its details were not disclosed. However, an oil-concessions map
put out by the UAE ministry of petroleum in June 1977, without any accompanying statement or explanation, depicted the Abu Dhabi–Saudi Arabia
frontier as starting on the coast some twenty miles west of the Sabkhat Matti
and following a course very similar to that of the original Saudi claim (the Red
Line) of 1935 (see map above and pp. 62–3). A month after the issuing of the
map the Saudi ambassador in Abu Dhabi was reported to have handed over a
cheque for the sum of $32.8 million – for what purpose is unknown, unless it

was to meet the cost of the construction of that section of the coastal highway which was to run through the Saudi corridor west of the Sabkhat Matti.

While Zayid, whether in his capacity as president of the UAE or in his role as ruler of Abu Dhabi, seems to have placed his trust in a policy of conciliation to secure the survival of the federation, Rashid at Dubai does not seem to care whether it lives or dies. Saqr ibn Muhammad of Ras al-Khaimah feels much the same way. Rashid, as already observed, does not trouble to conceal his exasperation with what he regards as the incompetence of the federal government at Abu Dhabi and the uselessness as well as the meddling propensities of the federal bureaucracy. He believes that Dubai could without much difficulty survive the collapse of the federation and make its own way as an independent shaikhdom. He has not bothered to cultivate close relations with any of the larger Arab states, nor does he waste his time in proclaiming his sympathy with the more popular pan-Arab causes. He sees little cause for alarm in any intentions Saudi Arabia may harbour towards the UAE, and until the fall of the shah he believed that, in the event of the federation's disintegration, he could confidently look to Tehran for help in preserving the independence and prosperity of Dubai. He may not feel so sanguine today.

Dubai, like Bahrain, is a modern replica of the city states that flourished along the shores of the Gulf in the middle ages – Siraf and Qais, Rishahr and Hormuz, Bahrain itself. They grew and prospered in the absence of any adjacent power strong enough to subdue them, while at the same time they depended upon the relative stability of the lands surrounding them to maintain their prosperity. Things are very different in the Gulf today. Just as Siraf and Qais, Rishahr and Hormuz were swept away by the tide of great events – the Qarmatian revolt, the fall of the Abbasid caliphate, the Mongol invasions, the rise of the Safavids and the appearance of the Portuguese – so, too, may Dubai and Bahrain be overtaken by calamities outside their power to avert. It is hard to escape the feeling that they, along with all the other little rich oil shaikhdoms along the Arabian shore, repose in the still eye of a steadily gathering storm.

Anyone who looks at all closely at the internal condition of the Arabian states of the Gulf today cannot fail to be struck by the uneasiness which lies beneath the atmosphere of carnival. Too much has happened too quickly – material affluence, the influx of foreigners, the impact of the outside world – for anything to have been digested thoroughly. It has been a most peculiar, even singular, transformation, in the sense that it has within the space of a single generation – and in some instances half that time – bridged the entire gap between a primitive, subsistence economy and the millenarian condition, where wealth is created without effort on the part of those who are its principal beneficiaries. The frenzy of activity which now grips the Gulf is not that associated in normal human experience with the stages of agricultural, industrial or technological revolution, leading to the creation of an increasingly complex economy which itself generates wealth by the production of goods. The frenzy is the frenzy of consumption, not of creation, the indiscriminate acquisition of the products of more advanced economies in the form of goods, skills and ideas, few of which are being put to use to lay the foundations of genuine economic progress.

To exorcize the demons of doubt and confusion that their hectic expenditure of oil revenues has brought in its train, the governments of these states have resorted to the hocus-pocus of statistics. They have, to give credibility to their claims to rule over polities worthy of international recognition as independent states, put out inflated figures for the size of their populations; and then, alarmed by the proportion of resident foreigners that these reveal, they have subsequently doctored the figures to show a higher percentage of native-born inhabitants than actually exists. To fend off the envious or the censorious among their fellow Arab governments (and those of the Afro-Asian world at large), they have made a great brouhaha about the sums they have donated as charity to needy lands or worthy causes; only to hurriedly amend their exaggerated estimates as they found the ragtag and bobtail of Asia and Africa beating a path to their doors, begging bowls outstretched. Ostentation and secretiveness, which reside uneasily together in the breast of the peninsular Arab, have combined to invest the statistical information issuing from the Gulf governments with a strong element of mendacity. Few if any of the figures quoted in this present chapter for populations, incomes or expenditures in the Gulf states can be regarded as reliable, since they are taken in the main from the pronouncements of the governments of these states or their fuglemen in the Western press. Finding refuge or solace in statistics, falsified or otherwise, is not, however, a weakness to which the Gulf Arabs alone are prone. As the well-known French Orientalist, Jacques Berque, has pointed out, it has been a common response among Arab governments throughout the Middle East to the unsettling effects produced by Western influences. 'Statistics', according to Berque, 'are the orison of the contemporary world ... [The] passion for enumeration ... gives the Arabs an intoxicating sense of modernity.' Hence the industrious compilation of all manner of figures (whether accurate or not) on population, trade, expenditure, transport, education and so forth. 'The Arab countries expect these figures [writes Berque] to supply direction and compensation, as well as expression, for the outburst of feeling, the expansive surge of heart and speech that is now agitating them.' Statistics, in other words, afford the Arabs both emotional and intellectual satisfaction. Or, as Berque puts it, 'We can trace a tendency to the old casuistic cult of abstractions in this passion for numbers, in so far as it is justified neither by the requirements of its subject matter nor the reliability of its information.'*

The constant invocation of statistics, however, has not served to lessen the fears, discontents and uncertainties which oppress one section or another of the populations of the Gulf states. Rulers and their families and close retainers fear

* *The Arabs: Their History and Future*, London, 1965, pp. 77–9.

political upheaval, the possibility of *coups* and revolts, and the machinations of their foes without. The *Uitlanders*, lacking all rights, fear the loss of their livelihoods through sudden, arbitrary deportation. The native inhabitants fear that the *Uitlanders* will overwhelm them with numbers. Discontent is perhaps more widespread than fear. Some rulers envy their richer neighbours, others their more powerful subjects. *Emigré* Arabs resent the privileges of the native tribesmen; the tribesmen resent the *hauteur* of the *émigrés*. Non-Arab *Uitlanders* chafe at their inferior status, and the poorer amongst them covet the greater rewards enjoyed by the unskilled native Arabs. They in their turn despise these *Uitlanders* for not being Arab, even while they profit from their labour and skills. There are, of course, as observed earlier, gradations of feeling among the several immigrant groups, and between them and the indigenous inhabitants, gradations which do not necessarily correspond to differences in financial reward or status. Persian, Pathan and Baluchi labourers, who work the hardest and are paid the least, are not unduly troubled by the degree of wealth possessed by the ruling families and their circles, or by the discrimination practised against them because they are not Arabs. Neither experience is novel to them or to the ways of Oriental society in general. Omani and Yemeni labourers fare a little better because they are Arabs, but the improvement is hardly noteworthy. The Indians and skilled Pakistanis, who tend to live in close-knit communities, secure in their self-regard, are content with their roles as merchants, clerks and craftsmen, making substantial profits and a comfortable living from the profligacy of others.

It is the *émigré* Arab community in each state which most exhibits discontent with its lot. Whatever the differences that divide them, Palestinian from Egyptian, Egyptian from Iraqi, Iraqi from Syrian, the northern Arabs are united in their belief in the superiority of their attainments, intellectual, social and political, over those of the Gulf Arabs. Being of such a mind, it galls them that they possess no civil or political rights, no legal standing, no customary recourse in these states, but are victims of the same exclusivism which dictates the lop-sided distribution of the oil revenues. The rulers of the Gulf states have made it extremely difficult for immigrants, whether Arab or non-Arab, to obtain local nationality, although the government of the UAE, alarmed at the declining proportion of native Arab inhabitants to *Uitlanders* in the population, has of late been granting citizenship to Omanis and other peninsular Arabs after three to five years' residence. Citizenship, however, is still strictly denied to Arabs from outside the peninsula.

As if the fears and troubles already mentioned were not enough to preoccupy the governments and peoples of the Gulf states, they have exposed themselves to further vexation by allowing themselves to be dragged into the Palestinian imbroglio. Until the June war of 1967 the Arab–Israeli dispute had impinged very little, if at all, upon the lives of the Gulf's inhabitants. That the dispute existed they could hardly but have been aware, whether from the vociferations of the *émigré* Palestinians in their midst or from the propaganda ceaselessly broadcast from Cairo and Baghdad and elsewhere. The dispute itself, however, had not touched them directly, and their attitude to it consequently was apathetic. Ritual condemnations of Israeli perfidy and professions of solidarity with Israel's Arab neighbours were uttered from time to time by some of the Gulf's rulers or their more excitable retainers, but there was no substance behind these pronouncements, except perhaps in Kuwait where the local *jeunesse dorée* took up the cause of Palestinian irredentism as politically *chic*, and the presence of thousands of Palestinians made it advisable for the government to show a comparable degree of enthusiasm. Even here, however, there was little fire beneath the smoke, and the further one travelled down the Gulf, through Qatar to the Trucial Coast, the harder it became to detect a spark of interest in the subject – except, of course, in Bahrain where the youthful firebrands from the schools and clubs might occasionally squeak and gibber in the streets in imitation of their fellows in Cairo or Damascus – until in the fastnesses of the Oman mountains one would be hard put to it to find a tribesman who had ever heard of Israel, let alone know in which direction it lay.

In Saudi Arabia, on the other hand, which in its north-western corner faced Israel across the Gulf of Eilat, there was a greater sense of involvement, though only in governmental circles. The populace, for the most part, was either unaware of or uninterested in Israel's existence. Saudi Arabia had been drawn into the Palestine question in the late 1930s, when the British government of the day decided to widen the scope of the quarrel between the Arab and Jewish communities in Palestine to include the independent Arab states. Ever since that time the Saudi government could not afford to appear less than wholly *engagé* in the Palestine issue, especially as any sign of wavering would have exposed it to vilification, and even sedition, from the revolutionary regimes in Cairo, Damascus and Baghdad.

The humiliation inflicted upon Arab arms in June 1967 brought the conflict with Israel into the politics of the Gulf for the first time, souring the political atmosphere and tinging it with hysteria. In part, the change was wrought by the Palestinian *émigrés*, whose activities, after the foundation of the Palestine Liberation Organization in 1964, had become more conspicuous and better orchestrated. After June 1967 they not only became more vociferous but, what is more to the point, they were paid more heed to by the Gulf rulers and their subjects. The consequences for the Gulf states of their involvement in the Arab–Israeli dispute have been, without exception, unfortunate. The language of politics in the Gulf, never at the best of times particularly elevated, has been immeasurably coarsened by the injection into it of the invective which customarily surrounds discussion of the Palestine question in the larger Arab states. Local standards of political conduct, again never very high, have been further degraded by the example set the Gulf tribesmen by the intrigues and peculations of their northern Arab mentors. The northern Arabs, however, were not the sole agents of change, or even the most effective. Every Gulf ruler, either because he felt so inclined or because he believed it to be expedient, gave voice to bellicose sentiments of one kind or another, or made conspicuous donations to the war chests of the Arab states in direct conflict with Israel. The only one who remained silent was the sultan of Muscat, Saiyid Said ibn Taimur, who, closeted in his palace in far-away Salalah, ignored the entire furore.

As far removed from him in attitude as he was in distance was the late King Faisal ibn Abdul Aziz of Saudi Arabia. Austere in his personal life, stern in his administration of his people, and intensely aware of his position as imam of the Wahhabiya, Faisal abhorred Israel and all that it represented, religiously and politically. To him the conflict with the Jewish state was a *jihad*, a holy war. *Delenda est Judaea*, and the land which the Israeli state had usurped must be restored to the *dar al-Islam* (Muslim territory). Incapable of intervening militarily in the fighting in June 1967, Faisal had expressed his anger by cutting off oil shipments to the United States and Britain. He afterwards subsidized Egypt's economy and helped to re-equip its armies. Because of the preponderance of Saudi Arabia in the politics of the peninsula the Gulf rulers were forced to take their colour on the Palestinian issue from Faisal. Hence the air in the Gulf became clamorous with denunciations of *perfide* Israel and demands for Palestine *irredenta*. Propaganda poured forth from government-controlled radio stations up and down the Gulf, branches of the Arab Boycott Office were opened in the various shaikhdoms, organized demonstrations of the type depressingly familiar in the Levant cities were mounted at frequent intervals, and the bravoes of the Palestine Liberation Organization were fêted as heroes and given large subventions – as much, it should be added, to dissuade them from threatening the established order in the Gulf as to support them in their operations against Israel. Yet for all the late Saudi ruler's implacable hatred of Israel, and for all the agitation created in the Gulf by the *émigré* Arabs and their local disciples, the Arab–Israeli conflict remained an artificial one so far as the people of the Gulf were concerned. Their real interests were unaffected by it and would remain unaffected until the day that they were placed in hazard by the utilization of the Gulf's oil as a political weapon in the conflict.

Because the dispute was extraneous to their lives the arousal of popular sentiment against Israel among the Gulf's inhabitants depended, and still depends, almost exclusively upon the stimulation of Muslim or Pan-Arab feeling. Islamic beliefs and practices, needless to say, have long regulated society in the Gulf states, but far greater prominence is now given in public life to the observance of Muslim occasions and the expression of Muslim sentiment than in years gone by. One sign of the increased emphasis upon religiosity is the presence of a growing number of Muslim Brethren (*al-ikhwan al-muslimin*), most of them Egyptians who fled to Saudi Arabia some years ago after the *ikhwan* had been proscribed in Egypt during Nasser's presidency. From Saudi Arabia a number of them later drifted, with Saudi blessing, to the Gulf shaikhdoms, where they were accorded an uneasy welcome by most of the rulers. Recently their influence and activities have increased considerably, under the pressure of the Arab–Israeli conflict and the example of Muslim obduracy set by the late Faisal ibn Abdul Aziz. They have also been helped by the fact that the doctrines they preach are calculated to appeal to the fears and prejudices of the recipients, especially in the general atmosphere of suspicion which hangs over the Gulf.

To the local governments this arousal of Muslim feeling is a mixed blessing: on the one hand it compels them to tolerate a certain degree of interference in the administration of their shaikhdoms by Muslim vigilantes; on the other hand, it is useful to them in countering the propaganda of Marxist groups like the PFLO by branding them irreligionists and even atheists. The charge has been applied with particular force to the National Front in South Yemen, which is regarded as being virtually beyond the pale of Islam. Yet for all the anathematizing of Arab revolutionary movements by Muslim conservatives, it is extremely doubtful whether these movements are *au fond* anti-Islamic or irreligious. Marxist dogma sits very lightly and uncomfortably upon the few semi-educated peninsular Arabs who have ostensibly adopted it. Their thoughts and their lives are still shaped by Islam, they themselves are still fundamentally Muslim. Nor could it be otherwise, since, as we have had occasion to observe already, Islam is the only real source of moral and intellectual guidance available to the Arabs of the peninsula. The present evidence of Islamic revivalism, therefore, may be a more significant indication of the drift of events in the Gulf than sporadic troublemaking by self-styled Marxist revolutionaries.

Most of the Gulf's inhabitants obtain their view of the world around them from radio, television and the cinema. What they hear and see through these media is almost exclusively Arab and Muslim in content as well as context, and what is not Arab or Muslim in origin is transformed and presented to them in Arab or Muslim terms. Thus it appears to them – and increasingly so since the oil embargo of 1973 – that the political map of the world is constructed upon an Arab projection, that the Arab lands are at the very centre of the globe, and that the affairs of the Arabs are of supreme moment to mankind. The self-esteem that this impression engenders in them has been inflated even further in the past few years by the regular arrival on their doorsteps of the world's statesmen, financiers and industrialists, come to pay them court; by the attention and flattery they receive when they travel abroad; and by the appearance in their midst of thousands upon thousands of 'white coolies', sent to serve their every need and indulge their every whim. Before the 1960s the Arabs of the Trucial Coast had encountered few Europeans, and these were mainly British political, military or naval officers, oil company men, bankers and the representatives of old-established trading and shipping companies. Most of these Europeans were familiar with the Gulf and the ways of its inhabitants. Their own callings, as well as their training and inclinations, had imposed upon them a certain code of personal conduct in their relations with the Arab shaikhs and tribesmen, a code which was also required by the legacy of Britain's historical responsibilities in the Gulf.

Now the Trucial Coast, or the UAE, along with the other Gulf shaikhdoms, is inundated with Europeans and Americans of every kind, and the old code of conduct has been discarded. It has gone because the age of the political residents and agents, the naval and military officers, and the pioneer oilmen has passed. In its place has dawned the age of the plumbers. The new arrivals care not in the slightest for the traditions, history or customs of the shaikhdoms themselves: they are there for a limited time, to construct, to service or to sell, and in so doing reap themselves substantial rewards. Having no real interest in the native Arabs, other than that of making money from them, and little respect for their mores, beyond the minimum necessary to avoid jeopardizing the attainment of their own ends, the Europeans and Americans lead their lives very much as they would if they were still residing in the more open and unrestricted societies of the West. Many aspects of their behaviour – whether it is their copious consumption of liquor, the cheerful vulgarity of some of their pleasures, their careless profanity, their casual sexual improprieties, or the heedless freedom they accord their own women and the lack of restraint these show in their dress and deportment – have, in one way or another, shocked or offended, and in some cases corrupted, the local Arab inhabitants.

It is extremely difficult for untutored Arabian tribesmen, accustomed to keep their own women in seclusion, to regard the inviolability of the *harim* as a matter of the deepest personal and family honour, and to punish with death any sexual infidelity by their womenfolk, to understand, still more to respect, the contemporary Western attitude towards women. And when they experience for themselves, as many now have done on visits to Western countries, the easy availability of Western women, their contempt for Western Christendom, for a civilization in which men hold their women in such low regard as to allow them to hire themselves out to men of alien race and hostile creed, becomes absolute. Rooted though it may be in ignorance and misunderstanding, it is a contempt which has dangerous implications for both the Arabs and the West.

Yet in all fairness it cannot be said that the Western communities in the Gulf shaikhdoms have been the prime agents in the corruption of the indigenous Arab inhabitants, turning them overnight into 'the hollow pamper'd jades of Asia'. This dubious honour belongs first and foremost to their own rulers, who have given them too much, too quickly and for nothing, and to the northern Arabs who have so rapidly taught them Levantine ways. Some credit, too, must go to those Western governments, and especially the British and French, who by their obsequious conduct towards the Gulf oil states have enlarged even further their inhabitants' conviction of their own importance. The same can be said of those sections of the Western press which have assiduously pandered to the craving of the governments of these states for recognition and repute, not only by reporting upon their affairs with a delicacy and tact which they do not display in their coverage of events elsewhere, but also by issuing an unending stream of supplements publicizing and lauding the wisdom and achievements of these governments. These supplements, whether put out by *The Times*, *Le Monde*, the *Financial Times* or the *International Herald Tribune*, have much in common: a plethora of large advertisements from Arab and Western enterprises doing business in the Gulf, whether as construction companies, banks or purveyors of plumbing equipment; page after page of overripe verbiage, stuffed with redundant and often suspect statistics; and a decorous avoidance of any topic whose inclusion might possibly give offence to the advertisers' Arabian paymasters. With the passage of time an air of desperation has crept into the supplements, as production has outstripped invention and the regurgitation of drearily familiar material has brought on editorial flatulence. The ceaseless search for novel forms of blandishment even led *The Times* in April 1978 to coin an ungainly neologism, 'The Gulf', written thus regardless of where it occurred in a sentence. One can only conclude those responsible for this vulgarism were under the impression that the capitalization of the initial letter of the definite article somehow invested the Gulf with an almost transcendental significance and importance, elevating it far beyond the world of ordinary men into a kind of shimmering Arcadia, the radiant repository of mankind's noblest dreams and aspirations.

It is more or less taken as axiomatic these days, especially after the upheavals in Persia in the winter of 1978–9, that political change is bound to come in the Gulf. Where disagreement arises is over the form this change will take. Most Western observers attach considerable significance to the introduction of elected assemblies in Kuwait and Bahrain (the suspension of which is generally deplored) and to the emergence into prominence of the younger generation of Gulf Arabs (to whom the epithets of 'educated', 'sophisticated', 'vigorous' and 'enlightened' are usually applied). But if the experience of elected assemblies in Kuwait and Bahrain shows anything, it shows that such assemblies are unworkable in the Gulf. They are simply not compatible with the temperament, mentality or background of the Gulf Arabs, even of the youthful sophisticates among them.

The history of constitutional government in every Arab country over the past sixty years is a melancholy one. Only in the Lebanon did constitutional government meet with even partial success, and the Lebanon, it must be recalled, has a large Christian minority resolutely orientated towards Europe. The conclusion is inescapable that parliamentary government, elected legislatures and constitutional restraints will not take root in Arab lands: it is as if there is something in the Arab character, in the Arab historical tradition or in the essential nature of Islam that militates against the adoption of Western parliamentary forms of government. Nor is it a coincidence that in every Arab country where constitutional government on the Western model has failed, the constitutions subsequently introduced have declared the country to be an Islamic state with the *sharia* as the basis of the law, which fact alone would serve to render democratic government as we know it in the West an impossibility. The one Arab country whose constitution contains no such provision, the Lebanon, has paid the price for its singularity by being ravaged by civil and confessional conflict, instigated and conducted by the Palestinian guerrilla forces to whom it has afforded sanctuary, while the guerrillas themselves have in turn been incited and supported by the more militant Islamic republics.

Given the failure of representative and constitutional government in the advanced Arab states, as well as its demise in most of Asia and Africa; given, also, the progressive extinction of liberal democracy in all but a handful of countries around the globe (and, indeed, the disappearance of civilized government over large tracts of the earth), it would be absurd beyond measure to expect any form of democratic government to emerge and flourish in the political backwaters of Arabia and the Gulf. Were the potential revolutionaries in the Gulf states ever to gain power (either through the feebleness and imbecility of their present rulers, or by their own exertions), they would promptly deny to their luckless fellow citizens any say in their own affairs, and ruthlessly suppress any and all expression of discontent, as their like have done elsewhere in the Arab world over the past twenty-five years or more. The existence of a legally constituted opposition offering an alternative programme of government is a *sine qua non* of parliamentary democracy. Without it, the system is meaningless. Where, one might justifiably ask, is such an opposition to be found in the Arab world today? Why therefore expect the Gulf shaikhdoms, of all the Arab states, to prove the exception?

Should the present system of traditional and hereditary rule be swept away in one or more of the Gulf shaikhdoms, presumably some form of republican government would succeed it. What the exact nature of such a government would be it is impossible to predict. A centralized bureaucracy under the direction of a president, backed by the army and a widespread police network, might serve to govern Egypt, but the peninsular Arabs are not the submissive, patient and malleable people the Egyptians are. What are the alternatives at present visible in the Arab world? A military junta, as in Libya, where Colonel Qaddafi holds his subjects in check with rifle and bayonet while bewildering them with an incongruous blend of Islamic fundamentalism and quasi-socialism? A full-blown socialist state, run by a powerful engine of repression, as in Algeria? The authoritarian and semi-socialist prescriptions of the Baath, which the peoples of Syria and Iraq have been forced to swallow? Or the doctrines of Marxism–Leninism as preached by the Palestinian Fronde and practised by the National Front in Aden?

Which of these examples attracts the potential revolutionaries in the Gulf it is difficult to say, just as it is hard to determine which of the political ideas these regimes embody excite them most. Baathist ideas have been circulating in the Gulf from the late 1950s onwards, and Iraqi agents have been trying to penetrate the Arabian states since the early 1960s. Neither they nor their teachings had much success until after the triumph of the main wings of the Baath party in Iraq and Syria later in the decade, when they began to win some converts in Kuwait and Bahrain, and in two or three of the Trucial Shaikh-doms. Baathism, which is virtually the only indigenous political movement in the Arab world with some doctrinal pretensions and a measure of practical success to its credit, has exerted for the restless and semi-educated youth of the upper Gulf states the same fascination at the intellectual level as the latest imported gadgetry from the industrial world exerts at the material. Stronger meat than Baathism has been purveyed by the wilder fringes of the Palestinian movement, whose cause progressed by leaps and bounds in the Gulf after the 1967 war. While many of the older generation of Gulf Arabs regarded the more atrocious crimes committed by the PFLP, Black September and some con-stituent groups of the PLO as abhorrent, their sons and grandsons failed to share their abhorrence, electing instead to regard the perpetrators of these crimes as heroes. As several of the terrorist groups professed Marxist–Leninist beliefs, some of their admirers in the Gulf states sought to emulate them by subscribing to the same political faith. As a further stimulus, they had before them the example of the PDRY, which was not only a full-blown Marx-ist–Leninist state but probably the most ardent supporter of the Palestinian guerrilla movement in the Middle East.

Along with the more radical wing of the ANM, the government of the PDRY has tried over the past decade to infiltrate the Gulf states through the agency of PFLOAG (or PFLO) and other extremist groups inspired by Marxist–Leninist doctrines, such as the Popular Revolutionary Front. The aim of these various groups is to exploit the discontents of the immigrant population in the Gulf states so as to bring about a revolutionary movement of a Marxist–Leninist kind. Their propaganda plays down sectarian and racial differences, and even nationalist aspirations, which formed the basis of much earlier agitation. It is framed instead in Marxist universal terms – the corrup-tion of existing institutions, the tyranny of the traditional orders, the parasit-ism of the bourgeoisie, the oppression of the masses, the unending struggle, the permanent revolution and so forth. Shaikhs, religious leaders, merchants, bureaucrats are lumped together with Western governments and oil companies as forming a monolithic capitalist and imperialist structure dedicated to the exploitation and suppression of the urban and rural proletariat. While the targets of this propaganda among the Gulf labourers may not be aware of its

ideological origins, or appreciate its doctrinal distinctions, its crude simp-
licities nevertheless hold some appeal for them, as they would for many men in
similar depressed economic circumstances.

They would be mistaken, however, if they believed that the installation of
republican regimes, of whatever variety, in the Gulf states would release them
from their present subjection and exploitation. Radical Arab regimes are
nowhere noted for their benevolence and magnanimity towards foreigners, or
non-Arabs in general. Traditional regimes, in fact, display greater tolerance.
Nor would the cause of political freedom prosper if the present malcontents
and conspirators among the Gulf and *émigré* Arabs were to emerge into the
daylight and occupy the Capitol. For their *beau idéal* of government is not the
gentle and noble vision attributed to them by credulous Westerners, of popu-
larly elected legislatures graced by the grave and dignified figures of so many
Oriental Ciceros, Scipios and Gracchi. On the contrary, their paragons of
political virtue are the self-perpetuating oligarchies and politburos of the kind
that rule in Baghdad, Tripoli and Aden, composed of men of flinty and vulpine
visage, backed by the apparatus of the thumbscrew and the rack, and animated
by a virulent mixture of Marxist bigotry and Muslim fanaticism – the contemporary expression, in short, of age-old Oriental despotism.

The key to the survival or subversion of the shaikhly system of government
would seem to lie with the northern Arab *émigrés* and the new *effendi* class
among the Gulf Arabs. Should the latter attempt a *coup d'état* in one or more of
the shaikhdoms (backed either by a 'street' or by the local defence force or by
both), they will, whether they fully realize it or not, be acting upon directions
and to a script supplied by their northern Arab mentors, and drawn up long
before by men of whom they know nothing, not even perhaps their very
existence. For this reason alone the ultimate consequences of their actions may
be far removed from those they envisage; for revolutions do not stand still and
their initiators all too often become their victims. The revolutionaries among
the Gulf Arabs, in other words, if they ally themselves with the northern
Arabs, are apt to find that they have exchanged one set of masters for another.
For the northern Arab *émigrés*, as remarked previously, are by and large
uninterested in the Gulf states from which they at present derive their livelihoods, they are disdainful of both the native and the non-Arab inhabitants of
these states, and they care not a jot about the true welfare of either. They are, in
short, true *émigrés*, whose intellectual and emotional energies are consumed by
the intricacies of Egyptian, Syrian, Lebanese or Iraqi politics, the multifarious
twists and turns of the Arab–Israeli dispute, and the ceaseless wranglings of the
various factions of the Palestinian movement. The current superfluity of
wealth in these small states, together with its prodigal consumption, must
present them with a constant and powerful temptation to take steps to appropriate this wealth to themselves, and to employ it, and the oil reserves which
have generated it, in the service of their own countries and causes. The

temptation must be doubly potent in the case of the Palestinians, a people dispossessed of their homeland, dispersed into exile and destitute of any real hope of return. Idle though it is to speculate – and even more pointless to dogmatize – about the likely course of Arab politics anywhere, least of all in Arabia and the Gulf, it is yet worth recalling that it was the loyalties of the *Uitlanders* in the Transvaal to alien lands and causes which set in train the sequence of events which terminated in the extinction of the Transvaal's independence at the turn of this century.

CHAPTER V
'Araby the Blest'

'The winds of Paradise are blowing. Where are ye who hanker
after Paradise?'

War chant of the Saudi *ikhwan*

The kingdom of Saudi Arabia is, to all intents and purposes, a theocracy, ruled on absolutist principles by the Al Saud dynasty. From its very beginning in the second half of the eighteenth century the Saudi state, together with its ruling house, has been identified with the puritanical movement of Islamic revival known to the outside world as Wahhabism, after the Muslim reformer who instituted it, Muhammad ibn Abdul Wahhab. A native of Ayaina in Najd, Ibn Abdul Wahhab spent much of his life up to the age of forty in travel and study abroad, returning to his birthplace in the early 1740s. What he had seen and learned on his travels had convinced him that the practice of Islam everywhere had fallen into a grievous state, which could only be remedied by a return to the austere simplicity of early Islam and a thoroughgoing purge of the superstitions, heresies and other pernicious accretions which over the centuries had come to sully the purity of the faith. He formulated his arguments in a work entitled *Kitab al-Tawhid*, 'the Book of the Unity (of God)', and set forth on a self-imposed mission to win his fellow Najdis back to a proper observance of their religious duties.

Initially, he made little headway with the townsmen of Najd, who were rather attached to the habits and customs that Ibn Abdul Wahhab condemned – among them adultery, hagiolatry and the worship of sacred trees, stones and springs. The Bedouin were even greater religious backsliders, almost incorrigible in their addiction to superstitions and animistic beliefs. At Dariya, some miles to the south-eastwards of Ayaina and a little to the north of Riyad, the reformer had better fortune, converting to his cause Muhammad ibn Saud, the chief of the Al Saud clan of the Anaiza tribal confederation. With Muhammad ibn Saud's armed support, Ibn Abdul Wahhab was able to spread his teaching more widely among the tribes; so that by the time of the Saudi chieftain's death in 1765 most of Najd had sworn dual allegiance to the Al Saud and to the doctrines of Ibn Abdul Wahhab. The theocratic compact was ratified when Muhammad ibn Saud's son and successor, Abdul Aziz, who had married a daughter of Ibn Abdul Wahhab, assumed, at the latter's urging, the title of *imam* – spiritual and temporal leader of the Muslim community.

The followers of Ibn Abdul Wahhab styled themselves *muwahhidun*, 'believers in the oneness (of God)', after the principal doctrine expounded by the reformer. It has been well said that the essence of his teaching was that he took the basic precept of Islam, 'There is no God but God and Muhammad is the Prophet of God', and enhanced the force of the first proposition by suppressing that of the second. As God is one and indivisible, as well as being the sole possessor of divine power, it follows (so Ibn Abdul Wahhab argued) that prayer to anyone other than God is tantamount to polytheism (*shirk*), the ultimate sin. Even the Prophet himself could not be excluded from this blanket admonition. To pray to him – as to any other prophet, saint or spirit – to intercede for the suppliant with God was to merit condemnation as a *mushrik*, a polytheist. A like abomination was the excessive veneration of past saints and prophets, especially when it took the form of erecting costly and elaborate tombs or mosques over their graves. To worship at such shrines – worse still, to seek blessings from the shrines themselves – was nothing short of idolatry, as heinous in its way as was the attribution of a spiritual or sacred quality to stones, trees and springs. In place of these odious and degenerate practices Ibn Abdul Wahhab preached a reversion to the pristine prescriptions of Islam, with especial emphasis being placed upon the performance of the obligatory acts of devotion, the so-called 'five pillars' of the faith – the *shahada*, or profession of faith; the *salah*, or daily ritual prayers; the *zakah*, or alms giving; the *sawm*, or fast during the month of Ramadan; and the *hajj*, or pilgrimage. The Koranic prohibitions and penalties were also to be strictly enforced, especially those applying to murder, theft, adultery, usury, gambling and the drinking of wine. To these proscribed acts Ibn Abdul Wahhab added the enjoyment of tobacco, music and fine apparel.

What, in sum, he was propounding was a fundamentalism of the narrowest and harshest kind. All knowledge other than that contained in the Koran and the *hadith* (traditions), construed at their face value, was, according to Ibn Abdul Wahhab, to be rejected. All philosophical or legal innovations (*bida*) introduced into Islam after the third century AH were to be discarded as excrescences. Only the four Sunni law schools – Hanbali, Hanafi, Maliki and Shafi – could be recognized as legitimate (the Shia were simply dismissed as *mushrikun*), and of these the Hanbali rite, the severest of the four, was that most worthy to be followed. It was the sacred duty of the *muwahhidun*, those who had accepted the Najdi reformation, to induce other Muslims to follow suit. If the latter failed to mend their ways, they were to be treated as *kafirs*, unbelievers, and the holy war (*jihad*) was to be waged against them as fiercely as against all infidels and non-Muslims.

It was this last element in Ibn Abdul Wahhab's dogma that accounted as much as anything for its spread in central Arabia, and along with it the extension of Saudi power. Nothing tempts the Bedouin like the prospect of plunder, especially if it is laced with an appeal to their innate fanaticism. The desert tribesmen flocked to the war banners of the Al Saud as they advanced through Najd and the Qasim, less out of an urge to open the eyes of the settled inhabitants of these districts to the truth and beauty of the reformed faith than to slit their purses. Nor was this motive by any means incidental to the spirit of Wahhabism; for, as one knowledgeable student of the movement in the nineteenth century has observed of it:

It may be defined as a politico-religious confederacy, which legalises the indiscriminate plunder and thraldom of all peoples beyond its own pale . . . [as] is fully borne out by the intolerant proceedings of its adherents, not only in Nejd, but wherever they succeeded in establishing their ascendancy.*

Even that most assiduous of Western apologists for the movement, Harry St John Philby, has been forced to concede that the driving force behind it was 'constant aggression and expansion at the expense of those who did not share the great idea'.† Small wonder, then, that by the time of Ibn Abdul Wahhab's death in 1792, the town dwellers of Najd and the Qasim, whether out of conviction or prudence, had all submitted to the Al Saud. From this time forward they, and not the fickle Bedouin, were to be the backbone of the Saudi state.

Most of central and eastern Arabia was, by the turn of the century, under Saudi dominion. Al-Hasa in the east, along the Gulf coast, had fallen, the shaikhs of the Bani Khalid, its former rulers, had been made to submit, and the Shia dwelling in the Hasa oasis and the coastal settlements, who formed the bulk of the indigenous population, had been brought into subjection. The next few years saw the Wahhabis burst the bounds of Najd and Hasa, marauding northwards into Turkish Iraq and Syria, south-eastwards into Oman and westwards into the Hijaz. The holy Shii city of Karbala was devastated in the spring of 1801, thousands of its inhabitants were put to the sword, and the shrine of Husain, the grandson of the Prophet, was looted and desecrated. Two years later the Wahhabis overran much of the Hijaz and captured Mecca. Madina fell the following spring and, like Mecca before it, was scoured and purged of all that the Wahhabis found offensive. Even the tomb of the Prophet himself was broken open in 1810 on the orders of the Saudi imam and its jewels and relics sold or distributed among the Wahhabi soldiery. This ultimate act of desecration finally stirred the Ottoman sultan, the sovereign protector of the holy places, to action. At his behest the *vali* of Egypt, Mehemet Ali Pasha, landed an expeditionary force in the Hijaz in 1811, which drove the Wahhabis from Mecca and Madina two years later and subsequently advanced into the heart of Arabia to lay siege to and capture the Wahhabi capital of Dariya in the

---

* G. P. Badger, *History of the Imams and Seyyids of Oman*, London, 1871, p. lxv.
† *Arabia*, London, 1930, p. 181.

autumn of 1818. Dariya was razed to the ground, its inhabitants dispersed and the Saudi imam sent a prisoner to Constantinople, where at the close of the year he was publicly beheaded in the square of Aya Sophia.

The Wahhabis rapidly recovered from their defeat. Within little more than a decade they had reasserted their authority over central and eastern Arabia and established a new capital at Riyad, a few miles to the south of the ruins of Dariya. Then, in 1837–8, they were vanquished a second time by an Egyptian army sent to subdue them as part of Mehemet Ali's grand design to establish an Egyptian *imperium* over the Arab provinces of the Ottoman empire, from Syria in the north to the Yemen in the south. A member of the Al Saud, Khalid ibn Saud, who had been taken a prisoner to Cairo in 1818, was set up as a puppet ruler in Riyad in place of the legitimate imam, Faisal ibn Turki, who was sent a captive to Egypt. When Mehemet Ali was forced in 1841 to give up all his conquests outside Egypt and restore the Hijaz to Ottoman rule, Khalid ibn Saud was deposed by one of his relatives. The latter was himself deposed and imprisoned for life when Faisal ibn Turki was released from captivity and returned to Riyad in 1843.

Faisal ibn Turki's reign over the next twenty years was the most tranquil experienced by a Saudi ruler in the nineteenth century. He had no rivals within Najd or among the numerous members of the Saudi clan, and he averted the hostility of the Sublime Porte by continuing to acknowledge his status as an Ottoman dependant, in token of which he paid an annual tribute to the Hashimite sharif of Mecca, who governed the Hijaz in the name of the Ottoman sultan. To compensate for the inactivity he was compelled to observe on the western limits of his territory, Faisal tried at intervals to extend his authority over Bahrain, Qatar, Trucial Oman and the sultanate of Oman. On each occasion he ran into opposition from the British government in India, which, as we have seen, was determined to prevent the extension of Wahhabi influence over the maritime tribes of the Arabian littoral.

When Faisal died in 1865 he was succeeded by his son, Abdullah. Almost from the day of his accession Abdullah ibn Faisal had to contend with the unrelenting efforts of his younger brother, Saud, to unseat him, an ambition in which Saud ibn Faisal succeeded at the outset of 1871. In desperation Abdullah sought the assistance of the Ottoman *vali* of Baghdad, who responded by dispatching a military expedition to Hasa in May 1871. Although the Turks occupied the coastal districts and the Hasa oasis without much difficulty, it became obvious with the passage of time that they had neither the resources nor the stomach for an advance into Najd. Not until the death of his brother Saud of smallpox in January 1875 was Abdullah ibn Faisal able to regain and resume the imamate.

It was a much truncated realm that he now ruled. Hasa had been annexed in full sovereignty by the Turks earlier in the year and incorporated in the newly created *vilayet* of Basra. Over most of the Qasim the shadow of Saudi rule fell but lightly. To the northward a new power was arising in Arabian politics in the shape of the Rashidi dynasty of Hail in Jabal Shammar. Abdullah ibn Faisal held on in Najd for ten uncertain years, until in October 1885 he was overthrown and imprisoned in Riyad by the sons of his late brother, Saud. He was saved from probable death by the intervention of Muhammad ibn Rashid, the head of the house of Rashid, who drove Saud's sons from Riyad, bore Abdullah off to Hail to recover from his ordeal, and appointed his own governor to rule the Wahhabi capital. It was the beginning of the eclipse of Saudi power in Arabia. Abdullah ibn Faisal was only permitted to return to Riyad in the autumn of 1889 so that he might die (as he did within weeks of his return) in the house of his fathers. Although his younger brother, Abdur Rahman, declared himself imam in his place, he remained at Riyad only on the sufferance of Muhammad ibn Rashid. Fifteen months later, in 1891, the Rashidi ruler foreclosed on Abdur Rahman's precarious mortgage. Riyad and the whole of Najd were added to the Rashidi domains, and Abdur Rahman and his family were driven into exile. The former imam appealed for succour to the Turks, who gave him a monthly stipend for his support and allowed him to settle with his family in Kuwait.

The downfall of the house of Saud now seemed complete. From being at the start of the century masters of half of Arabia they no longer held even their family domains, but survived only on the charity of their former enemies. The religious movement which had initiated their rise to power and sustained it thereafter still endured, however; for the Al Rashid followed the Wahhabi creed and identified themselves with the aspirations of the Wahhabi community, even to the point of assuming the imamate. The recovery in the fortunes of the Al Saud began a decade after Abdur Rahman ibn Faisal's flight to Kuwait, when, in January 1902, Riyad was captured and the Rashidi garrison expelled by a raiding party led by his son, Abdul Aziz, at that time twenty-one years of age. In the next three years Abdul Aziz restored Saudi rule over Najd and drove the forces of Ibn Rashid from the Qasim, to the northwest. The recovery of Hasa was a more daunting task, especially as his relations with the Turks had been compromised by his father's acknowledgement of Ottoman suzerainty and his investiture by the Porte with the title of *qaim-maqam* of Najd. After endeavouring unsuccessfully to secure help from the British authorities in the Gulf in ejecting the Turkish garrison from Hasa, Abdul Aziz accomplished the task by himself in the summer of 1913. Wisely he did not attempt to provoke the Turks further but agreed, in an engagement concluded in May 1914, to acknowledge Ottoman suzerainty in return for recognition as *vali* of Najd, with the rank of pasha, and the guaranteed succession of his sons and grandsons after him. Six months later war broke out between the British and Ottoman empires, opening up to Abdul Aziz bright new opportunities for political and financial advancement.

The first was that of casting off his lightly worn allegiance to the Turks and obtaining recognition from the British as independent ruler of Najd and Hasa. The second was that of gaining the mastery over his old enemies, the house of Rashid, and of bringing Hail and Jabal Shammar under his sway. Luckily for him, Ibn Rashid was to remain loyal to the Turks throughout the war, so that Abdul Aziz could argue plausibly to the British that by underwriting a campaign by him against Ibn Rashid they would be striking indirectly at the Turks themselves. It took some time for the bargain to be struck. The British wanted Abdul Aziz – or Ibn Saud, as we might henceforth call him, after the style by which he, like his predecessors, was known to his people, and was to become known to the rest of the world – to take a more active role in the field against the Turks than simply raiding into Shammar territory. On his side, Ibn Saud refused to disavow his status as an Ottoman dependant until he had a formal guarantee of the security and future independence of his possessions. After a leisurely negotiation conducted at intervals over twelve months an Anglo-Saudi treaty was signed on 26 December 1915. It recognized Ibn Saud as the independent ruler of Najd, Hasa and their dependencies, obliged the British government to assist him in the event of aggression upon his territories, and bound him to refrain from entering into relations with foreign powers or alienating any portion of his territories. He was also required to safeguard the pilgrim routes to the holy places and to abstain from aggression upon Kuwait, Bahrain, Qatar and Trucial Oman.

Arms and money were supplied to Ibn Saud by the British throughout the war, to no readily measurable advantage. The truth was that Ibn Saud was not strong enough to make any appreciable contribution to the defeat of the Turks and their Arab allies. His own attitude to the Turks, moreover, was highly equivocal. While his dislike of them was genuine, he did not actually carry it to the point of open conflict. Thus supplies from Jabal Shammar and Kuwait continued to reach the Turkish garrison at Madina by way of the caravan routes through the Qasim right up to the closing days of the war. Against the Rashidi allies of the Turks Ibn Saud was similarly ineffective. A few skirmishes apart, he did not take the field against them in any force until the summer of 1918, and the results of his campaign were inconclusive at best.

Ibn Saud's equivocations were due in no small degree to his hatred of the sharif of Mecca, Husain ibn Ali, the head of the Hashimite family, *de facto* ruler of the Hijaz, guardian of the holy places, putative leader of the Arab Revolt and self-styled King of the Arabs. The animosity between the house of Hashim and the Al Saud extended back to the late eighteenth century and the early years of the first Wahhabi expansion. It arose as much from territorial and economic rivalry as it did from religious friction, for what was at issue between the two rival dynasties was dominance over the Qasim and the other districts intermediate to Najd and the Hijaz, and hence over the valuable merchant traffic and pilgrim caravans which passed through them. Husain ibn Ali viewed the resurgence of Wahhabi power under Ibn Saud in the first and second decades of the twentieth century with much the same moody apprehension as previous sharifs of Mecca had felt at the rise of the Wahhabi confederacy a century or more earlier. Any real trial of strength between the two contenders for hegemony in Arabia was deferred by the war, which brought Husain a considerable accession of influence and money, if not of actual political power. While Husain was engaged in fighting the Turks, Ibn Saud stayed his hand. He had little choice in the matter: not only was he incapable at this stage of launching any kind of decisive offensive against the Hijaz but he was also beholden, as was Husain, to his British paymasters, and they forbade any open conflict between their two Arabian protégés. It also suited Ibn Saud's book for Husain to expend his resources upon the campaign against the Turks (at least to the extent that the sharif was expending them); since Husain would then be less capable of opposing the challenge from Najd, when in due course it was made.

The goal that Ibn Saud had set himself from the night in January 1902 when he scaled the walls of Riyad and expelled the Rashidi garrison was nothing less than the re-establishment of the Wahhabi realm as it had been at the furthest extent of its territorial expansion in the first decade of the nineteenth century. The means by which he intended to attain this goal was the same as that employed by his ancestors to achieve their conquests – the arousal of the latent fanaticism of the Bedouin tribes, its harnessing to their predatory and warlike instincts, and the launching of the resultant engine of destruction upon his neighbours. To organize this religio-military brotherhood (*al-ikhwan*) Ibn Saud had begun sending out, perhaps as early as 1910, Wahhabi preachers (*mutawiyah*) to the desert tribesmen to instruct them in their religious duties and to kindle in them a zeal for the holy war. He had also resolved that the only way to bring the Bedouin more firmly under control for the strategic purposes he had in mind was to settle them in military colonies. The first of these military settlements, to which was given the evocative name of *hijar* (*hijra* in the singular), was established in 1912 at Artawiya, some 150 miles to the north of Riyad, in the *dirah* of the Mutair tribe. A second *hijra* was started in the same year at Ghatghat, in Ataiba country to the west of Riyad. Dozens of *hijar* were founded in the next few years in Najd and Hasa and further north, as more and more Bedouin enthusiastically embraced the *ikhwan* ideal, lured as much by the vision of war and rapine in the name of Islam as they were by the arms, money, dwellings, grants of land and agricultural help provided by the authorities in Riyad.

From the very outset the *ikhwan* exhibited a self-righteousness about themselves and an intolerance towards others, whether Muslim or infidel, of excessive proportions. To distinguish themselves from the unregenerate of their fellows they abandoned the ordinary head-dress and head-rope of the Bedouin and adopted a loosely wound white turban. They pronounced an anathema upon all *bida*, or innovations, however harmless, since the days of the Prophet, shaved their moustaches, and grew their beards long to demonstrate their contempt for adornment and self-indulgence. One innovation they did not scorn, however, was the rifle, an exception which reveals rather more about their shrill insistence upon their unworldliness than they would perhaps have found comfortable. They called themselves *mujahidun*, fighters in the holy war, and when they rode forth on their camels they bore with them green and black banners inscribed with the *shahada*, the declaration of faith. They courted death in battle as martyrs to the cause of Islam. 'The winds of Paradise are blowing', ran one of their war chants. 'Where are ye who hanker after Paradise?' To those who defied them they were merciless in their ferocity, often putting every male prisoner, regardless of age, to the sword. On more occasions than one their bloodlust led them to slaughter women and children – a strange fulfilment of the mission of Ibn Abdul Wahhab and an even grosser violation of the code of the desert tribes.

The *ikhwan* had their blooding as an organized force in Ibn Saud's inconclusive campaign against the Rashidis in 1918, when they failed to distinguish themselves to any appreciable degree. They had more success the following year when they prevented the forces of Sharif Husain of the Hijaz under the command of his son, Abdullah (later the amir of Transjordan), from reasserting Hashimite authority over the oasis town of Khurma, which lay in the undefined and disputed borderland between the Hijaz and the Qasim. Thereafter the town, many of whose inhabitants, including the former Hashimite governor, had embraced Wahhabism, remained a Saudi outpost on the edge of the Hijaz, the tip of a dagger aimed at the vitals of the Hashimite kingdom. *Ikhwan* contingents rode with Ibn Saud's forces to the conquest of the northern Asir – the coastal region to the south of the Hijaz – in 1920. In the autumn of that year a large *ikhwan* force under Faisal ibn Sultan al-Dawish, the paramount chieftain of the Mutair, attacked Kuwait. It was repulsed in a bloody engagement at Jahra, a few miles from Kuwait town, early in October, in which some 200 Kuwaitis and 1,200 *ikhwan* were slain.

The attack on Kuwait arose from the Kuwaitis' objection to the establishment of a *hijra* by Mutairi *ikhwan* in territory which the Kuwaitis regarded as rightfully theirs. It lay within the frontiers assigned to Kuwait in the unratified Anglo-Ottoman convention of July 1913, frontiers which Ibn Saud refused to accept – if he even knew of their existence. The need to define the northern limits of Ibn Saud's territories became more pressing a year after the *ikhwan* attack on Kuwait, when Ibn Saud finally overthrew the Rashidi dynasty of Hail and annexed the principality of Jabal Shammar. This latest conquest removed the barrier which Jabal Shammar had interposed between the Saudi domains and the newly created British mandates of Iraq and Transjordan, exposing the southern flanks of these two territories to *ikhwan* marauding. Almost immediately after the fall of Hail the *ikhwan* began raiding the tribes of lower Iraq. Sir

Percy Cox, the British high commissioner in Iraq, told Ibn Saud that a permanent frontier would have to be drawn between Najd and Iraq, regardless of the unsuitability of the concept of a fixed frontier in a desert region frequented only by nomadic tribes in their seasonal migrations in search of grazing. At a meeting of Iraqi and Najdi representatives at Muhammarah in May 1922 a treaty laying down the principles upon which the proposed frontier was to be based was drawn up and signed under Cox's supervision. Ibn Saud refused to ratify it, alleging that its effect would be to allow his Hashimite rivals – Sharif Husain in the Hijaz, Husain's son, Abdullah, the amir of Transjordan, and his other son, Faisal, the newly enthroned King of Iraq – to hem him in. It was rather like the wolf expressing apprehension of the sheep grazing around him.

At the end of November 1922 Cox summoned Ibn Saud to a meeting at Uqair, on the Hasa coast south of Bahrain, to settle once and for all the question of the Kuwait and Iraq frontiers. Cox was accompanied by an Iraqi delegation and by the British political agents from Kuwait and Bahrain. Ibn Saud argued passionately against the idea of a fixed frontier, declaring magniloquently that the boundaries of Najd had since antiquity been the furthermost points reached in their wanderings by its Bedouin tribes – northern Syria and the edge of the Anatolian plateau. The Iraqi delegation was equally extravagant in its pretensions, claiming a western frontier on the Red Sea and a southern frontier that reached, give or take a few leagues, as far as the Rub al-Khali. Exasperated by all the rodomontade, Cox told Ibn Saud that he would simply have to accept the frontier that he, Cox, would lay down. With that, Cox drew a line on the map, beginning at Jabal Anaza, roughly 200 miles east of Amman in Transjordan, and running, with occasional changes of course, in a south-easterly direction to end at the western frontier of Kuwait as defined in the Anglo-Ottoman convention of 1913. To the west of Kuwait Cox created a rhomboid-shaped neutral zone over which Najd and Iraq would exercise joint sovereignty, and where tribes from both sides would enjoy freedom of movement and grazing rights. To the south of Kuwait he created another neutral zone under joint Nadj–Kuwait sovereignty, his object being equally to compensate Ibn Saud for those stretches of territory he claimed he was being forced to cede to Iraq, and to penalize Kuwait for her equivocal behaviour towards the Turks during the war.

It has never been entirely clear why Cox thought it necessary to compensate Ibn Saud for the alleged sacrifice of his territorial rights in the vicinity of the new Najd–Iraq frontier by assigning him a half-share in territory which Cox himself, at the time of the conclusion of the Anglo-Ottoman convention of 1913, when he was political resident in the Gulf, had acknowledged to lie within Kuwait's orbit. The truth is that Ibn Saud had no historic title to the districts he was forfeiting to Iraq, and the frontier that Cox awarded him was as generous as historical and political reality could sustain. These considerations apart, Ibn Saud had no option but to accept whatever frontiers Cox laid down. He had consented in the treaty of December 1915 to the delimitation of his territorial possessions by the British government, he had placed the conduct of his foreign affairs in British hands, and he was still in receipt of an annual subsidy from the British exchequer, paid him on condition that he observed his treaty obligations and heeded Britain's counsel. On her side, Britain, as the conqueror of the Ottoman empire, as the mandatory power in Iraq and as the protecting power in Najd and Kuwait, had the inherent right as well as the legal authority to apportion frontiers to these states as she saw fit.

Ibn Saud recovered with remarkable rapidity from his initial dismay at Cox's *diktat*. At the height of the summer of 1922 an *ikhwan* force, some 3,000–4,000 strong, had set out from Jabal Shammar, skirted the Great Nafud and advanced up the Wadi Sirhan to within a dozen miles of Amman, the chief town of Transjordan. It was stopped and virtually wiped out by aircraft and armoured cars of the Royal Air Force stationed in the amirate. The setback did not in the least deter Ibn Saud from his resolve to bring the whole of the Wadi Sirhan, a great depression extending for nearly 200 miles from the Jauf oases in the south-east to the Qaf oases in the north-west, under his authority, on the grounds that it was the principal avenue of trade and communication between Najd and Syria, and its people had already expressed their ardent desire to submit to his rule. The first point was true, the second was not – although Wahhabi *mutawiyah* were hard at work among the tribes of the Wadi Sirhan trying to make it so. The British were prepared to concede control of the Jauf oases and the southern half of the wadi to Ibn Saud, but not the northern half and the Qaf oases. To do so, they thought, would be to create a permanent threat to the stability of Transjordan. It would open up the possibility of Wahhabi interference in Syria as well as driving a wedge between Transjordan and Iraq, not only unsettling these two Hashimite principalities but also disrupting Britain's lines of communication between the Mediterranean and the Gulf.

Ikhwan of the Mutair launched a savage raid upon shepherd tribes across the Iraq frontier in the spring of 1924. The raid was made with the full knowledge of Ibn Saud, who had clearly decided that the time had come to throw caution to the winds and to stake all upon the swords and rifles of the *ikhwan*. Two events in March 1924 had helped him to make up his mind. The first, at the beginning of the month, was the action of the Turkish Grand National Assembly in abolishing the Ottoman caliphate following the inauguration of the Turkish republic in November 1922. Sharif Husain of the Hijaz, who had already in January 1924 had himself proclaimed *amir al-muminin* ('commander of the faithful'), promptly assumed the caliphate himself, thereby outraging not only the Wahhabi *ulama* but much of the Muslim world besides. The second occurrence which swayed Ibn Saud was the termination at the end of March of his annual subsidy from the British government. He was now free, he believed, to act as he pleased towards Britain's Hashimite protégés in the Hijaz and Transjordan. At a conference of tribal chieftains, *ikhwan* leaders and Wahhabi *ulama* convened at Riyad in the first week of June 1924 by Ibn Saud's father, the Imam Abdur Rahman ibn Faisal, the conquest of the Hijaz and the overthrow of Sharif Husain, the *soi-disant* caliph, were decided upon.

Ibn Saud launched his campaign at the end of August. Three expeditionary forces were despatched to the north-west and the north-east, to cut the Hijaz railway north of Madina and to raid up the Wadi Sirhan and across the Iraq frontier with the object of distracting Husain's sons, Abdullah in Transjordan and Faisal in Iraq, and so prevent them from coming to their father's assistance. The main attack was directed from Khurma and Turaba upon Taif, the oasis town in the highlands some forty miles to the east of Mecca, where the notables of that city were accustomed to spend the summer months. Taif fell in the first week of September without a fight, and its townsfolk paid dearly for their pusillanimity. The *ikhwan* ran amok, slaying hundreds of people before they were brought under control. Panic followed in Mecca, its citizens fleeing in their hundreds to find safety in Jiddah. Sharif Husain appealed to Britain for help, harking back to his wartime sacrifices on Britain's behalf. The appeal went unanswered. It was judged out of the question for Britain, as a Christian power, to send troops to the holy land of Islam to intervene in what was, as much as anything, a Muslim religious war. To send Indian Muslim troops would assuredly have provoked upheavals in India. Bowing to the inevitable, Husain abdicated as King of the Hijaz at the beginning of October and went into exile, leaving his son, Ali, to succeed him as so-called 'constitutional sovereign'.

Mecca was occupied by the Wahhabis in the second week of October. Ibn Saud proclaimed that he had no intention of annexing or dominating the Hijaz. Its future status would be determined by a congress of the whole Islamic world. He had undertaken the campaign against the Hashimites, he asserted, because Husain had neglected the holy places and debarred the people of Najd from making the pilgrimage. There was no place in the Hijaz for the family of Husain, and the war would continue until they had been expelled. Henceforth he, Ibn Saud, would guarantee the security of the holy places, the pilgrimage and the pilgrim routes. For all his confident assertions, however, he had to pick his way with care in the next few months. The acts of savagery by some of his soldiery, the destruction of shrines and sacred monuments by Wahhabi zealots, and the forcible interdiction of the cult of saints, which was both widespread and deeply rooted in the Hijaz, had all unsettled Muslim opinion abroad and turned much of it against him. For the next twelve months, therefore, Ibn Saud stayed his hand, declaring to the world at large that he wished to spare the holy land any further strife. More to the point, he was counting upon the respite to drain away what little support for the Hashimite dynasty remained among the townsmen of the Hijaz, whose inconstancy was as notorious as was their reputation for deceit and rapacity. His confidence was not misplaced, as the testimony of the British consul at Jiddah at the time, R. W. (later Sir Reader) Bullard, bears out. Writing on the eve of Husain's abdication, Bullard described the Hijazi townsman as

a mean-spirited and cowardly creature whose doughty deed is the swindling of a live pilgrim or the robbing of a dead one. His hatred of King Husain had hitherto been concealed under an effusive servility, but at the sight of the Wahhabis, about, as he thought, to set him free from King Husain, he began to talk treason boldly.*

Ibn Saud resumed his campaign in the Hijaz in the closing weeks of 1925. Only three towns of any importance remained in Hashimite hands – Madina, Jiddah and Yanbu. Madina fell in the first week of December, Yanbu a fortnight later. Meanwhile King Ali ibn Husain had signified his intention of giving up the struggle and leaving the Hijaz. He did so in the middle of the month, and on 19 December the Wahhabi forces entered Jiddah peacefully. Three weeks later Ibn Saud assumed the title of 'King of the Hijaz' proffered him by the notables of Mecca on 8 January 1926. Although he had publicly announced several times during 1925 that the Hijazis would be left to govern themselves and that it would be left to an Islamic congress to elect a ruler for the Hijaz, there was never any doubt that Ibn Saud intended to be master of the country and to add it to his dominions. An Islamic congress was held later in 1926, but it confined its discussions primarily to matters relating to the pilgrimage, the care of the holy places and sectarian ritual observances. As for the Hijazis, although they were initially granted permission to elect consultative councils for the country's principal towns, so many ordinances were enacted and enforced by their conquerors without consulting them that the concession soon amounted to nothing. The power and influence of the Hijazi nobility, the *ashraf* (*sharif* in the singular), were systematically undermined by expropriation, persecution and personal degradation, which gave great offence to many Muslims within Arabia and outside. Despite undertakings which had been given to the Muslim world at large that the other schools of Islamic law – the Maliki, Hanafi and Shafi – would be respected, it rapidly became plain that the Hanbali school (to which the Wahhabis alone adhered in any numbers) was not only to be accorded precedence but would in fact regulate every aspect of Hijazi life. For years to come there was to be tension and ill-feeling between the Hijaz and Najd, the Hijazis looking upon the Najdis as little better than barbarous Bedouin, while the Najdis viewed the Hijazis with contempt as *munafiqun* – hypocrites and libertines.

While the Wahhabi occupation of Jiddah and Madina and the obliteration of Hashimite rule in the Hijaz were still some weeks away, the British government had sent an envoy to Ibn Saud to settle the issue of the Najd–Transjordan frontier before the Wahhabi ruler's impending victory in the Hijaz tempted

* Bullard to Foreign Office, 28 September 1924, quoted in Gary Troeller, *The Birth of Saudi Arabia*, London, 1976, p. 232.

him subsequently to direct his forces northwards against the adjacent Hashimite principality. The envoy, Sir Gilbert Clayton, arrived in Ibn Saud's camp, located between Bahrah and the oasis of Hadda on the Mecca–Jiddah road, in the second week of October 1925. Three weeks later he and Ibn Saud put their signatures to two instruments. One, the Bahrah agreement, covered tribal movements across the Najd–Iraq frontier and the apprehension of raiding parties and their punishment. The other, the Hadda agreement, laid down a similar tribal regime for the Najd–Transjordan frontier and defined that frontier. Although Clayton had been instructed to draw the frontier across the Wadi Sirhan so as to include the Qaf oases at its northern end in Transjordan, he let himself be bamboozled by Ibn Saud into surrendering the whole wadi, including Qaf, to Najd. In return, Ibn Saud gave his consent, which he was in no position to withhold, to the creation of a territorial corridor linking Transjordan with Iraq and cutting off his dominions from southern Syria. As the conquest of the Hijaz was not yet complete the Hadda agreement did not take in the Hijaz–Transjordan frontier; but Clayton told Ibn Saud that the British government would insist upon the assignation of Aqaba and Maan to Transjordan, so as to give the amirate access to the sea. Ibn Saud refused to accept the stipulation – he had other things in mind for Transjordan – and the frontier remained undemarcated for forty years afterwards, until his son, Faisal, formally acknowledged the *de facto* frontier in 1965.

The great accession of power which Ibn Saud had won since the end of the First World War obviously invalidated on practical grounds his status as a British dependant under the terms of the Anglo-Saudi treaty of 1915. He was now the dual monarch of Najd and the Hijaz, and his title of 'Sultan of Najd and its Dependencies' (which had been conferred upon him by a congress of tribal notables and religious dignitaries at Riyad in the summer of 1921) had been changed by acclamation to that of 'King' at a similar gathering at Riyad in January 1927. So Clayton was sent out again in the spring of that year to conclude a new Anglo-Saudi treaty which would give proper recognition to Ibn Saud's new dignity and importance. The treaty was signed at Jiddah on 20 May 1927. It acknowledged Ibn Saud as 'King of the Hijaz and of Najd and its Dependencies' and recognized 'the complete and absolute independence' of his dominions. The body of the treaty was concerned with the security of the persons and property of British subjects and pilgrims in Ibn Saud's territories, reciprocal protection being accorded to Saudi subjects in British territories. Ibn Saud also undertook to co-operate fully with the British government in the suppression of the slave trade, and to maintain peaceful and friendly relations with Kuwait, Bahrain, Qatar and the Trucial Shaikhdoms.

The pilgrimage aside, Ibn Saud's observance of his treaty obligations in the years ahead was frequently subordinated to his own aims or objects. From 1922 onwards he kept up a blockade of Kuwait in an endeavour to divert the trade of Najd and Jabal Shammar to his own ports of Qatif, Jubail and Uqair on the

Hasa coast. The blockade was not removed until the British made an issue of it at the time of the treaty's first renewal – it was subject to confirmation every seven years – in October 1936. Towards the slave trade and its suppression Ibn Saud consistently exhibited torpor and indifference, while towards the petty shaikhs of the lower Gulf he displayed, as we have seen, both a contempt for their independence and an unseemly hunger – all the more unseemly in view of the large territorial acquisitions he had already ingested – for their few lands. Yet in the face of this conduct the British government and its officials, throughout the 1930s and the period of the Second World War and beyond, continued to treat him with an exaggerated deference which was warranted neither by his actual importance nor by his supposed attachment to their interests.

At the height of his many triumphs Ibn Saud found himself confronted in the winter of 1927–8 with a revolt of the most formidable *ikhwan* chieftains, led by Faisal ibn Sultan al-Dawish of the Mutair, who had been growing restive ever since their raids into Iraq and Transjordan had been blocked by British treaties and British arms. Further irritation was caused by the curbing, after the massacre of Taif, of their zeal to cleanse the Hijaz with fire and sword. Many of the *ikhwan* leaders had shown their disgust with Ibn Saud for accepting the title of 'king of the Hijaz' – a title which was, in their eyes, not only a worldly indulgence abhorrent to religion but one besmirched by its former possessors, the heretics of the house of Hashim – by refusing to attend the congress at Riyad in January 1927, at which he was proclaimed 'King of Najd'. Even his assumption of the dignity of imam of the Wahhabiya on the death of his father, Abdur Rahman ibn Faisal, in 1928 failed to mollify them. Ibn Saud, in the view of the *ikhwan*, had had too much truck with infidels, and with the British in particular. He was besotted with accursed innovations, like the motorcar, the telephone, the telegraph and the railway. He had failed to treat the idolators and polytheists of the Hijaz as such *mushrikun* deserved to be treated. He had been similarly remiss, the *ikhwan* zealots charged, in his attitude to the Shii apostates of al-Hasa after its reconquest in 1913.

How the poor Hasawis could have been more harshly treated by their Wahhabi overlords it is hard to imagine. From the time that Hasa fell under Wahhabi domination in the last decade of the eighteenth century its inhabitants had been treated as a subject people, inferior to the Najdis. On the few occasions when they managed to throw off Wahhabi rule, they were made to pay a heavy price for their boldness when the Wahhabis returned. More than half the population of Hasa – most of whom resided in the town of Hufuf and its satellite settlements in the Hasa oasis, or in the coastal towns of Qatif, Uqair, Dammam and Jubail – was Shii Muslim, and the majority of the Sunnis followed the Maliki rite. To the Wahhabis the Shia were objects of especial hatred, and they expressed this hatred in a number of oppressive ways, including the levying upon them of the *jizyah*, or poll tax, which in Islamic law is only to be exacted from Christians, Jews and other 'people of scripture' (*ahl al-kitab*). When Ibn Saud regained Hasa in 1913 the Hasawis were again subjected to persecution – though not enough, to be sure, to slake the *ikhwan*'s thirst for vengeance – a persecution which was not eased until many years later when the discovery of oil in the Eastern Province (as Hasa came to be called after 1950) made it the most valuable part of the Saudi realm. It was the Hasawis' misfortune that only a handful of outsiders knew of their sufferings after 1913; whereas it was the Hijazis' comparative good fortune that the world was watching the conduct of the Wahhabis in the Hijaz in the 1920s.

The *ikhwan* took matters into their own hands towards the close of 1927, raiding into southern Iraq in defiance of the treaties of Muhammarah, Uqair and Bahra, and of the injunctions of Ibn Saud himself. Behind their fierce insubordination lay their deep antipathy for the Shia of Iraq, who comprised half that kingdom's population, and their anger with Ibn Saud for refusing to unleash them in another sack and massacre of Karbala and other odious Shii shrines. When Ibn Saud summoned a congress of tribal chieftains at Riyad in October 1928, the leading *ikhwan* commanders refused to attend. Insubordination had become rebellion, and Ibn Saud was faced with the most dangerous challenge he had yet met, or was to meet, during his reign. He took the field against the rebel chieftains in March 1929 and defeated them at Sahala, not far from Artawiya. Those of the *ikhwan* leaders who did not die by the sword ended their days in prison.

Between 1930 and 1934 Ibn Saud tidied up the south-western borders of his dominions by annexing additional territory along the marches of the Yemen. He then turned his gaze to the one area where he had so far neglected to press his ancestral claims – Qatar and Trucial Oman. The story of his efforts in the 1930s (and later) to make good these claims has already been told. They were inspired in equal measure by his obsession with planting the Saudi flag wherever in the past, and however fleetingly, it may once have flown, and by his determination, after his grant of an oil concession for the eastern portion of his dominions to the Standard Oil Company of California in 1933, to make these dominions as far flung as possible. Oil was struck in Hasa in 1938, and the first consignment was shipped from Ras Tanura a year later, on the eve of the Second World War. The onset of war delayed the development of the fields, and it also drastically reduced the pilgrim traffic to the Hijaz, from which Ibn Saud normally derived a not inconsiderable revenue. Britain came to his aid with an annual subsidy, the payment of which was assumed later by the United States. It did not require a great deal of perspicacity for Ibn Saud to grasp that the United States was bound to exercise a preponderant influence in world affairs after the war, and by the time of his death in November 1953 Saudi Arabia was well on the way to forming that special relationship with the United States which has reached full bloom in our day.

Abdul Aziz ibn Saud's immediate successor, his son, Saud, was not the ruler his father had been. He seemed to be cast rather in the mould of Abdullah ibn Faisal, who had paved the way for the dynasty's eclipse two generations earlier. He did not possess the authority over the tribes or over his family that his father had wielded, nor was he blessed with the grace and ease of manner which might have earned him his people's affection. Yet Ibn Saud had left the ruling house so well entrenched and buttressed in the country that it could afford, for a time at least, the luxury of a lack-lustre monarch. Not only was the dynasty large but it included a number of men of ability and talent. During his lifetime Ibn Saud had drawn the shaikhly families of the major tribes into alliances with his house by the simple expedient of marrying their daughters. While the marriages in most cases lasted only a brief period, they produced an impressive number of progeny. As the Al Saud were already pretty numerous, and philoprogenitive, it is not surprising that today they are to be counted in the thousands rather than the hundreds.

The inner or ruling circle, however, was and has remained much smaller, consisting of Ibn Saud's surviving brothers, of whom there had originally been ten, and his sons, of whom there were at least thirty-seven, from fourteen different mothers. The Al Saud married, in the main, either within the clan itself or into a handful of families which had been so intimately associated with the ruling house since the eighteenth century as to be virtual extensions of it – the Thunaiyan, the Sudairi, the Jiluwi, the *ahl al-shaikh* (the 'family of the shaikh', i.e. the descendants of Ibn Abdul Wahhab). Ibn Saud's mother, Sara, was a Sudairi, and so, too, was the best known of his wives, Hassa bint Ahmad al-Sudairi. Her sons, among them Fahad, Sultan, Turki, Nayif, Salman, Ahmad, are today, as we shall have occasion to notice in due course, the most prominent members of the Saudi government. The mother of Saud ibn Abdul Aziz was of the Al Araiar, the shaikhly family of the Bani Khalid who once ruled Hasa. Faisal ibn Abdul Aziz, Saud's half-brother and eventual successor, was born of a mother from the *ahl al-shaikh*. His half-brother and successor, Khalid, had a Jiluwi mother.

Saud ibn Abdul Aziz reigned for barely a decade, during which time he managed to dissipate the entire fund of political capital which his father had bequeathed to him, as well as to bankrupt the Saudi treasury (despite its continual replenishment by oil revenues every year) through his own extravagance and his inability to curb the avarice of so many of his relatives. While much of the blame for the incompetence and corruption which were the order of the day in Saudi Arabia during Saud's reign could properly be laid at his door, he was not responsible for many of the tribulations which were visited upon him from abroad, the principal source of which was the government of Egypt under the presidency of Gamal Abdul Nasser.

It was obvious from the late 1950s onwards that Nasser had resurrected Mehemet Ali's grand design of making himself master of a federation of Arab states stretching from the Nile to the Euphrates, and thereby to dominate the routes from Europe to India and the Far East. Nasser's successful seizure of the Suez Canal in 1956 put him in possession of what was known a century earlier as the 'overland' route via Egypt and the Red Sea. Two years later the union of Egypt with Syria in the United Arab Republic, and the revolution in Iraq which swept away the Hashimite monarchy and placed a military regime in power in Baghdad, promised to place him in control of the old 'direct' route from the Mediterranean to the head of the Gulf. At that golden moment, in the autumn of 1958, it seemed that Nasser was on the threshold of attaining Mehemet Ali's dream; with the added prize of the Gulf's oil shimmering on the horizon and opening up the breathtaking prospect of both enriching Egypt and holding the West in pawn. Arabia played very much the same part in Nasser's calculations as it did in those of the old viceroy of Egypt, a part that grew in importance after the collapse of the Syro-Egyptian union in 1961 and the estrangement of the military regime in Baghdad from that in Cairo.

King Saud had tried hard in 1958 to destroy the newly formed union of Egypt and Syria by means of bribery and even by attempted assassination. His activities in this direction, combined with his mismanagement at home, brought on a crisis in the government of Saudi Arabia and in the ruling family itself in the spring of 1958, which resulted in Saud's being forced to hand over his powers to his brother, Faisal, in the capacity of prime minister. Despite Saud's hostility to Nasser, the Egyptian leader's strident propagation of Arab nationalist and anti-Western sentiments struck a responsive chord in some Saudi Arabian circles, including the royal family itself, which Nasser did not neglect to exploit by putting agents to work to promote unrest where they could. A group of younger amirs in the Saudi family, led by three of the late Ibn Saud's sons, Talal, Fawwaz and Badr, began agitating for the 'democratization' of the Saudi political system, the introduction of a national assembly and the conversion of the Wahhabi imamate into a constitutional monarchy. When they failed to make any headway against Faisal and the senior members of the family supporting him, they decamped in the summer of 1962, first to the Lebanon and then to Egypt.

When Nasser embarked upon his expedition to the Yemen in the autumn of that year – a project he had had in mind at least since 1958 – he hoped to make use of Talal ibn Abdul Aziz and his brothers to aggravate the disquiet which his intervention in the Yemen was bound to cause in Saudi Arabia. It was all very reminiscent of Mehemet Ali's tactics 130 years earlier. The viceroy of Egypt had undertaken the subjugation of the Yemeni lowlands in the early 1830s before ordering his military commander in the Hijaz to advance into central Arabia and depose the Saudi ruler of the day, Faisal ibn Turki, who was to be replaced by his cousin, the pro-Egyptian Khalid ibn Saud. The objective of Mehemet Ali's army in the Yemen was Aden, possession of which would allow him to command the passage of the Red Sea and the 'overland' route to the

East. He was baulked of his object by the British occupation of Aden in January 1839, just as he was to be denied command of the 'direct' route by the opposition of the major European powers and the British intervention in Syria the following year. In Nasser's scheme the Yemen was to be the forward base for the subversion of British rule in Aden, opening up an avenue of approach through southern Arabia to the oilfields of the Gulf.

It did not quite work out in this way. The Egyptian campaign in the Yemen certainly had its repercussions in both Saudi Arabia and Aden; but in Saudi Arabia it brought about the deposition of Saud ibn Abdul Aziz in November 1964 and his replacement by his far more capable half-brother, Faisal; while the British withdrawal from Aden in 1967 came after Nasser's armies had been decisively defeated by Israel and his political reputation had been dealt a blow from which it never fully recovered. He was saved from utter disgrace, and Egypt from certain bankruptcy, by Faisal's offer in August 1967 to underwrite him financially, the condition for his deliverance being a total Egyptian withdrawal from the Yemen.

Nasser tried one last gambit in Arabia. The Amir Talal ibn Abdul Aziz and his brothers had made their peace with Faisal after his accession and returned home, but the ex-king, Saud, after his forced abdication had taken up residence in Egypt. He had in the two or three years before his abdication affected to espouse the cause of constitutional reform in Saudi Arabia, not, it need hardly be remarked, out of any profound or even shallow conviction of its desirability but simply as a tactical measure in the contest for power with Faisal and his coterie. Now, in the apparent hope that it might help prepare the path for his return, he began preaching the doctrine of reform from exile in Egypt. His activities provoked heated protests from Faisal to Nasser at this abuse of his financial generosity, protests to which the latter responded by declaring his innocence of any collusion with Saud, least of all of casting him in the role of pretender to the Saudi throne. The affair was resolved by the death of the hapless ex-king, long a prey to illness and failing sight, in Athens in February 1969.

For the first two decades after the Second World War Saudi Arabia remained much as it had been before the coming of oil, an enclosed, inward-looking country inhabited by some three and a half million people scattered over thousands of square miles of desert, plateau and mountain range. The greatest concentrations of population were in the Hijaz and Asir in the west, in Hasa in the east, and in the towns and settlements of the Qasim and the central uplands of Najd. Smaller groups dwelt in what were basically oasis towns, like Hail in the north, Najran in the south and Jabrin in the east, while a sizable proportion of the population (perhaps as much as a third) was Bedouin. Most of the inhabitants derived their living from agriculture or pastoralism, much of it at subsistence level. Society was still organized along rigidly tribal lines. Illiteracy was almost total, arts and skills were rudimentary and medical facilities unknown. Communications were mediaeval, so that communities lived largely in isolation from one another and in ignorance of all but their immediate surroundings. Inevitably, as time passed and the oil revenues grew in volume, a measure of benefit began to reach the bulk of the population, usually in the form of larger government subventions for the tribes and the greater availability of imported commodities in the *suq*s. But the Saudi people as a whole remained unaware of the extent of the riches from oil being enjoyed by the ruling house, and of the ways in which those riches were being squandered.

Foreign influences, the inescapable accompaniment of the new oil wealth, touched the mass of the Saudi people hardly at all. These influences were only present to any appreciable degree in the coastal towns adjacent to the Hasa oilfields and, on the other side of the peninsula, at Jiddah, the chief port of the Hijaz. Jiddah was a more cosmopolitan town than any in Saudi Arabia: it had long been the port of entry for pilgrims to the holy cities as well as the site of foreign trading houses and diplomatic missions. Consequently the surge of mercantile activity and government expenditure which accompanied the expansion of oil production disturbed its inhabitants less than it would have disturbed those of the inland towns. The American and European communities were kept apart from the general population and away from the interior, being confined in the main to Jiddah and the Hasa hinterland. There were, however, a goodly number of Egyptians in the country, and smaller groups of Palestinians, Syrians and Lebanese, who had been engaged to staff the embryo educational system and ministries, as well as to provide the technical and professional services that the Saudis could not provide for themselves. Some of these newcomers had brought with them the gospel of Nasserism – of Arab nationalism, republicanism and socialism – although they had to be discreet almost to the point of muteness in propagating it. Those who were not, who through zealotry or on the orders of Cairo exercised a prerogative which they did not enjoy in their own country, viz. that of voicing alien political thoughts, were promptly deported. The lesson was quickly learned, and most of the Egyptians confined themselves to their work, pocketed their salaries and saw their contracts out. But in case they should chance to forget that they were in the country on sufferance, the Saudi authorities would occasionally expel numbers of them at a moment's notice and without explanation.

The presence of these *émigrés*, then, did little to disturb the prevailing political order. Power remained firmly in the hands of the Al Saud and their intimates. The country had no constitution; or, rather, its constitution was said to be the Koran. Unlike the rulers of Kuwait and Bahrain, the Al Saud made no gesture in the direction of the devolution of power or the broadening of the basis of government through the establishment of representative political institutions. There was no reason why they should have done so. The Saudi people knew no other system of government than the one they had, which in their eyes was ordained by God and sustained by time and tradition. It would never have occurred to them, or to their rulers, that it should be altered. So, too, with the religious establishment, the *ulama* and *qadis*, who regarded it as their solemn duty to support the authority both of the king in his capacity as imam of the Wahhabiya and of his house; while in return the house of Saud upheld the primacy of Islam in the state and gave heed to the pronouncements of the *ulama* where these did not intrude upon matters of high policy or personal indulgence. Obedience to the commands of God and compliance with the edicts of the king-imam were held by the *ulama* to be inseparable; and so the particular body of religious functionaries, to whom the duty of keeping the populace to the proper observance of its spiritual and moral obligations was delegated (the felicitously named 'Committee for the Commendation of Virtue and the Condemnation of Vice') was as much an arm of the state as it was the rod of the Almighty. Throughout the land the private as well as the public lives of the citizenry came under the scrutiny of the Committee's agents, the *mutawiyah*, who were quick to discipline any backsliders and to demand that the Koranic penalties be exacted for any transgressions of the severe Hanbali rite. Together with the myriad informers and spies who infested the country, the *mutawiyah* constituted a network of surveillance which was of inestimable value to the regime in detecting and suppressing discontent.

Riyad was and still is – for everything that has just been said of Saudi Arabia in the years up to the late 1960s remains true, *mutatis mutandis*, today – the sole source of authority. Centralization is the keynote of government, and the governors of the towns and provinces are all drawn from the ranks of the Al Saud or closely associated noble families like the Jiluwis and the Sudairis. Thus, for example, one son of Ibn Saud, Salman, is governor of Riyad, another son, Abdul Muhsin, is governor of Madina, a son of the late King Faisal, Khalid, is governor of the Asir, while the governorship of Hasa is virtually a hereditary office in the Jiluwi family. As with the urban and provincial governorships, so also with the ministries which have grown up over the years. At the time of writing, Fahad ibn Abdul Aziz, the heir apparent, was deputy prime minister (King Khalid held the premiership); his half-brother, Abdullah ibn Abdul Aziz, the commander of the National Guard, was second deputy prime minister (and, presumably, second in line for the throne). A brother of Fahad, Sultan, was minister of defence, and another brother, Turki, deputy minister. Nayif ibn Abdul Aziz was minister of the interior and Saud ibn Faisal, a son of the late king, minister of foreign affairs. Only two of the important ministerial portfolios were held by non-members of the ruling family – the ministry of petroleum and mineral resources by Shaikh Ahmad Zaki al-Yamani, and the ministry of finance by Shaikh Muhammad Aba al-Khail, whose family seat is at Buraida in the Qasim. The Aba al-Khail figured prominently in the history of Najd and the Qasim in the eighteenth and nineteenth centuries, usually as Saudi loyalists, although in the late nineteenth century they became Rashidi partisans.

The Amirs Fahad, Sultan, Turki, Nayif and Salman ibn Abdul Aziz are all uterine brothers, the sons of Hassa bint Ahmad al-Sudairi, Ibn Saud's senior wife. Together with two other uterine brothers (Ahmad, the deputy governor of Mecca, and Sattan, the deputy governor of Riyad) they make up the reputedly indivisible clique, the 'Sudairi Seven'. The eldest surviving son of Ibn Saud, Muhammad, is a uterine brother of King Khalid (their mother was a Jiluwi). He was twice passed over for the succession – once at the time of Faisal's accession, and again at Khalid's – reputedly because of his unstable character and irascible disposition. How much personal rivalry and factionalism exists within the upper ranks of the Al Saud it is impossible to say, since all one has to go on is rumour. Some members, in particular Abdullah, the second deputy prime minister, whose mother was of the Shammar tribe, are said to resent the ascendancy of the Sudairi fraternity. It may well be so. The history of the Al Saud is riddled with feuds, conspiracies, betrayals, violent deaths and the exploits of pretenders, a fact largely obscured by the relative absence of dynastic troubles during Ibn Saud's long reign. What has occurred within the family in the years since his death – events like the dethronement of Saud in 1964, the defection of Talal and his supporters to Egypt, the assassination of Faisal – has been more in keeping with the past conduct of the dynasty.

For all their quarrelsome and sanguinary proclivities, however, the Al Saud have shown, and still show, a remarkable resilience in times of adversity, along with a redoubtable capacity for self-preservation and cohesion, qualities which were much in evidence at the time of Faisal's assassination by one of his nephews, Faisal ibn Musaid, in March 1975. The comparatively minor repercussions that the crime occasioned in the kingdom were probably due as much to the solidarity displayed by the ruling house as they were to the absence of any subsequent signs that the murder was the product of a political conspiracy. The assassin's father, Musaid ibn Abdul Aziz, was an inoffensive and relatively obscure personage, a son of Ibn Saud and the uterine brother of Abdul Muhsin, the governor of Madina. From the limited information that reached the outside world about the assassin, it would seem that he was a somewhat unbalanced as well as over-indulged young man, whose mind may have become further disturbed by his exposure to radical political notions while a student in the United States and as an *habitué* of Beirut's political *demi-monde*. There was said to be a streak of insanity in his family: his elder brother, a devout Wahhabi, had been killed while leading a violent demonstration against the opening of a television station in Riyad. Faisal ibn Musaid's mother was of the house of Rashid which Ibn Saud had overthrown in 1921. He himself was engaged to be married to a daughter of the late King Saud and was said to have been incensed by King Faisal's refusal to increase his financial allowance to enable him to meet his matrimonial obligations. Yet despite these considerations, and notwithstanding the dissatisfaction felt by King Saud's family over the way in which they have been pushed into the background since his deposition, it seems in all probability that Faisal ibn Musaid acted alone and primarily out of a desire for vengeance.

Following the immense increase in her oil revenues after the oil-price rises of 1973–4, Saudi Arabia embarked upon much the same carnival of consumption and construction as did the minor oil states of the Gulf. As in their case, the massive expenditures and grandiose undertakings of the Saudi government have been exhaustively chronicled by the world's press – with much the same expressions of awe and deference as those with which the native chroniclers of Najd were wont, in years gone by, to celebrate the exploits of the house of Saud. An economic development plan had originally been introduced by the late Faisal ibn Abdul Aziz in the autumn of 1970. It was to be implemented within five years and to cost 4,100 million riyals ($911 million). Although a shade ambitious, the plan was not entirely divorced from the realities of Saudi Arabian society or the limitations of its native economy. Improvements were to be effected in agriculture, education, medicine and communications, the country's defences were to be strengthened and a start was to be made with industrialization. Some progress had been made towards achieving these ends by the time the five years were up, but too many of the funds which had been expended (aside from the large sums spent on arms and military equipment) had gone on urban construction of an unproductive kind – palaces, hotels, office blocks, apartment buildings and so forth – while industrial investment had been limited to petro-chemical works and a steel mill, the iron ore for which had to be brought half-way around the world.

Not in the least deterred by this experience, and captivated by the vision of apparently limitless sums of money at its disposal in the years ahead, the Saudi government announced in the latter half of 1975 the inauguration of a second five-year plan of awe-inspiring dimensions. Its cost would be 498,000 million riyals ($142,000 million), and it was intended to bring Saudi Arabia with one gigantic leap into the last quarter of the twentieth century. At the heart of this prodigious enterprise – conceived with the disinterested guidance of the Saudi government's American consultants – would be two huge industrial complexes located respectively at Yanbu, a small port on the Red Sea, and at Jubail, a fishing village on the Gulf coast. Jubail was to become a city of 175,000 souls, with oil refineries, petro-chemical plants and a steel mill with an eventual productive capacity of 5,000,000 tons per annum, the ore being supplied from deposits recently discovered in the Wadi Fatima, near Jiddah. Jubail was also to be developed as a major port, with a loading jetty that would stretch some five to seven miles out into the Gulf. Near by a huge new airport was to be constructed at a cost of some $2–3,000 million. A comparable future was

planned for Yanbu, whose population was to be expanded to 115,000 souls.
Other airports on an impressive scale were to be constructed elsewhere,
including one at Jiddah to handle the pilgrim traffic. When completed, it
would be the largest in the world. An aluminium smelter, a car-assembly plant,
a dozen desalination and electric power installations and several cement factories were also to be built. Pride of place, however, was given to the construction of an extensive gas-gathering system, which would provide the abundance
of energy upon which the industrialization of Yanbu and Jubail was projected.
As if all this were not enough, it was also announced that some 270,000 new
housing units, 2,000 new schools and 11,500 new hospital beds were to be
constructed by 1980.

What on earth, one might well ask, had these technological marvels, which it
was airily proposed to erect upon the desert sands at a cost of milliards of
dollars, to do with the people of Saudi Arabia, most of whom were still living
much as their forebears had lived for a thousand years previously, and hardly
one of whom over the age of twenty-five or thirty could read or write? The
answer, of course, is very little. It was all part of the 'numbers game' which we
have encountered in the Gulf states, the purpose of which is to provide
emotional and intellectual catharsis. Just how far removed are the Al Saud's
industrial fantasies from the people they rule may be judged from the fact that
while half the working population of the country is engaged in agriculture and
pastoralism, these pursuits were allocated a mere 0.8 per cent of the development programme's budget. The euphoria was shortly to be dissipated. By the
spring of 1977, barely eighteen months after the programme had been
unveiled, the Saudi government was forced to prune it drastically. Inflation,
incompetence, corruption and the sheer multiplicity of projects, along with the
physical and technical difficulties encountered by foreign construction firms
working in Saudi Arabia, had all helped to send costs soaring. So, too, had the
loss of financial control over the development programme, with different
factions in the royal family and the ministries committing and spending funds
as they wished. Millions, perhaps milliards, of dollars literally went missing,
although as we shall see later, much of the money may have been siphoned off
for other objects. By the early months of 1977 it was reckoned that the
programme would require twice the original sum estimated for its implementation, some $56,800 million a year instead of $28,400 million. Oil revenues were
simply not running at that level, so the axe had to fall. The planned aluminium
smelter was cancelled, the car-assembly plant was cancelled, five desalination
and electric power installations were cancelled, and the steel mill was scaled
down to a projected productive capacity of 300,000 tons per annum instead of
5,000,000, with the possibility that it might not even be completed. The cost of
the elaborate gas-gathering system was now estimated at four times the original
figure, and its completion date at 1985 instead of 1979, a revision sobering
enough to make potential foreign participants in the venture back hurriedly

away. With the gas-gathering project in jeopardy, the whole ambitious scheme for the industrialization of Yanbu and Jubail fell under a cloud.

What these retrenchments signify at one level is that the Saudi government has been forced to acknowledge the inescapable fact that the cost of constructing anything in Saudi Arabia is three or four times what it would be in Europe or North America, a consideration which of itself (without introducing the question of future operating costs) throws doubt upon the ability of any Saudi Arabian industrial enterprise to compete on economic terms with similar enterprises abroad. The acknowledgement, however, has not been made with good grace, nor have the Saudis been weaned from their attachment to technological ventures on a grand and impressive scale. Instead, the realization of the financial risks inherent in such ventures, especially those of uneconomic competition with similar enterprises in the industrial world and, in the case of the petro-chemical industry, of saturating the market, has led the Saudi government to try to minimize or spread the risks by putting pressure upon oil companies and large foreign industrial firms operating in Saudi Arabia to participate in these ventures. As a means of securing their compliance, the Saudis have shadowed forth the threat of a possible interruption of oil supplies at some time.

Saudi Arabia's targets for the provision of educational and medical services under the second five-year plan are as ambitious as those for the country's industrial development. According to the Saudi government's own figures, there were in 1970 some 370,000 pupils in primary schools, another 40–50,000 in secondary schools, and a few thousand more in the universities at Riyad and Madina and the technical colleges at Dhahran and Jiddah, which were soon to be elevated to the status of universities. By the time of the expiration of the first five-year plan in 1975 (again according to the Saudi government) the number of pupils in primary schools had risen to 615,900 (214,600 of them girls), in secondary schools to 150,200 (45,800 of them girls), and in higher education to 11,900. Under the second five-year plan this total of 778,000 pupils is to be almost doubled by 1980 – to 1,030,900 (including 353,400 girls) in primary schools, 305,700 (including 103,900 girls) in secondary schools, and 31,200 in higher education. If an interim report put out by the Saudi government in January 1978 is to be believed, remarkable progress has already been achieved in the implementation of the educational plan, to wit, 928,000 students in primary and secondary schools, 23,000 in the country's six universities (two at Riyad and one each at Madina, Jiddah, Dhahran and Dammam), and another 20,000 at educational institutions abroad – all this from a population of perhaps three and a half million souls.

The Saudi government is not alone in being impressed by its own accomplishments. A special supplement on Saudi Arabia put out by the *International Herald Tribune* in February 1978 carried an ecstatic description of the marvels being performed by the University of Petroleum and Minerals at

Dhahran, which began life as a technical school started by the Arabian American Oil Company. 'Sleek concrete towers and serene rows of Islamic arches rising from the sands mark UPM, Saudi Arabia's temple of higher education', the report starts off, and it goes on to list, with the respect that such matters naturally call forth, the benefits to which the students are entitled – free tuition, meals, accommodation, medical services and air fares, in addition to a monthly stipend and bonuses for obtaining good marks in their courses. Only the most advanced pedagogical methods are employed, the report emphasizes, quoting one of the institution's professors. 'We tap data bases. If we are working on structural research, we can tap by telex into a computer at Lockheed in California, search the departments there and answer problems quickly.' Such techniques come naturally, the report goes on to remark, to Saudi Arabs.

The greenest freshman delights in using the school's own IBM 370/158 computer and quickly becomes familiar with the remote processing terminals and other equipment in the data processing center. A $91 million building under construction will house projects in all fields of energy research under the direction of Dr William Pickering, the ex-chief of the U.S. Viking probes to Mars.

As if these costly baubles for the intellectual diversion of the students were not enough, lavish provision has also been made for their physical recreation.

The latest innovation in an already remarkably equipped physical education department is a $430,000 environmental chamber where 17 full-time European coaches of as many different sports plan to subject their young protégés to varied humidities, temperatures and simulated altitudes. 'This way, if we have a team which is going to play in Switzerland, we can put them in the chamber and freeze them for three or four weeks,' says the physical education director.

While such wide-eyed reportage may have some entertainment value, it tells us nothing of the nature and quality of the education in general being received by the hundreds of thousands of children at school in Saudi Arabia – if, indeed, they are at school. Since Saudi Arabia cannot provide teachers of her own, the schools have to be staffed by teachers from abroad. Most of those in Saudi schools are Egyptians, who come on short-term contracts and return home after three or four years. Apart from the question-mark that hangs over the academic ability and professional competence of the teachers themselves, the lack of continuity inherent in this arrangement means that the standard of education provided must be less than adequate. There are considerable restrictions, also, upon what can be taught in the schools. The religious establishment frowns upon secular education as it frowns upon most innovations, and its tentacles reach into every classroom. Even the glowing report just cited on the university at Dhahran noted, *en passant*, 'Textbooks are banned from mentioning Darwin's theory of evolution, anthropological photos of bare-breasted Pacific islanders are covered with black ink.' The ruling house is itself in two minds about the desirability of education for its subjects. On the one hand it acknowledges the country's need for technicians and clerks, and the desirability of showing an enlightened countenance to the world. On the other hand, it is suspicious of the tendency of secular education to arouse the political consciousness of the young. Considerable emphasis is placed, there-fore, upon the religious content of what is taught in the schools, to the extent that, for the majority of pupils, the instruction they receive is barely distin-guishable from that imparted in Koranic schools in the past.

Foreign observers are inclined to make much of the segregation of male and female pupils into separate schools, and to criticize it as both a reflection of the inferior status accorded women in Saudi Arabian society and a wasteful dupli-cation of educational resources. It is difficult to see the logic in such criticism. Separate schooling for girls and boys is hardly a rarity in the Western world – or anywhere around the globe, for that matter – nor does it involve much, if it involves any, duplication of resources. This is also true of higher education, where the only duplication of any consequence that arises is in the provision of libraries and expensive scientific equipment. The position and treatment of women in Saudi Arabia is a separate question. Yet here again, distressing though the lowly status and legal disabilities of Saudi Arabian women may appear to Western eyes, and regrettable though the waste of the talents of the educated among them may be (through their exclusion from public life and most forms of employment), the right of a society to raise its young in the way it sees fit is undeniable. What is more pertinent to any inquiry into education in Saudi Arabia is, as remarked already, the quality of this education, and the available indications are that it is not good at any level. The College (now University) of Petroleum and Minerals at Dhahran, for instance, the longest-established as well as the best of the institutions of higher learning, was always considered to be well below the standard of similar colleges in Europe and North America, and it is doubtful whether the situation has altered – whatever glutinous fudge Western reporters may choose to write about it. A comparable doubt extends to the standard of education being attained by the 20,000 or so Saudi Arabians studying abroad, the great majority of them in the United States. While a small proportion of these may be enrolled in Ivy League colleges or the major state universities, the greatest number is to be found in institutions of lesser academic distinction. Wherever they may be, moreover, a certain indulgence is extended to them in the matter of scholastic attainment, so that the qualifications with which they proudly return home are of question-able value.

What has been said of education in Saudi Arabia applies *pari passu* to the country's medical services. Twenty years ago these did not exist. The only doctors were those in attendance upon the royal family, the foreign community and the richer merchants of Jiddah. The only hospital deserving of the name was that operated by ARAMCO at Dhahran. Under the current five-year plan dozens of hospitals are to be built, to a total of 11,400 beds; the number of medical clinics is to be doubled to over 452; and the ratio of doctors is to be increased to one to every 357 inhabitants, double the figure for Great Britain. How much of this has been achieved is uncertain. Few Saudi Arabian doctors have as yet been trained, and nearly all of them have been absorbed into the bureaucracy. Most of the doctors in the country, perhaps some 2,500 in number, are foreigners, and the highest proportion of these are Egyptians. The King Faisal Memorial Hospital lately built at Riyad, the costliest and most lavishly furnished hospital of its size in the world, is operated by foreigners and serves only a privileged segment of Saudi Arabian society. How many less opulent hospitals and clinics have been built, and what improvements there have been in medical care for the mass of the population, remains a mystery.

Saudi Arabia not only refuses to open its doors very widely to Western newspaper correspondents, but it keeps them firmly shut against independent scholars and travellers – against all, in fact, who do not come to trade or sell their skills. What little news seeps out of the country concerns events in Riyad or Jiddah, Dhahran or Dammam. Nothing is heard of life in Buraida or Anaiza, Shaqra or Russ or elsewhere in the Qasim; nothing of Hail and Jabal Shammar, of Jabrin and the Dahana; nothing of Asir in the south or the Wadi Sirhan in the north; little even of Mecca and Madina. It is as if a shroud of silence lies over the greater part of the country. Only at the edges, on the Gulf coast and at Jiddah, is there to be heard a slight sound – the faint and fitful chatter of typewriters as visiting journalists dutifully transcribe what the spokesmen of the Saudi government have seen fit to tell them.

The ambivalence manifest in the Saudi regime's attitude to secular education is shared by the recipients of this education. Like other Arabs and Muslims – indeed, like most Asiatic peoples, whatever their religion – the Saudi Arab is convinced of the superiority of his own culture over that of the West and of the industrial world in general. He believes that he can acquire and use whatever the West has to offer in the way of material goods and technological methods, and at the same time reject the culture which produced them. It is, quite literally, incomprehensible to him that the products and skills of the West are inseparable, in their genesis and development, from the West's empirical and scientific traditions; from its historical experience, its modes of thought, its ethical values; from the Graeco-Roman and Christian-Judaic origins of its civilization; from its philosophical principles and systems, Socratic, Cartesian, Kantian or Hegelian – from everything, in fact, that has gone to shape the Western mind and the way in which it regards the universe and man's place in it. The result is that in Saudi Arabia today, in a society which before the second half of this century had been acquainted with only the most rudimentary mechanical aids to labour, the educated and semi-educated members of the population take it for granted that the most advanced technology in the history of mankind is at their disposal for the mere asking – to serve their needs and sustain them in their ease without their being required to understand, let alone to adapt to, any of the philosophical attitudes and cultural values which brought this technology into being.

There is little desire among the thousands of Saudi Arab students in the secondary schools or universities for technical or vocational training, still less for careers as veterinarians or agriculturists. Of the 2,900 students at Riyad University in 1970 only ninety were studying agriculture, and there is no reason to believe that the proportion is any greater today. The only professional occupations that Saudis consider suitable to their station are medicine and engineering: perhaps a quarter of Saudis who have been educated abroad have qualified in these fields. Too many of these, however, tend to end up within a short time in administrative posts in the bureaucracy, so that the benefit to the country of their training is minimal. As for the rest, whether they have attended universities at home or abroad, the subjects they elect to study are mostly the social sciences, which are of scant use in a country at Saudi Arabia's stage of development. Like their fellows in the secondary schools, Saudi university students value education primarily as a means of obtaining government employment. They have little urge to engage in productive work requiring technical skills. The life of the bureaucratic *flâneur* is their ideal. Although the 'drop-out' rate at the Saudi universities and the secondary schools alike is high, failure does not close the doors of the bureaucracy to those whose ambition it is to secure remunerative employment as government clerks, functionaries and administrators, and thereby lead a life of dignified indolence.

The aversion to sustained exertion is by no means confined to the multitudinous ranks of Saudi officialdom. The true Saudi cultivator of the soil, however mean his condition, shuns the more menial tasks, which in the past were performed by slaves – of whom there were anything from 500,000 to 750,000 in the country – and which are performed today by emancipated slaves or poverty-stricken Yemenis. The Bedouin will not soil his hands with work he considers beneath him. He is not greatly interested in improving the health and care of his flocks and herds, but would rather wander off to the towns or oilfields in search of diversion or temporary employment. Almost the only non-traditional pursuit he considers worthy of his station in life is driving cars or trucks. Servicing them is another matter, best left to lesser beings. In due course, when he feels he has had his fill of the sophisticated delights of Riyad or Dhahran, he returns to his tribal *dirah*. Most of the hard manual work involved in the welter of construction going on in Saudi Arabia is done by imported labourers, mostly Yemenis, of whom there are anything from 250,000 to 750,000 in the country, according to the available estimates. There are also about 100,000 Pakistanis, many of them Baluchis, employed as labourers and skilled tradesmen, and some 200,000 Egyptians, most of them working as teachers or clerks. Other northern Arabs are not present in large numbers since the regime regards them, and especially the Palestinians, with suspicion.

Nearly all the technical, architectural and engineering skills that the Saudis require at the present time are supplied by foreigners – by several thousand 'white coolies' and by several more thousand Pakistanis and northern Arabs. The winds of Paradise are assuredly blowing through Saudi Arabia today, if not in quite the way that the old *ikhwan* once envisaged.

If the first pillar of the Saudi state has been the Wahhabi religious movement, the second has been the Arabian American Oil Company. Virtually from the day in 1933 when the first of ARAMCO's four parent companies, Standard Oil of California, obtained a sixty-year concession for the Eastern Province, the company has served the house of Saud as guide, confidant, tutor, counsellor, emissary, advocate, steward and factotum. Indeed, it is doubtful whether in the entire history of Western enterprise in the East, even the heyday of the English East India Company, a great commercial corporation has so placed itself at the service of a foreign state as ARAMCO has done in Saudi Arabia. Without its loyal and devoted assistance the kingdom would certainly not be what it is today.

Standard Oil of California operated its concession through an affiliate, the California Arabian Standard Oil Company (CASOC), to which the Texas Oil Company (Texaco) was admitted as an equal partner in 1936. As mentioned earlier, oil was discovered in 1938 and the first shipment was loaded at Ras Tanura in May 1939. The war brought about a run-down of operations, and as it progressed it also caused CASOC a certain amount of apprehension about its own future. Ibn Saud was not only indebted to Britain for a substantial loan she had made him but he was also heavily reliant upon the British subsidy which had been paid to him since the early days of the war to keep the Saudi Arabian economy afloat. CASOC feared that this reliance might correspondingly incline Ibn Saud to invite the British to participate in the exploitation of Saudi Arabia's oil, perhaps even to abrogate CASOC's concession and transfer it, in part at least, to a British-controlled oil company. To counter this imagined danger, CASOC used every opportunity it could to undermine Britain's standing at Ibn Saud's court, even to the extent of suggesting that the subsidy from Britain was in reality American money paid through the medium of the British exchequer.

Whispered innuendoes about British guile, however, were not considered sufficiently effective to safeguard CASOC's future, so the company turned to Washington and the State Department for help. The animosity borne by the Roosevelt administration for the British empire in Asia was paralleled by the irritation felt by the State Department at Britain's political ascendancy in the Middle East. The twin sentiments found expression in a joint determination to undermine Britain's rule in the East. An approach by CASOC to the administration and the State Department for aid was sympathetically received by those responsible for American policy towards Saudi Arabia, and in February 1943 the Saudi kingdom was made eligible for lend-lease assistance – despite the legal requirement that recipients of such assistance should be active belligerents on the Allied side. The funds which subsequently flowed into Ibn Saud's coffers made the continuance of the British subsidy unnecessary, and CASOC's fears of being outflanked by British oil diplomacy were stilled.

The company, which renamed itself in January 1944 the Arabian American Oil Company, perhaps in acknowledgement of a subtle shift in its political orientation, had a few bad moments during the war as a result of its soliciting of lend-lease funds for its Saudi clients. For a time in 1943 it seemed as though the price of this aid might be the participation of the United States government in its oil concession, perhaps even as a controlling partner. No sooner had this spectre been banished by the invocation of the American capitalist ethos than another apparition took its place in the shape of a proposal for the construction, under the auspices of the United States government, of an oil pipeline from the eastern region of Saudi Arabia to the Mediterranean. Its cost was to be borne in the first instance by the United States government and repaid over a twenty-five-year period by ARAMCO. The company would also remain under an additional obligation to set aside 20 per cent of its oil reserves for the use of the United States armed forces. ARAMCO successfully evaded the government's embrace, and went on to build the Trans-Arabian Pipeline (TAPline) itself between 1947 and 1951. It also enlarged its shareholding by taking in Standard Oil of New Jersey (Esso) and Socony-Vacuum (afterwards Mobil) as partners in 1947–8, the former with a 30 per cent interest, the latter with 10 per cent.

From its earliest days in Saudi Arabia ARAMCO had set out to be a model company. It not only made itself responsible for such obvious matters as the training, safety, health, housing and proper remuneration of its workers, but it extended its responsibility to the people of Hasa in general. It built and maintained a modern road network; it encouraged local commercial enterprise by assisting in the establishment of service industries to meet its own many needs; it improved the general health of the population of Hasa by eradicating malaria and reducing the incidence of fly-borne and water-borne diseases; and it developed a comprehensive system of hospitals, clinics and dispensaries to care not just for its own workers and their families but for thousands of Hasawis as well. By the mid-1960s, in fact, ARAMCO was spending more on hospitals and health programmes to gratify the Saudi authorities than it was on oil exploration. The company also helped to plan or execute a miscellany of public works projects for the Saudi government, including irrigation schemes, wireless stations, airports, water pipelines and the construction of modern docks and jetties at Dammam and Jiddah. When Ibn Saud in 1947 expressed his desire for a railway to be laid from the Gulf coast at Dammam to Riyad, 350 miles away in the interior, ARAMCO had one built, even though it was a highly uneconomic venture.

Towards the Saudi government ARAMCO consistently pursued what a leading historian of the Middle-Eastern oil industry has categorized as 'a policy of complacent liberality, of concession in preference to bargaining, in the face of successive and various government demands'.* When the Saudis in 1950 demanded, in place of the fixed royalty they were receiving on oil production, a 50 per cent share of the company's profits, such as the Venezuelan government had successfully negotiated with the oil companies operating in its territory only a short time previously, ARAMCO hastened to accommodate them. Although ARAMCO's original and supplementary concessionary agreements of 1933 and 1939 had specifically exempted it from the obligation to pay income tax to the Saudi government, it now accepted such an obligation and agreed to pay the Saudi government (in addition to the royalty on every barrel of oil produced) income tax to the amount required to bring the government's total receipts up to one-half of the company's operating profits. What eased the way to ARAMCO's acceptance of this formula was the agreement of the United States government to the classification of these extra payments as foreign income tax, not as a distribution of profits, thereby enabling the company to offset the payments against its income tax liabilities in the United States. As might be imagined, the US Treasury lost a great deal of revenue in the next twenty-five years, more, in fact, than would appear at first sight; for the Saudis soon insisted that ARAMCO should sell its oil at a publicly fixed price, a demand which led to the introduction of the device of the 'posted price', a price which, from 1958 onwards, was appreciably higher than the actual selling price. Income tax payments to the Saudi government, however, were calculated on the basis of the posted price, so that they remained on the whole artificially inflated, with a corresponding further loss of revenue to the US Treasury.

Renewed demands by the Saudi government led in 1952 to the appointment of Saudi directors to the board of ARAMCO, and to the transfer of the company's headquarters from New York to Dhahran. Now ARAMCO could truly describe itself, as its public relations department was quick to do, as a Saudi Arabian company, situated in Saudi Arabia and working for the benefit of Saudi Arabia. There was a little more substance to the claim – for all that it passed over the obvious financial reasons why ARAMCO's parent companies were involved in Arabia in the first place – than is usually the case with such flummery. The rationale behind the United States government's grant of tax relief to ARAMCO in respect of the income tax it paid to Saudi Arabia was that the revenues lost to the US Treasury would probably have been paid out to Saudi Arabia, in any case, in the form of foreign aid. From the point of view of the State Department the advantage in the arrangement made with ARAMCO was that it allowed Saudi Arabia to be subsidized without the necessity of first obtaining Congressional approval, as was normally the practice in the allocation of foreign aid.

* S. H. Longrigg, *Oil in the Middle East*, p. 209.

The function of surrogate banker, however, was not the only one the State Department delegated to ARAMCO. To all intents and purposes it also resigned – whether it was fully aware of it or not is beside the point – the conduct of American relations with Saudi Arabia into the company's keeping. Naturally ARAMCO saw this delegation as only logical and fitting, since its management firmly believed that there was a broad coincidence of interests between ARAMCO and Saudi Arabia, between Saudi Arabia and the United States, and between the United States government and American oil companies operating in the Middle East. It was far from being alone in holding this view. Since as far back as the inter-war years there had existed a general consensus of opinion in those governmental, commercial and philanthropic circles in the United States which had close connexions with the Middle East that the sooner Britain and France were made to abandon their residual positions in the region the better it would be for all concerned – for the West as well as for the Middle East. The doctrine – for it was no less than an article of faith – was posited upon two assumptions: the first, that the days of the European empires were numbered anyway, and the West as a whole could only retain some positive influence in this vital strategic area by recognizing the force of Arab nationalism and fostering the national independence of the Arab countries; the second, that the demise of British and French power in the region would open up new and profitable avenues to American commerce – not least to American oil companies.

It was a doctrine to which the State Department was a fervent subscriber – as was only natural, since it had been one of its begetters. Well before the doctrine found its most triumphant expression in the humiliation of British and French arms at Suez in 1956, the State Department had applied it with enthusiasm to the Arabian peninsula, and it continued to do so, with undiminished ardour, in the years afterwards. Writing in 1966, in the light of his experiences as commander of the United Nations observer force in the Yemen during the civil war, Major-General Carl von Horn observed of the State Department's policy: 'Basically, I had the impression that, under a cloak of a benefactor and supporter of national aspirations in the Middle East, there was the desire to cut the throat of British influence in the Persian Gulf.' Certainly this was true of ARAMCO, and it had been ever since the day that the company began to see the presence of Britain in Arabia as an obstacle to the realization of its own ambitions in the peninsula. Over the years it had developed an almost obsessive resentment of Britain's special treaty relationship with the littoral shaikhdoms of eastern Arabia, and of her long and intimate connexion with the sultanate of Oman. There were even some in the senior ranks of ARAMCO (those who had constituted themselves, as it were, the company's *ikhwan*) who wanted to re-write the historical record, so as to obliterate all trace of Britain's past relations with the Gulf.

Behind the resentment, however, lay down-to-earth commercial considerations as well as doctrinaire convictions. The original oil concession granted to ARAMCO was, according to the proclamation issued by Ibn Saud in 1933, for the eastern portion of the Saudi kingdom, the limits of which had not at that time been defined. By the terms of both the 1933 concessionary agreement and the supplementary agreement of 1939, ARAMCO was required to surrender in stages its rights to those parts of its concessionary area which it had not explored or which it did not intend to develop. It was obviously in the company's interest, therefore, that it should survey within the period available to it those parts of its concessionary area where the possibility of oil being found seemed strongest, and that the limits of the concessionary area itself should be drawn as widely as possible. These two considerations inevitably led ARAMCO at the end of the Second World War to direct its attention southwards and eastwards, beyond the Jafurah desert to the great uncharted expanse of the Rub al-Khali and the coastal region to the north, where the frontier of Saudi Arabia was undefined.

Whether it was at the prompting of ARAMCO that the Saudi government resurrected and reasserted its territorial claims after 1945, or whether ARAMCO's impatience to extend its exploratory operations to the coast and hinterland east of Qatar merely coincided with the reawakening of Ibn Saud's old ambition to extend his rule over the territory in question, the mutuality of interests was obvious. Moreover, just as twenty years earlier Ibn Saud had reasoned that the termination of the subsidy paid to him by Britain during and after the First World War freed his hands for the conquest of the Hijaz, so the replacement of the British subsidy paid him during the Second World War by financial aid from the United States similarly freed him, he believed, from his obligation under the Treaty of Jiddah of 1927 to respect the integrity of Qatar and the Trucial Shaikhdoms. He had also decided by this time – or perhaps it would be more accurate to say that his son, Faisal, to whom he had largely entrusted the conduct of the kingdom's foreign relations, had decided – that the United States would be a stronger as well as a more tractable and accommodating ally in the post-war world than Britain, whose star was on the wane and whose interests, especially in Arabia and the Gulf, did not always coincide with those of Saudi Arabia. It scarcely needs to be said that he was strongly encouraged in this way of thinking by senior officials in ARAMCO, motivated by the considerations of self-interest and hostility to the British presence in the Gulf just noted.

The hand and, on occasions, the countenance of ARAMCO were all too clearly visible throughout the successive stages of the frontier dispute from 1949 onwards. No one in the company appeared to experience any qualms – at least none were expressed publicly – about the morality or wisdom of its co-operation with the Saudi government, even when the latter, as recounted earlier, showed its contempt for the process of arbitration (and indeed for legal restraints of any kind) by engaging in large-scale gun-running, bribery, subversion and attempted assassination. Nor did any senior official of ARAMCO evince the slightest doubt in public about the propriety of the company's involvement in an attempt to despoil the shaikhdom of Abu Dhabi of the greater part of its territory, to impair the concessionary rights of the Iraq Petroleum Company, British Petroleum and the Compagnie Française des Pétroles, and to injure the political interests in the Gulf of the United States' principal ally. That ARAMCO felt itself free to act in such cavalier and unprincipled fashion was a measure not only of the extent to which the State Department had abdicated its responsibility for the conduct of American relations with Saudi Arabia, but also of the confidence ARAMCO reposed in the effectiveness of its influence in Washington.

The confidence was not unfounded. When Sir Anthony Eden, the British prime minister, visited Washington in January 1956 for consultations with President Eisenhower, he found that the version of the origins and course of the frontier dispute that ARAMCO had circulated in the United States had been swallowed, hook, line and sinker, by the American administration. John Foster Dulles, the secretary of state, had some weeks earlier told both the Netherlands and the Australian ambassadors in Washington that the British eviction of the Saudis from the Buraimi oasis in October 1955 had been 'an act of aggression'; while Eisenhower himself solemnly informed Eden that 'people in general ... tended to think that the whole Arabian peninsula belonged, or ought to belong, to King Saud'. That such ideas should enjoy the currency they did was eloquent testimony to the success of the propaganda campaign ARAMCO had been conducting for many years on its own behalf and that of its Saudi patrons. It had constituted itself the interpreter of Saudi Arabia – its people, its history, its culture and, above all, its ruling house – to the United States at large, and because there were no other sources of information about that country open to the American public, ARAMCO could put across its version of recent Arabian history and politics with almost insolent ease.

Its propaganda was framed in a manner likely to strike a sympathetic response in the American people. The principal theme was that of 'manifest destiny'. The conquests of Ibn Saud were depicted as the culmination of his dynasty's quest for dominion over Arabia from sea to sea; his subjugation of Hasa, the Hijaz, Jabal Shammar and Asir was represented as 'nation-building'. Much emphasis was laid upon the spiritual nature of the Wahhabi movement, upon its puritanical aspects (with Riyad cast in the image of Salem), upon the felicitous alliance of religion with secular power, and upon the harmonious blend of piety and statecraft inherent in the person of the Saudi king-imam. To make the analogy more familiar, the term by which the Wahhabis distinguished themselves, *muwahhidun* ('believers in oneness'), was consistently rendered as 'Unitarians', a usage which must have puzzled the adherents of the American Unitarian Church and their fellow Americans in general. Naturally, little prominence was accorded in ARAMCO's publicity to the fanatical nature of Wahhabism, or to its dark and bloody excesses. To imbue its message with more widespread appeal, ARAMCO also propounded the notion that some kind of natural affinity existed between Americans and Saudi Arabs, an affinity which transcended the mutuality of economic interests represented by the harnessing of American technical expertise and commercial dynamism to Saudi Arabia's natural resources. The Saudi Arab, it appears, was also a great lover of liberty, one of nature's democrats, so that it was hardly surprising that he should feel a sense of kinship with Americans, and Americans with him. The irony implicit in this inventive attempt to create the fiction of a community of outlook and a spontaneous *camaraderie* between the citizens of the world's most advanced democracy and the subjects of one of its most unenlightened despotisms never seemed to dawn upon the industrious fabulists of Dhahran.

Over the years, beginning in the mid-1930s, ARAMCO had developed a close relationship with Harry St John Bridger Philby, the British Arabophile, explorer, entrepreneur, Wahhabi convert, historian and confidant of Ibn Saud. The two parties had many things in common, not the least being an abiding admiration for the house of Saud and an equally abiding hostility to Great Britain, which in Philby's case ran bone-deep. He used his influence with Ibn Saud before, during and after the Second World War to try to injure Britain's interests in Arabia and the Middle East, sailing on occasion fairly close to the wind of treason, although he never carried his hatred of his own country to the savage lengths that his son Kim was to go. Whatever his achievements as an explorer, and these were of an undeniably high order, Philby was a man of highly unpleasant character – mercenary, arrogant, irascible and untrustworthy. Though he had been an agnostic, perhaps even an atheist, since his schooldays, and was in old age to profess materialist beliefs, he became a Muslim so as to improve his standing with Ibn Saud and to further his own private objects. He was an admirer of Hitler, yet also a vociferous pacifist – although his pacifism did not embrace Ibn Saud's conquests or inhibit him from trafficking in arms himself. In later life he became an avowed if muddled communist, given to uncritical commendation of the beneficent influence exercised by the Soviet Union in the world, while reviling Britain for all the wrongs she had supposedly done the Arabs since the First World War. That ARAMCO should have seen fit to cultivate the intimate acquaintance of such a man places its own corporate character in an interesting light.

Since the publication of his first book, *The Heart of Arabia*, in 1922 Philby had constituted himself the court historian of the Al Saud, as well as the dynasty's principal apologist in the English-speaking world. His preoccupations and those of ARAMCO therefore meshed with one another very conveniently. From Philby ARAMCO initially learned a great deal about Arabia, past and present, while Philby in turn was able to profit in later years from the mass of information about the peninsula which ARAMCO gradually accumulated in its research division at Dhahran. The fruits of their collaboration are visible in Philby's last major work, *Saudi Arabia*, published in 1955 when he was seventy. Between them, Philby and the research division of ARAMCO evolved an interpretation of modern Arabian history that owed much more to the example of Scheherazade than it did to the guidance of Clio. All considerations of objectivity, balance and a proper regard for factual evidence were subordinated to the aim of hymning the 'right praise and true perfection' of the house of Saud. Its dynastic importance was inflated, its virtues extolled, its exploits celebrated, its excesses concealed and its rivals calumniated. To set out a list of the distortions, suppressions and falsifications of the historical record for which the Philby–ARAMCO school of Arabian history is responsible would require a chapter in itself. Suffice it to say that the publications for which this school is responsible outdo in sycophancy and sanctimony even the works of the Najdi chroniclers upon which they are largely based; for whereas the principal chroniclers often related in their writings incidents which revealed the Al Saud in an unflattering light, our latterday annalists have been careful to rigorously exclude such evidence from their own writings. Their reticence is understandable, if hardly admirable, for the Al Saud do not take kindly to candour, or to anything short of adulatory exposition, as the example of Othman ibn Bishr, one of the major Arabian chroniclers of the nineteenth century, attests. Ibn Bishr, who had had the temerity to record in his history of Najd the barbarities inflicted by the Al Saud upon the people of Hasa after their conquest, deemed it prudent to lay down his pen in 1851 and never to take it up again, even though he was to live on for another twenty-two years. Ibrahim ibn Isa, who in this century set down the history of the Al Saud from 1851 to 1922, had the latter part of his work, covering the years 1884–1922, suppressed on the orders of the Saudi court.

It was also due in some measure to Philby's example that ARAMCO adopted a particular literary style and imagery, the better to express the spirit and substance of its teachings. For all his vilification of his native land, Philby never completely lost his Englishness or erased the mark of his early years at Westminster and Cambridge. Consciously or unconsciously, he wrote primarily for an English readership, and his literary style, though highly idiosyncratic, reflected this fact. It reached its efflorescence in his *Saudi Arabia*, which was studded with phrases of the order of 'the barony of Dariya', 'the sturdy yeomen of Najd' and 'grave Wahhabi prelates', all of which tended to convey a picture of some sun-baked Plantagenet England. For their part, ARAMCO's publicists had early on shown a certain wistful preference for the contrived and stilted cadences of Charles Doughty and T. E. Lawrence, the school of the 'great, boundless, over-arching vault of the Arabian sky' and the 'vast, empty, silent, cathedral-like solitudes of the desert'. Such literary conceits, however, were soon deemed too high-flown for the mundane purpose in mind: a more down-to-earth style was needed. Nor was the Plantagenet England of Philby's invention the right metaphorical medium through which to present Saudi Arabia to an American audience: to be effective, the historical analogy would have to be a recognizable one. The one eventually chosen was the American West in pioneer times, presented in suitably homespun prose. So the American public was introduced to the sheep-herders of Najd, driving their flocks to watering-holes and high pastures, to Wahhabi circuit-riders bringing the 'good news' of the reformed faith to outlying settlements, and to posses of *ikhwan* pursuing outlaws into hostile territory. It was a highly evocative theme: Saudi Arabia as a mirror-image of the Old West, a wide, unfenced land where nature was unsubdued, where religion was simple and fundamentalist, and the law of the gun prevailed – the desert of Arabia, in short, as America's last frontier.

With no rival school of Arabian history in the United States to challenge it, ARAMCO had no difficulty in gaining acceptance for its interpretation of the modern history of the peninsula. The situation has not changed up to the present day. It was, and it still is, virtually impossible for any independent Western scholar to visit Saudi Arabia. The Saudi government does not welcome foreign inquirers after knowledge, and almost the only way in which a foreign scholar can enter the country – unless he is there at the government's request to serve it in some specific capacity – is to be sponsored by ARAMCO. Needless to say, the company exercises great care in its selection of those to whom it is prepared to give its seal of approval. Independence of outlook and an enquiring mind are not on the company's list of desirable qualities in applicants. The depressing results of these twin policies are all too evident in the dearth of European scholarship, and the current quality of American scholarship, on Saudi Arabia.

Over the past three decades the ARAMCO version of Saudi Arabian history and politics has been firmly implanted not only in those American universities which offer programmes in Middle-Eastern studies, but also in learned societies, philanthropic organizations and other institutions interested in the Middle East, such as the Middle East Institute in Washington which is (or was) partially subsidized by ARAMCO. The company's influence has been especially apparent in universities and colleges where Saudi Arabs are sent to study, whether situated on the eastern seaboard or in states like Texas and California where the parent companies have their homes. It has also been apparent in the scholarly publications issuing from these diverse sources, all of which have exhibited an uncritical, not to say reverential, attitude to the Al Saud and their doings. The company's propaganda on behalf of its Saudi clients even invaded the chaste pages of the new edition of the *Encyclopaedia of Islam*, where supposedly disinterested articles contributed by ARAMCO scholars proved, on closer inspection, to be semi-devotional exercises in honour of the Al Saud or disguised arguments in support of their territorial and dynastic ambitions. If

ARAMCO could successfully evangelize in such aloof surroundings, it is hardly surprising that it has found the propagation of its gospel to the American press and public an easy matter.

The political legacy bequeathed by ARAMCO to the United States was twofold: the company had shaped the way in which Americans looked upon Saudi Arabia, its rulers and its people; and it had also, by the manner in which it had comported itself in Arabia, led the Saudi regime to expect the government of the United States to exhibit a similar demeanour – accommodating, pliant, deferential and gullible. Thus, when the State Department was eventually forced by the Egyptian intervention in the civil war in the Yemen late in 1962, and the alarm this occasioned in Riyad, to assume a more active role in Saudi-American relations than it had hitherto played, it found its room for manoeuvre closely circumscribed by the assumptions and expectations which ARAMCO over the years had fostered in the minds of the Saudi ruling house. It was also hampered by the disposition of some of its officials to view the Arabian peninsula in much the same way as ARAMCO viewed it – which was a further tribute to the efficacy of ARAMCO's proselytizing. Having previously neglected to work out a coherent and logical policy of its own towards the region, the State Department had to proceed after 1962 on an *ad hoc* basis, which inevitably produced inconsistencies, confusion and not a few ironies.

One of these concerned the attitude to be adopted towards Britain's presence in the peninsula. Officially the Gulf was recognized as a British preserve where the United States was content to leave the protection of Western interests in British hands. Aden and South Arabia were another matter. The administration in Washington had welcomed the revolution in the Yemen in 1962 as advancing the cause of republicanism and Arab nationalism, and before the year was out it had granted recognition to the revolutionary government in return for an undertaking from Nasser to remove his troops from the Yemen within a short time. Needless to say, the undertaking was never honoured, and all that the action of the United States achieved was to unsettle the Saudis and offend the British. 'I have always thought, and I still do,' wrote Major-General von Horn, the UN commander in the Yemen, some time later, 'that beneath this apparently logical decision by the Americans [to recognize the republican regime] lay a baser policy aimed at embarrassing the British in southern Arabia, linked with a desire to further their own oil interests in the Arabian peninsula.' But while the United States administration might see fit to applaud both the revolution in the Yemen and the nationalist struggle against the British in Aden, the house of Saud viewed them in a different light, as posing a threat to its own continued existence. Over the next few years, and especially after the accession of Faisal ibn Abdul Aziz late in 1964, the United States was left in no doubt that what the Saudi government wanted was that the Egyptians should evacuate the Yemen and the British should stay in South Arabia. At the same time, however, Faisal expected the United States to exert pressure upon the British to compel them to concede his right to his 'ancestral domains' in eastern Arabia, i.e. to make over slices of Qatar, Abu Dhabi and Oman to him.

It was all very bewildering for the administration and the State Department, and their perplexity was not eased by developments in Arabia in the late 1960s and early 1970s. Rather late in the day the realization began to dawn in Washington that Britain's abandonment of Aden and her retreat from the Gulf had removed the major stabilizing influence from the peninsula. Over the same period of time, by a further irony, ARAMCO's position in Saudi Arabia had begun to deteriorate, as the Saudi regime, taking at face value ARAMCO's pious avowals for years past that it was, in reality, a Saudi Arabian enterprise, embarked upon the creeping nationalization of the company's assets through the device of 'participation' in its shareholding. Second thoughts were now very much the order of the day in Dhahran, though they seemed to yield nothing more than the desperate counsel of continued appeasement. Thus, as we shall see in a later chapter, ARAMCO carried out to the letter the Saudi government's orders on the implementation of the oil embargo of October 1973, even to the withholding of supplies from the United States navy. The company had travelled a long way since the proposal made thirty years earlier that it should earmark a proportion of its reserves for the use of that same navy.

With Britain gone from the Gulf and the days of ARAMCO's ascendancy in Saudi Arabia numbered, the United States was, and still is, hard put to provide for the protection of its own and the Western world's interests in the region. *Faute de mieux*, it had to settle in the early 1970s for the pretence that these interests could be adequately safeguarded by Saudi Arabia and Persia, acting in tandem and with the encouragement and support of the United States. The overthrow of the shah has now removed Persia from this arrangement, leaving the United States in a position of trying to exercise some control over events in the Gulf from behind an Arab façade, i.e. through her 'special relationship' with Saudi Arabia. What has yet to emerge is whether the United States actually has any clear idea of the course upon which she has embarked, or whether she has merely taken ARAMCO's place at the wheel of the Saudi chariot.

Oil and money are at the heart of the American involvement in Saudi Arabia – the guaranteed supply of oil to the United States, in the first instance, and the safe disposal of the financial surpluses Saudi Arabia has accumulated from her oil revenues, in the second. The problems that the surplus revenues of the Organization of Petroleum Exporting Countries pose to the Western world in general will be considered more fully in a later chapter. For the moment it may be noted that the total accumulated surplus revenues of OPEC were estimated by the United States Treasury in October 1977 to be of the order of $133,000 million, the bulk of which was owned by only three countries – Saudi Arabia, Kuwait and the United Arab Emirates (i.e. Abu Dhabi). Some $50,000 million were said to be invested or on deposit in the United States, more than half of which belonged to Saudi Arabia, whose total financial surpluses amounted to $50,000 million or more. Private Saudi investment in the United States probably matched that of the Saudi government, so that Saudi Arabia's total investment in the United States may have exceeded $50,000 million. Moreover, it could be expected to grow in the years ahead, since OPEC's surplus revenues for the years 1977–80 were expected to average $40,000 million annually, 90 per cent of which would accrue to the same three countries – Saudi Arabia, Kuwait and the UAE. The implications for the United States economy and treasury were obvious.

Imports of oil into the United States during 1977 and the first half of 1978 greatly exceeded in volume not only the imports of previous years but the country's nominal requirements as well. Almost half the oil came from three countries, Saudi Arabia, Nigeria and Persia, with Saudi Arabia providing the largest amount. It was clear that the United States government was building up a strategic oil reserve which would enable it to withstand any future constriction of supplies by the imposition of another Arab oil embargo like that of October 1973. To succeed in this aim, while staving off the grave financial risks involved, required the fulfilment of three conditions: an adequate and uninterrupted supply of oil, the maintenance of oil prices at a constant level, and an assurance against any substantial withdrawal of the surplus oil revenues deposited in the United States. Saudi Arabia was clearly considered to occupy a key position in this strategy. As early as the spring of 1974 the United States and Saudi governments had reached initial agreement upon the desirability of close economic and military co-operation between their two countries. On 7 June 1974 it was formally announced that joint commissions on military and economic relations were to be established, specific reference being made in the announcement to the 'special relationship' subsisting between the United States and Saudi Arabia. In the next few months the United States Department of Defence made a study of Saudi Arabia's defence needs, and its findings were accepted by the Saudi government towards the close of the year. Large orders for arms followed. Slower progress was made with the implementation of the agreement on economic co-operation; but by the latter months of 1976 the joint commission had agreed upon the methods by which it would oversee the investment of Saudi Arabia's surplus oil revenues in the United States, on the one hand, and assist with the economic and social development of Saudi Arabia, on the other. When the Saudi crown prince, Fahad ibn Abdul Aziz, visited Washington in May 1977 the arrangement was confirmed by the new administration of President Carter.

What is plainly implicit in this joint arrangement is that, in return for an undertaking from the Saudi government to meet the three conditions set out above, the United States government has committed itself to a guarantee of full political, economic and military support to maintain the independence and integrity of Saudi Arabia under its present rulers. Following Fahad's visit the United States–Saudi joint commission reached agreement that Saudi Arabia's oil production should be increased from June 1977 from 8,500,000 barrels per day to 9,900,000 b/d for the remainder of 1977, and to 10,400,000 b/d from 1 January 1978. The excess of production over 8,500,000 b/d – of which the United States already took a considerable share – was to be placed at the disposal of the United States. Like so many agreements in the delusive world of Middle-Eastern oil, this one hardly lived up to its promise. Saudi oil production throughout 1977 never exceeded an average of 8,500,000 b/d, if it actually attained this level. Excuses were made for the deficiency – bad weather in the Gulf early in the year, a fire in the Abqaiq oilfield in May – but the fact remains that the agreed level of production was not attained.

Meanwhile the United States has become more deeply involved in Saudi Arabia than ever before: ARAMCO's vision of a natural Saudi–American partnership has become flesh. According to the United States embassy in Jiddah in 1978, there were some 30,000 Americans in Saudi Arabia employed on commercial contracts, in government work or as military instructors and specialists. Unofficial estimates put the number at double this figure, and their presence was directly linked with the Saudi government's elaborate plans to expand and modernize its armed forces. The first steps to provide the country with a partial air-defence system had been taken after the Egyptian intervention in the Yemen in 1962. For a number of reasons, some of them political, the initial contracts were shared between American and British aircraft companies and armaments manufacturers, the Americans supplying Hawk surface-to-air missiles while the British set up a radar screen with missile support to cover part of the Red Sea region, and equipped the Saudi air force with theoretically operational squadrons of Lightning fighter aircraft. From 1970 onwards, and more particularly after the oil-price rises late in 1973, the Saudi government placed large orders for weapons and aircraft with Britain, France and the United States. Between 1973 and 1977 the Saudis purchased or contracted to buy, among other things, 735 medium tanks; 250 light tanks; 700 armoured cars and personnel carriers; Hawk, Rapier and Crotale surface-to-air missile systems; 75 and 100 mm field guns and anti-aircraft batteries; ninety F–5 (Tiger) fighter aircraft; thirty-eight Mirage III fighter-bombers (for subsequent transfer to Egypt); forty-five transport aircraft; over 500 military helicopters; and an assortment of naval craft, some equipped with guided missiles. To this actual and potential arsenal was added an order in the summer of 1978 for sixty F–16 (Cobra) fighter aircraft.

While British companies have been awarded substantial contracts (to a value of some £250 million in 1973 and £500 million in 1977) for the development, training and maintenance of the Saudi air force, the major task of equipping and expanding Saudi Arabia's armed forces is being performed by American defence contractors. Under the supervision of the United States Army Corps of

Engineers a new military academy and headquarters for the National Guard are being built at Riyad; naval bases are being constructed and equipped at Jiddah and Jubail, military and air bases at Tabuq, in the north-western corner of the country, and at Khamis Mushait, in the south-west, near Najran; while in the north-east, at al-Batin near the border with Kuwait, an entire military town is planned, on what would appear to be the model of an *ikhwan hijra*. The estimated cost of these establishments runs into thousands of millions of dollars. A United States military mission some 150 strong is advising the Saudi armed forces, its cost ($4,600,000 in 1977) being met, virtually *in toto*, by the Saudi government. In addition, the Bendix Corporation is engaged in organizing logistics support for the Saudi army; the Vinnel Corporation is training the National Guard; the AVCO corporation is supplying vessels and a training depot for the Saudi coastguard; the Lockheed Corporation is operating the air-defence network; the Raytheon Corporation is providing Hawk missile systems.

An air of unreality bordering upon lunacy hangs over the whole of this martial extravaganza. The Saudi defence budget for 1977–8 was $7,530 million (26,690 million riyals), a sum out of all proportion to the size of the country's population and the strength of its armed forces, which number some 61,500 men (or 103,000, if the para-military National Guard and the Frontier Force are included). The budget for the previous year was of the same order of magnitude – $6,343 million. (By way of comparison, Britain's defence expenditure was £4,548 million, or $9,974 million, in 1975–6, and £6,330 million, or $10,880 million, in 1977–8.) Moreover, the Saudis cannot operate most of the advanced weapons and highly complex defence equipment and installations they are acquiring, let alone maintain them properly. It will be years – perhaps well beyond the foreseeable future – before they are sufficiently skilled to do so, and in the meantime the Americans and others will have to supply the skills required. Yet the assistant secretary of state for Near Eastern and South Asian Affairs, Alfred L. Atherton Jr, blandly informed the Committee on International Relations of the House of Representatives in February 1976 that he considered the Saudis' arms orders to be 'reasonable and rational, albeit limited and relatively small, and well within their capability to absorb and employ effectively'.

It does not require oracular gifts to discern the dangers inherent in the policy which the United States is now pursuing towards Saudi Arabia. If the United States government entertains the cynical belief that it can sop up a goodly part of Saudi Arabia's surplus oil revenues by encouraging the Saudis to a wanton and prodigal expenditure upon arms, it may find itself in the situation of the biter bit. For the Saudi ruling house and its immediate circle are no strangers to chicanery and sharp practice, and it would be highly impolitic to count greatly upon their forbearance and good faith. While the Saudi government may be willing to spend several milliards of dollars upon armaments, it is not going to pour them all in the direction of the United States. It has already, over the past few years, made large purchases from Britain and France, and even since the confirmation of the mutual economic understanding with the United States in the spring of 1977, it has placed further substantial arms contracts with these two countries. It may have good political and practical reasons for doing so, but this is precisely the point being made here. Moreover, the same or similar political and practical considerations may at any time dictate not only the liquidation of Saudi Arabia's financial investments and deposits in the United States, but also the depositing of the bulk of her future surplus oil revenues elsewhere.

So far as oil supplies are concerned, the Saudi minister of petroleum, Shaikh Ahmad Zaki al-Yamani – who has publicly denied the existence of any mutual economic understanding between his country and the United States – has huffed and puffed mightily about Saudi Arabia's ability to lower or raise her oil production at will, whenever political considerations may call for it. It is not exactly a well-founded boast: Saudi Arabia cannot drop her oil production to 4 million b/d – the figure Yamani has mentioned as sufficient to meet the country's financial needs – without imperilling her ambitious development programme. Likewise, experience has shown that production cannot be raised above 8.5 million b/d for any sustained period of time because of technical difficulties, as will be seen in a later chapter. Despite the fall in world demand for oil in 1977 and 1978 Saudi Arabia kept her production at the highest possible level, to the detriment of the share of the world market enjoyed by the majority of the other members of OPEC. If the Saudi government is prepared to treat its partners in OPEC in this fashion, in order to safeguard or even increase its income from oil, what grounds are there for assuming that it will behave otherwise in its relations with the United States? Or, since its need for money seems so pressing, that it will not increase the current price of oil even further so as to raise its revenues?

One of the conditions referred to earlier as necessary to the successful working of the economic relationship the United States has established with Saudi Arabia, viz. that oil prices should remain constant, has already been set at nought. Should Saudi Arabia continue to go back on her undertakings to the United States government, it is difficult to visualize that government, on its record to date, taking any effective countermeasures to enforce compliance. The habit of accommodation is too strong, the legacy of ARAMCO too influential. Whenever in past years the Saudi government has demanded additional revenue payments from ARAMCO, payments not provided for in the concessionary agreements, ARAMCO has unfailingly found a way to satisfy those demands. What was at stake – access to the largest pool of oil in the world – was considered too valuable for questions of principle or honour to be allowed to jeopardize it. (There was also the sobering example of the expropriation of the Anglo-Iranian Oil Company's assets in Persia to be considered.) The gospel of expediency and appeasement preached by ARAMCO, along with its meretricious corollary of a natural Saudi–American partnership, has conditioned the thinking and moulded the attitude of the State Department for years now. It has also spread, helped in no small measure by the State Department's own evangelistic efforts – and, to only a slightly lesser extent, those of the Defence Department – to the United States Congress and the American public at large. Between 1972 and 1976 official after official appeared before the Senate Foreign Relations Committee and the House Foreign Affairs and International Relations Committees to testify to the stability of the Saudi regime, the beneficent use it was making of its oil revenues, the rapid strides it was making towards the social and economic betterment of its people, the moderation it exercised in the councils of the Arab nations and the deliberations of OPEC, its dedication to the ideals of the free world, its unrelenting opposition to communism, its constructive role in international affairs, its generosity to the less fortunate of the earth, its warm and protective concern for the small Gulf states and its anxious solicitude for the maintenance of peace and security in the Gulf – all of which was said to point not only to the vital necessity but also to the eminent desirability of a close alliance between the United States and Saudi Arabia. As a former United States ambassador to Saudi Arabia, James E. Akins, put it in an article in the *International Herald Tribune* in February 1978:

There is good reason to look forward to the development of a flourishing new relationship between these two unique countries. The United States' strength and technology working together with Saudi energy [*sc.* oil] and capital can be of immense benefit, not only to the two countries themselves, but to the world.

The State Department's judgement of Saudi Arabia was endorsed by a parade of non-governmental witnesses who appeared before the Congressional committees in these years. Most of them came from the universities, from research institutions or from the business world, and they appeared, with only one or possibly two exceptions, to know little, if anything, about Saudi Arabia and the Gulf. Instead, they based their submissions to the committees upon their knowledge of the Middle East in general, or of the armaments industry, or upon geo-political abstractions and theories of international relations. Even here they offered little in the way of independent analysis and conclusions, their statements and answers being shaped by their awareness of the prevailing consensus of official opinion, to which (whatever the reasons that may have moved them to do so) they were patently anxious to conform. A handful of senators and congressmen expressed scepticism or uneasiness about the arguments being offered in support of a more intimate relationship with Saudi Arabia and the need for arms procurement on the scale being advocated. Most, however, were prepared to accept them, along with the State Department's prognostications of an equitable and fruitful Saudi–American partnership.

A less complacent evaluation of the situation would yield the sobering conclusion that the United States, in return for a handful of undertakings of doubtful value and duration, has assumed commitments to Saudi Arabia of a potentially far-reaching character which may lead it one day into some very strange waters indeed. For this the United States government has only itself to blame. It has disdained the experience of Britain in Arabia over the past century and a half, as it has disdained the imperial experience of the European powers in Asia and Africa generally. And, like British governments themselves of late years, it has seen fit to spurn the lessons which this experience taught – among them the necessity to hold aloof from entangling alliances with the Al Saud, and the futility of propitiation as a mode of treating with that dynasty. Instead, the United States government has placed itself in an ignominious position *vis-à-vis* the Saudis, having confused the role of cicerone with that of *cicisbeo*. Not only is it tied to the Al Saud and to the preservation of the *status quo* in Saudi Arabia, but it is also, to all intents and purposes, committed to upholding the integrity and independence of the kingdom against its foes from without. What this may portend is anyone's guess.

What degree of political discontent may exist in Saudi Arabia it is impossible to judge for want of sufficient information about the country's internal affairs. Saudi methods of government have always been severe, partly of necessity, given the turbulent nature of the tribesmen, partly from inclination, given the character of the Al Saud and the spirit of Wahhabism. Wealth has slightly tempered this disposition so far as some sections of Saudi society are concerned, though not for the bulk of the population. The Wahhabi *mutawiyah*, the zealots who constitute the religious police, remain as vigilant as ever, and the prescriptions of Islam according to the Hanbali rite are still enforced with severity. Public floggings, mutilations and beheadings for crimes of mounting degrees of seriousness are normal practice, while the conditions in Saudi prisons and the punishments meted out to those confined in them remain as barbarous as ever. Some tardy realization of these aspects of Saudi government and society has come to the outside world as a result of the occasional punishment of Europeans or Americans who have offended against Saudi laws or Islamic prohibitions, and through the putting to death in November 1977 of a female member of the royal family for adultery and the public execution of her lover. (The adultery may have been no more than technical. The women of the Al Saud are forbidden to marry outside the family, unless into the closely related Thunaiyan clan. Marriage to a man not of the Al Saud, therefore, is classified as adultery. The men of the Al Saud may marry outsiders, though they usually confine themselves, as noted earlier, to the *ahl al-shaikh* or the Sudairi or Jiluwi clans.) Women and Westerners can, by and large, be chastised with relative impunity; women because they are accounted lesser beings, both before the law and in the eyes of men; Westerners because their governments are normally so fearful of jeopardizing the lucrative contracts they or Western industrial and commercial companies have won from the Saudi government that they will offer only token objections to the mistreatment of their own nationals. For the Saudis there is undoubtedly a double satisfaction to be gained from the infliction of humiliating punishments upon Westerners; for not only are they an expression of the power and independence of Saudi Arabia but they also demonstrate, as they are intended to demonstrate, contempt for Christianity and the pre-eminence of Islam. The most unfortunate victims of the merciless quality of the Saudi judicial system, however, are not Westerners but those wretched Yemeni labourers who happen to fall foul of the Saudi authorities.

The prescriptions of the Hanbali rite are not applied with the same rigour to all aspects of Saudi life or to every class of society. The Koranic injunction against usury, for instance, has been circumvented, notably in the case of Saudi banks, by the redesignation of interest as bank charges or disbursements. This happy expedient, duly enshrined in a *fatwa*, or legal ruling, from the Wahhabi *mufti*s, has proved even more felicitous of late, following a fiat from the Saudi government compelling all foreign banks operating in the country to accept a controlling Saudi shareholding. No legal restraints hinder the avid solicitation by the Saudi commercial community, government officials and influence pedlars alike of substantial bribes from foreign businessmen in return for introductions, permits and contracts. So vast is the scale on which this organized corruption is practised that its beneficiaries are said to have accumulated greater financial reserves (most of them held outside the country) than the Saudi government itself. A similar judicious indulgence regulates the application of the sterner ordinances of the *sharia* to the Al Saud and their intimates, to the more prominent tribal and merchant families, and, more recently, to the emergent educated and semi-educated classes.

The degree of immunity enjoyed by the last is the result of a conscious effort on the part of the Al Saud to broaden the support for their rule – from that traditionally provided by their own extensive ranks, by the religious establishment and by the shaikhs of the major tribes – by conciliating the new technocrats and their numerous acolytes. These have been won over to the maintenance of the *status quo* chiefly by the allocation to them of highly paid posts in the bureaucracy, and by allowing them a certain latitude to indulge the tastes that prosperity and Western influences have led them to cultivate. So far as is known, these new allies of the regime are content with their lot. Though they may lack some of the diversions available to their counterparts in the less puritanical societies of the minor oil states of the Gulf, they show no conspicuous tendency to compensate for the deprivation by taking an active interest in politics – other than to engage in the usual rhetoric about Islam, Arabism, imperialism and Zionism which is the standard fare of contemporary Arab political discourse. Even here, however, they have to exercise caution in expressing their opinions, for there is a widespread network of informers keeping watch on all activities, and every strand in this network leads to Riyad.

The presence of underground political organizations of one kind or another in Saudi Arabia has been reported for two decades now. At least as early as 1961 there was a 'National Front for the Liberation of Saudi Arabia', whose political complexion was murky but which appeared to gain a Marxist tinge as time went by. During the latter years of the reign of Saud ibn Abdul Aziz this group was allied with the dissident members of the royal house led by Talal ibn Abdul Aziz, who took refuge for a time in Egypt. Another group, with the *recherché* name 'Federation of Democratic Forces of the Arabian Peninsula', emerged in 1964, rather more radical in character and possibly incorporating some elements of the National Liberation Front. Almost at once it found itself with a rival, the 'Arabian Peninsula People's Union', a Nasserist organization based in the Yemen. Over the next three years the two clandestine movements were responsible for a series of sporadic bombing incidents in a number of Saudi Arabian towns, which in turn occasioned a sequence of public executions by the Saudi authorities, although it was not clear whether the persons executed were the actual perpetrators of the bombings. After the Egyptians withdrew from the Yemen in 1967 the Arabian Peninsula People's Union more or less faded from the scene. Cells of the Arab Nationalists' Movement were founded from the early 1960s onwards, usually by converts to the movement returning home from study abroad. Their connexion, if any, with the National Liberation Front was obscure. So, too, was the identity of the 'Popular Democratic Front' which made its presence felt in 1969, declaring itself to be 'a workers' revolutionary movement embracing the path of mass violence'. Its origins seemed to go back to 1965, yet its name and its distinctly Marxist pronouncements seemed to align it with the Popular Democratic Front for the Liberation of Palestine, which broke away from the PFLP and the ANM in February 1969.

The Popular Democratic Front, the National Front for the Liberation of Saudi Arabia and the Federation of Democratic Forces all appear to have been implicated in a revolutionary conspiracy – or perhaps two separate conspiracies – which was uncovered in June and July 1969. (So sparse is the information available about these revolutionary groups that it is not certain whether the last two were separate organizations or one organization under different names.) The Popular Democratic Front seems to have recruited mainly army and air force officers and men to its ranks, while the National Front for the Liberation of Saudi Arabia (and the Federation of Democratic Forces) had a membership composed largely of clerks, teachers and other government employees, along with individuals from some prominent Hijazi families. Differing accounts, none of them very illuminating, have been given of the nature of the conspiracy, its aims and the reasons for its failure. (One of the more interesting explanations is that it was designed to achieve an independent state in the Hijaz.) Hundreds of people were arrested, though few were brought to trial before the first half of 1973, by which time several of the ringleaders had been tortured to death in prison, while others reputedly had been disposed of by being tossed out of aircraft high over the Rub al-Khali with the macabre valedictory injunction to walk home. Report has it that 135 officers and men in the army and air force were sentenced to death, and 305 to life imprisonment. Another 752 officers, soldiers and civilians received sentences ranging from ten to fifteen years' imprisonment. Others again were released, with or without a trial, including, so it is said, the dean of the technical college at Dhahran.

Apart from the occasional defection of a Saudi air force pilot with his aircraft, there was little evidence of political unrest in the Saudi armed forces in the next few years. It may be that the Arab–Israeli war of 1973, though Saudi Arabia played only a minute military part in it, had a sobering influence for a time. However, in the summer of 1977 reports began filtering through to the outside world of the unmasking of another conspiracy, apparently centred upon the military base and airfield at Tabuq. It was said to involve air force officers and men at Tabuq and Dhahran, and army units at Taif, near Mecca. Trouble was also reported to have occurred at the military base and airfield at Hail. What substance there may be in these reports, and in others alleging Libyan and Iraqi involvement in the conspiracy and its suppression with the aid of Egyptian and Jordanian military intelligence, as well as Jordanian troops, it is impossible to say. On the face of it, and in the light of recent history, the Saudi armed forces would appear to be the natural spearhead of an uprising in Saudi Arabia. Yet the incidence of military *coups* in other Arab countries is not necessarily an infallible guide to the likely course of future events in Arabia. There is, moreover, a counterbalance to the regular armed forces in the National Guard, the para-military organization of armed tribesmen who number, according to different reports, 25–30,000 men, or about half the strength of the regular army and air force combined. This 'white army' (so called from the white turbans its members affect, after the style of the old *ikhwan*) is drawn from the townsmen and Bedouin of Najd. Its members also call themselves *mujahidun*, and the force still has something of the spirit of a religious brotherhood about it. It is commanded by Abdullah ibn Abdul Aziz, the second deputy prime minister, and its loyalty to the ruling house is said to be intense. A mark of its reputed reliability is that it, and not the regular army, has been entrusted with the protection of the oilfields in Hasa province.

If there is any restlessness in the Saudi armed forces, it could just as well proceed from suspicion about the manipulation of the Saudi defence budget for non-military purposes as from the ambitions of any potential Nassers within the officer corps. Early in 1978 the defence estimates for 1977–8 were revised upwards from 26,690 million riyals ($7,530 million) to 32,000 million riyals (about $9,050 million). Why this revision was considered necessary was never explained, and it appeared even more mystifying when the revised defence budget was compared with those of Saudi Arabia's neighbours. Egypt, for instance, with armed forces of 345,000, had a defence budget for 1977–8 of $4,370 million. Persia, with armed forces of 342,000 had a budget of $7,900 millions. It may be that the revision had some connexion with reports emanating from Saudi Arabia in the early months of 1978 both of gross mismanagement of the country's finances and of rifts within the ruling family as a consequence – or even as a possible cause. The minister of finance, Muhammad Ali Aba al-Khail, was said to be particularly concerned at both the rate of expenditure and the fall in real income brought about by the decline in value of the United States dollar. At the time the conclusion seemed inescapable that the defence budget was being used to cover either financial miscalculations on a monumental scale or pecuniary transactions of a questionable nature.

How much should be read into the reports of disaffection in the Saudi armed forces over the past decade, or into the real or rumoured activities of underground political organizations, it is impossible to say. Arab armies at all times and in all places have shown restive tendencies for one reason or another – and never so much as when they are idle. As for the subversive political groups, Marxist, Baathist or whatever, their menace has yet to assume definite shape. It is not easy for Maoist fish, or fish of any revolutionary species, to swim in the shallow political waters provided by Saudi Arabia's sparse population. At the same time it would be remarkable if there were to be no political repercussions from the social and economic convulsions of the past few years – the prodigious flood of wealth from oil, the frenzy of consumption and construction it has provoked, and the extravagance, waste and corruption which have been its accompaniments; the great influx of foreigners; the drift to the towns and cities; the murder of King Faisal; the expansion of education; and the involvement as never before with the world outside. The *ikhwan* flame still burns in the breasts of many tribesmen: it could yet flare up, as it did fifty years ago, in bursts of pious outrage and acts of disobedience against the ruling house over its profligacy and its dereliction of its religious duties. There are, as already noticed, indications of actual or impending financial difficulties which could pose a further threat to the country's stability. Domestic inflation, running as high as 40 or 50 per cent annually, has forced the government into ever higher expenditure upon wages, perquisites and subsidies, which in turn have stimulated further inflation. With the cost of the five-year development plan now doubled, and oil revenues, despite recent increases, perhaps insufficient to meet it, something has to give. Retrenchment, however, if it is to be at all effective, would require a drastic reduction – by as much as 75 per cent, according to some estimates – of expenditure upon education, health services and housing, as well as upon the more costly programmes of industrial innovation and military expansion. Expectations, at least among the favoured classes, have been raised so high by the prodigality of recent years that any serious financial pruning could well provoke serious unrest.

Finally, there is a potential if deep-lying source of political instability in the resentment that persists in some parts of the kingdom at the predominance of the Al Saud. The feeling runs most deeply in the Hijaz, and more particularly among the descendants of its former rulers, the *ashraf*, the several dozen families of the tribe of Quraish claiming descent from the Prophet in the house of Hashim, the best known of which were the sharifian families of Mecca. As we have seen, after the conquest of the Hijaz by Ibn Saud and its absorption into Saudi Arabia the *ashraf* were treated with contumely, to the distress of many Muslims, both within Arabia and outside. The *ashraf*, although outwardly resigned to Saudi rule, have never ceased to regard the Al Saud as other than interlopers, upstarts of undistinguished lineage and uncivilized ways who have usurped the guardianship of the *haramain*, the holy places, which rightfully belongs to the house of Hashim, and have deprived its members of their patrimony, the Hijaz itself. That the spirit of Hijazi separation exists there can be no doubt; whether it has a firmer basis than the grievances of the *ashraf* is unascertainable. Much the same kind of animosity towards the Al Saud, arising from comparable historical causes, exists in the Asir, in Jabal Shammar, and in Hasa. Hence, it is far from improbable that, in the event of some upheaval occurring at the centre of government (whether brought on by a contest for the succession among the Al Saud, by a revolutionary attempt upon the regime or by some external crisis), these regional discontents might assert themselves, precipitating a civil war and threatening the disintegration of the kingdom. What role the United States might be required to play in such an eventuality, as a consequence of her growing commitment to Saudi Arabia, is an interesting matter for speculation. Speculation, unfortunately, is what one is all too often driven to when considering the contemporary condition of Saudi Arabia. So little information is available about the country's internal affairs, or even its external relations, that it is pointless even to attempt to form a judgement about the likely course of events there in the years ahead.

CHAPTER VI
Mene, mene, tekel, upharsin

...MENE; *God hath numbered thy
kingdom, and finished it.*
TEKEL; *Thou art weighed in the
balances, and art found wanting.*
PERES; *Thy kingdom is divided, and
given to the Medes and Persians.*

Book of Daniel, *v, 26–8*

*La Perse peut lever et entretenir un assez grand nombre de troupes;
mais dans ses armées il y a des hommes et point de soldats.*

Charles Maurice de Talleyrand, 1807

The dismantling of the treaty relationship between Britain and the minor Gulf
states, which began with the abrogation of the British protectorate over Kuwait
in 1961 and ended with Britain's withdrawal from the Gulf ten years later, also
demolished the foundations of the states system which had existed in the Gulf
since the early years of this century, and in some of its aspects for even longer.
This system had ensured the prevalence of the rule of law in the conduct of the
Gulf's affairs over the ingrained preference of the peoples and principalities
around its shores to settle their differences with one another by the sword. No
comparable system has yet emerged to replace the former dispensation upheld
by Britain, nor is there the faintest sign of such a system emerging in the
foreseeable future. The peace of the Gulf, and with it the security of shipping
upon its waters, hangs precariously in a void, unsupported by any formal or
even tacit arrangement among the Gulf states for its protection. Instead, it is
dependent solely upon their sense of self-interest, and upon whatever feelings
of responsibility they may possess towards the international community at
large. In effect, this comes down to the willingness and the ability of the three
major states, Saudi Arabia, Iraq and Persia, to curb their mutual antagonisms
and preserve the status quo. They are not entirely free, however, to determine
their attitudes to one another or their general policies in the region as they
might wish; for two of them are, in varying degree, client states – Saudi Arabia

of the United States, Iraq of the Soviet Union – while the third, Persia, which until the close of 1978 was in a client relationship to the United States, has experienced so much domestic turmoil of late as to cast a cloud of uncertainty over her future role in the politics of the Gulf.

Iraq and Persia, for the most part, lie beyond the province of this book. What will be said about them here, therefore, will be confined in the main to those aspects of their internal affairs and their relations with each other which bear upon their activities and influence in the Gulf. A rigid dividing line, obviously, cannot be drawn in these matters, which makes such a treatment unsatisfactory in more respects than one. To attempt anything more, however, would be to exceed not only the appropriate limits of this study but also the competence of its author.

Iraq has never in modern times wielded the power and influence in the Gulf to which her position as the second most populous of the littoral states would appear to entitle her. To a considerable extent this failure has been due to her lack of maritime power, the possession of which has more often than not in the past determined political supremacy in the Gulf. During the period of Ottoman rule in Iraq, from the sixteenth to the twentieth century, control of the Gulf's waters was exercised and contested primarily by the maritime powers of Europe or the petty states of the Arabian shore. It was not until the closing decades of the nineteenth century, when the building of the Suez Canal facilitated the dispatch of ships from the Mediterranean into Arabian waters, that the Sublime Porte made a serious bid to extend its influence along the Arabian littoral of the Gulf. Although it succeeded in bringing the coastal region of al-Hasa under its control after 1871, and in imposing a tenuous suzerainty over Kuwait and the Qatar peninsula, the Porte was incapable by itself of posing an effective challenge to the preponderance enjoyed by Britain in the Gulf as a whole.

Turkish sovereignty over Iraq ended with the defeat of the Ottoman empire in the First World War, and Turkish suzerainty over Kuwait, Hasa and Qatar lapsed with it. The common boundaries of Iraq, Kuwait and the sultanate of Najd, as we have seen, were defined in a series of agreements drawn up in the 1920s on the initiative of Britain as the mandatory power in Iraq and the protecting power in Kuwait and Saudi Arabia. In the same decade the western and northern frontiers of Iraq – those with the amirate of Transjordan, the French mandate of Syria and the new Turkish republic – were defined in engagements concluded between Britain, France and Turkey and in the mandatory instruments issued by the League of Nations. The frontier of Iraq with Persia had been laid down three-quarters of a century earlier, in the treaty of Erzerum between the Ottoman and Persian empires concluded in 1847 under British and Russian auspices. The actual demarcation of the frontier, however, was not completed until the eve of war in 1914.

While Iraq remained under British tutelage there was little disposition, or opportunity, for her to engage in political activities in the Gulf. Her attention, in any case, was fully occupied with internal difficulties and with troubles along her border with Najd caused by the irregular movements of tribes and raids by Ibn Saud's *ikhwan*. There had never been any love lost between the Hashimites and the Saudis, and King Faisal of Iraq deeply resented the expulsion of his family from the Hijaz by Ibn Saud in 1924–5 and the subsequent incorporation of the kingdom of the Hijaz in the Saudi dominions. By 1930, however, the frontier troubles had died down, and relations between Faisal and Ibn Saud had improved sufficiently for them to conclude in that year an agreement of *bon voisinage*. Two years later Iraq became independent, and the following year Faisal died. The agreement, however, survived, and in 1936 it was converted by his son and successor, Ghazi, into a treaty of friendship and alliance between the two kingdoms.

Ghazi ibn Faisal took a much greater interest in the affairs of the Gulf than his father had done. At his instigation an 'Association of Arabs of the Gulf' was founded at Basra in 1936, with the object of disseminating propaganda in the Gulf states in favour of union with Iraq. Much of the propaganda was directed towards Kuwait, where it struck a responsive chord. Kuwait had had close economic ties with Iraq ever since the foundation of the shaikhdom in the early eighteenth century. Iraq supplied Kuwait with grain, vegetables, fruit and even water from the Shatt al-Arab. The Al Sabah shaikhs of Kuwait owned date groves and other property around Basra, and Kuwaiti shipping carried a fair proportion of the trade of lower Iraq. Iraqi propaganda towards Kuwait bore fruit at the close of 1938 and the beginning of 1939 in the form of resolutions passed in the advisory council of the ruler of Kuwait, unfavourably contrasting the poverty of Kuwait with the wealth of Iraq, and advocating union between the two. The resolutions found little favour with the British government. King Ghazi was reminded that when Iraq became independent in 1932 the Iraq–Kuwait frontier (as delineated in 1923) had been confirmed in an exchange of letters between the Iraqi prime minister and the ruler of Kuwait. At the same time the ruler, Ahmad ibn Jabir Al Sabah, was made to dismiss his advisory council and disown the resolutions. Riots followed in Kuwait, and Ghazi wanted to intervene and occupy the shaikhdom. Pressure was exerted upon him to refrain from doing so, and the affair came to an abrupt end in April 1939 when Ghazi killed himself in a motorcar accident.

More than twenty years passed before the question of a possible union between Iraq and Kuwait was again raised in serious form. In these years Kuwait's economic condition had been radically transformed by the discovery and exploitation of oil on a large scale, so that the desire for union on economic grounds no longer existed. Nor did the prospect of union hold any attraction for Kuwait politically, for the Hashimite monarchy had been swept away by violent revolution in 1958, and Iraq was now ruled by a military junta. The situation, in fact, had been reversed: republican Iraq now coveted Kuwait's wealth and abominated her shaikhly form of government. Iraq's opportunity to move against Kuwait came in June 1961 when Britain formally acknowledged Kuwait's independence and terminated her agreements with the shaikhdom. Half-a-dozen days later, on 25 June, the Iraqi prime minister, Major-General Abdul Karim Qassim, announced his intention to incorporate Kuwait in the republic of Iraq. He claimed, as justification for his action, that the shaikhdom had once been part of the Ottoman empire, that it had been administered until 1914 as a district of the *vilayet* of Basra, that sovereignty over it had passed to Iraq as a successor state of the Ottoman empire, and that Iraq had wrongfully been deprived of her inheritance by the arbitrary separation of Kuwait from Iraq by Britain after the First World War. Qassim's entire case was spurious. Kuwait had never been an integral part of the *vilayet* of Basra nor had it ever been administered from Basra, despite frequent attempts by Ottoman *vali*s of Basra, acting on their own initiative, to bring the shaikhdom under their control. Legally, the shaikhdom had been regarded by the Sublime Porte as an autonomous *qaza*, or district, of the empire, and the ruling shaikh up to 1914 had been invested by the Porte with the rank of *qaim-maqam*, or district governor. The validity of the Iraq–Kuwait frontier of 1923, moreover, had been recognized by the Iraqi government in 1932.

Qassim's move was frustrated by the dispatch of British troops to Kuwait at the request of the ruler. They were later replaced by a mixed force provided by Saudi Arabia, Egypt and other Arab states. The crisis passed and the issue became dormant, although Qassim never ceased, up to the time of his overthrow and death in February 1963, to proclaim his intention of annexing Kuwait. His successors were prepared to let the matter rest, and on 5 October 1963 they publicly acknowledged the sovereignty and independence of Kuwait within the frontiers confirmed in 1932. Less publicity was given to the price exacted – a 'loan' of $85 million from Kuwait and an undertaking that the 1961 agreement with Britain would be abrogated at the first favourable opportunity. Few observers really believed that the issue had been truly buried, if only because of the character of post-revolutionary politics in Iraq, where every *coup d'état* or *émeute* at Baghdad seemed to bring to power a regime more extreme and sanguinary than its predecessor. There were also the inescapable facts of geography: Iraq's seaboard on the Gulf was exceedingly narrow, a mere few dozen kilometres in length, in comparison with Kuwait's coastline of three hundred kilometres. Kuwait had far and away the best harbour in the upper Gulf, while Iraq's only outlet to the sea had for centuries been the Shatt al-Arab, the waterway formed by the confluence of the rivers Tigris and Euphrates, and, in its lower reaches, the Karun. Even before the Second World War Iraq's control over the Shatt al-Arab had been challenged by Persia, and it was to be contested again with increasing vigour from the late 1950s onwards.

It was this question of maritime access, and the related issues of maritime jurisdiction and sovereignty, which was to be largely responsible for the reopening of the Iraq–Kuwait frontier question in the latter months of 1972. Before turning to this phase in the dispute, therefore, it is necessary to look at the origins and growth of the Perso–Iraqi contest over the Shatt al-Arab; for it is along this waterway, and in the waters around the coasts and islands in its vicinity, that the interests of the three littoral states, Iraq, Persia and Kuwait, overlap and conflict.

The second and third articles of the treaty of Erzerum of 31 May 1847, which defined the frontier between the Ottoman and Persian empires, invested the Sublime Porte with sovereignty over the whole of the Shatt al-Arab, while recognizing Persian sovereignty over the left or eastern bank of the river and over the town and anchorage of Muhammarah (now Khurramshahr), at the junction of the Karun river and the Shatt al-Arab. The actual delimitation of the frontier was deferred again and again, and it was not until 1911, when a protocol was signed at Tehran by the four powers concerned (Britain, Russia, Turkey and Persia), that a delimitation commission was established. A further protocol was signed at Constantinople two years later, and the delimitation commission began its work in 1914. In the region of the Shatt al-Arab it demarcated the frontier (from the point where, coming from the north, it struck the river about twenty kilometres downstream from Basra) as running along the low-water mark on the Persian side, except in the vicinity of Muhammarah, where it was made to follow the thalweg, or line of deepest flow.

When Iraq achieved independence she made it clear that she considered herself entitled, as a successor state of the Ottoman empire, to succeed to full sovereignty over the Shatt al-Arab and to the frontier demarcated in 1914; and she believed her rights to have been reinforced by the transfer to her of responsibility for the security of navigation in the Shatt al-Arab, through the medium of the Basra Port Authority which had been set up by the British during the First World War. Persia, on the other hand, after the accession of Reza Shah and the reduction of Muhammarah and the adjoining province of Khuzistan to his authority in 1924–5, found the frontier regime prevailing in the Shatt al-Arab increasingly irksome, especially as it affected Abadan Island, the port of shipment for Persian oil, where ships had to berth and load in Iraqi waters. After some sharp exchanges between the Persian and Iraqi governments the dispute was referred to the League of Nations at the close of 1934. Iraq took her stand on the treaty of Erzerum and the Constantinople protocol of 1913. Persia declared both instruments to be null and void because they had been concluded under pressure from Britain and Russia. They had no force, the Persians contended, either in law or in equity in determining the frontier. On the contrary, they claimed, the frontier should be delimited according to the recognized principle of international law obtaining in cases

Kuwait and the Shatt al-Arab

where a river separated two states, which held that the frontier should run down either the thalweg or the median line. Eventually a compromise was reached between the two positions, and was incorporated in a treaty signed by the two sides on 4 July 1937. Persia was accorded as a frontier in the vicinity of Abadan the thalweg of the Shatt al-Arab for a distance of eight kilometres. Otherwise the previous frontier along the waterway was left unchanged.

Relations between Persia and Iraq remained distant in the years after the Second World War, and they deteriorated further after the Iraqi revolution in 1958. Muhammad Reza Shah regarded the new regime in Baghdad with distaste, and he was irritated by Iraqi attempts to stir up irredentist feeling in Khuzistan, where many of the inhabitants were of Arab descent. Another source of irritation was the treatment accorded the hundreds of thousands of Persians who dwelt in Iraq, particularly in the holy cities of Najaf and Karbala. The Shatt al-Arab, however, was the principal bone of contention, and after an acrimonious dispute over pilotage in 1959, and again in 1961, the Persian government embarked upon the construction of a major oil terminal at Kharq Island, off Bushire on the Gulf coast, so that the exportation of Persian oil should not be subject to interference by Iraq in the Shatt al-Arab. The Kharq terminal was completed in 1965, and in the same year trouble again flared up over what the Persians considered to be the Iraqis' excessive officiousness in exercising their rights in the Shatt al-Arab.

Although Abadan was no longer as important as it had been for the export of Persian oil, Khurramshahr further up the river was still a major port of entry for goods destined for the interior of Persia, and the Persian government was determined to control its approaches. It expressed its determination in 1965 by threatening to renounce the frontier treaty of 1937 if Iraq continued its provocation, and four years later it carried the threat into execution. On 19 April 1969 the Persian government pronounced the treaty of 1937 null and void. As grounds for the renunciation the Persians contended that the treaty had in the first place been forced upon Persia by Britain, and that for more than thirty years subsequent to its conclusion Iraq had misappropriated the dues collected from shipping, most of it bound for Persian ports, to purposes other than the improvement of navigation in the Shatt al-Arab. The only frontier Persia would now accept along the river was the median line. Iraq refused to accept the unilateral abrogation of the treaty, declaring that Iraqi sovereignty over the Shatt al-Arab was incontestable and that she would continue to regard the waterway as part of her territory.

A war of words followed between Baghdad and Tehran, accompanied by some sabre-rattling along the frontier. Centuries-old religious and racial antipathies expressed themselves in the expulsion of thousands of Persians from Iraq, in the harassing of Persian pilgrims to Najaf and Karbala, and in noisy threats by Baghdad to 'unleash' the 'Front for the Liberation of Khuzistan'. Though the tumult and the shouting gradually subsided the incident left its mark upon the Baathist government in Baghdad. Conscious of Iraq's inferiority to Persia in terms of population, wealth and military strength, alarmed by what they saw as a display of belligerence by the shah when his troops occupied Abu Musa and the Tunbs at the end of 1971, and all too aware, also, of their own friendless condition in the Arab world, the Baathists began a hasty search for wealthy and powerful allies. They found one in the next two or three years in the Soviet Union, whose interest in the Gulf had been growing ever since the British government at the beginning of 1968 had declared its intention of abandoning its political and military position in the region. The principal attractions for Russia of a foothold in Iraq were twofold – access to Iraqi oil and access to the Gulf. As the Soviet government was not anxious to be drawn into the dispute over the Shatt al-Arab, thereby needlessly antagonizing the shah and his government, and as that waterway was in many respects, practical as well as legal, unattractive as a means of egress to the sea, it was hardly surprising that, as Iraq's contacts with the Soviet Union became more intimate, the Baghdad regime began to show signs of preparing to reopen the frontier dispute with Kuwait.

While a number of agreements concerning trade, technical assistance and the supply of arms had been concluded between Iraq and the Soviet Union before 1969, they were as nothing compared with the hectic succession of agreements which now followed. Some of the more significant of these provided for Russian assistance in the development of Iraq's oil industry, in association with the Iraq National Oil Company. Payment for this assistance was to be made in crude oil. Particular attention was given in these agreements to the exploitation of the North Rumailah field, south-west of Basra, which had been discovered by the Iraq Petroleum Company some years earlier and expropriated by Qassim in 1960. With Russian help North Rumailah was expected to come on stream in 1972, with an initial annual output of 5 million tons rising to 20–25 million by 1975. The Russians also undertook to build a pipeline from North Rumailah to Fao, near the mouth of the Shatt al-Arab, and to construct storage tanks and loading facilities at that port to handle the increased flow of oil for export.

Fao, however, had its deficiencies as an oil-loading port. It lay upstream of the bar at the mouth of the Shatt al-Arab, and could be reached only by vessels of under thirty-five feet in draught. A second oil-loading terminal at Khaur al-Amayah, to the westward, was restricted to vessels of under fifty feet in draught. A deep-water terminal for large tankers was thus badly needed, and there was no suitable site for one along the brief span of coastline between the Shatt al-Arab and the Kuwait frontier. That frontier struck the coast at a point just below Umm Qasr, which had been developed as a port by the British and Americans during the Second World War to aid in the trans-shipment of goods to Russia. Afterwards it was dismantled and abandoned, but in 1960–61 the Iraqi government began to restore it, first as an alternative port to Basra and later as a naval base. Like Fao, however, Umm Qasr had its drawbacks, one of the principal being that its approaches lay in Kuwaiti waters; for the maritime frontier began below Umm Qasr and ran eastwards along the Khaur Abdullah, north of the islands of Warbah and Bubiyan which were under Kuwaiti sovereignty (see map p. 279). A further disadvantage of Iraq's narrow coastline was that it severely limited both the extent of her maritime jurisdiction and her share of the contiguous sea-bed, along with any oil deposits the latter might contain. For this reason Iraq had strenuously objected to the attempts which had been made by Persia and Kuwait to fix the location of the median line between their coasts for purposes of offshore oil exploration.

For Iraq, then, the whole situation at the head of the Gulf was highly unsatisfactory, and the temptation to make a forward move correspondingly strong. It needed only the close connexion forged with the Soviet Union in the spring of 1972 to make that temptation irresistible. On 7 April 1972, the twenty-fifth anniversary of the official creation of the Baath party, the first shipment of oil from the North Rumailah field was loaded at Fao in the presence of the Soviet prime minister, Alexei Kosygin. Two days later Kosygin and Ahmad Hasan al-Bakr, the Iraqi president, signed a treaty of friendship and co-operation. It was to run initially for a period of five years and thereafter it would be automatically renewed at five-yearly intervals. Article 8 of the treaty bound each side, in the event of a threat to the other, to 'hold immediate contacts to co-ordinate their positions in the interests of eliminating the developing danger and re-establishing peace'; while in article 9 they undertook 'to develop co-operation in the strengthening of the defence capabilities of each'. Taken together, these articles could be construed as constituting a limited offensive and defensive alliance, with Iraq providing military and naval facilities to Russia in return for a guarantee of protection. That such was their intention was subsequently confirmed publicly by the vice-president of the Revolutionary Command Council in Baghdad, Saddam Husain al-Takriti.

The Iraqi government clearly saw the alliance as intended to operate primarily against Persia, a view evidently shared by the Persian government, which responded to the news of the treaty's signing by sending an armoured column to attack an Iraqi border post ninety miles north-east of Baghdad. It is less certain that the Iraqi interpretation of the treaty's purpose was subscribed to by the Russians, whose behaviour towards Persia since the mid-1960s, as will be seen later, had been marked by caution and outward cordiality. As things turned out, the first target of the Iraqi government's new-found bellicosity was the Iraq Petroleum Company, whose concession was revoked and its assets nationalized by the Baathists in June 1972. The second target was Kuwait.

Relations between Iraq and Kuwait had gradually improved in the mid-1960s, reaching their optimum point in 1968 after Kuwait had, in May of that year, given notice of the termination of the 1961 defence agreement with Britain, and the Kuwaiti prime minister two months later had publicly declared that Kuwait would not accept 'any foreign presence, British or otherwise, in the area'. Thereafter, however, relations deteriorated, as the Baathists in Baghdad grew more militant and reckless – and more irritated by Kuwait's granting of asylum to their political opponents. Late in 1972 they demanded a large financial loan from Kuwait. The demand was rejected, and the Baathists replied by ostentatiously moving troops to the frontier at the beginning of 1973. Negotiations between the two governments followed, culminating in the presentation of an Iraqi ultimatum, couched in the form of a draft treaty of friendship and co-operation, to a Kuwaiti delegation in Baghdad in March 1973. The treaty provided for the grant to Iraq of the right 'to build, operate and maintain one or more pipelines on Kuwaiti territory extending to a terminal on the Arabian Gulf; also the right to build, maintain and operate offices, pumping stations, refineries, depots and tanks for the storing of oil and water, bridges, harbours, airports and railway lines' – and all without the payment of dues. Another article in the treaty gave Iraq the right to 'enlist the services of a third party to undertake studies and exploration operations or implement any part of the project', and granted this third party the same facilities and privileges as Iraq was to enjoy.

The site Iraq had in mind for the proposed oil terminal was the deep water off Bubiyan island, with pipelines running across the island and thence to the mainland. Obviously, if the concession were to be granted, it would be only a matter of time before Bubiyan, and the adjoining island of Warbah, became Iraqi territory. Umm Qasr could then be developed further as a port and naval base, and its maritime approaches would be wholly under Iraqi jurisdiction. Iraq's coastline on the Gulf would be tripled in length, and the extent of sea-bed to which she was entitled would be greatly enlarged. That these considerations lay behind the proposed treaty was publicly confirmed by the Iraqi foreign minister on 4 April 1973, when he stated that Iraq wanted Bubiyan and Warbah islands so that 'Iraq would become a Gulf state'. What was left unsaid was how much Russia would gain as Iraq's ally from the attainment of this object, especially from her role as the 'third party' in the proposed Kuwait–Iraq treaty, and from the increased usefulness of Umm Qasr, where, under the treaty of 9 April 1972, she was entitled to enjoy naval facilities.

The draft treaty of March 1973 was rejected by the Kuwait government, virtually on sight. On 20 March Iraqi tanks and infantry attacked two Kuwaiti border posts in the north-eastern corner of the shaikhdom. Small detachments of troops were also reported to have landed on Warbah and Bubiyan islands. Saudi Arabia moved troops to the Kuwait border in a gesture of support, and the Arab League appealed to the two sides to seek an accommodation. Iraq asserted, against all the evidence to the contrary, that she had never accepted the frontier delimited fifty years earlier, although she was now ready to consider renouncing her claim to sovereignty over Kuwait as a whole in return for the cession of Warbah and Bubiyan islands. In the first week of April the Iraqi forces withdrew from Kuwaiti territory, a withdrawal which was not wholly unconnected with the subsequent payment to Iraq of several million Kuwaiti dinars. The Baathist junta had made its point, and if any doubts about it remained, they were removed by the arrival in Baghdad in mid-April of Admiral Sergei Gorchakov, the Soviet chief of naval staff.

The Russian grip on Iraq was strengthened in July 1973 when, after more than eighteen months of negotiations, a 'national action pact' was concluded between the Baath and the Iraqi communist party which admitted the communists to a share in the government. It was the first official recognition of the party as a legal political body since its foundation in 1934, and it had come about as a result of Russian pressure. The pact provided for the formation of a 'national front', with the Baath in a 'privileged' position. The front was to be open to all 'progressive' political groups in the country, including the Kurdish Democratic Party, a provision which again reflected Russian influence, for the Russians had encouraged the cause of Kurdish separatism on and off for fifty years. The inclusion of the Kurds, however, was more easily decreed than achieved. The bitter war between them and successive governments in Baghdad which had dragged on, with occasional respites, for most of the previous decade, had been brought to a halt in March 1970 by the conclusion of an agreement conceding autonomy to the Kurds in those areas of Iraq where they predominated. The agreement broke down through the bad faith of the Baathist government, and the Kurds were still in a state of passive revolt at the time of the drawing up of the 'national action pact'. New discussions were now opened with them, and on 11 March 1974, the fourth anniversary of the original Kurdish compact, the Revolutionary Command Council in Baghdad announced that autonomy would henceforth be granted to the Kurds in those areas which were wholly Kurdish – but not those where, as in the original compact, they constituted a simple majority. The Kurds were given fifteen days in which to accept the settlement. They rejected the ultimatum, and under their venerable leader, Mullah Mustafa al-Barzani, they broke out once more in open revolt.

For the Russians the intransigence of their Kurdish protégés was an embarrassment. While they appreciated the value of the Kurdish national movement as a destabilizing force in Iraq, their preferred instrument for turning that country, if possible, into a Soviet satellite was the Iraqi communist party. The Russians' attitude to the Kurds, therefore, was determined, as much as anything, by the fluctuating fortunes of the Iraqi communists. While the latter were tolerated and even allowed a role in government, as they were by Qassim and in 1973 by the Baath, the Kurds were made the target of Russian obloquy. When the Baghdad regime clamped down on the communists, as it did at the time of Qassim's fall and periodically afterwards, the Kurdish struggle was commended and assisted by Moscow. It was *real-politik* that was to triumph in the end. When the Soviet government decided that its interests in Iraq might be better advanced by cultivating the Baathists than by continuing its ambiguous policy towards the Kurds, as it now did in the spring of 1974, it cast away the ambiguity and joined wholeheartedly in the destruction of Kurdish resistance. There followed a brutal and murderous campaign, which perhaps more than anything else revealed the repulsive character of the Baghdad regime and the shabby nature of the Russo–Iraqi alliance. Not, of course, that such considerations bothered the Russians; they could afford to be insouciant about them since the stakes for which they were playing in Iraq were very great – access to Iraqi oil in increasing quantities and a corresponding diminution of supplies to the West; a lodgement at the doorstep of Kuwait with its large oil reserves and splendid harbour; an avenue to the Gulf and a base at Umm Qasr from which to sustain a naval presence in its waters; the opportunity to turn to good account the Iraqi Baath's penchant for subversive activities against its neighbours; and the chance to exploit Iraq's animosity towards Persia to exert pressure upon the shah.

A set-back, at least in the short term, to this last hope was afforded by the accommodation reached between the Persians and Iraqis, through the mediation of the Algerian president, Houari Boumedienne, at the OPEC summit conference at Algiers in March 1975, when the world was treated to the affecting spectacle of the shah embracing before the assembled delegates Saddam Husain al-Takriti, the Iraqi vice-president and the most ruthless member of a government which the shah had previously seen fit to describe as a group of 'crazy, bloodthirsty savages'. At the heart of the *rapprochement*, however, lay not so much the discovery of a mutual attachment as a cynical agreement to resolve the differences between them at the expense of the Kurds. In return for Iraq's concession of the median line of the Shatt al-Arab as the Perso–Iraqi frontier along that waterway, the shah agreed to cease forthwith from assisting the Kurds with arms and supplies, and to close the Persian border adjacent to the Kurdish-held districts in northern Iraq by the end of March. It was the end for the Kurds. With their supply routes closed, they could not keep up the spirited resistance which had kept the Iraqi army at bay for years. Those who could not escape to Persia were hammered into submission by the Baghdad government, with a ferocity it had not dared (even had it been able) to muster only a short while earlier. As a means of destroying the last vestiges of Kurdish nationalism, thousands upon thousands of Kurds were uprooted from their homes in the northern mountains and forcibly resettled in the deserts and marshlands of lower Iraq.

The Kurdish struggle for autonomy, which has gone on for well over half a century, is symptomatic of the political instability of Iraq, and of the centrifugal forces within Iraqi society. Iraq is an artificial state, with no sense of historical continuity between its previous existence as three distinct *vilayets* of the Ottoman empire and its modern metamorphosis as a unified nation-state. Even the appearance of nationhood is illusory, for the population of Iraq is made up of a number of separate communities, each distinguished from the others by racial, religious or even national differences. There are Sunni Arabs and Shii Arabs, Kurds and Yazidis, Turcomans, Jews and Christians, none of whom, in the judgement of one of the most knowledgeable and thoughtful scholars of recent Iraqi political history, 'accepts the State of Iraq in its present form, and to all of [whom] it remains an artificial political entity'.* Because there is no general political community there is no common basis for the rule of law, so that political differences are resolved by violence, coercion and revolt. The Shiis, who constitute at least half the population of roughly eleven million souls and inhabit the lower half of the country from Baghdad southwards, resent the Sunni supremacy in the government. The Kurds and Turcomans, who are Sunni and live mainly in the north and north-east, chafe under the Arab ascendancy; while the scattered groups of Jews and Christians are kept in subjection as non-Muslim minorities.

One reason why a proper sense of Iraqi nationhood has not developed is that many in the Sunni community, which comprises about a quarter of the population and is concentrated principally in a territorial triangle whose apexes are Mosul, Baghdad and Rutha (in the west towards Syria), assert that their prime loyalty belongs to the Arab nation as a whole. Arab nationalism, however, is inseparable from Islam, and Sunni, or orthodox, Islam at that. Thus, to quote the opinion of the scholar just mentioned:

It has meant that nationalism as advocated by the Iraqi political élite could appeal to only one community, and in that sense it has become sectarian and divisive. In a mosaic society like that of Iraq the introduction of the concept of national autonomy linked to religion, as it is in the Arab nationalist ideology, could hardly encourage national cohesion.

For the greater part of the past twenty years, ever since the destruction of the monarchy, Iraq has been ruled by a military junta, and for the last decade at least this junta has been dominated by the leaders of the Iraqi branch of the Arab Baath Party. The army and the police, and more especially the officer corps, are traditionally recruited from the Sunni communities dwelling along the Tigris north of Baghdad, and along the middle reaches of the Euphrates. For the Sunni army and air-force officers drawn from these communities the pan-Arab and socialist ideology of the Baathist movement held a strong appeal, and it was they who overthrew Qassim in 1963, largely in the name of pan-Arabism. Though they had to wait another five years before achieving absolute power in the state, they succeeded in those years in purging the higher ranks of the armed forces of all Shii and other non-Sunni officers.

The purges did not stop there, however, but have continued down to the present day. Like so many revolutionary movements, the Baath party is

* Abbas Kelidar, 'Iraq: the search for stability', *Conflict Studies* no. 59.

riddled with factionalism, which in turn breeds cliques and conspiracies, rebellion and repression. Despite their pan-Arabism, the Syrian and Iraqi wings of the Baath are at daggers drawn, not least over their rival claims to ideological purity. Though the Baathist government in Baghdad gained power through the army, it has attempted in recent years to present itself at home and abroad as essentially a civil regime. Its motives for doing so have been twofold: firstly, to give the outward appearance of conforming to Baathist dogma, which holds that the armed forces should be the military arm of the party, i.e. a 'people's army' at the vanguard of the revolutionary struggle but subordinate to the party hierarchy; and, secondly, to make the dogma a reality so far as the party's actual control of the Iraqi armed forces is concerned. Hence the repeated purges of the latter's ranks. Yet the fact remains that the Baath seized power by force of arms and it is dependent upon the same force of arms to stay in power. All its cosmetic efforts to give the illusion of civil rule cannot disguise this fact, or invest the regime with the political legitimacy it has lacked from its inception.

Supreme authority in Iraq is wielded by a tightly knit group of army officers and civilians, the Revolutionary Command Council, which also incorporates the ruling apparatus, or regional command council, of the Iraqi Baath. The chairman of the RCC and president of the country was until recently Ahmad Hasan al-Bakr, a former major-general. The former vice-president, and secretary-general of the Iraqi Baath, who succeeded him as president in July 1979, is Saddam Husain, a civilian. Both men come from Takrit, a town on the Tigris about 100 miles north of Baghdad, in the heart of the Sunni 'triangle'. So also do the sixteen other members of the Baath's regional command council. Almost from the outset Saddam Husain al-Takriti's power in the government equalled, if it did not supersede, that of al-Bakr, and it was he who was largely responsible for the conclusion of the alliance with the Soviet Union in 1972. The alliance, and the compact with the Iraqi communist party which followed it, was a measure of the regime's sense of insecurity, for the Baathists at heart look upon communism with distaste as a threat to Arab nationalism and to Islam. What they gained from the Russian alliance they were to lose in large measure from their compact with the Iraqi communists; for the compact not only alienated many of their pan-Arab Sunni supporters but it also gave encouragement to the communists themselves and to the non-Sunni sections of the population, who saw in the communist party a vehicle for the expression of their disaffection with the Sunni supremacy. The uncomfortable suspicion that communist influence was penetrating ever deeper into the ranks of the disaffected was one of the reasons for the execution of a score of communists by the junta in the first half of 1978, and for the eventual expulsion of the communists from the government a year later. The latter measure, in particular, was indicative of the acute anxiety felt by the junta over the mounting civil disobedience being manifested by the Shii community, whose sectarian fervour had been raised to fever pitch by the triumph of Shii fundamentalism in Persia in the winter of 1978–9. Taken in conjunction with the deterioration in Iraq's relations with Persia since the fall of the shah, the growing restlessness among the Iraqi Shia has forced the Baathist regime to resort to ever more severe measures of repression to maintain itself in power.

Outside Iraq the Baath has preached revolution, promoted subversion and encouraged terrorism, all in the name of pan-Arabism and socialist ideals. Baghdad has been a haven and a base for the most ruthless of the Palestinian extremist factions, and for a number of other exponents of revolutionary violence. At one time or another the Iraqi Baath has tried to foment sedition in every one of the Gulf states, not stopping at assassination in its attempts to procure its ends. It has supplied weapons, money and training to insurgents in Oman and Dhufar, often playing the political pander between them and their Russian or Chinese patrons. In company with the Libyan junta it has been the most consistent, and at times the most vocal, apologist for the gruesome Marxist dictatorship in Aden. The Baath's policy in the Gulf has had two main objectives: to undermine the traditional shaikhly system of government in the Gulf states, thereby paving the way for the emergency of leftist, revolutionary regimes similar to its own; and to win acceptance as the champion of Arabism in the region, especially against Persian attempts at hegemony and the supposed 'neo-imperialist' designs of the Western powers. Saudi Arabia, of course, is seen as a major obstacle to the attainment of these ends. Iraqi antipathy to the Al Saud goes back a long way, well beyond the days of the Hashimite monarchy to the time of the Wahhabi incursions into Iraq at the turn of the nineteenth century. It has both religious and political elements in it, and it has been intensified since the Baath's advent to power by the party's ideological animosity against hereditary and monarchical forms of government. Yet while the Baath may keep up, as it has, a ceaseless barrage of seditious propaganda against the Saudis, and lend surreptitious support to subversive groups within Saudi Arabia in the hope of bringing down the ruling house, it is too tightly constrained by its own internal and external difficulties to venture upon an armed conflict with the Saudi kingdom. It has already alienated not only the Saudis but the minor Gulf states as well by its alliance with the Russians, and by its underhand attempts to foment insurrection within these states. Almost without exception – and the only obvious one has been Shaikh Saqr ibn Muhammad of Ras al-Khaimah – the Gulf rulers look upon the Baghdad regime with abhorrence. Wary though they may be of the Saudis, they would almost certainly take their side in a clash with Iraq.

What hampers the Iraqis perhaps more than anything else – and here we return full circle to the point where we began – is their lack of naval power. Without it they can never hope to command the Gulf, or even to make their weight felt there. Any forward move they might make would bring them up against the naval strength of Persia, which, however illusory it may be in real terms, is still superior to that of Iraq. To reduce this disadvantage the Iraqi government has only one recourse – to turn to the Soviet Union.

In the autumn of 1971 the 2,500th anniversary of the Persian monarchy was celebrated with great pomp and circumstance at Persepolis in southern Persia. It was Muhammad Reza Shah's way of announcing the re-emergence of Persia as a great power upon the world's stage. Rather more pointedly, perhaps, it was also an expression of satisfaction at the impending withdrawal of Britain from her role of guardian of the peace of the Gulf, and an intimation of the shah's intention to assume that role himself. The character and personality of Muhammad Reza Shah have been decisive in the shaping of Persia's policy in the Gulf over the past decade. From the moment of his accession in the summer of 1941, when he was placed upon the throne by the British and Russian envoys in Tehran following the joint occupation of Persia by British and Russian forces, he had nursed a galling resentment against the two powers for the dual humiliation they had inflicted upon him by deposing his father, Reza Shah, and setting him up in his stead. That Reza Shah had himself abdicated, out of a fear that the Russian troops advancing on Tehran were bent upon his deposition, was ignored by his son, as it was by most Persians. Muhammad Reza Shah's whole reign was spent in an attempt to erase the memory of this humiliation, and to release his country from the dominance which Russia and Britain had exerted over it from the early decades of the nineteenth century.

The iron circumstances of geography, and of military and economic power, however, combined to frustrate his efforts. Like his predecessors on the Peacock Throne, he was compelled, simply to ensure the continued existence and integrity of his country, both to seek accommodations with those he could not resist and to obtain assurances of support from those whose goodwill he could not afford to spurn. Thus the withdrawal of Russian troops from Persia after the Second World War had been partially secured for him by the United States and Britain, his throne was saved for him by American intervention in the early 1950s, and the security of his country was afterwards assured by American economic, military and political aid. The awareness of these past debts did not sit well with Muhammad Reza Shah: it served more to irritate than to chasten, especially as it did not harmonize with his own plans and ambitions. Conscious of the humiliations Persia has had to bear in the past as an economically backward country, he proclaimed his determination to make it the most powerful industrial nation in Asia, outside Japan, within two decades. Unquestioning in his belief in the superiority of Persian civilization over that of his Muslim neighbours, whether Turks, Afghans or Arabs, scornful of the apparent frivolity of the West (which he saw as sliding hopelessly into decadence), and unalterable in his conviction of the soaring destiny which awaited him and his country, he regarded it as nothing short of axiomatic that the other governments of the Middle East should look to Tehran for inspiration and leadership, just as the satraps of the East had looked to the court of Cyrus the Great 2,500 years ago.

Notwithstanding his exalted vision of himself and his destiny in this world, he was nagged through his reign by an anxiety to invest his dynasty with the legitimacy which, in his heart of hearts, he knew it lacked. His father, Reza Khan, had been a near illiterate soldier in the Persian Cossack brigade (the only military unit worthy of the name in the Persian army before the First World War), who had risen to command of the brigade after its Russian officers had been dismissed in the aftermath of the Bolshevik revolution. Reza Khan overthrew the government of the reigning Qajar shah by means of a military *coup d'état* in 1920–21, and at the close of 1925 he proclaimed himself shah. To confer some kind of historical legitimacy upon his rule, Reza Shah adopted the factitious patronymic of 'Pahlavi', the name given to the archaic form of the Persian language before the admixture of Arabic. In a further attempt to link his regime with Persia's remote past, and especially the glories of the Sassanian empire, he changed the name of the country in 1935 to 'Iran', which derives from the same root as 'Aryan', the generic term for the group of Indo-European languages of which Persian is one. Muhammad Reza Shah continued his father's efforts at legitimization, carrying them often to extreme lengths.

Like his father – upon whom in later years he bestowed the cognomen of *al-Kabir*, 'the great' – he assumed the titles of *shahanshah* ('king of kings', the style affected by ancient Persian monarchs to denote their sway over the subject rulers of Georgia, Kurdistan, Arabistan and Afghanistan), 'centre of the universe' and 'Shadow of God upon earth', the Muslim dignity accorded in days gone by to, among others, caliphs of Islam, Ottoman sultans and Mughal emperors. Not content with this impressive array of titles, Muhammad Reza Shah invented a new dignity for himself at the time of his coronation in 1967 (an event he had postponed until after the birth of a male heir) – *Aryamehr* or 'light of the Aryans'. The institution of kingship in Persia was imbued with a sacred quality, a survival from the distant days of the Achaemenian and Sassanian kingdoms and the religion of Zoroaster. It was also invested with a strongly theocratic character through its association with Shii Islam, the monarch being looked to as the active head and defender of the faith. Muhammad Reza Shah chose to emphasize the ancient Persian conception of kingship, with its concomitant doctrine of the divine right of kings, rather than the Shii interpretation of the nature and duties of the office. The choice was dictated by his own inclinations and his passion for modernity but it was one which offended the more devout Shii mullahs, who firmly believed that he should rule in strict accordance with the prescriptions of Islam.

Reza Shah is said to have modelled himself and his endeavours to transform Persia into a modern state upon Mustafa Kemal, Ataturk, and his deliberate Europeanization of Turkey after 1923. Muhammad Reza Shah would appear to have taken as his exemplar Louis XIV, *le roi soleil*, both in his personal conduct and in the absolutist nature of his rule. The guiding principle of his government was centralization: every artery and sinew of the country's administration led ultimately to the royal palace in Tehran. The Persian parliament, the *majlis*, was ignored. So, too, was the constitution enacted under the Qajars in 1906, which had created the *majlis* and, in theory, placed limits upon the power of the monarch. The judiciary suffered the same fate, the administration of justice being conducted, for all practical purposes, by executive tribunals, often under military direction. No political institution, in short, was suffered to function other than that of the sovereign in mystical communion with his people. To supervise the workings of the sprawling bureaucracy necessitated by such a highly centralized and personal system of government the shah relied upon a series of overlapping and interlocking agencies, all of them responsible to him alone. The most important was the imperial inspectorate, whose power of investigation, as well as its reach, was almost unlimited. It worked hand-in-glove with a large and ubiquitous secret police force, the National Information and Security Organization or SAVAK (*Sazman-i Ettelaat va Amniyat-i Keshvar*), whose particular function it was to detect and suppress political unrest, a function which led it eventually to extend its tentacles into nearly every corner of the nation's life. The attention of the military intelligence service was as much directed towards internal security as it was towards the safety and integrity of Persia's frontiers, for the first and overriding duty of the army was to keep the shah in power. The immediate protection of the shah's person was entrusted to the imperial guard, some 2,000 strong, which was backed up by élite units of the Persian army stationed in and around Tehran.

Political activity of any real kind was effectively suppressed by the *de facto* banning of political parties and the vigilance of SAVAK. Muhammad Reza Shah never forgot the brief but distressing experience of being forced into temporary exile in 1953 by the *majlis* under the leadership of Muhammad Musaddiq, who two years earlier had boldly nationalized the Anglo-Iranian Oil Company's concession in Persia. After being restored to the throne by an army *coup*, largely engineered by the Americans, the shah forbade those members of the *majlis* who had constituted the National Front (a loose coalition of various nationalist parties who had united behind Musaddiq as prime minister) ever to engage in active politics again. He was even more ruthless with the *Tudeh* ('Masses') party, a more radical movement under communist leadership which purported to represent the Persian masses but in reality was thoroughly subservient to the Soviet Union. Its leading members were executed, imprisoned or exiled and the party itself was outlawed. Denied any kind of legitimate political outlet, the educated classes in Persia more or less turned their backs on politics for the next two decades, knuckling under to the regime and contenting themselves with the improvement of their material circumstances. In this they were actively abetted by the shah, who sought as a deliberate act of policy to secure their political quiescence by conferring more and more economic benefits upon them, a policy made possible by the steady augmentation of Persia's oil revenues from the mid-1960s onwards.

The policy of buying the loyalty of his subjects by economic rewards, at the same time as he compelled their obedience by the sword, was also applied by the shah to the Persian people at large. In 1962 he inaugurated a programme of land reform, the object of which was both to improve the country's agriculture and to benefit the peasants by increasing the proportion of landholders among them. Though observers differ in their estimates of the degree of success achieved by the first stage of the land reform – which concentrated upon the distribution of crown lands and the reduction of the holdings of absentee landlords – there is general agreement that some progress was made. The second stage of the programme, which began in 1965, brought further redistribution of land through sales, although large landholders were permitted to keep their estates on condition that they improved their farming methods and productivity. Agricultural co-operatives were also set up and loans made available to the peasant shareholders. The success of this stage was more problematical, as we shall see later in looking at the performance of Persian agriculture over the past decade. What is more certain is that the motive for the land reform was political rather than economic, being designed to cement the bond between the shah and the rural population, upon whose fealty he, like preceding shahs, ultimately depended to give legitimacy to his rule. It was a relationship commonly found in all Oriental despotisms, including those which exist, in one form or another, elsewhere in the Middle East today. There was, moreover, a further purpose apparent in the institution of the land reform at this time. The Kennedy administration was in power in the United States, and the shah was anxious to curry favour with it by playing the liberal monarch.

Land reform was only part of what the shah presented to his people and the world as his 'white revolution', which was officially inaugurated in 1963 with the promulgation of the third five-year development plan and which was intended to transform Persia smoothly and swiftly into a replica, at least, of a modern state. Ten years later the spectacular rise in oil prices vastly increased Persia's oil revenues, and the shah's ambitions soared with them. The fifth economic development plan announced in January 1973 had envisaged the expenditure of $35,500 million over the next five years to expand Persia's industry and improve the country's agriculture. This figure was almost doubled to $69,600 million in the revised version of the plan which the shah ordered to be drawn up in August 1974 and which was eventually published in May 1975. In it Muhammad Reza Shah proclaimed his intention to build a 'Great Civilization' in Persia and to make his country the fifth industrial power in the world before the end of the century. The miracle was to be accomplished by the spending of money, which in turn would be furnished by the industrial West in the form of bounteous oil payments.

Unfortunately, Persia lacked nearly every prerequisite necessary for the transition to an industrial economy in so short a space of time as the shah had decreed. Her people were in the main illiterate (perhaps as many as three-quarters of them), devoid of the technical skills and experience needed for an industrial labour force. The country had no economic infrastructure in the form of adequate roads, railways, ports, communications or power and water supplies to support the rapid development of industry. There was only one steel mill in existence, the Aryamehr complex at Ispahan, which the Russians had undertaken to build in 1966–7. It was completed in 1973 but three years later it had still not achieved its planned output of 600,000 tons per annum. Although in the decade from the late 1960s to the late 1970s Persia's gross national product grew at a remarkable rate, averaging some 13–14 per cent per annum, most of the industrial growth was in activities deriving from the oil industry. Only the barest start was made with the manufacture of intermediate and heavy (i.e. capital) goods, which demands greater technical skills and managerial talents than light manufacturing. Instead, the bulk of the national output was either in construction or in what might be termed 'Coca Cola' manufacturing, i.e. the production of light consumer goods intended as substitutes for imports.

What the economic activity of the 1970s lacked in achievement it more than made up for in extravagance. At least 40 per cent of the money invested in any project, it has been estimated, was wasted. Much of the waste was caused by the inability of Persia's ports and transport system to handle the vast quantities of imports which had been ordered with senseless abandon. At Khurramshahr in the middle of 1975 there were some 200 ships waiting to unload their cargoes, and the average waiting time was five months. In one year alone (1974–5), demurrage charges cost Persia over $1,000 million, or 5 per cent of her oil revenues. Although half the imports were government purchases, they, like every class of import, were held up by the lethargic and elephantine workings of the Persian bureaucracy and by the systematic peculations of customs officers. There were not enough vehicles to transport the goods from the docks to their destinations; so the government purchased several thousand lorries, only to find that there were not enough Persians capable of driving or maintaining them.

There were reasons other than the inadequacy of the country's economic infrastructure to account for the frustration of the shah's efforts to industrialize his country overnight. Among Persia's landowning and mercantile classes there was no tradition of long-term investment in industrial undertakings, or any disposition to take the risks that such investment involved. Even when money was made available to the landowners in the form of over-generous compensation for the estates they had been made to surrender in the first and second stages of the land reform, they did not invest this capital, as the shah had intended they should, in industrial development. Instead, they employed it in the purchase of urban land and property, and in speculative construction of an unproductive kind (office buildings, apartment blocks, shops, housing, etc.) with the aim of continuing to live, as they had in the past, off their rents. It was much the same with the merchants and local manufacturers who accumulated fortunes during the consumer boom of the early 1970s. They, like the landowners and other beneficiaries of the flood of oil money among the professional and bureaucratic classes, preferred to sink their gains in real estate or to transfer them out of the country, usually for investment in the West. From the latter part of 1975 onwards some $100 million of private capital on average left Persia every month, sometimes even more, as in the autumn of 1975 when $2,000 million at least was estimated to have been remitted abroad, and again in the autumn of 1978 when a similar sum was said to have left the country.

Another cause of the stultification of the shah's grand design was the sheer shortage of skilled labour already alluded to, a shortage made all the more severe by the competition from, and priority given to, military construction projects. Throughout the 1960s and increasingly in the 1970s the shah had encouraged the migration of workers from the countryside to the towns so as to create the pool of labour necessary for Persia's industrial revolution. On the eve of the Second World War three-quarters of Persia's population of some fourteen and a half million souls lived either on rural estates or in villages and towns of fewer than 5,000 inhabitants. Forty years later some 46 per cent of the population, which by this time had grown to about forty million, lived in the cities and larger towns, and this urban population was expanding at three times the rate of growth of the rural population. The economic boom of the 1970s was virtually confined to the main cities – Tehran, Tabriz, Ispahan, Mashhad, Shiraz, Kirmanshah, Ahwaz and Abadan – and to Tehran above all, the population of the capital growing from something over half a million in 1939 to more than four million by the mid-1970s. Most of the peasants who poured into the cities, however, were mechanically unskilled (the great majority of them unlettered as well), so that they were fit for no more than basic physical labour or the simplest kinds of factory work.

Their expectations, however, had been raised by the excitement of the oil boom and by the shah's exhortations to them to build the 'Great Civilization'. Aware that such a fast-growing urban proletariat, newly uprooted from its traditional way of life, could prove politically dangerous, especially in Tehran, the shah sought to buy off its potential enmity, as he had bought off that of the upper and middle classes, by economic *douceurs*. By royal decree the wages of factory workers were constantly increased, and employers were required to pay bonuses to their employees at regular intervals. A further populist measure devised by the shah was that of workers' shares – the urban equivalent of the land reform programme – which he introduced in July 1975. Every commercial and manufacturing enterprise over a specified size was required to divest itself of 49 per cent of its equity to its employees over a period of three years, the funds for the purchase of these shares being made available to the workers from the state treasury. It was a purely political gesture by the shah to appease a section of the urban work force, particularly in Tehran, and as such it misfired, economically as well as politically. The employers, after their initial dismay, realized that the scheme afforded them an opportunity to rid themselves of unwanted or wasting assets for sums far exceeding their actual worth and their own expectations. When they received their compensation, instead of reinvesting the capital they promptly transferred it out of the country. From a political standpoint the scheme brought the shah scant reward, for it did not touch the mass of the urban working class which was employed in small firms outside the scope of the scheme. Within two years or less of its inception, the scheme had joined the growing pile of Muhammad Reza Shah's discarded fiscal inspirations.

Veritable torrents of money were poured into the Persian economy by the shah between 1974 and 1976 in an effort to achieve his dual object of stimulating industrial activity and procuring popular content with his rule. Between March 1974 and March 1975 the money supply in Persia increased by 61 per cent. The previous year it had risen by 27.7 per cent, and it was still growing at an annual rate of 36 per cent at the end of 1975. Such a massive increase in so short a time was bound to generate equally massive inflation, and so it did. The unchecked speculation in land and building, notably in Tehran, only drove the rate of inflation higher, to 40 per cent or more in 1974, 1975 and 1976. As the cost of living rose, more money was pumped into the economy in the form of wage increases, workers' bonuses and food subsidies, fuelling the engine of inflation still further. Refusing to admit any responsibility for creating the monster, the shah blamed its emergence upon the Western industrial nations for unwarrantably increasing the cost of their exports to Persia (any suggestion that the steep rise in oil prices, which he had been largely instrumental in engineering, might have had a bearing upon these increases was brushed aside as unworthy of consideration), and upon Persian merchants and entrepreneurs for profiteering at the expense of their fellow citizens. To curry favour with the city masses, he encouraged anti-profiteering demonstrations against local merchants and foreign businesses, which only served to create greater economic uncertainty, leading in turn to further flights of capital from the country.

If what has been said so far about the shah's attempt to modernize Persia overnight seems unduly harsh, it is because he more than any man was responsible for the chaos, waste and corruption which accompanied that attempt. As the source of all power within the state, he insisted upon retaining control of the direction taken by the economy and the way in which the oil revenues were spent. So far as he was concerned, the chief purpose of this expenditure was to consolidate and aggrandize his own power, any benefits that might accrue to the Persian people being incidental or subordinate to that purpose. Persia, her oil and natural gas resources notwithstanding, is a relatively poor country, and the Persians, whatever their native talents, are a poor and backward people. Malnutrition is widespread among them, the infant mortality rate is tragically high and life expectancy is correspondingly low. Only 25 per cent of them, as we have seen, are literate, and their general standard of living is a meagre one. What they needed above all was improvements in agriculture. Persia was, and still is, predominantly an agricultural country, with 40 per cent or more of her people engaged in farming of one kind or another. Fairly substantial sums were allocated to the improvement of the country's agriculture in the fourth and fifth quinquennial development plans (i.e. from 1968 to 1978), but the overall results were hardly impressive. Experiments were made with large-scale commercial farming, on the American 'agribusiness' model, with substantial capital and the assistance of foreign experts. Four such ventures in Khuzistan in the early 1970s all proved financial disasters. At the other end of the scale, there was little more success with the small individual farms of eleven hectares or less, to which the majority of landholdings had been reduced by the land reform programme. The burden of the past, whether in the form of social distinctions, religious prejudices, the grip of the landholders upon the peasant cultivators, disease, ignorance, illiteracy, corruption or resistance to innovations, proved almost impossible to shift – which only went to show how irrelevant, in the end, the land reforms had been.

The achievements of the 'white revolution' in the fields of health and education were not much more encouraging. That there was some improvement was undeniable – as well as unavoidable in view of the sums of money expended. But the results hardly matched the shah's claims that he had lifted his people out of a slough of disease and ignorance. A single instance may perhaps suffice to illustrate the wide gap between promise and fulfilment in the Persia of the 1970s.*

In 1974 the Persian government announced that it intended to provide 20,000 new hospital beds by 1978. The initial phase of the programme envisaged the construction of fifteen hospitals with a capacity of 6,000 beds. As the shah insisted that only the best that Western technology could supply would suffice, the estimates submitted by Western contractors were of a commensurate order. Drift, delay and indecision on the part of the Persian ministries concerned caused the estimated cost per bed to rise, by the time the final bids were submitted, to 38.8 million rials, or over $500,000. The Persian government's reaction to this unwelcome news was to cancel the contracts on

* It is one of many recounted by Robert Graham, a correspondent of the *Financial Times* stationed in Tehran during the boom years, in his valuable study, *Iran, the Illusion of Power*.

the grounds that the foreign contractors were cheating them. As a result, construction of the first fifteen hospitals had not even begun by 1978.

Even if the hospital construction programme had by some miraculous means been implemented, there was not the slightest chance that the Persians themselves could have staffed the hospitals. Medical education in Persia was in no better condition than higher education in the country generally. A relatively high proportion of the thousands of Persians studying at universities and colleges abroad were reading medicine, though less, it seems, out of a sense of vocation than because it offered the promise of a highly lucrative career on their return home, whether they entered practice or obtained a post in the bureaucracy. Not all the Persian medical students at American or European universities, however, succeeded in graduating, and of those who did a fair proportion elected not to return to Persia. As the output of Persia's own medical schools was limited, there was a fairly desperate shortage in the country of qualified doctors, as well as of nurses and medical technicians, a shortage which could not be erased simply by the recruitment of foreigners. What made the situation even worse was the low level of professional competence (and in the eyes of foreign observers, of professional ethics also) displayed by a high proportion of the Persian medical fraternity. Most of them, furthermore, refused to consider practising anywhere except in the major cities – or, for that matter, anywhere outside Tehran. Taken together with the high cost of medical treatment, the insufficiency of urban and rural health clinics, and the general inefficiency of those who staffed them, these various drawbacks made the prospect of adequate medical care for the great mass of the Persian population little more than a mirage.

Higher education in Persia presents much the same picture as it does elsewhere in the Middle East. There are far too many students for either the size or the needs of the country, and too many of them are motivated not by a desire to acquire knowledge but by the conception of a university degree or college diploma as the passport to an agreeable sinecure in the bureaucracy. While Persia has a far larger number of students abroad than any other Middle-Eastern country, she has at the same time fewer students than most of them at her own higher institutions of learning. To recover the loss of face which he believed he suffered by this circumstance, Muhammad Reza Shah decreed a major expansion of the Persian student body, which was accomplished in large measure by the foundation of several new universities and technical institutions, most of which were graced with either his name or that of his father, or with one of his several titles. Between 1970 and 1977 the student body almost trebled in size, from around 65,000 to over 170,000, by the simple expedient of lowering academic standards, which had never been high at the best of times. The expansion of higher education was all of a piece with the shah's other ostentatious endeavours to portray himself as a patron of learning, such as his donations to American and European universities to promote Persian studies, donations which ran into millions of dollars and which might have been better spent in trying to eradicate illiteracy among the Persian peasantry.

Far from laying the foundations of an industrial economy in Persia in the decade between 1968 and 1978, the shah, through his vanity, his impatience and his intemperate ambitions, succeeded in erecting only the papier-mâché façade of such an economy. The boom in Persia's economy lasted only two years, from the early months of 1974 to the early months of 1976. Oil revenues had failed to keep up with the Persian government's expectations, as the world's consumption of oil steadily fell after the quadrupling of prices in 1973. By the spring of 1976 Persia was faced with a reversion to the financial situation she had been in at the beginning of the decade, that of running an annual deficit on her external balance of trade. (At the end of 1972 her outstanding foreign public debt had stood at $5,900 million, the servicing of which consumed 18 per cent of her total export earnings every year.) Still the shah refused to reduce expenditure, resorting instead to foreign loans and barter deals in an effort to keep the party going. In a way, he had no choice but to continue to ride the tiger of avarice which he had created by his unheeding expenditures and his lavish disbursement of subsidies upon imports, especially foodstuffs – of which Persia had produced an exportable surplus a decade earlier. For if he did not keep up the supply of sops, the beast might well unseat and devour him.

Yet for all his foolish vaunting, for all his prodigious extravagance and even more prodigious errors, Muhammad Reza Shah's ambition to modernize his country's economy and to earn for his people a respected place among the nations of the world was by no means an unworthy one. That he failed to achieve it was due as much to what are the seemingly ineradicable vices of Persian society – vanity, self-deception, inconstancy, nepotism and venality – as it was to his own personal failings and *folie de grandeur*. 'The Persians', wrote Sir John Malcolm, an early British envoy to Tehran, in his *History of Persia* a century and a half ago, 'are the vainest people on earth', and ample evidence of this attribute, as well as of the other prime constituents of Persian behaviour, is to be found in James Morier's tales of the estimable Hajji Baba of Ispahan. (It is not, perhaps, entirely incidental that the symbol of royal authority in Persia should be the Peacock Throne, or that the throne itself is not the fabled Peacock Throne of the Mughal emperors, which in popular legend was brought back by Nadir Shah from the sack of Delhi in 1739–40, but was in fact named after a wife of the first Qajar shah who was known by the soubriquet of the 'Peacock Lady of Ispahan'.) *Pishkesh*, the system of bribery, is entrenched in every layer of Persian society, and has been since time immemorial. Combined with the deep streak of vanity in the Persian character, and the ingrained disposition to view public office as an opportunity for personal enrichment and family advancement, it practically ensured that the windfall of wealth from oil in the 1970s would be consumed in a blaze of corruption, folly and ostentation at every level of official and commercial life, from the royal court down to the humblest clerk in the bureaucracy and the meanest shopkeeper in the *suq*.

Little else could have been expected when the shah himself and his family set an example of peculation on a breathtaking scale. His father had been possessed of only modest means when he came to power in 1921; but by the time of his abdication twenty years later Reza Shah owned over 830 villages, standing on 2.5 million hectares of agricultural land. Not only was he the largest landowner in Persia but he was the leading entrepreneur also, as a result of having insisted that he himself should participate in every important commercial undertaking in the country. Following his father's example, Muhammad Reza Shah treated Persia as his personal fief and, like him, enriched himself at his country's expense. The assets of the royal family were vested in and administered by the Pahlavi Foundation, which was set up by the shah in 1958, ostensibly for charitable purposes. The principal recipients of the charity it disbursed, however, were the Pahlavis themselves, a family numbering several dozen members, whose upkeep, in a style only befitting their rank and distinction, required as many millions of dollars each year as there were Pahlavi relatives. The chief purpose of the Pahlavi Foundation was to protect and augment the political and economic power of the shah, which was achieved by the distribution of *pishkesh* wherever it might prove advantageous, by influencing the direction taken by the Persian economy and by investing in profitable ventures at home and abroad. Most of the charitable activities supported by the foundation were, in fact, paid for out of state revenues.

Just how large the assets of the Pahlavi Foundation were there is no way of knowing with any exactness, for its affairs were, as far as possible, shrouded in secrecy. They could not have been less, however, it has been estimated, than $3,000 million, of which the shah's personal share is said to have been around $1,000 million. For all his insistence upon the necessity to give priority to industrial expansion, the shah did not hazard the Pahlavi fortunes by investing in heavy industry. That risk was to be borne by the state treasury. Instead, the Pahlavi Foundation directed the greater part of the funds it invested in Persia into activities promising quick returns or a rapid appreciation of capital – banking, insurance, speculative urban construction, cement and building materials, hotels, sugar factories, casinos and tourist resorts. One of the more bizarre projects, in which SAVAK, the security force, had the majority share, was the development, at a cost of more than $100 million, of a luxurious holiday resort on Kish island (off the Persian coast of the Gulf), where the rich and privileged of Persia might take their ease and indulge their fancies, most of which were obligingly imported from Europe. Abroad, the Pahlavi Foundation's known investments – what others there may have been can only be guessed at – included a new skyscraper in New York and a property development scheme in New Orleans. How these exotic ventures were meant to benefit the Persian economy, which had, in the last analysis, provided the original

funds for them, was not entirely clear. What they and all the other extensive
funds remitted abroad by the Pahlavi Foundation in recent years would
ensure, however, would be a comfortable exile for the shah should he ever be
forced to seek it.

Of all Muhammad Reza Shah's follies and extravagances none was more
ridiculous, and in the end more ruinous, than his attempt to make Persia a
great military power. Between 1972 and 1978 the strength of the Persian armed
forces rose from 191,000 men to 413,000, and expenditures upon defence were
commensurate with this expansion. The Persian defence budget in 1970 was
$880 million. It rose steadily every year thereafter until 1973 when it reached
$2,095 million. Under the impact of higher oil revenues it was inflated to
$3,224 million in 1974, $10,405 million in 1975, $9,500 million in 1976, $7,900
million in 1977 and $9,940 million in 1978, making a grand total for the six
years, 1973–8 inclusive, of well over $43,000 million. The Persian army, some
285,000 strong, was larger than the British Army. It was equipped with 760
Chieftain tanks, 860 medium tanks, 250 Scorpion light tanks, almost a
thousand armoured personnel carriers and innumerable armoured cars. On
order in 1978 were a further 1,300 Chieftains with Chobham armour and a
more powerful engine, and 110 Scorpions, which would have eventually given
the Persian army an armoured strength three times as great as that of the
British Army. In addition, the Persian army possessed, or had on order, a
formidable array of artillery (1,500 field guns, 2,000 anti-tank and anti-aircraft
guns), anti-tank and surface-to-air missiles, motorized transport on a large
scale and an army air wing of 60 light aircraft and over 600 helicopters (with
another 500 on order).

The Persian air force, of more than 100,000 men, was larger than the Royal
Air Force. It had well over 400 combat aircraft, including 200 F–4s (Phan-
toms), 150 F–5s (Tigers) and 56 F–14s (Tomcats), the last-named being one of
the most advanced fighters in the world. Another 24 F–14s and 160 of the
newly developed F–16s (Cobras) were on order. In addition, the Persian air
force was equipped with surface-to-air missiles, nearly a dozen transport
squadrons, and 160 helicopters, with more helicopters, transport planes and
missiles on order. The Persian navy, to which we shall turn our attention
shortly, was being developed along comparably lavish lines.

What did this panoply of arms really amount to, and whom was it meant to
frighten? The Persian army has not won great renown on the battlefield in
modern times, or even had much experience of actual warfare. Apart from
brushes with the British and the Bolsheviks during and after the First World
War, and with the Soviet and British forces which occupied Persia in 1941, the
Persians have not faced European troops in battle since the Anglo-Persian war
of 1856–7, in which they scarcely acquitted themselves with distinction. The
rest of the Persian army's service in the field has been limited to campaigning

against rebellious tribesmen or chasing marauders along the Afghan border. Its unremarkable performance against the guerrillas of Dhufar in the early 1970s has been referred to already. European military missions have been trying to train the Persian army since the end of the eighteenth century (and European adventurers for even longer), without notable success. The reason for failure lay not so much with the Persian soldier (who was as likely, in any case, to be an Afghan or a Turcoman) as with his officers, who regarded the profession of arms primarily as a means of advancing their personal interests and lining their own pockets, so that the men under their command were treated as mere objects for exploitation. While this attitude, which obtained up to the end of the Second World War at least, may have improved of late years, the general level of efficiency in the Persian army has remained fairly low, due in large measure to the lack of education and the want of technical competence throughout its ranks. Little, in short, would appear to have changed since Talleyrand in February 1807, in the course of persuading Napoleon of the futility of enlisting Persia in an alliance directed against the British in India, observed of Persia's military capacity: 'La Perse peut lever et entretenir un assez grand nombre de troupes; mais dans ses armées il y a des hommes et point de soldats.'

The Persians' military shortcomings were only underlined by the shah's insistence upon equipping his armed forces with the most complex modern weaponry; for as time went by they became more and not less dependent upon American and British military advisers and technicians, not merely for training in the use of the new weaponry but for its actual operation and maintenance as well. This dependence was particularly marked in the case of the Hawk and Rapier missile defence systems which the Persian army and air force were acquiring, and over the introduction of the F-14 fighter into service with the air force. The installation of the Hawk missile system, one of the most expensive and complicated programmes upon which the Persians had embarked, fell increasingly behind schedule with each passing month, as a result of delays in the construction of missile sites, grossly inadequate logistics and a dire shortage of qualified Persian technicians. Even before the overthrow of the shah cut the ground from under the programme it had become clear that the system would never have been able to function without the continued assistance of American technicians.

It was the same story with the Persian air force, whose real as opposed to assumed capabilities were very much in doubt. The backbone of the air force was its American F-4 (Phantom) and F-5 (Tiger) aircraft, of which Persia had purchased some 360, many of them equipped with missiles. Although sufficient air crews had been trained to fly these aircraft, there was a serious shortage of ground crews to service them, with the result that maintenance was largely carried out by American contractors. The necessity for American assistance was even more strikingly apparent in the case of the highly complex

Grumman Tomcat, the F–14, with its integrated Phoenix missile system. So advanced was this fighter, which had been developed to master the Russian MiG–25 (Foxbat), that it was known as 'the flying computer'; yet the shah had purchased fifty-six of them and contracted to buy a further twenty-four. (He had also undertaken to buy 160 of the simpler, but still advanced, F–16, with the option of acquiring 140 more, and he was looking to purchase 250 of the new F–18s which were barely off the drawing-board.) While a certain amount of progress was made with training air crews for the F–14s – mainly by transferring the best air crews from the Phantom squadrons, which left these inadequately manned – there was no question but that their maintenance and logistics support would require the services of American technicians for years to come. Much the same situation obtained with regard to the dozens of helicopter squadrons with which the Persian army and air force were being provided. As late as September 1978 a hundred military helicopters were sitting uselessly on the airfield at Ispahan, where they had been mouldering for two years for want of crews to fly and service them. Even in the matter of the tactical use of their aircraft and helicopters the Persians were still reliant upon the instruction and support of American military and air force advisers.

What this all implied was summed up in the conclusions of a staff report to the United States Senate Foreign Relations Committee in July 1976 on the subject of American arms sales to Persia.

The Government of Iran [the report stated] is attempting to create an extremely modern military establishment in a country that lacks the technical, educational and industrial base to provide the necessary trained personnel and management capabilities to operate such an establishment effectively. Iran also lacks experience in logistics and support operations and does not have the maintenance capabilities, the infrastructure (port facilities, roads, rail nets, etc.), and the construction capacity to implement its new programs independent of outside support.... Iran will not be able to absorb and operate within the next five to ten years a large proportion of the sophisticated military systems purchased from the US unless increasing numbers of American personnel go to Iran in a support capacity. This support, alone, may not be sufficient to guarantee success for the Iranian program.

The blame for this sorry state of affairs rested equally with the shah and with the United States government. Carried away by dreams of glory, the shah insisted that only the most up-to-date weapons of war were good enough for his armed forces. Although he possessed no military qualifications or experience worth speaking of, he regarded himself as an expert in matters of strategy and military technology, in need of no advice or instruction from others. He demanded, as much for reasons of *amour propre* as anything else, the latest and most powerful armaments the West had to offer, and he would not suffer himself to be thwarted. What the United States had, what NATO had, was what Persia should have, and as soon as they had it, if not sooner. What he chose to overlook was that the introduction of new and advanced weapons into the armoury of NATO was facilitated as much by the existence of a comprehensive industrial and technological infrastructure in the countries of Western Europe as it was by their lengthy military experience. Both prerequisites were lacking in the case of Persia. In consequence, the shah burdened his country with a massive programme of arms procurement without having taken the trouble to determine whether the Persian economy had the capacity to underwrite it, whether the skilled manpower was available to implement it or whether the arms in question were suited to Persia's real defensive needs.

The cost of the arms programme to the Persian economy did not end with the acquisition of the weapons. Resources and manpower which would have been better employed in improving Persia's industrial and agricultural performance were diverted into the martial extravaganza. Between 1974 and 1977 a total sum of $3,200 million over and above the actual defence appropriations was spent on the construction of military bases, housing and other facilities connected with the defence programme. The salaries, allowances and upkeep of American technicians and advisers with the armed forces consumed a disproportionately large slice of the defence budget – some $100,000 per annum for every man, and there were 20,000 such technicians and advisers in Persia. In fact, it was reckoned that more than half the cost of each defence contract was absorbed by the expenses of the training, maintenance and advisory personnel associated with it. For this, however, the shah could not be held wholly or even largely responsible. On the contrary, he was being brazenly exploited by American and British defence contractors, spurred on by their own governments.

When President Nixon and his secretary of state, Henry Kissinger, visited Tehran in May 1972, on their way back from disarmament talks in Moscow, they told the shah that the United States would be willing to sell him the advanced F–14 aircraft (which had had its first proving flight barely eighteen months previously) so as to counter both the Russian MiG–23 and MiG–25 which, the shah alleged, had been making surveillance flights over northern Persia. Two months later Nixon instructed the Departments of State and Defence to comply with virtually any request from the shah for the supply of conventional weapons. It was an unprecedented act of policy by the United States with respect to arms sales to any non-Western country. Moreover, it ran directly counter to the advice given by Nixon's own secretary of defence, James Schlesinger, that the provision of advanced weapons to countries like Persia carried with it a security risk, as well as a danger of political entanglement, since the acquisition of such weapons would require the services of American technicians and advisers for training and maintenance purposes for a long time to come. Why Nixon chose to ignore this warning and effectively to exempt the shah's arms orders from the scrutiny normally accorded requests for arms from non-Western countries by the Departments of State and Defence is not entirely clear. The only immediately obvious explanation is that he and his secretary of state had accepted the shah's argument that Persia was the natural successor to Britain as the guardian of the security of the Gulf. What was not foreseen at the time was the fourfold increase in the price of oil which was to come eighteen months later, and the subsequent augmentation of Persia's oil revenues to an extent which encouraged the shah to believe that he could purchase whatever armaments his heart desired.

A free-for-all developed as the governments of the United States, Britain and France competed strenuously with one another to sell him the most expensive and lethal weapons in their armouries, regardless of whether he was fit to be entrusted with them or whether they would be of any benefit to his country. Common sense was thrown to the winds, ethics went out of the window and all parties – the shah, the Persian general staff, the commission agents and influence pedlars, the Western defence ministries and the Western aircraft and arms manufacturers – had a marvellous time. Apparently considering that it was absolved by the presidential directive of July 1972 from any obligation to examine the implications of the shah's spending spree for the United States or Persia, the Department of State gave its full support to American arms salesmen touting for orders in Tehran. Although the assistant secretary of state for Near Eastern and South Asian Affairs, Joseph J. Sisco, told the Committee on Foreign Affairs of the House of Representatives in August 1973 that 'in arms sales to Persia and other Gulf states political and economic ramifications are carefully examined as are military and strategic considerations', and furthermore that he and other officials 'naturally remain alert to ensure that only those arms which the recipients can reasonably be expected to operate and maintain are sold', the Senate Foreign Relations Committee staff report of July 1976 on the Persian arms sales stated flatly:

If senior officials in the State Department were concerned about reports in the last two years that Iran was experiencing problems in absorbing the equipment it had purchased, it was certainly not evident in the public and semi-public statements about Iranian military programs and the US involvement.... Senior State Department officials appear not to have been prepared to tolerate open debate on the possible adverse implications of unrestricted arms sales to Iran.... The State Department has not formally reviewed US arms sale policy to Iran since the 1972 decision and continues to support it wholeheartedly.

There was a disposition on the part of the Department of Defence, also, to play down (in public at least) any suggestion that the weapons the Persians were acquiring were too advanced for their needs and capabilities. Asked by the Senate Foreign Relations Committee in September 1976 to comment upon allegations in the committee's staff report that the Persian air force was experiencing serious difficulty in adapting to the F–14 fighter and its associated missile system, the deputy Secretary of Defence, Robert F. Ellsworth, replied that, on the contrary, much less trouble had been encountered than had been expected. In fact, he added, the whole Persian training programme was going swimmingly, which seems a little odd seeing that the United States Navy itself was experiencing problems in adjusting to the F–14. Ellsworth, however, was not in the least put out by the implications of the contrast. The reason why the Persians had been successful, he told the Senate committee in all seriousness, was that 'the government of Iran is turning to innovative and modern management to stay on top'. It need hardly be said that the Defence Department had reasons of its own to present as flattering a picture as possible of the arms-training programme. Ever since it received the presidential directive of 1972 it had consistently omitted Persia from the list of Middle-Eastern countries whose requests for arms were subject to regular review by the department, concentrating instead upon the more rewarding work of meeting the shah's wishes. Within the department the individual armed services competed among themselves to sell him weapons, largely with an eye to recouping some of the research and development costs of the weapons in question and to reduce, by means of longer production runs, the cost of the weapons to their own services. Thus, the United States Air Force and the Navy both strove to persuade the Persian government to purchase their respective versions of the F–14.

The case of the F–14 purchase is a highly instructive one for the light it sheds upon the way in which arms contracts were negotiated with the shah's government. The F–14 Grumman Tomcat is the most advanced and expensive fighter ever produced in the United States. With its associated Phoenix missile system and ground control each fighter costs, by all reports, around $20 million. The Grumman Corporation, which had a contract for the development of the aircraft for the United States Navy, had almost bankrupted itself in putting the plane into the air: it lost $18 million on the project in 1971, $70 million in 1972. Desperate to recoup its losses and to make the plane a financial success, Grumman undertook to pay commissions amounting to $28 million to individuals who promised to secure purchase orders from the Persian government. The first such order, for thirty aircraft, was obtained in 1973 through an acquaintance of General Muhammad Khatami, the commander-in-chief of the Persian air force and a brother-in-law of the shah. A second order for a further fifty aircraft, bringing the value of the total contract to about $2,000 million, was secured in the summer of 1974. To help Grumman overcome the financial difficulties it was experiencing at this time, the Persian state bank, Bank Melli Iran, loaned the corporation $75 million.

General Khatami was killed in a water ski-gliding accident in September 1975. Whether the timing was significant or merely incidental, the Persian vice-minister of war, General Hasan Toufanian, began to make noisy protests in public about Grumman's large payments to commission agents. 'This shows that the foreign companies want to loot us,' he exclaimed at a press conference in February 1976. 'We will not allow this and we will pull the extra money out of their throats.' What the general forbore to mention was that he himself had demanded, at the time of the signing of the second F–14 contract, that

Grumman should dispense with their original agent and deal directly through him. Toufanian, who was in charge of the Persian arms procurement programme, was merely acting, however, as in other instances, on his master's orders. The latter now intervened in person to castigate Grumman for resorting to bribery (a practice unheard of in Persia), and to demand that the aircraft company deduct from the cost of the F–14 contract the $28 million paid out in *douceurs*. The shah's own family, however, was not exactly immune to the lure of commission money: according to testimony given before the Senate Foreign Relations Committee later in 1976, the Northrop Corporation, for example, paid several hundred thousand dollars to one of his nephews for services rendered. Meanwhile Grumman had unhappily complied with the shah's edict, without anyone, it would seem, knowing for certain where the $28 million, or the bulk of it, eventually wound up. What made the loss (which was $5 million more than Grumman's total profits for the previous year) doubly hard to bear was that the company had to put up with a good deal of unctuous moralizing by the shah's ministers – in particular by the prime minister, Amir Abbas Hoveida, who piously protested when the matter became public, 'For God's sake, foreign businessmen should be more ethical in our country!' In November 1978, on the eve of the shah's departure from Persia, Hoveida was himself indicted on charges of corruption on a grand scale.

A fall in oil revenues in 1975–6 caused a temporary lull in the pace of arms procurement, although some $12,000 million was budgeted from all sources for expenditure upon weapons and related services, construction and equipment in 1976–7. At the time of his indignant outburst against Grumman, General Toufanian somewhat heavy-handedly suggested that Persia might have to cut back her arms purchases if the price and volume of her oil exports were not increased. His remarks did not go down well in Washington, where Congress was growing more and more uneasy about the scale of arms sales to the Gulf countries, and to Persia and Saudi Arabia in particular. There had been hearings on the subject by either the Senate Foreign Relations Committee or the House Foreign Affairs Committee in nearly every session since 1973, hearings which had revealed a sharp difference of opinion between those senators and congressmen who suspected that the arms race was getting out of control and officials from the State Department who exhibited considerable equanimity, not to say complacency, about the whole business. At the Department of Defence, however, doubts had begun to arise over the wisdom of the Persian arms procurement programme, especially as United States military advisers and technicians in Persia had begun to report on the difficulties which the Persian armed forces were experiencing in assimilating the advanced weaponry they were receiving. At the end of 1973 the secretary of defence, Schlesinger, had sent a retired army colonel to Persia in an unofficial capacity to act as an independent adviser to the shah on arms procurement and to keep Schlesinger himself informed about the shah's views. To judge from the volume and nature of Persia's arms purchases in the next two years, it would hardly seem that the colonel exercised much of a restraining influence at the Persian court. He was replaced in September 1975 by an official representative appointed by Schlesinger to act as an 'honest broker' in arms transactions. A few months later it emerged that the late unofficial appointee, the retired colonel, was being employed as an adviser on arms procurement by General Toufanian.

What the Department of Defence was increasingly prepared to admit – for all its enthusiastic promotion of arms sales between 1972 and 1975 – but which the State Department seemingly preferred to obscure, was that the Persian arms programme held serious political and strategic implications for the United States in the Middle East. Persia had become the biggest single purchaser of American arms, military equipment and services in the world, outside the United States herself. The American security assistance operation in Persia was by far the largest in any country: in 1976 it involved over 2,000 military advisers and specialists. Several thousand more Americans were working on military contracts for American companies. Whereas all sales of weapons to another country carry with them an obligation to maintain the supply of spare parts, ammunition or whatever is required to keep the weapons operational, it was the sheer size and complexity of the American arms programme in Persia which marked it out from other transactions of this nature. So deeply committed had the United States become in Persia that it seemed doubtful whether she would be able to disengage from her role as armourer to the shah for years to come.

It was equally doubtful whether she would be able to dissociate herself from whatever purpose to which he might choose to put these arms in the future. There was general agreement among qualified military observers up to the time of the shah's fall that the Persian armed forces were incapable of mounting a major military operation without the assistance of American technical specialists, whether military or civilian, or without American logistics support. A similar disability applied with respect to the armour and missile systems supplied by Britain. If, in the event of the Persian armed forces becoming involved in hostilities, the United States had refused to permit her military and technical specialists to support the Persians in the field, or to fulfil her own contractual obligations for the supply of arms, not only would Perso–American relations have been seriously damaged but the relations of the United States with other countries with whom she had entered into arms contracts would have been adversely affected. There was also the possibility that the American technicians and advisers in Persia might have been held hostage to ensure the fulfilment by their government of its contractual obligations. If, despite these hazards, the United States had decided to register her disapproval of any action taken by the Persian government by shutting off military supplies and thereby immobilizing the Persian armed forces, the shah would have found himself in a serious predicament. He could not promptly switch to another power for arms, for the replacement of the aircraft and weapons he had acquired over a period of time would have taken roughly the same amount of time to accomplish. The cost would probably have been more than the Persian treasury could bear, and besides, at the end of the changeover he would have found himself in the same situation of dependence as before. It was no doubt with thoughts like these in mind, and remembering the abrupt discontinuance of the supply of American arms to Pakistan in 1965 and to Turkey in 1974, that the shah embarked upon an ambitious scheme of arms production at Ispahan, primarily with British help, at a reputed cost of $1,400 million.

The situation of dependence created by the furnishing of American arms to Persia, however, was not entirely one-sided. The close integration of the Persian arms procurement programme with that of the armed forces of the United States themselves carried with it some disturbing implications, the outlines of which had become increasingly apparent by 1976. For example, the shah's insistence upon early delivery of the F–14s he had ordered led to delays in delivery of the aircraft in the numbers required to the United States Navy. New weapons developed by the United States had by then, as their order of priority for delivery, the United States armed forces, NATO and Persia. Even this, however, was not good enough for the shah, who demanded that Persia be moved up the list, ahead of NATO. He also attempted, by indicating his preference for particular weapons at the development stage, to influence the selection of arms by the United States government for its own forces. The Grumman Tomcat, as we have seen, was a case in point. Moreover, as we have also seen, the United States was ready, even anxious, to gratify his desire for preferential treatment in arms procurement. The readiness can partly be ascribed to apprehensions that the shah might retaliate against a constriction of arms supplies or the withholding of advanced weaponry by reducing Persia's oil exports to the West; although this would have been a desperate expedient in view of his utter dependence upon oil exports to finance his 'Great Civilization'. A less dangerous and probably equally effective device would have been to play upon the fears of the American aircraft and armaments manufacturers that they might suffer financially from any diminution of Persia's oil revenues. The trouble with all this, so far as the wider interests of the Western world were concerned, was that it created a vicious circle, in which expensive armaments that required mounting oil revenues to meet the cost of their purchase generated pressure for increased oil prices, leading in turn to the need for the West to sell even greater quantities of ever more expensive weapons in order to meet the soaring cost of oil.

Most of all, however, the American attitude was determined by the policy laid down by Nixon and Kissinger of entrusting the security of the Gulf and its oil reserves to Persia and, to only a slightly lesser extent, Saudi Arabia, a policy that required that nothing be done to impede the building up of the Persian armed forces. Testifying before the foreign assistance sub-committee of the Senate Foreign Relations Committee in hearings held in September 1976 to approve or disallow the proposed sale of 160 F–16 aircraft to Persia, Philip C. Habib, the under-secretary for political affairs at the State Department, described the policies pursued by the shah over the preceding decade as having been 'generally compatible with our own'. Quoting from statements made by Kissinger, the secretary of state, at various times, to the effect that the policies of the United States and Persia 'have been parallel and therefore mutually reinforcing' and that there was 'a parallelism of views on many key problems', Habib proceeded to drive the point home to the sub-committee by emphasizing yet again that the United States and Persia 'have generally seen our respective interests as parallel, at times congruent, and we share many objectives'. Hence the sales of advanced weapons to Persia. As Habib explained,

These sales add to the strength of a valued ally and to that nation's ability to continue to carry out a policy on which we and the Iranians agree. They also provide the essential assurances that the United States has not changed its mind about Iran, that we remain committed to a close relationship in all fields and that close co-ordination with the United States on the part of the Iranians is still justified.

Despite the scepticism evinced by the members of the Senate sub-committee about the wisdom of allowing the sale of the F-16s to proceed, it was eventually sanctioned by the Senate. Any misgivings that might have been felt by some senators were not strong enough to prevail against the special pleading of others from states in which the major aircraft and armaments industries were located. The F–16 contract, after all, along with its associated missile order, was worth around $3,800 million. By this time, however, considerable doubts were arising about the shah's ability to finance the arms purchases he was making with such abandon. He had already fallen behind in his payments for arms already acquired, to an extent it is impossible to determine but which has been put as high as $2,000 million. One of the casualties of the financial straits in which he now found himself was a highly complex and extremely expensive electronic surveillance system, code-named 'Ibex', which was being developed by the Rockwell Corporation for installation along the borders of Persia to monitor signals traffic, especially beyond the Russian frontier. The project was shelved in 1977, as much, it would seem, for reasons of political prudence as through financial stringency.

Mere insolvency, however, was not sufficient to cure the shah of his obsession with the piling up of arms. In October 1976 he sent General Toufanian to Moscow to conclude an agreement worth some $550 million with the Soviet Union for the supply of tank-transporters, armoured personnel carriers and surface-to-air missiles. Payment was to be made, as with a previous arms agreement ten years earlier, in gas supplies. The following month the shah informed the British government that henceforth it would have to accept payment in crude oil for the Rapier missile system being installed in Persia. The British government hastened to comply with the edict, being nervously aware of the value to the ailing British economy of the Persian arms contracts. (The price of a Chieftain tank, for example, had been increased from £295,000 to £450,000 by August 1976 and it was still rising.) It was crystal clear by this time, though no one would say so publicly, that the shah's infatuation with the deadly playthings of war had reached the pathological stage, just as his lofty vision of himself and his country's place in the world had passed the limits of reason. 'I hope my good friends in Europe and the United States and elsewhere will finally understand', he told Anthony Sampson in an interview at St Moritz in February 1975, 'that there is absolutely no difference between Iran and France, Britain and Germany. Why should you find it absolutely normal that France will spend that much money on her army, and not my country?'*

From the decline of the Safavid empire in the late seventeenth century to the fall of the Qajar dynasty in the early twentieth century no Persian government had been able to control for any length of time the entire Persian coastline from Khuzistan in the west to Makran and Baluchistan in the east. The reason, apart from the prevalence of corruption, incompetence and feebleness in the administration of the empire, was the lack of seapower at the disposal of Persia's rulers. Much of the coast was inhabited by Arabs, in whose hands the entire shipping resources of Persia were concentrated. Secure in the knowledge that they could, as a last resort, take to the sea and from there inflict consider-able damage upon Persia's trade, they were able for generations to set the will of provincial governors at naught. Nadir Shah in the eighteenth century attempted to remedy the deficiency by constructing navies for both the Caspian Sea and the Gulf. The Caspian project, which involved the transfer of part of the Arab population of the Gulf coast to the shores of the Caspian, came to nothing, and from the early nineteenth century onwards Persia was forbidden by Russia to maintain any naval vessels in that sea. In the Gulf, Nadir Shah managed to assemble a force of some twenty to thirty ships, built in Europe and in India, which were manned by Indian Muslims and Portuguese renegades. The Indians, however, when ordered to sea to destroy Arab shipping, refused, on the grounds that they were Sunni Muslims and would not fight their fellow Sunnis. Instead, they turned on their Persian officers, who were Shii, butch-ered them and made off with the ships. Not only was this the end of Nadir Shah's attempt to create a Persian navy but it was virtually the end of all such attempts – apart from the purchase of a couple of German steamers in the late nineteenth century – for 200 years.

   Though Persia possessed no navy to enforce her will in the Gulf, she more than made up for the lack by the extravagance of her pretensions to dominion

* Anthony Sampson, *The Arms Bazaar*, p. 256.

in the area. Indeed, the history of Persia's relations with her neighbours and with the two European powers most intimately connected with her, Russia and Britain, revolved in the nineteenth and early twentieth centuries around Persian claims to various slices of *terra irredenta* – in the Caucasus, beyond the Caspian, along the marches of Afghanistan and Baluchistan, across the mountains of Kurdistan, down the rivers, valleys and plains of Iraq and throughout the length and breadth of the Gulf. While a few of these claims may have had some solid foundation, the rest were merely fanciful, the fruit of illusion and of memories of infinite durability. Like their Safavid predecessors, the Qajar shahs held as an article of faith that wherever in the world a Persian foot had trod became from that moment onwards irrevocably Persian, however long the place in question may have lain under foreign domination. Such delusions, combined with the frustration engendered by the reality of Persia's impotence, supplied the fuel which stoked a thousand protests, *démarches* and other diplomatic pinpricks throughout the nineteenth century, and made Persia, after the Saudi amirate of Najd, the greatest source of disruption and disorder in the Gulf region.

Incapable of policing their own waters or controlling their own coastline, successive shahs and their governments consoled themselves by doing their utmost to hinder Britain in her efforts to suppress piracy and maritime warfare in the Gulf. They refused, also, for many years to close Persian ports to the slave trade, to grant rights of search and seizure to British naval vessels for the apprehension of Persian slavers, or to discourage the slave trade within their own dominions. When eventually they yielded to British representations on the subject, they did so not out of any conviction of the evils of the traffic or of the institution of slavery itself, but for the sake of political advantage. Their co-operation later in the century in the restriction of the arms traffic, where it was not withheld completely, was grudging and meaningless. Their territorial demands and claims to sovereignty over Bahrain and other islands, over the delta of the Shatt al-Arab and Kuwait, over parts of Makran, Baluchistan, Seistan, Oman and the Trucial Shaikhdoms, were a source of irritation to all concerned, and might have been more disturbing if they had been less absurd. Whatever improvements were introduced to the Gulf, whether they were the charting of its waters, the laying of telegraph cables, the provision of aids to navigation or the establishment of quarantine stations and regulations, they were invariably interpreted by the court of Tehran as affronts to its dignity, and used as pretexts for renewed bombast about Persia's sacred and immutable rights.

These same shrill complaints about violations of Persia's sovereign rights were to be heard again in the 1970s. The shah and his ministers let slip no opportunity to impress upon anyone who cared to listen that they regarded the safeguarding of the peace of the Gulf as the exclusive responsibility of the states around its shores. Although the shah denied that he was trying to declare a

Monroe Doctrine for the Gulf, he equally and more frequently denied that any outside power had the right to maintain a naval presence in its waters. This right, he asserted dogmatically, belonged to Persia alone. According to a statement made by his prime minister, Amir Abbas Hoveida, in April 1973, 'two considerations of paramount significance have governed and will continue to govern' Persia's policy in the Gulf.

Firstly, that the Persian Gulf and the Sea of Oman constitute our southern borders; and, secondly, that they form the artery through which daily over five million barrels of Persian oil pass today and more than 10 million barrels will pass by the 1980s. . . . We cannot and we will not tolerate any subversive activity that would endanger the security of the Straits of Hormuz or the freedom of navigation in the Persian Gulf. This artery must remain open to international commerce and we in Iran have the determination and the capacity to see that it does.

The sentiments rang rather hollow when tested against Persia's failure up to that time to subscribe to any of the conventions on the law of the sea which had been concluded in 1958. They sounded even more hollow when set against the record of Persian intransigence and mischief-making in the Gulf over the past two centuries, the latest instance of which had been the shah's occupation of Abu Musa and forcible seizure of the Tunbs at the close of 1971. The object of this move had been to enlarge the extent of Persia's maritime sovereignty and with it her rights to the submarine shelf and any oil deposits it might contain. At the same time, the acquisition of Abu Musa and the Tunbs brought the main track of Gulf shipping, for a distance of 100–150 miles west of the Straits of Hormuz, wholly within Persian territorial waters. In so doing, the shah ignored, or brushed aside as of little consequence, the fact that the straits were also a major outlet to the world outside for the other Gulf states, none of which was anxious to see them under exclusive Persian domination.

Nor would the world at large have necessarily benefited, as the shah would have it believe it would, from Persian control of the straits. The straits are an international waterway, through which the ships of all nations have right of passage without let or hindrance, a status which has been established, as the whole corpus of international law has been established, by the nations of the West, almost invariably against the opposition, or at least without the active assistance, of the states of the East. There have already been dangerous indications on the part of some Middle-Eastern countries of a desire to exert the kind of command over the narrow seas adjacent to their coasts which is incompatible with international rights of free passage. (Perhaps the best-known instances are the closure of the Straits of Tiran by the Egyptian government in 1967, and the attempted closure of the Straits of Bab al-Mandab by the government of South Yemen at intervals before, during and after the October 1973 war.) It is the interest as well as the responsibility of the major maritime powers of the world to resist this tendency, particularly in an area of such singular economic importance as the Gulf. While the shah reigned, there was a disposition on the part of the Western powers to indulge his fancies in this respect, and to accede to his claims to stand sentinel over the Straits of Hormuz. The dangers of retreating from the firm ground of international law in determining the Western position on the status of the straits have become all too apparent with the change of regime in Persia.

To turn the Gulf into a Persian sea, to make it once again the *sinus Persicus* of antiquity, the shah expended considerable efforts, and even more considerable sums of money, to create a Persian navy. On paper the results looked impressive: three destroyers, four frigates, four corvettes, twenty patrol boats, a dozen or so hovercraft, and an assortment of minesweepers, landing craft and support ships. There was also a naval air wing of three squadrons of aircraft and two dozen or more helicopters. On order in 1978 were six more frigates, nine submarines and four *Spruance*-class destroyers, the most modern and powerful warships of their kind, the first of which was only then entering into service with the United States Navy. There could have been only one intention behind the projected acquisition of the submarines and *Spruance*-class destroyers, and this was to extend the range of Persia's naval capability beyond her own territorial waters into the Arabian Sea and the Indian Ocean. To carry this plan into effect would have required more extensive facilities than those available at the existing naval base at Bandar Abbas, where a dockyard had already been built at a cost of £60 million. So the shah ordered the construction of a huge naval, military and air base at Chah Bahar on the Makran coast outside the Gulf proper, where, so report had it, he envisaged the possible use of the base by American nuclear submarines, a possibility which, if it had ever existed, became exceedingly remote as time went by. When the initial contracts for Chah Bahar were signed in November 1975 the estimated cost of the base was $2,500 million. The figure kept rising over the next couple of years, in roughly the same proportion as Persia's oil revenues declined; so that by 1978 only the air base was anywhere near completion, while work on the naval station had barely begun.

While the shah plainly regarded his fledgling navy as a glittering instrument of his will, the reality was somewhat different. The sea has never been the Persians' natural element. Persia has no indigenous naval or maritime tradition, and seamen cannot be conjured from the waves by royal command. Though the shah spent a great deal of money in buying ships, creating naval facilities and recruiting naval advisers from Britain and the United States, the legacy of the past could not be overcome. While he posed as the guardian of the maritime peace of the Gulf, he had to rely upon the ships of the Royal Navy to carry out a hydrographic survey of its waters. His admirals proved themselves more adept at lining their pockets than at mastering the arts of seamanship. In February 1976 the commander-in-chief of the navy, Rear-Admiral Ramzi Abbas Atai, was tried on charges of corruption, fined £3.7 million and sentenced to five years' imprisonment. Ten other naval officers were tried with him on similar charges and found guilty. The following year five more flag-officers were dismissed the service after being accused of financial malpractices connected with the development of the port of Bandar Abbas.

There was, in short, something decidedly Gilbertian about the Persian navy and the shah's dreams of admiralty.

> When I sally forth to seek my prey,
> I help myself in a royal way:
> I sink a few more ships, it's true,
> Than a well-bred monarch ought to do;
> But many a king on a first-class throne,
> If he wants to call his crown his own,
> Must manage somehow to get through
> More dirty work than ever *I* do,
> For I am a Pirate King.

Nothing, in fact, has changed since Lord Curzon, well over eighty years ago, delivered his slighting verdict on the concept of a Persian navy – the subject of the shortest chapter in his monumental *Persia and the Persian Question* – with the words: 'In these few pages I have come to both the beginning and the end of all that there is to be said about the naval strength of Persia. *Ex nihilo nihil fit*; and I am even surprised at my own tale of bricks, with so modest an allowance of straw.'

It was only its nuisance value that gave, and may yet give, the Persian navy significance. However mediocre in calibre it may be, it is still superior to the naval forces of the other Gulf states. How the shah may have intended to use it is now only a matter of academic interest. The historical tendency of Persia in a period of strong central government, as with many states, has been towards expansion, and Muhammad Reza Shah plainly considered himself the equal in might and lustre of any Qajar or Safavid monarch. He never troubled to conceal his contempt for his Arab neighbours, Iraq included, or that he found their continued survival somewhat ridiculous. 'It must be said', he told a correspondent of *L'Express* in 1970,

that in the Near East there are countries which have been created after the First World War with the stroke of a pen by Britain. These countries have no value and are worthless.... All these make life difficult in our region and force us to spend more in the field of defence.

He expressed the same sentiments in his conversation with Anthony Sampson in 1975.

We don't want the land of others, we don't need the wealth of others, we have enough: furthermore, we could have crushed all those nuisance people much more: we never did it ... [though] the strength that we have now in the Persian Gulf is ten times, twenty times more than the British ever had.

Whatever may have been the case in 1975, however, by 1977–8 the shah was becoming sore pressed for sufficient funds with which to fulfil the expectations he had aroused in his subjects, to keep up the pace of rapid industrialization and modernization, and at the same time to equip his armed forces with ever more splendid armaments – which brings us back to the question with which we began this section, viz. to what use, apart from his own protection, did the shah intend to put his expensively equipped forces? While his own revenues were inadequate to meet his extensive needs, and while Persia's oil reserves were expected, at the rate at which oil was being extracted up to the latter months of 1978, to run dry before the end of the century, across the Gulf such inconsequential places in his eyes as Kuwait and Abu Dhabi were swimming in oil revenues which they could not usefully employ. The temptation to bring them under Persian control was one which would undoubtedly have grown with the passage of time, along with the opportunities for such a move. There are large Persian communities in all the minor Gulf states, whose protection and welfare might well have afforded the pretext for armed intervention. The Iraqi claim to Kuwait could well have provided the shah with an excuse to offer his protection to Al Sabah shaikhs, even to force it upon them, although such an action would have embroiled him not only with Iraq but also with Saudi Arabia and the other Arab states. Again, he might have taken advantage of a renewal of the guerrilla war in Dhufar, or of other possible insurgent activity in Oman, to extend aid to the sultan with the object of converting the sultanate into a Persian satrapy. Yet a further pretext for interference might have been a *coup d'état*, or threatened *coup d'état*, by Marxist or other revolutionaries in one of the Gulf shaikhdoms.

While the shah's departure from the scene now makes further speculation along these lines somewhat pointless, the danger of an eventual Perso–Arab conflict in the Gulf has by no means wholly receded. Doubtless much depends upon the type of regime which eventually succeeds in establishing itself in Persia after the dissolution of the Pahlavi monarchy; but it would be a mistake to assume that a conservative or centre government would be less likely than one of radical disposition to adopt a forward policy in the Gulf. After all, few regimes could have been more conservative than the absolute monarchy of Muhammad Reza Shah. It was the religious and conservative sections of Persian society, moreover, which objected to his renunciation in 1970 of the long-standing Persian claim to Bahrain. If a future government in Tehran were to take the offensive in the Gulf, Bahrain might well be its first objective. The shaikhdom's strategic location and commercial importance would make it a valuable acquisition, especially if a prolonged Persian command of the Arabian shore were in contemplation. Bahrain also has a large Shii minority, and sectarian sentiment, after the violent upsurge of religious fervour in Persia in 1978–9, may well play a larger part in the determination of Persian policy in the Gulf in the future than in recent years. Apart from the expatriate Persian Shia in the Gulf shaikhdoms, there is a sizable native Shii community in Hasa, which for generations has suffered disabilities under Saudi rule. While the shah still reigned, some kind of understanding was said to exist between Persia and Saudi Arabia for the maintenance of peace in the Gulf and the suppression of political elements hostile to the prevailing political order. It would have been exceedingly strange if any such accord had existed, for the two countries were more divided by their differences – religious, racial, cultural, historical and political – than they were superficially united by a shared anxiety to uphold the monarchical principle of government. The shah never bothered overmuch to conceal his contempt for the Saudi ruling house, whom he regarded as backward Bedouin and religious fanatics; while the Al Saud in their turn looked upon him as a coxcomb and an upstart, and upon the Persian Shia as little better than *mushrikun*, polytheists.

The establishment of any kind of theocratic government in Tehran would obviously strengthen the mutual Sunni–Shii antipathy already present in the Gulf region. Nor would the effect be any different if a radical or even Marxist regime were to gain power in Persia. On the contrary, as recent events in Persia have indicated, such a regime would not scruple to exploit Shii zealotry to promote subversion in the Arab states of the Gulf, directed, in the first instance, against the existing shaikhly regimes. What is more in doubt, whatever the political complexion of the successor government in Tehran, is whether the Persian armed forces, after their demoralization and partial disintegration at the time of the shah's downfall, would be capable of undertaking offensive operations. On the other hand, if the new rulers of Persia were of radical persuasion, they might choose to accomplish their ends in the Gulf, not by conventional military means but by the tactics of guerrilla warfare and popular sedition. Amid all the uncertainties about Persia's future rule in the Gulf, however, one thing is clear, and this is that her actions will be strongly, perhaps decisively, influenced by the relationship of her new rulers with the Soviet Union.

The Russians have played a careful game in Persia these last two decades or so, with the result that Russo-Persian relations have pursued a fairly tranquil course. A number of economic agreements were concluded between the two countries in the mid-1960s, revolving mainly around the sale of natural gas by Persia to Russia and the provision of technical and economic assistance by the Russians in the development of Persian industry, the most important contribution being the construction of the Aryamehr steel mill at Ispahan. A further economic convention was concluded in 1976, providing for the export of industrial goods from Russia to Persia over a five-year period, in exchange for gas, minerals and textiles. A minor arms agreement was negotiated in 1966–7 for the supply of Russian anti-aircraft guns and military transport, though the Russians refused a request for surface-to-air missiles for the defence of Persia's oil installations, presumably out of deference to the feelings of their clients among the Arab states. Ten years later, as we have seen, the Russians withdrew their objections to the supply of missiles in the new arms agreement negotiated in October 1976, the Persians by this time having obtained surface-to-air missiles from Britain and the United States. The Russians do not appear to have been at all put out by the shah's expansionist ambitions in the Gulf. On the contrary, because they disturbed the stability of the region they served the Kremlin's purposes. Thus the Russo-Iraqi treaty of April 1972 had its immediate origins in the alarm aroused in the government of Baghdad by the shah's truculent behaviour over the Shatt al-Arab and Abu Musa and the Tunbs. Six months after the signing of the treaty the shah paid a state visit to the Soviet Union. At the end of his visit a joint communiqué was issued which proclaimed the determination of both parties to ensure 'that matters concerning the Persian Gulf region should be dealt with by the countries of the region on the basis of the United Nations charter and without any outside intervention'.

There was more than a little irony in the shah's quest for approval of his ambitions in the Gulf from the power which had for two centuries consistently encroached upon Persia's sovereignty and independence, relenting only when the pressure of events within Russia or elsewhere distracted it. But there were historical precedents for both the shah's soliciting of Russian approval and his receipt of it. Throughout much of the nineteenth century Persian rulers were wont to turn to St Petersburg rather than to London for aid and counsel in furthering their aggressive designs upon their neighbours, and upon the Afghans in particular. For their part, the Russians were only too happy to encourage the Persians to aggrandize themselves at the expense of their neighbours, since by doing so the Persians would be diverted from brooding over the losses they had suffered at Russia's hands in the form of large war indemnities and territorial concessions in the Caucasus. What Muhammad Reza Shah overlooked, however, or perhaps preferred to ignore as incompatible with his dignity, was that his country's survival as an independent state depended up to the Second World War upon the backing of Russia's principal rival in Asia, Britain; and that since that time Persia has continued to enjoy an independent existence because of the friendship and support of the United States.

The shah's presumptuous pronouncement in Moscow in October 1972, made with the smiling approval of his Russian hosts, was issued only five months after President Nixon's visit to Tehran, when he had assured the shah of continued American support and virtually unrestricted access to American arms. The pronouncement was directed primarily against the United States and against her stationing of a small naval force in the Gulf, based by agreement with the shaikh of Bahrain at the former British naval station at Jufair. At the time of the signature of the agreement in December 1971 the shah had protested (in the curious company of Iraq, Kuwait, Egypt and Saudi Arabia) against the introduction of the American naval presence, on the grounds that it would encourage the Russians to follow suit – as if the Russians needed any instruction in such matters. Over the next half-a-dozen years the American naval agreement with Bahrain was subject to the customary vagaries of Arab politics, with the shaikh of Bahrain announcing at times of tension the imminent cancellation of the agreement, and then, after the vociferations of his nationalist critics had died down, quietly allowing it to continue. The shah's petulant complaints about the American naval squadron persisted, inspired by his irritation at the thought that it might one day inhibit his own navy's movements. He would not have dared to bait the Soviet Union in the same fashion, but he was emboldened to do so in the case of the United States because of the irresolution which that country had been displaying in the conduct of her foreign policy since the débâcle in Vietnam. He was also encouraged by the way in which his complaints were endorsed by gullible or foolish Western politicians. For instance, in November 1975 the British foreign secretary, James Callaghan, gave it as his opinion, during a brief stop in Bahrain, that the United States would be well advised to relinquish its rights of visit and supply at Jufair. 'There is no real justification for an American presence in the Gulf,' he declared rotundly, 'especially if the Gulf can co-operate to protect its own areas.' Neither Callaghan nor the shah, it might be remarked in passing, is on record as having criticized the use by the Soviet Union of naval facilities at the Iraqi port of Umm Qasr.

Western opinion in general throughout the 1970s was content to accept the shah at his own valuation, even to the point of acquiescing in his claim that the best guarantee for the preservation of Western interests in the Gulf lay in the establishment of a Persian ascendancy. The evident military and economic superiority of Persia over the other states of the region was constantly cited by Western politicians, government officials and professional pundits as solid grounds for this belief; and the argument was frequently bolstered by optimistic assertions about the Soviet Union's having an equal interest with the West in promoting a Persian paramountcy in the Gulf, since the Russians, so it was alleged, were anxious to remain on good terms with the shah so as to safeguard their own economic interests in Persia, especially in the continuing supply of natural gas from the Khuzistan and other fields. Such speculation was merely whistling in the dark. Persia was not a power of any consequence, nor could her ability to command the Gulf be taken as self-evident. As for Russian policy towards Persia, this could only be deduced from the history of the past two centuries, not from the events of the last two decades. For the Soviet Union, Persia represents a far superior means of access to the Gulf and the Indian Ocean than any other, and in the final assessment Persia as a power is incapable of denying the Russians anything.

The fates never permitted Muhammad Reza Shah to win the guerdon of wide renown and far dominion that he craved, still less to achieve his dream of recreating the Persian empire of old and bestriding western Asia like a Colossus. In the end his regime proved no match for the anti-monarchical forces which have been loose in the Middle East these past twenty-five years and more. He was, to a considerable degree, responsible for his own downfall; and to the extent that he was the victim of circumstances, these circumstances were in large measure brought about by the conduct of the Western powers, and of the United States in particular.

It is from the loyalty of the rural and religious classes that the legitimacy of the institution of monarchy in Persia fundamentally derives. The shah, by deliberately encouraging the growth of an industrial proletariat and a technocracy in a primarily agricultural country, by employing the financial resources of Persia so as to allow the cities and towns to reap the principal benefits from the recent burst of prosperity, succeeded in undermining the loyalty of the peasants without gaining that of the urban population. Although the standard of living of the inhabitants of Tehran and the other major cities – many of whom, and especially the unskilled and semi-skilled labourers, were recent migrants from the rural areas – materially improved during the 1970s, the improvement was bought at the cost of considerable disruption to their family lives, their social habits, their religious feelings and their ties to their traditional communities. The familiar and inevitable temper produced by heightened expectations appeared among them – of sullen dissatisfaction with what had so far been gained and a fractious insistence upon acquiring yet more, and quickly. Such feelings among the urban masses were only strengthened by the sight around them of the official, merchant and landowning classes ostentatiously, and in many cases corruptly, enjoying the spoils of the oil boom. When declining oil revenues forced financial retrenchment upon the shah, it was the urban masses, already smarting from real and imagined grievances (the most galling being galloping inflation and cynical exploitation by property speculators), who were the most rapidly and adversely affected. Their mood was scarcely improved by the sight of the shah continuing to lavish money upon his armed forces, money which might have been better spent, for instance, in providing Tehran with a sewerage system, something which it, alone among the major capitals of the world, entirely lacked.

An urban proletariat in such a mood was highly susceptible to political agitation, especially as legal outlets for the expression of discontent were closed by the ban on political parties, by censorship, by the intimidation of intellectuals and by the constant surveillance exercised by SAVAK. The *majlis* was a cipher, and so, too, was the only permitted political organization, the Rastakhiz or 'Resurgence' Party, which was brought into being by the shah in March 1975. Although it was presented to the Persian people as a vehicle through which they could make their voices heard, the Rastakhiz Party, which was alleged to have a membership by the end of 1976 of some five million, was solely intended to serve as a means of drumming up mass support for the regime. Like so many rulers of Persia before him, the shah considered the Persian people to have only one political function, viz. to offer him unquestioning obedience. Popular participation in government, as he was so fond of pointing out to Western visitors, inevitably led to instability, unrest and the kind of moral decadence he professed to see in the Western world. Having denied his people any kind of representative political institutions, and therefore the chance to acquire even the rudiments of a political education, he could scarcely complain if they turned elsewhere for guidance and release.

Where they turned, in the main, was to the mosque and to the Shii religious establishment, which had its own bones of contention to pick with the shah and his regime. In the view of the Shii mullahs, the prime duty of a Persian sovereign is to uphold the *sharia*, and to govern according to the interpretation of the sacred law handed down by the Shii *mujtahids*, the jurisconsults. While the sovereign is regarded as the visible head of the Persian Shia, he is also considered as no more than a *locum tenens* for the 'Hidden Imam' – the *mahdi*, or 'rightly guided one' – whose coming is ever awaited by the Shii community and who alone will rule by divine right. Though belief in the *mahdi* is also shared by many Sunni Muslims, they do not accord to the belief, or to the divine mission of the *mahdi*, the same fervent significance as do the Shia. It is the conviction of salvation, along with the concepts of martyrdom and redemption which are so strongly present in Shii Islam, that gives Shiism so decided a fanatical tinge. The religious authority of the Shii *mujtahids*, moreover, is far more substantial than that of their counterparts, the Sunni *ulama*, in other Muslim lands, where they are regarded primarily as servants of the state.

The power of the Shii *mujtahids* to influence the actions of the Persian sovereign had been on the wane since the latter half of the nineteenth century. Whereas in theory the edicts and ordinances of the monarch were subject to the imprimatur of the *mujtahids*, in practice successive shahs increasingly spurned their pronouncements, even to the point of permanently silencing the more obstreperous divines. The declining importance of the religious establishment in national life was in direct proportion to the progressive introduction of Western practices and ideas into Persia, against which the mullahs and *mujtahids* were constantly inveighing. They were treated with contumely and sometimes with brutality by Reza Shah, whose attempted relegation of Islam to the sidelines of Persian life outraged the ranks of pious Shia to the core of their being. His son seemed determined to continue the tradition, to forge even closer links with the infidel West than his father had done, and to introduce even more innovations which were anathema to the *mujtahids*.

Although there had been outbreaks of religious disaffection in the major cities of Persia at intervals since the Second World War, the first concerted upsurge of protest against the shah's modernizing programme came in 1963. It was set off by his land reform programme and more particularly by his forcible appropriation and distribution of *waqf*, i.e. religious endowment, lands. Riots broke out in several cities, incited by the mullahs who stood to lose financially from the alienation of the *waqf* lands. The worst rioting was at Qum, a city noted for its theological schools, where the disturbances were led, if not directly instigated, by a singularly austere and obdurate *mujtahid*, the *ayatollah* ('sign or token from God') Ruhollah Khomeini. The riots were suppressed with great severity by the army and police, and Khomeini was banished from the country. From this time onwards, however, the mosque became more than ever a forum for the articulation of popular grievances, particularly of the urban masses' dissatisfaction with the fruits of the 'white revolution' and their resentment of the disorientation it had caused in their lives. As for the religious classes themselves, they viewed the process of Westernization with abhorrence, fearing the introduction of alien moral and intellectual standards and all that these implied for the reduction of their own influence. Whatever other agencies and forces may have helped to stoke the fires of insurrection in Persia in 1978, it was in the mosques that the basic tinder was fashioned. The rage that vented itself in the streets of Tehran and other major cities in the winter of 1978–9 in a carnival of blood and destruction was not just the fury of a citizenry in revolt; it was also the reverse side of the coin of Shii fanaticism, which commonly expressed itself in the displays of hysterical grief and self-flagellation seen at religious festivals such as that of 10 Muharram in the Muslim calendar, which commemorates the martyrdom of Husain, the son of Ali and the third rightful imam of the Shii succession.

These intense and deep-seated religious emotions fused readily with the excitation aroused in the Persian masses by the seditious slogans and revolutionary propaganda circulated before and during 1978 by agitators of every stripe. The amalgam of Islamic fundamentalism and radical political ideas, whether of Marxist or other provenance, is by no means a new phenomenon in the Middle East: it has been observed before in this century, most recently in countries as diverse as South Yemen and the Lebanon, where in both cases the ideological alchemists have been the extremist factions of the Palestinian movement, with the PFLP in the van. What part they and other outsiders may have played in laying the powder train in Persia in 1978 has yet to emerge with any clarity. So, too, has the identity of the revolution's paymasters. Uncertainties of every kind, in fact, cloud the tumultuous events which brought the reign of the Pahlavi dynasty to an end in the winter of 1978–9, and it is much too soon after its demise to hold the kind of inquest which might determine with any finality the relative lethality of the numerous blows dealt the Persian monarchy in its final months – by the Shii religious establishment, by disaffected politicians and intelligentsia, by the merchants and guilds of the Tehran *suq*, by the underground guerrilla organizations and their foreign backers, by the swift collapse of the Persian armed forces, by Soviet intrigue, French meddling or American vacillation, or by any one of a hundred other contributory circumstances.

What the outcome will be for Persia is even more uncertain. Every time in the past that a dynasty has fallen the country has been rent by civil war and subjected to foreign invasion. With the disintegration of the central government, regional loyalties are bound to assert themselves with varying degrees of vigour. The Persians are not yet a nation, however long the ghost of the Persian empire has endured. They are, on the contrary, a miscellany of Persians, Afghans, Kurds, Turcomans, Arabs, Baluchis and other peoples, set apart from one another by ethnic, cultural or religious differences. Beyond the frontiers of Persia dwell larger communities of all those non-Persian minorities, each of them with irredentist claims of some sort upon Persian soil. Nor does the prospect of a turbulent future arise solely from the diversity of Persia's population, or from the danger of interference from without, or even from the doctrines of political violence preached of late by Muslim and Marxist revolutionaries. It derives also from the character of the Persians themselves, and from the singular talent they have displayed throughout their history for devising bizarre and gruesome methods of exacting vengeance or compelling obedience.

The founder of the Qajar dynasty, Agha Muhammad Khan, after defeating the last of the Zand rulers of southern Persia in 1795, erected a pyramid of skulls from the slaughtered bodies of the Zand ruler's followers over the spot where he was slain. To punish the men of Kirman for supporting the Zand cause, Agha Muhammad Khan ordered their eyes to be torn out. It was not until 7,000 eyes had been delivered to him that he declared himself satisfied. Manuchehr Khan, the governor-general of Fars, after suppressing a tribal revolt in 1841, built a tower of 300 living men, packed in layers of mortar, near Shiraz. After the defeat of the Persian army at the battle of Muhammarah during the Anglo–Persian war of 1856–7 the officers of one regiment were taken in chains to Tehran, where they were dragged, by ropes attached to rings inserted in their noses, through the ranks of their men before being publicly flogged and cast into prison. Common methods of punishment for criminals up to the early years of this century included crucifixion, impalement, live burial, mutilation, flaying alive and the bastinado. Against such a background of horrors, the treatment meted out by SAVAK to political prisoners of late years appears almost mild. It will be instructive to see how it compares with the penal regime instituted by the new rulers of Persia, whoever they may eventually be.

There was about the latter years of the reign of Muhammad Reza Shah an air of grim inevitability, of hubris and nemesis and the 'Gods of the Copybook Headings'. He would brook no dissent, heed no advice, listen to no voices but those uttering his praises. Vanity was his overriding weakness, and too much flattering unction was laid to his soul over the years by foolish or thoughtless Western statesmen. 'Iran, because of the great leadership of the Shah, is an island of stability in one of the more troubled areas of the world,' gushed

President Carter at a state banquet in Tehran on 31 December 1977. 'This is a great tribute to you, Your Majesty, and to the respect and the admiration and the love which your people give you.'

Muhammad Reza Shah accepted such blandishments at their face value. Although he was reputed to possess a strong sense of history, he used the past solely as an adjunct to his rule, as if its whole purpose had been to furnish a prologue to the accession of the Pahlavi dynasty. A more unassuming approach, a little sober reflection upon the imponderables and accidents of history, might have served him better. He might even have derived some profit (and a timely warning) from heeding what one of the most astute observers of Persian society and history, George Curzon, had written some eighty years or so earlier (in *Persia and the Persian Question*) about the fate that was bound to attend any fanciful plans for the rapid modernization of Persia:

Persia is neither powerful, nor spontaneously progressive, nor patriotic. Her agriculture is bad, her resources unexplored, her trade ill-developed, her government corrupt, her army a cypher. The impediments that exist to a policy of reform, or even to material recuperation, are neither few nor insignificant. . . . Colossal schemes for the swift regeneration of Persia are not in my judgment – though herein I differ from some other authorities – to be thought of, and will only end in fiasco. Magnificent projects for overlaying the country with a network of railways from north to south, and from east to west, and for equipping it with a panoply of factories and workshops and mills, can only end in financial disaster, and bring discredit upon their promoters. Hot-headed concessions for making or exporting or importing every article under the sun, from telephones to tobacco, and from rose-water to roulette-tables, contain no element of durable advantage, and are seldom devised with any other object than to put money into the pocket of the originators of the scheme.

CHAPTER VII
The Masquerade

*Members shall demand that oil companies maintain their prices
steady and free from all unnecessary fluctuations.*

First resolution of the Organization of Petroleum Exporting
Countries, September 1960

Masquerade: ad. Sp. mascarada, *f.* máscara *mask; usually taken
as a. Arab.* maskhara – *laughing-stock, f. root* sakhira *to ridicule.*

Shorter Oxford English Dictionary

There used to be a certain amount of argument in the 1960s, in those circles
where the subject was of interest, about whether or not the British political and
military presence in the Gulf was a help or a hindrance to the international oil
companies in their operations, and especially in their relations with the
governments of the oil-producing states. The argument was never resolved,
partly because it was clouded from the start by the personal or ideological
predilections of many of the disputants, partly because the oil companies
themselves were reluctant or unable to express a definite opinion one way or
another, but mostly because the only conclusive way in which the issue could
be decided was the empirical one of putting it to the test. This, it need hardly be
said, has now been done, and the years that have passed since the British
withdrew from the Gulf have seen not only a great erosion of the oil companies'
position *vis-à-vis* the governments of the oil-producing states, but also the
imposition of a selective embargo upon oil exports, arbitrary cutbacks in
production without reference to market requirements, enormous increases in
the price of crude oil, the disappearance of any effective control by the
countries of Western Europe over their principal source of oil supplies, and the
dislocation of their economies to a highly dangerous extent. It would be
erroneous, however, to conclude that a simple cause-and-effect relationship
linked the British withdrawal and the developments which succeeded it, even
though the withdrawal undoubtedly contributed to them. The decline in the
oil companies' fortunes in the Gulf had set in some years earlier: it was only

hastened from 1970 onwards by Britain's growing infirmity and by the increasingly feverish condition of Arab politics.

With every change of regime that has occurred in the Arab lands of the Middle East in the past two decades or so there has been a further deterioration of respect for law and civilized processes, and a corresponding reinforcement of the propensity to resort to violence to gain whatever ends may be in view. It is hardly surprising, therefore, that as time has gone by the international oil companies have become less and less of a match for the governments with which their operations compel them to deal. Indeed, it is doubtful whether, in the quarter-century which has elapsed since the settlement of the Anglo-Persian oil dispute in 1954, the companies have been in a position to put up any determined opposition to a Middle-Eastern government. To say this, however, is really to raise a false issue, for at almost no time during these twenty-five years have the major companies engaged in the production of Middle-Eastern oil–Standard Oil of New Jersey (Esso), Standard Oil of California (SOCAL), Socony–Mobil (Mobil Oil), Gulf Oil, Texaco, British Petroleum, Royal Dutch Shell and Compagnie Française des Pétroles – shown any firm disposition to run the risks to their concessions and investments which such opposition would have entailed. The companies' primary interest was in obtaining access to the oil reserves of Libya, Persia, Iraq and the Gulf in the quantities they wanted and at prices the market would bear. Whenever this interest was threatened, or appeared to be threatened, by complaints from the concessionary governments about the workings of the concessionary agreements or by allegations about the companies' manipulation of the international petroleum market, the companies were normally at pains to remedy the complaints or disprove the allegations. In short, the response was placatory, and as often as not it took the form of increasing the host governments' share of profits from the production of crude oil.

The first such accommodation after the Second World War took place late in 1950, when, following the precedent set two years earlier by the government of Venezuela, the Saudi government demanded and received from ARAMCO an undertaking to share its profits with Saudi Arabia on a fifty–fifty basis. ARAMCO's willingness to meet the Saudi demand was inspired not just by the size and importance of its oil concession in Saudi Arabia but also (as related in a previous chapter) by the readiness of the United States government to compensate the company for the reduction in its earnings by classifying the increased revenue payments as foreign income tax and, as such, allowable against ARAMCO's tax liability in the United States. Other oil companies operating in the Gulf were forced to follow ARAMCO's lead, and their home governments to adopt the same tax procedure. It seemed at the time, despite the serious loss of tax revenue to the Western governments concerned, a reasonably painless means of satisfying the desire of the oil-producing states for more money; but in fact, by implanting in the minds of the rulers of these states the notion that the Western world was prepared to subsidize their oil income, it established a most unfortunate and dangerous precedent.

Parity of profit-sharing having been achieved – without parity of investment and hence of risk-taking – the governments of the oil-producing countries now demanded that the companies publicly fix the price for crude oil and not conceal it (as had hitherto been the practice) in the complexities of their accounting procedures. Prices were to be fixed, furthermore, without over-much consideration being given to production costs. The companies conceded the demand, thenceforth posting the price at which they would offer their oil for sale and upon which the revenues paid to the concessionary governments in the form of tax would be calculated.

The effects of the fifty–fifty profit-sharing agreements and the introduction of the posted price system upon the income of the oil-producing countries quickly became apparent. Between 1950 and 1955 their revenues rose more than fourfold, from $193.5 million to $898 million per annum. It was in part an artificial growth, for their 50 per cent of profits was based not upon actual profits but upon the difference between production costs and the posted price. The producing countries also insisted that output be continually increased, so as to push their revenues even higher, with the result that towards the end of the 1950s a world surplus of crude oil began to develop. Although the surplus had the inevitable effect of forcing down oil prices in the international market, the posted price remained the same; so that the fifty–fifty balance of profits between the companies and the producing countries actually began to tilt in favour of the latter. Something had to give, and in February 1959 the companies made a cut of 18 cents a barrel in the posted price. The producing countries promptly protested at the reduction in their revenues, ignoring the fact that it was their insistence upon increased output which had created the glut and the consequent fall in market prices. Eighteen months later, in August 1960, Esso, acting alone, made a further cut of 10 cents a barrel. The other major companies, although they had not been consulted, had no option but to reduce their posted prices also.

The reaction of the producing countries was angry and vengeful. Iraq, which since the accession to power of the military regime under Abdul Karim Qassim in 1958 had been locked in an acrimonious dispute with the Iraq Petroleum Company over the operation of its concession, called a meeting of the four leading Middle-Eastern oil-producing states – Saudi Arabia, Kuwait, Persia and Iraq – at Baghdad in September 1960 to determine how best to retaliate against the seven major international oil companies – the 'Seven Sisters', *le sette sorelle*, as Enrico Mattei, the head of the Italian state oil company, ENI, had dubbed them. Venezuela, the pace-setter in most of the innovations which had been introduced into oil company and concessionary government relations over the previous decade, was also invited to attend. The upshot was the creation, by the 'Five Furies of Baghdad', of the Organization of Petroleum

Exporting Countries. The first resolution passed by the new organization outlined its immediate aims, viz. 'that members shall demand that oil companies maintain their prices steady and free from all unnecessary fluctuations; that members shall endeavour, by all means available to them, to restore present prices to the levels prevailing before the reductions . . .'. One of the most active personalities in the new organization was the director-general of petroleum and mineral resources in Saudi Arabia, Abdullah al-Tariki. He had been a prominent participant in the first Arab Petroleum Congress held in Cairo in April 1959 to discuss the implications of the initial reduction in posted prices in February of that year. The conference had been attended by delegates from all the Arab League states except Iraq (then in the throes of one of her innumerable quarrels with Egypt) and by unofficial delegates from Venezuela, Persia and the minor Gulf states. At the second congress held in Beirut a month after the foundation of OPEC, Tariki vehemently castigated the oil companies for their arbitrary conduct over posted prices, accusing them of cheating the oil-producing states of their rightful revenues by concealing the true amounts of their profits in recent years.

Tariki was a man of considerable ability and initiative, passionate by temperament, fervently nationalist in sentiment, and governed by an overweening sense of his own righteousness. He had been educated at the University of Texas and trained by Texaco, and in his years in the United States he had acquired a good deal of information about such matters as oil-depletion allowances, conservation and cartels, much of it by courtesy of the anti-trust hearings conducted by Congress into the activities of the major American oil companies in the 1950s. Many of the ideas about profit-sharing, participation, conservation, price-fixing and production levels which were to become the common coinage of Arab oil negotiations later in the 1960s and 1970s, if they did not actually originate in Tariki's fertile mind, owed their wide circulation to his vigorous and tireless promotion of them in the oil capitals of the Middle East. Although he fell from grace in 1962 and was replaced as Saudi Arabian oil minister by Ahmad Zaki al-Yamani, his ideas and his influence persisted for years afterwards, with consequences which he doubtless found highly gratifying.

Tariki wanted OPEC to operate as a cartel, fixing not only prices but production levels as well. The times were out of joint, however, for such an ambitious enterprise, because the world in the early 1960s was nowhere near as dependent for oil supplies upon the handful of member countries that made up OPEC as it is today. Moreover, the market for oil remained comparatively depressed, so that real prices continued to decline. OPEC's twin goals, of restoring posted prices to their previous levels and restricting production so as to keep the purchase price of oil buoyant, were not attained, largely because each member state was anxious to obtain as big a share of the market as possible for itself, and therefore refused to limit its production to a quota fixed by mutual agreement. Yet, while posted prices were not raised to their pre-1959 level, neither were they lowered in these years, despite the fact that at one stage selling prices were some 30 per cent below the posted price. It need hardly be said that the benefit of a constant posted price to the governments of the oil states, whose revenues were calculated on the basis of the posted price, was considerable. Moreover, the companies agreed in 1964 (though not without misgivings, since the oil market was well down) to deduct the royalty payments they made to the concessionary governments *before* reckoning their profits, half of which were paid to the governments in tax. As partial compensation to the companies for increasing their revenues, the concessionary governments agreed that posted prices should be reduced by 8.5 per cent from 1 January 1965, diminishing to 7.5 per cent in 1966 and to 6.5 per cent in 1967 – a concession which was an implicit recognition by these governments that posted prices were in excess of market prices. The effect of the expensing of the royalty payments by the companies was to divide their actual profits, not in the proportion of fifty–fifty as provided for in the tax agreements, but more of the order of sixty–forty in favour of the concessionary governments.

For all this, the governments in question were still dissatisfied, having long since convinced themselves that they were being fleeced by the oil companies with the active encouragement of the governments of the Western industrial countries. Against all factual evidence to the contrary, they refused to believe that fluctuations in the price of oil or the volume of consumption had anything to do with world demand or the normal workings of the market. Small matters like the dumping of large quantities of oil on the international market by the Soviet Union in the 1960s were dismissed as mere irrelevancies. Instead, the governments of the producing states preferred to attribute any fall in production, and any consequent decline in revenues, to the workings of a grand conspiracy on the part of the oil companies to deprive them of their economic heritage. Despite the rise in their annual revenues from $1,861 million in 1963 to $3,370 million in 1968, they were still avid for more, their appetites being stimulated by the need to finance the costly schemes of development upon which some of them, and Persia in particular, had lately embarked. They were consequently on the look-out for any opportunity to augment their revenues, and such an opportunity came their way with the Arab–Israeli war of 1967 – although it was an opportunity that was not without its risks and disquieting moments.

Up to 1967 the major Arab oil-producing states, Saudi Arabia, Kuwait and Iraq, had consistently refused to entertain the notion, which every year was given a ritual airing at the convening of the Arab Petroleum Congress, of using their oil resources in the Arab campaign against Israel. Even Iraq, which under its Baathist rulers had become one of the most vocal advocates of Arab solidarity and war *à outrance* with Israel, preferred to keep the subject of oil out of the pan-Arab political arena. When war broke out in June 1967, however, the wave of emotion which swept the Arab world compelled the governments of the oil states, despite their private misgivings, to make a gesture of sacrifice in support of the common cause. They did so by ostentatiously declaring an embargo upon the export of oil to the world outside. Hardly had the embargo been proclaimed, however, than it was quietly ignored by the governments concerned, which were well aware of the financial losses they could expect to incur if the embargo were really to be put into effect. Within a week or ten days of the declaration of the embargo, Saudi Arabia, Kuwait and Iraq were again permitting the shipment of oil to other countries, with the sole exception of the United States, Britain and West Germany, who were accused of actively supporting the Israelis. Since these were three of the biggest customers for Middle-Eastern oil it was obvious that the embargo against them could not be sustained, except at an unsupportable cost. At the summit conference held at Khartum in August 1967 to decide upon the policy to be followed by the Arab states in the aftermath of the war, the consent of Egypt, Jordan and Syria, the countries which had suffered most in the conflict, to the lifting of the embargo was obtained in exchange for a promise by the major oil states (Saudi Arabia in the main) to make good the trio's loses by annual financial contributions.

The experience had been an unnerving one for the three most conservative oil states, Saudi Arabia, Kuwait and Libya, and shortly afterwards they proceeded to take steps to protect themselves against its recurrence. In January 1968 they founded the Organization of Arab Petroleum Exporting Countries with the object of insulating the production and sale of oil from politics – Arab or international. Membership of the new organization was confined to Arab countries whose principal export was oil, a requirement which operated to shut out those with radical governments, like Egypt and Algeria. As an additional precaution, it was also laid down that membership should be dependent upon the approval of the three founding members, a condition which served to keep the refractory Iraqis out. A more encouraging aspect of the events of 1967 for the oil-producing countries was that they afforded them an opening to press for increased revenues. Saudi Arabia's output had not really been hit by the embargo: in fact, by the end of the year production had risen by 9 per cent over the preceding year. Iraq, in contrast, had suffered a decline in production of 15 per cent as a consequence of the closure of the Mediterranean pipeline by Syria. It was a loss which gave the Saudis and Kuwaitis not a little cheer.

The closing of the Suez Canal and the consequent increase in the transport costs of oil led Saudi Arabia and Iraq, though not in concert, to press the companies for a premium to be paid on oil delivered at Mediterranean ports through TAPline and the pipeline from Mosul and Kirkuk. The companies agreed. Meanwhile the Persians had been taking full advantage of the dislocation caused by the Arab oil embargo to increase their own exports of oil, and the shah was reluctant to lose the additional income he was receiving and which he needed to translate his dreams of glory into something approaching reality. He had professed great indignation in public over the revelation that the oil companies which comprised the consortium producing Persia's oil had an agreement among themselves to restrict the amount of oil each of them could lift every year. The limitation, as he knew full well, was essential if the price of oil was not to be driven down even further in the depressed world market. Despite this knowledge he proceeded to insist at the close of 1967 that the companies raise their output by 20 per cent annually, justifying his demand by a pious reference to his selflessness in allowing production to be increased from June 1967 onwards to compensate for the shortage caused by the ephemeral Arab oil embargo. To mollify him, the consortium companies offered to give up a quarter of their concessionary area and to increase the volume of oil supplied to the National Iranian Oil Company for subsequent sale to Eastern bloc countries. All concerned, however, were well aware that it was only a stop-gap measure; the shah's appetite had been whetted and he would be back for more.

Although OPEC's measures against the oil companies had so far been of a minor order only, its ambitions were growing larger. The organization's membership had expanded and eventually was to include, along with its five founders, Algeria, Libya, Qatar, Abu Dhabi, Indonesia, Nigeria, Ecuador and Gabon. Its confidence was mounting, step by step, as that of the West wavered, and the turn of events in the Middle East and elsewhere in 1968 offered the chance to make further gains. At the start of the year the British, after abandoning Aden, had announced their intention of quitting the Gulf by the end of 1971. The Americans, distracted by the war in Vietnam, by domestic turbulence and by the approach of a presidential election, were unlikely to give much thought to the implications of the British withdrawal. Western Europe had its own distractions – the Russian occupation of Czechoslovakia, the student *événements* in Paris, and the fleeting spectre of red revolution that these conjured up in impressionable minds. With an agreeable feeling that wider and rosier horizons were opening up before them, the oil ministers of OPEC gathered in Vienna in June 1968 for their sixteenth conference. After only a modicum of discussion the delegates passed a resolution (the ninetieth in a line stretching back to 1960) setting out the policy they intended henceforth to pursue towards the oil companies operating in their territories.

The resolution enunciated a novel doctrine of 'changing circumstances' to justify not only the revision ('at predetermined intervals') of the terms and conditions of any concessionary agreements, but also the acquisition by the governments of the oil-producing countries of 'a reasonable participation' in existing concessions and 'progressive and more accelerated relinquishments' of concessionary areas by the concessionaires. Tax and royalty payments were to be based upon posted or tax reference prices, and these in turn would be determined by the governments concerned. Although the latter might be prepared to grant the oil companies guarantees of stability of revenue payments for a limited period, they reserved to themselves the right to renegotiate concessionary agreements at any time to recover what they considered to be 'excessive net earnings' by the companies. If a company refused to negotiate, or to agree upon a figure for excessive profits, the host government would decide the sum unilaterally. Any disputes between governments and companies were to fall exclusively within the legal jurisdiction of the competent courts of the oil-producing country in question, or within that of any special regional court which might be established in the future.

Taken as a body, these claims amounted to a renunciation of formerly recognized principles of international law in the conduct of relations between the oil companies and the OPEC governments. If the claims were enforced, then any hope of stable company–government relations would fly out of the window – as the delegates doubtless realized. The strongest advocate of 'participation', i.e. the acquisition by the concessionary government of a portion of an oil company's assets and equity shareholding, was the youthful oil minister of Saudi Arabia, Ahmad Zaki al-Yamani, who had picked up the germ of the idea from his predecessor, Abdullah al-Tariki. It was on all counts a thoroughly unscrupulous device – though, not surprisingly, in an age of increasingly debased standards of international behaviour, it was soon to be regarded as unexceptionable – for it opened the way for a concessionary government to reap the benefit, at relatively little cost to itself, of an oil company's labours over the years, without taking any of the risks, financial or otherwise, which the company had run in prospecting for and extracting oil. Participation was all too clearly the first step along the road to complete nationalization, which Tariki was at that time, in his capacity as oil consultant to more than one Arab government, strenuously urging (although he was later to temper his enthusiasm in the light of experience). While some oilmen saw resolution XVI–90 as the writing on the wall, the companies as a whole were reluctant to believe that it spelled a real danger to their position. They doubted that OPEC would ever attain the cohesive strength to challenge their prerogative to fix posted prices and to determine the amounts of crude oil they would lift. Still less were they disposed to credit OPEC with the capability to enforce the other provisions in the resolution, including that on participation. Where the companies erred in their calculations was in regarding price-fixing and participation primarily as economic questions. If they ever had been, which is doubtful, they certainly were no longer. Now they were almost exclusively political issues, and the political mood in the Arab world in 1968 was sullen and captious, soured more than usual, after the events of 1967, by hostility towards the West. Sooner or later the oil companies, as the most conspicuous representatives of Western influence and interests in the Middle East, were bound to feel the weight of this baleful nationalism. The only uncertainty was where the first blow would be struck.

On 1 September 1969 the government of King Idris of Libya was overturned by a group of young army officers. The monarchy was abolished and Libya was declared an Islamic socialist republic, with the Koran and the *sharia* as the basis of its constitution. Power was concentrated in the hands of a Revolutionary Command Council headed by a thirty-year-old colonel, Muammar Qaddafi. Although the Western powers, and especially the United States and Britain, were taken by surprise by the military *coup d'état*, they were not on the whole disconcerted by it. The general view in Washington and London was that the reign of King Idris had been feeble and corrupt, and there was a lingering belief in both capitals (a legacy from the early days of Nasser's regime in Egypt) in the cleansing and therapeutic powers of revolutions conducted by ardent young officers of austere habits, stern demeanour and patent rectitude. If change meant progress, so the accepted theory went, then arbitrary change meant even greater progress. Colonel Qaddafi's ascetic ways, his conspicuous piety and his relentless vigour greatly impressed the British and American governments, so that when he peremptorily demanded the immediate removal of their military and air bases from Libya they hastened to accommodate him. They also felt obliged, when a number of *émigré* Libyans organized an expedition to release some political prisoners from a fortress in Tripoli with the object of overthrowing the revolutionary regime, to inform Qaddafi in advance of the intended attack and to intervene themselves to frustrate it. The British Foreign Office, running true to the form it has increasingly shown of late years, also tried to ingratiate itself with him by counselling British nurses in a hospital in Benghazi, when Libyan soldiers went on an anti-European rampage through the town, to submit to rape rather than provoke the Libyans' ill-will.

Oil was the only natural attribute that gave Libya any significance in the world, and Qaddafi was resolved to use it to make his mark upon history. The timid deference shown him by Britain and the United States convinced him that he could conduct an economic *jihad* against the West without inviting severe retaliation. He had a number of overlapping aims in view: to increase Libya's oil revenues by ignoring existing agreements with the oil companies; to acquire, as soon as possible, control over the companies' operations so as to be able to manipulate oil supplies for political and financial purposes; to demonstrate to the Arab world, by his audacity and success, that revolution and the Libyan brand of Arab socialism were the wave of the future; and to employ Libya's oil reserves and its revenues to promote the Palestinian cause and encompass the destruction of Israel. There were several factors working to his advantage, in addition to the radical policy adopted by OPEC in 1968 and the prevailing mood in the other Arab states. One was the growing dependence of Western Europe upon Libyan oil, particularly since the closure of the Suez

Canal. Another was the severity of the winter of 1969–70 in Europe, which had rapidly depleted existing stocks of oil. A third factor was the presence in Libya of a number of independent oil companies which, unlike the majors, had no alternative sources of supply if their Libyan operations were interfered with.

Towards the end of January 1970 Qaddafi summoned the representatives of the various oil companies in Libya to their first, and what was to prove their last, personal meeting with him. He told them that they would have to alter their pricing policy for Libyan oil, otherwise they would find themselves cut off from it. 'People who have lived for 5,000 years without petroleum', he proclaimed loftily, 'are able to live without it even for scores of years in order to reach their legitimate right.' At a subsequent meeting with Qaddafi's nominee as oil minister, the companies' representatives were informed that higher prices for Libyan oil were justified not only by Libya's proximity to Europe, which reduced transport charges, and by the low sulphur content of Libyan oil, but also because Libya had been underpaid for her oil ever since exports began in 1961. It was clear from this last allegation that the domestic political motive for demanding a substantial increase in oil prices was to discredit the previous regime by showing that it had sold its oil too cheaply. The increase the Libyan junta wanted was 44 cents per barrel, which was about 40 per cent up on the current posted price. Interestingly enough, the amount was close to the figure the Algerian government was demanding in the negotiations it had embarked on with the French government over oil and other matters late in 1969. Indeed, as time went by, it became more and more apparent that the two North African states were closely co-ordinating the tactics they were using to bring pressure upon the oil companies and their home governments.

In an endeavour to intimidate the companies, Qaddafi pointedly dispatched his oil minister to the Soviet Union, and in April 1970 he called upon the Libyan people to mobilize for the battle with the oil companies – the allies, so he asserted, of world Zionism and local forces of reaction. He made his intentions even plainer by putting the negotiations with the companies in the hands of his prime minister, Mahmud Mughrabi, a Palestinian exile who had obtained a doctoral degree in economics at Georgetown University in Washington, and who had been imprisoned by the monarchical regime for his extremist activities. At first Mughrabi, who had called in Abdullah al-Tariki as an adviser, directed his attack upon only two companies, Occidental Petroleum and Esso. Early in May Occidental was ordered to cut its production from 800,000 barrels a day to 485,000 b/d, and Esso was at the same time forbidden to commence the export of liquefied natural gas from the plant it had built at Marsa al-Brega at a cost of $350 million. The fiat to Occidental was justified by the Libyan RCC on the grounds of the need to 'conserve' Libya's oil reserves, a notion which Libyan reservoir engineers had picked up during their training in the United States. The real reason was that Occidental, like the other small independent companies, which by the early summer of 1970 were producing half of Libya's oil exports, was highly vulnerable to the RCC's chosen tactic of imposing restrictions upon production as a means of forcing up prices. If the independents could be made to yield, so the junta reasoned, the majors would have to follow. Amoseas was ordered to reduce its production by 31 per cent in June, Oasis by 12 per cent in July, Mobil/Gelsenberg (the West German oil company) by 20 per cent in August, and finally Esso by 15 per cent in early September.

It was largely the play of forces elsewhere which had both allowed and encouraged Qaddafi to behave as boldly as he had. A rather mysterious 'accident' to the Syrian end of TAPline in May had cut off the flow of Saudi Arabian oil to its Mediterranean terminal. Civil war broke out in Nigeria in the summer over the attempted secession of Biafra, interrupting the supply of Nigerian oil. A shortage of tankers, combined with a high demand for oil in Europe, drove up the spot market prices for both oil and tankers. From the Libyans' point of view it was an excellent moment to force a renegotiation of the posted prices, since the inflated rates for tanker charters could be used to raise the premium paid for Libyan oil because of its lower transportation cost. Once the new premium had been fixed, Qaddafi intended to compel the companies to continue paying it, regardless of whether or not tanker rates and transport costs fell. For this very reason, and also because the other oil-producing countries were bound to demand the same posted price as Libya achieved, the companies were inclined to stand their ground and to put off all negotiations. While the majors could afford to take this stand, having alternative sources of oil supplies to fall back on should the going become rough, the independent producers were without any such protection, and it was on them that the Libyan RCC now concentrated its fire.

In the third week of August Occidental was instructed by Major Abdul Salem Jallud, the deputy prime minister and Qaddafi's right-hand man in the RCC, to reduce its production further, from 485,000 to 425,000 b/d. Qaddafi was clearly keeping a close eye on the Algerians, who in July had unilaterally raised the posted price of Algerian oil by some 37 per cent. As a warning to the French companies not to resist, the Algerians had at the same time nationalized the assets of Shell, Phillips and Atlantic Richfield. With the first anniversary of his own revolution approaching, Qaddafi was eager to show that he, too, could triumph spectacularly over his Western adversaries. Occidental, whose humiliation was obviously to be the *pièce de résistance* of the celebratory games, was caught in a trap. If it yielded to the Libyans and raised its posted price, it ran the risk of pricing itself out of the European market, especially if tanker rates for Persian Gulf crude were to drop as a consequence of the reopening of the Suez Canal, or for other reasons. On the other hand, if it stood up to the junta and as a result was deprived of even more of its share of Libyan crude, it would lose most of its European customers anyway. Earlier in the summer the company had tried to persuade Esso to guarantee its supplies of crude, virtually at cost, so that it could hold out against the Libyans. Esso refused to sell at less than the market price. As a result, when in the last week of August the Libyans produced the ultimate threat, nationalization, Occidental was defenceless.

The company capitulated. On 2 September it concluded an agreement with the Libyan junta which raised the posted price of crude lifted by Occidental from $2.23 to $2.53 a barrel, effective from September 1970. The price was to be increased by a further 2 cents a barrel each year for five years, starting on 1 January 1971. The tax rate was to be increased from 50 to 58 per cent, to compensate, so Occidental was told, for the under-payment of revenues in previous years. In return for its capitulation, Occidental was to be allowed to raise its production from 425,000 to 700,000 b/d. 'Conservation', it seemed, had been swept away on the wings of the sirocco.

With Occidental vanquished, the junta turned to the other independents. Continental, Marathon and Amerada-Hess (the partners with Shell in the Oasis Consortium) were all forced in the latter half of September to concede a 30 cents a barrel increase, a tax rate of 54 per cent (again to compensate for alleged under-payment of revenues since January 1965) and a 10 cents per barrel annual increase for five years. They were allowed no more than a token restoration (some 5,000 b/d) of the production cut they had suffered in July. With half of Libya's oil production now covered by the revised agreements, the RCC felt strong enough to tackle the majors (Esso, BP, Texaco, Shell, SOCAL and Mobil) and the remaining independents (Hunt, Arco, Grace and Gelsenberg). On 22 September Texaco, SOCAL and the four independents were given five days to accept the new posted prices and tax rates. Esso, Mobil and BP did not wait for a similar ultimatum but increased their posted prices by 30 cents a barrel on 28 September. This was not good enough for the RCC. It wanted not only a new 55 per cent tax rate but also a public *mea culpa* from the companies in the form of an explicit written acknowledgement that the increased rate was part compensation for the under-posting of oil prices since 1965. The companies gave in: Texaco, SOCAL and the four independents on 30 September; Esso, Mobil and BP on 8 October. Only Shell had the courage to refuse, and as a punishment it was forbidden to lift oil from 22 September.

Shell's refusal was based not only upon principle but also upon the consideration that if Libya got the increases it was demanding and by the methods it was employing, then the other Middle-Eastern oil-producing states would make similar demands, using like methods. If these demands were conceded, Libya was bound to 'leap-frog' over them and demand yet further increases, citing as justification for them the differential freight rate for Libyan oil. The same thought had, of course, occurred to the other majors, but it would seem that it was outweighed in their minds by the fear that they would lose their Libyan concessions altogether if they defied the RCC. The fear was not without foundation. By subduing the independents the Libyans had assured themselves of a sufficient level of production and revenue to sit out a shut-down of the majors' production for an indeterminate period. On the other hand, however, by submitting to the Libyan junta's extortion, the majors were laying up more serious trouble for the future. Already the junta had made it clear that it would tolerate no restraints upon its behaviour. It had walked roughshod over the arbitration provisions in the concessionary agreements, declaring them null and void, and had then gone on to abrogate the agreements themselves. As a justification for its conduct it had put forward a meretricious argument concocted from assorted bits and pieces taken from the recognized doctrine of state sovereignty in international law, the unrecognized and highly dubious propositions about 'changing circumstances' advanced in OPEC's resolution XVI–90 of June 1968, and a number of sweeping accusations of corruption (especially over oil prices and revenues) against the former monarchical regime. What was perhaps of greater moment than this legalistic sleight-of-hand was the fact that the Libyans were closely co-ordinating their actions with those of the Algerian government in its negotiations with the French oil companies. Indeed, the Libyan RCC's tactics were almost a carbon copy of the Algerians', down to the throwing of tantrums, hurling of insults and snarling of threats which were a feature of the Libyans' conduct at nearly every negotiating session with the companies. The conclusion was inescapable that, if the Libyans were permitted to go on playing the yahoo as they wished, and to treat the concessionary agreements as so much waste paper, then not only would the whole Western oil industry in the Middle East be placed in jeopardy but respect for international law everywhere was bound to be seriously diminished.

Obvious though this conclusion might be, it was equally obvious (and had been almost from the outset of the Libyan offensive) that the Western governments most concerned were not going to offer the Libyans any resistance worthy of the name. Although American companies had the lion's share of Libya's oil, the United States government displayed a curious reluctance to support them against the junta. Its attitude was conditioned in part by its anxiety to re-establish diplomatic relations with the Algerians next door, and to obtain an assured supply of Algerian natural gas. For this reason, therefore, the United States government had sought to appease the Algerian government by muting its protests over the expropriation of Phillips's and Atlantic Richfield's assets in Algeria. The new Conservative government in Britain, for all its resounding election pronouncements, was no more prepared than its predecessor had been to protect British interests in the Middle East – or anywhere else, for that matter.

The attitude of the United States government, or at least of the officials charged with responsibility in the matter, was made clear at a meeting convened at the State Department on 25 September 1970, while Qaddafi's *putsch* against the oil companies was at its height. Nearly all the major and independent companies operating in Libya were represented at the meeting, which was presided over by U. Alexis Johnson, the under-secretary of state, assisted by the director of the office of fuels and energy in the Department, James E. Akins. Soon after the meeting began, the company representatives, to their astonishment, found themselves subjected to a lengthy harangue about the misfortunes of the Palestinians and the tribulations that their guerrilla forces were then undergoing at the hands of the Jordanian army. The Palestinian question, the oilmen were told, was intimately linked with the difficulties they were experiencing in Libya, and it followed, therefore, that a settlement of the Palestinian problem would lead to a resolution of the oil companies' difficulties. It was an interesting contention, not only because of the source from which it issued, but also because it was a faithful echo of the argument which the Libyans had been propounding over the previous months.

Why should it have been brought forth at this juncture and under these particular auspices? The answer would seem to reside in the personal and political convictions of the State Department's oil expert, James Akins. Akins took a rather favourable view of the Qaddafi regime, at least in comparison with its predecessor, the government of King Idris. 'The Idris regime', he told a sub-committee of the Senate Foreign Relations Committee in October 1973, 'was certainly one of the most corrupt in the area and probably one of the most corrupt in the world. Concessions were given, contracts were given on the basis of payments to members of the royal family.' What lends interest to these otherwise commonplace observations is that they were made after the complicity of Qaddafi's government in terrorist activities in Europe had become known to the whole world. They were also made after Akins had been appointed to the post of American ambassador to Saudi Arabia, a country where the securing of concessions and contracts by bribery and other corrupt practices had almost attained the status of a national industry. That Akins felt strong sympathy for – one might almost say, identification with – the beliefs and aspirations of Arab nationalism is now more or less public knowledge. Certainly he himself is reputed to have made little if any attempt to conceal his thoughts and feelings on the subject. As with so many American Arabophiles and partisans of Arab causes, especially that of Palestinian irredentism, it is possible to detect in the opinions he espoused the formative influence of the propaganda on behalf of Arab causes, and particularly that of Arab nationalism, which American Protestant missionaries in the Levant had been disseminating to their fellow-countrymen for a good century past.

Although Akins himself does not appear to have had any strong missionary connexion with the Middle East, he was a Quaker, and the Quakers have been among the most active and dedicated workers in the Levantine vineyard for several generations. From 1948 to 1950, as a young man in his early twenties, Akins was engaged in charitable work with the American Friends Service Committee in Europe, helping to repair the ravages of the Second World War. He then went on to Beirut, where he taught in a school for a year and spent a further year or two in educational work of a charitable nature. In 1954, at the age of twenty-eight, he entered the US Foreign Service, and in the course of the next dozen years he served (apart from posts in Europe) in Damascus, Beirut, Baghdad and Kuwait, before being appointed in 1967 to the office of fuels and energy in the Department of State. He was, from all accounts, a man consumed by a sense of mission, stiff in opinions to the point of inflexibility, an ardent Arabophile, and utterly convinced of the correctness of his own views concerning the proper relationship which the West should cultivate with the Arab states.

To return to the State Department meeting of 25 September, where Akins held forth so passionately on the plight of the Palestinians and its connexion with the problems the oil companies were experiencing in Libya. Akins was inclined to dismiss the companies' apprehensions about the implications of the severe increases in oil prices and tax rates which the Libyans had forced upon Occidental at the beginning of September. Although they constituted the largest increases in the revenues of a concessionary government to have taken place for twenty years, Akins thought them no more than 'reasonable'. 'It was also to our interest', he explained to the oil companies' representatives, '. . . that the companies have a reasonable working relationship with the Libyans and with other producers. If the Libyans concluded they were being cheated, this . . . guaranteed a breakdown in relations with the companies and all sorts of subsequent problems.' Sir David Barran, the chairman of Shell, promptly took Akins up on this score. He said that he strongly resented both the categorization of the Libyan demands as 'reasonable' and the insinuation that the Libyans were being 'cheated', with its underlying suggestion that the companies should therefore concede these demands. 'The dangers to our own and the consumers' interests lay much more in yielding than in resisting the demands being made upon us . . .', Barran argued. 'Our conclusion was that sooner or later we, both oil company and consumer, would have to face an avalanche of escalating demands from the producer governments and that we should at least try to stem the avalanche.'

What the United States government should do, Barran suggested, was to dare the Libyans to nationalize the companies' operations in Libya and then see what happened. Akins was greatly alarmed by the suggestion. 'If Libya moves in and takes over the companies,' he said, 'Europe, one way or another, is going to get Libyan oil, and if the companies then try to block the sale of Libyan oil, as they said they would, . . . they would find themselves nationalized in Europe as well.' It was an entertaining conceit, this forecast of the nationalization of every American oil company operating in Europe, especially as it came from the State Department's expert on oil and fuels. What made it more intriguing was that Akins, according to his own testimony three years later, did not feel similar alarm at the prospect of the nationalization of American oil companies by Arab or African or Asian governments. Testifying before the Senate Foreign Relations Committee in October 1973, he said: 'If, say, country X nationalizes an American company, there is full, prompt and adequate compensation and this country then sells its oil or its copper or whatever, we would certainly have no grounds whatsoever to make the protest, none, and we would not.'*

Was there no way, then, in which pressure could be brought to bear upon the Libyans to moderate their demands upon the companies? The opinion of the State Department, as expressed at the meeting of 25 September, was that there was none. According to the under-secretary of state, Alexis Johnson, the United States government had little or no influence with the Libyans; its intervention, he said, would be 'ineffective at best'. But what if the Libyans went so far as to nationalize the companies' concessions, and Libyan production was shut down as a result? Would not the Libyans soon begin to feel the pinch financially? Akins dismissed the possibility, pointing out that the Libyans had some $2,000 million in reserves which would keep them going for four years, at least. But surely, he was asked, it was logical to assume that Libyan deposits in American and European banks would automatically be frozen? 'It was an assumption', Akins later recalled with some satisfaction in an article he wrote for *Foreign Affairs* in April 1973, 'hardly likely to be realized.' He was equally certain that the countries of Western Europe would not have been prepared to endure the hardships which would result from the loss of Libyan oil simply 'to protect the Anglo-Saxon oil monopoly, which they had long sought to break'. 'As for the possibility of using force (actually suggested since by a handful of imperialists *manqués*),' he added with amused condescension, 'suffice it that it was never for a moment considered.'

With support like this from their home governments, the oil companies must have concluded that they scarce had need of the Libyan RCC as enemies. Every suggestion put forward at the State Department meeting of 25 September of ways in which the companies might fight back was rejected as impracticable, dangerous or (that most modish of the weasel words of our day) 'counter-productive'. The State Department would countenance no course of action except surrender. Yet three years later, in his article in *Foreign Affairs*, Akins was indignantly to deny, in the face of all that had flowed in the interim from the Libyan surrender, 'that the State Department by its inaction was to blame for creating a new monster'. 'The Libyans were competent men in a strong position,' he asserted; 'they played their hand straight, and found it a winning one.' It certainly was, seeing that the cards had been obligingly dealt to them by the State Department. A similar infirmity of spirit pervaded the British Foreign Office. On his way to Washington in late September, Barran,

* For these remarks and those in the foregoing paragraph, see the hearings of the sub-committee on multinational corporations of the Senate Foreign Relations Committee. One of the most valuable contributions to the hearings was the narrative of events from the spring of 1970 to the spring of 1971 supplied by Henry Mayer Schuler of Bunker Hunt. I have drawn upon his narrative at length for the account given here of the oil companies' negotiations with the OPEC governments in 1970–1.

in company with Sir Eric Drake, the chairman of BP, had talked in New York with Sir Alec Douglas Home, who was attending a session of the United Nations. They told the British foreign secretary that they believed that the oil companies should defy the Libyans, even at the risk of losing their concessions. Home said he would have to consult his fellow European foreign ministers before giving an opinion on the matter. According to what he is said to have reported back later, he found the foreign ministers unprepared to run any risk of losing their oil supplies. It would have been surprising if they had responded in any other way; which is not to say, however, that they would necessarily have refused to countenance any action if the consequences of a surrender in Libya had been adequately explained to them. Nor were they being asked to take inordinate risks, for Barran and Drake had assured Home that if they were deprived of Libyan oil, the companies could still supply 85–90 cent of Europe's oil requirements.

Whether Home made all this clear to the foreign ministers is not known. Even if he had, however, they may still have taken their cue in framing their response from his attitude and demeanour; and the British foreign secretary was not exactly spoiling for a fight with the Libyans, or any other Arabs for that matter, in defence of British interests in the Middle East in the autumn of 1970. The Conservative administration of Edward Heath was already showing its metal by its supine response to the wave of hijackings of civil airliners by Arab terrorists in September 1970, and by its furtive preparations to abandon its responsibilities in the Persian Gulf. The price of its disingenuousness and pusillanimity was to be paid by BP fifteen months later, in December 1971, when Qaddafi expropriated the company's concession and assets in Libya, ostensibly in reprisal for the British government's complicity in the Persian occupation of the Gulf islands of Abu Musa and the Tunbs.

Denied support by the British and American governments, the oil companies, as we have seen, had no recourse but to concede the Libyan junta's demands. Even Shell, the most valiant of the Seven Sisters, was compelled in the end to settle on similar terms to those forced upon the others. The ripples from the Libyan surrender were swift to make their appearance. Iraq and Algeria, claiming parity with Libya as Mediterranean oil exporters, demanded a similar 30 cents a barrel increase in the posted price of their crude. The Iraq Petroleum Company responded by offering Iraq 20 cents a barrel on oil delivered by pipeline to the Mediterranean and additional payments connected with royalty expenses. (The course of the Algerian negotiations will be described later.) Kuwait, Persia and Saudi Arabia all pressed for higher posted prices. While the Kuwaitis and the Persians proceeded to settle for an increase of 9 cents a barrel, the Saudis held back. To raise the producing countries' revenues further, the companies offered Persia, Kuwait, Nigeria, Iraq and the Gulf shaikhdoms the 55 per cent tax rate which had been conceded to Libya. The offer met with virtual silence, a silence which began to look all the more ominous when, at the beginning of December 1970, the government of Venezuela raised its tax rate to 60 per cent and arrogated to itself the right to set posted prices unilaterally.

A week later, on 9 December, the twenty-first meeting of OPEC opened at Caracus. Half a dozen resolutions were passed, of which the key one was Resolution XXI–120. It provided for a minimum 55 per cent tax rate for all member countries, the elimination of disparities in posted prices by taking the higher price as the norm (with allowances for gravity factors and geographic location), a uniform increase to reflect the improvement in the world petroleum market, the adoption of a new gravity escalation system and – somewhat inconsistently – the abolition of all differential allowances among OPEC members. There were other resolutions. One provided for the establishment of a committee to discuss production levels; another for the compulsory reinvestment of oil company earnings in the producing countries; and yet another for two factors of recent origin to be taken into account in determining the level of posted prices, viz. the decline in the international value of the US dollar and the rise in the cost to OPEC's members of imported manufactures. The attainment of these various aims was entrusted to a negotiating group of Gulf oil-producing countries which was to begin discussions with the oil companies at Tehran within thirty-one days. The Gulf group was to report to the full body of OPEC no later than seven days after the end of the negotiations, and OPEC was to meet to evaluate the results within a further fifteen days. Should the negotiations 'fail to achieve their purpose', the relevant resolution concluded, the member countries of OPEC would take 'concerted and simultaneous action' to secure the desired results.

The Caracas resolutions signalled the end, for all practical purposes, of separate agreements between oil companies and individual governments over oil prices and tax rates. Henceforth, any concession granted to one country would rapidly and inevitably be demanded by another, starting a chain reaction which would eventually bring in every member of OPEC. The Caracas Conference also made plain – to anyone, that is, whose eyes were not clouded by trust or hope – that the distinction which supposedly existed between moderate and radical members of OPEC was an illusion. The representatives of the so-called 'moderate' Arab governments at the conference were fully as vocal as those of the 'radical' regimes in their acclamation of the Libyan junta's triumph a few months earlier, and in their approval of the new demands formulated by the conference. Whether they were driven to assume this position, as has been alleged on their behalf by their apologists in the West, by fear of the consequences of appearing less aggressive and anti-imperialist than the revolutionary Arab governments is really beside the point. (It might as easily be argued that the whole 'moderate/radical' business was merely a pantomime staged to gull an impressionable Western audience.) What is more to the point is that the Caracas demands revealed with brutal clarity the lamentable consequences of allowing transitory market conditions (in the case of the Libyan capitulation, the temporarily severe demand for oil in Europe in the spring and summer of 1970) to bring about the abandonment of principle and logic in treating with the oil-producing states of the Middle East. Not only the oil companies but the oil-consuming countries as well were now faced with the prospect of repeated 'leap-frogging' of prices by the members of OPEC, backed by threats of curtailed production, appropriation of assets and disruption of oil supplies.

As might have been foreseen, the Libyans, cock-a-hoop over their victory in the autumn, decided to pre-empt the outcome of the negotiations due to begin at Tehran in the middle of January 1971. On 3 January the representatives of the oil companies in Libya were summoned by Major Abdul Salem Jallud, Qaddafi's closest confidant in the RCC, and told that, in conformity with the Caracas resolutions, Libya's tax rate was to be raised to between 59 and 63 per cent – figures which were said to represent the new tax rate of 55 per cent laid down at Caracas plus the increase to which the companies had agreed the previous autumn as compensation for 'under-payment' of oil revenues since 1965. The folly of allowing themselves to be browbeaten into signing explicit written acknowledgements of this alleged under-payment was now brought home to the companies. These 'confessions' were henceforth to be used by the junta to ensure that, whatever tax rate OPEC might decide upon, the Libyan tax rate would remain above it by a margin of several percentage points, as compensation for previous 'under-payment'. Jallud also stated that the posted price of Libyan oil was to be raised by 69 cents a barrel to eliminate what he called 'excessive windfall profits' earned by the companies as a result of replenishing Europe's oil stocks. Payment, or an appreciable part of it, was to be retroactive to the closing of the Suez Canal in 1967. The companies were also told that they would be required to reinvest in Libya the sum of 25 cents for every barrel of oil they exported, and to pay taxes and royalties by the month instead of by the quarter. Finally, even though the effect of the new payments was to double the price of Libyan oil from that fixed only three months earlier, after Qaddafi's offensive against the companies, the Libyan government, Jallud announced, would also expect to receive any increases agreed in the forthcoming negotiations at Tehran. So much for the five-year agreement on posted prices which his government had signed the previous September – but, then, circumstances had changed.

As in its initial offensive, the RCC picked upon the independent companies as soft targets. On 9 January Occidental and Bunker Hunt were told by Jallud that they had one week in which to accept the new terms. The ultimatum was accompanied, as in the case of the *diktat* to the companies a week earlier, by the familiar threats of curtailment of production and nationalization. At both meetings Jallud had been insistent that the coercion of the oil companies was motivated by the RCC's determination to force the United States to adopt a pro-Arab policy in the Middle East. The claim needed to be taken with a pinch of salt. There were as many good reasons for ascribing the Libyans' behaviour to sheer rapacity as there were for believing that it derived solely or even largely from Qaddafi's known Islamic fundamentalism, his hatred of Israel and his detestation of Western civilization. Whatever the explanation, the companies had little time to spare at the close of 1970 for speculation about the psychopathology of the Qaddafi regime. What preoccupied their thoughts were the serious dangers posed to the Western industrial nations, and to the oil-consuming countries of the non-communist world in general, by OPEC's avowed intention to assume exclusive control over oil pricing and the fixing of tax rates.

If the leap-frogging or ratchet tactics of OPEC over oil prices were to be defeated, the oil companies would have to act in concert, to present a united front to the organization just as it presented one to them. Late in December 1970 Shell took the initiative and set about persuading the other companies, majors and independents, to form a joint negotiating body. 'Our view', the chairman of Shell, Barran, explained later, 'was that the avalanche had begun and that our best hope of withstanding the pressures being exerted by the members of OPEC would lie in the companies refusing to be picked off one by one in any country and by declining to deal with the producers except on a total, global basis.' For the American oil companies to act together, without rendering themselves liable to prosecution under existing United States anti-trust laws, would require an undertaking from the United States government that proceedings would not be instituted against them if they took a joint stand against OPEC. An approach to the US Department of Justice to secure its consent was made early in January 1971 by the veteran lawyer, John J. McCloy, who had acted as counsel for the Seven Sisters on anti-trust matters on several occasions in the past. McCloy was a man of considerable distinction and influence who had been in his time assistant secretary of war, United States high commissioner in Germany, president of the World Bank and chairman of the Chase Manhattan Bank. He had foreseen the potential dangers to Western interests from OPEC soon after the founding of the organization in 1960, and he had warned successive administrations in Washington that the day would come when the oil companies would have to act together for their own and the Western world's protection.

On 11 January the representatives of twenty-three oil companies – the Seven Sisters, the independents, Compagnie Française des Pétroles, the Arabian Oil Company of Japan, Petrofina of Belgium and Elverath of West Germany – met in New York to decide upon the substance of a combined message to OPEC. The text that was finally agreed on 13 January set out courteously but firmly the view of the companies that the long-term interests of both oil-producing and oil-consuming countries required that there should be stability of financial arrangements between the companies and the OPEC governments. As the continuous series of claims being made by individual members of OPEC made the attainment of such stability impossible, the companies had decided that the only basis upon which they were henceforth prepared to negotiate was 'one which reaches a settlement simultaneously with all producing governments concerned'. To this end the companies proposed 'that an all-embracing negotiation should be commenced between representatives of ourselves, together with such other oil companies as wish to be associated with this proposal, on the one hand, and OPEC as representing all its member countries, on the other hand, under which an overall and durable settlement would be achieved'. To ensure both stability and mutual respect for contractual arrangements, and at the same time to demonstrate their genuine desire to achieve a comprehensive and lasting settlement, the companies were prepared to offer a revision of posted prices for all member countries of OPEC, together with a further provision for a 'moderate annual adjustment' to reflect any world-wide inflation that occurred. They were also willing to agree to a further, variable, temporary adjustment for Libyan and other 'short-haul' crudes. These offers were contingent upon there being no increase in the tax rate percentage beyond that already in force, no imposition of retroactive payments and no new provision for the obligatory re-investment of earnings. The offers were also subject to the settlement's remaining in force for five years from the date of its signing.

Unsure of what the Libyan government's reaction to this joint statement might be, but fearing it might take a drastic form, the companies operating in Libya quietly concluded among themselves a 'safety net' agreement. They undertook, if any one company was forced (as a consequence of refusing to comply with the Libyan government's demands) to reduce or halt production, that the other Libyan producers would replace the crude lost at cost, or near cost. It was further agreed that, under certain circumstances, those Libyan producers with Persian Gulf concessions would share their Gulf production with any Libyan producer whose wells had been shut down. The agreement, which was mainly designed to protect the independent producers, was for this very reason a measure of the anxiety felt by the companies over the situation which confronted them. For there was no love lost between the majors and the independents, whom the former had often accused in the past of poaching on their preserves and concluding arrangements with local governments which adversely affected the majors' interests. (Esso, it will be recalled, had only the previous summer refused to guarantee supplies to Occidental.)

Shortly after the drafting and signature of the message to OPEC and the conclusion of the Libyan producers' agreement the Justice Department issued business review letters to the American oil companies involved, assuring them that proceedings would not be taken against them under the anti-trust laws in respect of their actions. Other oil companies, including Gelsenberg of West

Germany and Hispanoil of Spain, were already beginning to range themselves alongside the original signatories of the message to OPEC. In the third week of January two groups of company representatives were assembled, one in London, the other in New York, to co-ordinate the companies' moves. The London Policy Group, as it was called, was made responsible for drawing up terms of reference for the representatives who were to negotiate with OPEC on behalf of the companies in Tehran and Tripoli, and for modifying the negotiators' instructions and answering their queries. The New York group was to review and comment upon policy proposals made in London, and to provide technical information. Diplomatic exchanges had also taken place among the United States, British, French, Dutch and Japanese governments. The French were then undergoing their own trial by fire, as will be seen later on, over their oil concessions in Algeria, while the Japanese were alarmed by the prospect of yet higher oil prices. There was, however, no co-ordination of efforts by these governments comparable to that being made by the oil companies. What was more disturbing, there was no evidence of any strong governmental disposition to back the companies' stand.

On 15 January the chief executive officers of the major companies and the leading independents, with McCloy in attendance, had a meeting at the State Department with the secretary of state, William Rogers, and the under-secretary, John Irwin II. The oilmen emphasized the necessity of maintaining a collective approach to OPEC and the desirability of the United States government's supporting the companies, especially by persuading the OPEC governments to moderate their demands and to follow fair bargaining practices. Rogers accepted the advice, along with the further proposal that a personal envoy from President Nixon should be dispatched without delay to the shah, King Faisal of Saudi Arabia and the shaikh of Kuwait, carrying with him letters from the president to the three rulers. It would be the envoy's task, firstly, to explain why the United States government was permitting the American oil companies to negotiate jointly; secondly, to prevent the possible interruption of oil supplies should negotiations reach an impasse; and, finally, to seek assurances from the Gulf oil states of the continued supply of oil at reasonable prices to the free world. At the suggestion of Akins, who was present at the meeting, the under-secretary of state, Irwin, was selected for the mission. He left for Tehran the next day, accompanied by Akins. Since Irwin was not conversant with the oil industry, and there had been no time to brief him adequately, it was obvious that he would have to rely for guidance on oil matters upon Akins.

Meanwhile the representatives of the companies had had a preliminary meeting in Tehran on 12 January with the Gulf Committee of OPEC, which had been charged with implementing the resolutions adopted by the organization at Caracas in December. The Gulf Committee, representing Saudi Arabia, Persia, Iraq, Kuwait, Qatar and Abu Dhabi, was made up of Ahmad Zaki al-Yamani, the Saudi minister of petroleum, Jamshid Amuzegar, the Persian minister of finance, and Saadun al-Hammadi, the Iraqi oil minister. The deadline laid down at Caracas for the completion of negotiations was still operative; so, too, was the threat of a shut-down of oil production if satisfactory terms had not been agreed by 3 February. At the preparatory meeting the companies' representatives explained that they were not yet empowered to negotiate on the increases demanded by OPEC, and the meeting was thereupon adjourned. On 16 January the collective message to OPEC was delivered to the organization's constituent governments. The initial reactions to it were fairly muted. Amuzegar in Tehran challenged the validity and practicability of an attempt to negotiate with OPEC as a body, saying that if the companies persisted in it the organization would respond by adopting what he called the 'crazy demands' of the Libyans as a common denominator.

Much the same reception was accorded the joint message in Tripoli. The oil minister, Izzedin Mabruk, summoned the representatives of Bunker Hunt and Occidental on 16 January to remind them of the ultimatum delivered to the independents earlier in the month, and to threaten and cajole them alternately in an effort to persuade them to break away from the combined negotiations. He and Major Jallud tried the same approach three days later, when they harangued the representatives of Esso about the 'poisoned letter', as they called the joint message. There was no doubt that they were shaken by it, to such an extent that they allowed three consecutive ultimata to Bunker Hunt to expire without taking punitive action. In conversations with the companies' representatives they revealed that what worried them most was the companies' refusal to entertain any demands for retroactive tax payments or new reinvestment obligations, two desiderata which were close to the Libyans' hearts. They could rake up no plausible reasons for objecting to a collective OPEC settlement: indeed, Jallud was reduced to complaining feebly that he was being asked to negotiate with oil companies which did not operate in Libya. This was a palpable lie: all the Persian Gulf producers at that time, with the exception of Gulf Oil, also operated in Libya. What clearly emerged from what was, for the Libyans, a meek and mild response to the companies' joint message was that Jallud and his *rais*, Qaddafi, were taking their colour from the Algerians with whom they were in close touch and who had also reacted to the companies' message in subdued fashion. All the signs indicated that a critical juncture had been reached in the contest between the companies and OPEC, and that a firm approach by President Nixon's special envoy could well prove decisive.

Irwin arrived in Tehran on 17 January. Accompanied by the American ambassador to Persia, Douglas MacArthur (nephew of the general), he had a meeting with the shah, the Persian prime minister, Ardeshir Zahedi, and the finance minister, Amuzegar. What transpired at this meeting, and at a further meeting between Irwin and Amuzegar, is not entirely clear, although its general content can be deduced from evidence which has subsequently come to light. Testifying before a sub-committee of the Senate Foreign Relations Committee three years later, Irwin recalled that he had begun by explaining to the shah and his ministers 'that the US government was not in the oil business and did not intend to become involved in the details of the producing countries' negotiations with the oil companies'. He had gone on to say 'that the United States had urged the companies to be co-operative and reasonable, and . . . that the companies had already agreed in their message to OPEC of January 16 to negotiate the substantive demands included in the Caracas OPEC resolutions'. He had then emphasized that the companies as well as the oil-consuming countries were worried by the thought of the incessant rounds of price increases that were bound to follow if the members of OPEC negotiated in separate geographic groups. Finally, he had pointed out that, as the United States Department of Justice had not given its permission until 13 January for the American oil companies to act in unison, the companies had been unable to commence negotiations before then. They would therefore require more time to negotiate a settlement than that allowed by the deadline laid down in OPEC's Caracas resolutions.

To this the shah and his ministers replied that they considered the companies' decision to negotiate *en bloc* was 'a most monumental error'. It meant that the 'moderate' members of OPEC (with Persia naturally in the van) would not be able to restrain the Libyans and Venezuelans, the 'wild men', as Amuzegar called them. Consequently the increase that would eventually emerge would be the highest common denominator. What would make far better sense, the shah argued, would be for the companies to adopt the suggestion made by the Persian representative at the Caracas conference and conduct separate negotiations with the Gulf members of OPEC, the Mediterranean members and the non-Middle-Eastern members. The greatest importance, so the shah and his ministers contended, attached to the conclusion of a satisfactory settlement with the Gulf states, since they would be the principal suppliers of oil to the industrial world in the years to come. The companies should not require as a condition of arriving at such a settlement that the rest of OPEC should also subscribe to it. Should they do so, it would be taken as a sign of 'bad faith' on their part and 'serious trouble' would follow. The Gulf countries could not impose their will upon Libya, Algeria or Venezuela, and the companies would be making a grave mistake if they tried to play one member of OPEC off against another, or to prolong the negotiations unduly. It was patently obvious, the shah added testily, that this was exactly what the companies were attempting to do by their insistence upon negotiating with OPEC as a whole. If they were seeking to stir up dissension within the organization between its 'moderate' and 'radical' members and thereby to hasten its disintegration, they were, the shah proclaimed grandly, seeking in vain. OPEC would stand united, even to the point of closing down oil production altogether. On the other hand, the shah affirmed (so Irwin later reported), 'if the companies dealt with the Gulf producers as a separate group, the latter were prepared to sign an agreement and stick to it for the length of its term, even though producers in other areas obtained better terms from the companies'.

Another version of the meeting, based upon a verbal account rendered by the American ambassador, MacArthur, a couple of days afterwards, has it that the shah categorized the oil companies' joint approach to OPEC as 'a dirty trick' and warned that if they persisted in it, 'the entire Gulf would be shut down and no oil would flow'. MacArthur subsequently claimed, however, that the shah had not even discussed the question of separate negotiations for the Gulf states, let alone threatened an oil embargo in support of them. Instead, the threat was attributed to Amuzegar. The discrepancy is immaterial: Amuzegar was merely his master's voice. What matters is that the threat of an embargo was made.

The following day, 18 January, Irwin cabled the State Department recommending that the oil companies should be advised to negotiate separately with the Gulf and Mediterranean oil states. He gave as his reasons the strong objection of the shah and his ministers to the companies' insistence upon negotiating *en bloc*, and the willingness of the Gulf oil states (of which, Irwin said, he had not previously been aware) to enter into an agreement on prices for five years and to abide by it, even though oil-producing states elsewhere might later succeed in obtaining higher prices. It was an astonishing *volte face* on Irwin's part, all the more so because it occurred within twenty-four hours of his arrival in Tehran. What had prompted it?

In his testimony before the Senate Foreign Relations Committee in January 1974 Irwin explained that he had made his recommendation 'in view of the assurances which the Persian Gulf producers were prepared to give on future price ratcheting'. But on 18 January 1971 Irwin had visited only one Gulf oil-producing country, Persia, and had talked with only one Gulf ruler, the shah. The sole 'assurance' he had received, therefore, was that conveyed, or intimated, to him by that monarch and his ministers. Why did Irwin not wait until he had completed his mission by visiting Riyad and Kuwait before submitting his recommendations? Why, also, when no one at the time (as he himself was later to testify) believed for a moment that any agreement with OPEC on prices would last, did he accept the Persian government's assurance that it would honour such an agreement for five years and make this assurance the basis for his recommendation to Washington? There is no doubt that the shah and Amuzegar could be both forceful and persuasive in argument. But even a diplomatist as inexperienced as Irwin (he had joined the State Department from a prominent New York law firm only the previous September) should never have allowed himself, after only two or three hours' conversation, to be inveigled into precipitately abandoning the object of his mission and to bow to the wishes of those with whom he had been sent to treat. It has to be remembered, furthermore, that it was not the purpose of Irwin's mission that he should negotiate with the Persian government over the oil companies' joint approach to OPEC: his task was simply to impress upon the governments of Persia, Saudi Arabia and Kuwait that the United States wholly supported the companies in their combined stand against the ratchet tactics of OPEC over oil prices. Instead of confining himself to this object in his exchanges with the shah and his ministers, he elected to dwell – as his own testimony revealed three years later – upon the injurious effects which any interference with oil supplies would have upon the Western industrial nations.

Apart from the arguments put to him by Muhammad Reza Shah and Amuzegar, what other considerations may have persuaded Irwin to alter the purpose of his mission? By his own admission, it seems that he was not very well informed about the Middle East or about the oil industry. Nor does he appear to have grasped precisely and thoroughly what was at stake in the impending confrontation with OPEC. (In his recollections before the Senate Foreign Relations Committee, for instance, he categorized the oil companies' decision to negotiate with OPEC *en bloc*, a decision which was the very foundation stone of the whole strategy to checkmate OPEC, as a 'procedural issue'.) It is difficult to resist the conclusion that Irwin was unduly swayed, especially in his judgement of the urgency of the situation, by the views of others at Tehran – MacArthur in particular. MacArthur was in no doubt that the oil companies should, in their own interest and that of the Western industrial nations, concede the Persians' desire for separate negotiations with the Gulf oil states. He strongly impressed this opinion upon the State Department. Why he should have taken the Persians' part in this matter is no great mystery: partisan sympathies of this kind were, and still are, almost *de rigueur* among American and British diplomatists in the Middle East. John J. McCloy, for instance, described MacArthur to the Senate Foreign Relations Committee in February 1974 as being 'more Persian than the Persians sometimes'. Henry Mayer Schuler of Bunker Hunt expressed a similar opinion: 'Oftentimes the representative of the United States becomes the representative of the country to which he is accredited. His primary interests are in bilateral relations between the United States and Iran and he could not care less about multilateral oil negotiations. . . .'

Presumably much the same kind of recommendation as MacArthur made to Washington was sent to the Foreign Office by the British ambassador in Tehran, Sir Denis Wright, and for much the same reasons. Wright, who spent the eight years before his retirement from the diplomatic service as ambassador to Persia, was a passionate admirer of the shah and much attached to the Persian people. He was also at this time deeply involved in negotiations with the Persian government over the pending British withdrawal from the Gulf, negotiations which included the satisfaction of the shah's claims to Abu Musa and the Tunbs. Not surprisingly, there was little disposition on his part or that of the Foreign Office to disturb the even tenor of these negotiations by thwarting, or even questioning, the shah's wishes over the manner in which the discussions between OPEC and the oil companies were to be conducted. Only the Dutch ambassador at Tehran doubted the wisdom of yielding to the shah's wish to split the negotiations into two, for he recognized that capitulation on this score would immediately rob the companies' combined message to OPEC, delivered only two days previously, of its entire force. What part James Akins may have played in Irwin's *volte face* is not ascertainable from the evidence available, although it would not be illogical to assume that it was in keeping with the complaisant attitude he had adopted towards the Libyan *putsch* some months earlier. Nothing, it would seem, least of all the turn of events, would alter Akins's faith in the virtue and seemliness of acceding to whatever demands OPEC might make. At the meeting of oil company representatives held at the State Department the previous September he had pooh-poohed the idea that the other Middle-Eastern oil states would be encouraged by Libya's example to demand higher prices and tax rates. He was, as one of the British oilmen recalled with some disgust, 'hypnotized by the Saudi Arabians. He said that there was no question of Saudi Arabia following Libya. I said you must be joking, and nearly walked out.'* At the Caracas conference Saudi Arabia *had* followed Libya, yet Akins's ardent belief, both in the reasonableness of the Saudis and in propitiation as the cardinal principle of diplomacy, remained, and was to remain, unshaken.

Perhaps the most remarkable aspect of Irwin's decision at Tehran was that he took it without making any effort to consult the oil companies. George T. Piercy, a director of Esso, and Lord Strathalmond, managing director of BP, were due to reach Tehran early on 19 January to lead the oil companies' side in the negotiations with OPEC. Irwin did not see fit to wait the few hours until their arrival before sending his recommendation to Washington. Indeed, he did not even wait to see them *after* he had sent it, but flew off instead to Riyad. Piercy and Strathalmond were apprised of the outcome of Irwin's mission when they met MacArthur, Wright and the French and Dutch ambassadors on their arrival. They were also told that word had been received from Washington that the secretary of state, Rogers, had endorsed Irwin's recommendation in favour of separate negotiations with the Gulf States, and was urging the oil companies to comply with it. Piercy immediately protested that to do so would set at naught the message to OPEC delivered only three days earlier. Furthermore, he questioned whether the past history of oil agreements in the Middle East gave cause for confidence that the Gulf States would honour any price settlement they might reach, especially if the companies were subsequently to be forced to concede a ludicrously high price for Libyan oil. MacArthur, to whom these views were expressed, seemed incapable of grasping what was at stake. Instead, he kept urging upon Piercy and Strathalmond that they should content themselves with a separate negotiation with the Gulf states.

* Anthony Sampson, *The Seven Sisters*, p. 227.

Thus, within the space of forty-eight hours, Irwin, MacArthur and Rogers – to mention only the principals – had managed to undermine the entire strategy of the combined approach worked out by the oil companies in consultation with the State Department and the Justice Department, and in exchanges among the United States, British, French and Dutch governments. The State Department now proceeded to guarantee the failure of the combined strategy – whether it intended to do so or not is a moot point – by hurriedly convening a meeting of the member countries of the Organization of Economic Co-operation and Development in Paris on 20 January. Its purpose, it would seem (for the record of the meeting was not made public), was to persuade the other OECD governments to adopt the placatory approach to OPEC that the State Department had obviously decided upon. The United States representative is said to have assured the meeting that if no resistance were offered to higher oil prices, they could count upon at least five years' supply of oil at stable or only slightly rising prices. (According to one account, the oil company representatives who were present as observers echoed the assurance. On the face of it, it seems improbable, unless they and their companies had got their wires crossed.) After the meeting an OECD spokesman announced that 'contingency arrangements for coping with an oil shortage . . . were discussed' – a statement which was as good as an open signal to the shah and the other members of OPEC to persist with their threat of an oil embargo as a means of attaining their ends. It is not even certain that Irwin himself had not unwittingly planted the germ of the idea of an embargo in the shah's mind in the course of their conversation by dwelling upon the plight to which Western Europe and Japan would be reduced were oil supplies to be seriously disrupted. Even an inadvertent hint was enough to set the shah's fertile brain ticking, especially as statements along the same lines had begun to issue, and were to continue to issue, from American official sources elsewhere.

Unlike the State Department, the oil companies were not yet ready to throw in the towel. Late on 19 January, Piercy and Strathalmond held preliminary talks with the three members of the Gulf Committee – Amuzegar, Yamani and Hammadi. They explained that the companies' combined approach had been rendered necessary by the resolutions adopted by OPEC at Caracas, especially in support of the exorbitant demands being made by Libya. It was essential, the companies believed, to put an end once and for all to the leap-frogging of prices by negotiating with OPEC *en bloc*. Amuzegar said in reply that OPEC had only authorized the Gulf states to enter into negotiations. It was up to the companies, therefore, to alter their terms of reference, not for the member governments of OPEC to alter theirs. If the companies insisted upon an overall negotiation, it could only result in the adoption of the highest common denominator for oil prices. Piercy countered these arguments by pointing out that the joint approach had been arrived at in consultation with, and with the approval of, the United States and other Western governments. The companies were therefore obliged to respect the compact which had been made. Amuzegar blithely dismissed this objection. 'If you think you have a problem with your government,' he said airily, 'I am quite confident that they will agree to a regional or Gulf approach.'

The shah was equally confident about the matter when he spoke to Wright, the British ambassador, the next day. He was 'under the impression', he said, 'that the Americans accepted the "Gulf only" procedure'. Such confidence as both he and his finance minister displayed could only have been generated by their conversations with Irwin and MacArthur; for the State Department's adoption of the latter's recommendations had not yet been formally communicated to Tehran. Here, if anywhere, is confirmation of what Senator Frank Church of the Senate Foreign Relations Committee was later to condemn, at a hearing of the sub-committee on multinational corporations of which he was chairman, as 'waffling' (in its American sense of shilly-shallying) on the part of the United States government in its support of the oil companies. What was more, the confidence exuded by the shah and Amuzegar was merely a reflection of MacArthur's own confidence that his recommendation that the negotiations be split would be endorsed by the State Department, a confidence which could only have proceeded from the knowledge that the views he held on the proper posture for the United States to adopt in the Middle East were in the ascendant at the State Department. Small wonder that John J. McCloy, the counsel for the oil companies, was to remark laconically to Church's sub-committee three years later: 'We weren't too much impressed, if I may say so, by the attitude of the US government.'

After the preliminary meeting of 19 January Piercy and Strathalmond cabled their impressions to the London Policy Group.

It is not easy to advise what should be done. If we commence with Gulf negotiations we must have very firm assurances that stupidities in the Mediterranean will not be reflected here. On the other hand, if we stick firm on the global approach, we cannot but think . . . that there will be a complete muddle for many months to come. Somehow we feel the former will in the end be inevitable.

The Tehran negotiators' pessimism communicated itself to the London Policy Group. Support from the United States government had evaporated (if it had ever existed in solid form); the French and British governments had all along been half-hearted in their backing for the combined approach; and the State Department was constantly urging the companies to be conciliatory. In these circumstances, the London Policy Group decided there was no alternative but to split the negotiations. Strathalmond would lead the Gulf negotiating team in Tehran, Piercy the Mediterranean team in Tripoli. It was still the companies' intention, however, that the two teams should operate as one: neither was empowered to negotiate terms independently of the other, and any proposal or counter-proposal that might be put forward would have to be considered by both teams. These precautions, however, could not conceal the fact that the companies had, within a brief space of time, backed down from their first and most vital principle – a single combined negotiation with OPEC. With this concession the slide began, and it was not to stop until the companies had given way on nearly every issue.

Strathalmond informed the Gulf committee – Amuzegar, Hammadi and Abdur Rahman al-Atiqi (the Kuwaiti oil minister who was standing in for Yamani) – of the new arrangements on 21 January. Amuzegar and his fellow triumvirs immediately rejected the condition that a price settlement in the Gulf should be linked to one in the Mediterranean. Instead, they said, they were prepared to give 'all the assurances' the companies might require against future leap-frogging, and Amuzegar volunteered to set down these assurances, along with a number of other provisos and conditions, including a stipulation that negotiations should end by 1 February so that the results could be presented to a full conference of OPEC on 3 February, in a letter to Strathalmond.

The London Policy Group promptly instructed Strathalmond not to accept such a letter. If it was forced upon him, they said, he should reply to it in writing, to the effect that the companies' view was that it was 'in the long-term interest of both producing and consuming countries alike, as well as that of the oil companies, that there should be stability in the financial arrangements with producing governments', and that the companies consequently 'cannot agree to a settlement in the Gulf which would be independent of other areas'. Strathalmond, however, chose to reject these instructions at the urging of the British and American ambassadors, Wright and MacArthur, who feared an immediate breaking-off of negotiations if Strathalmond were to act on them. Instead, on their advice, he accepted on 23 January a letter signed by Amuzegar, Yamani, Hammadi and Atiqi repeating much of what Amuzegar had said to Strathalmond two days before, and insisting that a price settlement be reached with the Gulf countries in isolation. Negotiations towards such a settlement were to begin within the week.

The next day the shah gave a press conference – his first in twelve years. It lasted for two and a half hours, a good deal of which was taken up with an abusive tirade against the oil companies. He condemned the idea of an overall negotiation with OPEC, vilified the companies for their stand, saying that they should be got rid of, and warned the Western powers not to support them. 'If the companies form a powerful cartel in the belief that they can put pressure on the producing countries,' he declaimed, 'and if industrial nations stand behind them, we will have the most detestable expression of economic imperialism and neo-colonialism.' He went on to threaten that if the companies persisted in their combined approach, the Gulf states would legislate to raise the tax rate to 60 per cent. Nor would this be all. At the forthcoming OPEC conference he himself would make sure 'that the question of cutting off the flow of oil will be definitely considered'. However, he concluded, with a show of magnanimity, if a five-year agreement on prices were concluded with the Gulf states, 'we shall stick to the agreement' – provided, he added quickly, that the companies did not raise their selling prices for oil and oil products.

Muhammad Reza Shah could well afford to wax belligerent in front of the world's press, for he knew full well (had he not been privately assured of it?) that the oil companies could not count on the backing of their own governments. Other excitable spirits in OPEC took courage from his vapouring. Izzedin Mabruk, the Libyan oil minister, announced that Libya would not accept any five-year agreement, and that if the oil companies did not accede to OPEC's terms, Libya would cut off oil to the West. Not to be outdone, the Venezuelan oil minister inveighed against the Irwin mission, adding somewhat obscurely, 'If the British or the US governments had anything to discuss, they should have adopted a more direct line rather than resort to other ways'.

The two halves of the companies' negotiating team, which had returned to London for consultations, left for Tehran and Tripoli on 27 January. They had been instructed to adhere to the separate but connected approach and, in the case of the Tehran team, to try to get the Gulf states to agree to a posted price for Iraqi and Saudi Arabian oil delivered at the eastern Mediterranean terminals of their respective pipelines. Such postings would then act as a 'hinge' between the Gulf and Mediterranean negotiations so as to forestall any leap-frogging of prices. The Tripoli negotiation was very short-lived. The Libyan oil minister rejected the joint letter presented by Piercy, indignantly and (considering what OPEC was up to) rather quaintly accusing the oil companies of acting as a 'cartel'. Obviously the Libyans were going to await the outcome of the Tehran negotiations and then leap-frog over the terms agreed there. Piercy therefore returned to London.

In Tehran, Strathalmond and his team found the Gulf negotiators brimming over with confidence, as well they might be; for, the Western governments having forsaken the fight, the contest between the companies and the Gulf governments was an unequal one. At the very outset of the talks the Gulf committee refused to agree to set the eastern Mediterranean postings, which effectively destroyed the 'hinge'. Although Yamani promised that Saudi Arabia would not 'leap-frog back from Sidon [the TAPline terminal] to Ras Tanura [the Gulf loading terminal]', the very fact that he volunteered this assurance was a strong indication that this was exactly what he and his fellow oil ministers had in mind. He may also have volunteered it to weaken the companies' solidarity, which was already showing signs of cracking. It cracked wide open on 30 January, when the Tehran team returned to London for consultations. Its members left again for Tehran the same evening without waiting for the arrival of the Tripoli team which was due at any moment. So much for separate but connected negotiations and the concerted approach. That same day the London Policy Group and a rump section of the New York 'back-up' group decided to abandon the letter to OPEC and to recognize the total separation of the Gulf and Libyan negotiations. Gone now was all hope of achieving a reasonable settlement. In its place was a fatalistic acceptance that any agreement with Libya would be unrealistic, and that all that might perhaps be salvaged from the collapse was some kind of undertaking from the Gulf states that they would not leap-frog over the Libyan settlement.

Suffice it to say that in the negotiations that followed none of the assurances that the companies had previously deemed essential was obtained – or if it was, it was not worth the breath of air expelled in its utterance. A major reason for the companies' failure was the obvious disarray in their ranks, especially in contrast to the solidarity displayed by OPEC. Unlike the companies, OPEC made skilful use of publicity and press conferences, with the shah as the star turn and Amuzegar and Yamani orchestrating the performances. At one stage in the negotiations the companies were greatly embarrassed by the leaking of their so-called 'irreducible terms' – sent by way of the Foreign Office to the British embassy in Tehran – and their subsequent publication in the government-controlled Tehran press. Scarcely able to contain his glee, Amuzegar seized upon the leak to berate the company negotiators for their 'duplicity'. 'The British government was running negotiations!' he cried, in a touching affirmation of the enduring legend of a British hand in every intrigue in Persia. All talk of assurances now, he exclaimed, would only serve to make him and his colleagues 'absolutely furious'. They would present their terms to the companies on 3 February on a take-it-or-leave-it basis. If the companies did not accede to them, the shah would legislate to impose a 60 per cent tax rate unilaterally and he would ask the rest of OPEC to follow suit. Any company which refused to accept the new tax rate would be told to cease production.

The companies made one last effort to dig in their heels. Without the required assurances, they indicated, they could not reply to the Gulf committee's terms by 3 February, when the OPEC conference was due to convene. The warning was brushed aside. On the opening day of the conference the shah addressed the delegates and exhorted them to gird themselves for battle. Thus encouraged, the next day, 4 February, the conference adopted two defiant resolutions. The first required the Gulf oil states to introduce legislation on 15 February to implement Caracas resolution XXI–120 which provided for, among other things, a 55 per cent tax rate and the elimination of posted price disparities. If the companies had not signified their acceptance of the legislation by 22 February, all OPEC members were to take 'appropriate measures, including a total embargo on shipments of crude oil and petroleum products'. The resolution also called for the enactment of similar legislation by Libya and Algeria, threatening an OPEC embargo if the oil companies did not grant these two states the new Gulf posted prices plus a premium for lower freight costs. Further support was given to the Libyans in the second resolution, which endorsed any action the Libyan government might take to protect itself against 'any collective act that might be exercised by the oil companies' – in other words, the safety-net sharing agreement. Outside the conference hall Amuzegar made it clear that the resolutions constituted a *diktat*. 'There is no question of negotiations or resuming negotiations,' he declared. 'It's just the acceptance of our terms or we will go ahead with legislation.'

Legislation by all the members of OPEC, however, was by no means a foregone conclusion. Each of them separately, in their capacity as sovereign states, would have to bear the brunt of the consequences of legislation, not OPEC as an organization. There was, therefore, a strong possibility that OPEC's unity would crumble if the companies stood firm and their own governments showed the slightest disposition to back them. The shah was confident that they would not. 'The major governments happily, after my warning two weeks ago,' he observed at a press conference late on 3 February, 'have shown not the slightest sign of any interference or support for the companies.' He was, of course, right, especially so far as the British and American governments were concerned, since neither of them wished to run the risk of provoking him and thus jeopardizing the attainment of their own separate goals – the British to make as smooth and comfortable an exit as possible from the Gulf at the end of the year, the Americans to build the shah up as the guardian of the Gulf's security after the British departure.

The oil companies capitulated on 14 February, twenty-four hours before the expiry of the deadline set by OPEC. The principal terms of agreement worked out with the Gulf states were:

(i) the posted price of Gulf oil was to go up by 30 cents a barrel from an average of $1.80 to $2.10 a barrel for the marker crude (Arabian light);

(ii) it was to increase thereafter by 5 cents a barrel per annum (to match the increased profits the companies might expect to receive on refined products);

(iii) there was to be a further increase of $2\frac{1}{2}$ per cent every year to offset inflation in the price of industrial goods (indexing for inflation rather than a fixed percentage had been offered to OPEC but was rejected);

(iv) the tax rate was to be raised to 55 per cent; and

(v) the agreement was to run for five years from 1 January 1971, with the Gulf states undertaking to refrain from leap-frogging should other OPEC members obtain higher prices.

At the same time, the parent companies of the Iraq Petroleum Company were compelled to issue a separate notification to the Iraqi oil minister, Hammadi, stating that the Tehran agreement 'is applicable solely and exclusively to crude oil exported from Gulf terminals, and contains no obligation or commitment whatsoever on Iraq or any of the said companies in respect of crude oil exported from Mediterranean terminals'. It was a humiliating end to the brave hopes of only six weeks earlier.

The shah pronounced his benediction upon the Tehran settlement from Switzerland, where he had gone to ski. Whatever the Libyans and others might gain from their negotiations with the companies, he declared grandly, he himself would honour the new agreement. 'Whatever happens, there will be no leap-frogging.' A more demonstrative reaction to the St Valentine's Day massacre of the Western oil companies was that of the irrepressible Jamshid Amuzegar: 'I was so happy I had tears in my eyes!' And why not, indeed? After all, the agreement would net Persia an additional $450 million in 1971 alone. He and his royal master could now boast that the boardrooms of the international oil companies were, in the words of their celebrated fellow countryman, Omar Khayyam, 'the courts where Jamshyd gloried and drank deep'. As for the State Department, which throughout the whole inglorious episode had been telling its beads and intoning supplications about 'stability', 'orderliness' and 'durability', it rushed to profess its faith in the Tehran settlement with indecent haste and convenient myopia, owlishly opining that it 'expected the previously turbulent international oil situation to calm down following the new agreement'.

Predictably, the Libyan settlement resulted in much higher posted prices. At first the Libyans refused to negotiate with the companies *en bloc*, and had a series of separate meetings with representatives of the individual companies. Threats and tantrums were the order of the day, most of them issuing from Major Abdul Salem Jallud, the *soi-disant* 'strong man' of the regime. The other Arab governments involved in the Mediterranean settlement backed the Libyans, knowing that they themselves would profit from a high posted price for Libyan oil. Algeria, which had worked hand-in-glove with the Libyans all along and which was, as we shall see shortly, still embroiled in an acrimonious contest with France over oil production and prices, joined with Iraq in threatening the companies with embargoes and other dire happenings. Nor were the 'moderate' Saudis slow to throw out dark hints of cut-offs and other penalties if their Libyan 'brothers' were not satisfied. Eventually the Libyans agreed to a combined negotiation. Several lengthy bargaining sessions followed, marked on the Libyan side by boorishness and malevolence and on the companies' part by misplaced civility and forbearance. Towards the end of March Colonel Qaddafi tried to hurry things along in his own inimitable way by threatening to nationalize the companies' assets in Libya if they refused to concede his terms. At length, on 2 April, a settlement was agreed. It gave the Libyans a posted price of $3.30 a barrel (77 cents up on the September 1970 price of $2.53), plus freight and gravity premiums which pushed it to $3.45 – a total increase of 30 per cent on the prices exacted from the companies only six months earlier, and 130 per cent up on the August 1970 prices.

Iraq and Saudi Arabia both tried to get comparable prices for their oil delivered at Mediterranean terminals. The exchanges between the Iraqis and the Iraq Petroleum Company were almost of the same order of churlishness on their side and patient meekness on the company's as they had been in the case of the Libyan negotiations. Relations between IPC and the Iraqi government had been strained for a decade, ever since the military government of Abdul Karim Qassim had expropriated 99½ per cent of the company's concession areas by the notorious Law 80 of December 1961. Since the accession of the Baath to power these relations had grown worse with each passing month, in spite of a series of accommodations made by the company to mollify the Iraqi government. A price rise of 80 cents a barrel was finally agreed in the first week of June 1971, bringing the Mediterranean price of Iraqi oil to $3.21 a barrel. The Saudis also settled with ARAMCO for an increase of 81 cents a barrel, which raised the Mediterranean price of their oil to $3.18 a barrel. The other provisions of the two agreements followed those of the Libyan settlement, and the whole Tripoli agreement, as it was called, was to remain in force for five years.

As soon as he learned of the terms of the settlement the shah was almost beside himself with anger and chagrin. Gone was the air of statesmanly reasonableness which had marked his recent gracious assurance to the Western powers that he would honour the Tehran settlement for five years. The 'Shadow of God upon earth' had been overshadowed, and immanent majesty as well as regal avarice required that the situation be promptly put to rights. Before relating how he went about doing so, however, we must first turn to the Franco-Algerian oil dispute and its outcome; for at its core lay the very notion that the shah had propounded during the Tehran negotiations, to the effect that the OPEC governments should by-pass the oil companies and conclude agreements on oil supplies and prices directly with the governments of the oil-consuming nations.

The basis upon which French oil companies would continue to operate in Algeria after independence had been agreed during the negotiations at Evian in 1962 which ended French rule in the colony. The regime laid down for the operation of the oil industry was supplemented by an agreement concluded in July 1965 which set a tax rate for Algeria of 55 per cent, and a price per barrel for Algerian oil of $2.08, a high figure for those days. Algeria was also granted effective control over sales of natural gas. On the French side, it was hoped that the arrangement would eventually provide France with up to one-third of her oil supplies (she already drew almost a quarter of them from Algeria) by way of a direct agreement with the Algerian government, thereby reducing her dependence upon sources of supply in the Middle East controlled by the major international companies.

The arrangement was not seriously called into question until November 1969, when a series of what were to prove long-drawn-out discussions between the French and Algerian governments was initiated to resolve a number of differences which had arisen over the implementation of the Evian accords as a whole. Among the main topics for discussion were sales of Algerian wine to France, freedom for Algerians to work in France, the supply of French teachers to Algerian educational institutions and the exploitation and sale of oil and natural gas. From the outset, the talks between the Algerian government and the French oil companies involved in Algeria – the partly state-owned Compagnie Française des Pétroles and the wholly state-owned Entreprise de Recherches et d'Activités Pétrolières (ERAP) in association with the ELF company – were compromised by the collaboration going on at the time between the Algerians and the Libyans to take advantage of the temporary oil shortage in Europe early in 1970, and the proximity of the North African oilfields to European markets, to force substantial price increases from the producing companies. Libya, as we have seen, made the first move in the spring of 1970, and then in July the Algerians unilaterally raised the posted price of their oil from $2.08 to $2.85 a barrel, the increase to be retroactive to 1 January 1969. The Franco-Algerian discussions were broken off and they did not resume until December 1970, by which time much had occurred that was ominous from a French point of view, notably the Libyan junta's triumph over the oil companies in September, the arbitrary enactment of a 60 per cent tax rate by the Venezuelans at the outset of December and the OPEC resolutions at Caracas soon afterwards, which had both endorsed and adopted Libyan methods of negotiation.

In the last week of December 1970 CFP and ELF–ERAP tabled a set of proposals which represented considerable concessions to the Algerians' wishes. They offered retroactive royalty payments to 1 January 1969 on the basis of an oil price of $2.65 a barrel, an offer which would cost them FF700 million, and a posted price of $2.75 for five years from 1 January 1971. One-third of the companies' oil production would be set aside for the use of Algeria, and 50 per cent of the companies' profits on oil sales to the Algerian state oil and gas corporation, SONATRACH (Société Nationale de Transport et de Commercialisation des Hydro-Carbures), would be repatriated to Algeria for investment. SONATRACH would also be awarded the majority share-holding in joint oil and natural gas undertakings. The Algerians rejected the proposals almost without reading them, demanding instead a posted price of $3.24 a barrel and the reinvestment in Algeria of 90 per cent of the companies' profits on Algerian oil sales. To reinforce their demands they barred ELF–ERAP tankers in the second week of January 1971 from loading crude at Arzew terminal.

Stung by the Algerian government's unreasonable and uncompromising attitude, CFP reacted by associating itself that same week with the joint initiative of the other major companies and the independents against OPEC, putting its signature to the message to OPEC delivered on 16 January. Yet even as CFP was taking this action the French foreign minister, Maurice

Schumann, let it be known that France would not be bound, in arriving at a settlement with Algeria, by any agreement that might be reached with OPEC at Tehran. The French government, he said, would still seek to conclude a bilateral engagement, so as to preserve the 'special relationship' between France and Algeria.

As might have been foreseen, all that Schumann's statement succeeded in doing was to encourage the Algerians to persist in their campaign of harassment against the oil companies, and to extend it to Franco-Algerian relations in general, as they did by such tactics as refusing to grant exit visas to some 10,000 French technicians, teachers and others working in Algeria. The tactics worked. Talks were reopened in Paris on 19 January between the French minister for industrial development, François-Xavier Ortoli, and the Algerian foreign minister, Abdul Aziz Bouteflika. On 24 January ELF–ERAP announced that it would not align itself with the united front which the major and independent oil companies were presenting to OPEC. Instead, a day or so later it joined with CFP in making a new offer to the Algerian government, the main features of which were a posted price of $2.77 a barrel and the sum of FF675 million as an advance on back taxes for 1969 and 1970. (As the two sides had not yet agreed upon the exact amount owed, the proffered payment was purely an act of goodwill on the part of the French companies.)

The response of the Algerian president, Houari Boumedienne, was to tell the French government at the beginning of February that France had better start looking elsewhere for her oil supplies if she did not want to pay what Algeria considered to be a fair price for her oil. It was transparently clear that Boumedienne was simply filling in the time with a little sniping at the French while he awaited the outcome of the Tehran negotiations, when he would know just how high to go with his demands. The Tehran settlement was everything that his heart could desire. Henceforth, with the Western oil companies and the Western governments in ignominious retreat, he knew that he could be as outrageous in his behaviour as he wished. With a melodramatic flourish he announced on 24 February 1971 'the entry of the revolution into the oil sector', and he proceeded to embellish this statement with some familiar crypto-Marxist rhetoric.

We consider that questions of nationalization and control . . . are part of the sovereignty of our country and its fundamental options. . . . We will never trade away these options. Today the hour has come for these fundamental options to be turned into accomplished fact.

After a good deal more of this dreary newspeak Boumedienne at length got to the point. Algeria, he said, would be taking an immediate 51 per cent shareholding in CRP's and ELF–ERAP's operations. The country's natural gas resources would be nationalized, along with the pipelines which ran from the oilfields to the coast.

Boumedienne's ultimate aim – as well as the utter pointlessness of the negotiations up to date – was now plain. He intended to take total control of the French oil industry in Algeria, while retaining French technicians to run it. The revenues from oil production, most of which would go to Algeria, were to be used to finance a highly ambitious programme of Algerian industrialization. In an interview published in *Le Monde* on 2 March 1971 the Algerian president made no secret of his intentions.

If we have not nationalized [the oil companies] 100 per cent, it is so as to take account of the interest of our partners and of the important relations which exist in other fields. We have sought only one objective: to acquire control. . . . Having acquired control, we will respect the interests of our partner. If he finds the situation uncomfortable for various reasons, if he does not accustom himself to what the Arabs require in this respect, then he will have to find other solutions. But this would mean that on the other shore of the Mediterranean a decolonization of attitudes is still far distant.

The 'partnership', in short, consisted in the French supplying the skills and the money and the Algerians giving the orders. It was nationalization 'on the cheap' and ELF–ERAP had said so on 25 February. The company was not prepared to play the ox to the Algerian plough. On the contrary, it demanded that the Algerian government nationalize its assets in the country outright, and pay a proper indemnity, which ELF–ERAP defined as FF4,000 million. The French government made a show of supporting the companies. It informed the Algerians early in March that they would be expected to pay FF4,000 million as compensation for the 51 per cent shareholding they had taken in CFP's and ELF–ERAP's operations in Algeria. In addition, the companies' share of future crude oil production was to be made available to them at a reasonable price and without restrictions upon its sale; and the companies were to be entitled to retain their profits from production in hard currencies and to be freed from any obligation to reinvest them in Algeria. If the Algerian government refused to accept these conditions, so the French official statement continued, it must proceed to nationalize the companies' operations in Algeria completely and pay full and fair compensation, payment to be made in crude oil should Algeria not possess the necessary reserves of foreign currency.

For all its brave words, however, the French government betrayed an almost palpable lack of determination in its demeanour, a fact which did not escape Boumedienne's notice. After waiting to see the outcome of the Tripoli negotiations between the companies and the Libyans, he announced on 13 April that the new posted price of Algerian crude was $3.60 a barrel, i.e. 15 cents more than the Libyans had achieved. He offered the derisory sum of 500 million francs in compensation for the 51 per cent participation he had taken in CFP's and ELF–ERAP's operations, and at the same time he cancelled all other foreign-held exploratory concessions. Moreover, he insisted upon the payment of retrospective taxation, a demand which, if it had been complied with, would

have more than absorbed the 500 million francs he was offering in compensation to the companies. All this was too much for even the French government
to stomach. Negotiations were again broken off, and the French declared the
whole system of economic co-operation between France and Algeria established by the Evian accords of 1962 and by the oil agreement of 1965 to be at
an end. Henceforth, the French government stated, all economic relations
would be conducted on a purely commercial basis: the oil companies would
resume sole charge of any negotiations with the Algerian government on
matters affecting them, and it would be up to them to decide whether there was
any future for them in Algeria.

As was to be expected, the Algerians responded by making life miserable for
the French employees of the oil companies in Algeria. The harassment led
CFP and ELF–ERAP to withdraw their technicians and to declare a boycott
of Algerian oil. Legal action, they said, would be taken against any purchasers
of Algerian oil while the issue of proper compensation for the nationalized 51
per cent of their operations was still undecided. CFP and ELF–ERAP also
informed the World Bank and private American banks of the existence of the
dispute, with a view to halting the negotiations which were then going on for
the provision of financial and technical assistance to Algeria to develop her
natural gas industry. Some support for the companies' stand was given by the
United States government, which was by now growing a little uneasy over the
course that events had been taking since the Tehran settlement the previous
February. On its advice, the completion of the contract between the Algerian
SONATRACH and the El Paso Natural Gas Company for the exploitation
and sale of natural gas was put into cold storage. In contrast, little positive
support for the Algerian position was forthcoming from most of the members
of OPEC, or even from OAPEC, the Organization of Arab Petroleum Exporting Countries. Apart from the obligatory avowals of solidarity from these
organizations, the only belligerent noises came from Libya and Kuwait, who
threatened retaliatory action against any oil company which complied with the
French boycott. For their part, CFP and ELF–ERAP had no difficulty in
obtaining supplies of oil elsewhere to make up for the loss of Algerian crude,
whereas the Algerians were hard put to it to find buyers willing to break the
boycott.

In these circumstances it seemed only sensible for the French companies to
continue to hold out until the Algerian government had second thoughts about
the blessings to be gained from 'bringing the revolution into the oil sector' and
exercising its 'fundamental options'. Yet, surprisingly, in mid-May 1971 CFP
extended an invitation to the Algerians to resume talks. Whether the company
did so at the behest of the French government or not is unclear, though it is far
from unlikely. The Algerians accepted, and on 17 June CFP and SONAT-
RACH came to an agreement about their future relationship. SONATRACH
would retain a 51 per cent shareholding in CFP's Algerian operations, paying

as compensation the sum of 300 million francs over a period of seven years. CFP in its turn undertook to pay retrospective taxes to Algeria and to repatriate a substantial proportion of the profits it earned from sales of oil for investment in the development of Algeria's oil reserves. The posted price of Algerian crude was fixed at $2.95 a barrel. The agreement between the two partners was to run for five years in the first instance, and to be renewed for a further five years by mutual agreement.

Unless CFP was under pressure from the French government to give in to the Algerians it is not easy to see why it did so, especially over the question of proper compensation. ELF–ERAP certainly put up a better fight, for all that ERAP was a state enterprise. It was not until the end of 1971 that the company reached an understanding with SONATRACH. While it had originally sought to obtain the sum of 185 million francs as compensation for the nationalization of 51 per cent of its shareholding, it agreed in the end to forgo payment in return for the cancellation of the Algerian demand for retrospective taxes – which only went to show that the demand itself had no basis in legality. In an agreement signed on 15 December 1971 ELF–ERAP was guaranteed a yearly quota, at a posted price of $2.75 a barrel, of six million tons of crude oil, which was about one-third of what it might have expected to receive if it had not lost its majority shareholding. The agreement, like that with CFP, was to run for five years and to be renewed by mutual consent. What it all amounted to, in effect, was a decision by ELF–ERAP to write off its Algerian assets as not worth holding on to.

The obvious moral to be drawn from the experience of the French oil companies in Algeria was that it was utterly pointless, from the point of view of an oil-consuming country, to try to ensure security of oil supplies by direct arrangements with the government of an oil-producing state. The arrangement had failed primarily because of the bad faith of the Algerian government, which had broken every agreement it had freely entered into, whether with the French government or with the French oil companies. France's experience in Algeria offered little comfort to the Western industrial nations or Japan. On the contrary, it provided them with good reason to treat with extreme caution the kind of suggestion thrown out by the shah during the Tehran negotiations early in 1971 – that the oil companies should be excluded from the process of determining oil prices and production levels, leaving these to be agreed by direct arrangement between consuming and producing countries. The shah, of course, saw his own role in such government-to-government arrangements as that of final arbiter, laying down terms in lofty magisterial fashion. There was also a lesson for OPEC, however, in the sour and sullen way in which the Franco-Algerian arrangement ended; and this was that sudden and precipitate moves towards nationalization as a means of obtaining higher oil revenues could produce such unstable conditions in the international oil market that an oil-producing country might find its economic interests considerably shaken and bruised as a consequence.

Though the ink on the Tehran agreement was barely dry it was patently obvious that OPEC was already hungry for higher oil revenues. The shah, in particular, irritated by the advantageous settlement Libya had won, was determined for reasons of prestige as well as cupidity to equal or even better it. Lip-service, however, had still to be paid to the Tehran settlement if only to prevent the United States government from becoming uneasy. After his departure from Tehran in January 1971 John Irwin had visited Kuwait and Riyad where he had obtained assurances from both the ruler of Kuwait and King Faisal, similar to the one he had been given by the shah, that there would be no interruption of oil supplies to the consuming countries, and that the settlement reached with the oil companies at Tehran would be honoured for its full term. Evidently the State Department attached considerable weight to these assurances; for in testimony before the House Foreign Affairs Committee in July 1971 Akins expressed his conviction that the Tehran agreement would last the full five years. How, then, the shah and his fellow Gulf rulers must have asked themselves, were they to find a way of increasing their oil revenues still further without violating their promises and thereby disappointing the State Department's hopes in them?

They found the answer in 'participation', a device by which they could acquire a share in the assets of the oil companies operating in their territories, and with it a higher proportion of the earnings from oil production than they received from royalties and taxes alone. Saudi Arabia's oil minister, Ahmad Zaki al-Yamani, was particularly taken with the idea of participation and not just because of its financial allurements. Although he sat on the board of ARAMCO as a Saudi government nominee, he had no real voice in the company's operations or in the determination of its policies, a deprivation which he found irksome. Like his predecessor, Abdullah al-Tariki, Yamani was an ARAMCO protégé, who had been sent for his higher education to American universities. He had emerged from the business school at Harvard convinced that his grasp of economics, of the oil industry, and of the legal questions associated with it was such as to put him on an equal footing with the chief officers of the major international oil companies. While Yamani had derived many of his notions about government–company relations from Tariki (perhaps more than he was in later years prepared to acknowledge), he was more circumspect than his exemplar had been in putting them into practice. While Tariki's intemperate pursuit of his plans to reverse the balance of power between companies and governments had led to a steady deterioration of his relationship with ARAMCO and to his own eventual dismissal and expulsion from Saudi Arabia, Yamani preferred the subtler approach and so kept his relations with ARAMCO intimate and warm. Tariki still travelled the OPEC circuit as an adviser on oil questions, preaching the doctrine of complete nationalization and winning some converts, especially among the radical Arab governments. Yamani, however, was more inclined to heed the warning signals put out by such experiences as that of Algeria with CFP and ELF–ERAP, and to proceed to the goal of nationalization by stealth, i.e. through participation.

One obstacle to the introduction of participation at this stage was the unfavourable impression it would have created in the world at large of the producing countries' greed, coming so soon after the tax rate, i.e. their share of the oil companies' earnings, had been raised to 55 per cent. Another more serious obstacle was a provision in the Tehran agreement itself which ran: 'The existing arrangements between each of the Gulf States and each of the Companies, to which this Agreement is an overall amendment, will continue to be valid in accordance with their terms.' In other words, existing concessionary and contractual arrangements were not to be disturbed. A demand for participation would constitute a violation of these arrangements and, therefore, a breach of the Tehran agreement. That Yamani was aware of this potential obstacle is clear from a statement he made to Irwin at the time of the Tehran negotiations, to the effect that he and the other Gulf oil ministers would never sign the agreement if, by doing so, they were precluded from pursuing the goal of participation afterwards. That he also intended to ignore it emerges from his remark to Piercy of Esso, on the same occasion, that the companies were being unrealistic if they truly expected the agreement to give them price stability for five years. The conclusion is unavoidable that Yamani and his fellow Gulf ministers signed the Tehran settlement in the full knowledge that they intended to break it. So much for the 'moderate/radical' theories about OPEC's membership subscribed to then and since by trusting Westerners; so much, too, for the assurances of the 'moderates' in which the State Department reposed such faith. Perhaps the best verdict on the charade played out at Tehran was that rendered at the time by the chairman of Bunker Hunt, the partner of BP in Libya and the doughtiest of the independent producers:

I take little stock in the theory that certain so-called moderate producing countries desire to isolate certain more radical countries in their demands for excessive increases. To the contrary, it would seem that the so-called moderates and radicals are now playing a rather unmelodious duet.

The OPEC orchestra struck up the overture to 'La Partecipazione' at Beirut on 22 September 1971, when the organization met and passed resolutions calling for 'effective participation' by member states in the assets of the producing companies. The conference also called for an adjustment of posted prices to offset the decline in the purchasing power of oil revenues caused by the depreciation in the international value of the United States dollar since the beginning of the year. Once again the oil companies reacted by attempting to form a united front. John J. McCloy, as legal counsel for the Seven Sisters, sought and obtained business review letters from the United States Department of Justice in October to enable the companies to negotiate jointly. The safety-net sharing agreement of the previous January was also reactivated to protect any oil company which might suffer a cut in production (or even be denied oil supplies altogether) as a punishment for opposing OPEC's demands. Yamani had raised the possibility that one or more members of OPEC might resort to a cut-off of supplies to get its way in one of his conversations with Piercy at Tehran in January. Drawing the latter's attention to the lack of spare producing capacity available to the companies anywhere outside the OPEC area, compared with the state of affairs a few years earlier, Yamani remarked: 'You know the situation better than I. You know you cannot take a shut-down.' Whatever limits there might be to spare producing capacity, however, there was no actual shortage of crude oil in the world in the last quarter of 1971 – certainly none that, in normal market conditions, would have justified an oil price increase, even to compensate for the slight fall that had occurred in the value of the dollar. Yet in the years that have elapsed since 1971 OPEC and its apologists have alleged that there was a surge in demand for oil in 1970–71 which transformed a buyer's into a seller's market. The facts of the case are different. The increase in consumption in 1970 over that of 1969 was *below* the average annual increase for the decade 1960–69; and the increase in 1971 over 1970 was only about half the average yearly increase for the same decade. As supply actually exceeded demand, prices should correspondingly have fallen. That they did not was due, not to the transition from a buyer's to a seller's market but to OPEC's success in forcing an upward revision of prices at Tehran at the beginning of 1971 by the threat of an embargo upon oil exports.

Following the OPEC conference at Beirut it was arranged that talks between the organization and the companies over equity participation and the dollar-depreciation adjustment should open in Geneva in January 1972. Before they could begin, however, the Libyans again upstaged their fellow OPEC actors. The RCC had tried in November 1971 to effect an indirect revaluation of the Libyan dinar, in which Libya's oil revenues were normally paid and which the oil companies were obliged to purchase from the Libyan central bank, by requiring the companies to obtain their dinars at the rate of $2.94 instead of $2.80 per dinar. As the dodge, if it had succeeded, would have cost the companies an extra $75 million a year in revenue payments, they naturally dragged their heels in complying. To intimidate them, the Libyan government froze a portion of Esso's Libyan bank deposits. Something more spectacular, however, was called for before the Geneva meeting, if Libya was to maintain her reputation as the holy terror of OPEC. Opportunity fortunately knocked at the end of November, when the shah's troops seized the Tunbs and occupied Abu Musa Island. Qaddafi, arrayed in all his effulgence as the champion of Arabism and Islam, smote the imperialist British for their underhand collaboration with the Persians by nationalizing BP's assets in

Libya. He also announced his intention of withdrawing the sterling deposits held by his government in London.

British official reaction to the expropriation was mild, almost indifferent. Libya provided only 5 per cent of BP's production world-wide; there was a glut rather than a shortage of oil on the world's markets; and Britain's financial reserves were deemed to be healthy enough to withstand the withdrawal of Libya's funds. Indeed, such was the confidence of the British government of the day in the robust state of Britain's economy that the withdrawal was held to be a blessing in disguise, since it helped to prevent sterling from rising too high against the dollar and other currencies. For BP, however, the loss of its concession for the Sarir field, the largest in Africa, which it shared with Bunker Hunt on a fifty–fifty basis, was not entirely an occasion for imperturbability. Still less was it so for BP's co-concessionaire, Bunker Hunt, to whom Qaddafi's *coup de théâtre* looked uncomfortably like the penultimate step in the liquidation of its own concession.

Events at Geneva in January 1972 were a repetition of those at Tehran a year earlier. The oil companies yielded to the arguments of the OPEC ministers about the depreciation in the international value of the dollar and agreed to increase the posted price of oil by $8\frac{1}{2}$ per cent, which would give the Gulf oil states alone a further $700 million in revenue in 1972. Libya, naturally, refused to accept the settlement, which indicated that a further turn of the screw was to come, doubtless of sufficient degree to provoke the admiration of the rest of OPEC and excite their cupidity. The companies resignedly agreed to play their part in the forthcoming spectacle by undertaking, when the time came, to adjust the prices they had only just fixed so as to reflect any higher settlement they might reach with Libya. They had progressed from *post hoc* to *ante hoc* price 'ratcheting'. On participation, OPEC, running true to form, set its initial demands high – 20 per cent ownership of the companies' producing assets immediately, rising by progressive annual increases to a 51 per cent shareholding, the whole to be obtained at the net book value of the companies' assets, i.e. at virtually nominal cost. The OPEC ministers also insisted that agreement between the companies and the individual member states on the implementation of the proposals would have to be reached by the end of 1972.

For the companies, the prospect opened up by participation was a dismal one. From being the arbiters of the international oil market they faced relegation to the position of bondservants to the oil states, compelled to produce oil on the latter's behalf and to purchase it at prices they laid down. The sole purpose of participation was to aggrandize the wealth and power of the producing states. It was, as the experienced oil consultant, Walter J. Levy, has accurately defined it,

mainly a device through which they [the OPEC governments] smoothly and by arrangements with the international oil companies plan to obtain complete control over their countries' total oil operations. It represents a grand design by the producing countries to forge an alliance with the oil companies in which the producing countries, while pursuing their national objectives, would still be able to take advantage of the larger distribution outlets, the investment capabilities and the technical know-how of the oil companies.

Under a participation regime competition would be stifled. The OPEC governments would agree production levels among themselves with the object of guarding against excessive production in any one country and thus preventing any fluctuations in oil prices such as would occur in an open market. Partnership with the major international oil companies was essential if OPEC's designs were to be successfully carried into execution. If the oil states themselves took complete charge of oil production, they would become sellers and brokers of oil, with the companies as its purchasers and distributors. Since there was no shortage of oil, and the companies would naturally seek to strike the best possible bargain, oil prices were bound to drop, as the producing countries were forced to compete with one another to sell their oil.

There were other good reasons why OPEC preferred participation to outright nationalization. Although the organization's secretary-general, Nadim al-Pachachi, claimed at the outset of the Geneva talks in January 1972 that the demand for participation 'is based on our conviction that such direct participation would reinforce and render more effective our right to permanent sovereignty over our resources', six months earlier he had, rather more frankly, explained that 'the main objective of our participation is to gain know-how rather than to increase revenue'. None of the producing countries was in a position to take over production from its own fields, still less to undertake exploration or marketing. Saudi Arabia, the largest producer in the Middle East, was particularly vulnerable in this respect, which was why Yamani, her oil minister, walked so carefully around the jagged edges of the nationalization issue, preferring the smoother outlines of participation as being better suited to his government's purposes.

The very aspects of participation which made it attractive to the oil-producing countries were those which the oil companies, in general, found so repugnant. Sir David Barran, the outspoken chairman of Shell, in June 1972 condemned the idea of 51 per cent participation as 'intolerable', and said that he would even prefer full nationalization. If so (and the managements of several other companies shared Barran's view), why, it may be asked, did they not use the one powerful weapon they had at their disposal at the time, viz. the threat to abandon their concessions and throw the onus of operating them upon the governments of the oil states, to force those governments to drop the demand for participation? None of the companies did so, presumably out of a sense of responsibility to their customers, but also, perhaps, because they were subjected to pressure from their home governments to keep the oil flowing. With some companies, however, and they may well have constituted a majority, it would seem that the desire to retain access to their oil reserves, at whatever cost, weighed more heavily than the need to stand up to OPEC on a vital and fundamental matter affecting not only their own welfare but that of the entire Western world as well. As events were to prove, it was a most short-sighted view to take.

By late May 1972 the major oil companies had conceded the principle of 20 per cent participation to most of the Arab oil-producing states of the Gulf. The concession had not been made without the companies having been subjected to threats, particularly from Saudi Arabia, of compulsory acquisition of majority shareholdings if the companies were unco-operative. That the threats were not necessarily idle was demonstrated at the eighth Arab Petroleum Congress in Algiers at the end of May, which was attended by all the members of the Organization of Arab Petroleum Exporting Countries. Two months earlier, Iraq, Syria and Egypt had been admitted to membership of OAPEC, the latter pair by means of a revision of membership requirements. With the recruitment of Iraq and Syria to its ranks, OAPEC's character as a predominantly political organization was confirmed, though not in the way that its founders, Saudi Arabia, Kuwait and pre-revolutionary Libya, had originally intended. It was now, and would be increasingly, a militant and radical body. As its bridal gift or membership fee, Iraq made a contribution of truly Libyan proportions – the nationalization of the Iraq Petroleum Company. The sour and fretful state of relations between the company and the Iraqi government over the preceding decade has already been mentioned. At the time of the Tehran negotiations in January 1971 the Iraqi oil minister, Saadun al-Hammadi, had indicated that a settlement of differences might be expected as a consequence of the 'atmosphere of mutual trust' which had developed at Tehran between the company negotiators and the Gulf committee of OPEC. His purpose in saying so, it soon transpired, was simply to induce the company negotiators to concede OPEC's demands at Tehran by dangling before them the prospect of better times for IPC in Iraq. Once the Tehran agreement had been signed, the Baghdad government reverted to its customary disagreeable habits.

IPC had accepted the principle of 25 per cent participation – an advance of 5 per cent on OPEC's figure – in March 1972, but this was not good enough for the Iraqis. Not only had they grown very fierce as a result of the treaty of friendship they had concluded with the Soviet Union in April, but they were further emboldened by the discreet encouragement they were receiving from the French government in their dispute with IPC. The conduct of the French in this instance – CFP, after all, was one of the major partners in IPC – defies reason, especially in a people for whom reason is said to be the supreme virtue ('Ce qui n'est pas logique n'est pas français'). Apparently undeterred by its experience in Algeria, the French government had set out to conclude an understanding with the Iraqis which would assure France of a stable supply of oil for years to come. The Iraqis were naturally delighted by the readiness of the French to place their necks once more in a noose of Algerian design, and to lure them in they held out the prospect of French oil companies working the North Rumailah field in southern Iraq, which had been discovered and proved by the Basra Petroleum Company, a subsidiary of IPC. (Because North Rumailah was in the areas covered by Law 80 of December 1961 its development had unavoidably been held back.) When the Franco-Iraqi agreement was eventually concluded, at a cost to France of $80 million in credits to Iraq, it committed CFP to lift its full share of Iraqi oil (to which it was entitled anyway as a partner in IPC) for the next ten years – a commitment which CFP had earlier rejected as too expensive. France also acquired the right to buy additional oil at higher prices. As for the North Rumailah field, the Iraqis kept it for themselves and called in the Russians to exploit it.

The nationalization of the Iraq Petroleum Company (which was not unconnected with the Iraqi government's irritation at the declining volume of oil being lifted at the Mediterranean terminal) was announced to the other Arab delegates at the petroleum congress in Algiers on 1 June 1972. Elated by the Iraqis' audacity, the delegates sent a joint message of congratulation to Baghdad on 2 June. Later that day they were addressed by James Akins of the State Department, who was attending the congress as an observer. Although he counselled the delegates against rushing impetuously into schemes of nationalization, Akins also expressed his personal opinion that the expropriation of IPC's concession was not necessarily 'the unmitigated disaster which I'm sure is being predicted in London, Paris, The Hague and New York'. 'I'm also certainly not going to say that the old concessions were writ on tablets of stone,' he went on,

or that they couldn't or shouldn't ever be changed. The companies themselves have been remarkably flexible . . . [they] have yielded under the sledge-hammer blows of the producing countries. All the changes have been in the favor of the producing countries. I don't think you have any reason to be ashamed of your success so far. I'm just suggesting that it might continue to be of benefit to the producing governments to continue to bend, not to break, this steel rod [i.e. the companies].

So mild a reaction from a senior official in the United States government to the nationalization of IPC, in which American oil companies had almost a quarter-interest, can only have surprised and delighted the assembled Arab oil delegates. There was further cheer for them both in the implicit acceptance by Akins of the validity of the doctrine of 'changing circumstances' (with which OPEC sought to cloak both its rapacity and its contempt for the sanctity of contracts) and in his tacit encouragement of their continued use of the device of participation to secure larger revenues without doing anything to earn them. To leave them in no doubt of his belief that they were entitled to continue to seek ever higher prices for their oil, Akins volunteered the further comment that 'on this question the consumers have had their heads in the sands, like a collection of especially stupid ostriches . . .'. A few of his hearers must surely have wondered whether they had heard aright, and if this was the same man who only eleven months earlier had told the House Committee on Foreign Affairs that he expected the Tehran and Tripoli agreements on prices to run their full five years.

A nod was as good as a wink to the magnates of OPEC. At the end of June they met in Vienna and drew up an ultimatum to the oil companies. If the exchanges between the companies and the governments of the oil-exporting countries failed to arrive at a satisfactory settlement of the terms on which compensation for participation was to be assessed and the prices at which the governments' share of oil production was to be bought back by the companies, OPEC would take 'definite concerted action' to force a settlement. Two months later, in the last week of September, Ahmad Zaki al-Yamani warned a gathering of oilmen in London that the choice before them was simply 'nationalization or participation'. The latter, he added disarmingly, was 'our substitute for nationalization'. As the warning was not well taken, Yamani felt obliged to sweeten it by assuring his audience that any participation agreement would extend, without any renegotiation, for the designated life of existing oil concessions, i.e. to the end of the century or beyond. A few days later, in an address at the Middle East Institute in Washington (which served more or less as ARAMCO's regimental chapel), he put forward a visionary scheme of an enduring partnership between the United States and Saudi Arabia in their respective roles as the world's largest consumer and the world's largest producer of crude oil. In return for the lifting of all taxes upon the importation of Saudi oil into the United States, Yamani proposed, Saudi Arabia not only would supply as much oil as the United States required but would, in addition, invest money in the American oil industry, more particularly in its 'downstream' operations.

The proposal was not exactly a spur-of-the-moment inspiration. Some time previously, in testimony given before a committee of the United States Senate in February 1972, James Akins, in his capacity as director of the office of fuels and energy in the State Department, had assured the committee that the United States could confidently rely upon stable and secure supplies of oil from Saudi Arabia. Talks between Yamani and ARAMCO since the beginning of the year had resulted in the concession by ARAMCO of Saudi participation in its operations in return for assurances regarding future levels of oil production. Thus, when Yamani made his big splash in Washington in September he was already aware of the temperature of the water. The other purpose of his mission to the United States was to conclude a general participation agreement on behalf of Saudi Arabia, Kuwait, Qatar and Abu Dhabi with the parent companies of ARAMCO (Esso, SOCAL, Texaco and Mobil) and the other majors operating in the four Gulf States. The agreement was signed on 5 October. It provided for 25 per cent government participation in existing concessions, starting in 1973, and rising by stages to 51 per cent participation by 1983.

Payment for the initial government shareholding was to be spread over three years: it would be made in crude oil and based upon the 'updated book value' of the companies' assets in the countries concerned, that is to say, upon the historical value of their investments in current monetary terms. A formula was also worked out for the disposal of the participation crude, the proportion of it that the companies would be entitled to buy back and the prices they would pay for it. All in all, the effect of the agreement was to deprive the companies of roughly half the profits they might have expected to earn on the host governments' 25 per cent share of oil production.

It was left to the individual Gulf states to work out in direct negotiation with the companies operating in their territories detailed terms for the implementation of the proposals embodied in the general agreement. The critical discussions, obviously, would be those between Saudi Arabia and ARAMCO. Saudi Arabia had the largest reserves of oil of any country, and the parent companies of ARAMCO were four of the legendary Seven Sisters. Whatever agreement they reached on the implementation of participation, and the price at which the companies would buy back participation crude, would set the pace for the other Middle-Eastern members of OPEC. ARAMCO had plans to increase productive capacity to 13.4 million b/d by 1976, and 20 million b/d by 1983, the year in which the Saudi government was due to acquire a majority shareholding in the company. Although ARAMCO's 49 per cent share in production after that date would bring it – provided, of course, that the production target had been reached – roughly as much oil as it was receiving in 1972, the amount would still not be sufficient to enable its three principal parent companies, Esso, SOCAL and Texaco, to dominate the international petroleum market in the way that they had. For this they needed continued exclusive access to the Saudi government's share in oil production. It became ARAMCO's prime concern in the participation negotiations, therefore, to secure such a preferential right to government crude.

Price scales for 'buy back' crude had been drawn up when the general agreement on participation was concluded in October 1972; but by the time negotiations between ARAMCO and the Saudi government resumed in December the Saudis had changed their minds. As George Piercy of Esso, the chief negotiator for the Persian Gulf majors, reported:

Yamani has made the decision to break the agreement made in New York on prices. Individual country negotiations, firming markets, various attacks on him have all contributed. But perhaps it is all part of a plan. He has decided to grab for big price increases.

Piercy recommended that the companies make a firm and final offer on prices which would allow for substantial but not excessive increases for future participation crude. His position was supported by Gulf Oil, which had no interests in Saudi Arabia but which held a half-share (BP had the other half) in the Kuwait Oil Company. Gulf Oil believed that ARAMCO's strategy of trying to keep exclusive control of Saudi Arabia's oil reserves, almost regardless of cost, was mistaken. Price was just as vital a consideration as access, and guaranteed access could prove in the end to be tantamount to a legal obligation upon the companies to buy back participation crude at inflated and irrational prices. In Gulf Oil's view, there should be no mandatory buying back of government crude: instead, if agreement on its price should prove unattainable, the government in question should be left to market the crude itself.

ARAMCO rejected Gulf Oil's arguments and went ahead with its offer of higher prices in return for guaranteed access to participation crude. The other companies had little choice but to follow suit. Between 20 December 1972 and 22 January 1973 interim participation agreements were concluded by the companies concerned with Saudi Arabia, Abu Dhabi, Qatar and Kuwait, all of which were to take effect from 1 January 1973. They provided for a 51 per cent government shareholding to be attained by 1982, rather than 1983, and they obliged the companies to buy back any and all participation crude that the governments might wish to sell them. Far from clearing the air, the agreements only created fresh uncertainty. The Kuwait national assembly refused to ratify the agreement with Gulf Oil and BP, its assorted Robespierres and Dantons calling variously for 60 per cent participation, complete nationalization and a *jihad* against the West. The Saudis, too, treated the agreement they had just signed as a dead letter, and the neighbouring small fry down the Gulf dutifully aped their lead. In truth, none of the Gulf governments really had its mind upon the actual agreements, being too enthralled by the fascinating goings-on in Libya and Persia in the early weeks of 1973.

Indulgent though the terms of the Gulf participation agreements had been, they were looked upon with derision by Qaddafi and his fellow praetorians. They wanted 50 per cent participation in all oil company operations in Libya, and they wanted it immediately. They would pay compensation for this compulsorily acquired shareholding only at the net book value, not the current value, of the companies' Libyan assets, and they were not prepared to give any assurances to the companies about future access to participation crude. Once again Qaddafi singled out the smaller, independent companies for attack because they had few, if any, alternative sources of supply. Starting with Bunker Hunt, he demanded that the company make over half of its producing concession in the Sarir field. As the Libyans already controlled half the original concession, which they had expropriated from BP in December 1971, compliance with their demand would have left Bunker Hunt with only a quarter of the field. The company refused to budge, offering instead to treat with the Libyan government on the basis of the October 1972 general agreement on participation. Qaddafi thereupon turned his fire on the other independents, preferring upon them similar demands to those made upon Bunker Hunt.

They temporized, hoping rather wistfully that something might materialize which would save them from the fate looming before them.

To the east Muhammed Reza Shah, who had been watching the participation quadrilles *de haut en bas*, decided disdainfully that what was good enough for the Arabs was not good enough for him. Persia had dropped out of the group of Gulf states negotiating with the companies in June 1972, when the shah let it be known that he was not greatly interested in acquiring a percentage of the assets of the companies which made up the Persian consortium – BP, Shell, Esso, Mobil, Texaco, Gulf, SOCAL and CFP. Instead he indicated that he was prepared to confirm the companies' existing option to extend their concession by three consecutive five-year periods from 1979 – when the original concessionary term of twenty-five years was due to expire – in return for the consortium's undertaking to double its oil production to 8 million b/d and to make part of it available to the National Iranian Oil Company for marketing independently. It was, on the shah's part, a Punic pledge. In the last week of January 1973 he announced abruptly that when the 1954 consortium agreement terminated in 1979, the provision for the extension of the concession to 1994 would lapse with it. After publicly reviling the companies in his now familiar fashion for what he alleged was their neglect of Persia's interests, he went on to offer them only two choices. They could continue to operate up to 1979, on condition that they doubled Persia's oil-producing capacity and paid for the oil they shipped at rates not less than those obtaining elsewhere in the Gulf, after which, as he graciously put it, 'they would have to stand in a long queue of customers for Iran's oil'. Or they could agree to the termination of the concessionary agreement there and then, hand over all oil facilities and installations not already under Persian control, and undertake to expand their export capacity to 8 million b/d – in which case they would be accorded preferential treatment in the purchase of Persian oil for the next twenty to twenty-five years.

The companies temporized in framing their reply to the ultimatum, conscious that they were fast approaching the end of the road in Persia. Declaring his patience to be at an end – and also with an eye to upstaging a special OPEC conference which was to open at Beirut in two days' time – the shah announced on 20 March 1973 that his government was taking charge of the consortium's operations and transferring control of the oil industry to the National Iranian Oil Company. Weary of coping with the Lion of Persia rampant, the oil companies surrendered the next day. A new agreement was signed which was ratified by the Persian *majlis* on 16 July 1973. The companies would be permitted to buy oil over a period of twenty years, but only in amounts that Persia was willing to deliver and at prices not lower than those current elsewhere in the Gulf. They were both ominous reservations. The companies were also required to provide technical staff and expert advice for the operation and development of the Persian national oil industry. Nothing was said in the agreement about the provision of capital for new investment in the oilfields, which was another ominous omission in view of the shah's commitment of every penny of Persia's oil revenues to the realization of his over-ambitious schemes of industrial expansion and armed might. Instead, the companies were placed under an obligation to participate (up to as much as a 40 per cent share) in new projects of unspecified extent and duration for the development of Persia's oil resources under the overall direction of the National Iranian Oil Company. In other words, they would be dragged ever deeper into investments over which they had no control and from which they could only expect to reap continually mounting losses.

By the early weeks of 1973 the great deterioration which had taken place in the Western oil companies' position in the Middle East over the previous two years was plain for all to see. Since the Tehran and Tripoli agreements the companies had given up, or were to give up before 1973 was out, a whole succession of valid rights – among them the right to fix crude-oil prices in response to market demand; the right to share profits with the governments of the host countries on an equitable basis; the right to determine for themselves the shareholding of their operating companies and the disposition of their assets in the host countries; the right to sell crude oil or refined oil products in markets and to customers of their own choosing; the right to fulfil their contracts of sale to governments, commercial enterprises and individuals; the right to prospect for and extract oil under the terms of their original concessions; and the right to expect those concessions to be honoured by the governments which had awarded them. None of these rights was surrendered as a consequence of fair and orderly negotiation, or as a voluntary act on the part of the companies. On the contrary, every single right was given up under duress, or abandoned in response to threats of shut-downs or expropriation from governments which were animated as much by their detestation of Western values and enterprise as they were by their unassuageable appetite for more and more revenue. Increasingly the companies had fallen into a situation of economic thrall to the governments of the oil states, becoming, as the chairman of BP, Sir Eric Drake, acidly put it, mere 'tax-collecting agencies'. Wholly dependent upon the goodwill of these governments for access to the oil reserves upon which the industrial world relied so heavily, the companies felt themselves obliged to pander increasingly to their whims, however ludicrous or extortionate these might be. The cost of the companies' submissiveness and the host governments' avarice, needless to say, was paid by the oil-consuming countries of the world.

All these melancholy consequences flowed from the failure of the Western powers to back the oil companies to the hilt from the early months of 1970 onwards, to stop Qaddafi in his tracks in the summer of that year, to prick the bubble of the shah's insensate illusions about his own power and consequence, and to help the companies gain the upper hand of OPEC at Tehran at the outset of 1971. The companies lost the contest, not because their adversaries were stronger but because their own governments were indecisive and they themselves were enfeebled by their own disunity. Too many of the companies, and the American majors in particular, were preoccupied, not with the objects for which the grand alliance of majors and independents had been formed, but with the jealous preservation of their individual concessionary privileges, or with stealing a march upon their rivals, or with warding off the evil eye of accusations of collusion. As a result, they were irresolute or equivocal in their reaction to OPEC's bombast and shrill menaces. Yet, for all that their defeat was partly self-inflicted, at least it can be said of them that they made an effort to oppose the OPEC cartel, which is more than can be said of the governments of the West, then or in the years to follow.

The argument that was used at the time, and which has been used *ad nauseam* ever since, to justify the supine behaviour of the Western powers, and of the United States and Britain in particular, towards OPEC from the spring of 1970 onwards was that any show of firmness over oil prices would have brought retribution in the form of an oil embargo, something that the peoples of Western Europe and the United States were in no mood to tolerate. It is not an argument that reflects much credit upon those who made it, or upon those on whose behalf it was made. If the assertion is true, it says little for the spirit and temper of the peoples of the West; if it is false, it indicates in what low esteem they are held by their own governments. But in any case, how well in the long run did the timid and feeble reaction of the United States and British governments to the leap-frogging tactics of the OPEC governments from 1970 onwards serve the interests of the American and British peoples or those of the rest of the Western industrial world? Did it save them from further price increases, or did it merely ensure that these increases when they came would be more exorbitant than before? Is it not possible that a determined stand, especially in Libya in 1970 or at Tehran in 1971, with all the attendant risks of an embargo – risks that were in all probability far less real than the faint-hearted advocates of appeasement have made them out to be – would have injected a measure of sanity into the fevered colloquies of OPEC and averted the economic dislocation which overtook the industrial world after October 1973?

Questions of this kind are usually answered, or evaded, by reference to those twin hobgoblins, the 'energy gap' and the 'oil shortage', whose existence was discovered late in 1971 and thereafter frantically proclaimed to a bewildered world by a weird miscellany of Western sages, oracles and environmentalists. That the 'energy gap' and the 'oil shortage' were then, as now, spectral fancies was of little moment to the Western governments most concerned. Belief in them, real or assumed, offered a splendid excuse to the United States, British and French governments to do what they wanted to do anyway, viz. to bend the knee to the Arabs and Persians. All three governments suffered, and suffer still, from delusions regarding the rationality of contemporary political regimes in the Middle East: they believed that conciliation and fair dealing would prompt the Arabs and Persians to reciprocate, to act with good faith and moderation over oil prices and supplies. The French were sublimely confident, despite all their unhappy experiences in the past, that they knew the secret of handling the Arabs. The British persevered undismayed with the same conceit, heedless of the depths of ignominy into which it had dragged them. For those in the Foreign Office who clung to this belief, the presence of the oil companies in the Middle East had long been a matter for regret, since the companies' sordid commercial activities were seen as tending to sully what might otherwise have been the pure and limpid waters of Anglo-Arab amity.

While such sentiments were not entirely unknown in the State Department, they would seem to have played a less decisive part in determining official policy towards the oil companies. The State Department certainly had its quota of officials smitten with the *furor arabicus*, earnest souls who believed that they had unravelled the mysteries of the Arab psyche, and that the understanding they had gained as a consequence, combined with the sympathy they felt for Arab aspirations (or, rather, what they thought these aspirations to be), gave them an incomparable advantage over their French and British counterparts in treating with Arab governments. Such illusions aside, there were some grounds for the relative equanimity with which Washington viewed the rising level of oil prices in the Middle East after the Tehran *diktat* and, in the early months of 1973, the prospect of higher levels yet. The United States was herself a not inconsiderable producer of oil, and domestic oil prices were a good deal higher than those prevailing in the Middle East. American oil companies were not only the main producers of Middle-Eastern oil but they also had the largest share of the world market for crude oil and refined products. Financially, therefore, the United States could expect to derive substantial benefit from the greater profits which American oil companies would reap from passing on to their customers whatever increases in the price of crude oil were obtained by the Middle-Eastern oil states.

Politically, too, higher oil prices were not unwelcome to the United States. They helped to soothe the feelings of the Arabs, ruffled by some aspects of American policy in the Middle East, particularly concerning Israel. More directly, they helped to smooth the path of Saudi–American co-operation, which had by the latter half of 1972, if not before, become a principal strand in American policy towards the Arab states. Furthermore, as Saudi Arabia and Persia were now conceived of as the two local powers which would, with the blessing of the United States, guard the peace and security of the Gulf after Britain's withdrawal, Washington naturally wished to ensure the continuance in power of the Saudi and Pahlavi dynasties, and ample financial resources were a necessary means to this end. They were also necessary if the two states were to equip their armed forces with expensive weaponry, to the incidental benefit of the American aircraft and armaments industries. Mounting oil revenues, bolstered by rising oil prices, would ensure that these financial resources were plentiful.

While European oil companies followed the same practice as American companies in passing on price increases in crude oil to their customers, they had to take into account that their principal market was Europe itself, and to consider, therefore, the impact of higher prices upon the European economy, of which they themselves were an important part. The higher the prices Europe paid for oil and petro-chemicals, the more European manufacturers would be placed at a disadvantage in competing with American manufacturers in the markets of the world. Europe's appetite for oil, though sizable, was not as great as that of the United States. Nor could Europe as a whole afford to pay the prices that the United States could pay. There was, in sum, a fundamental divergence of interests between the United States and Europe over Middle-Eastern oil. The United States was primarily concerned with the volume of supply, Europe with the level of prices. At the outset of 1973 it was uncertain which of these two interests – which were far from being incompatible – would prevail. What was certain was that the outcome would largely be determined by what happened in Saudi Arabia over the twin issues of participation and prices. Saudi Arabia had the largest resources of oil in the Middle East and in the world. ARAMCO's four parent companies were amongst the biggest oil companies in existence, and one of them, Esso, was the biggest of all. What ARAMCO and the Saudis did in concert would set the terms upon which negotiations between OPEC and the Western oil companies would be conducted – and ARAMCO had already indicated that it reckoned the volume of oil supplied to be of greater moment than the price paid for it.

CHAPTER VIII
The 'Sting'

We shall ruin your industries as well as your trade with the Arab world.

Muammar Qaddafi, *October 1973*

The Arab oil producers with their massive reserves are the true friends of the West.

Ahmad Zaki al-Yamani, *November 1976*

It is our revenge for Poitiers!

Arab oil official, *December 1973*

By the winter of 1972–3 the 'energy crisis' was all the rage in the intellectual salons and political pavilions of the West. The student radicalism of the 1960s – the 'hippy movement', the 'youth revolt' and the 'New Left' – had spawned a number of fashionable causes which were swiftly taken up by politicians on the make and lark-brained leaders of contemporary thought, who affected to hear in the raucous complaints of the young the very music of the spheres. Prominent among these various causes were the preservation of the ecological balance, the protection of the environment and the conservation of the world's natural resources. On the basis of predictions of what the energy requirements of the industrial world were likely to be in five, ten or twenty years' time, it was discovered and solemnly proclaimed around the globe that mankind faced an imminent and perhaps catastrophic shortage of crude oil supplies – if, indeed, the shortage had not already materialized. What lent the discovery its particular piquancy was that it harmonized so agreeably with the reigning liberal canon on the subject of Western guilt for the economic backwardness of Asia and Africa and the need for the West to purify itself by self-abnegation and atonement. Now, it seemed, the day of retribution had dawned, and the temples of the higher thinking in the West rang with solemn prophecies of the economic wrath to come as a requital for the West's extravagant and heedless consumption of the earth's irreplaceable resources.

The tumult and the clamour were observed with some puzzlement and not a little excitement by the Arabs and Persians. They knew that there was no real shortage of oil supplies, then or in the foreseeable future. Output in all the Arab oil states except Saudi Arabia had, in fact, dropped in 1971 and again in 1972, reflecting a fall in the world market despite a rise in European, American and Japanese consumption. Still, if the nations of the West insisted upon working themselves into a hysterical state over a looming 'oil crisis', the Arabs were not going to pass up the opportunity to unsettle them further. Soon such learned and amiable students of the human predicament as Colonel Qaddafi and the oligarchs of Kuwait began prating, in the jargon made fashionable by Western discourse on the subject, about 'conservation', 'diminishing assets', 'finite resources' – everything, in fact, short of 'caribou crossings on the Alaskan pipeline' – demurely portraying themselves as disinterested benefactors holding their oil reserves 'as a sacred trust for mankind'. ('Conservation' was the pretext used by the Kuwaiti government in the spring of 1972 to impose a limit on oil production of 3 million b/d, in the hope both of disguising the falling sales of Kuwaiti crude and of preparing the ground for a price increase.) So many solemn dunces in the West were swift to applaud these pieties that the Arabs began to wonder whether the time was not ripe for a further round of price increases. They were further encouraged in this line of thought by the shah's high-handed treatment of the Persian consortium companies in January 1973, and by Qaddafi's truculent behaviour towards the Libyan oil producers in the same month.

A new devaluation of the United States dollar by 11.11 per cent in February 1973 gave the Arabs and OPEC their opening. An extraordinary congress of OPEC was convened at Vienna on 15 March 1973, ostensibly to consider the impending oil-supply 'crisis'. Its real purpose, however, as the burden of the discussions made clear, was to push for a price increase on the grounds of the dollar's devaluation. (The situation was not without the touch of irony which customarily graced OPEC's deliberations. A major contributory factor in the decline of the dollar's fortunes was the substantial speculation against it by those members of OPEC, Saudi Arabia and Kuwait in particular, which had large financial surpluses.) According to the formula agreed at Geneva in January 1972, an 11.11 per cent dollar devaluation called for a maximum increase in oil prices at the end of the first quarter of 1973 of between 6 and 6½ per cent. At the Vienna conference, however, Algeria demanded an immediate increase of 10 per cent. Saudi Arabia opposed the motion and the conference adjourned, to be reconvened in Beirut on 22 March. As a reminder to the Western industrial nations of the purported reason for the conference, a warning was issued by the OPEC secretariat that any 'concerted action' by them to keep prices down 'would have negative effects on the present energy situation'.

When the OPEC conference resumed at Beirut in late March it decided to set up a committee of three members, Libya, Iraq and Kuwait, to conduct the negotiations with the oil companies over prices. (The choice of this particular trio was also tinged with irony; for Kuwait and Iraq were then at loggerheads over an Iraqi military incursion into Kuwait territory. Squabbles of this kind, it was obvious, faded into insignificance before the prospect of oil price increases.) The committee – Izzedin Mabruk of Libya, Saadun al-Hammadi of Iraq and Abdur Rahman al-Atiqi of Kuwait – met the oil companies at Cairo in the latter half of April, when the companies were reported to have made an offer of a 6 per cent price increase in accordance with the Geneva 1972 formula, together with an additional 1.2 per cent as a sweetener. The three oil ministers rejected the offer on 24 April and gave the companies ten days in which to come up with 'positive proposals', which would be submitted to another special OPEC conference said to be due to commence in Tripoli in early May. The putative special conference was a blind, a ruse to put pressure upon the companies. When the latter came forward with their proposals, the conference was consigned to limbo. However, the committee of three declared the new proposals also to be unsatisfactory, and the secretary-general of OPEC, the Algerian Abdur Rahman Khene, chided the companies for their 'negative' attitude, saying that they had offered only the upper limit of the Geneva formula, 6.6 per cent. This was not true: the companies had offered 7.2 per cent at first, raising it to 8.1 per cent afterwards.

The fact of the matter was that the three OPEC ministers were not really interested in reaching an amicable settlement. They had sensed, especially after the shah's bold and successful initiative against the Persian consortium, that the companies were ripe for the plucking, and they were further whipped into an aggressive mood by the exhortations and actions of the Libyan RCC, working hand in glove with the Algerians. In the second week of May Qaddafi threatened three of the Libyan operators – Oasis (Continental, Marathon, Amerada–Hess and Shell), Amoseas (SOCAL and Texas) and Occidental – with total nationalization at the net book value of their assets, adding that thereafter they would only be able to buy Libyan oil at market prices. His oil minister, Izzedin Mabruk, spoke of the companies' 'underhand man-oeuvres' and warned that OPEC would not hesitate to use every means at its disposal ('and our means are numerous') to get better prices for its oil. Hinting not too subtly at the possibility of a curtailment of production, he bade the companies confine themselves to the role of 'middleman' between producing and consuming countries – 'if they do not want to become bankrupt'.

It was against this background of threats and blackmail that an article was published in the April 1973 issue of *Foreign Affairs* by James Akins of the State Department under the alarmist title of 'The oil crisis: this time the wolf is here'. Its principal theme was that everything that had happened between OPEC and the oil companies in the preceding years had really been for the best, and that the oil-consuming countries had better begin to adapt themselves to the irreversible changes that had taken place in the oil market-place. In the course of the article Akins made a special point of defending the State Department against the charge of passivity in the face of the Libyan junta's conduct in 1970, which, it will be recalled, had ushered in the yahoo phase in the history of oil negotiations. The oil companies, according to Akins, 'had little choice' but to yield to the threats made by the Libyans of a shut-down in production if their demands for increased prices were not met. 'The Libyans', he explained, in words which have been quoted in the previous chapter, 'were competent men in a strong position; they played their hand straight and found it a winning one.' ('Competent men', it might be remarked in passing, seems a peculiarly anodyne description to apply to a boorish *camarilla* whose sordid implication in international terrorism was well known by the spring of 1973.) Suggestions made at the time and afterwards, Akins continued, for countering the Libyans' threats by challenging them to nationalize the oil companies' assets outright, or by blocking Libyan funds in European or American banks, were simply 'unrealistic'.

The task of self-exoneration agreeably accomplished, Akins proceeded to devote the major part of his article to a detailed description of current and projected levels of oil consumption in the United States, Western Europe and Japan, the distribution of oil reserves between the eastern and western hemispheres, and present and future rates of output in the principal oil-producing countries. The impression produced was that of the utter dependence of Western Europe and Japan upon Middle-Eastern oil, and of the impotence of the industrial countries in the face of OPEC's resolution and might. Nothing demonstrated this more, in Akins's view, than the relief displayed by Europe at the conclusion of the Tehran agreement in February 1971, which, he said, 'guaranteed' oil supplies for five years. 'The underlying bargaining position of the European consumers was weak, and they knew it full well.' However, he went on, tossing a crumb of comfort to his readers, there was no need for the industrial nations to be unduly pessimistic about future supplies of oil, provided that they were prepared to pay the prices asked for it. Still less was there reason for alarm over the possibility that supplies would be cut off for political rather than financial reasons. 'King Faisal [has] said repeatedly', Akins affirmed, 'that the Arabs should not, and that he himself would not, allow oil to be used as a political weapon.' Satisfied that he had amply demonstrated, at one and the same time, the helplessness of Western Europe and Japan before the iron solidarity of OPEC and his own staunch faith in the moderation of the governments of the Middle-Eastern oil states, Akins departed from Washington the following autumn to take up the post of American ambassador to Saudi Arabia. Doubtless Jiddah was dressed over-all for his arrival.

Hard on the heels of Akins's article, the next issue of *Foreign Affairs* in July 1973 carried a further disquisition on the subject of OPEC and the West entitled 'The oil story: facts, fiction and fair play'. Its author was Jahangir

Amuzegar, the head of the Persian economic mission in Washington and a man of similar outlook to that of his namesake, the doughty Jamshid. Living up to its title, the article contained a fair amount of fiction and some not inconsiderable playing with facts. It opened with a sermon on the wickedness of the West and Japan for having consumed oil at a prodigal rate over the preceding three decades, and for having achieved their industrial growth 'by subsidies from oil-producing countries, mostly poor and struggling countries, at the expense of *their* irreplaceable assets'. In contrast, Amuzegar claimed piously, all that OPEC had done in return had been to secure proper recognition and representation of the producing countries' interests, and to ensure that 'the price of crude oil like other energy prices reflects its true cost'. Considering that the price of crude oil at the time that Amuzegar was writing was at least twenty times its marginal cost, and that within the next eighteen months it was to rise to over one hundred times, the claim set something of a record for effrontery. It was, however, by no means the limit of the Persian ambassador's audacity. OPEC's strength, he went on to explain, lay in 'the awareness, wisdom and determination of its members', and any move by Western consumers to try to break the organization's ranks would be 'incredibly naïve'. Nor would it do them any good to set up a counter-organization ('innocuous', 'swashbuckling', 'impractical and counter-productive'), still less to toy with the notion of taking over the oilfields ('preposterous'). In fact, Amuzegar declared darkly, if the consuming countries tried to act in concert against the producers, all manner of evils would result, including the cutting off of all oil supplies. The consumers had no choice, he concluded, in a distinct echo of Akins, but to pay whatever price for oil OPEC asked of them. 'Any attempt to hold down OPEC's oil revenues by "drastic measures" may not only result in fruitless and even dangerous reprisals and counter-reprisals, but would indeed be self-defeating.'

This was the authentic voice of OPEC, not the mellifluous sounds being diffused in the West by OPEC's apologists. It had, moreover, been heard earlier in the year, in February 1973, when Ahmad Zaki al-Yamani had declared, in response to a suggestion that the consuming countries might act in concert to defend their interests, that such a move would mean 'war'. If the consumers dared to combine, he said, OPEC would 'destroy their industries and civilization'. It was this mood of belligerence exhibited by OPEC in the first half of 1973 that lent Akins's article more significance than it intrinsically possessed. Whether he was writing to a State Department brief or whether he was merely expressing his own view was immaterial. The fact remained that he wrote in his capacity as the State Department official responsible for oil policy, and what he had to say was as clear a signal as could be sent that the United States government would not resist the pressure then being exerted by OPEC for higher oil prices. At an extraordinary general meeting of the organization at Vienna on 26 May it was resolved to seek a straight 12 per cent increase (twice that warranted by the Geneva formula) when negotiations resumed with the oil companies later that week. 'In the case of failure of the forthcoming negotiations,' the secretary-general, Khene, warned, 'the conference will resume its meeting to decide on sanctions to be taken.'

At the negotiations which followed at Geneva the OPEC representatives were in contentious form, despite the addition to the negotiating committee of two so-called 'moderates', Yamani and Jamshid Amuzegar. The companies, at cross-purposes among themselves, gave in within the week. Yet another agreement was signed on 1 June raising the price of oil by 11.9 per cent, effective immediately. It would net the producing states a further $1,000 million a year. Posted prices were to be adjusted monthly instead of quarterly (as under the Geneva 1972 formula), so as to take account of any fluctuations in the international value of the dollar. The agreement was to run for the remaining period of the Tehran settlement, i.e. until the end of 1975. After the signing Amuzegar went around assuring anyone who would listen that posted prices would fall if the international value of the dollar were to rise. As an assurance, it was worth exactly nothing.

The Geneva 'agreement' shattered once and for all the pretence which had been maintained since the Tehran settlement of 1971 that oil prices were decided by negotiation. It was not an agreement but a *diktat*, as indeed had been every decision on prices since 1970. It also revealed as something of a sham the grounds upon which the oil companies were continuing to negotiate with OPEC as one body. The justification urged by the companies for the issue of successive business review letters by the United States Department of Justice, to protect them from possible anti-trust actions, was the public interest. But the public interest at stake in the combined negotiations was the stability of oil prices, not their constant augmentation. What the companies were doing was interpreting, or reinterpreting, the public interest to accord with their own priorities, and in this the lead was taken by the parent companies of ARAMCO. For reasons which will be described shortly (and which were as much political as they were economic), the ARAMCO partners were far more concerned at Geneva with ensuring continued and unhampered access to Saudi Arabian crude than they were with holding down prices for the sake of the consumers. It was their insistence upon pursuing this object as their foremost priority which was as responsible as any other factor for the feebleness of the companies' resistance to the OPEC ukase.

One did not have to be a dyed-in-the-wool cynic to regard the Geneva 'settlement' as settling nothing. The only function that it served was to mark the opening of the 1973 leap-frogging season. Naturally, the Libyans were the first off the mark. At a public assembly in Tripoli on 11 June, ten days after the signing of the 'settlement', Colonel Qaddafi melodramatically announced the nationalization of Bunker Hunt's assets and operations in Libya. It was a theatrical performance to rival that of his hero and exemplar, Gamal Abdul Nasser, when in July 1956 he announced the nationalization of the Suez Canal

Company. Flanked by President Sadat of Egypt and President Field-Marshal Idi Amin Dada of Uganda, the Libyan Pericles harangued the assembled throng at length about the evil machinations of the Western oil companies and the wickedness and rapacity of the United States. Tossing into the wastepaper basket of history the assurances he had given at the time of his nationalization of BP's concession ('We nationalized BP for political reasons. . . . We have no intention of nationalizing American oil companies'), he declaimed:

The time has come for the Arabs to face up to the United States. The time has come for the Arabs to take serious measures to undermine American interests in our region. . . . No power in the world can impair our right to nationalize our own oilfields, or to stop pumping oil to the world. . . . It is about time the Americans took a hard slap in their cool, arrogant faces. American imperialism has exceeded every limit.

To everyone's surprise (not least Qaddafi's) the United States reacted promptly to the nationalization of Bunker Hunt, condemning both the act and the motives behind it, which were categorized in a formal note to the Libyan government on 5 July 1973 as 'political reprisal against the United States Government and coercion against the economic interests of certain other U.S. nationals in Libya'. Gone, it seemed, at least for the moment, was the complacent attitude towards nationalization personified by Akins only the previous year. Instead, the State Department protested strongly against the action of the Libyan government which, the note of 5 July insisted, violated established principles of international law. 'Measures taken against the rights and property of foreign nationals which are arbitrary, discriminatory, or based on considerations of political reprisal and economic coercion are invalid and not entitled to recognition by other states.' It was little use, however, quoting international law at Qaddafi. He acknowledged only one system of law, the *sharia*, the law of Islam, and then only when it suited his mood or purpose. He spurned the State Department's protest, confident from his observation of the United States's ineffectual reaction to every one of his swashbuckling stunts over the preceding three years that nothing would be done to give the protest teeth. To emphasize his contempt for the protest, and for the United States in general, the following month he unilaterally assumed a 51 per cent interest in all the independent oil companies operating in Libya, declaring at the same time that he intended to acquire a similar shareholding in the assets and operations of the other Libyan producers – Esso, Mobil, Shell, Texaco and SOCAL. Though the State Department called upon the customers of the companies whose assets had been expropriated to refrain from purchasing oil from the Libyan government, nothing was actually done, when it came to the point, to prevent domestic American fuel companies from rushing, as they did, to buy the nationalized oil.

Greatly excited by the frolics going on in Libya, the Kuwaitis rushed to join in the fun. It may be recalled that at the beginning of the year the Kuwaiti national assembly had refused to ratify the agreement with BP and Gulf, which gave Kuwait a 25 per cent share in the companies' operations, on the grounds that it affronted the sovereign dignity of the people of Kuwait. The opposition to the agreement was led by Ahmad al-Khatib, the founder of the Kuwaiti chapter of the Arab Nationalists' Movement and the darling of the radical faction in the assembly. The government of Kuwait, anxious as always to show its radical-chic colours, and at the same time to neutralize the growing influence of Khatib and his followers, in the second week of July proclaimed the agreement it had signed in January null and void. Nothing less than an immediate 51 per cent share in BP's and Gulf's operations, it declared, would satisfy the aspirations of Kuwait. BP and Gulf must have recalled rather wryly the assurance given by Abdur Rahman al-Atiqi, the Kuwaiti oil minister, less than eighteen months previously when he had stated unequivocally (or so it seemed at the time):

Effecting an increase in the oil revenues of an oil-producing country depends on a state's awareness of its legal commitments under a concession granted to a company to operate on its territory, and the ability and willingness of such a state to keep its agreements. I would say that it would not be possible to realise such an increase by issuing unilateral legislation.

The events of June and July were followed with keen interest by the Saudi Arabian oil minister, Yamani. Up to date no progress has been made with the implementation of the participation measures worked out between the Saudi government and ARAMCO the previous December. In part, the delay was due to the Saudis' reluctance to agree on future production levels and the basis of compensation; but it was also occasioned by the Saudis' desire to temporize until they had seen what was happening elsewhere. Now, with the Libyan and Kuwaiti examples to hand, Yamani told the ARAMCO representatives when talks were resumed early in August, 'You [i.e. the oil companies in general] will have to improve on the Kuwaiti deal if you are to avoid nationalization [in Kuwait] and then I'll have something even better than Kuwait.' On 1 September Qaddafi took by fiat what he could not obtain by fair negotiation – a 51 per cent share in the Libyan operations of Esso, SOCAL, Texaco, Mobil and Shell, the first four being, of course, the parent companies of ARAMCO. A fortnight later Yamani expressed the view to ARAMCO that Kuwait was bound to demand more than the 51 per cent participation achieved by Libya. Saudi Arabia, naturally, would not be outdone by either Libya or Kuwait but would require something more, especially as Persia across the Gulf was now in full possession of her own oil resources.

Participation was only one of the strings to OPEC's bow: another, and just as strong, was prices. Throughout July there had been rumblings from the organization about the need to increase oil prices further so as to keep pace with inflation in the industrial nations. They culminated in a statement from OPEC on 27 July warning the oil-consuming countries against contemplating any concerted action to keep oil prices static. 'To seek a direct confrontation with OPEC', the statement said, 'may have a damaging effect upon the world economy.' In the course of his talks with ARAMCO the following month Yamani went out of his way to emphasize that the Tehran agreement, which still had nearly two and a half years to run, would soon have to be renegotiated. (The fact that the latest revision of that tattered document had taken place at Geneva only two months previously was brushed aside as of no consequence.) The next price increases, Yamani told the ARAMCO representatives, would be very large, and they would be imposed by OPEC, not negotiated with the oil companies. It would be the same with the determination of the prices at which ARAMCO would be permitted to buy back the Saudi government's share of oil production: the prices would be set by Petromin (the Saudi government corporation under the direction of the department of petroleum and mineral resources), and if ARAMCO did not accept them it would be ordered to cut back production.

How real Yamani's threat was, and how seriously it was viewed by ARAMCO, are questions to which it is not easy to supply the answers from the scanty evidence it is possible to gather about Saudi–ARAMCO relations in 1973. It could have been that the two sides were merely dancing an elaborate minuet – to music played in Washington – for the diversion of those who cared to watch. On the other hand, there was in 1973 a growing demand for oil on the world market, deriving in part from fears of a possible shortage. ARAMCO was doing its best to raise production, although it was encountering difficulties in the process, not only with the Saudi government but also for technical reasons. At one stage there were rumours that the future life of the Saudi Arabian fields, in particular the Abqaiq and Ghawar fields, was being endangered by the rate and manner of their depletion. ARAMCO publicly dismissed the rumours as unfounded, pointing to the problems it was experiencing with water injection, pressure reductions and unsatisfactory pumping equipment. It was fairly obvious, however, that ARAMCO could not have sustained for very much longer the production levels it was achieving by September 1973 (8.3 million b/d as compared with 6.5 million b/d in February 1973) without the risk of doing permanent damage to the fields. This knowledge must have removed much of the sting from Yamani's threat of a production cut-back.

There was rather more substance to his warnings about price increases, although here again, as observed earlier in connexion with the Geneva agreement of 1 June, ARAMCO was more concerned with access than with prices. The world-wide demand for oil had driven the market price of oil during the summer steadily upwards towards its posted price, and in September market prices actually overtook posted prices. There was, therefore, an apparently strong case in purely commercial terms for an increase in posted prices in the near future. But it was not the market, or even its own concern with production levels, that was preoccupying ARAMCO's attention in the late summer of 1973. There was something else in the wind, of a far more disturbing character.

As 1973 wore on, politics was coming to exercise more and more of a baleful influence upon the Middle-Eastern oil scene. That influence had always been present, of course, whether in the form of the enduring and deep-seated resentment felt by the Muslim states for the Christian West, or in the shape of their own regional, dynastic or ideological rivalries, ambitions and antipathies. But it was the particular attribute of the year 1973 that it should bring forth, at one and the same time, a growing aggressiveness on the part of OPEC towards the Western industrial nations and an even more marked distemper in the Arab attitude to the Western powers, especially in connexion with the unending and unrelenting Arab quarrel with Israel. Inevitably, the two sentiments nourished each other, the more so since their roots were intertwined. When they eventually fused in the early autumn of 1973 they engendered a convulsion in the oil markets of the world the like of which had not been seen before. Somewhere near the epicentre of that convulsion was the singular and tangled relationship that subsisted between ARAMCO and the government of Saudi Arabia.

Talk of the possible use of Arab oil as a weapon in the Arab–Israeli dispute had been in the air for some years. As we have seen, a short-lived embargo upon the shipment of oil to the United States, Britain and West Germany had been imposed by Saudi Arabia at the time of the Six-Day War in June 1967. It was lifted within a month, partly because other oil-producing countries like Persia and Venezuela had promptly taken advantage of the temporary deficit in supplies to increase their own oil exports, partly because Saudi Arabia could not afford to sustain the financial losses which the embargo was causing. By the close of 1967 Saudi Arabia's oil production had risen by 9 per cent over the preceding year. Thereafter the likelihood of another oil embargo was viewed in the West with scepticism. The conventional wisdom was that expressed, for example, in the *Guardian* in October 1967: 'The quick resumption of oil supplies after the June war has discredited the idea that oil – which the Arabs cannot drink – is an effective weapon against the West.' As late as January 1972 the *Financial Times* was still assuring its readers, 'These moves [e.g. participation] need not necessarily disrupt either oil prices or oil flows – nor, indeed, have the Gulf countries shown any sign they wish to do so.'

The subject was aired at intervals over the years, usually in the context of the Arab–Israeli dispute, only to be lost to sight on each occasion in the dust and smoke raised by one or other of the successive *bouleversements* which normally mark the progress of Arab politics. Early in 1973 there was a renewal of rhetoric about the use of the 'oil weapon' in the event of a 'fourth round' between Israel and the Arab states, much of it issuing from Kuwait. On 6 January the Kuwaiti national assembly passed a resolution calling upon the government 'to use our oil resources in the battle once the fighting begins, or even before that'. The following month the prime minister and heir apparent, Shaikh Jabir ibn Ahmad Al Sabah, stated publicly that Kuwait would not hesitate to use her oil as a weapon in another war with Israel. Shaikh Sabah ibn Salim Al Sabah, the ruler of Kuwait, declared in mid-March, 'When zero hour comes, we shall use the oil as an effective weapon in the battle.' He went on to say that he was also prepared to manipulate the supply of oil to bring pressure upon the United States to diminish its support for Israel. During the discussions between the three-man OPEC committee and the oil companies' representatives in Cairo in April there was some talk of the use of oil for political purposes, most of it, however, coming from Egyptian officials outside the conference room. On a visit to Washington in late April, Yamani spoke of the possibility that Saudi Arabia might not agree to raise oil production to meet the needs of the United States unless 'the right political atmosphere' was created. Three weeks later, on 13 May, Colonel Qaddafi asserted, in the course of a six-hour press conference, 'Undoubtedly the day will come when oil will be used as the last weapon.'

The suggestion that the Saudi government might be contemplating a restriction of oil supplies for political reasons was much more disturbing than the gasconade issuing from Kuwait and Tripoli, particularly as it seemed to originate with King Faisal himself. When the chairman of ARAMCO, R. W. Powers, and the company president, Frank Jungers, paid a courtesy call upon the king at the beginning of May, they were treated to a long lecture on the subject of the worsening situation in the Middle East and the dangers to American interests in the region presented by the continuing stalemate between Israel and the Arabs. It was 'absolutely mandatory', Faisal told the two oilmen, that the United States should do something to alter the course which events were taking. Saudi Arabia was the only Arab country where American interests were safe, but Saudi Arabia could not hold out much longer against the anti-American feeling that prevailed in the rest of the Arab world. He was, he said, 'utterly amazed' by the failure of the United States to recognize where its true interest lay, especially as a 'simple disavowal of Israel policies and actions' by the United States would go a long way towards improving her image in Arab eyes. It seemed to him urgently necessary for those Americans, whether individuals or corporations, who were friends of the Arabs to bring their influence to bear within the United States to secure such a disavowal.

What Faisal was driving at was made more explicit after the audience by the king's chamberlain and confidant, Kamal Adham, who told Powers and Jungers that Saudi Arabia was becoming increasingly isolated from the other Arab states because of her friendship with the United States. Adham himself believed that President Sadat of Egypt intended to go to war against Israel, hopeless though the Egyptians considered their chances of military success to be, in a last desperate attempt to break the stalemate. If he did so, Saudi Arabia could not afford to stand aloof from the battle. Inevitably the question of oil supplies would arise, and when it did, Adham said, he was 'deeply concerned' that the tide of events might prove fatal to American interests in the Middle East, even in Saudi Arabia itself. How confident, he asked, was ARAMCO about the safety of its oil installations in Hasa, and about public security in that province in general? 'Good security', he added, seemingly as an afterthought, 'was not a matter of a lot of sophisticated equipment.'

These unsettling hints and veiled warnings were followed by a rather more direct admonition in the last week of May when Powers and Jungers, together with the directors responsible for Middle-Eastern operations in ARAMCO's parent companies – C. J. Hedlund of Esso, W. J. McQuinn of SOCAL, A. C. De Crane of Texaco and H. C. Moses of Mobil – were received by Faisal in Geneva, where the oilmen had arrived for the negotiations with OPEC and to discuss participation questions with Yamani. In the interval Faisal had visited Cairo, where Sadat had importuned him for greater financial and political support. The comparative cordiality with which Faisal had expressed his opinions to the chairman and president of ARAMCO at the beginning of the month was absent on this occasion. 'Time is running out with respect to United States interests in the Middle East,' he told the oilmen with some asperity. Saudi Arabia, the only friend the United States had in the area, was in danger of being isolated because the Americans had failed to give her positive support by taking the initiative over Israel. He was not prepared to allow Saudi Arabia to be isolated. 'You will lose everything', he warned Powers and Jungers, apparently referring to the possibility that he would, if driven to it, revoke ARAMCO's concession as a means of disproving his critics' allegations that he was subordinating Arab to American interests. What ARAMCO must do, he insisted, was, firstly, to inform the American public, which was being misled by biased news reports and propaganda, where its 'true interests' lay in the Middle East; and, secondly, to impress upon the United States government the urgent need for action. 'Time is running out,' he repeated. 'You may lose everything.'

Whatever apprehension ARAMCO might feel about the situation in which it now found itself, it could not blink the fact that it was a situation largely of its own making. From the very first, the company had made much ado about its identity as a Saudi company, located in Saudi Arabia and advancing Saudi interests. It had, as related in an earlier chapter, given devoted service to the Saudi royal house as counsellor, major-domo, intermediary and propagandist. In the United States it had, through the discreet exercise of patronage and influence in universities, foundations, learned societies, political and cultural organizations and the press, shaped the American outlook upon Saudi Arabia, her rulers, her people and her place in the international order. Less discreetly, ARAMCO had sought to win over every American of any importance who visited Saudi Arabia, whether politician, bureaucrat or military officer, to the Saudi view of Middle-Eastern politics and of the Arab–Israeli question in particular. A notable instance of this practice came to light during the hearings of the sub-committee on multinational corporations of the Senate Foreign Relations Committee in June 1974. It seems that in January 1973, while he was still director of the office of fuels and energy at the State Department, James Akins had invited the ARAMCO lobbyist in Washington, Michael Ameen, to his home, where he had told him in confidence that John Erlichman, the presidential assistant, might be visiting Saudi Arabia the following April. The transcript of the hearings goes on: 'Akins wanted Ameen to tell Yamani it was very important that he, Yamani, take Erlichman under his wing and see to it that Erlichman was given the message we Saudis love you people but your American policy is hurting us.'

A week after their conversation with Faisal in Geneva, Hedlund, McQuinn, De Crane and Moses went to Washington to pass on the king's warning to the Nixon administration. They spoke to the assistant secretary for Near-Eastern affairs at the State Department, Joseph J. Sisco, to the acting secretary of defence, William Clements, and to members of the presidential staff at the White House. Their representations met with a sceptical reception. Although the depth of Faisal's feeling over the Arab–Israeli question was acknowledged, there was no disposition to believe that a drastic move on his part was imminent. There was no need, it was felt, for the United States to do any more than what was already being done to prevent such a move. Faisal was crying wolf where none prowled. Saudi Arabia in the past, so the official thinking went, had been subjected to far greater pressure from Nasser than she was now experiencing from Sadat: she had successfully withstood such pressure then, and no doubt she would do so on the present occasion.

The administration's scepticism probably had another source. ARAMCO's real solicitude was not for the Arab–Israeli dispute *per se*, or for the direction and emphasis of United States policy in the Middle East, or even for the susceptibilities of the Saudi government. The company's real preoccupation was with the rate at which it could extract oil from the Saudi Arabian fields. Ultimately, of course, it was solicitous for its own concession, though it was confident that if the Saudis ever evinced a serious intention to revoke it unilaterally, the United States government would intervene on the company's behalf. Moreover, the value of the concession had already been reduced by the Saudi government's decision to acquire a substantial interest in the company's assets and operations, a decision to which ARAMCO was becoming increasingly resigned. To this extent, therefore, Faisal's veiled threat about the company's 'losing everything' could be viewed less as the writing on the wall than as a tactical move, designed to spur ARAMCO's parent companies into using their influence in Washington to bring about a change in American policy towards Israel, while providing them at the same time with a plausible reason for urging the adoption by the United States of a pro-Arab position. Where Faisal's words did contain a suggestion of coercive measures of a kind to worry ARAMCO was in their implication that a limitation might be placed upon the level of oil production which ARAMCO would be permitted to reach and sustain, if the Saudi monarch's wishes were not met in the near future.

Having failed with their direct approach to the administration in Washington on Faisal's behalf, ARAMCO and its parent companies embarked upon an extensive campaign of propaganda and political lobbying to try to bring about a change in American policy. The propriety of this campaign was sharply questioned a year later by the Senate sub-committee referred to above, whose counsel criticized the companies for acting as 'instruments of the Saudi Arab government and carrying out Saudi orders in terms of influencing U.S. foreign policy'. The same accusation had been levelled at the companies on other occasions, though in less public circumstances, and the ARAMCO partners had each time shrugged it off. In their own eyes they saw little cause for reproaches against them, and in any case they felt that they had bigger problems to contend with than allegations of pro-Saudi bias.

These problems almost exclusively related, as noticed already, to production targets and the retention of preferential access to the Saudi government's share of oil production in the future. Output from the Saudi fields had been raised in 1971 by 26 per cent over the previous year's figure, and the same increase had again been achieved in 1972. As seen earlier, ARAMCO was endeavouring to achieve as great an increase, or even greater, in 1973. To reach this goal, and to ensure preferential access to future participation crude, ARAMCO was prepared, as has also been remarked already, to give way on prices. The extent to which it gave way was revealed in the price settlement reached by the company with Yamani in San Francisco on 17 September 1973, a settlement so generous that it prompted suspicions that ARAMCO's parent companies had actively encouraged Yamani to bid up prices, especially for participation crude. Whether there were solid grounds for these suspicions is uncertain. All that the counsel to the Senate sub-committee on multinational corporations could conclude after his investigations the following year was that 'the documentary record is ambiguous'; although, as he went on to remark rather drily, 'the record would seem to indicate that they [the ARAMCO partners] are, indeed, trading off price for preferential access to this Saudi crude'.

ARAMCO's lavish settlement with the Saudis was to have a vital bearing upon the new round of price negotiations which OPEC had been calling for almost from the moment that the Geneva agreement of 1 June 1973 was signed. The recurring complaints of the cartel's members about the insufficiency of the revenues they were receiving were primarily directed against the profits made by the oil companies from their 'downstream' activities, i.e. refining, distribution and retailing. Whereas, as OPEC never tired of pointing out, the price per metric ton of crude oil had only risen from $7 to $13 between 1970 and the latter half of 1973, the price of petroleum products had risen from $29 to $52 per metric ton. Likewise, the revenue derived by the governments of the industrial oil-consuming countries from duties and taxes levied upon petroleum products greatly exceeded those obtained by the governments of the producing states from the extraction of crude oil. As an argument, it had about as much sense and worth as a complaint from a farmer about the profits made by a whisky distiller to whom he had sold barley. The only valid test of the justice of the price received for a raw material is its relationship to the cost of its production, especially in terms of capital investment, skill and effort. The contribution of the Middle-Eastern members of OPEC to the production of crude oil was, in all three respects, exactly nil.

A further complaint voiced by OPEC was that inflation in the Western industrial countries was eroding the value of the price increases obtained by and since the Tehran settlement of February 1971. That these increases may have been a contributory cause of that inflation was conveniently ignored. In any case, the original Tehran settlement provided for dual increases of 5 cents a barrel and $2\frac{1}{2}$ per cent on posted prices each year to compensate for inflation in the cost of goods imported from the West. Moreover, the United States dollar, in which oil prices were calculated, had in the summer of 1973 regained ground against other major currencies and was still rising. Under the terms of the Tehran settlement such a development called for a reduction in the price of crude oil, not an increase. (It also called for Jamshid Amuzegar, the Pangloss of OPEC, to live up to the assurance he had so eagerly proffered to all and sundry at Geneva in June.) Such considerations, however, were as thistledown in the wind that was blowing in September 1973. OPEC was due to meet on 15 September to set a date for the start of new price negotiations with the oil companies. On 7 September Yamani pronounced the Tehran settlement to be 'dead or dying'. 'If we fail to obtain the co-operation of the oil companies in amending the Tehran price agreement,' he said, 'we will have to exercise our rights on our own.'

At its meeting in Vienna on 15–16 September OPEC designated Monday, 8 October as the date for the opening of talks with the companies at Geneva. The mood of the meeting left no doubt that the new prices would be dictated, not negotiated, and that the instrument of coercion OPEC had in mind to enforce its will was a threatened restriction upon oil production, the same threat that had recently been used with effect by Saudi Arabia against ARAMCO. Again, as in the case of the Saudis, the aims of the Arab members of OPEC were as much political as they were financial. The world was well aware of the nature of these aims from the incessant and insistent proclamation of them by Arab governments over the years, and they were again being expounded with great fervour by the spokesmen of Arab oil interests in the summer of 1973. One such exponent was a former secretary-general of OPEC, Nadim al-Pachachi, who, in an address given at the American University of Beirut in the second week of June, made no secret of what the Arab oil states would like to do if they thought they could bring it off. He repeated his remarks at a conference in London organized by the *Financial Times* in the third week of September. The Arabs, Pachachi told his audience, were fully prepared to exploit the world's pressing need for their oil to achieve not only ever higher financial returns but also their political ends, chief among which was the withdrawal of Israel from occupied Arab territory. 'The Arabs now hold the keys to the energy and monetary crisis,' Pachachi declared. 'They will know how to use both as a political weapon to enforce a just settlement in the Middle East on the United States administration that still believes might is right.' The method used would be the imposition of restrictions upon crude-oil production. As Pachachi saw it,

The balance between demand and supply has become extremely delicate and precarious. Interruption of supply or a slow-down in the expansion of production of one major supplier could cause a serious energy crisis in a short time. . . . The present crude oil production levels in the Arab countries are sufficient and adequate to meet the economic and financial needs of the Arab producing countries, particularly in the current situation of rising prices. Is there a better investment for any Arab oil-producing country than conserving the oil wealth which they do not need at present for future generations? Oil in the ground is more valuable as an investment than bonds and securities in the present uncertainties prevailing in the world monetary system.

For all this, however, Pachachi went on to assure his listeners.

Arab oil, considering the current political and economic challenges of the West, might be regarded as the most secure source of imported energy. I do not need to remind you that even at the height of the pre-Tehran crisis, when oil companies refused to comply with the reasonable demands of OPEC countries, no interruption of supplies to consumers was ever contemplated.

As an assurance it was cold comfort, as well as a striking departure from the true facts concerning OPEC's behaviour in December 1970 and January 1971 – as Pachachi, who had been secretary-general of the organization at the time, was in a better position than most to know. In view of this, his further assurance on the subject of a possible embargo – 'We need not deny oil supply to any country in the world. We do not need to impose an oil embargo or a boycott against any country. An embargo against one or more countries is neither practical nor effective' – was not of a nature to inspire confidence, or even credence, in his listeners.

At the time that Pachachi was hawking his hollow promises around the capitals of Europe, Egypt and Syria were making their final preparations for war with Israel. Oil had already been selected as one of the principal strategic weapons in the Arab armoury, particularly to deter the Western powers from intervening in the conflict on Israel's behalf. On 26 August Anwar al-Sadat had paid a visit to Faisal to apprise him of his military plans and to seek assurances of financial aid. At the meeting the use of Saudi Arabia's oil to bring pressure to bear upon the United States, should the need arise, was also discussed, with what definite result is not known for certain. From the subsequent actions of the Saudi government, however, and from Faisal's own conversations with the heads of ARAMCO in May, it is logical to infer, at the very least, that Faisal did not reject the idea of a resort to this expedient. At the end of August he was visited by the ruler of Kuwait, Sabah ibn Salim Al Sabah, who afterwards went on to Cairo to see Sadat. Before he left Cairo Shaikh Sabah indicated his willingness to throw Kuwait's oil into the balance in the forthcoming battle with Israel.

For all these furtive comings and goings, clandestine preparations and surreptitious undertakings, what was still uppermost in the calculations of the governments of the Arab oil states in the early autumn of 1973 was substantial price increases. The financial cutting edge of the oil weapon was as vital to its effectiveness as the imposition of restrictions upon production. Principle and profit, they reckoned, could be combined in harmonious union: oil production would be reduced to persuade the Western powers to turn against Israel; and prices could be increased to compensate for any loss of revenue from reduced output – and at the same time provide the funds with which to exert further economic pressure upon the industrial nations. It was an enchanting prospect and the auguries all seemed favourable.

The Yom Kippur war broke out on 6 October and two days later the Gulf members of OPEC met the representatives of the oil companies at Vienna. The first move against the companies had already been made on 7 October when Iraq had nationalized the shareholding of Esso and Mobil in the Basra Petroleum Company – a move which was, in a legal sense, nugatory, since BPC was a British company. At Vienna the delegates of the six Gulf oil states, led by Yamani and Amuzegar, demanded an immediate increase in the government tax rate which would have been equivalent to doubling the posted price of Gulf oil from around $3 to $6 a barrel. The oil companies' representatives, still negotiating as one under business review letters from the United States Department of Justice, were empowered to offer no more than a 25 per cent increase in the posted price. Yamani and Amuzegar came down to $5 a barrel, which the companies' chief negotiators, Piercy of Esso and André Bénard of Shell, passed on to their boards in New York and London. The companies as a whole were appalled by the financial implications of such a huge increase, implications which, they believed, were potentially so momentous that they could not by themselves take the responsibility for reaching a decision. Such a decision could only be made in consultation with the governments of the industrial nations, and Piercy and Bénard were instructed to reply in this sense to the OPEC delegates. The two negotiators conveyed the message to Yamani on the night of 10 October. It was, for all practical purposes, the end of the discussions. It was also to be the last occasion on which the companies were to go through the motions of negotiating oil prices with OPEC. Henceforth, as Yamani had predicted two months earlier, prices would be laid down by OPEC alone.

The day before the talks collapsed the government of Kuwait had called for an urgent conference of the Arab oil-producing states to discuss 'the role of oil' in the war now raging. At their last meeting Yamani warned Piercy that ARAMCO could expect, at the least, to be ordered to cut back its production from 8.3 million b/d to 7 million b/d. The warning caused consternation in the boardrooms of ARAMCO's four parent companies, and on 12 October their chairmen – J. K. Jamieson of Esso, Rawleigh Warner of Mobil, M. F. Granville of Texaco and Otto N. Miller of SOCAL – sent a joint memorandum to President Nixon expressing their alarm at the dangerous situation they saw developing. It was a unique occasion in the oil world, in that it was the first time that the chairmen of the four major American international companies had put their signatures to a joint message. They expressed their alarm at two developments in particular: the huge increase in posted prices demanded by OPEC, which, they said, was of such magnitude that its impact 'could produce a serious disruption in the balance of payments position of the Western world'; and the looming threat of a cut-back in oil production by Saudi Arabia and Kuwait. 'We are convinced of the seriousness of the intentions of the Saudis and Kuwaitis', they wrote, 'and that any actions of the U.S. government at this time in terms of increased military aid to Israel will have a critical and adverse effect on our relations with the moderate Arab oil-producing countries.' The four chairmen went on to express their apprehensions not only of the immediate danger of an oil-supply crisis but also of the serious possibility that American oil interests in the Middle East would suffer permanent damage. 'The bulk of the oil produced in the Persian Gulf goes to Japan and Western Europe. These countries cannot face a serious shut-in. . . . We believe they will of necessity continue to seek Middle East oil and that they may be forced to expand their Middle East supply positions at our expense.'

Beyond the bare acknowledgement three days later of its receipt the memorandum seems to have elicited no response from the White House. In the interim President Nixon had authorized the dispatch of military supplies by air to Israel. The meeting of the Arab oil-producing countries (OAPEC) called for by Kuwait was due to take place in that shaikhdom on 16 October. The same place and date had been chosen by the Gulf members of OPEC – Saudi Arabia, Persia, Kuwait, Iraq, Qatar and Abu Dhabi – at Vienna on 12 October for their meeting to decide, as their public statement put it, upon 'a course of collective action to determine the true value of the crude oil they produce'. There was little doubt about what was foremost in the minds of the oil ministers when they assembled in Kuwait on the 16th. The war, now ten days old, afforded OPEC the most plausible pretext it had ever had to push up prices, with the absolute assurance, furnished by the supine conduct of the Western powers over the preceding three years and by the current agitation in the West at the thought of an oil shortage, that the industrial nations would swallow any increase.

The day of 16 October, therefore, was given over to excited discussions about the levels to which prices could be raised, with Amuzegar reportedly pushing for the topmost limit. That night the decision was made public. The posted price of the Gulf marker crude (standard Arabian light) was raised from $3.01 to $5.11, an increase of 70 per cent, effective immediately. The Tehran agreement was scrapped, and with it the obligation to vary posted prices in accordance with the international value of the US dollar – then still moving upwards. Henceforth the posted price was at all times to be 40 per cent above the market price of oil, so as to ensure continued high government revenues. All manner of variables were introduced for the calculation of the tax-reference prices – the specific gravity of oil as it came from the ground, sulphur content, distance from markets and so on. Partly these were designed, as in the past, to provide Libya, Algeria and other OPEC members with the price differentials which their geographical location and the quality of their oil warranted. Partly, however, they arose from the atmosphere of confusion and emotion in which the discussions were conducted.

The following day the Arab oil ministers turned their attention to the associated issue of restrictions upon oil production. While they deliberated, in Washington the acting Saudi minister for foreign affairs, Omar Saqqaf, handed President Nixon and the secretary of state, Henry Kissinger, a letter from King Faisal stating that, if the United States did not within forty-eight hours halt the dispatch of arms to Israel, an embargo would be placed upon the shipment of oil to the United States. Saqqaf was told in reply that the United States was committed to aiding Israel. Late that same night in Kuwait, after seven hours of debate, the Arab oil ministers issued a communiqué announcing that all members of OAPEC would reduce their oil production by 5 per cent each month. The measure would be back-dated to the end of September, and the September production figures would be taken as a basis for calculating the reduction. Any member of OAPEC would be free to make greater reductions, if it so desired. The process of reduction would continue at the same rate, the communiqué stated, 'until the Israeli forces are completely evacuated from all the Arab territories occupied in the June 1967 war, and the legitimate rights of the Palestinian people are restored'. There would be no respite from the progressive hardship imposed by these measures,

unless the world community arises to put matters in order, compel Israel to withdraw from our occupied lands and make the United States aware of the exorbitant price the great industrial states are paying as a result of its blind and unlimited support for Israel.

A crumb of comfort, however, was held out to those countries which might decide to take the 'correct' attitude to the conflict – or, as the communiqué phrased it, 'any friendly state which has helped or will help the Arabs in a fruitful and effective manner'.

They will continue to be supplied with the same quantities of oil they used to obtain before the reduction. The same special treatment will be given to every state which adopts an important measure against Israel to persuade it to end its occupation of the usurped Arab territories.

Everything about the communiqué, including the way in which it was issued, was muddled and obscure. Only one copy of it was made available to the newspaper reporters crowding the Kuwait Sheraton Hotel where the meeting was held, and this was handwritten in Arabic, with phrases crossed out and others inserted in pencil – including the reference to the rights of the Palestinians. No translation into any other language was offered: indeed, the OAPEC secretariat refused outright to produce an official English version, either of the communiqué or of the actual resolution passed by the OAPEC ministers. It was a pity that the two documents could not have been compared, for there was an interesting discrepancy between them. The original resolution stated that the recurrent 5 per cent cut in production every month would continue

until such time as the international community compels Israel to relinquish our occupied territories or until the production of every individual country reaches the point where its economy does not permit of any further reduction without detriment to its national and Arab obligations.

There was no mention of this last prudent reservation in the communiqué. In its place was a piece of flim-flam about the 'economic sacrifices' the Arabs had been making for the sake of the rest of the world in 'producing quantities of their valuable oil wealth in excess of what is justified by the economic factors in their states'.

The obfuscation surrounding the communiqué was to some extent calculated, so as to create bewilderment and disquiet in the West. But it was also a reflection of the oil ministers' own turbulent state of mind as a result of developments on the fighting fronts in the previous forty-eight hours. The fortunes of war were now turning steadily in favour of Israel. Israeli forces had cleared the Golan Heights and were well into Syria, where their forward elements were only twenty-five miles from Damascus. On the night of 15–16 October Israeli troops launched a counter-attack across the Suez Canal, and by the 17th Israeli armour was over the Canal in strength. As Egyptian arms suffered progressively severe reverses from this point onwards, the measures taken by the Arab oil states to raise oil prices and restrict supplies came to appear less and less like bold and resolute strokes in the tumult of war, and more and more like peevish requitals for Arab defeats on the field of battle – even, perhaps, as an underhand attempt to exploit the fortuitous circumstance of war as an opportunity to fleece the West.

The sequence of reprisals began with an announcement by Abu Dhabi on 19 October that she was imposing a complete ban on oil shipments to the United States. For connoisseurs of international drollery the gesture had an especial charm; for at that very moment Abu Dhabi was anxiously trying to raise a large loan in US dollars through the agency of a London merchant bank. On the same day Colonel Qaddafi proclaimed a similar embargo, adding *en passant* that the price of Libyan oil was being raised from $4.90 to $8.92 a barrel, effective immediately. The other Arab oil states waited to see what Saudi Arabia would do. On 18 October President Nixon had asked Congress to approve the expenditure of $2,000 million to cover shipments of arms to Israel. King Faisal took the request, coming as it did so soon after his warning of a few days earlier, as a personal insult. On 20 October he let the world know the measure of his wrath. Declaring a *jihad* against Israel and calling upon Muslims everywhere to join it, he ordered the cessation forthwith of all oil shipments to the United States, including supplies to the American armed forces wherever they might be. The next day Yamani summoned the heads of ARAMCO to Riyad and gave them detailed instructions about the implementation of the embargo. Not only were there to be no direct shipments of oil to the United States, but indirect shipments through American refineries in Canada, the Caribbean and elsewhere were also banned. In addition to the cut in production resulting from the embargo upon the supply of oil to the United States, there was to be a general cut of 10 per cent, based upon the output for September. The total reduction would amount to roughly 1.8 million b/d, i.e. from almost 8.3 million b/d in September to 6.5 million b/d in October.

A series of further instructions from the Saudi oil minister followed. Countries which subscribed, or were deemed sympathetic, to the Arab cause were to be spared the adverse effects of reduced production. They were to receive supplies equivalent to their average daily consumption over the previous nine months. In this category were included Britain, France, Spain, Jordan, Lebanon, Malaysia, Pakistan, Tunisia and (somewhat superfluously) Egypt. Other countries, not specifically placed on the embargo list, would share the remaining crude oil available on a *pro rata* basis, according to their previous respective volumes of consumption. When the ARAMCO representatives pointed out that this ruling would bear harshly upon countries like Japan and Italy, Yamani responded by saying that this was the intention. (At the OAPEC meeting in Kuwait on 17 October one of the delegates had referred to Japan's position in the Arab–Israeli conflict as one of 'odious neutrality'.)

The lesser oil states hastened to join the dance. Within a couple of days Kuwait, Bahrain, Qatar, Dubai and Algeria had all banned the shipment of oil to the United States and cut their production by 10 per cent. Iraq, while ready to forbid the sale of oil to the United States, refused to cut production, not because she was any less impatient for the fray (Iraqi troops, after all, had been committed to the Syrian battlefront) but because she felt that such measures were not sweeping enough. At the OAPEC meeting in Kuwait the Iraqi oil minister, Saadun al-Hammadi, had argued passionately for the expropriation of American oil interests in every Arab country and the withdrawal of all Arab investments in the United States. When this was rejected the Iraqis went their own way, increasing their oil production during the period of the embargo and cut-backs, and selling it for whatever prices they could get. They even managed a further feat of pious larceny by 'nationalizing' Royal Dutch Shell's share of the Basra Petroleum Company, allegedly as a punishment for Dutch support of Israel.

The seizure of Shell's assets, which took place on 21 October, was prompted by the action of Algeria the previous day in banning the shipment of oil to the Netherlands. Kuwait scrambled to follow suit on 23 October, and before the month was out all the other Arab oil states had joined in. Ostensibly the reason for the embargo on the shipment of oil to the Netherlands was the 'hostile' attitude of the Dutch to the Arab cause, especially as demonstrated by their allowing volunteers on their way to Israel to travel *via* Schiphol airport, and by the contributions made by Jewish diamond brokers in Amsterdam to the Israeli cause. But a more pertinent reason was the function of Rotterdam as one of Europe's principal ports of entry for crude oil and the site of a great complex of refineries, which made it a major source of petroleum products for Western Europe. To impede the flow of oil through Rotterdam would make the effects of the restrictions upon production felt more quickly throughout the countries of the European Economic Community. Political calculations of a similar kind underlay the decision, first taken by Saudi Arabia on 20 October and later by the other oil states, to cut off oil supplies to South Africa. Such a move, it was confidently believed, would help persuade the black African states to take the Arab side in the conflict, particularly if it were to be accompanied by a liberal disbursement of funds, something the oil states could now well afford. The confidence was not misplaced: the dual appeal to prejudice and venality sufficed to obscure the centuries-old record of Arab spoliation in Africa and to unite the black African states in denunciation of Israel.

The same aim lay behind the grandiloquent announcement in early November that Portugal was to be included in the embargo, as much for her wickedness in holding on to her colonial possessions in Africa as for her perfidy in permitting the Azores to be used as a staging point in the American airlift of arms to Israel. There was one other state on the Saudi Arabian 'black list' – coupled with South Africa in the instructions given by Yamani to ARAMCO on 21 October – and this was the People's Democratic Republic of Yemen. Why such a rabid supporter of the Palestinian cause, which had armed, succoured and given refuge to all manner of Palestinian terrorists, should have been put under the ban of Riyad appears, at first sight, something of a mystery. But when it is recalled that the embargo, like the cut-backs, had as much contrivance as spontaneity in its composition, and also that it was designed to secure numerous ends and achieve multiple satisfactions, it becomes clear that the Saudis simply seized the chance to deal a blow at a regime which was ideologically repugnant to them. (It is possible, of course, that they were also influenced in their decision by the fact that – strange though it may seem – the Marxist government of South Yemen was continuing to allow the refinery at Aden to supply fuel to the American forces in Vietnar..)

For the implementation of the embargo and its associated restrictive measures the Saudi government relied wholly upon ARAMCO. The company was not only required to allocate oil in specified quantities to countries exempted from the embargo and others, like West Germany, Italy and Japan, to which limited amounts of oil were being supplied on sufferance; but it was also instructed to ascertain from its off-takers of crude what amounts of refined products they were supplying to the United States armed forces from their refineries outside the United States, e.g. in the Caribbean and the Pacific. ARAMCO was then obliged to subtract from the allocations of crude to the countries in which these refineries were located an amount equivalent to the aggregate amount of refined products supplied from these countries to the United States armed forces; and to make a further reduction in its production of crude from the Saudi fields by the same amount. The intention behind this purely vindictive measure was to prevent ARAMCO's parent companies from continuing to supply the United States forces overseas, and in particular the Sixth Fleet in the Mediterranean.

ARAMCO faithfully carried out the Saudis' instructions, never questioning, it would seem, either the propriety of such co-operation or the Saudis' right to require it. ARAMCO's prime concern appeared to be with its own fortunes, with the safety of its concession and with the preservation of its special relationship with the Saudi ruling house. It was also, to some extent, secretly relieved by the imposition of the cuts in production. For although in September it had set itself output targets of approximately 8.76 million b/d for October and 9.1 million b/d for November 1973, it was encountering, as indicated earlier, more and more technical difficulties in reaching and maintaining higher levels of production from its fields. As one of its senior engineers candidly confessed some months afterwards, ARAMCO was 'taken off the hook' by the embargo: without it, the company would have had to cut back production or risk doing permanent damage to the fields. What this admission leaves unanswered, however, is why ARAMCO allowed itself to be impaled on the hook in the first place; that is to say, why it strove so mightily to raise its production from 6.5 million b/d in February 1973 to 8.3 million b/d in September, an increase so spectacular as to raise fears, well before September, that the fields were in danger of being damaged. It certainly suited the Saudi government's book for production to reach a peak in September; for it was upon the September production figure that the subsequent cuts were to be based, and a high volume meant that output would still continue to be substantial – as well as profitable, in view of the near doubling of oil prices. As things turned out, even with a production cut which eventually reached 25 per cent at least, Saudi Arabia's oil output in the last quarter of 1973 was 3 per cent higher than it had been in the last quarter of 1972.

So far as Western Europe and Japan were concerned the oil weapon was designed to accomplish two general objects: firstly, to push the Europeans and Japanese towards a pro-Arab stand or, failing this, to a neutral position in the Arab–Israeli conflict; and, secondly, to arouse them to such a state of anxiety over whether or not adequate supplies of oil would be forthcoming that they would swallow without protest the simultaneous exorbitant increase in oil prices. The panic with which Western Europe (with one or two honourable exceptions) and Japan reacted to the oil restrictions could not have been more gratifying to the Arabs. Public figures of high and low estate fell over themselves in their eagerness to affirm their understanding of and indignation at the insupportable tribulations which had driven the Arab states to take up arms against Israel. The air above the capitals of Europe positively vibrated with the peal of platitudes about retribution and reconciliation and the trilling of rondeaus to peace and justice. Leading the antiphony were Britain and France, the two powers possessed of an implicit faith in their singular ability to get on with the Arabs. Moreover, they had good cause to bend the knee gladly, for they, along with Spain, had received assurances from one or another of the Arab oil potentates that they would continue to receive their accustomed supply of oil if they comported themselves properly. And so they did. Not long after the outbreak of hostilities the British foreign secretary, Sir Alec Douglas Home, announced the imposition of an embargo upon the shipment of arms from Britain to the combatants, a measure which, although blandly presented as fair and even-handed, happened, with agreeable fortuity, to bear more heavily upon Israel than upon the Arab states. For France no comparable step was necessary, since a virtual embargo upon the shipment of arms to Israel had been in effect since the 1967 war. Thus, in the last week of October the British prime minister, Edward Heath, was able to inform the House of Commons, with ample satisfaction, that the oil supply position for the United Kingdom was far from critical.

What was accorded less prominence was the undertaking which the British and French governments had given, in return, to those states which had provided the assurances of oil supplies (Saudi Arabia, Kuwait and Abu Dhabi) that they would not allow the re-export of oil elsewhere, least of all to the Netherlands. If any oil was diverted to the Dutch, the British government had been warned, Britain would suffer an immediate 25 per cent cut in supplies. It was further made clear that all the EEC countries would incur the same penalty if they attempted to pool supplies to help the Dutch. However, much though the British and French governments would have preferred it otherwise, the question of oil supplies to the Netherlands could not simply be swept under the carpet. The Dutch themselves were annoyed at being singled out by the Arabs for retaliatory action, and they rightly felt that they were entitled to help in their difficulties from their EEC partners. A meeting of the foreign ministers of the European Community was convened at Brussels on 5 November – not, it might be said, on British or French initiative – to discuss the oil crisis and the Netherlands' appeal for solidarity, particularly over the sharing of oil supplies. Ireland apart, the EEC states were also members of NATO, and the military as distinct from the economic repercussions of the embargo and restrictions on oil supplies should have been of no small consequence to them. Joseph Luns, the secretary-general of NATO, had expressed the opinion three weeks earlier that any stoppage of oil supplies to Western countries by the Arabs would be tantamount to a 'hostile act'. Since then oil supplies had been stopped to two NATO members, the United States and the Netherlands. Few of their allies, however, seemed to feel as strongly about the affront as did Luns; or, if they did, they managed most successfully to conceal their feelings in public. Their silence on the issue was in striking contrast to the sentiments of irritation and indignation, born of sheer funk, which they manifested over the actions of the United States during October in replenishing Israel's armoury and calling a strategic alert in response to muted sabre-rattling by the Soviet Union. Britain, West Germany and Italy all let it be known to their senior partner in the Atlantic Alliance that they were peeved by the use of American air bases in their territories – bases whose prime purpose was the defence of Western Europe – as staging-points for the American air-lift to Israel.

It was against this background that the Brussels meeting of foreign ministers took place on 5 and 6 November. Under the circumstances it was not in the least surprising that Sir Alec Douglas Home and the French foreign minister, Michel Jobert, should have made it their first, indeed almost their sole, concern to steer the attention of the conference away from the purpose for which it had been summoned and to direct it instead into the devising of obsequious gestures with which to appease the Arabs. Home made his intention clear on the night of 5 November when he said that

in the light of suggestions by Arab oil producers that they would impose an embargo on those countries who agreed to furnish the Netherlands with oil, it would be much better to see how Europe could influence a political settlement in the Middle East.

'Much better' for whom? For the Netherlands? For the EEC? Or for Britain and France, with their *sub rosa* guarantees of oil supplies, given on condition that they toed the Arab line and, by implication, persuaded the rest of the EEC to do likewise?

Home and Jobert got their way at Brussels, despite some initial opposition from the Danes and the Germans who wanted the conference to consider what it had been convened to do. The declaration issued in the names of the nine EEC states when the conference ended at midday on 6 November contained not a word about the oil crisis or the predicament of the Netherlands. Instead, it was wholly taken up with mawkish appeals to the Israelis and Arabs to respect the resolutions passed by the United Nations Security Council in the last week of October, to return to the cease-fire lines of 22 October and to enter into negotiations to secure a just and lasting peace between themselves. It ended with some sickly fudge about the states of the EEC recalling 'on this occasion the ties of all kinds which have long linked them to the littoral states of the south and east of the Mediterranean'.

The signatories of the declaration were pleased to describe it as a 'first contribution' by the EEC 'to the search for a comprehensive solution' to the Arab–Israeli problem, while Home extolled it as a 'success for the process of political consultations of the Nine'. In truth, it was something far less grand, being little more than a pathetic and contemptible attempt by the majority of the EEC to wriggle out of the obligations inherent in the Treaty of Rome, and to save themselves from any discomfort that a reduction in oil supplies might bring. How Israel was to regard such a biased concoction as a 'contribution' to 'a comprehensive solution' of her conflict with the Arabs defies understanding, especially as the admonition to the adversaries to retire to the cease-fire lines of 22 October was all too transparently a device to help the Egyptian Third Army to extricate itself from the trap on the east bank of the Suez Canal into which it had been forced by the Israelis since that date. It is equally incomprehensible why a document reeking of servility and pusillanimity should have had any effect upon the Arabs, other than to confirm them in the contempt in which they already held the powers of Europe. What other outcome could have been expected from the Brussels meeting when, in the same week, the Egyptian foreign minister called upon the British prime minister in London to proffer reassurances of the continued flow of oil and to receive in return assurances of an unrevealed nature? Or when, the day before the meeting began, the new arbiters of Europe's economic destiny, OAPEC, met in Kuwait and increased the cut-back in oil production from 10 to 25 per cent, with Yamani driving the message home with the ominous reminder that 'if any other European country tries to supply oil to the Netherlands, we will reduce our oil shipments to them in an equivalent amount'?

None of the major Western European powers saw fit openly to challenge the legality of the Arab oil embargo. Yet the embargo was a direct violation of a United Nations declaration of 1965 on the inadmissibility of intervention in the affairs of states, and of a further declaration in 1970 on the principles of international law governing relations between states in conformity with the charter of the United Nations. Both declarations affirmed in part:

No state may use or encourage the use of economic, political or any other type of measures to coerce another state in order to obtain from it the subordination of the exercise of its sovereign rights and to secure from it advantages of any kind.

Among the countries which had pressed hard for the adoption of these resolutions in the General Assembly on both occasions had been Algeria, Iraq,
Kuwait, Saudi Arabia, Libya, Syria and Egypt. (All seven were to be equally
vigorous in their support for another resolution – concerning permanent rights
of sovereignty over natural resources – adopted by the General Assembly on 17
December 1973 while the embargo was still in force. Two clauses in this
resolution, it is worth remarking, specifically deplored 'acts of States which use
force, armed aggression, economic coercion or any other illegal or improper
means in resolving disputes'.) Kuwait, the only signatory among the Arab oil
states of the General Agreement on Trade and Tariffs (1947), was in breach of
at least four provisions of that agreement – relating to restraints upon international trade – as a consequence of her participation in the embargo and her
allocation of oil supplies to consuming countries according to their arbitrary
classification by OAPEC as sympathetic, neutral or hostile to the Arab cause.
Needless to say, in all the tedious hours of partisan debate in the United
Nations unleashed by the Arab–Israeli war not a single member state so much
as raised the subject of these violations of that body's own statutes by the
governments of the Arab oil countries.

No Arab government, then or since, has publicly attempted to justify the
embargo and its accompanying punitive measures in the context of international law. The one lonely attempt to do so was made by the legal adviser of
the Kuwait Fund for Arab Economic Development, Ibrahim Shihata, in an
article in the *American Journal of International Law* in 1974. It was not a very
convincing presentation. According to Shihata, Arab oil production up to
October 1973 was 'an economic sacrifice that could only be interpreted as a
political favor to the consuming countries'. The embargo and the restrictions
on production were intended to put an end to 'the practice of doing favors for
countries whose foreign policy made them unworthy, in Arab eyes, of receiving such favors'. The categorization of concessionary agreements and contracts
between Arab governments and oil companies, not as solemn and binding legal
obligations but as 'political favours' is a novel concept in international law, and
a most illuminating one. It was by no means the limit, however, of Shihata's
inventiveness. The embargo, he explained, in an equivocation to make the
shade of Oppenheim blench, was 'an instrument of flexible persuasion meant
only to ensure respect for the rules of international order in the Middle East' –
by which he meant the end of the Israeli occupation of Arab lands and the
restitution of the rights of the Palestinians. The claim might have carried
slightly more conviction if the plight of the Palestinians had at any time figured
prominently in the negotiations conducted by the Arab governments with the
oil companies before October 1973. It is hardly necessary to say that it did not:
the subject under discussion was always and exclusively money. Moreover,
Shihata himself, in developing his case, confounded his own argument.
Discussing the decisions taken by the conference of Arab heads of state at

Algiers at the end of November 1973 (which will be described shortly), he stated: 'In response to a decision of the OAU Ministerial Council held in Addis Ababa on November 21 and attended by 42 African countries, the Arab Summit Conference decided also to impose an oil embargo against Portugal, South Africa and Rhodesia.' This act alone revealed that the political purposes of the embargo had gone well beyond the exercise of 'flexible persuasion' to bring pressure upon Israel in the Palestinian interest; and it is significant that Shihata makes no attempt in his article to justify it.

The failure of the United States to arraign the Arab oil-producing countries in the United Nations or elsewhere on charges of violating resolutions of that body to which they themselves had subscribed is perhaps more understandable, if no less reprehensible. For one thing, the United States had herself resorted to economic coercion against other states – notably, in recent times, Cuba and North Vietnam – and she was, therefore, vulnerable to taunts of *tu quoque*. For another, she was intimately involved in the efforts to resolve the Arab–Israeli conflict and consequently had to tread a careful diplomatic path. Yet again, the United States, with her own substantial oil production, was better situated than any of the other Western industrial nations to withstand an interruption of oil supplies from the Arab Middle East. For all this, however, the fact remained that the embargo imposed by Saudi Arabia was a contravention of the provisions of the Saudi–American commercial treaty of 1933, which stipulated that both parties should accord each other most-favoured-nation treatment in matters of trade, that is to say, neither party could impose discriminatory regulations or tariffs upon the other. The oil embargo, which was not applied to Britain, France, Spain or a number of other countries, was a discriminatory measure, yet the United States government took no legal action to contest it.

According to testimony given to the Senate sub-committee on multinational corporations two years later by James Akins, the American ambassador to Saudi Arabia in 1973, it was not until the embargo had been in operation for some months that the United States government contemplated taking a sterner line with the Saudis over its removal. Akins was instructed by the State Department (apparently in late February or early March 1974) to deliver an 'ultimatum' to the Saudi government, the nature of which he refrained from disclosing to the sub-committee. He thought it, however, 'inept and stupid', and told the State Department so at the time. He also took it upon himself to divulge his instructions unofficially to the Saudi deputy foreign minister, Omar Saqqaf, whose reaction to them, said Akins, 'was very strong and very negative'. Akins reported in this sense to the State Department, and the upshot was that the ultimatum was withdrawn, 'a very conciliatory message' was substituted for it and the embargo was lifted within two weeks. Omar Saqqaf had in the meantime (he later told Akins) shown the original instructions to Faisal, who had responded to them by saying that if the ultimatum had been presented he would have broken off diplomatic relations with the United States. It seems, all things considered, a fairly innocuous threat.

The action taken by Akins on this occasion would appear to have been consistent with his behaviour throughout the period of the embargo. Four days after its imposition he had urged ARAMCO to impress upon its parent companies in the United States the need 'to hammer home' to the United States government the point that 'oil restrictions are not going to be lifted unless [the] political struggle is settled in [a] manner satisfactory to [the] Arabs'. The message, he said, should be delivered in a 'clear unequivocal way'. Apart from being a most peculiar recourse for an ambassador to employ to influence the policy of his own government, Akins's advice to ARAMCO clearly indicates that the thought then uppermost in his mind was the necessity to placate the Saudis. He can only have been confirmed in this opinion by what he heard from Faisal's own lips less than a fortnight later, when he presented his credentials. The embargo and the restrictions on production would continue, Faisal told him, until Israel withdrew from all Arab territory. Furthermore, the king added, any increases in oil production in the future would be considered only in the 'right political atmosphere', i.e. when all the Arab lands had been recovered, the Palestinian problem had been resolved and an Arab flag flew over the Arab quarter of Jerusalem. 'I am an old man,' he told Akins dolefully. 'Before I die I want to pray in the Mosque of Omar.'

If the United States and the powers of Western Europe funked their duty in 1973, the major and independent oil companies did not. True to their character as international companies, they discharged their responsibilities to their customers conscientiously and fairly, allocating what oil was available on an equitable basis so that no consuming country was made to suffer more than another. The Netherlands was supplied with crude from Persia, Nigeria, Venezuela and elsewhere – including, interestingly enough, Libya, and (so rumour has it) the Soviet Union. Western Europe as a whole suffered a drop in supplies of only 11 per cent during the period of the embargo, while the United States experienced a fall of 6.9 per cent. The companies had to withstand a good deal of pressure from countries on the Arabs' 'white list' which saw no reason why they should suffer any diminution of supplies at all. Canada, for example, hinted at a curtailment of exports from her own oilfields to the Middle West of the United States if she did not receive the quantity of imported oil she wanted. She had her way, and her consumption of oil during the embargo actually rose 6.5 per cent over what it had been before. So, also, did Japan's, though only by 1 per cent. Little appreciation of the sense of responsibility and spirit of co-operation demonstrated by the oil companies was expressed by the British or French governments, both of which fondly believed that they had secured themselves against any reduction in supplies by their furtive exchanges with the Arab oil potentates. Edward Heath, who was running into domestic political difficulties as a consequence of his own mis-management of the British economy, was so incensed by the thought that Britain would fare no better for oil than her partners in the EEC that he summoned the chairmen of BP and Shell at the end of the third week of October to demand that they see to it that Britain was supplied with her normal needs. He was given in reply a curt lecture on the ethics and operations of the international oil industry.

For all its fawning upon the Arabs, Heath's government was still regarded with some suspicion by the fire-eaters in the Arab camp. When the Arab oil ministers met at Kuwait on 4–5 November to review the working of the embargo and, as we have seen, to increase the cut-back in oil production to 25 per cent, the Kuwaiti minister, Abdur Rahman al-Atiqi, vehemently expressed his dissatisfaction with the British attitude to the Arab cause. 'We appreciate the stand taken by France,' he said.

I personally do not appreciate the British position. The British government has allowed the collection of contributions to Israel and as many as £40 million have already been sent to Israel. To me, and as long as I live, Britain will remain the country which had permitted the founding of the State of Israel when it granted the Balfour Declaration.

It would have been useful to remind Atiqi that Britain was also the country which had enabled the state of Kuwait to come into existence and which for many decades had safeguarded it from its enemies. But perhaps it was too much to expect of any British government in recent years that it should venture to reproach a functionary of a minor Arab state for his impertinence. A week later the irrepressible Atiqi was vapouring again, this time against the countries of the EEC. 'Should they defy the Arab States by announcing solidarity with Holland publicly,' he blustered, 'then we shall take measures against them.' No European government had sufficient spirit to respond by pointing out that, if it was in order for the Arab oil states to band together to restrict oil supplies and raise prices for political and mercenary ends, it was equally in order for the Western industrial countries likewise to combine to resist such extortion.

While the fear and disarray among the Western nations were an undiluted source of gratification to the OAPEC ministers gathered at Kuwait in the first week of November, at the same time the ministers themselves were slightly apprehensive about the direction in which their policy might be taking them. Figures of 37.8 per cent and 31 per cent were being bandied about as the amounts by which Saudi Arabia and Kuwait respectively were said to have cut, or were about to cut, their oil output. (Neither figure was remotely true, as the production figures for both countries in the last quarter of 1973 eventually revealed.) Yet the original resolution passed by OAPEC on 17 October had required each member state to reduce its oil production only to a level which would not cause 'detriment to its national and Arab obligations' – which, translated, meant when a serious fall in revenue might result. While the greatly increased prices acted as a cushion against such a fall, the smaller oil states could not bring their production down to the levels of which the Saudis and Kuwaitis were boasting. A compromise, therefore, was necessary, and it was found in the 25 per cent reduction – in which, significantly, the proportion of oil normally exported to the United States and the Netherlands was included, thereby diminishing the impact of the cut. A further reduction of 5 per cent was scheduled for December.

A degree of uncertainty also reigned over the quantities of oil some consuming countries were to receive. (Kuwait and Abu Dhabi, for instance, had not yet supplied lists of approved countries to the oil companies.) France, Spain and Britain were on the 'most-favoured' list, along with certain Muslim countries. West Germany, Italy, Japan, India and Brazil were in the 'limbo' category, subject to a 10 per cent reduction in supplies. Denmark, Belgium and Luxembourg had apparently been overlooked. A good deal of attention was given to Japan's position, since the Japanese relied almost exclusively upon the Middle East for oil, and they were fearful of the possibility of any diminution in supply. In the last week of October the Japanese foreign minister had told the Arab ambassadors in Tokyo collectively that his government supported Arab demands for the restitution of territory occupied by Israel. This, however, was apparently not enough to satisfy the Saudis, who subsequently informed the Japanese government that it must break off diplomatic relations with Israel, and all economic ties as well, if it wished to acquire 'most-favoured' status for oil supplies. The Saudis also calculated that the Japanese, if they grew desperate at the prospect of an oil shortage, would importune the United States to diminish its support for Israel.

Japan was still in limbo in the third week of November when the OAPEC ministers assembled in Vienna for another meeting. By this time their governments had had time to digest the EEC declaration of 6 November, which they evidently found to their taste. For after the meeting on 18 November OAPEC announced that the additional 5 per cent cut in production due in December would not affect supplies to the EEC countries (the Netherlands, of course, apart) but would be deferred until January. The exemption, it was explained, was 'in appreciation of the political stand taken by the Common Market countries regarding the Middle East crisis'. The governments of Europe sighed with relief and turned to other preoccupations. They would have been wiser to have kept their eyes fixed on Vienna, where on 19–20 November OPEC held its regular semi-annual conference. On this occasion, as on others, the most strident voice to be heard was that of Jamshid Amuzegar, the Persian minister of finance. Conscious of his fiscal responsibilities, he assailed the oil companies for their miserliness, angrily complaining that since the beginning of October they had not come forward with any new proposals to ensure the onward and upward march of posted prices. 'We asked them for suggestions', he exclaimed indignantly, 'but they only talked to us about chaotic market conditions!' Quite understandably, for someone wholly absorbed in his portrayal of a man suffering the keenest umbrage, Amuzegar overlooked the fact that the chaotic conditions in the market had been caused not only by the Arab embargo and production cuts but also by OPEC's own action at Kuwait on 16 October in setting out a host of variables which were to be used in the calculation of posted prices.

It was decided at Vienna to hold an extraordinary conference of OPEC in a month's time, when the level of oil prices would be looked at again in the light of current market conditions. Meanwhile, Yamani and the Algerian oil minister, Belaid Abdessalem, were to undertake a tour of Europe's capitals with the ostensible object (which had been agreed at the OAPEC meeting in Kuwait on 4–5 November) of explaining the Arab position on oil to the EEC governments. Less obtrusively, they were to size up the chances of Europe's acquiescing in a further price rise. The arrival of the two ministers in Copenhagen, their first stop, coincided with a statement by the American secretary of state, Henry Kissinger, on 21 November that the United States would have to consider counter-measures if the Arab boycott continued for too long. Angered by this impiety, Yamani appeared on Danish television to denounce the United States and to say that the Arabs would respond to such provocation by reducing their oil production by 80 per cent. Saudi Arabia would not suffer any discomfort by doing so, he asserted, because with production at 20 per cent of capacity she would get $20 a barrel for her oil. 'It is the law of supply and demand.'

Yamani also had a word of warning for the industrial nations of the free world. 'I don't know to what extent Europe and Japan will get together to join the Americans in any kind of measures, because your whole economy will definitely collapse all of a sudden. If the Americans are thinking of a military action, this is a possibility, but this is suicide. There are some sensitive areas in the oilfields in Saudi Arabia which will be blown up.' Questioned the next day about the seriousness of this threat, Yamani hurriedly backed away from it, saying, 'That was not a threat.' His Kuwaiti counterpart, Atiqi, who was at the time gracing Paris with his presence, scorned such equivocation. The Arabs, he said, were ready to paralyse the economy of the Western world to secure their aims in the Middle East. 'Europe will suffer terribly if it does not help us.' And Saudi Arabia's representative at the United Nations, Jamil Baroody, whose oratorical incontinence had become a legend, demanded in the General Assembly on 28 November that Kissinger explain the 'sneaky, hypocritical terminology' of his allusions to counter-measures. 'What does he mean by counter-measures?' Baroody fulminated. 'Why doesn't he spell them out like a man of the third part of the twentieth century?'

This minor passage of arms was soon forgotten amid the jollifications which attended Yamani's and Abdessalem's progress through Europe. From

Copenhagen, where they had diplomatically refrained from suggesting that Denmark should be black-listed for its open support of the Netherlands, they went on to Paris and London. 'Paris is our friend number one and London our friend number two,' Yamani had announced expansively before he left Vienna, adding, by way of explanation, 'Any country to be qualified as a friendly country must assist in a very significant manner the Arab cause.' In Paris he and Abdessalem were banqueted at the Crîllon by senior ministers of the French government, and in London they were lunched by the foreign secretary in the state dining-room at Lancaster House. Everywhere ministers and functionaries scurried to attend upon them, to court their favour and seek their approbation. The press and the luminaries of television and radio hung upon their slightest word, their most inadvertent aside or subtlest inflexion, even the occasional weighty pause – all of which were breathlessly transmitted, with instantaneous oracular embellishments, to the anxious masses, mute and perplexed spectators of the hubbub and the fêting. It was a spectacle worthy to be captured on a vast and crowded canvas in the style of Tiepolo, depicting a throng of gorgeously attired dignitaries all pressing forward with beseeching gestures towards two proud figures standing sternly aloof, the whole tableau perhaps to be grandly entitled 'The Plenipotentiaries of Arabia and Mauretania receiving the submission of Britain and Gaul'.

Recrossing the Channel, Yamani and Abdessalem made for Brussels, where, Yamani had let it be known, they would be prepared to entertain any petition the Dutch might make for the restoration of oil supplies from Arab sources. However, he stipulated, if the Dutch wanted to be taken off the black-list, they would have 'to take a very clear-cut position condemning Israeli occupation of Arab ground and demand complete withdrawal from all Arab territory'. Furthermore, they would have to make some 'special gesture to repair the damage done' by their 'hostile action' against the Arabs in the early days of the war. On 1 December the Dutch minister of economic affairs, Ruud Lubbers, had a meeting with Yamani and Abdessalem. He refused to concede their demands and said that a 'special gesture' was out of the question. He told them that although the Netherlands had endorsed the EEC declaration of 6 November, the endorsement had caused his government 'some trouble and pain to achieve'. 'Holland's position', he said flatly, 'is the same now as it was on that occasion.' After the heady excitements of Paris and London the Dutch minister's uncompromising words came as something of an unpleasant surprise to the two envoys. Yamani suddenly complained of feeling unwell and retired to his hotel bed.

While he and Abdessalem had been tripping gaily through Europe the Arab heads of state had been in conference at Algiers. There were a few absentees. King Husain of Jordan did not attend, nor did President Ahmad Hasan al-Bakr of Iraq, who was disgusted with Egypt's acceptance of a cease-fire in the war. Muammar Qaddafi also boycotted the conference, ostensibly for the same reason, calling the gathering 'a rotten sell-out' and 'a bad musical comedy'. It was perhaps prudent of him to stay away, for he had tended to play the chocolate soldier during the war, breathing great gusts of fire and uttering blood-curdling threats but doing very little to actually aid the battle. Smarting from snubs received from both Sadat and Faisal, he had responded by imposing only a 5 per cent reduction in Libya's oil production and by turning a blind eye to the shipment of Libyan oil both to the Netherlands and to American refineries in the Caribbean. (He may also have decided that discretion was the better part of valour, out of a fear of possible Western retaliation against Libya, the nearest Arab oil state to Europe and the most defenceless.) Instead of going to the conference at Algiers he flew to Paris in the last week of November to attend a colloquium on the Middle East sponsored by *Le Monde*, *The Times*, *La Stampa* and *Die Welt*. Before he arrived he hinted that he would like his stay to be considered a state visit. Although this was refused, the French prime minister, Pierre Messmer, met him at Orly airport with a guard of honour, the ceremony being enlivened by the playing by the military band of the old, royal, Libyan national anthem. When Qaddafi departed a couple of days later he was seen off by Jobert, the French foreign minister. Before he left the Libyan leader tossed a characteristic apple of discord in the direction of the conference at Algiers. 'Any Arab country calling on Russian forces does not merit freedom,' he told a group of newspaper reporters. 'Better to have Israeli colonialism than Soviet troops in the area.'

The Algiers conference ended on 28 November. Among its decisions, most of which were concerned with the aftermath of the war, it confirmed the continuance of the full oil embargo against South Africa, Portugal and Rhodesia, so as to consolidate black African support. Japan, which had by this time made sufficiently humiliating amends for her sins of omission regarding Israel, and the Philippines, whose oil supplies had been reduced because her oil refineries were American-owned, were both exempted from the proposed additional 5 per cent cut in production due to take effect in December. Western Europe, which had already been exempted from the proposed cut, was put on notice that if it was to continue to receive adequate supplies of oil, it would have to 'take a clear and impartial position towards our just cause'. What was meant by 'impartial' was made clear by the secretary-general of the Arab League, Mahmud Riad of Egypt: 'Europe must therefore find every possible means to move away from its present position towards a recognition of Arab rights.'

Two days later, at a conclave of OAPEC ministers in Kuwait, it was agreed that the additional 5 per cent cut in production should be deferred to January. African and Muslim countries would not be subjected to the new restriction but would continue to receive their full quota of oil – so long as there was no possibility of re-exportation to countries on the black-list. The lifting of the embargo against the United States would be conditional upon the conclusion of an agreement, the implementation of which was to be guaranteed by the United States, providing for an Israeli withdrawal from Arab territories occupied in 1967 – 'including first and foremost Jerusalem', a proviso expressly inserted at the insistence of Faisal ibn Abdul Aziz. The withdrawal was to proceed according to a strict timetable, and the rate at which oil production would be restored to its previous levels would be geared to the progressive stages of the withdrawal.

All this was announced largely with an eye to the impending meeting of heads of government of the EEC due to take place at Copenhagen on 14 December. Although Europe had continued to display subservience to Arab wishes, there was always a faint chance that one or other of its governments might begin to sicken of the bread of servility and start behaving like a responsible power. The possibility agitated more than one Arab leader, and prompted an hysterical outburst from the president of Algeria, Houari Boumedienne, in the first week of December. 'If the West tries to be arrogant or to act by force,' he raved,

it will be subjected to a catastrophe; every single oil well will be set on fire. All the pipelines will be destroyed and the West will pay for it. . . . It takes only a few of our *fedayeen* to trigger a world catastrophe if the West gets too headstrong.

The Algerian president's philippic emboldened the ineffable Abdur Rahman al-Atiqi of Kuwait to pronounce his own fearsome malediction upon the West the following week. Categorizing Israel as 'a spoilt child' whom 'it was the West's duty to punish', he upbraided Western Europe and Japan for failing to come down firmly on the side of the Arabs.

These countries have been content until now to throw us kisses from afar. . . . We want a clear attitude and real co-operation. . . . If the West does not modify its attitude, it must expect the worst. . . . We will destroy everything in a short time if anyone tries to occupy our oil wells.

Atiqi knew full well, of course, that he was on safe ground in ranting thus. Only a few days earlier the ruler of Kuwait had received an impassioned plea from the British prime minister, now confronted with a national coalminers' strike, for a larger allocation of oil. It was hardly likely that the government of Edward Heath would have contemplated a desperate *coup de main* against the oil wells of Arabia. It was just not its style, then or at any time.

Most of this rodomontade in the first fortnight of December – there was more of it gushing forth from other Arab states – was designed, as indicated already, to soften up the EEC governments before the Copenhagen conference. There was little need for it: the European spirit was still palsied, despite the efforts of the American secretary of state to invigorate it, as he did in a public speech in London on 12 December when he proposed the creation by the Western industrial nations and Japan of an international energy agency to ensure their fuel supplies. The reluctance of the EEC governments to work together in resisting the extortive tactics of the Arab oil states was demonstrated all too plainly when the Copenhagen conference opened on 14 December. Originally the conference had been called on the initiative of President Pompidou of France to discuss the political development of the EEC. No real preparation had been made for it, however, even in the shape of prior consultations at lower levels of government. In any case, the general feeling seemed to be that its *raison d'être* had been eclipsed by the events of the previous two months. The minds of all the participants were preoccupied with the oil crisis, though not with plans to do anything constructive about it. Matters were made worse by the receipt of news on the eve of the conference that the foreign ministers of six Arab countries – Saudi Arabia, Algeria, Morocco, Tunisia, Sudan and the United Arab Emirates – were on their way to Copenhagen for the purpose, so it was said, of informing the heads of government of the EEC of the decisions of the Algiers conference.

The first two of these gate-crashers descended upon Copenhagen on the opening day of the conference. They were Abdul Aziz Bouteflika, the Algerian foreign minister, and Adnan al-Pachachi, a former foreign minister of Iraq (and cousin of Nadim al-Pachachi) who was temporarily acting as foreign minister of the UAE. It could scarcely be said of them that they represented countries of whose might the globe lived in dread, yet their mere appearance sufficed to cause consternation among the statesmen of Europe. What was their true mission? How were they to be received? What was to be said to them? (That they might simply have decided to come after hearing reports from Yamani and Abdessalem of the splendid hospitality dispensed by Europe's governments never seemed to occur to anyone.) The two envoys let it be known that they wanted an exchange of views with the EEC countries. Britain and France eagerly supported their request, but West Germany, Denmark and the Benelux countries were not prepared to do more than accord them a hearing. On the evening of 14 December the foreign ministers of the EEC waited upon Bouteflika and Pachachi at the Danish foreign ministry. What passed there was not made known publicly, although Pachachi afterwards told the press, 'We don't want to hurt Europe and create hardship. We do not want to blackmail you' – which was a droll interpretation, to say the least, of the existing situation. The rest of his message was a familiar one, which was repeated by Bouteflika at a crowded press conference the following day: Europe must take Israel severely to task for her sins; 'Europe must urgently reconsider its policies'.

Europe, in fact, in the persons of its assembled heads of government, had been doing so for the previous two days, and had only succeeded in confounding itself further. The German chancellor, Willy Brandt, tried to promote the idea of a common energy policy, as Kissinger had done a few days earlier, and to persuade his partners in the EEC to share the burden of oil shortages equitably by pooling their reserves. Heath and Pompidou had little room in their minds for any thought other than how best to propitiate the Arabs, who, they suggested, might be persuaded to enter into arrangements for the steady supply of oil in return for technical and industrial aid and a copious flow of European manufactures. Heath's attitude, which was largely instrumental in frustrating any hope of European solidarity, defies understanding. He sorely needed, and the ailing British economy even more, the financial assistance which would have been forthcoming from the regional development fund the Community was endeavouring to establish. The bulk of the money for the fund was to be subscribed by Germany; yet Heath refused to heed Brandt's call for equality of sacrifice in dealing with the oil crisis. Instead, he bent his efforts, as did Pompidou, towards appeasing the Arabs.

Nothing of the remotest consequence was accomplished at Copenhagen, except a further demonstration of Europe's infirmity of will. Even after the conference had ended uncertainty remained as to why Bouteflika and Pachachi had made their journey, especially as the foreign ministers of Saudi Arabia, Morocco and Tunisia never put in an appearance. The Sudanese foreign minister turned up when the conference was over, delivered himself of some *blague* about the Western world gobbling up the Arabs' oil as it had gobbled up Africa's grain ('bringing death and famine to millions') and disappeared into the *bled*. The dithering at Copenhagen, however, was immensely cheering to the oil ministers of OPEC, who were due to gather at Tehran the following week to decide how best to profit from the seller's market in oil. At auctions of participation crude held in early December bids of $16 a barrel, and even in one instance of $17.90 a barrel, had been made (although in some cases the buyers later revoked their offers). Europe and Japan were plainly sheep ready for the fleecing, and to this agreeable task the OPEC ministers applied themselves at Tehran on 22 December.

Before the proceedings opened, however, there was the customary, obligatory abjuration by Ahmad Zaki al-Yamani of any avaricious intent on the part of OPEC, a ritual patter which was an essential prologue, as well as a frequent epilogue, to any performance of OPEC's peripatetic sacred drama. While in London, Yamani had stated that the Arab oil states wished to establish an oil-pricing system which was 'fair and reasonable' to producing and consuming countries alike. 'We will be more than happy', he assured his respectful listeners, 'to sit down with the consumers and listen to their views and discuss with them our problems.' Three weeks later, while passing through Beirut on his way to Tehran, he graciously expressed his solicitude for the consuming countries' welfare. The high prices that oil was fetching at auction, he declared by way of comfort, should not be taken as a basis for determining the price of oil. '[They] reflect to a large extent the effects of the oil embargo and cut-back measures taken by the Arab oil-producing countries, and since these measures are of a political nature, they should not have an economic effect.' Yamani was prepared to go further to demonstrate the essential moderation of his views:

If we were to take these prices as a basis for revising Gulf postings we would ruin the existing economic structure of the industrialised countries, as well as of the developing countries, and very soon the entire amount of money available for financing international trade would not be enough to pay for our oil. We must be reasonable and act responsibly as members of the international community.

Dominus vobiscum: the blessing had been pronounced, only, alas, to prove so much mellifluous humbug a mere forty-eight hours later. OPEC met in conclave throughout 22 and 23 December, and when its meditations were over the shah called a press conference and spoke, as was his wont, *urbi et orbi*. The price of the Gulf marker crude was to go up on 1 January 1974 from $5.11 to $11.65 a barrel. Prices of other varieties of crude would be raised proportionately, according to the differentials laid down by the producing countries. The shah, who was rumoured to have pressed for a marker price of $20 a barrel, graciously explained that the new prices had been arrived at 'on the basis of generosity and kindness' – a delicate allusion, perhaps, to the season of the year in the West. However, he went on, launching into one of his familiar homilies, the Western industrial nations would have to mend their ways from now on.

They will have to realise that the era of their terrific progress and even more terrific income and wealth based on cheap oil is finished. . . . They will have to find new sources of energy, tighten their belts. If you want to live as well as now, you'll have to work for it.

To help the West adjust to a new regime of austerity, the shah advanced a new formula for the future determination of oil prices.

We must compare the price of oil with the other sources of energy – what is the real price for the extraction of shale, the extraction of gas, the liquefaction of coal? The price should be the minimum that you would have to pay to get shale, for example, or the liquefaction of gas or coal. . . . How much it costs you to exploit these other sources should be a basis for the cost of oil.

Two days later, on Christmas Day, the Arab oil ministers meeting in Kuwait announced, with a nice sense of occasion, the cancellation of the further 5 per cent cut in oil production projected for January. Instead, production would be increased by 10 per cent. The obvious connexion between the increase in prices and the increase in production was virtually ignored by government and press in Europe. Far from protesting against the 'whip-sawing' they had received, they submitted to it abjectly. The spinelessness of Europe's reaction was epitomized by an editorial which appeared in the *Financial Times* on 24 December. 'The new price level', it gushed, 'is designed to encourage the development of substitute sources of oil and energy.' The new price level was designed to do nothing of the kind; its sole purpose, whatever hypocritical balderdash Muhammad Reza Shah might utter, was to mulct the Western industrial nations of their treasure and to enrich OPEC. To see it as anything else was to indulge in fantasies, to make the cardinal error, to which the West was becoming increasingly prone, of attributing Western modes of thought to Eastern minds. Thus the same editorial went on: 'One reason for believing that the new policy is based on long-term thinking is the fact that many of the OPEC countries have no immediate use for the revenues that they will now earn.' Apparently it did not occur to the *Financial Times*, a newspaper devoted to the study of finance and economics, that money is power. Or that the Middle-Eastern oil states had a very good use to which to put their surplus funds, viz. to manipulate the economies of Western Europe and Japan and thereby influence their governments to do their political bidding. In any case, how often has the accumulation of substantial, or even vast, wealth inhibited individuals, corporations or governments from endeavouring to acquire yet greater riches? Certainly the shah, who had been the guiding spirit behind the redoubling of oil prices, had need of every dollar he could get to accomplish his grand designs. Hence his bizarre suggestion that the price of oil be determined by reference to the cost of its extraction from other mineral or natural sources. One wonders how he might have reacted to a counter-suggestion that the price of Western manufactures, and more particularly the advanced weaponry and aircraft he delighted in, should be equated to what they would cost if they were to be produced in Persia by the Persians themselves.

While the price increases of October 1973 had raised the estimated annual revenue, at 1972 levels of production, of OPEC's members to $30,000 million (it had been $7,000 million in 1970), those of December 1973 would, it was reckoned, net them an annual income of $80,000 million, or over eleven times what it had been three years earlier. Still OPEC was not satisfied, and when the organization held its first meeting of 1974 at Geneva on 7–9 January the delegates' first item of business – after congratulating themselves on the success of their spectacular 'sting' – was to see whether oil prices could not be raised even higher by the use of the Geneva agreement of June 1973, whereby the oil companies had undertaken to adjust posted prices monthly in accordance with fluctuations in the international value of the US dollar. Jamshid Amuzegar made his customary speech about the current strength of the dollar actually calling for a reduction in prices, then quickly passed on to the more pleasurable duty of declaring that any such reduction was rendered impossible by the rising cost of imported goods from the industrial countries. In his opinion the December oil-price increase was no more than 'adequate', and the rest of the delegates gravely agreed with him. They decided that there should be no downward adjustment of oil prices to compensate for the current value of the dollar, and that future price movements would depend upon the measures taken by the industrial nations to prevent the cost of their exports from rising. The latter condition was pretty cool, seeing that the fourfold increase in oil prices since October was bound to have an inflationary effect upon the economies of the oil-consuming countries.

A further decision of the conference was to abandon the principle adopted at the Kuwait meeting of 16 October that posted prices should always be 40 per cent above the market price of oil. Although the delegates would not admit it publicly, the decision was an acknowledgement of the impossibility of adhering to the formula in the chaotic market conditions which they themselves had created with the oil embargo, the production cuts, the huge price rises and a mass of complicated differentials for calculating the posted prices of the various crudes.

Finally, the OPEC delegates refused to institute a two-tier system of prices for the benefit of the poorer Afro-Asian oil-consuming countries. After all the impassioned rhetoric which had poured forth from the OPEC governments about unrestrained exploitation by Western 'imperialists' and the crying need to redress the economic balance between the rich industrial nations and *les damnés de la terre*, the refusal came as a great disappointment to those in the West who had set any store by this rhetoric. Yet if they had followed OPEC's actions at all closely over the years, instead of accepting its verbal outpourings at face value, they would not have had cause for disenchantment. When the plight of the poorer Afro-Asian countries in the face of rising oil prices had been brought to the attention of the OPEC delegates at Tehran in February 1971, with the suggestion that they be permitted to buy oil at a lower price, the delegates replied that a two-tier system of prices would lead inevitably to much of the cheaper oil ending up in Western hands through its re-sale by the Afro-Asian states. What the West had to realize, the OPEC delegates argued, was that the member states of OPEC were themselves 'under-developed' and had need of all the revenues they could get for their own use. If Europe, the United States and Japan were so concerned about the welfare of India or Tanzania or Colombia, the delegates added, they had ample means of their own with which to assist these countries. The reply left no doubt that, in the minds of the OPEC governments, considerations of magnanimity or compassion, if they existed at all, took second place to calculations of political and financial advantage. The Geneva conference of January 1974 and subsequent events merely confirmed the fact. All that the OPEC governments were prepared to do, in response to appeals made to them by the less affluent Afro-Asian states in the months which followed, was to offer loans and establish investment funds to help mitigate the adverse effects of higher oil prices on the latter's economies. In other words, they were prepared to return some of the money they had extorted from the poorer countries, taking good care as they did so that they received a *quid pro quo* in the form of political support at the United Nations and elsewhere.

There was no rising up in their wrath by the powers of Western Europe against this latest instance of OPEC's rapacity – far from it. Unnerved by the embargo and the production cuts, they could think of little else but ensuring future supplies of oil, regardless of cost. In vain did the United States secretary of the treasury, George Schultz, argue at a meeting of the industrial nations at

Rome in mid-January 1974 that the only way to avert an economic recession was for the oil-consuming countries to press in concert for a reduction of oil prices to sensible levels. In vain did the United States government urge its European allies to refrain from taking separate initiatives over oil supplies before they had discussed the possibilities of co-ordinated action at the conference which the United States was arranging in Washington for early February. Self-respect was thrown to the winds as the governments of Europe and Japan rushed to court the Arabs and the Persians, jostling and shoving one another in their eagerness to be the first to pay the Danegeld and to receive in return knowing nods and winks about future oil supplies.

On 9 January 1974 the French government announced that a preliminary agreement had been reached with Saudi Arabia (upon whom France relied for about a quarter of her oil supplies) for the supply of thirty million tons of oil over the next three years in exchange for refining and petro-chemical equipment. The agreement, between CFP and ELF–ERAP on the one side and Petromin, the Saudi government agency, on the other, was described as a 'pilot' scheme for a much more extensive arrangement between the two countries for the exchange of oil for industrial goods, including arms. While the French government obviously believed it had pulled off something of a *coup* by the arrangement, the sober truth was that the French oil companies had agreed to pay $10.80 a barrel for participation crude which they could have purchased through ARAMCO for $8.40 a barrel. On 24 January the French foreign minister, Jobert, arrived in Saudi Arabia on the first stage of a tour which was to take him, after Saudi Arabia, to Kuwait, Syria and Iraq. All manner of topics were discussed by him on this tour during the next fortnight – oil supplies, technical aid, economic co-operation, liquefied gas tankers, power stations, aircraft, and armaments galore. Everywhere he went Jobert urged the desirability of an early conference between the EEC countries and the Arab oil states to discuss both oil supplies and the need for close economic co-operation between the two blocs, a proposal which his listeners could not fail to interpret, as they were intended to, as a pointed snub to the United States and the forthcoming Washington conference.

While Jobert was on his travels, French ministers and officials elsewhere were feverishly negotiating a positive farrago of agreements, each one more wondrous than its predecessor. A Franco-Libyan protocol signed by the French premier, Messmer, and Major Abdul Salem Jallud (now prime minister in Qaddafi's 'cabinet') on 19 February envisaged the construction of nuclear power stations along the Libyan littoral, its transformation into a great agricultural region, and the creation of harbours, docks, desalination plants and telecommunications systems, all to be provided in return for certain quantities of oil, the price of which, as Jallud was careful to stipulate, would be fixed by the Libyan government alone. Even more sublime wonders were to be wrought by Franco–Persian collaboration, if a protocol signed on 9 February by the French minister of finance, Valéry Giscard d'Estaing, and the Persian minister of economy, Houshang Ansari, was to be taken at its face value. Contracts initially worth $3,000 million, and potentially $5,000 million over a ten-year period, were to be placed by the Persian government with French industries. Five nuclear power stations would be built, along with desalination plants, a gas liquefaction plant, a fleet of liquid-gas tankers, a petro-chemical complex, a giant steel mill and a natural-gas pipeline to Europe. Though oil supplies were not specifically mentioned, the whole purpose of the elaborate charade – which even referred to joint Franco–Persian ventures in oil exploration and exploitation in third countries – was to ensure a flow of oil to France.

What was more remarkable than these dreams of cloud-capp'd industrial Xanadus arising in the Middle East was that the French, after their recent experience in Algeria of the fragility of agreements of economic co-operation with Middle-Eastern governments, should have sought so eagerly, and with such haste, to repeat their mistakes. Perhaps, if the truth were known, they did not in their hearts believe that anything substantial would ever eventuate from these hurried transactions. Whatever the explanation, their behaviour was all too representative of the frenzy which gripped the governments of Western Europe and Japan in the early months of 1974. Along the golden roads which led to Riyad and Tehran, Kuwait and Baghdad, the dust swirled in unending clouds over the heads of Frenchmen, Britons, Germans, Italians, Japanese, Belgians and others, hastening in their thousands to attend at the courts of the oil dynasts. Vast and chimerical projects were floated in the shimmering air over these distant, sun-baked capitals – nuclear reactors generating limitless power, huge industrial complexes spewing forth steel and cement and aluminium, giant desalination plants ceaselessly gushing oceans of water to transform the deserts into gardens of Eden, great refineries and petro-chemical works, huge dry-docks and splendid harbours, where glittering argosies freighted with the world's treasures rode at anchor under the ensigns of old, Umayyad red and Abbasid black and Alid green – all conjured up by the *gulli-gulli* men of the industrial West and East for the delight and diversion of oriental princes, in whose hands lay the power to reward with streams of yellow gold from their overflowing treasuries and torrents of black gold from their capacious reservoirs.

Not all the Western ministers, officials, industrialists, merchants and entrepreneurs had to undertake the lengthy journey to remote parts to pay their respects to the new arbiters of their destinies. For some the road led merely to St Moritz, where the 'Shadow of God upon earth', Muhammad Reza Shah, had taken up residence in early January, to enjoy the skiing, as was his custom, and, on this occasion, to play the Grand Sophy receiving the homage of a cowed and timorous Europe. One after another the legates and emissaries of the defeated powers came, the West Germans, the French, the British, all with deferential step and anxious countenance. None sought the shah's goodwill with more zeal than the British chancellor of the exchequer, Anthony Barber, who, in company with the secretary of state for trade and industry, Peter Walker, flew to St Moritz on 24 January. The strike of coalminers and electricity workers, combined with the oil shortage, had compelled the Heath government to introduce a three-day working week in British industry on 1 January. Heath plainly felt his administration to be tottering, a belief which was perhaps more a reflection of his own gravelled state than it was of the actual political situation. There was an air of desperation, even of panic, in his dispatch of two of his senior ministers to intercede with the shah for help in overcoming his domestic economic difficulties.

Barber and Walker were accorded a fitting reception. They were met at the airport by a Persian who, according to an eye-witness, said he was not important enough to give his name. He was dressed, 'more suitably for the garden in rollneck sweater and baggy, brown trousers', and he had arrived in an unwashed Cadillac in which he was to escort the ministers to St Moritz. The shah, he said, was out skiing, and the finance minister, Amuzegar (the 'shadow of the Shadow of God'), was 'around – I think'.

The shah, when the two ministers were admitted to his presence, was most affable. He would grant Britain an extra five million tons of oil in 1974–5, he said, in exchange for British goods valued at something over £100 million, including chemicals, synthetic rubber and fibres, paper, newsprint and steel. He was also prepared to contemplate the development of a more intimate and extensive economic relationship between Persia and Britain, which would include Persian investment in British industry. A jubilant Walker returned to London to inform Parliament of his triumph. He drew special attention to the fact that the price for which he had obtained the oil, just over $7 a barrel, was much less than that paid for Persian oil at auction a few weeks earlier. So it was, but the auction prices were generally acknowledged to be freakish, and the price of $7 a barrel was what the Persian government would have received in tax and royalties from the new posted price of $11.65 a barrel, and exactly what BP, who were forced to accept this oil whether they wanted it or not, would have paid for it anyway. The other side of Walker's 'bargain' was even less of an accomplishment. Some of the goods to be bartered in exchange for oil, notably chemicals and rubber, were in short supply in Britain herself. Moreover, the goods as a whole were to be supplied at prices fixed at the time of the agreement's signing, regardless of any fluctuations thereafter. By the time that the last shipment had been dispatched the total cost of the goods had risen to £123 million, exclusive of the administrative expenses incurred by the British government in handling the whole transaction. So the real cost of the 'cut-price' oil was around $9 a barrel, or about $2 a barrel more than it would have cost if it had been purchased from BP or one of the other partners in the Persian consortium.

While Walker had been demonstrating to the House of Commons his grasp of oil economics Barber had been closeted with the shah and Amuzegar discussing high finance, including the possibility of the Persian government's increasing its holdings of sterling in London. Whether anything more was discussed, such as an outright loan by the shah to the British government, was not immediately apparent. Barber was evasive afterwards about the topics of conversation, and the shah denied to a newspaper correspondent ten days later that he had promised the chancellor a direct loan of $1,000 million. While there was doubtless substance to his denial, nevertheless before many weeks had passed the sum of $500 million had been made available to the British government, the first *tranche*, so it was said, of a larger loan. It came much too late to restore Edward Heath's political fortunes. Unnerved by the intransigence of the coalminers, he called a general election on the issue of 'Who governs Britain?' – a question which must have provoked a high degree of mirth in Riyad and Tehran. The election brought defeat for Heath and the eclipse of his political career. Yet, if he had cared to reflect upon it at all objectively, he might have seen that he had himself sown the seeds of that defeat in his first few months in office, when he and his Cabinet failed to back the Western oil companies in their stand against OPEC at Tehran in January 1971, and at the same time allowed themselves to be persuaded by their advisers in the Foreign Office to retract their undertakings about the maintenance of a British presence in the Gulf – electing instead to strike 'a *suq* bargain' with those who, for their own purposes, wanted the British to leave. Less than two years after the British withdrawal came the Arab oil offensive of October 1973, which exacerbated the effects of the coalminers' strike in Britain and in turn brought nemesis down upon Heath's own head.

It is hard to see any injustice in the outcome. For in their years in office, and more especially in their final months, Heath and Home, together with the officials who stood in the shadows and advised them, dragged the name of British foreign policy in the dust. Despite all their highly publicized protestations of adherence to the ideal of a united Europe, theirs was not an England which, in the weeks between October 1973 and February 1974, saved herself by her exertions and Europe by her example. Blinkered self-interest was what largely motivated British foreign policy in the critical years of the Heath administration – as it had, for the most part, animated the foreign policy of the Wilson administration which had preceded and now was to succeed it. Never, perhaps, in British history has the reputation of Britain in the world been brought so low as it has been in the last dozen years or so. The conduct of the nation's affairs abroad and at home has been marked by futility, duplicity and cowardice; the political air is rank; and the lion and unicorn have yielded place on the arms of the kingdom to the weasel and the natterjack.

It would serve little purpose to rehearse in any detail here the ebb and flow of relations between the Western industrial nations and the Middle-Eastern members of OPEC since the early weeks of 1974. While the sequence of events over the past five years is well known, they do not form sufficient of a pattern to give shape to a narrative. The remainder of this chapter, therefore, will be given over to reflections upon some of the dilemmas which continue to face the Western world in treating with the oil-producing states of the Middle East.

The embargo upon the shipment of oil from Arab countries to the United States was lifted on 18 March 1974, and that upon oil exports to the Netherlands, Portugal and South Africa some time later. The memory of the embargo, however, and of OPEC's successful double 'sting' in the latter months of 1973, persisted, especially in the Arab world, where it served to heighten the mood of Muslim revivalism which has been sweeping the Middle East this past decade and more, and of which the embargo and the 'sting' themselves were an expression. The reaction of Western Europe to the oil offensive, as we have seen, was an unedifying exhibition of *sauve qui peut*. Old alliances, mutual obligations, common decencies, all were trampled under foot in the headlong rush of the powers of Europe to propitiate the Arabs and ingratiate themselves with the shah. It must rank as the most humiliating episode in the history of Western Christendom since the collapse of the last Crusade – which is exactly how the Arabs saw it. 'It is our revenge for Poitiers!' exulted an official of an Arab oil state in December 1973, harking back over twelve centuries to the defeat of the Arab armies by Charles Martel in 732. 'We shall do as Samson did: we shall destroy the temple with all its occupants, ourselves included!' spluttered Colonel Qaddafi in late October 1973, adding, in an echo of Ahmad Zaki al-Yamani's threat of the previous February, 'Europe should watch out for the catastrophe which lies in wait for it. . . . I have made my preparations – as have the other Arabs – to deprive Europe completely of oil. We shall ruin your industries as well as your trade with the Arab world.' Similar rodomontade, it will be recalled, was to be heard in the remaining weeks of 1973 from, among others, Houari Boumedienne, the Algerian president, and Abdul Rahman al-Atiqi, the Kuwaiti oil minister.

Outbursts like these reveal the true nature of the emotions and aspirations which underlay the oil embargo, the production restrictions and the quadrupling of oil prices, emotions which still continue to govern the conduct of the Arab oil states and Persia in their intercourse with the West. Stripped of their specious justifications about past Western exploitation and the intolerable affront to Arab susceptibilities afforded by the existence of Israel, the actions of the Arabs and the Persians before, during and since 1973, if placed in their historical, religious, racial and cultural setting, amount to nothing less than a bold attempt to lay the Christian West under tribute to the Muslim East. To the Arabs, the peculiar conjunction of economic circumstances since the autumn of 1973 has offered a singular opportunity to behave as though the power and grandeur of the Umayyad and Abbasid caliphates has been restored. For the former shah it provided a chance to behave as though the Safavid empire still held gorgeous sway over a submissive East. Far removed though these extravagant fancies may be from the realities of the international balance of power, the yearnings and passions which give rise to them are actual enough, and infinitely more potent and seductive to those who experience them than the cooler intimations of reason.

These dreams and expectations were given full rein at the conference of heads of state of member countries of OPEC at Algiers in March 1975. The participants in the conference made no secret of their determination to use their control of the greater part of the proven reserves of crude oil in the world to force, if they could, a massive shift of wealth and resources from the Western industrial nations and Japan to the economically backward countries of Asia and Africa, and to widen the area of conflict between the two groups of nations from that of oil alone to embrace all the raw materials produced by the Afro–Asian states. The temper of the conference was shown by the 'solemn document' issued at its close, which harped upon the necessity for the 'adequate and timely' transfer of modern technology from the industrial countries to the 'developing countries', and for 'the removal of the obstacles that slow the utilization and integration of such technology in the economies of the developing countries' – a programme which seemed to call for the education and technical training of the greater part of the populations of Asia and Africa at the expense of the West and Japan.

'The price of petroleum', the document continued,'must be maintained by linking it to certain objective criteria, including the price of manufactured goods, the rate of inflation, the terms of transfer of goods and technology for the development of OPEC member states.' To remind the West of its dependence upon the goodwill of OPEC, and of its need to tread carefully if it wished to retain this goodwill, the document also recorded the displeasure of its signatories at 'the threats, propaganda campaigns and other measures' which had been mounted in some quarters in the West in an endeavour to affix blame on OPEC for the economic depression then overtaking the industrial world. Such campaigns, the document warned, should cease forthwith, along with 'any grouping of consumer nations with the aim of confrontation' – a reference to the International Energy Agency which had been established by sixteen of the OECD nations in November 1974 with the prime object of ensuring adequate oil supplies for its members in the event of any future embargo or politically motivated cut-backs in production. The OPEC governments were also displeased with the authorization by the United States Congress a short time earlier of the creation of a National Strategic Petroleum Reserve of 1,000 million barrels by 1981, a move which they characterized as 'aggressive'. However, they were prepared to overlook these transgressions and to continue to meet the 'essential requirements' of the industrial countries for oil, provided that these countries did not erect 'artificial barriers' to impede the normal operation of the laws of supply and demand – which was a pretty conceit coming from the world's most brazen cartel. Finally, the OPEC governments affirmed that they were prepared to approve in principle the convening of a conference of industrial and under-developed countries to consider the question of future oil prices and supplies; but only on condition that all the producers of raw materials in the world were represented and that the agenda included both the prices of raw materials and the reform of the international monetary system.

The Algiers conference merely enunciated once again the argument which OPEC had been using since the Tehran 'settlement' of February 1971, and is still using, to justify the continual raising of oil prices. It rests primarily upon two assertions: one, that inflation in the industrial countries has increased the cost of imports to OPEC's member states; the other, that compensation must be afforded for past exploitation by Western oil companies. Neither of these meretricious simplifications has any validity. The mean rate of inflation in the OECD countries in 1971 was 4 per cent. It rose to 7 per cent in 1973 and to 12 per cent, its highest point, in 1974. By 1976 it was down to 8 per cent, yet in that year alone OPEC's revenues increased by 16 per cent, and a further 10 per cent price increase was imposed by the organization at its conference in Qatar in December. Taken as a whole, the increase in the posted prices of crude oil between 1970 and 1974 was of the order of 800 per cent. By January 1977 it was approaching 1,000 per cent, and in July 1979 it exceeded 1,500 per cent.

Muhammad Reza Shah was one of the foremost proponents of the argument that the price of oil (as well as the prices of all the commodities produced by the economically backward countries of the world) should be geared both to the prevailing level of inflation in the industrial countries and to the cost of production of the goods which the oil-producing countries and other producers of raw materials were importing. Yet it is interesting to note that while the consumer prices index in the United States rose from 100 in 1955 to 187 in 1974, the index price of Persian oil rose during the same years from 100 to 621, and has kept rising ever since. As for the cost of raw materials, it might be remarked that while in some cases, notably those of sugar and copper, prices have dropped dramatically in recent years, there has been no fall, but rather the opposite, in the posted price of Persian and other OPEC oil. Moreover, there was never any sign of the shah's insisting that the price of oil be tied to that of the sugar Persia imported, or of his offering to reduce the price of oil exported from Persia to sugar-producing countries. To take another example of the selective application of the theory that the cost of imports and exports should be regulated by the cost of their production. The marginal cost of production of Saudi Arabian oil is roughly 15 cents a barrel, that of Kuwaiti oil about 10 cents a barrel. A posted price of $18.00 a barrel, such as obtained in the case of Saudi Arabia from 1 June 1979, is equivalent to 12,000 per cent of the cost of production; while a posted price of $19.50, such as Kuwait imposed from 1

July 1979, is equivalent to 19,500 per cent. It is hard to think off-hand of any Western manufacture which is priced comparably.

The inflation of which the OPEC governments complain has to a large extent been generated in their own countries. The thousands of millions of dollars that have flowed into the oil states of the Gulf since 1970–71 have pushed up the prices of goods and the cost of skilled labour to giddy heights. This was inevitable, given the huge sums of money involved, the carelessness with which they were spent, and the determination of all sections of the populations of these states to profit from the vast windfall. It did not require a rise in the cost of imports from the industrial countries to create inflation in these states: it was a home-grown product, brought about by an impatience to possess in profusion, and in the shortest possible time, not just the manufactures of the West but also, if possible, the entire infrastructure and superstructure of a modern Western economy. Skilled labour was scarce, so that construction costs soared. Foreign firms were forced to take on local partners who contributed nothing of value to any enterprise but added greatly to its cost. A reckless multiplicity of orders and contracts for every imaginable artefact and service generated follies by the score, as epitomized by the importation of a shipment of sand from England to equip a swimming resort in Saudi Arabia. So great were the quantities of goods and materials purchased that the rudimentary port facilities of the Gulf states were overwhelmed by them. The charges for their transport soared, as ships waited off-shore for weeks, or even months, on end to discharge their cargoes, the intrinsic value of which was, in many cases, a mere fraction of the cost of their shipment. When to these countless mercantile follies and the administrative blunders which accompanied them are added the millions upon millions of dollars, dirhams, riyals and dinars – how many millions no one will ever know, though the total must be enormous – absorbed by the swarm of middlemen, commission agents, influence pedlars, courtiers, placemen, touts and pimps of every hue and description frantically engaged in the soliciting and obtaining of contracts, the charge that inflation has been exported to the Gulf oil states from the West may be seen for the *canard* it is.

The argument based upon past exploitation by the oil companies and the compensation due in consequence is equally false. One could argue with as much validity that the oil industry in the Middle East is virtually a gift from the West, that before the coming of the oil companies the Arabs and Persians knew neither what they possessed nor what to do with it if they had known, and that the discovery and exploitation of their oil amounted to a charitable enterprise on the part of Western philanthropists. Whatever flavour of moral lollipop one elects to suck upon when contemplating the development of the oil industry in the Middle East, the fundamental truth cannot be avoided that since the end of the Second World War the governments of the Middle-Eastern oil states have, without contributing a scintilla of effort, capital or skill of their own, acquired vast fortunes and been treated by the rest of the world with gratifying deference. Their accusations of exploitation stem almost wholly from a comparison between the prices paid for crude oil from the Gulf fields with those obtained by domestic producers in the United States, a comparison which, for obvious reasons, not the least being the relative costs of production, is both illogical and irrelevant.

Although the great number and variety of oilfields in the United States makes it difficult to estimate the average cost of production of a barrel of American oil, a figure of between $1.50 and $2.00 would not be too wide of the mark. The cost of production in Kuwait, as we have seen, is 10 cents a barrel (a few years ago it was about 6 cents), while in the Middle East as a whole it is 25 cents. The official selling price of the Gulf marker crude in the summer of 1979 was $18.00 a barrel, which was equivalent to 180 times the cost of production in Kuwait, and over seventy times the average cost in the Middle East in general. A comparison of the financial returns enjoyed respectively by the Middle-Eastern oil states and the oil companies reveals a like imbalance. In 1960 these states received a total of $1,720 million in revenues, while the companies earned a similar sum. In 1970 the oil states received $4,500 million in revenues, the companies $1,685 million. In 1974 the oil states received $76,500 million, the companies $1,516 million. Later figures show an even more monumental imbalance. One can only conclude that if the oil states of the Middle East have been exploited in any way, it is surely the type of exploitation which the great mass of mankind would welcome with open arms.

The extent of the riches which the Middle-Eastern oil states have accumulated during the present decade is well-nigh impossible to ascertain, for the owners are conspicuously shy of revealing the degree of their wealth and may even, in some cases, be uncertain themselves of exactly how many millions or milliards they command. From time to time figures are put out by government bodies and other institutions in the West – among them the United States Treasury, the Bank of England, the International Monetary Fund, the Bank for International Settlements, the major international commercial banks and the oil companies – as estimates of the size of the financial surpluses built up by these states. While the figures, not surprisingly, do not agree, they approximate sufficiently to permit some tentative conclusions to be reached about the extent of these surpluses. It must be recalled, furthermore, in assessing the significance of these surpluses, that they represent the residual disposable funds of the oil-producing countries after all expenditures have been met, expenditures which, in the case of the Gulf states, are among the highest *per capita* in the world.

According to the United States Treasury in May 1977, the thirteen members of OPEC had total reserves of $6,000 million before 1973. By the end of the first quarter of 1977 these reserves had grown to $145,000 million. Another estimate from the same source in September 1977 put the combined surplus of the OPEC member states from the beginning of 1967 to the end of 1973 at $15,000 million, and their combined surplus for the three years 1974–6 at $140,000 million. United States government witnesses before a sub-committee on foreign economic policy of the Senate Foreign Relations Committee in September and October 1977 reckoned the surpluses for these same three years at $133,000 million, with a further $45,000 million being added during 1977. The Bank of England in April 1978 put the three-year total slightly lower, at $128,600 million, of which $56,400 million was accumulated in 1974 (out of revenues of $94,500 million), about $36,400 million in 1975 and $35,800 million (out of revenues of $113,000 million) in 1976. There is reason to believe, however, that the surplus for 1976 was higher, viz. $42,000 million, out of combined revenues of $116,600 million. The rate of growth of the financial surpluses of OPEC's member states varied considerably. At the end of 1970 Persia's foreign exchange reserves stood at $208 million; by July 1976 they were $8,426 million. Saudi Arabia in 1970 had international reserves of $662 million; in June 1976 they were estimated at $24,700 million. Even this large figure was a gross underestimate, for the country had received oil revenues of $22,600 million in 1974, $25,700 million in 1975 and some $17,000 million in the first six months of 1976. The true extent of Saudi Arabia's foreign currency reserves, as we shall have occasion to notice later, must be in the region of $50,000–$60,000 million, unless some spectacularly scandalous mis-appropriation of the country's finances has occurred of late years. What Kuwait has built up in foreign exchange reserves is difficult to ascertain, for the Kuwaitis are highly sensitive about such delicate matters. But it must be a sizable amount, since the shaikhdom's oil revenues rose from $1,581 million in 1970 to $10,686 million in 1974, dropped to $8,565 million in 1975 and again reached over $10,000 million in 1976.

The foregoing figures for the OPEC financial surpluses apply almost exclusively to the Middle-Eastern members of the organization, and the bulk of these surpluses of late years has been accruing to only three countries – Saudi Arabia, Kuwait and the United Arab Emirates (which means, in effect, Abu Dhabi). In 1976 these three states received oil revenues of $47,000 million, or 41 per cent of the OPEC total, of which they retained as surpluses anything between $32,000 million and $37,000 million. What they retained in 1977 is not known with any exactness: OPEC itself estimated the surplus for the year at $35,000 million, while the United States Treasury put it at $45,000 million. Whatever the case, the three Gulf states in question were expected to accumulate 90 per cent of the surplus. If oil prices and rates of production continued at their then levels (so both the OECD secretariat and the US Treasury forecast in 1977), the total disposable surpluses of the Middle-East members of OPEC would reach something like $250,000 million by 1980, most of it in the treasuries of Saudi Arabia, Kuwait, Libya and Abu Dhabi.

By the same calculation, the corresponding deficit incurred through the purchase of oil by the twenty-four nations of the OECD would be about $110,000 million, and that of the non-oil-producing countries of Asia and Africa some $160,000 million. If oil prices increased before 1980 (as they have), the surpluses and the deficits would grow proportionately; for at the average annual rates of oil consumption in the world an increase of one per cent in the price of oil operates to raise the OPEC surplus by $1,000 million. The essential inference to be drawn from these figures is plain, viz. that the enrichment of the Middle-Eastern oil states is being achieved by the gradual deterioration of the trading position of all but the economically strongest nations of the world.

According to the testimony cited earlier, given before the foreign economic policy sub-committee of the United States Senate in September 1977, the aggregate deficit between 1971 and 1973 of all countries in the world on their current trading accounts was, on average, $15,000 million per annum, making a total deficit for these three years of $45,000 million. In the three years 1974–6, that is, after the fourfold increase in oil prices, the annual aggregate deficit rose to an average of $75,000 million, which added up to a total of $225,000 million for the three years. The significance of this rapidly growing deficit might perhaps be made clearer by showing its impact upon individual countries. Denmark's foreign trade deficit, which was $715 million in 1972, rose to $2,400 million in 1974 and exceeded $3,000 million in 1976. New Zealand, which had a trade deficit of only $16.6 million in 1971, registered a deficit of over $1,000 million in the year July 1974–June 1975 alone. Spain recorded a deficit of $5,700 million in the first eight months of 1976, Britain owed its creditors over $22,000 million in the spring of 1977, while Italy admitted debts of $16,000 million and probably owed more.

The grievous effects of the oil-price rises upon the less fortunate countries of Asia and Africa requires little emphasis. OPEC, as noted earlier, has consistently refused to operate a two-tier system of prices for the benefit of the poorer Afro–Asian nations, on the pretext that oil sold at the lower price would eventually find its way into the hands of the Western industrial powers. OPEC has also, in the main, fought shy of contributing to international or regional funds established to provide financial aid to economically backward countries hard hit by the surge in oil prices. The reluctance is due primarily to the objections of the richer members of the organization to the lack of control they would exercise over the selection of recipients and the way in which the funds would be expended. They prefer, and this is particularly true of the Arab oil states, to decide for themselves individually to whom to extend financial aid, if any.

Obviously the motives behind this attitude are political, or religio-political, and this is borne out by what is known of the grants, loans and investments made by the Arab oil states to African and Asian countries in the past few years. The principal recipients of these disbursements have been the so-called 'front-line' Arab states, Egypt, Syria and Jordan, the money going to shore up their economies and defences in the struggle against Israel. Next in line have been poorer Arab countries like the Sudan and the Yemen Arab Republic, and Muslim states like Pakistan and Malaysia. Pakistan, in particular, enjoys considerable favour in the eyes of the Gulf states. Grants and loans to black African states have been of far smaller dimensions, and their apportionment has been decided almost exclusively on political grounds, some of them of a highly dubious character, as in the case of Uganda, where the execrable Idi Amin was kept in power largely by Libyan money and Palestinian mercenaries.

OPEC's aggregate revenues in 1975 amounted to $94,700 million, of which more than three-quarters were received by the Arab oil states and Persia. The amount loaned by these states to black African countries in the same year was under $500 million, or about 0.5 per cent of the OPEC total. It was reported in 1976 that a total of $5,200 million in aid had been promised or committed by the Middle-Eastern oil states to other Afro–Asian countries. In fact, actual disbursements barely reached $2,000 million, 90 per cent of which went to Arab or other Islamic countries, with the 'front-line' Arab states receiving the largest portions. Saudi Arabia's aggregate oil revenues for the years 1974, 1975 and 1976 were in excess of $80,000 million. Her loans and grants to black Africa in the same period were said to total nearly $1,000 million, or 1¼ per cent of her revenues. At the Afro–Arab conference in Cairo in March 1977 Saudi Arabia undertook to provide the African states with a further $1,000 million over an unspecified period of time. Whether the money was to be in the form of investments, loans or outright grants was not explained. Within two months the Saudi government had had second thoughts about honouring its pledge, and the outcome of the whole affair is shrouded in mystery. At the same conference Kuwait, Qatar and the UAE engaged to invest $350 million in black Africa over a term of five years. (Over the preceding three years these states had received an aggregate of $46,800 million in oil revenues.) Whether the engagement is fulfilled remains to be seen.

The total indebtedness of the countries of Asia, Africa and Latin America (the ill-named 'Third World') at the end of 1976 was estimated by the United States Treasury in September 1977 to be, at the very least, $150,000 million. It could be as much as $30,000–$40,000 million higher. The Bank for International Settlements in Basle, which arrived at much the same figure as the US Treasury, added the rider that it had omitted from its calculations the private external debt of the countries concerned, which, it said, might amount to as much as $30,000–$40,000 million. It also made the highly pertinent comment that the governments of some economically backward countries were unsure of exactly how much money they had borrowed. The cost to the countries of Asia, Africa and Latin America of servicing their external debt increased between 1973 and 1976 from $13,000 million to $26,000 million per annum. Yet while a considerable portion of their total indebtedness was directly attributable to the steep increase in oil prices in these years ($78,000 million was added between 1974 and 1976), the OPEC governments, as we have seen, have refused by and large to help solve the financial problems which they have had a major hand in creating. Instead, it has been left to the Western banking system to underwrite the financial deficits of the indigent Afro–Asian countries. Up to the middle of 1977 Western commercial banks alone had loaned almost $75,000 million to these countries – some of which have been teetering on the edge of bankruptcy for years. Should they be driven through any reason to repudiate their foreign debts, the financial consequences for the Western world would be serious in the extreme.

Meanwhile OPEC's member states have been investing the bulk of their surplus funds in the West. A rough and ready calculation of the several ways in which these funds have been invested was submitted to the United States Senate sub-committee on foreign economic policy in September 1977. It showed that the member governments of OPEC (which meant, in effect, the Middle-Eastern members) had invested $48,000 million in Western government securities, stocks and real estate; $49,000 million in Western commercial bank deposits; $9,750 million in loans to international financial organizations; $16,000 million in loans and grants to 'developing countries' (mainly, that is, to other Arab and Muslim states); and an unascertainable sum in loans to Eastern European countries. At least $10,000 million – and possibly as much as $15,000 million – was unaccounted for.

The investment of their financial surpluses in the industrial West by the Middle-Eastern members of OPEC has been accompanied by a sustained effort on their part, either directly or through the medium of Western financiers, politicians and publicists, to persuade an uneasy Western public that no potential danger or conflict of interests resides in the injection of these surpluses into the Western economic system. The arguments deployed in support of this proposition have become sufficiently well known by dint of assiduous repetition to require no extensive restatement here. The surpluses are represented either as the proceeds of normal trading, or as the natural consequence of high prices being obtained for a commodity in limited supply, or even as a form of compulsory saving imposed upon the Western industrial nations by OPEC out of a disinterested solicitude for their economic welfare. Some Western apologists go so far as to suggest that the mulcting of the West is a punishment for its sins – for its affluence, for its materialism, above all for its indifference to the less fortunate masses of Asia and Africa. Others counsel us to regard the unrelenting extraction of vast sums from the coffers of the West by the Arabs and Persians, and their expenditure of them as they see fit, as an act of Providence, the only seemly response to which is unquestioning submission; or as akin to a force of nature, to the existence of which we must adjust ourselves with a decent fatalism. At the same time, and without any apparent conscious appreciation of the contradiction, the governments of Britain,

France and the United States, among others, have assured their peoples that the foreign and finance ministries of the West, along with the international financial community, are diligently applying their not inconsiderable alchemical powers to the task of transforming the surpluses into a golden windfall for the West. Through the occult process of 'recycling', it seems, a substantial part of the money poured out for the purchase of oil over the past half a dozen years is to be recouped by inducing the magnates of OPEC to invest in the West, to embark upon expensive projects in their own countries, and to consume the greater part of their oil revenues in lavish expenditures upon Western goods, armaments and services.

A few observers – a very small minority, if their number is to be judged by the rarity with which their views appear in the public prints – are far from sanguine about the feasibility of coping with the OPEC surpluses by 're-cycling', or other forms of Western financial sorcery. Although the reduced world demand for oil in 1977 and 1978, and the consequent surreptitious price-cutting by OPEC members hungry for revenue, may have reduced the financial surpluses for these years below the figures predicted by the OECD secretariat and the US Treasury in September 1977, the reduction may well prove to have been a transient phenomenon. The surpluses accumulated so far do *not* represent a once-for-all transfer of income from the industrial countries to the OPEC cartel, but are part of a continuing and cumulative process. This was pointed out with some force by Thomas O. Enders, assistant secretary of state for economic and business affairs at the Department of State, in an article in *Foreign Affairs* in July 1975.

The real costs of the cartel [Enders wrote] – the long-term transfer annually of goods and services, and the potential deterioration of the security and political position of the industrial countries – have yet to be fully faced. As long as the cartel is effective, the central element of energy in the industrial economies will be subject to manipulation, both as to prices and availability, by the supplying countries which do not have, and may well not develop, an inherent interest in their prosperity.

If the process was allowed to continue, Enders feared, it would within a comparatively short time do serious harm to the security and economic interests of the industrial states, as well as to their political coherence. 'It is in the interest of the industrial countries, indeed, of all consuming countries,' he concluded, 'that conditions be created in which OPEC loses and cannot subsequently regain the power to set oil prices at artificially high levels.'

There is, in short, only one way to cope with the OPEC surpluses, and this is to reduce them to marginal limits – if not to erase them completely – by breaking up the cartel and forcing down the price of oil. All other expedients designed to soak up the surpluses are bound to prove, as they are proving, unavailing. The surpluses are little more than ill-gotten gains, accumulated by the unscrupulous use of monopoly power. To encourage the Middle-Eastern members of the OPEC cartel to employ these gains, this veritable 'Monopoly' money, in the purchase of Western industrial and commercial assets is tantamount to making them a gift of these assets. Equally, for the West to try to recoup the sums it has paid out for excessively over-priced oil over the past few years by contracting to sell the Arabs and Persians great quantities of industrial manufactures, including an inordinate amount of costly armaments, is a policy as dangerous in practice as it is objectionable in principle. If the orders for such manufactures and weapons are cancelled, as they so often are, the Western world will still be burdened with high oil prices without being able to offset them by means of increased exports.

It is just as futile to attempt, as some Western governments have attempted, to evade the financial consequences of paying too high a price for oil, and at the same time to ensure their oil supplies, by entering into barter arrangements with Middle-Eastern governments – oil in exchange for manufactures, armaments, raw materials and help with industrialization – along the lines of those concluded in recent years by the Soviet Union and her Eastern European satellites. Barter arrangements, of their very nature, must be of long duration, with the price of oil fixed accordingly, usually on a sliding scale, ostensibly to allow for inflation but really to act as a *douceur* to the Middle-Eastern government concerned. Such arrangements only serve to hamper the operation of the market in crude oil, impeding any fall in prices which might otherwise occur through competition, a decline in consumption or the discovery of new oil deposits outside the Middle East. Even Muhammad Reza Shah, who strongly favoured barter agreements, confirmed this fact when in February 1977 he rejected suggestions that the exchange of oil for goods tended to undercut OPEC prices. 'We sell our oil at OPEC prices,' he said. 'Whoever buys our oil would have to pay the price set by OPEC.'

Aside from their economic drawbacks, barter arrangements entail very real risks of undesirable political entanglements. The volatile political condition of the Middle East makes it a virtual certainty that sooner or later a situation will arise in which a Western oil-consuming country will be faced with a demand for political support from a Middle-Eastern oil state, under pain of forfeiting its access to oil supplies. Middle-Eastern governments do not distinguish in their relations with other states between purely commercial arrangements and political engagements. Far from exempting commercial agreements with other states from the scope of any dispute in which it may become involved, a Middle-Eastern government will regard these agreements as reinforcing the obligations of those states to take its side and lend it active assistance. The discontents and irritants which abound in the Gulf and in the Middle East as a whole are a constant potential source of political upheavals and armed hostilities. Who can foretell when one of these discontents or irritants will erupt into insurrection, war between states, or violent dissension just short of war?

How would a Western nation, say Britain or France or West Germany, which was tied by barter arrangements to Saudi Arabia or Persia or Iraq, fare in such an eventuality? It could well find itself dragged willy-nilly into a remote quarrel, in the making of which it had no hand, in the outcome of which it has no real interest, yet in the conduct of which it is required to participate – and all for the sake of essentially (or even exclusively) Arab or Persian or Muslim objects.

The nerveless acquiescence of the Western nations in the frequency of oil-price rises since the Tehran confrontation of 1971 has been prompted in the main by the hope that the acquiescence will gain them security of oil supplies. It will, of course, do nothing of the kind. All that continual surrender does is to strengthen the financial weapon in the economic armoury of the Middle-Eastern oil states. But there are even more insidious dangers to the West in the inexorable accumulation of great wealth by these states than the threat to its economic health. Because this wealth has been obtained without effort on the part of the states in question, it has had a profoundly corrupting influence upon their governments and upon numbers of their subjects, a corruption made all the more inevitable by the nature of Arab and Persian society. As greater riches are amassed, the process of corruption will intensify, hastening the spread of instability in Arabia, Persia and the Gulf. It is doubtful whether at any time in the history of mankind a group of intrinsically insignificant polities, at a comparatively primitive stage of economic, political and social development, has possessed such enormous financial power as the handful of Gulf states now dispose of. As the governments of the Gulf states are moved to employ this power for political and other purposes abroad, the corruption will spread beyond the Gulf, influencing and disturbing governments and societies in lands far removed from them in customs, culture and religion.

It is beyond the scope of this book to examine at any length the injurious effects of Arab and Persian oil money upon the West. That the contagion has already entered the body of the West can be confirmed by the merest glance about one. It is present in financial and commercial circles, though its workings are rarely exposed to public view. It has penetrated politics and government, especially in Britain, France and the United States, where the spectacle of high-ranking ministers, officials and politicians wheedling, flattering and fawning upon the plutocrats of Arabia and Persia has become a daily occurrence. To the Western public, growing increasingly uneasy and dejected at the progress of the contagion, it is glibly explained by their rulers and by those in public life to whom they look for instruction and guidance that the contagion does not exist; or, if it does, that it is benign; or if it is not benign, then there is naught to be done about it.

It is difficult, indeed impossible, to believe that the governments of Britain, France and the United States are not fully aware of the nature of the Middle-

Eastern regimes with which they are treating and of the corrupting effects which Arab and Persian oil money is having in Western society. This being so, their indifference to what is happening – one might almost say their encouragement of it – is presumably occasioned by fear and greed: fear of offending the Arabs and Persians lest they reduce oil supplies or raise oil prices; greed for the expenditure and investment of their oil revenues in the ailing economies of the West. How else is one to account for the obsequious contortions performed by British, French or American politicians and officials to ingratiate themselves with the rulers of the Gulf states and, until his fall, the shah? How else to interpret the insensibility of the British and French governments to the feelings of the citizens of London and Paris as they watch the more select parts of their cities being turned into Middle-Eastern caravanserais, bazaars and bagnios? Or are forced to witness assassinations and gun-battles in their streets between warring Arab factions, whose presence in their capitals, along with the arms and money with which they are amply furnished, has largely been made possible by the excessive oil revenues paid to the Arab oil states?

The lure of Arab and Persian oil money has also exerted its attraction outside Western financial and political circles. Its influence is discernible in publishing and journalism, in the professions, in the universities and learned societies, most of it unnoticed and unrealized by the Western public at large. Throughout the past decade, as we have seen, newspapers like *The Times*, the *Financial Times* and *Le Monde* have shown themselves increasingly ready to cater to the desire of Saudi Arabia and the petty states of the Gulf for self-esteem and self-advertisement by publishing a seemingly endless stream of supplements about the vigour, wisdom and capacity of the governments of these countries, the charm and talents of their peoples, the giant strides they are making towards the millennium, and the gratifyingly large sums of money they are spending in the process upon Western goods and services. The content of the articles which appear in these supplements, hemmed in by acres of advertising, is, as indicated in an earlier chapter, best passed over in silence. A reminder of what it is like, however, may not be out of place here.

A special supplement on King Abdul Aziz University, Jiddah, put out by the *Times Higher Educational Supplement* in October, 1977, had this to say about the aims of this new seat of learning. 'The main campus of King Abdul Aziz University one day ... will house one of the most prestigious centres of learning in the Middle East – and, it is hoped, the world. Named after the charismatic monarch who earlier this century welded the ancient warring tribes of Arabia into today's modern nation state, ... its expansion is really taking off.' Airborne himself on a flight of rhetoric, *The Times*'s correspondent goes on to enthuse over 'the Master Plan' to spend £3,000 million on buildings and equipment, the recruitment of a distinguished academic staff ('in large numbers from Europe and North America: salaries are high and this is reflected in the quality of applicants') and the high standards of scholarship students will be expected to attain. The presiding genius over all this, the correspondent informs us, is 'Sheikh Ahmad Salah Jamjoom, one of the founding fathers of the university', who is 'keenly concerned about the preservation of quality during expansion. He is insistent that the flood of students and staff into the university should not water down the ideals of academic excellence. The university is aiming to ensure undergraduate excellence by laying down tight entry qualifications. . . .' Nor is this the limit of Shaikh Jamjoom's vision. 'Knowledge must not only serve society: it must also serve good,' he told his interlocutor from *The Times*, who himself goes on to embroider the theme rather richly in the concluding sentences of his article.

The Muslim world in general and Saudi Arabia in particular sees the wealth generated by the oil bonanza as a chance to reverse the eclipse by the west of learning. They are convinced of the possibility of developing highly sophisticated systems of, for example, 'Islamic' social science, 'Islamic' economics, 'Islamic' medicine and even 'Islamic' mathematics. The aim is the creation of a new Islamic Golden Age of culture and learning: Islam with a modern face. The de-westernization of knowledge is the first central task of the enterprise.

It is not only the savants and schoolmen of Saudi Arabia who see 'the wealth generated by the oil bonanza as a chance to reverse the eclipse by the west of learning'. A number of ambitious academics and administrators in universities and other institutions of learning in Europe and North America have also had their glimpse of El Dorado and made for it hot-foot. Sums of money, some of them of considerable proportions, have been solicited from the oil shaikhs and the court of the 'Shadow of God upon earth' for the establishment or expansion of programmes of Arab, Persian and Islamic studies in France, Britain, Canada and the United States. Georgetown University in Washington, a Jesuit foundation, has accepted, without any evident misgivings, several hundred thousand dollars of Arab oil money for the establishment of a chair of Islamic and Arabic studies. The donor is the government of Libya, the head of which, as is well known, is a fanatical Muslim, a supporter of terrorist movements and one of the principal paymasters of the Muslim *fidaiyin* who lately endeavoured to crush the Latin Christian community in the Lebanon. At institutions as different as McGill University in Montreal and the University of Exeter in Devon there are now chairs or lectureships in 'Arabian Gulf studies', endowed by one or another of the lesser Gulf governments. Indeed, it would almost seem as if Edward Gibbon's musings two centuries ago upon what might have been, had the Arab armies not been halted at Poitiers a thousand years earlier, were more of a prophetic than a visionary nature. 'Perhaps the interpretation of the Koran would now be taught in the schools of Oxford, and her pulpits might demonstrate to a circumcised people the sanctity and truth of the revelation of Mahomet.'

One could go on listing the ancient and modern foundations in the Old

World and the New, some members of which have been driven by the *auri sacra fames* to curry favour with the oil potentates of the Middle East by paying exaggerated deference to Islamic history and culture (not to mention 'Islamic' social sciences and 'Islamic' economics); but the exercise would be as depressing as it would be futile. The only point to be made is that the rulers of the Arab oil states are neither simple philanthropists nor disinterested patrons of the humanities. They expect a return upon their donations to institutions of learning and their subsidies to publishing houses; whether it be in the form of subtle propaganda on behalf of Arab or Islamic causes, or the preferential admission of their nationals, however unqualified, to Western universities and colleges, or the publication of the kind of sycophantic flim-flam about themselves and their countries which now clutters sections of the Western press and even respectable periodical literature.

If the peoples of the West do not take heed of what is happening and act to halt it, they will inevitably suffer a debasement of their national lives, standards and institutions from the penetration of their societies by Arab and Persian oil money. It is worth recalling in this connexion that Muslim jurisprudence views the world in uncompromising terms, dividing it arbitrarily into the *dar al-Islam* (Muslim territory) and the *dar al-harb* (hostile territory), of which Western Christendom is the principal constituent. Between these two territorial entities there can exist only a state of active warfare or a condition of latent hostility. If the West continues in its present abject and infirm posture towards the Arabs and the Persians, it may well contribute a third category to the Islamic order – the *dar al-abid,* or land of slaves.

Oil is, and has been since the beginning of its use industrially in the West, a strategic commodity, and secure control over adequate sources of supply was until recent years deemed essential by the Western industrial nations. The origins of the quest by the major powers of Europe for strategic control over reserves of oil go back to the eve of the First World War, when Britain and Germany competed for oil concessionary rights in the Ottoman empire, and the British government acquired a majority shareholding in the Anglo-Persian Oil Company (afterwards British Petroleum) so as to have a direct supply of oil for the Royal Navy. Britain's dependence upon non-British sources of oil was sharply revealed in the course of the war, reinforcing the British government's determination to bring substantial reserves of foreign oil under British control. Thus, after the war, Britain obtained through Anglo–Persian an equal share in the Iraq Petroleum Company with Royal Dutch Shell, Compagnie Française des Pétroles and the Near East Development Corporation (five American companies led by Standard Oil of New Jersey and Mobil). The British government also arranged that the management of the company should lie in British hands. This principle of latent British official involvement in Middle-Eastern oil exploration and exploitation was extended into the Gulf between the wars, as Anglo–Persian and IPC obtained concessions in Kuwait, Qatar, the Trucial Shaikhdoms and Oman.

The French government, which held a minority shareholding in CFP, pursued much the same policy in Iraq and the lower Gulf, either through the agency of IPC or through CFP's direct association with British Petroleum, and later Shell, in concessionary ventures after the Second World War. The United States never sought to acquire the same measure of strategic control over Middle-Eastern oil reserves as did Britain and France, the most pertinent reasons for her abstention being her possession of considerable reserves of her own and the absence of any American interests of a vital nature in the Middle East. During the Second World War, as we have seen, the United States government seriously considered the acquisition of a shareholding in the major American oil companies operating in the region, and more particularly in ARAMCO's concession in Saudi Arabia. But with the termination of hostilities and in the face of strong opposition from the companies the idea was abandoned. Thereafter the United States virtually entrusted the protection of its strategic interest in Middle-Eastern oil to the major American companies, which meant, in effect, to the four parent companies of ARAMCO, whose Saudi Arabian concession eventually came to constitute the principal foreign oil reserves of the United States.

How and when in the past two decades the Western world's indifference to the retention of strategic control over its Middle-Eastern sources of oil took root is not readily determinable; although there is little doubt that it was the consequence, as Correlli Barnett has remarked, 'of following Keynes instead of Clausewitz' in the formulation of Western policy towards the Middle-Eastern oil states.* The erosion of British and French power in the Middle East went hand in hand with – indeed, was in large measure the direct consequence of – the growth of a debilitating conviction that the tides of history were flowing against the exercise by Western Europe of any power beyond its shores; that in the Middle East the Arabs' and Persians' hour had come; and that the whole question of access to oil was a purely commercial matter of supply and demand, an outlook summed up by the fashionable precept of the day, 'the Arabs cannot drink their oil'. With the departure of Britain from the Gulf at the close of 1971 the last pretence of maintaining any kind of physical hold over sources of supply was abandoned. Henceforth, Britain, France, Western Europe in general and Japan would have to rely for the bulk of their oil supplies upon the goodwill of the Gulf oil states and (to whatever extent it might prove effective) upon the influence and authority wielded in the area by the United States. The United States, however, as has already been observed, had entrusted the care of its strategic oil interests to ARAMCO, and ARAMCO had proved unequal to the trust when put to the test in October 1973. So the United States is now in

* See 'Oil – strategic importance and future supplies', a seminar report by the Royal United Services Institute for Defence Studies, June 1973.

much the same case as Western Europe and Japan, with no security of access to the oil reserves of the Gulf beyond what she can obtain by pursuing the hazardous policy, bequeathed to her by ARAMCO, of identifying herself and her interests with the present Saudi regime.

Now and for some years to come, Western Europe and Japan must draw their major supplies of oil from an area of extreme political instability, relying for the uninterrupted continuance of these supplies upon the good faith and good sense of regimes notorious for their fickle and contentious behaviour. It is not a comforting thought. The Middle-Eastern members of OPEC have broken almost every agreement they have entered into since 1970, whether it was the Libyan settlement in September of that year, or the Tehran agreement in February 1971, or the Geneva formula for the adjustment of prices against the international value of the dollar, or the provisions for the extension of the 1954 Persian consortium agreement, or the timetables for the implementation of participation, or the prices at which the oil companies could buy back participation crude. Nearly every pledge by an Arab oil state not to use oil as a political weapon has been dishonoured, nearly every undertaking to reduce oil prices or moderate price increases has been broken. In contrast, almost every threat to restrict or embargo the shipment of oil, to reduce production or to raise oil prices has been carried out. It is a sorry record; yet nearly every Western government continues to make public avowals of its faith in the essential reasonableness and good intentions of the OPEC cartel.

For Western Europe to have abandoned all vestige of strategic control over its major sources of oil is folly enough; but to compound this folly by offering further hostages to fortune in the shape of earnest predictions about oil shortages, embargoes and price rises to come can only be construed as evidence of a profoundly felt death-wish. Yet this is exactly what Western governments and the garrulous tribe of Western pundits have been doing for some time now, apparently oblivious of the part played by similar predictions in bringing about the OPEC offensive in the autumn of 1973. Whether oil shortages will occur in the years ahead it is beyond the power of anyone to predict with utter certainty. Much will depend upon the discovery and exploitation of new oil reserves, upon the rate of depletion of the known ones, upon the levels of oil consumption in the industrial and non-industrial countries of the world, upon the development of alternative sources of energy and the increased utilization of existing ones – in short, upon a long list of variable and even unforeseeable factors. What can be said with some assurance is that it is unwise in the extreme for the West to shape its current policy towards OPEC upon the basis of hypothetical oil shortages in the future. To do so is to play straight into the cartel's hands, allowing it to manipulate the West for its own political and financial purposes. What these purposes are has already been indicated. Whether OPEC, and its Middle-Eastern members in particular, has the power and the skill to go on accomplishing them is again dependent upon a number of variable circumstances which it would require a book in itself to examine properly. Here we can do no more than glance at a few of them.

Reduced demand for oil after the price rises late in 1973 caused a slight drop in production world-wide in 1974, and a bigger drop of 5.4 per cent in 1975, the first of this magnitude since 1942. The fall in OPEC's production in 1975 was much larger – 12 per cent, with Venezuela (21.3 per cent), Nigeria (20.9 per cent) and Kuwait (19.2 per cent) suffering the heaviest losses. Iraq, in contrast, raised her output by 12.8 per cent, mainly through price-cutting. While there has been some recovery in world consumption since 1975, it has not returned to the average annual increase recorded in the years 1955–73, viz. 7 per cent, but has persisted at around 1 per cent. With new oil discoveries coming on-stream (North Sea, Alaska, Mexico), the result has been a net decline in consumption, and therefore production, of OPEC oil. So many fluctuations in the production of Middle-Eastern oil have occurred in the past five years that it is impossible to discern any significant pattern to them. Producers of heavy and high sulphur crudes like Persia, Kuwait and Saudi Arabia seem to have suffered the largest falls, though in the case of Saudi Arabia the fall has been mitigated by other circumstances. Some of the fluctuations were caused by the oil companies' stock-piling in advance of expected price increases, as was the case before the OPEC meeting in Dauhah in December 1976 when prices were raised by 10 per cent. Others, however, can only be attributed to falling demand. Thus, Saudi Arabia's production in the first six months of 1978 was down 17.5 per cent on that of the comparable period in 1977. Persia's production was down 7 per cent in the first quarter of 1978 on that of the first quarter of 1977. Kuwait was 36 per cent down in January 1978 on January 1977, and 40 per cent down in February 1978 on the previous February.

It would be unwise to read much into these figures: as just remarked, there is more confusion than clarity in the recent pattern of oil production in the Middle East. What is fairly clear is that the fall in production and the decline in value of the US dollar means that only three states, Saudi Arabia, Kuwait and Abu Dhabi, can count upon a continuing surplus of revenue over expenditure in the immediate future, and even this surplus is diminishing – or it was until the oil-price increases of 1979. What this portends is as unpredictable as most occurrences in the Middle East, although Kuwait, as in other instances, may well prove to be the bell-wether. Up to 1973 Kuwait's oil production ran at roughly 3 million b/d. By the end of 1974 it had dropped to 2.5 million b/d, and Kuwait had become the leading proponent of 'conservation' as a means of extending the productive life of its oilfields and of maximizing the financial return on oil exports. The final nationalization of the Kuwait Oil Company (jointly owned by BP and Gulf) took place in December 1975, and even before then the Kuwaiti government had imposed a ceiling of 2 million b/d on production. It proved to be a flexible ceiling: late in 1976 production was averaging 3.3 million b/d as the companies stockpiled before the Dauhah meeting of OPEC in December. Thereafter production dropped to 1.3 million b/d early in 1976, recovering to 2 million b/d by the middle of 1977. A further fall, as we have seen, occurred in the early months of 1978. The effect of this stagnation, which should have gladdened the hearts of the Kuwaiti 'conservationists', was to provoke insistent calls from the Kuwait government in the late summer and early autumn of 1978 for an increase in oil prices.

Although it was a call calculated to arouse a natural response in the breasts of the other members of OPEC, things were not quite as they had been five years earlier, nor was 'conservation' the tactical weapon it had once promised to be. Demand for oil was still depressed, selling prices were well below posted prices, the depreciation in the value of the dollar had further reduced real income, and most of OPEC's members were having difficulty in covering their expenditures out of current revenue. Several, in fact, had either contracted, or were actively seeking, loans to cover their deficits. On the face of it, a price increase seemed only logical as a means of recovering lost financial ground. Yet there were sufficient imponderables in the situation to induce caution. A price rise could lead to a further drop in consumption, to a reduction of economic activity in the Western industrial countries, to a fresh decline in the value of the dollar and, at the end of the day, to diminished oil revenues. Even the adoption of proposals which had long been floating about to end the system of fixing posted prices in dollars and to peg them instead to a 'basket' of strong currencies might not alter the outcome.

'Conservation' was an equally sterile option. In the case of Kuwait, for instance, an absolute minimum of 1.5 million b/d of oil had to be produced to provide sufficient associated gas to run the shaikhdom's utilities, including the electricity needed for the thousands of air-conditioners to which the Kuwaitis had become addicted. OPEC's main problem, in any case, was to sell its oil in quantities and at prices sufficient to meet its members' current financial needs, rather than to conserve it as an asset for the future, an asset which might well turn out to be largely illusory. It was a problem which weighed more heavily upon countries like Persia, Algeria and Iraq, with large populations and ambitious programmes of modernization, than it did upon sparsely populated countries with limited potential for development, like Saudi Arabia, Libya and Abu Dhabi. A glut of oil on the market, as existed in the first half of 1978, could well have led the two groups to compete for buyers, thereby straining the unity of OPEC and perhaps even endangering its whole structure.

From this cheerless prospect the organization was rescued by the revolution in Persia in the autumn of 1978 which eventually unseated the shah and established a republic of sorts. Persian oil production dropped rapidly in the last two months of the year, from 5.2 million b/d to less than 0.5 million b/d and then ceased altogether for a time at the turn of the year. As usual, the industrial nations of the world panicked at the thought of an oil shortage, forgetting overnight that there had been a surplus of oil on the market only a short time previously, and that spare producing capacity had been some 5 million b/d, roughly equivalent to the normal output from Persia. A much relieved OPEC convened at Abu Dhabi in mid-December 1978 where it proceeded to wring what advantage it could from the changed situation. The posted price of the marker crude, standard Arabian light, was raised by 14.5 per cent, the increase to be imposed in four stages, commencing with 5 per cent on 1 January 1979, when the price would rise from $13.66 to $14.34 per barrel.

Western reaction to the increase was generally passive, being conditioned, as OPEC had intended it should, by the fact that the new price was to take effect in stages. The mildness of the reaction, together with the predictable cries of alarm about a looming oil shortage which issued from the usual pack of Western soothsayers, persuaded the magnates of OPEC that they were foolish to content themselves with a finger when an arm was theirs for the taking. One after another they proceeded to add surcharges of a dollar or more a barrel to the price of their oil until eventually, at an extraordinary session of OPEC called in the last week of March 1979, the organization resolved to bring forward the full increase for the year of 14.5 per cent to 1 April. What was perhaps more significant than OPEC's readiness to exploit any opportunity to raise prices was the abandonment of all pretence at regulating the official selling prices (as posted prices were now called) charged by individual members for their oil. All states, as the official communiqué delicately phrased it, were entitled to levy whatever surcharges or premiums 'they deem justifiable in the light of their own circumstances'. What this meant in practice was that, on top of the usual premiums for specific gravity, geographic location and other differentials, every member country was at liberty to impose whatever additional charge it wished.

A free-for-all followed, which entered its manic phase in May when price leap-frogging took place on almost a daily basis. Some peculiar incidents occurred of which the Western public was mostly unaware. The revolutionary government in Tehran demanded that BP and Shell pay *pishkesh*, in the form of the obligatory purchase of a quantity of Persian oil at spot market prices (up to $35 a barrel), if they wanted to qualify for six or twelve months' contracts; and then in late June it tore up the contracts it had signed, even though they were supposed to run to the end of the year. The Algerian government increased the price of its crude to $21 a barrel in the third week of May in direct violation of its contracts with the oil companies, which stipulated that prices could only be raised at quarterly intervals unless OPEC had authorized a mid-quarter increase, which it had not. To get around this obstacle the Algerians asked for the voluntary compliance of the companies with the increase, adding pointedly that if it was not forthcoming, oil prices would be revised at the outset of the next quarter in such a way as to compensate Algeria for any loss of potential revenue she might have suffered in the interim. There were also moments of light relief, such as that afforded by the oil minister of

Abu Dhabi and the UAE, and current president of OPEC, who solemnly averred on 9 May: 'Although the market can now justify more or less any size of increase in crude oil prices owing to the current imbalance between supply and demand, nevertheless I think we should not go for any further price increases this year. . . . This is a duty we have to fulfil.' Eight days later Abu Dhabi raised the official selling price of her oil by a further 80 cents a barrel.

At its semi-annual conference in Geneva in the last week of June 1979 OPEC unblushingly ratified the results of the prices' free-for-all of the preceding quarter. Saudi Arabia, which had for the most part kept her prices steady since April, agreed to raise the price of the marker crude, standard Arabian light, to $18 a barrel. To recover some of the revenue she had lost in the interim, the increase was made retrospective to 1 June and the period allowed for payment of purchases of Saudi crude, hitherto sixty days, was reduced to thirty days. The Persian delegation, perhaps unhinged by revolutionary zeal, promptly raised the price of Persian light crude, customarily pegged at 11 cents above the price of Arabian light, to $21 a barrel, thereby creating in effect a second Gulf marker price. All the delegates were agreed that in the prevailing condition of the market their governments were entitled to impose a surcharge of $2 a barrel on the Saudi marker price, and to charge whatever they saw fit for quality and geographic location premiums, up to a ceiling price of $23.50 a barrel. With the sole exception of Saudi Arabia every member state imposed the surcharge from 1 July, and, where applicable, the quality and location premiums. The effect was to bring the average price increase for a barrel of OPEC oil for the six months since December 1978 to an aggregate of 65 per cent, with Iraq (71 per cent), Libya (69 per cent) and Algeria (67 per cent) leading the field, and Saudi Arabia (42 per cent) trailing well behind. Such was the volume of Saudi Arabian production, however, that the Saudi government would be the principal financial beneficiary of the price increases. The total revenues of OPEC, which had been in the vicinity of $140,000 million in 1978, were expected to exceed $200,000 million in 1979.

Although the combined price increases of the first half of 1979 were by far the highest that had occurred since the quadrupling of oil prices late in 1973, they failed to elicit from the Western world any response other than a sustained bout of indignant bleating. The finance ministers of the OECD, meeting in Paris in the middle of June 1979, could propose no solution to the severe economic problems which the price increases would create for the industrial nations other than to say that their peoples should resign themselves to a lower standard of living. Just how excessive a price increase is needed to provoke some real resistance from the Western powers and Japan there is no way of knowing: their submissiveness seems boundless. However, should the improbable occur and they should find the modicum of courage required to resist some particularly outrageous demand, what measures could the Middle-Eastern members of OPEC adopt to force the West to resume its habitual obedient posture? The obvious ones are a reduction in output and the im-position of an embargo, probably under cover of redress for some political grievance or other to give it a spurious respectability. A reduction in output, needless to say, depends for its effectiveness upon the state of the market and the level of world consumption at the time. It also calls for the exercise by the Arab oil states of a degree of self-restraint and disciplined co-operation which, on the evidence of their past showing, they may not be capable of attaining.

In 1975 these states supplied 58 per cent of world imports of oil (outside the communist bloc) and 52 per cent of the requirements of the countries which make up the membership of the International Energy Agency. On the basis of these figures, to cause a 25 per cent loss of supply to the IEA countries (which would be equivalent to an import loss of 36 per cent), the Arab oil states would have to reduce their production by well over 60 per cent. If, for example, Libya and Iraq, which failed to participate in the embargo in 1973, refused to co-operate in the cut-back, the remaining Arab oil-producing countries would have to reduce production by between 80 and 90 per cent to achieve the same effect. Alternatively, if Saudi Arabia held aloof, all the other states together could not impose a 25 per cent reduction in IEA supplies even if they curtailed production completely.

The above calculations are based upon the stockpiles of oil which the IEA's member states have built up, or are supposed to have built up, since the end of 1974. The distinction is important. The average stockpile held by each member country in 1977 was said to be roughly equivalent to eighty days' consumption, and all members have undertaken to attain a ninety-day level by 1980. However, what is not clear from the IEA's returns is whether the figures represent actual reserves or whether they also include oil stocks *in situ*, i.e. oil held by industries or in the pipeline, which, though necessary to the efficient functioning of an emergency system, should not properly be reckoned part of a strategic reserve. Whatever the case may be, it remains that the industrial countries are in somewhat better condition now to resist intimidation by the Arab oil states than they were in 1973 – which is why Kuwait urged her fellow Gulf states in the early summer of 1979 not to increase production to offset the temporary shortages in the IEA countries but to force them instead to run down their stockpiles.

It has been estimated that it would take a cut-back in oil production by the Arab oil states of 60 per cent for a period of six months to exhaust the present IEA stockpiles. The loss of revenues which the Arab governments could expect to suffer as a consequence of such a cut-back would be formidable enough to make some of them, at least, hesitate before committing themselves to this course. On the basis of their output and revenues for 1976, for example, it has been reckoned that a 60 per cent loss of earnings for six months would have amounted in the case of Saudi Arabia to around $10,000 million, in those of Kuwait and Iraq to about $2,600 million each, and in that of Abu Dhabi to

$2,000 million. The loss to Persia, on the basis of her production and revenues for the same year, would have been about $6,600 million. Obviously, with the higher oil prices obtaining in the summer of 1979, the loss of revenue would be correspondingly greater, perhaps by as much as 50 per cent. While the richer oil states might be able to bear the strain, the less wealthy and more populous could not. Nor would the richer states' clients (notably Syria, Jordan and the various Palestinian organizations) forgo their accustomed subsidies with good grace.

That the Arab members of OPEC would have to resort to such extremes to secure the acquiescence of the West in any price rise is, however, highly unlikely. The inevitability of continual price rises is now accepted by the West with much the same fatalism as that with which an Australian aborigine, at whom the bone has been pointed, accepts the certainty of impending death. Indeed, most public commentators on the subject go further and take a perverse pleasure in enumerating the economic tribulations which are about to be visited upon the sinful and self-indulgent West by the avenging angel of OPEC. Two comparatively recent examples of these attempts at self-fulfilling prophecies of doom may suffice to illustrate the kind of thing to be found in most leading newspapers and journals of opinion in Europe and North America in any week of the year.

An article in *The Times* on 16 June 1978 – graced, naturally, with a large photograph of Shaikh Yamani – gloomily speculated about forthcoming oil-price rises, on the basis of predictions in the oil industry of a 6–10 per cent increase in world consumption of oil at the outset of 1979, and of a 15–20 per cent increase in the 1980s. That the former figure would equal and the latter greatly exceed the average annual rate of increase in the boom years up to 1973 was not mentioned by the writer. Nor did he attempt to reconcile the predictions with the existence of a surplus of heavy crudes on the market over the preceding eighteen months. Instead, he chose to wax indignant on behalf of the OPEC producers over the persistence of this surplus. 'The oil states, in short, are tired of carrying the brunt of the oil glut, fed up of being treated as free storage warehouses by Western consumers.' What, one might ask in some wonderment, had become of the arguments about oil in the ground being the best investment open to the oil states? What of the moral virtues of 'conservation'? To this, the writer had an answer of sorts. 'Conservation of reserves', he informed his readers '. . . inevitably means higher prices. As OPEC sees it, higher prices will both help to conserve reserves and encourage the development of alternative energy sources.' In confirmation of this agreeable prospect, he went on to quote from the annual report of OAPEC for 1978 on the question of higher world consumption in the 1980s. 'Production and price policies must be adopted which would create the necessary economic incentives to extend the lives of the present reserves and increase investments for creating new reserves.'

Six months previously, on 20 December 1977, another report had appeared in *The Times* which demonstrated even more forcibly the compulsive fascination exerted by higher oil prices over the minds of Western newspapermen. A German correspondent interviewed Shaikh Yamani during an OPEC meeting at Caracas, and the dialogue went as follows:

Q: Can you roughly tell us by how much the oil price will be increased in Caracas and what the Western world can expect?
A: There will be no increase.
Q: Do you believe that an increase in oil prices ranging to 15 per cent (which is the average inflation rate in the Western countries) could be borne by the oil consumer countries?
A: There will be no increase.
Q: Does the slackness of the world economy actually permit an increase in oil prices, perhaps from January 1, 1978 . . .?

The pathetic litany continued until Yamani – either goaded by the correspondent's persistence or perhaps out of pity for the poor fellow's yearning to feel the lash across his back – replied at last to his questioner's desperate plea of 'Could you attempt to guess at which level the price will be in 1980 and 1990?' with a grave and suitably Delphic pronouncement: 'There will be an increase in the oil prices in 1980 and a strong increase in 1990.' Needless to say, Yamani and his interlocutor were both off target: the increase came on 1 January 1979.

Ahmad Zaki al-Yamani and the country he serves are the principal focus of Western hopes, fears and speculations about oil supplies and prices. The Saudi oil minister's comings and goings about the world are devoutly chronicled by the Western press, his every utterance reverently recorded and sifted for hidden significance as if he were the Pythian oracle. Yamani, in his turn, has played the role assigned him with great verve, ceaselessly girdling the earth like a fretful Puck, scattering golden promises of price reductions and unfettered supplies, intermingled with dark allusions to possible embargoes and restrictions – and simultaneous assurances that they are a thing of the past.

> 'My conscience hath a thousand several tongues,
> And every tongue brings in a several tale . . .'

On a visit to Japan in January 1974 he startled the Japanese by offering them the same all-encompassing agreement for the provision of oil and finance for investment that he had offered the Americans in 1972. 'Japan is nation number one that is in the position to have a continuous supply of crude oil from Saudi Arabia on a long-term basis.' He astonished his hosts even further by proclaiming dramatically:

We sense our responsibilities, and therefore we want to reduce the present price of oil, although we believe it to be a fair and reasonable price. His Majesty, King Faisal, . . .

will take very important steps towards fulfilling this policy, and I hope he will succeed in doing it for the benefit of the whole world.'

A day later Yamani had second thoughts and beat a quick retreat from his pledge of unilateral Saudi action on prices. 'We always like to act as part of a group, not as an individual,' he explained. 'If we can convince the others [in OPEC], we will reduce our prices.' For good measure, he threw in his customary warning about the 'very serious trouble' that would ensue if the oil-consuming countries attempted to form a common front against OPEC. 'We are in a very strong position; you [the consuming countries] cannot afford any sort of confrontation.'

Three years later Yamani was still uttering the same melodious sounds, though by this time the theme of price reduction had been replaced by that of 'moderation'. In an address at the University of Edinburgh in November 1976 (such occasions have become commonplace, so eager is the scholarly world for the light of his discourse) he explained yet again the reasons for the 1973 embargo and the price increases which accompanied it. The explanation called for some strenuous reworking of recent history, but Yamani was equal to the task. Rejecting with some indignation the unworthy suggestions which had been put about that there was a connexion between the embargo and the price increases, he told his audience:

It is true that the oil restrictions did cause a shortage which in turn led to a rise in market prices, but that was not our aim nor were we the main beneficiaries. . . . The truth of the matter is that we did not for a moment seek to influence the market price of oil by enforcing our embargo.

He dismissed as misguided the frequently voiced criticism that the steep rise in oil prices had been detrimental to the poorer countries of the world. Such criticism, he said, 'conveniently overlooked the vast aid programmes established by the oil producers'. Furthermore, he contended, one of the 'blessings' which had flowed from the politicizing of the oil trade and the raising of prices to 'realistic' levels had been the awakening of those Asian and African countries which exported raw materials to the industrial world to the potentialities of obtaining 'realistic' prices for their exports, also. Saudi Arabia, in fact, was responsible for initiating the discussions on raw materials, technological aid and financial assistance between the industrial nations and the under-developed countries – the Conference on International Economic Co-operation, or the 'North–South dialogue' – which had begun in Paris in December 1975.

As for the huge financial surpluses which Saudi Arabia and the other oil states had amassed, they had never been employed, Yamani claimed, 'in a destructive or threatening manner. Speaking for Saudi Arabia, it is an established fact now that the excess funds that we recycled in the money markets of the West have been a source of stability if anything.' However, he continued, launching into his habitual minatory coda, this happy harmony of interests would be destroyed if the West persisted with such expedients as the International Energy Agency.

The very first result of the IEA oil-sharing plan, if implemented, would therefore be to offset the efforts of Saudi Arabia which involve using oil in a gradual and constructive manner, and to enable the other Arab producers to resort to much harsher measures which will lead to grave consequences.

If the ultimate aim of the IEA was, as the Arab oil states suspected it was, 'to ensure that Arab oil can never again be used to further the Arab cause . . . then the IEA and the Arab world and perhaps the whole of the Western and developing worlds will be set upon a collision course that can only lead to the destruction of everybody'. Assuming once more the air of a man who brought peace, not a sword, Yamani concluded:

I hope, as I suppose every person in his right senses would hope, that this will not be the case and that the IEA will not be used as an instrument of confrontation. . . . The Arab oil producers with their massive reserves are the true friends of the West. This is something they have proved on almost every occasion in the past, even in their differences with the West and in the way in which they enforced their embargo.

Yamani has been allowed to get away with this mixture of *blague* and gasconade for so many years that he must long ago have concluded that the West has taken leave of its senses. Not only are none of his protestations and admonitions ever challenged but instead they are accorded the utmost respect and credence. Thus, when he haughtily proclaimed in an interview on French television at the end of May 1979, 'You had a lesson in 1973 and you learned nothing from it. Now there is another lesson, and you are trying to avoid the meaning of this lesson in the West,' his interviewer practically fell off his chair in his eagerness to prostrate himself and to crave the oracle's forgiveness. It is the same with Yamani's melodramatic performances as the incarnation of sweet reason and gracious moderation at the conferences of OPEC. When, for instance, at the Dauhah meeting in December 1976 he refused, amid scenes of high emotion, to commit Saudi Arabia to the 10 per cent increase in oil prices adopted by the majority of OPEC, the Western world rang with jubilant encomiums to the new Horatius who had defied the fearsome ranks of Tuscany and saved the treasuries of the West from spoliation. When the tumult had subsided it emerged that the 5 per cent increase with which Saudi Arabia and the UAE had declared themselves satisfied worked out in practice at $7\frac{1}{2}$ per cent, while the 10 per cent which the cads in OPEC had insisted upon would be reduced by market conditions to $8\frac{1}{2}$ per cent. What is more, Saudi Arabia and Abu Dhabi greatly increased their oil production in the first six months of 1977, at the expense of their partners in OPEC, so as to offset the slightly lower prices they were receiving for their oil. Then, on 1 July 1977, they quietly raised their prices by the full 10 per cent to bring themselves into line with the rest of OPEC.

However captious and overweening Yamani may be – and he is by no means as captious and overweening as some of his ministerial colleagues in OPEC – he is by virtue of what others, and particularly ARAMCO and its parent companies, have made him. In evidence before the sub-committee on multinational corporations of the Senate Foreign Relations Committee in June 1974, a former chairman of Standard Oil of California, Otto Miller, gave this reply when the chairman of the sub-committee asked whether, if the political situation in the Middle East became inflamed, the Arabs might not again cut off oil supplies to the industrial nations, regardless of the consequences to themselves: 'They would do almost anything. . . . You are completely at their mercy and that is why I have always felt that it is extremely important to have friendly relationships with those countries. . . .' It was a view commonly elicited from representatives of the major American oil companies who testified before the sub-committee. Behind it lay the tacit admission that the companies regarded the governments of the Arab oil states as both wilful and mercurial, slaves of suspicion and emotion, whose words and actions alike were unreliable and unpredictable. The only way to handle them, so the companies had long ago concluded, was as one would treat fractious children, by indulging their whims, feeding their vanity and abstaining from provocation. That there are other and more beneficial ways of treating fractious children than by the tactics which the companies have employed (and which have been largely responsible for bringing them to their present unhappy and precarious situation *vis-à-vis* the governments in question) is a possibility which the companies would seem to have contemplated only for as long as it took them to reject it. The record of their negotiations with OPEC since 1970, with a few short-lived exceptions, only reinforces this conclusion.

Saudi Arabia, as indicated a page or two earlier, occupies a central place in the counter-strategy which the Western powers, and the United States in particular, have adopted in an endeavour to ensure stability of oil supplies and prices. The key element is the size of the Saudi Arabian oil reserves, and the extent to which production from them can be raised, both to meet the oil requirements of the industrial countries and to frustrate any moves by the rest of OPEC to raise prices. The success of the counter-strategy (the implementation of which is closely bound up with the Saudi–American 'special relationship') depends to a considerable extent upon the correct answers – 'correct', that is, from the standpoint of the West – being given to a number of questions. Does Saudi Arabia actually possess, or will she possess in the immediate future, the requisite spare producing capacity? Is she willing to act as 'residual supplier' in the Western interest, boosting her production, if required, to prevent the rest of OPEC from threatening a cut-back or even a shut-down as a means of forcing up the price of oil? Conversely, will she act as 'residual supplier' in OPEC's interest, lowering her output whenever a glut occurs on the market so as to enable those members of OPEC with the greatest need for revenue (Algeria, Persia, etc.) to keep up their oil exports as well as to prevent a fall in oil prices? Or, again, will Saudi Arabia simply consult her own interests, primarily if not exclusively, and adjust her production of oil to her own financial and political desiderata?

Saudi Arabian production, after the lifting of the previous winter's embargo, reached 8.5 million b/d in the summer of 1974, at which time ARAMCO predicted that production would rise to a maximum sustainable capacity of 11.2 million b/d by 1976, 16 million b/d by 1979 and 20 million b/d by 1980. When 1976 came, however, actual production averaged only 8.3 million b/d throughout the year, even though it reached a height of 8.8 million b/d in December, when the oil companies were stockpiling against the price increase expected to take effect from 1 January 1977. ARAMCO's maximum sustainable productive capacity was reported in the spring of 1977, and again in February 1978, to be between 11 and 12 million b/d. The later report admitted, however, that actual production in the first quarter of 1977 had been well below this level, averaging 9.2 million b/d. It rose to 10 million b/d in April 1977, before the fire which broke out in the Abqaiq field in the second week of May severely reduced output. Before the year was out ARAMCO had had to revise its estimate of future sustainable productive capacity (from the earlier figures of 16 million b/d by 1979 and 20 million b/d by 1980) down to 15.5 million b/d by 1983. Even this estimate had to be trimmed again in the first half of 1978 to 12 million b/d by 1983 – or even as late as 1987. Some doubt must attach, therefore, to the accuracy of the reports of ARAMCO's having achieved a sustainable productive capacity of between 11 and 12 million b/d in 1977.

According to testimony from ARAMCO sources given before the Senate sub-committee on multinational corporations in 1974, 9.2 million b/d was the level at which major technical difficulties would be encountered in raising the rate of production in the Saudi Arabian fields. To overcome these difficulties would require not only considerable engineering skill and perhaps technical innovations but also the investment of very large amounts of capital. Whether the figure of 9.2 million b/d was accurate or not, the Saudi government apparently seized upon it, and upon similar calculations from undisclosed sources, to impose in the latter half of 1978 a ceiling of 12 million b/d of sustainable capacity upon ARAMCO's future production levels. At the same time the Saudis reaffirmed the unchanging nature of the requirement that ARAMCO should finance any and all expansion of its production facilities from earnings – even though Saudi Arabia was on the verge of fully nationalizing the company. The upshot of these restrictions was that ARAMCO again revised its estimate of future production levels, from a maximum sustainable capacity of 12 million b/d down to 10.8 million b/d by 1983, and to 11.2 million b/d by 1987. Actual production during 1978 was limited by order of the Saudi government to a maximum of 8.5 million b/d, of which no more than 65 per cent was allowed to be drawn in Arabian light crude, i.e. primarily from the Ghawar and Abqaiq fields. While the limitation was temporarily suspended during the first few months of 1979 to help offset the loss of oil exports from Persia, it was reimposed after Persian production began to pick up. From a reported output of 9.5 million b/d in the first quarter of the year ARAMCO was made to cut back to the limit of 8.5 million b/d.

Even without the constraints imposed by the Saudi government and the problem of raising the large amounts of capital necessary to finance future development of the oilfields, the fields themselves present formidable technical obstacles, which there is not space to describe here, to the expansion of Saudi Arabian oil production.* Accidents like the Abqaiq fire, or unforeseeable Acts of God, moreover, underline the risks of basing Western policy upon predictions of future Saudi production levels. But there are other reasons for casting doubt upon the willingness or ability of Saudi Arabia to act as 'residual supplier' in the Western interest, particularly in order to keep oil prices down. Despite numerous promises of price reductions, usually conveyed through the mouth of Yamani, the price of oil has continued to rise and it has done so, however much the Saudis and their Western apologists may endeavour to camouflage the fact, with Saudi encouragement. William Simon, the United States secretary of the treasury, told the Senate sub-committee on multi-national corporations in July 1974 that Yamani had assured him that an auction of Saudi Arabian oil would be held the following month, the intention of the Saudi government being to demonstrate that the real market price of oil was well below its posted price, and thereby to induce the other OPEC governments to lower it. The auction never took place. Asked by the sub-committee in May 1976 why it had not, James Akins (who had been the American ambassador to Saudi Arabia at the time) explained that there was opposition to the move from within the Saudi government as well as from Persia, Iraq and Algeria. Because the United States government did not pursue the matter, Akins added, Yamani and his masters concluded that it was not really interested in bringing down oil prices. It is a pretty tale, its only flaw being that it omits to mention that a short time later, at an OPEC meeting in Abu Dhabi in November 1974, Yamani took the lead in pushing through a further price increase which was completely unwarranted by prevailing circumstances.

Two months later Saudi Arabia reduced her output of oil from 8.5 million to 7.6 million b/d. A further cut, to 6.5 million b/d, was made the following month, February 1975, and for the same reason, viz. to prevent a glut in the oil market, which was then in a depressed state as a result of the economic

---

* They are discussed in detail in a staff report to the sub-committee on international economic policy of the Senate Foreign Relations Committee in April 1979, from which much of the above information has been obtained.

depression in many industrial countries. To what degree the major oil companies may have co-operated in implementing this policy it is difficult to
determine. The companies themselves maintain that monthly production
levels are determined by market conditions, and that the market for oil early in
1975 was slack. There was no point, therefore, in producing at a higher level
than the market warranted, as excess production entailed additional costs, not
least in transport and storage charges. Yet the fact remains that the cuts in
Saudi Arabian output in 1975 were ordered by the Saudi government and
carried into effect by ARAMCO, even though the Saudis' motives in ordering
them were transparently clear, viz. to prevent the latest price increase from
being undermined by price-cutting in a buyer's market, and to allow the other
members of OPEC a sufficient share of the market so as not to tempt them into
discounting their oil in order to sell it. All could then expect to benefit from the
latest price increase when demand picked up.

   At first glance, Saudi Arabia's actions in 1975 would appear to indicate that if
she is to play the role of residual supplier at all, she will do so in OPEC's
interests, not the West's; and substance is lent to this view by Yamani's
frequently repeated claims in the past that Saudi Arabia's financial needs could
be met by a daily production of 4.5 million barrels. Yet the situation is not quite
as clear-cut as this. When world demand for oil fell in 1976 and 1977 Saudi
Arabia increased her production, from 7.1 million b/d in 1975 to 8.5 million
b/d in 1976 and to roughly 9 million b/d for the first six months of 1977.
Together, Saudi Arabia and the UAE (i.e. principally Abu Dhabi) increased
their oil exports in 1976 and 1977 by 120 million tonnes, while all the other
Arab oil states combined increased their exports by 30 million tonnes. Saudi
Arabia, in other words, at a time when demand was slack, raised her production as she saw fit, kept oil prices steady and increased her share of the market
at the expense of her Arab partners in OPEC. Her conduct has been a
repetition of what it was in 1971 and 1972, when she raised her output by 26 per
cent in both years while that of Iraq, Libya and Algeria declined. That she
intends to go on this way was indicated by the loquacious Yamani in September
1977, when he warned that Saudi Arabia would not increase her production
above 8.5 million b/d to meet the industrial world's needs unless some progress
was made towards a settlement of the Arab–Israeli dispute. As production at
that time was 7.65 million b/d the warning did not carry a great deal of weight.

   An even stronger pointer to Saudi Arabia's intended policy was the condition laid down by the Saudi government, in its negotiations with ARAMCO
for the complete nationalization of the company's concession and assets, that
the company should lift a minimum of 7 million b/d of Saudi oil. 'Significant'
penalties would be imposed if ARAMCO's off-take fell below this figure,
which was equivalent to 20–25 per cent of OPEC's total average daily output in
1976 and 1977. Yamani's nonchalant pretence that 4.5 or even 4 million b/d is
sufficient to meet Saudi Arabia's financial needs is plainly a thing of the past.

The Saudi government's appetite for revenue has grown in direct proportion to its lavish expenditure and the soaring costs of its current five-year development programme. The sum of $28,400 million per annum originally budgeted for the implementation of the programme has proved grossly inadequate. The oil revenues for 1978 were in the vicinity of $34,000 million, which at prices current in that year represented an output of around 8.4 million b/d. (ARAMCO's average production for 1978 is said to have been 8.1 million b/d. Production from Saudi Arabia's share of the former Saudi–Kuwaiti neutral zone averaged 300,000 b/d.) Perhaps as much as $20,000 million per annum more is needed to carry out the development programme in its original form. Where is the money to come from? Increased production of any significant dimensions seems out of the question, for the reasons already adverted to, including the fluctuating state of the market. To trim the programme to fit the financial cloth would require sweeping economies of expenditure upon industrial development, the armed services, the bureaucracy, education and other social services, economies which could not fail to produce adverse effects, especially in terms of political unrest. The only alternative, it would seem, is to seek higher oil prices.

All the indications are that the Saudi government intends to continue to impose restraints upon oil production so as to prolong the technical life of the fields – which in turn implies that it will seek to raise prices at intervals in order to maintain revenues at a desired level. The only way to achieve this aim is through the survival of the OPEC cartel, which is why Saudi Arabia, one of the principal founders of the organization, will strive to ensure its survival. How much, if at all, her 'special relationship' with the United States may hamper her pursuit of these aims has yet to be seen. Her equally special relationship with ARAMCO is unlikely to act as a brake upon her activities and ambitions, even though the Saudi government sorely needs the company's assistance, not only to operate its oil industry but also as an instrument with which to regulate or manipulate the volume of oil on the market, and its price. Under the terms that have so far been revealed of the arrangements worked out between the Saudis and ARAMCO for the continued operation of the Saudi oil industry, ARAMCO will remain a wholly American-owned services company, responsible for producing operations, exploration and development, as well as for marketing Saudi Arabian oil through its parent companies. Ownership of the oil reserves and the company's physical assets in Saudi Arabia, TAPline excepted, passes to the Saudi government, which will also control output, as it has done for some years past.

Much the same relationship has been established between the governments of the other Arab oil states and the companies operating in their territories. The companies' concessions and assets have been fully nationalized, or, if the companies have been permitted to retain a minority shareholding (as is the case, for instance, in Abu Dhabi), it is because the local government is reluctant to assume responsibility for matters beyond its competence to handle. (Because of the dearth of competent local personnel the Abu Dhabi National Oil Company is in effect run by Algerians, who may be counted upon, whenever the occasion warrants it, to find trumped-up reasons for restricting production.) Whatever the case, the companies have placed themselves at the service of the Gulf oil states, regulating oil production on their behalf and raising prices at their behest. Rivalry between the companies themselves nowadays takes less the form of competition for a larger share of the world market in oil than that of a contest for long-term contracts with the Gulf oil states and preferential terms of access to their reserves of crude. Until very recently the companies were wont to justify their progressive submission to the dictates of the governments of these states by arguing that their concessions, however much they might be modified by each successive participation agreement, still gave them access, albeit in ever diminishing degree, to their own reserves of crude. Now even this flimsy justification is denied them, and all that the companies have to fall back upon by way of excuse for their unfailing deference to the wishes of the governments of the Arab oil states is that it allows them privileged access to government-owned crude. It is a dubious privilege, as the companies know full well. For not only can it be revoked in an instant, at the whim of any one of these governments, but it has also been obtained at very high cost, viz. the abdication by the companies of their prime responsibility to their customers, the oil-consuming countries. This abdication, and the drastic diminution of their power over the past decade, has left the companies virtual prisoners of the Arab oil states. They are forced to be accessories to, or at best mute witnesses of, whatever economic follies and excesses the governments of these states may care to commit. They are not even any longer, as they were dubbed a few years back, 'mere tax-collecting agencies' for these governments; instead, they have become even lowlier functionaries, the bearers of tribute from the West and hostages for the good conduct of their own governments in Arab eyes.

Further tribulations doubtless lie in store for them. They may be forced, after the precedent set by the Saudi government in its negotiations with ARAMCO, to lift a minimum quantity of crude, whatever the state of the market. As the price of their preferential access to crude, they may be required – and some companies already have been – to enter into partnership with the host government (even to put up the major part of the capital needed) in huge and expensive schemes of industrialization, most, though not all, of them related to the oil industry, whose chances of economic success are problematical in the extreme. The Gulf oil states have made no secret of the fact that they intend to move more and more into the 'downstream' operations of the oil industry, to build more refineries, petro-chemical plants and other associated facilities in their own countries, to transport and market abroad crude oil, gas and refined products. In short, they are bent upon extending their control over the world oil market by expansion into the secondary and tertiary sectors. There is little chance that the Gulf oil states could compete on even terms in the market for refined products. The cost of building and operating refineries, petro-chemical plants and petroleum-related facilities in the Gulf is far higher than it is in the industrial countries. So also is the cost of transporting refined products as compared with that of shipping crude oil in bulk. Unless the governments of the oil states are prepared to sustain large losses on their investments, the prices they will have to charge for their refined products will make them uncompetitive. Faced with this unpalatable conclusion, they may well resort to intimidation to dispose of their unwanted output, by making it a condition of continued access to their reserves of crude that the oil companies accept a certain proportion of their off-take in refined products -- and transport them in host-government flag vessels.

How the oil companies view their present situation *vis-à-vis* the Arab oil states it is impossible to deduce from their rare and excessively sibylline utterances on the subject. It is hard to believe that they are content with it or that they are not apprehensive about the future. Perhaps it would be no bad thing, as some qualified observers have suggested, if the companies were to withdraw completely from direct operations in the Arab producing countries. After all, they have lost their *raison d'être* for being in these countries, viz. ownership of the oil reserves. If they were to become simply purchasers of crude at the pierhead, they could use their position as world-wide distributors of oil to negotiate sensible prices, instead of merely bowing to the caprices of the governments of the oil states and passing on arbitrary price rises to the consumers. The obvious drawback to this course of action is that the national oil companies which these governments have set up to assume ostensible control over oil production and 'downstream' activities in their countries are, most of them, incapable of running the oil industry by themselves. Unless the Western oil companies were to provide the necessary engineers and technical staff, they would quickly run the industry into the sand.

However chimerical the 'partnership' between the oil companies and the governments of the Arab oil states has become, the West in general is still relying upon it to ensure security of oil supplies and stability of prices. The IEA apart, the Western governments have made no real effort to co-ordinate their oil policies or to present a united front to OPEC. Instead, they are pursuing separate and often conflicting national policies, three of the worst offenders being the United States, Britain and France. The United States virtually doubled its importation of oil between 1973 and 1976, while that of most Western European countries remained constant or even declined. Oil imports into the United States in 1976 were 29 per cent higher than in 1975, and 46 per cent of the total volume of oil imported came from the Arab oil states, an increase from this source of 83 per cent over the previous year. The picture did not alter appreciably in 1977 and 1978. While some of the oil was acquired to build up a strategic oil reserve, too great a portion of it was simply consumed in profligate domestic use. It is really little short of scandalous that the United States should consume so disproportionate a share as she does of the oil produced in the world each year, and it is equally reprehensible that as the senior partner in the Atlantic Alliance she should have ignored the economic and strategic interests of Western Europe in committing herself to a comprehensive arrangement with Saudi Arabia over oil, the implications of which may well prove formidable. Britain likewise has shown a cynical indifference to the welfare of her European partners and allies by the restrictive practices she has followed with respect to the extraction and disposition of oil from the North Sea fields, and by insisting upon the maintenance of a substantial minimum price for it. It is wholly against the interest of Western Europe, and still more of that of the poorer countries of the world, that oil prices should remain at their present high levels.

What the United States, Western Europe and Japan should be aiming at in concert is the target indicated by Thomas Enders of the State Department in 1975, when he drew attention to the menace implicit in the mounting financial surpluses of the Arab oil states. 'It is in the interest of the industrial countries – indeed, of all consuming countries', Enders wrote, 'that conditions be created in which OPEC loses and cannot subsequently regain the power to set oil prices at artificially high levels.' A *sine qua non* of this strategy is that the industrial nations should reduce their excessive dependence upon Middle-Eastern oil by cutting their oil consumption in absolute terms, by intensifying the search for new oil reserves, and by developing and utilizing more efficiently existing alternative sources of energy. Even a sizable reduction in oil consumption, however, will not release the industrial nations, still less the economically backward countries of Asia and Africa, from the financial straitjacket into which they have been strapped by exorbitant oil prices. A fall in demand for oil will merely induce OPEC to raise prices, if it can, to compensate for the drop in revenues. The more aggressive members of the cartel, notably Persia, Libya, Kuwait and Algeria, have made this plain on several occasions. Yet any severe increase in prices might well prompt a correspondingly severe fall in consumption and a further loss of revenue.

OPEC is not a monolith. Its thirteen members – Algeria, Iraq, Kuwait, Libya, Qatar, Saudi Arabia, UAE, Persia, Nigeria, Indonesia, Venezuela, Ecuador and Gabon – all have divergent ambitions and requirements; none is the natural partner of the others, not even its Arab members. The very diversity of its membership, and the inevitable tensions that will arise now that the OPEC governments have taken full control of oil production, make the cartel vulnerable to disruption. Until recently the Western oil companies have served as a buffer to reduce or absorb potential causes of friction among the cartel's members. They still serve this function, although to a diminishing extent. They could, if they wished, abandon it altogether. As the natural antipathies among OPEC's member governments assert themselves, which they are bound to, the façade of unity will crack, particularly among the Middle-Eastern states. The entire course of Middle-Eastern history testifies to such an outcome. The day when the cartel disintegrates, however, will not be hastened by the Western powers continuing to adopt towards OPEC the posture of the rabbit faced with the stoat. If they act instead in unison to exploit the organization's patent vulnerability, using the diversity of economic and political weapons at their disposal and playing upon the antagonisms that divide OPEC's members, they will accomplish both the break-up of the cartel and their own release from financial bondage.

It is sometimes forgotten that the dependence of the industrial world upon oil from the Middle East is less than a generation old. Out of a total world production in 1939 of approximately 278 million tons, the United States produced 168 million tons, and Persia and Iraq between them only 13.62 million tons. In 1946, the first full year of post-war production, the United States produced 230 million tons out of a total world production of 371 million tons, while Persia produced 19.19 million, Iraq 4.60 million, Saudi Arabia 7.99 million and Kuwait 0.80 million tons. Even in 1950, by which time the Saudi Arabian and Kuwaiti fields were beginning to come into full production, the total amount of oil produced in the Middle East was only 86.60 million tons out of a total world production of 518 million tons. The industrial world, in brief, has done without Middle-Eastern oil before, and it can, if necessary, do without it again. The attraction which Middle-Eastern oil held for the West was not just its abundance but its cheapness. If it ceases to be cheap, if it becomes, as it has become, ludicrously expensive, it will lose its attractiveness, and the Western industrial nations and Japan, as soon as they are in a position to do so, will cease to buy it.

Indeed, if the Arabs and the Persians and their partners in OPEC continue on their present reckless course, they could well bring the age of oil in the world's history to a premature end. The Gulf would then revert to the backwater it has been for centuries past, its shores lined with the rusting carcasses of refineries, petro-chemical complexes and gas liquefaction plants, the skeletons of which may still be visible two or three millennia hence, to confound any archaeologist who may chance upon them and perhaps lead him to wonder, like Shelley's traveller in an antique land, whether he is not contemplating the vestiges of a once magnificent civilization.

> Nothing beside remains. Round the decay
> Of that colossal wreck, boundless and bare
> The lone and level sands stretch far away.

CHAPTER IX
Gazelles and Lions

*The Arab oil producers are militarily insignificant – gazelles . . . in
a world of lions.*

J. William Fulbright, *November 1973*

It is one of the intellectual conceits of our day that the scientific and technological advances of the past half-century, especially in methods of waging war,
have invalidated the strategic concepts which held good in the nineteenth
century and up to the First World War regarding the defence of the Middle
East against the expansionist aims of Russia. The old notions about the
safeguarding of the routes to India, the definition of spheres of influence in
western Asia, the maintenance of the independence of Turkey, Persia and
Afghanistan as buffer states or barrier powers for the defence of India –
everything, in fact, that went to make up the constituents of the 'Great Game'
played between Britain and Russia in the lands stretching from the Bosporus to
the Himalaya, has been rendered obsolete (so we have been told by the school
of strategic thought which has been in the ascendant these last two decades or
so) by the advent of nuclear weapons, by air power, by the passing of the
British raj in India, by the end of European dominion in Asia, by the emergence of the successor Asian nation-states, and by the ideological revolution
which has accompanied these great transformations. Changed political
circumstances, new techniques of warfare and advances in methods of transportation and communication, so the same authoritative voices have assured
us, have likewise undermined the older doctrines about the primacy of sea
power, the preservation of Western naval supremacy in the Indian Ocean, the
acquisition and retention of naval stations around its shores, and the necessity
to command the sea lanes from Asia to Europe.

There has been about this insistent denunciation of the strategic concepts of
an earlier age as hopelessly outmoded and irrelevant to our contemporary
condition more than a suggestion of despair, of a compelling need to rationalize
the dispirited retreat of the West from the world east of Suez by representing it
as the logical consequence of a revolutionary change in strategic imperatives,
and not (as it might otherwise be interpreted) as a manifestation of the

demoralization and deadly lethargy which has overtaken the West of late years. It is a compulsion which the Soviet Union evidently does not share; for her policy and conduct in the Middle East over the past thirty years, ever since she attempted to remain in possession of northern Persia at the end of the Second World War, bear all the hallmarks of a strategy inherited from imperial Russia, one which successive Tsarist governments had consistently adhered to since the early eighteenth century.

'Russia pursues the same system of strategy against Persia and Turkey,' observed Lord Palmerston, the British foreign secretary, in October 1835; 'she creeps down the Black Sea and wants to do the same down the Caspian and to take both Persia and Turkey on each of their flanks.' Russia's bid to dominate the Black Sea and secure an outlet to the Mediterranean began with Peter the Great, and by the time that Palmerston made his observation she had annexed Bessarabia, loosened the Turkish hold over the Danubian principalities of Moldavia and Wallachia, and played a major part in securing the independence of the Greek provinces of the Ottoman empire. She had also obtained the right, which she had not hitherto possessed, to maintain a navy in the Black Sea; and by the deliberate misconstruction of a treaty clause she claimed the further right to exercise a protectorate over the Orthodox Christian subjects of the Ottoman sultan throughout the empire.

The first three decades of the nineteenth century also saw a spectacular extension of Russia's frontiers in the Caucasus. In two wars with Persia, the first in 1804–13, the second in 1826–8, Russia obtained possession of Baku, Georgia, Daghestan, Erivan, northern Azerbaijan and part of Armenia – in fact, all of Persia's Caucasian territories as far south as the River Araxes. She also assumed for herself the sole right to keep warships in the Caspian Sea. The threat that might eventually develop to the security of the British dominions in India from Russia's penetration of Persia led in 1814 to the conclusion of a British defensive treaty with the court of Tehran. But owing to the neglect and parsimony of British governments in England and in India over the next twenty years the treaty fell into virtual abeyance. British interest in Persia only revived in the mid-1830s when the reigning shah showed signs of intending, with Russian encouragement, to compensate himself for the loss of his Caucasian provinces over the previous two decades by annexing Herat, one of the three major Afghan principalities. As any extension of Persian authority into Afghanistan at this stage was, in British eyes, tantamount to giving the Russians an advanced outpost on the approaches to India, pressure was applied to the shah to abandon his plans. His refusal to do so led the British government in India not only to mount an armed demonstration in the Persian Gulf but also (such are the curious inconstancies and contradictions of Oriental politics) to send an expedition to occupy Kabul a year or so later. For the assumption upon which British policy towards Persia was henceforth to proceed was that Afghanistan served just as much as Persia as a buffer state to

British India; and that neither, therefore, should be permitted, acting either on its own initiative or under inspiration or duress from Russia, to weaken the other.

For the rest of the century Russia's efforts against the Ottoman empire were directed primarily to the elimination of Turkish rule from the Balkans. These efforts were not opposed by Britain except when they threatened to secure for Russia direct access to the Mediterranean. Instead, British policy was directed towards the preservation of the Ottoman empire in Asia and the prevention of a Russian ascendancy at Constantinople. Although Russia wrested possession of Batum from the Turks in the Russo–Turkish war of 1877–8, there seemed less chance that she would make further inroads into the Ottoman dominions in Asia Minor in the last quarter of the century than that she might acquire further slices of Persian territory, as a consequence of having outflanked that power east of the Caspian by her advances into Central Asia in the twenty years between 1864 and 1884. As it happened, the Russians were quite content at this stage to pause and digest their new conquests, and not to continue their advance southwards into Khorasan and Afghanistan.

Two important consequences followed from the Russian conquest of Central Asia. One was that Russia, like Britain in India, had become a Muslim as well as a Christian power; the other was that, in addition to drawing much closer to the approaches to India, she had shown herself to be capable of undertaking arduous and sustained military operations deep in the heart of Asia. Hitherto the British had believed that the preservation of Turkey, Persia and Afghanistan as barrier powers to India could be achieved by diplomatic, political and economic means. Now they had to consider whether and by what routes the Russians might attempt an actual advance to the gates of India; whether it would be from Armenia by way of Lake Van or Persian Azerbaijan to the Tigris and thence to Baghdad and the Gulf; or from Transcaspia by way of Merv and Herat to Kandahar; or from Khiva to Bukhara and on over the Hindu Kush to Kabul; or by any one of a dozen alternative, if difficult, approaches. The Russians apparently regarded Persia as the key. Northern Persia in the thirty years between the conquest of Merv in 1884 and the outbreak of the First World War became virtually a Russian province. The Russians also evinced a growing interest in the Gulf, opening a consulate-general at Bushire and regularly dispatching warships to cruise in its waters. When Britain extended a veiled protectorate over Kuwait by means of the secret agreement of 1899, her action was influenced as much by reports of Russian endeavours to secure permission from the Sublime Porte to build a railway through Turkey to the Gulf as it was by Germany's bid to obtain a concession to extend the Berlin-to-Constantinople line onwards to Baghdad and Kuwait.

By the turn of the century, or even earlier, it was clear that Germany's growing penetration of the Ottoman empire and Russia's undoubted preponderance in Persia and Central Asia had made it impossible for Britain to continue to hold the line in Turkey and Persia. Taking advantage, therefore, of the mood of caution induced in the Tsarist government by the 1905 revolution and Russia's defeat at the hands of Japan in the Far East, Britain reached an accommodation with the Russians in 1907 over their respective positions in Asia. So far as Persia was concerned, the northern part of the country was acknowledged as lying within Russia's direct sphere of influence, the east as coming within Britain's, and the intervening southern and central portions as neutral territory. Unavoidable though the Anglo-Russian *détente* now seems in the perspective of history, the Persians not unreasonably condemned the 'partition' of their country out of hand, and they have never ceased to heap opprobrium upon Britain for consenting to it, while tempering their criticism of Russia's participation with a large measure of discretion.

The outbreak of war in 1914 and the decision of the Sublime Porte to align itself with Germany and Austria–Hungary spelled the end not only of the Ottoman empire's role as a barrier power but also of the empire itself. Early in 1915 Russia, Britain and France agreed that on the termination of hostilities the Ottoman dominions should be dismembered, with Russia being placed in possession of the straits and substantial areas of eastern Turkey. The revolution of 1917 and Russia's subsequent withdrawal from the war nullified the agreement so far as she was concerned; and the turmoil which followed within the Russian empire, as the Tsarist and Bolshevik forces fought for supremacy, brought to a halt for the time being the expansionist policy of the preceding century and a half. In the Caucasus, Georgia, Armenia and Azerbaijan rose in revolt against the Bolsheviks and Russian rule alike; while beyond the Caspian the subject khanates of Kokand, Khiva and Bukhara declared themselves independent once again. Though the Bolsheviks were to crush the revolts in the Caucasus and Transcaspia before very long, they were sufficiently unsettled by them, as well as distracted by the exigencies of the civil war, to seek to calm Muslim sentiment in the frontier regions by reaching an accommodation with Turkey and Persia respectively.

There was a further consideration which made the establishment of good relations with these two countries desirable. Russia was not merely a great power but she was also now a communist state. Henceforth her foreign policy was to be conducted in accordance both with her national interests and with her position as the centre and driving force of international communism. As time was to show, the national and ideological objectives of the Soviet Union rapidly merged (if they had ever been separate), and were to be pursued by means of the international communist movement as well as by conventional diplomatic and military means. One of Lenin's principal theses was that Western capitalism might be dealt a crippling and perhaps mortal blow by striking at it through its dependence upon its colonial possessions, overseas trade and distant sources of raw materials. At the Congress of the Peoples of the East at Baku in September 1920 a great deal of oratory was expended on the theme of fomenting revolutionary and nationalist discontent throughout Asia, directed against 'reactionary native rulers' and 'foreign imperialists' alike. Stalin, as Commissar of Nationalities, was much taken at the time with the attractions of this 'Eastern' strategy, and at the twelfth congress of the Soviet communist party in April 1923 he declared:

Two things are possible: either we succeed in stirring up and revolutionizing the far imperialist rear – the colonial and semi-colonial countries of the East – and thereby hasten the fall of capitalism, or we fail, and thereby strengthen imperialism and weaken the force of our own movement.

Although Leninist dogma had it that the destruction of capitalism and imperialism in Asia would be accomplished, as it had been in Russia, by the revolt of the masses under communist leadership, the Bolsheviks in time came to realize that the likelihood of native communist parties emerging in the states of Asia in sufficient strength to precipitate revolution in the foreseeable future was exceedingly remote. They fell back, therefore, upon the expedient alternative of co-operating with any nationalist movement, whatever its origins, which took up the struggle against Western imperialism. In the Middle East this meant any movement which was anti-British, since Britain was the dominant power in the area. It was with this in mind, as well as the need to stabilize the situation in the Caucasus and Transcaspia, that the Bolsheviks set out in 1921 to conciliate the provisional nationalist government in Ankara led by Mustafa Kemal, and the nationalist regime installed in Tehran by the military *coup* of Reza Khan. Treaties were concluded by the Bolsheviks with both governments in 1921, by which the Bolsheviks renounced the 'criminal policy' of their Tsarist predecessors and cancelled all existing treaties previously concluded with Turkey and Persia by Tsarist Russia. Further treaties of friendship and neutrality with the Soviet Union were signed by the Turkish and Persian governments in 1925 and 1927 respectively.

For all the fair phrases in the Soviet treaties with Persia and Turkey about the 'renunciation' of Tsarist ambitions, it is difficult to detect any measurable difference between Soviet aims in the Middle East after 1918 and those of Tsarist Russia before that date – whatever doctrinaire gloss the Bolsheviks might care to put upon their actions. Like the Tsarist regime before them, they were essentially concerned to eliminate British influence from Turkey and Persia, to destroy the function of these countries as barrier powers and to vanquish Britain in the ultimate innings of the 'Great Game' in Asia, whenever it might be played. Hence the conclusion of treaties in the 1920s with such unlikely partners as King Husain of the Hijaz, Ibn Saud of Najd and Imam Yahya of the Yemen. Notwithstanding occasional spurts of interest like these, the Soviet Union paid comparatively little attention to the Middle East between the wars, the energies of her rulers being primarily engaged in the task of substituting communist totalitarianism for Tsarist autocracy at home and teaching the peoples of the USSR to appreciate the distinction between the two. In fact, the strength of Soviet ambitions to spread Marxism throughout Asia fluctuated in accordance with developments inside the Soviet Union and in Europe. So, too, did the doctrinal approach towards the question of co-operation with nationalist movements opposed to the European powers in Asia. At the sixth congress of the Comintern in 1928, after the disappointing results of collaboration with the nationalists in China and the failure of communism to make progress in Germany had been made apparent, the decision was reached to withdraw support from bourgeois nationalism and to strive to bring about the revolution of the masses through the instrumentality of national communist parties alone. The decision had little effect upon the political scene in the Middle East, and especially in the Arab countries, where the local communist parties were of little account. At the seventh congress of the Comintern in 1935 the decision was reversed in the face of the ominous drift of events in central Europe. Co-operation with bourgeois nationalist parties in 'popular fronts' against the forces of 'fascism and imperialism' became the order of the day. Again, however, the ratiocinations of the ideologists in Moscow had no discernible impact upon the course of Middle-Eastern politics or the advancement of Soviet aims in the countries of the area.

While the Soviet government was prepared, subject to shifts in doctrinal emphasis, to tolerate or co-operate with bourgeois nationalism in Asia, it was resolutely opposed to any religious or racial movements which transcended national frontiers. Its hostility to such movements in the Middle East as pan-Islamism and pan-Turanianism (or pan-Turkism) arose from the fact that these movements appealed to Muslims and Turks in the Soviet Union to give their loyalty to an ideal or cause other than that of the USSR and Marxism–Leninism. Towards pan-Arabism, on the other hand, the Soviet attitude was equivocal. In so far as the movement was motivated by antagonism to the West it was to be welcomed; but to the extent that it was inspired by religious and racial sentiments it was to be deplored. What were considered to be more rewarding candidates for Soviet attention were the minority groups in which the Middle East abounded, and whose ethnic, religious and cultural grievances could be exploited to create difficulties for the governments under which they dwelt, as well as tension among these governments themselves. The fact that there were branches of these minorities living within the borders of the Soviet Union – among them Armenians, Kurds, Azerbaijanis and Turcomans – only increased the prospects for exploitation, although it also carried with it a danger of provoking disaffection with Soviet rule among these same Soviet minorities.

The Second World War, together with the opportunities for aggrandizement it afforded, stimulated the Soviet Union's interest in the Middle East anew. In September 1940 Germany, Italy and Japan concluded a tripartite pact defining their respective spheres of influence in Europe, Africa and Asia.

During negotiations in November 1940 to secure the Soviet Union's adhesion to the pact, the Soviet foreign minister stipulated that his government's concurrence was contingent upon the establishment of a Russian military and naval base 'within range of the Bosporus and the Dardanelles', and upon the recognition that 'the area south of Batum and Baku in the general direction of the Persian Gulf is the centre of the aspirations of the Soviet Union'. Before twelve months had passed the Russians had an opportunity to pursue these aspirations under rather different auspices. Following the German invasion of Russia in June 1941 and the refusal of Reza Shah to expel the numerous German agents in Persia, the British and Russian governments, now wartime allies, dispatched troops into Persia. Reza Shah abdicated, to be succeeded by his son, Muhammad Reza, and the country was divided into zones of occupation, the Russians in the north, the British in the centre and the south. Although Britain and Russia jointly undertook to respect the territorial integrity, sovereignty and political independence of Persia, and to cease their occupation of the country within six months of the termination of hostilities against Germany and her allies, when the war ended the Russians refused to evacuate northern Persia. The reason was fairly obvious.

The region south of Batum and Baku, which the Soviet foreign minister had spoken of in 1940 as constituting 'the centre of the aspirations of the Soviet Union', has as its strategic core a wedge of territory stretching southwards from Soviet Armenia to Diyarbakir in Turkey in the west and Tabriz, the capital of Persian Azerbaijan, in the east, and thence to Mosul and the upper reaches of the Tigris and Zab rivers. Enclosed within this wedge is the greater part of Kurdistan, that is to say, those parts of Turkey, Persia and Iraq which comprise the homeland of the Kurdish tribes. Kurdistan and Azerbaijan are the northern gates to Iraq and western Persia, to the valley of the Tigris, the oilfields of Kirkuk and Khuzistan and the approaches to the Gulf. If the Russians were to station themselves at either gate, they would be well placed to advance southwards at any time of their choosing. For this reason they had before the war expressed cautious sympathy for the cause of Kurdish independence (cautious because there were over a hundred thousand Kurds living within the borders of the Soviet Union). Separatist tendencies, though on a lesser scale, also existed among the Turkic-speaking inhabitants of Persian Azerbaijan, tendencies which the Russian occupying forces endeavoured to exploit in the closing stages of the Second World War. With their backing, the local communist *Tudeh* party in December 1945 proclaimed the inauguration of the 'Democratic Republic of Azerbaijan', linked by 'fraternal bonds' with the USSR. Almost simultaneously with their installation of a puppet regime at Tabriz, the Russians encouraged a revolt against the authority of the Persian government by the Kurdish tribes in and around Mahabad, in the mountainous region of western Persia south of Lake Urmia. Although the leaders of the putative 'Kurdish Republic of Mahabad' were not communists, the Russians proposed to control them by making them dependent for arms and other supplies upon the revolutionary government in Tabriz.

The Soviet attempt to detach the 'republics' of Azerbaijan and Mahabad from Persia and to erect them into strategic outposts for future use was accompanied by a determined Soviet diplomatic offensive against Turkey. In March 1945 the Soviet government denounced the Russo–Turkish treaty of friendship of 1925, and in the months that followed let it be known that it would not be satisfied with anything less than the grant of military bases in the Bosporus and Dardanelles, together with the institution of a new regime of the straits which would amount to their being placed under Russian control. A demand was also preferred for the cession of the provinces of Kars and Ardahan in eastern Turkey.

The dual Soviet offensive against Turkey and Persia failed, partly but not entirely because the Russians overplayed their hand. The Turks stood firm, encouraged by Britain and the United States; and when in February 1947 the British government informed the United States that it could no longer afford to supply military and economic aid to Greece and Turkey, President Truman announced the following month that the United States would assume the task herself. Five years later Turkey's accession to NATO made the question of the straits an issue central to the defence of Western Europe, thereby checkmating the Russians. The crisis caused by the retention of Russian troops in northern Persia was resolved in May 1946 when the troops were withdrawn, following remonstrances by the British and United States governments and an appeal by the Persians to the newly created UN Security Council. Exactly why the Russians chose to withdraw is not entirely clear, even today. The explanation usually offered is that they were swayed both by the strength of the British and American protests and by their desire to retain the oil concession for northern Persia, which they had extracted from the Persian government as the price of their leaving. It is also possible, however, that a decisive influence was exerted upon the Russians' calculations by the realization that their behaviour in Persia was having adverse effects upon their diplomatic activities elsewhere. What-ever the reason, the Russians evacuated northern Persia, and before 1946 was out the Persian government had reasserted its authority over Azerbaijan and Mahabad. The following October, emboldened by the decision of the United States government earlier in the month to send a military mission to the Persian army, the Persians cancelled the Soviet oil concession outright.

The dissolution of the Indian empire in 1947 brought an end to Britain's role as a Muslim and Oriental power. It also deprived Persia of her principal buttress against the encroachment of Russia. However, the assumption by the United States, through the promulgation of the Truman Doctrine, of responsibility for the military and economic support of Greece and Turkey, and the extension of this responsibility to Persia later in 1947, meant that the old system of barrier powers to restrain the southward advance of Russia still survived. Formal expression was given to the prolongation of the system by the inauguration in 1955 of the Baghdad Pact, a defensive alliance linking Turkey, Persia, Iraq and Pakistan. While Britain adhered to the pact as a full member, the United States deemed it prudent only to 'associate' herself with the alliance, so as not to offer too great a provocation to the Soviet Union. Iraq withdrew from the pact after the revolution of 1958, the alliance thereafter being reconstituted as the Central Treaty Organization in 1960. Meanwhile the United States had acted to counter the weakening of the 'northern tier' caused by Iraq's defection by entering into bilateral defence agreements with Turkey, Persia and Pakistan in March 1959.

While the Soviet Union objected strongly to the creation of the Baghdad Pact she did not try to break it up by direct means but set out rather to undermine it from behind and within. The Russians were greatly assisted in their aim by the activities of Gamal Abdul Nasser, the president of Egypt, whose capacity for spreading disruption in the Middle East, like that of Mehemet Ali Pasha a century earlier, created opportunities for rich political pickings for the Russians. The Russo–Egyptian *entente*, initiated by the arms agreement between the two countries in 1955, enabled the Soviet Union to hurdle the 'northern tier' in the same year as it was erected, and to effect a lodgement not only in Egypt but also, in the course of the next decade, in Syria, Iraq and Algeria. Further lodgements were made in the succeeding decade in South Yemen, Somalia and Ethiopia, placing the Russians, for the first time in their history, in a position to exert pressure upon the Middle East from its southern as well as its northern perimeter.

The gains made by the Soviet Union in the Middle East in the twenty years or so after 1955 had been achieved by the policy of supporting Arab nationalist governments against the Western powers. At the twentieth congress of the Soviet communist party in 1956 the doctrine of the class struggle as the fundamental and indispensable element in the progression to communism in the countries of Asia was played down. Cautious approval was given instead to the possibility of different and even non-violent paths to socialism, as well as to the notion of the 'national bourgeoisie' as an ally in both the struggle against Western imperialism and the victory of the national liberation movement. Traditionally, Soviet ideology regarded the 'national bourgeoisie' in the states of Asia under European dominion as necessary only at the stage of winning their independence from the powers of Europe. Thereafter, so the dogma had it, the national bourgeoisie was bound to become unstable, would lose its 'progressive' character and would compromise with its late imperial masters. It would therefore become the task of the proletariat, after initially supporting the national bourgeoisie in the struggle for independence, to turn upon it in due course, and, under the leadership of the local communist parties and with the backing of the Soviet Union and other socialist states, overthrow the national bourgeois governments as a preliminary to building the socialist state.

So much for Soviet theory. By 1960 the national bourgeois regimes which had emerged as the successors to European imperial rule in Asia had consolidated their positions and were, most of them, beginning to develop their own kind of socialist state. More often than not this process involved the intimidation or suppression of the local communist parties, a consequence which implicitly challenged (even if unwittingly) Soviet dogma that the transition from the national bourgeois to the socialist state should be directed by the communist party. For sound practical reasons – among them the weakness of the local communist parties and the lack of working-class cadres in most Asian countries – the Soviet government suppressed its ideological reservations and continued to support the national bourgeois regimes. They were, after all, accomplishing the Russians' objectives for them, by their unceasing display of hostility to the West and by their constant extension of state control over their own economies. Thus, in the Middle East, the Soviet Union followed the wholly pragmatic policy of supplying military, economic and technical assistance to the military dictatorships which ruled over Egypt, Syria, Iraq, and later Algeria, refusing to allow herself to be disconcerted by the deviations from the doctrinally legitimate path to socialism which they represented.

The subordination of dogma to expediency in the conduct of Soviet foreign policy was all too apparent, as we have seen in an earlier chapter, in the Russians' exploitation of the Kurdish separatist movement in Iraq from the mid-1950s to the mid-1970s. Soviet policy in Arabia in the same period likewise demonstrated the secondary role assigned by the Russians to ideology in the pursuit of their strategic objectives in the Middle East. A new treaty was concluded with the Yemen in October 1955 in which the Soviet Union recognized 'the full and absolute independence of Yemen and also the full independence and absolute legal sovereignty of the king'. It seemed to matter little that the king in question, the Imam Ahmad ibn Yahya, was an absolutist and theocratic sovereign, utterly aloof from, indeed, immovably opposed to, everything the Soviet Union stood for. What mattered, as in the case of his father, the Imam Yahya, with whom a similar treaty had been concluded in 1928, was that he was actively hostile to the British in Aden. Further agreements covering the supply of arms and economic aid followed in 1956 and 1957, their latent purpose being to underwrite the campaign of harassment which the Yemenis were conducting against the British along the borders of the Aden Protectorate. As late as 1961, a year before Imam Ahmad's death and the revolution which overthrew his successor, the Soviet propaganda machine was still grinding out encomiums to the aged monarch, particular stress being laid upon his unrelenting struggle against the 'imperialists' to the south.

In contrast, the Soviet attitude towards Saudi Arabia in these years became increasingly churlish. Although no serious attempt had been made after the

Second World War to renew the earlier diplomatic ties which had been abandoned in 1938, the Soviet government had observed a considerable degree of caution in its approach to the Saudi regime, exempting it from the kind of criticism to which governments of a monarchical or theocratic character were normally subject. When it seemed, however, in the late 1950s that Saudi Arabia was aligning herself with the 'imperialist' camp in the Middle East, the tolerance formerly accorded the Al Saud and Wahhabism in general vanished. Modern Wahhabism was accused of having discarded its 'positive' (i.e. egalitarian) attributes, and of having forsaken its original mission to restore the pristine simplicity of Islam. Instead, it had become a mere tool of the 'feudalists' for the exploitation of the Saudi people, part of the wider conspiracy to substitute religion for the growth of class feelings among the Arab masses. The criticism intensified when the revolution in the Yemen in 1962 brought a republican regime to power in Sana and the Saudis gave aid to the royalist forces in the ensuing civil war. The anti-Saudi propaganda did not diminish when Faisal succeeded his brother as ruler and instituted a programme of reform in Saudi Arabia. On the contrary, it reached new heights when Faisal organized the Islamic Pact in December 1965 as a counter to Nasser's influence in the Arab world. *Pravda* proceeded to denounce the Islamic Pact as 'an imperialist creation similar to the notorious Baghdad Pact, an instrument for combating the Arab national liberation movement . . . a means of bolstering the reactionary forces . . . a spearhead against the spreading of socialist ideas in the Middle East'.*

Much the same kind of hostility was evinced towards Kuwait in these years, partly for ideological reasons but mainly out of political calculation. The desire to preserve the influence it had acquired in Baghdad led the Kremlin both to adopt a more or less neutral stand over the merits of the Iraqi claim to Kuwait in 1961 and to curry favour with Qassim by vetoing Kuwait's application to join the United Nations. After Qassim's fall in 1963, however, the Russians responded favourably to an approach from Kuwait for the establishment of diplomatic relations, consented to Kuwait's admission to the UN and appointed an ambassador to the shaikhdom in June 1963. Pragmatism had smothered ideological misgivings. There was clearly more to be gained from acquiring a diplomatic foothold in Kuwait (the only such foothold the Soviet Union had in the Arabian peninsula other than that in the Yemen) than from indulging in denunciations of the Al Sabah's 'feudal' and 'reactionary' rule on the lines of that uttered by Khrushchev in 1964.

There was more to the Soviet Union's veering and tacking over policy in Arabia in the 1960s, however, than simply the growing ascendancy of pragmatism. The Kremlin's own ideological conceptions were in flux, largely as a consequence of the challenge that had been thrown down by the Chinese

---

* For this quotation, as for much useful background information on the development of Soviet ideology concerning the Arab world, I am indebted to Stephen Page's excellent study, *The USSR and Arabia*.

communists. Whereas the Soviet Union was prepared, in the interests of securing her own objectives as a great power, to accept the notion of gradualism – of separate and peaceful paths to socialism, of the role of the national bourgeoisie in effecting the transition to the socialist state and in fomenting and sustaining anti-Western sentiment in the Middle East as well as in Asia at large – the Chinese were not. They rejected all such compromises, declaring that the triumph of socialism in the world could only be achieved through the national liberation movement, a violent uprising of the urban and rural proletariat led by the communists and directed against the 'colonialists' and 'feudalists'. No trust or hope was to be reposed in the 'national bourgeoisie', however one defined, or failed to define, this anomalous body: its members were bound in the long run to throw in their lot with the 'imperialists' against the 'progressive' forces.

Under the impact of the Maoist assault the Russians were forced to revise some of their ideological formulations concerning the progression to socialism in the backward countries of the world. By the mid-1960s less emphasis was being placed upon the role of the national bourgeoisie as an instrument of political transformation, especially in countries where more than one political movement was active. More confidence was reposed instead in those one-party states where the governments, although not communist in complexion, were nevertheless strongly anti-Western, as well as interventionist in their national economic policies. In truth, however, the ideological arguments were becoming increasingly diffuse, contradictory and irrelevant as opportunism gained the upper hand in Soviet foreign policy. This became particularly evident in the Middle East after the disaster which befell Arab arms at the hands of the Israelis in the war of 1967, a disaster which grieved the Kremlin sorely. It had tied its fortunes to those of Nasser's 'Arab socialist' regime without having sufficient influence over the Egyptian dictator to ensure that his fortunes prospered. The Russians were not going to make the mistake again of allowing themselves to be ideologically identified with an Arab regime which claimed to be socialist. Thus Soviet commentary on the Arab world after 1967 made a point of emphasizing how far the states of the area were from making the transition to true socialism.

It was this attitude of caution which regulated Soviet relations with South Yemen in the years immediately following that country's attainment of independence in 1967. The Russians had been relatively slow to take notice of developments in Aden and the protectorates in the years after the Second World War. It was not until 1958, in fact, that they began to comment upon them, and then largely as a consequence of their own activities in the Yemen. The usual propaganda resulted. Britain was 'exploiting' Aden and the protectorates, using them as a base for 'aggression against the peace-loving countries and national liberation movements of Asia and Africa'. Over the next few years the Russians, in accordance with their theories about the national bourgeoisie, affected to regard, first the South Arabian League and then the Aden People's Socialist Party, as the leaders of the struggle for independence. They never seemed to grasp the fact that from 1963 onwards the running was being made by the NLF, and to a lesser extent by FLOSY; so that when the NLF emerged at the end of 1967 as the new masters of Aden and South Arabia, the Kremlin was taken by surprise. It was also uncertain of the character of the new regime, even though some of the NLF leadership were quick to show their Marxist–Leninist colours. Another factor inhibiting the Russians' approach to the NLF regime was the prompt appearance on the scene of their ideological rivals, the Chinese, with offers of technical aid for the new republic and support for the insurgency in Dhufar. Though the Russians lost little time in making comparable offers, they still hesitated to clasp the NLF leadership in a fraternal embrace, even after the Marxist–Leninist faction within it had overthrown its opponents and proclaimed its intention to build a society based upon the principles of 'scientific socialism' in South Yemen.

Moscow's reluctance to give its ideological imprimatur to the South Yemeni revolution was based primarily upon practical considerations. Ideological approval implied a willingness to provide economic, political and even military assistance, especially if the standing of the Soviet Union as the true and legitimate heir of Marx and Lenin, and the dynamic centre of world communism, was not to be impaired. Yet a commitment to a country such as South Yemen, virtually bankrupt and highly unstable, could well prove very costly financially and extremely embarrassing politically. The uncomfortable lesson of Cuba, with all that it had entailed in the way of incalculable economic and political liabilities incurred in haste, was still very much in the forefront of the Soviet government's mind a decade later. It was also uncertain of how the Western powers might react if it were to make a client of South Yemen. Moscow was still digesting the implications of Britain's withdrawal from Aden in 1967 and her proclaimed intention to leave the Gulf in 1971. It seemed to the Kremlin inconceivable that the United States would not compel the British to change their minds, still less that the Americans would sit idly by and allow the Soviet Union to occupy Britain's former base at Aden.

Britain's action in quitting the Gulf at the end of 1971 removed most of the Kremlin's doubts and hesitations about the wisdom of becoming involved in South Yemen. What few misgivings remained were completely dispelled two years later by the panic displayed by the Western powers in the wake of the Arab oil embargo of October 1973. Developments in South Yemen itself also played into the Russians' hands. The Aden regime had by this time managed to alienate not only the Western powers but the conservative Arab regimes as well, thereby cutting itself off from two potential sources of aid to alleviate South Yemen's desperate economic condition. The Chinese could not compete with the Soviet Union in the provision of material goods and arms, which left the radical Arab states, like Libya, and the Soviet Union and her European satellites as the only possible countries to which South Yemen could turn for succour. At the same time the Aden politburo was experiencing growing difficulty in maintaining its hold upon the country, especially as it was frequently distracted by outbreaks of feuding within its own ranks.

As every ruler of South Arabia since time began has learned, the only way in which order and authority can be imposed upon the country is by the ruthless and widespread application of force. The British never attempted, or wished to attempt, to enforce their rule outside Aden colony in this fashion, with the result that they have since been criticized for having left the hinterland, the former Aden Protectorate, in as backward a condition as they found it. Its perversion of the truth apart, the criticism is misconceived; for if Britain had employed the measure of severity necessary to subdue the inhabitants of South Arabia and cause them to abandon their age-old pursuits of rapine, slaughter and brigandage, not to mention their cherished superstitions, tribal customs and primitive social habits, she would have been execrated by enlightened opinion everywhere. Unlike the British, the NLF politburo had no compunction about endeavouring to crush the resistance of the tribesmen of South Yemen. Moreover, being Marxist–Leninist and therefore counted among the 'progressive' regimes of the world, it provoked no outraged protests in enlightened circles about the methods it used in erecting the grotesquerie of a Marxist–Leninist state in southern Arabia. Its only real problems were those created by its own limited economic resources, a lack of arms and deficiencies in modern techniques of repression.

All of these were supplied in increasing quantities by the Soviet Union and her allies from the mid-1970s onwards. For the Russians it was a small price to pay to secure access to Aden's incomparable strategic location, commanding at one and the same time the passage of the Red Sea, the southern gates of Arabia and the Horn of Africa. The benefits accruing to both partners to the arrangement were complementary. As the National Front regime was enabled to employ more brutal and effective methods for the subjugation of its people, so also the Soviet grip on Aden and South Yemen progressively tightened. The army was placed under the *de facto* command of Soviet officers, while the popular militia was trained by Cubans. East Germans, eventually to the number of 2,000, were brought in to take charge of the police and security services. They proceeded to introduce their own methods of dealing with political dissidents, including the setting up of concentration camps for the detention of real or suspected opponents of the regime. A South Yemeni air force was created, the aircraft being supplied by the Soviet Union, the air and ground crews by Cuba.

By the outset of 1978 South Yemen had progressed from being a client state of the Soviet Union to the status, for all practical purposes, of a Soviet colony. At the former RAF station at Khormaksar, outside Aden, now an operational base for the Soviet air force, were located the Russian military and intelligence headquarters for the Red Sea region. Aden itself furnished the Russians with naval facilities. A second naval station and air base had been established at Mukalla, in the Hadramaut, while on Socotra Island the Russians had installed communications and surveillance equipment. Whatever the Kremlin might privately think of the Marxist–Leninist pretensions of the National Front, it had now identified itself with the regime and with its fortunes. In any case, the ideological veneer on Soviet policy in this corner of the world, never very substantial at any time, had by now almost completely worn away. It mattered not in the least to the Kremlin that South Yemen was a pariah state, with an unsavoury reputation as a haven and training ground for the terrorist riff-raff of the world. On the contrary, her involvement in international terrorism only increased her attraction in Soviet eyes. Opportunism of the most flagrant kind was the governing factor in Soviet policy towards South Yemen, as it was towards her neighbours, Somalia and Ethiopia. Just how subject South Yemen had become to Soviet direction was amply demonstrated during 1977 and 1978 by the use of Aden as a logistics centre for the Ogaden and Eritrean campaigns, and by the employment of South Yemeni troops as Soviet auxiliaries in the latter conflict. It was displayed even more, however, by the Soviet intervention in the crisis which erupted in the leadership of the Aden politburo in the middle of 1978.

How the crisis came about and the course it took are still unclear, and doubtless will remain so for some time yet. Supreme power in South Yemen up to June 1978 had been wielded by a presidential council of three men – Salim Rubayyi Ali, the president, Ali Nasir Muhammad, the prime minister and Abdul Fattah Ismail, the chairman of the central committee of the National Front. The personal and political rivalry which had long existed between Salim Rubayyi Ali and Abdul Fattah Ismail attained violent proportions in late June 1978, when the presidential palace in Aden was assaulted by South Yemeni army units and militia detachments loyal to Abdul Fattah Ismail. They were supported by Cuban troops, five thousand of whom had been flown in from Ethiopia only the previous week. Cuban pilots flying MiG fighters attacked the palace and the defence ministry with cannon fire, while one or more Soviet warships off-shore shelled the same targets. The fighting lasted for most of 26 June, ending with the capture and swift execution of Salim Rubayyi Ali and his closest associates. Ali Nasir Muhammad was installed as acting president in his place, but the real victor was the fanatical Marxist ideologue, Abdul Fattah Ismail.

Fighting broke out at various places in South Yemen in the days and weeks that followed. It was probably inspired less by sentiment for the late president than by hatred for the victorious faction in the politburo, who called upon the Russians and the Cubans to help suppress the outbreaks. Russian naval vessels were reported to have shelled districts in the Hadramaut, while Cuban pilots flew sorties against rebel strongholds. Thousands of South Yemenis fled for safety to the Yemen, Saudi Arabia and Dhufar, among them army officers and police officials who feared the consequences of yet another vindictive purge of the army and police force. An entire battalion of the army in Beihan defected to the Yemen, its place being taken by an Ethiopian battalion brought in by the Russians. For students of history this last circumstance had a certain ironic interest; for in AD 525 the ancient Himyarite kingdom of Yemen was destroyed by invaders from Ethiopia, who remained in possession of south-western Arabia for the next fifty years, until they in turn were expelled in AD 575 by an expeditionary force sent from Persia. Thereafter Yemen was ruled as a Persian satrapy for half a century. The chances of such an historical episode recurring in our day would appear to be fairly remote.

Whatever other benefits the Soviet Union may have reaped from the ascendancy she has established at Aden, three at least are plain to see. She has acquired a base for the penetration of Africa; she has placed herself within striking distance of the Gulf oilfields; and she has gained control of one of the most important strategic outposts in the world, an importance which Aden has possessed ever since the early years of the sixteenth century when the great Portuguese captain, Affonso d'Albuquerque, sought to capture the trade of the Indies by seizing its traditional outlets, the Red Sea, the Gulf and the Straits of Malacca. Moreover, the Russians have learned the uses of sea power, which the West is in danger of forgetting, and they are ready to act upon this knowledge in the seas east of Suez.

How far the Soviet Union may desire access to the oil reserves of Arabia and the Gulf for her own sake, how far to deny them to the West, can only be matters for speculation. Much depends upon the Russians' reliance upon outside sources of oil to meet their own needs and those of their Eastern European allies. Up to about 1966 the Soviet Union produced sufficient oil each year to have a surplus after satisfying these requirements. Normally, the surplus was exported to the West in order to earn the hard currency needed to import industrial goods and machinery. After 1966, however, consumption of oil in the Soviet bloc began to exceed production, despite a rise in the volume of oil produced annually – from 148 million tons in 1960 to 353 millions tons in 1970 and perhaps as much as 520 million tons in 1976. Consumption has continued to increase in recent years and will probably go on doing so, though to what extent it will exceed production it is impossible to forecast with any precision. Western estimates of the probable size of the gap between the two have varied considerably: from 20 million to 100 million tons annually in the mid-1970s, up to as much as 160 million tons annually by the early 1980s. So far the deficiency has been made good by the importation of oil from the Middle East by the European satellite states, the transaction being arranged as a form of barter – oil in exchange for machinery and other industrial equipment. Barter deals of this kind have been concluded, for instance, between Persia on the one side and Rumania and Czechoslovakia on the other, and between Iraq on the one side and Hungary, East Germany and Czechoslovakia on the other. Although these transactions have been conducted with Soviet approval, the Soviet government is still anxious to retain the major part of the Eastern European market for itself, for obvious political purposes. It also wants to remain in a position to export oil to the West and Japan for the financial reasons outlined above.

There are only two ways open to the Soviet Union of meeting these various requirements: one is by expanding Soviet domestic production of oil; the other is by importing more oil from the Middle East. Most of the oil produced in the Soviet Union at present comes from the Volga–Urals region. It is doubtful, however, whether the deposits there will be sufficient to supply even half the volume of oil needed in the near future. There are large deposits in Siberia, especially around Tyumen in western Siberia, but their exploitation depends upon capital investment and advanced technological resources beyond the present reach of the Soviet government. Hence the Russian efforts in recent years to interest both the United States and Japan in the development of these oilfields. Even if these efforts were to bear fruit, there is little likelihood that oil would begin to flow from the Tyumen fields in any quantity for some time to come. Meanwhile the Soviet Union will become increasingly dependent upon Middle-Eastern oil to fill the gap between demand and supply and to provide the surplus needed for sale to Western Europe and Japan.

The Russians, however, are having to pay much higher prices for Middle-Eastern oil than they were before October 1973, and the extent to which they can increase their trade with the oil-producing countries to meet the bill is limited. Up to date the Russians have paid for Arab oil mainly with arms, to a value of $500–600 million annually over the past few years. Oil imports have been of comparable value, viz. 20 million tons in 1973 at a cost of $800 million at pre-October 1973 prices. The same volume of oil at prices obtaining in 1979 would cost anything between $4,000 million and $4,500 million. It seems unlikely that the Russians will be able to increase the value of their arms shipments to anything approaching these figures, and ordinary Russian manufactured goods have little appeal in the oil-producing countries, where there is a strong preference for Western and Japanese manufactures. The Soviet government's inability both to supply acceptable manufactures as substitutes for Western and Japanese products and to pay for oil in the requisite amounts of hard currency would appear to limit severely its power to purchase oil from the Middle East in appreciably larger quantities than those it is at present purchasing. Certainly it lacks the financial and economic means needed to induce the governments of the oil-producing states to divert oil exports from the West to the Soviet bloc on a scale sufficient to cause serious damage to the West's economy.

It would seem, therefore, in so far as any judgements are possible in such uncharted terrain, that the Soviet government is faced with an ever-widening margin between oil production in the Soviet Union and consumption of oil by the Soviet bloc; that the cost of developing the Soviet Union's own untapped oil reserves – a cost per barrel well above that for Alaskan or North Sea oil – is beyond her financial capacity, even if she had the technological skills and equipment required, which she does not; and that similar financial and economic constraints limit her ability to purchase Middle-Eastern oil in excess of what she now obtains through barter agreements and sales of arms. If this assessment is correct, the temptation for the Russians to acquire by political or military means what they cannot afford to purchase must be a strong one. It can only be made stronger by the consideration that the acquisition of preferential access to the Gulf's oil would enable the Soviet Union to dictate the terms upon which oil would thereafter be supplied to the West.

Soviet Russia is now in a stronger position than ever before in her history to accomplish her ambitions in the Middle East, whether they be to dominate the routes from Europe to the East, to command the landward and maritime approaches to the eastern Mediterranean, the Red Sea and the Gulf, or to lay hands upon the massive oil reserves of the region. She is entrenched in Iraq and Afghanistan by virtue of extensive arrangements for the supply of arms, the equipment and training of their military forces and the provision of economic and technical assistance, as well as by actual treaties of friendship with both countries. In the case of Afghanistan the treaty concluded in December 1978 was the direct outcome of the violent overthrow of the republican government in April 1978 and the subsequent installation, after further bloodshed, of a Marxist regime at Kabul. The opportunities which the Marxist *coup d'état* in Afghanistan and the civil turmoil in Persia in the latter months of 1978 opened up to Russia to advance her strategic interests in the direction of the Gulf and the Indian Ocean were almost infinite. Even to begin to enumerate them would take us well beyond the range and purpose of this book. Leaving to one side the implications of a Russian paramountcy in Afghanistan for the politics and security of the Indian sub-continent, the combination of radical governments in Kabul and Baghdad and domestic chaos in Persia directly threatens the political and territorial integrity of the latter country. For both Iraq and Afghanistan harbour deep animosities of a religious, racial and cultural kind against Persia, which, if they were to find active expression – whether under Russian inspiration or guidance is almost immaterial – at a time when Persia was torn by internal dissension, could lead to the disintegration of the Persian state as it is now constituted.

While the Soviet Union's favoured position in Iraq and Afghanistan has increased her strategic options, it is Persia which has been the focus of Russian attention since Tsarist times and which offers the Russians the richest potential rewards. Persia is by far the most important of the three states. She also possesses the greatest natural advantages, whether these consist in her oil and mineral resources or in her long coastline on the Gulf. The Russians have acknowledged this fact by maintaining at Tehran their largest embassy in the Middle East, twice as large in terms of personnel as the embassies at Ankara and Cairo, and with the biggest contingent of KGB and GRU officers. While the latter may have played little part in precipitating the collapse of the governmental authority in Persia in the latter part of 1978, there can be no doubt of the large benefits the Russians may expect to derive from that collapse, and conversely, of the grim harvest of troubles the Western world may expect to reap in consequence. The Russians are just as well placed to bring pressure to bear upon the Gulf region from its southern approaches, their obvious base of operations being Aden and the Hadramaut. From there they can proceed, under cover of reactivating the guerrilla war in Dhufar, to sow the seeds of subversion in a wide arc through Oman to the shores of the Gulf. It is a most promising line of advance, especially as the Russians now have the naval and air power to support a campaign of this nature fought by their South Yemeni auxiliaries. They may equally elect to initiate or encourage seditious activities, or *soi-disant* 'national liberation movements', within the Gulf states, where radical political elements of all shades, including Marxist–Leninist, are to be found, not least among the extremist factions in the Palestinian *émigré* communities. The clandestine running of arms to dissidents to raise rebellions has been a commonplace of political life in eastern Arabia since the Second World War, and there is no reason why the Russians should be any less successful at the activity than the Saudis, Iraqis, Egyptians and South Yemenis have been. Should the Russians decide to intervene more forcefully in any insurrection which may occur in one of the Gulf states, they have at their disposal a highly effective instrument, viz. naval power, the means by which dominion over Arabia's coasts and seas has been asserted and sustained down the centuries.

One could sum up the Soviet Union's position in the summer of 1979 by paraphrasing Palmerston: 'Russia pursues the same system of strategy against Arabia and Persia; she creeps down the Red Sea and wants to do the same down the Gulf, and to take both Arabia and Persia on each of their flanks.' Yet to present the situation in such literal terms would be an over-simplification. For one thing, the actual intentions of the Soviet Union towards the Gulf are inscrutable, and any attempt to divine them depends upon the interpretation of a host of considerations, the greater part of which have little or no direct connexion with Arabia and the Gulf. For another, it would be wrong to view the progress of Russia in the Middle East over the past sixty, or even thirty, years as a chronicle of uninterrupted successes, or as the preordained and irresistible fulfilment of some grand design. The necessity to compress historical material in an endeavour to achieve succinctness in the present narrative may have produced an impression of the ineluctability of this progress; but such an impression would be a misleading one. While there is undoubtedly a consistent central theme in Soviet policy towards the region, the Soviet Union is as prone to make *ad hoc* moves and decisions in the face of changing circumstances as are the Western powers. The Kremlin is far from being infallible in its political judgements, as the record of its relations with the Arab world since the Second World War bears witness. It has revealed no signs of possessing any unique insight into the hearts and minds of the Arabs, nor has it exhibited any unusual dexterity in handling them. What it has shown has been an unremarkable ability to exploit for its own purposes the numerous grievances held by the Arabs in general against the West.

Whatever view one may take of Soviet intentions towards Arabia and the Gulf, and of the Soviet Union's capacity to carry them into effect, it remains that the Russians now possess considerable strategic and tactical advantages in the region which they did not possess a decade ago. These advantages, moreover, have been gained as much through the ineptitude and infirmity of the Western powers as they have by the Soviet Union's own efforts. While the Russians may have miscalculated at times, they have at least attempted to ground their policy upon reality and not upon wishful thinking. Western policy, on the other hand, has been based upon illusions, upon self-deception and upon calculations of short-term advantage. Nowhere is this more evident than in the formulation and execution of American policy towards Arabia and the Gulf during the past decade.

However widely one may choose to define American interests in the Middle East, three are of obvious paramount importance, viz. the prevention, for strategic reasons, of Soviet domination of the region; the retention of the bulk of its oil reserves for the use of the Western industrial nations and Japan; and the preservation of the security and independence of Israel. While it may seem at first glance self-evident that the United States has successfully defended these interests over the past three decades, the fact remains that this defence has been wearing dangerously thin for some years now. One has only to compare the general Western position in the Middle East in 1945 with what it is today to appreciate how greatly Western power and influence in the area have been diminished in the intervening years, a deterioration which is in large measure attributable to the peculiarities and vagaries of the policy pursued there by the United States. While the undermining of British and French influence in the Middle East was a conscious early aim of that policy, it was also to some extent unconscious, the product of American unwillingness or inability to understand that the strength of Britain and France as European powers, and therefore as allies of the United States, derived in appreciable degree from their imperial and post-imperial interests overseas. The United States was so intent upon destroying these interests for reasons of anti-colonial sentiment and commercial advantage that she failed to realize the incongruity, let alone the injurious consequences, of supporting the British and French as allies in Europe and harrying them as rivals in Asia.

In Arabia and the Gulf, as we have seen, the United States government, having no real policy of its own to follow, allowed itself to be seduced – partly through its own promiscuity – into adopting and implementing ARAMCO's plans for the furtherance of that company's commercial ambitions and those of its Saudi Arabian clients. The key to the fulfilment of these ambitions was seen to be the removal of Britain from Arabia and the Gulf; and to the attainment of this end the State Department lent its unobtrusive support for twenty years or more after 1945, rationalizing its duplicity with catchpenny references to the United States' anti-imperialist traditions, American sympathy with Arab nationalist aspirations and the natural harmony of Arab–American relations. If the United States government had paused to look about it in the 1960s to see who else (besides ARAMCO and the Saudis) was eager to see Britain ousted from the Gulf – a *galère* which included Muhammad Reza Shah, the Baathist junta in Baghdad, the NLF politburo in Aden, the guerrillas of Dhufar and associated Marxist and terrorist groups – it might have had cause to think again. As it was, the realization of what might follow the British withdrawal from Aden and the Gulf came too late for the United States to throw the policy of the previous twenty years into reverse, even if the British had been prepared to swallow their bile and co-operate.

Since 1971 the United States has had to grapple by herself with the problem of devising and implementing a strategy to protect Western interests in Arabia and the Gulf. To date she has not found one, beyond the *faute de mieux* arrangement of entrusting the security of the Gulf to the joint care of Saudi Arabia and Persia. That such an arrangement was hopelessly inadequate even for the protection of the vital interests of the Gulf states, let alone those of the Western industrial nations and Japan, was obvious from the start; yet since the beginning of the decade successive administrations in Washington have persisted in believing, or affecting to believe, the contrary. Just how great a part illusion, self-deception and wilful obtuseness have played in fostering this belief is clearly revealed in the transcripts of hearings on the subject of American relations with the Gulf states held by the Senate Foreign Relations Committee and the House Committees on Foreign Affairs and International Relations from 1972 onwards. To read these transcripts is to enter a strange world from which reality has been resolutely banished, a world where ectoplasmic shapes variously labelled 'Persia' (or 'Iran'), 'Saudi Arabia', 'Kuwait', 'Oman' and so forth are solemnly and interminably described by a shuffling, endless procession of sages, oracles, sophists and sciolists, with all the perspicacity of an Arabian Bedouin discussing the finer points of the United States Constitution.

In the main, the witnesses appearing before the congressional committees belonged to one or another of three categories. There were government officials, usually from the Departments of State and Defence; representatives of the oil industry or other commercial undertakings; and professional students of the Middle East, most of them from academic institutions. In the case of the oilmen and other financial or commercial representatives, the object they had in view in presenting a case for the close identification of American interests with those of the oil-producing countries of the Gulf was fairly obvious, even if some of the representatives of the parent companies of ARAMCO revealed more than a hint of that devout sense of mission which has long marked ARAMCO's approach to the affairs of Arabia. The academic witnesses, by and large, seemed to be more concerned with burnishing their individual images and reputations than with presenting sober, lucid and informed assessments of the history, politics and societies of Arabia and the Gulf. This, perhaps, is understandable, for while a handful of them were scholars of genuine distinction in their fields, only one was an acknowledged authority on the area and he had acquired his expertise as an employee of ARAMCO. Because of their unfamiliarity with the subjects upon which they were called to discourse, the majority were driven to take refuge in pedestrian generalities or theories of international relations, in which the peoples and countries of the Gulf were reduced to mere symbols. A few of the cast of witnesses were instant experts, bright young men on the make, programmed with the fashionable ideas and jargon of the day, who awakened uncomfortable memories of the early years of 'Camelot' and the beginning of the American involvement in Vietnam.

What the academics and the officials expressed in common was a decidedly roseate view of the Gulf states, whether it was of their contemporary condition or of their future prospects. Every country was making rapid progress, some, of course, more rapidly than others. Their rulers were men of great vision and infinite resource, devoted to the welfare of their subjects and acutely conscious of their responsibilities to the world at large, not least as regards the continued supply of oil in adequate quantities and at reasonable prices. Every regime was firm and stable, shored up by the affection and esteem of its people. None, naturally, was more solid than that of the Al Saud, who enjoyed a special eminence and spiritual dominion as heirs of the 'Arabian Reformation'. Under the benign guidance of their rulers the peoples of the Gulf were evolving their own democratic institutions, as was only to be expected of tribesmen reared in the proud and fiercely independent tradition of the Arab of the desert and in the brotherhood of Islam. Economic miracles and wonders of all description were being performed to transform the coasts and deserts of Arabia into modern, dynamic, thriving economies (the clichés tended to tumble forth by the barrelful during the hearings) directed by eager, vigorous, resourceful local managers and entrepreneurs, many of them, of course, graduates of American universities and schools of business administration. There were, it hardly needed to be emphasized, enormous opportunities for the United States to profit from the ferment of economic activity going on in the area, opportunities which stemmed as much from the natural affinity and feelings of mutual affection and regard which existed between Arabs and Americans (an affinity so natural, in fact, that it must surely have been ordained by the Divine Creator himself) as they did from the normal determinants of trade between countries. One of the foremost of these opportunities, as nearly every witness was at pains to remark, was that of selling huge quantities of arms to the Gulf countries, all of which, so it was argued, had an urgent and legitimate need for them.

Such, here necessarily compressed, was the burden of the opinions vouchsafed to the congressional committees by the great majority of witnesses who appeared before them between 1972 and 1977. Nothing that occurred in Arabia and the Gulf in these years acted to wither or stale these Panglossian views, which were still in the ascendant in Washington in 1979. Yet for all the assurance with which they were enunciated, they had a markedly hollow ring to them – which was hardly surprising since they originated in a virtual vacuum. Unlike other areas of the world, Arabia and the Gulf were practically *terra incognita* to most Americans. They had no historical links with the region, no long record of travel and exploration, no political, military, or – before the advent of the oil era – mercantile contacts, no intimate experience, extending over generations, of its inhabitants and their ways, no tradition of American scholarship on Arabia and Persia. Despite these deficiencies, however, one may search in vain through the hundreds of thousands of words uttered by the succession of voluble witnesses who testified before 1972 and 1977 for even the most fleeting acknowledgement of the slightest feeling of inadequacy on the part of any speaker to pronounce with less than Olympian certitude upon the matters set before him. One can only wonder, in the circumstances, where this ease of exposition and conviction of omniscience derived from.

Where the witnesses possessed some knowledge of, or acquaintance with, Arabia and the Gulf (as in the case of the State Department officials) they seem less concerned to enlighten their hearers about the area than to urge upon them a particular interpretation of Arabian or Gulf politics, together with its implications for the correct policy for the United States to adopt in the region. To make their point, the State Department officials resorted to a good deal of obfuscation, and at times to downright misrepresentation. For instance, the standard version of the history of Saudi Arabia retailed by these officials was expurgated to a degree that might have been considered excessive even by ARAMCO's fulsome standards. From it the senators and congressmen would have learned nothing of the bloodier aspects of the Saudi conquests in Arabia, of the darker side of the Saudi family history, of the dour intolerance of Wahhabism, of the corruption and cruelty rampant at the Saudi court, of the colossal waste of oil revenues – of anything, in short, which might have indicated the true nature of the Saudi state, its expansionist tendencies and the dread in which it was held by its neighbours in Arabia. The same techniques of selection and omission were used to obscure the record of American involvement in Arabia, of ARAMCO's subservience to the Al Saud, of its active encouragement of Saudi Arabia's bid to subjugate Abu Dhabi, of the Saudis' efforts to subvert the sultanate of Oman, of the State Department's supine condonation of these activities and, indeed, of the entire campaign to undermine Britain's position in the Gulf. If the general drift of American policy in the peninsula during and since the Second World War was concealed from the Senate and House committees, how were their members to judge for themselves the real nature of the situation in which the United States now found herself, and where she might be headed on her present course? Reliable information on Arabia and the Gulf was much more difficult to come by than was the case, say, with European or Latin American countries, where the congressional committees could draw for information upon a multitude of independent and alternate sources. Newspaper coverage of the Arabian peninsula was thin and riddled with inaccuracies. Few books were published about its affairs, and fewer still which were reliable. The American oil companies operating in Arabia and the State Department alone possessed the resources to supply the committees with any volume of material, and the former, naturally, were extremely loath to reveal anything publicly which might possibly annoy or offend the governments of Saudi Arabia and the other Gulf states. Perforce, therefore, the senators and congressmen had to rely upon the State Department for full and accurate information about the affairs of Arabia, Persia and the Gulf, and it cannot be said that they were particularly well served in this respect by that arm of government.

The central recurrent theme in the State Department's evidence to the committees from 1972 onwards was that the departure of the British had left no resultant political vacuum in the Gulf. To substantiate this assertion it was necessary to demonstrate that the Gulf states were capable by themselves of ensuring the security of the Gulf, and this in turn required that they be depicted as sober, responsible and well governed political entities. Hence the portrait of Saudi Arabia drawn by the State Department along the lines already described. It was not only in the case of Saudi Arabia, however, that the State Department witnesses before the committees were prone to act more like publicity agents for the Gulf states than as servants of the United States government. They served up the same dish of flummery in describing the past and present condition of Kuwait, Bahrain, Qatar and the United Arab Emirates. Kuwait's surreptitious encouragement of Palestinian terrorism, the sanctuary she afforded to radical groups promoting sedition elsewhere in the Arab world, her government's shrill denunciations of the West, her prominent role in forcing the pace of oil nationalization and price increases were all passed over in silence. The shaikhdom was presented instead as the very model of a modern, welfare state, governed with benevolence and foresight, its riches disbursed for the benefit of all, its philanthropic endeavours transcending its

own frontiers. The Kuwait national assembly, like that of Bahrain, was extolled as the harbinger of democracy, a worthy facsimile, it might almost be said,
of the parliament at Westminster – or the Diet of Worms. Much the same kind
of nonsense was talked about the UAE and Qatar, with their 'constitutions'
and 'representative bodies' and 'growing political sophistication', as if what
was being discussed was the Athens of Pericles rather than the primitive
backwaters of Ajman and Umm al-Qaiwain.

A good example of this Pollyanna view of the Gulf was the statement made to
a sub-committee of the House Committee on International Relations on 10
June 1975 by Joseph J. Sisco, under-secretary for political affairs at the State
Department. According to Sisco, 'a spectacular transition' was under way in
the Gulf, 'where new political institutions have been formed and tested and
where traditional values are subject to modern social change'; 'where there has
been a dramatic evolution in relationships between international oil companies
and oil producer states'; and where 'the countries in the area have moved
toward greater regional co-operation'. None of this bore the remotest resemblance to reality. The two or three 'new political institutions' that had been
created, like the Kuwait and Bahrain national assemblies, were, even as Sisco
spoke, well on their way to oblivion, while the political structure of the UAE
had not even been tested. The 'dramatic evolution' in relations between the oil
companies and the oil-producing states consisted in the creeping nationalization of the companies and the arbitrary fixing of oil prices by the states. As for
'greater regional co-operation' among the Gulf states, it was then, and remains
still, a mirage. Yet the promotion of such co-operation in the interests of
collective security was, so Sisco asserted, the first object of American policy in
the Gulf. What he did not explain was why the United States had had no
success in achieving this aim, if the Gulf states were really of such a mind to
co-operate with one another as he claimed.

The other leading aims of American policy as enunciated by Sisco seemed
just as far from realization. They included the encouragement of 'orderly
economic progress' in the region, continued access to oil supplies 'at reasonable
prices', and the employment of surplus oil revenues 'in a constructive way,
supportive of the international financial system'. To attain these objectives,
Sisco explained solemnly, the United States 'has relied increasingly on a varied
mix and growing nexus of relationships'. What this meant exactly was not
clear, although it seemed to include the expansion of American diplomatic,
cultural, technical and commercial contacts with the Gulf, and particularly the
lower Gulf, where, so Sisco proudly informed the committee, 'we have lean,
hard-working, "shirtsleeve" Embassies, staffed with some of the best young
talent we have'. (An instance of this diplomatic talent at work was the wording
of invitations from the American embassy in Abu Dhabi in 1974 to foreign and
local dignitaries to attend a Fourth of July reception, to celebrate 'our independence from the British Empire'.)

At the heart of American policy in the Gulf, so Sisco affirmed, lay the conviction that 'the major burden for assuring security in the region must be borne by the gulf states themselves and in particular by the major nations of the region, Iran and Saudi Arabia'. He was pained by accusations that the United States was primarily motivated in its adherence to this conviction by the desire to sell large quantities of arms to these states. 'The impression that our military relationships with the gulf nations have dominated all other aspects of our relations is as erroneous as it seems to be persistent.' All that the United States was doing was to help Saudi Arabia and Persia to satisfy their essential defensive requirements. The shah, for example, although he had made substantial purchases of arms, had kept the Persian armed forces 'relatively small in number (about 350,000)' – that is, although Sisco never made the comparison, about as 'small' as Britain's. Nor, in Sisco's opinion, had the shah's expenditure upon weapons affected

the impressive strides which the government has made in economic development and in improving the welfare of its people. Iran's domestic investment program is more than twice what it spends on defense. . . . A substantial portion is for industrial growth, but $19 billion is earmarked for housing, free education, urban and rural development, and a massive increase in medical facilities.

If this were so, then Sisco must have been sorely disappointed by the misguided lack of appreciation shown by the Persian people in the closing months of 1978.

Nowhere in Sisco's disquisition on the Gulf was there the slightest suggestion that the headlong rush of the local states, led by Persia and Saudi Arabia, to acquire vast quantities of modern arms was highly revelatory of the kind of countries they were. Whether he saw the connexion or whether he deemed it politic to ignore it (since it hardly accorded with the case he was at pains to make for their progress) is uncertain. It is also significant, for the arms trade *was* at the very centre of the United States government's relations with these countries, and the State Department was being a good deal less than candid in accounting for the transactions which were then taking place. In his testimony before the House committee Sisco conveyed the impression that requests from the Gulf states for arms and related equipment and services were carefully scrutinized and responded to according to the State Department's judgement of the merits of each application. Yet within the next twelve months the scandal of the irresponsible sale of American arms abroad, in the Middle East as elsewhere, had reached such proportions that the Congress passed the Arms Export Control Act which was signed into law on 30 June 1976. The act did little, however, to break down the wall of equivocation behind which the Departments of State and Defence strove to conceal the fact that arms transactions with Persia and Saudi Arabia had got completely out of hand.

On 16 September 1976, two and a half months after the enactment of the Arms Export Control Act, the sub-committee on foreign assistance of the Senate Foreign Relations Committee reopened hearings on the proposed sale of 160 F–16 aircraft to Persia at a cost of $3,800 million. The sale was the initial stage of an eventual order for a total of 300 F–16 and 250 F–18 aircraft. At the start of the proceedings the chairman of the sub-committee, Senator Hubert Humphrey, remarked that, when the hearings had originally begun, the Committee on Foreign Relations had been inclined to ask for detailed information on each and every proposed sale of arms to the Middle-Eastern states concerned. At the urging of the State and Defence Departments, however, automatic reporting requirements had been held to a minimum, with the committee only asking for information as it required it. Until the more recent notifications of arms sales the practicality of the arrangement had not been seriously tested. Now, Humphrey said, he had to report that the performance of both the State and Defence Departments in responding to requests for information was nothing less than 'deplorable'. The committee had asked for details about Saudi Arabia's armed forces and had not received them. It had asked for an analysis of the military threats to several countries in the Middle East and had not received it. It had asked for inventories of the weapons possessed by Middle-Eastern countries. The information was delivered, Humphrey observed, 'in a totally unusable form'. Instead of requests for approval of specific arms sales coming in at intervals, a 'whole bucket' of requests, involving sales to a value of $6,000 million, had now been put before the committee for its approval, with only thirty days left before the ninety-fourth Congress was due to adjourn. The whole sequence of events, Humphrey concluded, 'indicates an almost total lack of respect on the part of the executive branch for the committee's role in considering arms sales matters'.

At the root of the State and Defence Departments' cavalier behaviour lay the calculations that each had made about how arms sales to Persia and Saudi Arabia might serve its own separate interests. For the Defence Department, as we have seen, there were considerable benefits for its own research, development and procurement plans in the continuing sale of large quantities of advanced weapons to the two countries. For the State Department the arms sales were an integral part of the financial and political compact into which the United States had entered with Saudi Arabia, one of the chief purposes of which was to absorb Saudi Arabia's surplus oil revenues. Much the same calculation applied in the case of Persia, also. But the main consideration, so far as the State Department was concerned, was the part that arms played, and were designed to play, in equipping Persia and Saudi Arabia to play the role which the State Department had devised for them as the guardians of the security of the Gulf. It was on these grounds that the State Department had sought, in the years from 1972 to 1976, to justify the increasing volume of arms sales to the two countries, and it did so again in the testimony it offered to the

Senate Foreign Relations Committee at the hearings of September 1976 in support of the sale of F–16 aircraft to Persia.

On that occasion, as we have noted already, Philip C. Habib, Sisco's successor as under-secretary for political affairs, spoke of the policies pursued by Persia since 1945 as having been 'generally compatible with our own'. '[We] have generally seen our respective interests as parallel, at times congruent, and we share many objectives,' he informed the committee. To reinforce his argument, he went on to quote statements that had been made at various times by the secretary of state, Henry Kissinger, to the effect that the policies of the United States and Persia 'have been parallel and therefore mutually reinforc-ing', and that co-operation between the two powers 'grew out of a leadership that is clearly independent, that pursues its conception of its own national interest based on a history of 2,500 years of Iranian policy'. To this Habib added his own gloss, declaring roundly, 'It is our belief that the imperatives of Iran's history, its geography, its location, its relationship with its neighbors, is such that it is not likely to result in any substantial change in the current policy lines.' To make such statements required a resolute indifference on the part of Kissinger and Habib to both the realities of Persian history and the conduct of Muhammad Reza Shah over the preceding few years. It would be interesting to know what interests, apart from keeping the Russians at bay, the secretary of state and his subordinate thought the United States and Persia had in common. The shah had already made plain to the world what some of his principal interests were by taking the lead in forcing up the price of oil, by his seizure of Abu Musa and the Tunbs, by his megalomaniac dreams of making Persia a great industrial power, by his lavishing of Persia's oil revenues upon his armed forces so that he might strut and posture as a new Cyrus or Darius, by his enrichment of the Pahlavi dynasty, and by his tolerance of the monumental corruption which pervaded the upper reaches of Persian society. Were these the interests which, according to the State Department, the United States had in common with him?

The testimony offered the Senate Foreign Relations Committee by the Department of Defence to justify the sale of the aircraft in question to Persia was no more convincing. Robert F. Ellsworth, the deputy secretary of defence, made the same treacly references to the natural affinity of interests between the United States and Persia, emphasizing the necessity for the Persians to be reassured of an uninterrupted supply of arms. 'For Iranian leaders, the willingness of the United States to remain a reliable supplier of military equipment to meet the threats which they perceive to their security is extremely important.' Ellsworth's vision of Perso–American military co-operation extended well beyond the immediate future. 'In the regional con-text,' he told the committee, 'the proposed sale would improve Iran's ability to carry out in the latter part of the 1980s and 1990s the major security missions on which we agree.' The prospect filled Humphrey with foreboding. Who could tell, he asked Ellsworth, what the national interests of the United States were likely to be in twenty or even ten years' time? To act upon the presumption of a continuing identity of interests would land the United States in the position of having armed Persia to the teeth without knowing what the future held for that country, or in which direction it might turn. Humphrey, though he would have been the last to claim any special knowledge of Persia and Persian history, showed a great deal more prescience than the State or Defence Departments. The chickens, whose far-off flutterings he had detected, were to come home to roost barely two years later.

How the Soviet Union was supposed to view the continued build-up of the Persian armed forces with the most advanced American military equipment and aircraft was a question to which officials of the two departments never seriously addressed themselves in their public testimony. It was obvious to even the most casual observer that, however many arms Persia accumulated, she could never by her own efforts ensure her defence against the Soviet Union, or even acquire sufficient military strength to give the Russians cause to hesitate before launching an offensive across her borders. If this was so, and if, as the Soviet government was prepared tacitly to concede (however much its official propaganda might assert the contrary), the continued independence of Persia depended, in the last analysis, upon the support of the United States, what were the Russians to make of this vast supply of modern weapons to Persia, especially when it was accompanied by frequent and fervent assertions about a close identity of American and Persian political interests and strategic objectives? By tying itself so closely to the shah and his pretensions, the United States government (so it must have seemed to the Russians) was running a serious risk of finding itself drawn further and further into the internal affairs of Persia, especially if the shah should find himself in domestic difficulties or at odds with his neighbours. If such an eventuality were to occur, and if by that time the connexion of the United States with Persia had attained anything like the proportions of the Soviet Union's involvement in Cuba, the two great powers would inevitably have been brought into close and exceedingly danger-ous proximity.

The Russians were not to know, of course, that when the moment of truth came the United States would desert the shah in the midst of his travails, even to the point of urging him to quit his throne and his country. All the fine words and noble sentiments expressed by the State Department's officials in 1976 swiftly evaporated in the civil conflagration that broke out in Persia late in 1978. It required only a growled warning from President Brezhnev in the third week of November 1978 – 'it must be clear that any interference, especially military interference, in the affairs of Persia, a state which directly borders on the Soviet Union, would be regarded by the USSR as a matter affecting its security interests' – to elicit a hurried disclaimer from the United States government of any thought of intervening to save the shah. After all, the

United States had other matters to absorb her attention in the closing weeks of 1978 – among them the abandonment of Taiwan, the restoration of full diplomatic relations with China and the strategic arms limitation talks – matters which closely affected Soviet–American relations and which could easily upset the delicate equilibrium governing these relations.

A mutuality of interests was similarly propounded by State Department witnesses before the congressional committees from 1972 onwards to justify the sale of large quantities of advanced American weapons and aircraft to Saudi Arabia. The tenor of the arguments used may be gauged from what has already been said of the State Department's determination to portray Saudi Arabia and her ruling house as arrayed like the lilies of the field. That the lilies had been festering for some time was just as resolutely concealed from the committee members. Thus, testifying before Senator Humphrey's sub-committee in September 1976 in support of requests from the Saudi government to purchase arms and aircraft to a value of $7,510 million, Alfred L. Atherton, Jr, assistant secretary for Near Eastern and South Asian Affairs, painted a glowing picture of Saudi Arabia as a country soberly aware of its duties as a regional power, eminently worthy to be trusted to employ sensibly and responsibly the panoply of weapons it had ordered, and above all a tried and true friend of the United States. The previous March, Atherton had made a like deposition in support of Saudi arms requests to a sub-committee of the House Committee on International Relations, on which occasion he had assured its members: 'We see their present requests as reasonable and rational, albeit limited and relatively small, and well within their capability to absorb and employ effectively.' Considering that these requests included F-5 fighter aircraft to a value of over $1,000 million, 440 helicopters and Hawk missile systems, they could hardly be described as 'relatively small'. Nor, in view of the elementary level of technical competence possessed by the Saudi armed forces, could it be claimed by any stretch of the imagination that the Saudis were capable of employing them effectively.

Atherton was equally misleading about the political implications of these arms sales. As he told the sub-committee,

We have looked carefully at the relative balance of forces in Saudi Arabia and its neighbors, and conclude that these sales would not significantly affect that balance. In fact, to the extent that strengthening Saudi ground forces in a limited way enhances the Saudi security role with respect to its smaller neighbors in the Arabian Peninsula, the impact would be positive.

(It might be remarked in passing that if the State Department had in fact 'looked carefully' at the relative strength of the Saudi armed forces, it was keeping its information carefully to itself. For, as we noticed a short while ago, Senator Humphrey, the chairman of the Senate sub-committee on foreign assistance, was still complaining in September 1976 about the department's

failure to provide him with information on this very subject.) For Atherton to
argue thus required either an overwhelming ignorance of the record of Saudi
Arabia's past behaviour towards her smaller neighbours, or a wilful blinking of
that record, or a cynical indifference to the continued independence of the
smaller Gulf states. That the last was the most likely explanation is borne out
by the burden of the State Department's evidence before the congressional
committees over the preceding five years. For at no time in those years had the
department's spokesmen attempted to examine, even in the most perfunctory
fashion, the threat that Saudi Arabia had presented and continued to present to
the littoral shaikhdoms. Instead, as we have seen, they treated the committees
to a well-laundered version of Saudi Arabian history, designed to accord with
their advocacy of Saudi Arabia's fitness to play the role of guardian of the
Gulf's security.

What the United States has done in helping to arm Persia, Saudi Arabia and
the minor Gulf states to the teeth has been to create an explosive situation of
potentially nightmarish proportions. It has been a policy – if one can dignify it
with the name – of unbelievable foolishness, culpable irresponsibility and
addled opportunism, which has done the gravest disservice to the peoples of
the Gulf and to Western interests there. The United States, however, is not
alone among the Western powers in bearing the blame for bringing the Gulf to
its present dangerous pass: she has been run a very close second by Britain and
France in the race to inundate the Gulf with arms. Upon the motives, other
than the obvious one of financial gain, which impelled the French to sell
massive quantities of arms to the Arab states, it is pointless to dwell; for the
processes by which the national interests of France are perceived and pursued
by her governments have for years now been unfathomable to non-
Frenchmen. It is almost as difficult, though for very different reasons, to
understand the behaviour of Britain in indiscriminately selling arms to anyone
in the Gulf who wanted them. For whereas it might be argued in partial
extenuation of the United States's delinquency in this respect that Americans
in general were unfamiliar with the Gulf and the nature of the peoples around
its shores, the British knew full well what the area was like and what the effects
of a sudden and huge injection of arms were likely to be.

It had been one of the principal objects of British policy in the Gulf from the
late nineteenth century onwards to limit the importation and distribution of
arms. By the time of the First World War considerable progress had been made
towards diminishing the size of the Gulf arms traffic by means of
treaties with the Gulf states, through the series of Hague conferences and
through direct engagements with the other European powers. After the war the
work was continued under the auspices of the League of Nations, meeting with
a good measure of success. No such accomplishment stands to the credit of the
United Nations, the League's successor, presumably because the majority of
its members would have considered any restriction upon their freedom to

accoutre themselves with whatever weapons they desired a derogation from their national dignity and sovereign independence. Britain, however, continued to regulate the flow of arms into the Gulf in the post-war years, restricting it to limited quantities of weapons for which the Gulf rulers could prove a legitimate need. Her policing of the arms trade ceased with her withdrawal from the Gulf in 1971, and so too, it would seem, did her sense of moral responsibility. From being the policeman of the Gulf she became within an indecently brief span of time one of the leading arms pedlars in the region, soliciting and supplying orders with all the moral sensibility of a racecourse tout, stooping readily to bribery and other *louche* practices (including the debasement of the Crown honours system) to further these discreditable transactions. If the questionable methods by which British aircraft and armaments manufacturers sought to secure large and lucrative contracts were not exposed to public scrutiny, as were those employed by a handful of American firms, it was only because the British parliamentary process did not operate to bring these matters out into the open in the way that the system of congressional inquiry in the United States did. Not once in this decade has the British parliament seriously debated the question of British arms sales to Arabia and Persia. Not a single committee of the House of Commons has inquired in any depth into Britain's involvement in this pernicious traffic. Instead, like France and the United States, Britain has found it expedient to try to recoup the costs of her oil purchases from the Gulf states, and at the same time to keep their governments happy so that they will not impede the flow of oil to the West, by catering to their obsession with military might, a policy which all three Western powers have attempted to justify, individually and in unison, on the contemptible grounds of *force majeure* – i.e. if the Arabs and Persians are precluded from buying arms from one Western power they will buy them from another or from the Soviet bloc.

To try to ensure the security of the Gulf's oilfields by pandering to the passion of the local governments for the deadly and costly trinkets of war is a policy so bereft of sense as to be unworthy of serious discussion. The extent to which Persia and Saudi Arabia have armed themselves has already been indicated in the chapters on those two countries. Iraq has armed forces of 212,000 men, upon whom she spent $1,660 million in 1977 alone. Her air force comprises well over 300 combat aircraft, organized in two bomber and eighteen fighter squadrons (with another forty or more aircraft on order), in addition to transport squadrons, helicopters and missile systems. Her army, 180,000 strong, has 2,000 tanks, 1,500 armoured fighting vehicles, artillery of every calibre and a variety of missile systems. It is much the same, allowing for the discrepancies in population, with the minor states of the Gulf. Kuwait, with total armed forces of 12,000 men, had a defence budget of well over $2,500 million for the three years 1975, 1976 and 1977. She has equipped herself with 125 medium tanks (with another 130 on order), 250 armoured cars, half-a-dozen squadrons of modern fighters, missile systems, transport planes, helicopters and naval patrol craft. The UAE (which is to say principally Abu Dhabi) spent the better part of $1,000 million on arms and aircraft between 1974 and 1978, equipping her armed forces of 25,900 men with four fighter squadrons, transport planes, helicopters, thirty light tanks, 150 armoured cars, artillery, missile systems and naval patrol boats. Oman has spent a comparable sum in the same period of time – though with better cause – to purchase for her armed forces of 20,000 men three fighter squadrons, four transport squadrons, helicopters, missile systems, naval craft, artillery and armoured cars. Qatar, while spending more modestly, has still acquired a goodly armament in addition to ordering thirty Mirage fighters for her air force. Over and above the flood of new and up-to-date weapons pouring into the Gulf there is also a brisk secondary traffic in arms going on (the Persians have been particularly involved in it), with many older weapons, procured only a decade or so ago, being sold off to a variety of customers, including Afghans, Baluchis and the poorer shaikhdoms of the UAE.

It is evident from even the most cursory glance that these extensive and elaborate armaments either will be used in the near future in conflicts among the Gulf states, or they will be left to deteriorate into huge piles of expensive junk, a fitting commemoration of one of the greatest acts of pecuniary folly in the history of the Middle East. Given the past record and ingrained disposition of the governments and peoples of the Gulf, the former eventuality is the more likely, and the destruction that will result will be on a scale never before experienced in the Gulf. For several reasons, among them the relative paucity of alternative worthwhile targets for bomber aircraft, oil installations and port facilities are bound to suffer heavy damage. If the Gulf states had been equipped according to their real defensive needs, as they were in the past, they would now possess little more than small arms, light artillery, armoured cars, helicopters, naval patrol craft and other military equipment of an equally modest order. What they have accumulated instead in the way of powerful and costly armaments will not serve to protect them from a major power bent on their subjection but will merely increase their capacity to inflict serious injury upon themselves and upon Western interests in the Gulf.

The dismal spectacle of the Gulf arms extravaganza is a reflection of the utter bankruptcy of Western policy in the region since the departure of the British in 1971. In place of a coherent strategy to safeguard the vital economic interests of the West there is only a pathetic reliance upon the doctrine of common interest to achieve the same purpose. The principal precepts of the doctrine are that the Arabs and Persians stand to benefit as much as the West from the uninterrupted supply of oil to the industrial world, that they have a mutual interest with the West in resisting the extension of Soviet influence in the Middle East, and that they will refrain, therefore, from weakening the West economically by manipulating oil supplies and prices, lest they thereby impair the West's ability to shield the Middle East against the designs of the Soviet Union. (A corollary to the doctrine is the necessity for the West to remove the irritation caused by the Arab–Israeli conflict by securing from Israel the political and territorial concessions which the Arabs desire.)

None of these arguments will stand up to close examination. Talk of Arab or Persian self-interest, and of common purpose with the West, must of necessity be conjectural. It is based, not upon an intimate knowledge of what is discussed and decided in the innermost councils of the Saudi ruling house, or the Libyan junta, or the shaikhly families of the lesser Gulf states, but upon divination and surmise. It presupposes the existence among Arabs, Persians and Westerners of a similarity of moral outlook, ethical values, political beliefs, modes of thought and ideas of international law which has no foundation in reality. It ignores the nature of the regimes, whether conservative or radical, in power in the Arab countries, and it glosses over those aspects of the Arab character which habitually impel these regimes to wilful and erratic behaviour. To argue that Persia and the Arab oil-producing states will tread the path of prudence and moderation in the knowledge that, if they weaken the West through the interruption of oil supplies and the imposition of excessively high oil prices, they are only exposing themselves to eventual Russian domination, is to credit these states with a preference for rational and responsible conduct for which their history (or even the record of the past decade) affords no substantial evidence. The Middle-Eastern members of OPEC, by their intemperate behaviour since 1970, have simply played the Russians' game for them, sometimes in ways which they may not have foreseen. When North Vietnam launched what was to prove to be her final offensive against the Saigon regime in January 1975, the resistance of the South Vietnamese forces to the invasion was severely hampered, not only by the refusal of the United States Congress to sanction the dispatch of arms to South Vietnam but also by the serious shortage of petrol for the South Vietnamese army and air force, a shortage which was a direct consequence of the quadrupling of oil prices by OPEC twelve months earlier and the further price rise of November 1974 engineered by Ahmad Zaki al-Yamani. It is highly doubtful whether the fall of Saigon to the communists in April 1975 was a cause for celebration in Riyad.

The plain fact is that the Russians are now well established in the Middle East and they are there by Arab invitation. It is immaterial that they have been helped on their way by the Arab–Israeli dispute: if Israel had never existed, some pretext or other would have been found by the Arabs to bring the Soviet Union as a political force into the Middle East. For the animosity borne by the Muslim Arab world for the Christian West is of such intensity that it was bound sooner or later to cause the Arab maxim of 'the enemy of my enemy is my friend' to operate to embrace the West's most powerful and malevolent foe. It is much the same with the Persian Shia. Fear of Russia failed to inhibit the outburst of anti-Western and Shii fundamentalist sentiment in Persia at the close of 1978, which led to the drastic reduction and eventual curtailment of the country's oil production, all the previous assurances of the shah's government notwithstanding. That outburst also exposed the irrelevance of another argument with which the West is accustomed to comfort itself, viz. the supposed incompatibility, philosophical as well as spiritual, between Islam and Marxism. The achievement of some kind of notional synthesis between Islam and Marxism is not an essential prelude to the undermining of Western interests in the Middle East: simply by indulging in vindictive acts against the West as they have been doing for years, the Arabs and Persians have served the Russians' purposes only too well.

All that the constant reiteration of the doctrine of common interest achieves is to convince the Middle-Eastern oil-producing states that the West needs them as much as (or even more than) they need the West, thereby confirming them in their *hauteur* and their illusions of power. These illusions are bound to lead these states sooner or later to threaten the West with further oil embargoes, boycotts or other sanctions. The secretary-general of OAPEC, the Arab oil organization, more or less gave notice of this intention in June 1976 when he upbraided the head of the United States federal energy administration, Frank G. Zarb, during a visit by the latter to Kuwait, for having instituted an oil-stockpiling programme. Such a move, so the OAPEC secretary-general claimed, could only lead to a 'confrontation' with the Arab oil states. Zarb replied that if OAPEC undertook not to use oil again as a political weapon but simply to treat it as an item of commerce, the United States would be prepared to re-examine her stockpiling measures. The OAPEC secretary-general made no response to the offer, nor has any response been forthcoming from OAPEC since then.

A similar malignity informs the outlook of OPEC. The behaviour of that organization over the past decade – its unilateral abrogation of agreements, its 'whip-sawing' tactics over prices, its arbitrary revocation of concessions and compulsory nationalization of oil company assets – has revealed its contempt for international law, indeed, for the whole concept of an international order based upon legal principles arrived at after long and arduous experience. In place of international law as a system for regulating the affairs of nations OPEC has tried to substitute a set of notions, made familiar by their constant iteration by Afro–Asian states, about historical injustice, inalienable rights (especially over natural resources) and the need for the West to atone for its past crimes against the peoples of Asia and Africa by paying them vast reparations. Leaving aside the questionable validity of these propositions, it is patent that they are the product of the intellectual and emotional fashions of our times. But times change, and circumstances with them, undermining the fashionable precepts of the day together with the situations which gave rise to them; so that what seems grounded in certainty today will seem hopelessly outdated and irrelevant tomorrow. For this reason, if for no other, it follows that only an international order based upon enduring principles evolved over the centuries, principles which have resisted the ravages of passing fashion and changing circumstance alike, offers any real protection against the buffets of fate – a protection, it might be said, which ultimately works to the benefit of the Afro–Asian peoples as well as to that of the rest of mankind.

There has been a strong tendency in the West for some time now to acquiesce in the arguments of OPEC and to abandon, or at least to compromise, the established principles of international law in treating with that organization, and more particularly its Middle-Eastern members. The lure of expediency, as we have seen, proved irresistible in October 1973, and nothing in the behaviour of the Western powers since then gives grounds for believing that their response to another Arab oil embargo, or the threat of it, would be any different. It is usually assumed that such a threat would be evoked by the Arab–Israeli conflict, and that it would be directed towards securing some advantage for the Arab governments or their Palestinian protégés in the form of territorial or other concessions by Israel. Yet a curious feature of the innumerable exchanges over the oil question which have taken place since October 1973 among the Arab oil states, Western governments, OPEC and the Western oil companies is that the Arab–Israeli question and the plight of the Palestinians have for most of the time been lost to sight in the brouhaha over oil prices, production levels, financial surpluses, arms transactions, 'recycling' of revenues, and the multifarious altercations to which these issues have given rise. Again, it is worth recalling that, although it was the October 1973 war which prompted the imposition of the Arab oil embargo and cuts in oil production, it was not the war which occasioned the doubling and redoubling of oil prices and their subsequent increase. While the Saudi government's winged messenger, the ubiquitous Shaikh Yamani, has proffered frequent assurances of the continuity of oil supplies to the West in exchange for Western pressure upon Israel to make substantial concessions to Arab demands, the honouring of such assurances, in the light of past experience, is highly problematical. What is more, no Arab government, including his own, has ever linked concessions by Israel with a reduction in oil prices, which is a matter of as much moment to the West as security of supplies.

For these and other reasons it would be unwise in the extreme for the West to assume that the Arab–Israeli dispute constitutes the sole or even the chief source of irritation which could provoke another Arab oil embargo. The acid test, after all, is to postulate an end to the dispute which would have satisfied every Arab aspiration, even down to the abolition of the State of Israel. Could the Western industrial nations and Japan thereafter rest easy in the serene expectation of untrammelled access to oil at reasonable prices? It is scarcely necessary to say that they could not. For the oil weapon, and particularly its financial aspects, has less to do with the Arab–Israeli conflict than with the powerful sentiments of grievance and resentment against the Christian West long cherished by the Arabs, who deem themselves a chosen people, the repository of the true faith, the race of the Prophet, ordained by Providence to receive the submission of others. These emotions, together with the fertility of the Arab imagination and the exhilaration induced in the Arab mind by the possession of vast oil wealth, virtually guarantee that the Arab oil states will be tempted to employ the weapons of embargo and boycott to achieve a variety of political and economic objectives at the expense of the West. It is equally likely, in view of the spasms of religious fanaticism which have racked Persia since the closing months of 1978, that the Persians, too, will experience similar temptations.

There is an almost palpable reluctance in the West to face squarely the likelihood that the Arab oil states, alone or in company with their fellow members of OPEC, will again attempt to constrict or curtail the flow of oil to the Western industrial nations and Japan. There is an even greater reluctance to consider the possibility that the West might be forced as a consequence to take active measures to secure its sources of supply in Arabia and the Gulf. On the rare occasions when the subject has been aired – and these, in the main, have been confined to the United States – it has produced guarded comments from government ministers, mixed opinions (mostly of an emollient kind) from prominent politicians, and a certain amount of excited discussion in the public prints, much of it dominated by the ideological outlook of the participants.

The possibility of Western counteraction was first shadowed forth on 21 November 1973, when the American secretary of state, Henry Kissinger, remarked, apropos of the embargo then in operation, that 'the United States would consider counter-measures if the oil embargo is continued indefinitely or unreasonably'. Innocuous though this statement seemed to be, it provoked some furious bluster from Yamani, who, it may be recalled, described the idea of American military intervention as 'suicide' and threatened to destroy the Saudi Arabian oilfields in advance of such intervention. A few weeks later, on 7 January 1974, the United States secretary of defence, James Schlesinger, ventured the opinion that the use of force could not be excluded if circumstances called for it.

We should recognize [he said] that the independent powers of sovereign states should not be used in such a way as would cripple the larger mass of the industrialized world. That is running too high a risk, and it is a source of danger, I think, not only from our standpoint, but also from the standpoint of the oil producing nations.

An angry protest followed from the Saudi government, which in a formal note warned the United States not to 'belittle' Yamani's remarks of the previous November about the possible destruction of the oilfields. A good deal of publicity was given during the remainder of January 1974 to the alleged wiring of the Hasa oilfields with explosives, and to the investiture of the Amir Abdullah ibn Abdul Aziz, commander of the National Guard and a brother of King Faisal, with responsibility for 'Operation Detonation', as it was called.

Little more was heard of the matter until the following December, when Kissinger dropped a remark during the course of an interview with a magazine reporter to the effect that a resort to force could not be ruled out 'where there is some actual strangulation of the industrialized world'. A certain amount of indignant comment and excited speculation ensued, which led Kissinger to amplify his remark in the course of a press conference on 17 January 1975, when he explained that what he meant was that 'in case of actual strangulation of the industrialized world, we would reserve our position'. 'Now, if you analyzed this,' he went on, 'no Secretary of State could say less. We cannot take the position that no matter what the producing countries do, we will acquiesce.'

One could hardly describe either Schlesinger's or Kissinger's remarks – or the occasional murmurs on the subject which were to be heard from President Ford during 1975 – as even mildly bellicose, still less as a stirring call to the colours to the nations of the West. Yet they caused flurries of outrage in the Arab world, where, as is well known, a recourse to force to secure one's ends is almost unheard of. They were received with scarcely less indignation by prominent liberals in the United States Senate. Senator George S. McGovern, the chairman of the Senate sub-committee on Near Eastern and South Asian Affairs, paid a visit to Saudi Arabia in March 1975, from which he returned greatly disturbed by the displeasure expressed to him by the Saudis at what they perceived to be threats of a military seizure of their oilfields. McGovern agreed with them. An American military expedition to the Gulf, he reported to his colleagues in the Senate, would be 'sheer stupidity': even talk of it was a 'political catastrophe'. 'Before an invading force could occupy the oil fields, demolition teams could and undoubtedly would sabotage machinery and set oil fires that would put installations out of production for many months.' The United States would earn 'the undying hostility of the entire Arab world, probably as well of the entire third world', from which all manner of horrors would result – Arab terrorism on an unprecedented scale, bomb attacks in American cities, security measures at American airports ('two-hour check-in times, friskings and double-checks').

Senator Mike Mansfield, the majority leader in the Senate, followed McGovern's trail out to Jiddah in August 1975. He, too, returned distressed by the damage which had been done to the harmony of Saudi–American relations by loose talk of a military occupation of the oilfields. In his view, he told his fellow senators, it would probably take 'years' to repair the damage to the oilfields done by Saudi sabotage in advance of an American invasion.

Saber rattling, in short, will do nothing to bring about a solution posed [*sic*] by the oil producers' cartel.... The best counter to arbitrary practices on the part of any economic combine, in my judgement, is not military threat, embargo or political manipulation. Rather, it is to be found in conservation at home, diversification of sources and the development of substitutes.

Senator Charles H. Percy was another who was horrified by Kissinger's veiled allusion to a resort to arms, which had been voiced when Percy also was on his travels in the Middle East, necessitating some rapid invention on his part to explain it away to his various interlocutors. He was as opposed as Mansfield and McGovern to military action. 'Is it practical?' he asked his fellow senators rhetorically, at a sitting of McGovern's sub-committee in June 1976. 'Set aside the moral aspect, which I don't think I can. Is it really a feasible, practical thing for us to use force or imply that force will be used in an oil-producing country?'

There were certainly a number of interested parties in Washington in 1975 and 1976 who were concerned to prove that a military seizure of any of the Middle-Eastern oilfields was a Herculean enterprise, doomed by its very nature to produce a Pyrrhic victory. A fair summary of the principal tenets of this school of thought is provided by a study entitled 'Oil Fields as Military Objectives', which was prepared by the Congressional Research Service of the Library of Congress in August 1975 for the House Committee on International Relations. The study runs to over a hundred pages and is decked out with all manner of impressive devices to lend it authority: some 200 footnotes; statistical tables of oil production, distribution and consumption; maps, appendices and comparisons of military strength; glossaries of oil industry and military terminology; and extracts from the United States Constitution, treaties with foreign powers and assorted United Nations charters and resolutions. The authors range far and wide in their search for apposite historical, legal and military precedents, delving into the arcana of international law, constitutional restraints and public opinion ('public opinion once again could be expected to provide key input to any "go–no go" decision'), invoking such historical parallels as the invasion of Normandy in 1944, the Arab Revolt of 1916–18 and the War of 1812, and illustrating their discourse with significant historical quotations (e.g. 'How many divisions has the Pope?').

As a case study to test the feasibility of a military operation the authors select what they call the 'Saudi core', i.e. that area of Hasa which contains the Abqaiq, Ghawar, Dammam, Qatif and Berri (off-shore) fields. They examine the climate, vegetation and terrain ('the stony soil around Dhahran lacks any cushion, but would suit seasoned [para]troopers'), and then draw up what they consider to be the essential components of an invasion force. So far as can be discerned through the fog of jargon in which they clothe their thoughts ('deliberations in the clutch would be conditioned by strong emotions on both sides. Money elements in the decisionmaking matrix ... would be magnified'; 'nevertheless, U.S. posture, tailored to fit special situations, would display peculiarities'), the occupation of the 'Saudi core' would require, in their view:

two airborne divisions,
one marine division,
two to four infantry divisions,
a marine air wing,
six squadrons of attack aircraft,
six squadrons of defence aircraft,
transport squadrons (number unspecified),
three to five Hawk missile battalions,
sixteen aircraft carriers,
128 cruisers and destroyers,
forty-eight assault craft, and
an undetermined number of transports and supply ships.

After this, the conclusions of the authors hardly come as a surprise:

U.S. parachute assault forces are too few to cover all objectives quickly. Amphibious forces are too slow. Skilled teams could wreck havoc before we arrived;
Two to four divisions, plus substantial support, would be tied down for a protracted period;
Direct intervention by Soviet air/ground forces, a distinct possibility, . . . might make our mission impossible;
U.S. strategic reserves would be stripped. Prospects would be poor, and plights of far-reaching political, economic, social, psychological, and perhaps military consequence the penalty for failure.

It is difficult to appreciate from all this that what is being discussed is the occupation of a corner of Saudi Arabia, a country which is not exactly a military power of the first dimension. It is equally difficult to take seriously the opinions of researchers who will postulate for this task an invasion force roughly the size of the American army corps which landed in Sicily in July 1943, or who talk of the Saudis as being bound to pursue a 'scorched earth' policy – in Arabia. Yet the authors of the congressional study were only articulating the prevailing opinion in political and intellectual circles in the United States at the time on the subject of possible military intervention to secure the Gulf oilfields. Much of this opinion was voiced in response to the publication of two articles stating the case for intervention, the first by Robert W. Tucker in *Commentary* in January 1975, the second by a pseudonymous author, 'Miles Ignotus' (whom our Library of Congress researchers classify in their study as 'Ignotus, Miles') in *Harper's* in March 1975. The general reaction of the politicians and pundits to the mere notion of intervention was one of fear and alarm. Visions were conjured up of the sky over Arabia aglow with the flames from a thousand blazing oil wells, of the ferocious hordes of Araby sweeping out of the desert to smite the Western interlopers and drive them reeling into the sea, of the gigantic figure of the Russian bear (snow on his paws, vodka on his breath and rape on his mind) lurching down the valleys of Mesopotamia, and of a subsequent scene of utter desolation along the Arabian shore, where only a few drops of oil seeping from a mass of mangled pipes and shattered machinery indicated the site of what had once been the world's greatest oil industry. The loquacious James Akins, ever alert for a chance to preach the doctrine of Western dependence upon Arab goodwill, found it impossible to hold his tongue, as he might reasonably have been expected to do in his capacity as American ambassador to Saudi Arabia. Instead, he let fall a few ill-chosen words in public about the iniquity of contemplating the use of force, an indulgence which earned him a prompt recall from his post and subsequently led to his resignation from the foreign service.

The most sensible comment on the subject from a public figure in the United States was that made by Senator William Fulbright eighteen months earlier, in November 1973, when he observed drily: 'The Arab oil producers are militarily insignificant – gazelles . . . in a world of lions.' As such, he went on, 'they should take account of the pressures and temptations to which the powerful industrial nations would be subjected if their economies should be threatened by severe and protracted energy crises'. What, in other words, we are speaking of here is not states of even the military capacity of Egypt or Syria, but of Saudi Arabia, Kuwait, Qatar and Abu Dhabi. The ability of these states to defend themselves is minimal, which is why their governments have taken refuge in extravagant threats to destroy their oilfields and installations in advance of Western military intervention. Whether they would actually do so, their braggadocio notwithstanding, is another question. (Whether they have the technical competence to sabotage the fields thoroughly is also problematical.) Without their oil these states are nothing, as they well realize – though it must be said of them, also, that they have a remarkable penchant for cutting off their noses to spite their faces. As for the tremulous predictions of the ferocity of the Russian reaction to a Western occupation of the Gulf oilfields, all that need be said of them is that the nature of that reaction is unforeseeable, probably even to the Russians themselves and certainly to the tribe of Western augurs confidently prophesying what it will be.

The poverty of resource and invention underlying the reigning American consensus of opinion on the subject of continued Western access to the Gulf's oil is almost as depressing as the infirmity of spirit which informs it. For years now the people of the United States, like those of Western Europe, have been led to believe that the only choice open to them lies between a docile submission to the dictates of the Middle-Eastern oil states and the outright occupation of the Gulf oilfields. On the contrary, it is well within the power and ability of the United States, Western Europe and Japan, should the Gulf oil states again interrupt the flow of oil to the industrial world or engineer another huge price 'sting', to bring such economic pressure to bear upon these states as to compel them to desist forthwith. If the Arabs of the Gulf think they can hold the West to ransom by suspending oil supplies, the West can as readily coerce them by withholding almost every single item they require to make their lives worth

living. When their governments threaten to destroy the oilfields and oil installations they overlook the fact that they, too, have hostages to fortune, whether
in the shape of their financial and commercial assets abroad or in the form of
power stations, water-distillation plants, oil refineries, docks, airports and
other facilities in the Gulf, all of which are vulnerable to technical disruption or
sabotage. They depend upon the West, also, for the bulk of their armaments,
for the training of their armed forces, for technical instruction, and for the
maintenance and replacement of the complicated weaponry, gadgetry and
aircraft with which they have equipped themselves. If these armaments and
services were denied them, the alternative would be to procure them from the
Soviet bloc, which is hardly an attractive prospect for the regimes in power in
the Gulf today, whose survival largely depends, in the last resort, upon
Western support.

If a Western embargo upon trade, or similar economic and political
measures, should fail to induce the governments of the Gulf oil states to lift any
restrictions they might have imposed upon the supply of oil, the Western
powers may have to resort to an occupation of the oilfields. Legally speaking,
they would be entitled to do so, under the doctrine of necessity in international
law, especially if they had by that time been reduced to desperate economic
straits. The likelihood that such a contingency might arise has increased with
every passing year during the last decade, as the elements of instability
present in Arabia and the Gulf have grown more threatening and diverse. As
any change of regime in one or more of the Gulf states is bound to be in a radical
direction, the consequences for Western interests are likewise bound to be
adverse, particularly if the new revolutionary order is of a Marxist tinge and
likely to involve the Soviet Union intimately in the Gulf's affairs. In such an
eventuality, the pressures upon the West to intervene to secure its vital oil
supplies may become irresistible. If a recourse to arms does prove necessary,
however, it will be because of the dismal policy of drift and propitiation the
West has followed for a decade past, instead of employing the hundred and one
political and economic weapons it had, and still has, at its disposal to impress
upon the Gulf states that it will not suffer its great strategic interests in the
region to be set at naught by their ill-intentioned antics and inflated pretensions.

There was a time, earlier in this century and in the last, when the powers of
Europe were inclined to look upon the realms and principalities of the Middle
East with a certain degree of wonder, not unmixed with disdain. While their
own interests, ambitions and rivalries might require them to treat with a
miscellany of sultans and amirs, sharifs and saiyids, bashaws and beglerbegs in
the lands between the Golden Horn and the Hindu Kush, they could not bring
themselves to take most of them seriously. To European statesmen these
Oriental potentates were at once sinister and absurd, their pretensions

ridiculous, their personal conduct repugnant, their administrations feeble and corrupt. A few earnest souls thought that Middle-Eastern societies and governments might possibly be regenerated by the application of Western political and economic specifics; others hoped that their rehabilitation might be accomplished through the agency of Islam, reformed and reinvigorated. Most Europeans acquainted with the ways of Middle-Eastern governments, however, regarded them as incorrigible, even though they were generally at pains to conceal this belief beneath layers of diplomatic *politesse*.

What then has happened in recent decades, we may well ask, to cause the derangement we now see about us, wherein the statesmen of the Western world scurry from one dusty Middle-Eastern capital to another, to attend anxiously upon our latter-day bashaws and beglerbegs, sultans and amirs, soliciting their indulgence, sympathizing with their complaints and listening gravely to their counsel? It cannot be that the nature of Middle-Eastern rulers and governments has changed, rendering them less corrupt, capricious or absurd, more worthy of the respect and approval of Europe. The cast of vizirs, sultans and sharifs may have altered and new props been brought upon the stage; but the play remains the same – a tragi-comedy of despotism in countless acts. Nor has any striking reversal taken place in the balance of power between Europe and the Middle East such as would justify the exaggerated deference which some European governments – notably those of Britain and France – now pay to polities of the stature of Kuwait or Saudi Arabia, Iraq or Persia. It is not enough to ascribe this deference to the issue of oil supplies and the financial problems generated by excessive oil prices. The process of appeasement began a good half-century ago, with the lowering of Europe's standards of judgement in treating with the major and minor states of Asia and Africa, and it has continued at an ever-accelerating pace over the past three decades.

What lies behind Europe's changed attitude to the countries of the Middle East is basically a loss of nerve. No longer does Europe possess the confidence to treat these countries in a manner consonant with its own importance and their relative insignificance. No Middle-Eastern state, least of all any of those bordering on the Gulf, is the peer of any of the major powers of Europe, and it is simply ridiculous that Europe should take their pretensions as seriously as it does, even to the point of jeopardizing its own economic and political well-being. For this is, in effect, what Europe has done by acquiescing in the presumptuous claims of Persia, Saudi Arabia and the other Gulf states to exclusive control over the Gulf's waters and sole responsibility for the security of its oil reserves. It is not sufficient to justify this acquiescence on the grounds that Persia and Saudi Arabia were actively encouraged by the United States to arrogate to themselves the guardianship of the Gulf. Whatever may have been the determinants of American policy in this instance, the interests of Europe and the United States in the Gulf region are not wholly congruent. In any case, Europe has had a far longer acquaintance with the Middle East and much greater experience of its governments and peoples than has the United States. This experience alone should have convinced the powers of Western Europe of the folly of resigning the care of their vital interests in the Gulf into the hands of Persia and Saudi Arabia. The Gulf and its oilfields are one of the great strategic prizes in the world, and Persia and Saudi Arabia are quite incapable of defending them, especially against the designs of the Soviet Union.

The precarious situation in which Western Europe and Japan now find themselves with regard to the supply of oil from the Gulf is in some measure due to the reluctance of the major oil companies operating in the Gulf in the 1960s to risk incurring the displeasure of the local regimes by demanding both strong support from their own governments and the continuance of a Western political and military presence in an area as unstable and primitive as the Gulf. Instead they subscribed – or, what was as ill-considered, affected to subscribe – to the reigning orthodoxy of the decade, which held that such support was a hindrance to them in their dealings with the local governments, that the Western political and military presence was an irritant to local feelings, and that the oil companies' continued access to the Gulf's oil might best be secured by treating its production and purchase as a purely commercial activity – Keynes again, instead of Clausewitz. Time has proved both the oil companies and the high priests of the orthodoxy to have been mistaken. If the companies had stood firm in their confrontation with OPEC at Tehran in 1971, and if the governments of the Western world – and those of Britain and the United States in particular – had backed them to the hilt, it is highly likely that the national-ization of the companies (as distinct from minority equity participation in them by the governments of the host countries) would not have been achieved, or even attempted, in so short a space of time; that the great oil-price rises of subsequent years would not have occurred; and that the resultant economic troubles of the industrial world would not have materialized in the form that they have.

Likewise, if Britain had not thrown away her position in the Gulf in 1971 but had converted it into a defensive alliance with the minor states of the lower Gulf, as was possible at the time, Western Europe and Japan would today possess some protection for their interests in the region, as well as some physical security for their nationals. Britain's position had always rested upon the lower Gulf, upon the trucial system and the long-standing connexion with Oman. It did not depend upon her relations with Saudi Arabia, Persia or Iraq, or upon her former protectorate over Kuwait. The Trucial Shaikhs did not want Britain to leave in 1971; nor did the shaikh of Bahrain or the sultan of Oman. It was the major Gulf states, notably Persia and Saudi Arabia, who for a diversity of reasons had long resented the British presence in the area, that wanted Britain to depart. The British government of the day chose to listen to them, allowing itself to be induced and coerced alternately by Faisal ibn Abdul Aziz and Muhammad Reza Shah into abandoning the responsibilities laid upon it by both the past and the present. Successive turns of fate, of a kind all too common in the Middle East, have since removed both monarchs from the scene, thereby rendering worthless the arguments about the necessity to propitiate them which were put forward in 1971 to justify Britain's withdrawal.

Yet to question the wisdom and propriety of that withdrawal in isolation is beside the point; for it was merely another step in the long retreat of Europe from Asia and Africa which has been going on since the Second World War, and which has been consistently represented in the West as the inescapable consequence of the rise and prevalence of Afro–Asian nationalism. That the one has led to the other is undeniable; but the explanation generally accorded the phenomenon – viz. that empires are intrinsically unstable because they are morally indefensible, that the rule of one people over another offends against a basic principle of nature, if not a higher edict, and that the transition from empire to nation-state is not only irresistible but also essential if mankind is to live in harmony – has been flatly contradicted by the events of the past three decades. For what has been lost to sight in all the tumultuous celebrations over the end of the imperial age is the crucial fact that the collapse of the European empires in Asia and Africa was due less to the might of the anti-colonialist forces than it was to the sapping of the European powers' will to rule.

> When the riotous set them at naught they said:
> 'Praise the upheaval!
> For the show and the word and the thought
> of Dominion is evil!'

It was primarily the loss of nerve and resolution on the part of the European imperial powers which brought to an end Europe's authority and dominion overseas. In turn, and ineluctably, the retreat from empire has endangered the foundations of order, security and good government in Europe itself; for, as the decline and fall of the Roman empire demonstrated long ago, the holding of the *limes*, the imperial frontiers, is vital to the maintenance of stability at the empire's heart. A precipitate abandonment of imperial responsibilities, such as we have seen take place within the span of a single generation, inevitably creates its own nemesis. For once the habit of authority begins to atrophy, as it has atrophied with each successive surrender of a colonial territory, the degenerative process becomes virtually irresistible. No sudden reversal occurs, no magical recapturing of the habit of authority, when the shores of Europe are reached. The habit of surrender, born of so many ignominious capitulations in Asia and Africa, has by then become too strong.

Thus Europe has reacted to the tactics of larceny and intimidation practised by the Middle-Eastern oil-producing states since 1970 in a spirit of abject appeasement. It is a reaction, needless to say, that can only yield bitter fruit, for it has served to heighten the mood of exultancy which of late years has gripped both Sunni and Shii Islam, a mood fraught with danger for the West, not only of economic dislocation but also, through the deployment of Arab oil money, of the corruption of Western society and its institutions. Yet Western governments have been reluctant to acknowledge the existence of this danger, preferring to seek refuge in optimistic arguments and predictions about the behaviour of Persia and the Arab oil states which are based, not upon their history, their political philosophies or their religious beliefs but upon Western ideas of moderation and good sense, reasonableness and sober judgement, power and responsibility, to none of which the states in question actively subscribe.

The same malaise of spirit has led Europe to resign the care of its strategic interests in Arabia and the Gulf, as well as in the Middle East at large, to the United States, even though the United States, for a generation and more, has considered herself as much the rival as the ally of the European powers in the area, and has regulated her conduct there in conformity with this view. Nor should it be overlooked that in the struggle between the European imperial powers and the forces of nationalism in Asia and Africa over the past half-century, the United States has unremittingly thrown her influence into the scales against the European empires. It is unwise, therefore, to say the least, for Europe to continue to rely upon the United States for the defence of its great interests in the Gulf and the Middle East. The United States government, as we have seen, has pursued a futile policy of entrusting the security of the Gulf to Persia and Saudi Arabia. Now one of these pillars has collapsed and the strength of the other is highly questionable. Since the United States does not have the same fundamental need of the Gulf's oil as do Europe and Japan, it is unlikely, in the final analysis, that she would be prepared to take the possibly desperate measures that may be required to retain control over it for the West, especially in view of both the neo-isolationist sentiment which has surfaced in the United States since the defeat of American arms in Vietnam, and the want of vigour and firmness which has in consequence characterized American actions abroad.

It is abundantly clear that Europe and Japan must themselves assume responsibility for the protection of their interests in the Gulf. They must do so as much for reasons of honour and self-respect as out of self-interest; for the United States cannot and should not be left to carry the burden alone. Determination, flexibility, resource and skill will all be required if the Western powers and Japan are to safeguard their very great economic and strategic interests in the Gulf against the arbitrary and violent shifts of political fortune which have always marked the course of the Gulf's history, and which will undoubtedly continue to mark it in the future. The key to mastery of the Gulf remains still, as it has always been, command of the sea. Britain and Japan, and to only a lesser degree, France and Germany, have in the recent past been naval powers of the first rank. There is nothing intrinsic in their condition today, other than their will and sense of purpose, to prevent them in combination from becoming so again. If the Soviet Union, which has never been a formidable naval power, can evolve into one in the space of a few years, so also can they, and much more effectively. It is to this end, and to ensuring (in alliance with the United States) Western naval supremacy in the Indian Ocean, the Red Sea and the Gulf that Western Europe and Japan should be directing their efforts, instead of wasting them in an endeavour to cajole the refractory and capricious regimes of the Gulf into acting with a sense of responsibility to the world at large.

How much time may be left to Western Europe in which to preserve or recover its strategic inheritance east of Suez it is impossible to foretell. While the *pax Britannica* endured, that is to say, from the fourth or fifth decade of the nineteenth century to the middle years of this century, tranquillity reigned in the Eastern Seas and around the shores of the Western Indian Ocean. An ephemeral calm still lingers there, the vestigial shadow of the old imperial order. If the history of the past four or five hundred years indicates anything, however, it is that this fragile peace cannot last much longer. Most of Asia is fast lapsing back into despotism – most of Africa into barbarism – into the condition, in short, they were in when Vasco da Gama first doubled the Cape to lay the foundations of Portuguese dominion in the East. What now seems destined to succeed is a struggle for supremacy in the Indian Ocean and the Arabian Sea among the naval powers of the world, along the lines of the campaigns periodically waged by Portugal, Holland, England and France in the centuries following da Gama's momentous voyage of discovery. For da Gama's successors the keys to command of the Arabian Sea and control of the maritime trade of Arabia, Persia and India were Muscat, Hormuz and Aden. Others after them, notably the British rulers of India in the nineteenth century, reached the same strategic conclusions and acted upon them accordingly. The paramountcy which Britain was eventually to establish in the Gulf and around the shores of Arabia had its beginnings in the defensive engagement concluded with the Al Bu Said sultan of Oman in response to Bonaparte's occupation of Egypt in the summer of 1798. Oman is still the key to command of the Gulf and its seaward approaches, just as Aden remains the key to the passage of the Red Sea. The Western powers have already thrown away one of these keys; the other, however, is still within their reach. Whether, like the captains-general of Portugal long ago, they have the boldness to grasp it has yet to be seen.

Bibliography

The oil embargo and the price rises in the latter months of 1973 unleashed a vast flood of publication in the Western world on Arabia, Persia and the Gulf, the bulk of it being concerned with oil supplies and the financial implications of the price increases. Much of the publication was, by the nature of things, of ephemeral interest or value, and much, inevitably, was repetitive or derivative in content. For these reasons, and because it would have been humanly impossible to do otherwise, I made no attempt while writing this book to keep track of everything that was being published relative to the subjects treated here. The list of books, articles, journals, etc. which follows, therefore, is a highly selective one, restricted (with only a few exceptions) to those works which were of direct use to me. Needless to say, I have also drawn for certain material upon unpublished sources.

I Books and articles:

Adelman, M. A., *The World Petroleum Market*, Baltimore, 1972.

Adelman, M. A., 'Is the oil shortage real?', *Foreign Policy*, Winter 1972–3.

Akins, James E., 'The oil crisis: this time the wolf is here', *Foreign Affairs*, April 1973.

Amuzegar, Jahangir, 'The oil story: facts, fiction and fair play', *Foreign Affairs*, July 1973.

Anthony, John Duke, *Arab States of the Lower Gulf: People, Politics, Petroleum*, Washington, 1975.

Bernier, T., 'Confédérations et tribus de Sud de l'Arabie', *Cahiers de l'Afrique et de l'Asie*, v (1959).

Beydoun, Z. R. and Dunnington, H. V., *The Petroleum Geology and Resources of the Middle East*, Beaconsfield, 1975.

Bharier, Julian, *Economic Development in Iran, 1900–1970*, London, 1971.

Boustead, Hugh, *The Wind of Morning*, London, 1971.

Bujra, A. S., 'Political conflict and stratification in Hadramaut', *Middle Eastern Studies*, iii (1966–7) and iv (1967).

Bujra, A. S., 'Urban elites and colonialism: the nationalist elites of Aden and South Arabia', *Middle Eastern Studies*, vi (1970).

Burrell, R. M., 'Britain, Iran and the Persian Gulf: some aspects of the situation in the 1920s and 1930s', in *The Arabian Peninsula: Society and Politics* (ed. Derek Hopwood), London, 1972.

Burrell, R. M., 'Rebellion in Dhofar, the spectre of Vietnam', *The New Middle East*, March–April 1972.

Burrell, R. M., 'The Cape route and the oil trade', *Round Table*, July 1973.

Bury, John A., 'Oil and Soviet Policy in the Middle East', *Middle East Journal*, Spring 1972.

Chisholm, Archibald H. T., *The First Kuwait Oil Concession Agreement*, London, 1975.

Crossman, Richard, *The Diaries of a Cabinet Minister* (ed. Janet Morgan), vol. 2, London, 1976.

Dostal, Walter, 'The Shihuh of Northern Oman', *Geographical Journal*, cxxxviii.

Edmonds, C. J., 'The Iraqi–Persian Frontier, 1639–1938', *Asian Affairs*, June 1975.

Enders, Thomas O., 'OPEC and the industrial countries: the next ten years', *Foreign Affairs*, October 1975.

Fenelon, K. G., *The United Arab Emirates*, London, 1973.

Fiennes, Ranulph, *Where Soldiers Fear to Tread*, London, 1975.

Gardner, Richard N., 'The hard road to world order', *Foreign Affairs*, April 1974.

Gavin, R. J., *Aden under British Rule, 1839–1967*, London, 1975.

Gordon, Edward, 'Resolution of the Bahrain dispute', *American Journal of International Law*, July 1971.

Graham, Robert, *Iran: the Illusion of Power*, London, 1978.

Halliday, Fred, *Arabia without Sultans*, Harmondsworth, 1974.

Hartshorn, J. E., 'From Tripoli to Teheran', *The World Today*, July 1971.

Hartshorn, J. E., 'Oil diplomacy: the new approach', *The World Today*, July 1973.

Hawley, Donald, *The Trucial States*, London, 1970.

Heard-Bey, Frauke, 'Social changes in the Gulf states and Oman', *Asian Affairs*, October 1972.

Heard-Bey, Frauke, 'Development anomalies in the Beduin oases of al-Liwa', *Asian Affairs*, October 1974.

Horn, Carl von, *Soldiering for Peace*, London, 1966.

Hudson Institute (Europe), *Iran: Oil Money and the Ambitions of a Nation*, Paris, 1975.

Ingrams, Harold, *Arabia and the Isles*, 3rd edition, London, 1966.

Ishow, Habib, 'Les relations entre l'Irak et le Koweit', *Politique étrangère*, 2–3 (1968).

Institute for the Study of Conflict, 'Soviet objectives in the Middle East', *ISC Special Report*, London, 1974.

Institute for the Study of Conflict, 'The security of Middle East oil', *ISC Special Report*, London, 1979.

International Institute for Strategic Studies, *The Military Balance*, London, annually.

Johnston, Charles, *The View from Steamer Point*, London, 1964.

Jukes, Geoffrey, 'The Indian Ocean in Soviet naval policy', *Adelphi Papers*, no. 87, IISS, London, 1972.

Kanovsky, Eliahu, 'Saudi Arabia's moderation in oil pricing – political or economic?', Shiloah Centre for Middle Eastern and African Studies, Tel Aviv University, *Occasional Papers*, April 1977.

Kazziha, Walid, *Revolutionary Transformation in the Arab World*, London, 1975.

Kelidar, Abbas, 'Iraq: the search for stability', *Conflict Studies*, no. 59, ISC, London, 1975.

Kelly, J. B., *Eastern Arabian Frontiers*, London, 1964.

Kelly, J. B., *Britain and the Persian Gulf, 1795–1880*, Oxford, 1968.

Kelly, J. B., 'A prevalence of furies: tribes, politics and religion in Oman and Trucial Oman', in *The Arabian Peninsula: Society and Politics* (ed. Derek Hopwood), London, 1972.

Kelly, J. B., 'Hadramaut, Oman, Dhufar: the experience of revolution', *Middle Eastern Studies*, xii (1976).

Krapels, Edward N., 'Oil and security: problems and prospects of importing countries', *Adelphi Papers*, no. 136, IISS, London, 1977.

Laliberté, Gerard (pseud.?), 'La guérilla du Dhofar', *Études Internationales*, March–June 1973.

Lambton, Ann K. S., *The Persian Land Reform, 1962–1966*, Oxford, 1969.

Levy, Walter J., 'Oil power', *Foreign Affairs*, July 1971.

Levy, Walter J., 'An Atlantic-Japanese energy policy', *Survey*, Summer 1973.

Lillich, Richard B., 'Economic coercion and the international legal order', *International Affairs*, July 1975.

Little, Tom, *South Arabia: Arena of Conflict*, London, 1968.

Longrigg, Stephen Hemsley, *Oil in the Middle East*, London, 1954.

Luce, William, 'Britain in the Persian Gulf', *Round Table*, July 1967.

Luce, William, 'A naval force for the Gulf', *Round Table*, October 1969.

Maull, Hanns, 'Oil and influence: the oil weapon examined', *Adelphi Papers*, no. 117, IISS, London, 1975.

Mazrui, Ali A., 'Black Africa and the Arabs', *Foreign Affairs*, July 1975.

Middle East Record, vol. one, 1960 (ed. Yitzhak Oron), Jerusalem, 1965. Vol. two, 1961 (ed. Yitzhak Oron), Jerusalem, 1967. Vol. three, 1967 (ed. Daniel Dishon), Jerusalem, 1971. Vol. four, 1968 (ed. Daniel Dishon), Jerusalem, 1973. Vol. five, 1969–70 (ed. Daniel Dishon), Jerusalem, 1977.

Mitchell, Colin, *Having Been a Soldier*, London, 1969.

Odell, Peter R., *Oil and World Power*, 3rd edition, Harmondsworth, 1974.

Odell, Peter R., 'The world of oil power in 1975', *The World Today*, July 1975.

Owen, R. P., 'Developments in the Sultanate of Muscat and Oman', *The World Today*, September 1970.

Owen, R. P., 'The rebellion in Dhofar – a threat to Western interests in the Gulf', *The World Today*, June 1973.

Page, Stephen, *The U.S.S.R. and Arabia*, London, 1971.

Paust, Jordan J., and Blaustein, Albert B., 'The Arab oil weapon – a threat to international peace', *American Journal of International Law*, lxviii (1974).

Price, D. L., 'Oman: insurgency and development', *Conflict Studies*, no. 53, ISC, London, 1975.

Rodolfo, Claudine, 'Le golfe persique: situation actuelle et perspectives d'avenir', *Politique étrangère*, no. 5, 1970.

Rodolfo, Claudine, 'Le golfe Arabo-Persique', *Maghreb-Machrek*, July–August 1973.

Royal United Services Institute for Defence Studies, 'Oil – strategic importance and future supplies', Report of a seminar, London, 1973.

Sampson, Anthony, *The Seven Sisters: the Great Oil Companies and the World They Made*, London, 1975.

Sampson, Anthony, *The Arms Bazaar*, London, 1977.

Shihata, Ibrahim F. I., 'Destination embargo of Arab oil: its legality under international law', *American Journal of International Law*, lxviii (1974).

Shwadran, Benjamin, *Middle East Oil: Issues and Problems*, Cambridge, Massachusetts, 1977.

Skeet, Ian, *Muscat and Oman: the End of an Era*, London, 1974.

Smiley, David, *Arabian Assignment*, London, 1975.

Thesiger, Wilfred, 'Across the Empty Quarter', *Geographical Journal*, cxi.

Thesiger, Wilfred, 'A further journey across the Empty Quarter', *Geog. Journ.*, cxiii.

Thesiger, Wilfred, 'Desert borderlands of Oman', *Geog. Journ.*, cxvi.

Thesiger, Wilfred, *Arabian Sands*, London, 1959.

Thomas, Bertram, *Arabia Felix*, London, 1932.

Townsend, John, *Oman: the Making of the Modern State*, London, 1977.

Tremayne, Penelope, 'Guevara through the looking glass: a view of the Dhofar war', *Royal United Services Institute Journal*, September 1974.

Trevaskis, Kennedy, *Shades of Amber: a South Arabian Episode, London*, 1968.

Trevelyan, Humphrey, *The Middle East in Revolution*, London, 1970.

Troeller, Gordian and Deffarge, Claude, 'Sud-Yémen, une révolution menacée?', *Le Monde diplomatique*, April 1972.

Viennot, Jean-Pierre, 'Aden: de la lutte pour la libération a l'indépendance', *Orient*, nos. 43–4 (1967).

Viennot, Jean-Pierre (trans.), 'Communiqué du front de libération du Zhofar, 9 Septembre 1968', *Orient*, nos. 43–4. (Article and translation are both dated 'November 1968'.)

Viennot, Jean-Pierre, 'La guérilla du Dhofar entre dans une nouvelle phase', *Le Monde diplomatique*, August 1972.

Viennot, Jean-Pierre, 'L'expérience révolutionnaire du Sud-Yémen', *Maghreb-Machrek*, September–October 1973.

Watt, D. C., 'Labor relations and trades unionism in Aden', *Middle East Journal*, xvi (1962).

Watt, D. C., 'The decision to withdraw from the Gulf', *Political Quarterly*, July–September 1968.

Watt, D. C., 'Britain and the Indian Ocean: diplomacy before defence', *Political Quarterly*, June 1971.

Wilkinson, J. C., 'The Oman question: the background to the political geography of South-East Arabia', *Geographical Journal*, cxxxvii.

Wright, Denis, 'The changed balance of power in the Persian Gulf', *Asian Affairs*, October 1973.

Zonis, Marvin, *The Political Elite of Iran*, Princeton, 1971.

II Official publications:

Saudi Arabia:

Memorial of the Government of Saudi Arabia: Arbitration for the Settlement of the Territorial Dispute between Muscat and Abu Dhabi on the one side and Saudi Arabia on the other, AH 1374/AD 1955.

United Kingdom:

Hansard, *Parliamentary Debates*.

Arbitration Concerning Buraimi and the Common Frontier between Abu Dhabi and Sa'ūdi Arabia: Memorial submitted by the Government of the United Kingdom of Great Britain and Northern Ireland, 1955.

United States:

Senate Committee on Foreign Relations: 'Multinational Corporations and United States Foreign Policy'. Hearings before the Subcommittee on Multinational Corporations, 93rd Congress, first and second sessions:

> Parts 4–9, 'Multinational Petroleum Companies and Foreign Policy', hearings of October, November 1973, January, February, March, June, August 1974.
> Part 10, Report of Subcommittee, 2 January 1975.

> Hearings before the Subcommittee on Multinational Corporations, 94th Congress, first session:

>> Part 11, 'Political and Financial Consequences of the OPEC Price Increases', hearings of January, February, March 1975.
>> Part 12, 'Political Contributions to Foreign Governments', hearings of June 1975.
>> Part 14, 'Lockheed Aircraft Corporation', hearings of February, May 1976.
>> Part 17, 'Grumman Sale of F–14s to Iran', hearings of August, September 1976.

Senate Committee on Foreign Relations: 'U.S. Oil Companies and the Arab Oil Embargo: the International Allocation of Constricted Supplies', report prepared by the Federal Energy Administration's Office of International Energy Affairs for the Subcommittee on Multinational Corporations, 27 January 1975.

Senate Committee on Foreign Relations: 'A Select Chronology and Background Documents relating to the Middle East', printed for the use of the Committee, February 1975.

Senate Committee on Foreign Relations: 'Realities of the Middle East', a report by Senator George S. McGovern, May 1975.

Senate Committee on Foreign Relations: 'Saudi Arabia', a report by Senator Mike Mansfield, October 1975.

Senate Committee on Foreign Relations: 'International Security Assistance and Arms Export Control Act of 1976', Report of Committee, 30 January 1976.

Senate Committee on Foreign Relations: 'International Security Assistance and Arms Export Control Act of 1976–77', Report, 14 May 1976.

Senate Committee on Foreign Relations: 'Middle East Peace Prospects'. Hearings before the Subcommittee on Near Eastern and South Asian Affairs, 94th Congress, second session, May, June, July 1976.

Senate Committee on Foreign Relations: 'U.S. Military Sales to Iran', a staff report to the Subcommittee on Foreign Assistance, July 1976.

Senate Committee on Foreign Relations: 'U.S. Arms Sales Policy: Proposed Sales of Arms to Iran and Saudi Arabia'. Hearings before the Committee on Foreign Relations and the Subcommittee on Foreign Assistance, 94th Congress, second session, September 1976.

Senate Committee on Foreign Relations: 'The Witteveen Facility and the OPEC Financial Surpluses.' Hearings before the Subcommittee on Foreign Economic Policy, 95th Congress, first session, September, October 1977.

Senate Committee on Foreign Relations: 'The Future of Saudi Arabian Oil Production', a staff report to the Subcommittee on International Economic Policy, 96th Congress, first session, April 1979.

House of Representatives Committee on Foreign Affairs: 'The Middle East 1971: the Need to Strengthen the Peace'. Hearings before the Subcommittee on the Near East, 92nd Congress, first session, July, August, September, October 1971.

House of Representatives Committee on Foreign Affairs: 'U.S. Interests in and Policy toward the Persian Gulf'. Hearings before the Subcommittee on the Near East, 92nd Congress, second session, February, June, August 1972.

House of Representatives Committee on Foreign Affairs: 'The United States and the Persian Gulf', Report of the Subcommittee on the Near East, 29 September 1972.

House of Representatives Committee on Foreign Affairs: 'New Perspectives on the Persian Gulf'. Hearings before the Subcommittee on the Near East and South Asia, 93rd Congress, first session, June, July, November 1973.

House of Representatives Committee on Foreign Affairs: 'U.S. Policy and the International Energy Agency'. Hearings before the Subcommittees on International Organizations and Movements and on Foreign Economic Policy, 93rd Congress, second session, December 1974.

House of Representatives Committee on International Relations: 'The Persian Gulf, 1975: the Continuing Debate on Arms Sales'. Hearings before the Special Subcommittee on Investigations, 94th Congress, first session, June, July 1975.

House of Representatives Committee on International Relations: 'Oil Fields as Military Objectives. A Feasibility Study', prepared for the Special Subcommittee on Investigations by the Congressional Research Service, Library of Congress, 21 August 1975.

III Newspapers and periodicals:
Daily Telegraph
Economist
Egyptian Gazette
Financial Times
Guardian
International Herald Tribune
Keesing's Contemporary Archives
Le Monde
Le Monde diplomatique
Middle East Economic Survey
New York Times
Petroleum Intelligence Weekly
The Times

Index